URBAN DESIGN

Seattle, Washington

URBAN DESIGN:
The American Experience

Jon Lang

VAN NOSTRAND REINHOLD
_____ New York

Library of Congress Catalog Card Number 93-15893
ISBN 0-442-01360-4

I(T)P Van Nostrand Reinhold is an International Thomson Publishing company.
       ITP logo is a trademark under license.

Printed in the United States of America

Van Nostrand Reinhold   International Thomson Publishing GmbH
115 Fifth Avenue   Königswinterer Str. 418
New York, NY 10003   53227 Bonn
                                     Germany

International Thomson Publishing   International Thomson Publishing Asia
Berkshire House,168-173   221 Henderson Bldg. #05-10
High Holborn, London WC1V 7AA   Singapore 0315
England

Thomas Nelson Australia   International Thomson Publishing Japan
102 Dodds Street   Kyowa Building, 3F
South Melbourne 3205   2-2-1 Hirakawacho
Victoria, Australia   Chiyoda-ku, Tokyo 102
                                     Japan

Nelson Canada
1120 Birchmount Road
Scarborough, Ontario
M1K 5G4, Canada

COUWF 16 15 14 13 12 11 10 9 8 7 6 5 4 3 2 1

Lang, Jon T.
      Urban design: the American experience / Jon Lang.
            p.   cm.
      Includes bibliographical references and index.
      ISBN 0-442-01360-4
      1. Architecture--Environmental aspects--United States.
      2. Architecture and society--United States. 3. City planning-
      -United States. I. Title.
      NA2542.35.L36 1194
      720' .47--dc20   93-15893
                                                   CIP

For Meredith, Benjamin, and Susannah with thanks

"The Modernists almost got it right."

Robert Venturi

CONTENTS

PREFACE

Urban Design is a relatively new term for an activity of long standing. It is concerned with the design of the four-dimensional physical layout of human settlements and their parts. It "is the art of relating: STRUCTURES to one another and to their NATURAL SETTING to serve CONTEMPORARY LIVING" wrote Clarence Stein in 1955. He should have added "in time" and "over time" to his observation. Urban design is a complex art for it strives to attain a multitude of ends simultaneously. These ends range from the provision of shelter for activities, to the creation of a sense of place, to the technological soundness of the built environment, to the health of the fiscal and biological environments. Urban design clearly overlaps the endeavors of many fields. It is thus also the art of relating one set of professional concerns to other sets.

The manner in which the term "urban design" has come into use in the professional design fields since the late 1950s says much about its development as a distinct field of professional activity, if not a profession, not only in the United States, but elsewhere. Urban design has its roots in the profession of architecture. More particularly, the roots are in the Modern Movement in architecture and, even more particularly, it has developed as a response to the failure of the Modern Movement to come to grips with the realities of human experience and of urban life.

The post–World War II need to rebuild the cities of Europe and the effect of the changing nature of manufacturing and transportation technologies on cities throughout the world led to the need for much urban rebuilding. Population expansion, new social policies, and changing social orders all contributed to an unprecedented building boom. The result was a series of new towns—capital cities, manufacturing/company towns, suburbs—and large urban renewal projects in almost all the countries of the world. Most of the work carried out by professional designers followed the tenets of one or another branch of the Modern Movement. The results varied in quality although the goal, contrary to some cynical observations, was the

admirable one of creating a livable and delightful new world. Some of the new work has indeed been a joy to all; some has proven to be uninhabitable even though it was highly esteemed by the design professions. The development of urban design as a field resulted from the widespread dissatisfaction among a number of architects, city planners, and landscape architects with the traditional substantive and procedural paradigms of contemporary work in the late 1950s.

The criticism varied. Some architects felt that the work was not artistic enough—that it followed too few Architectural precedents. Others shared the perceptions of the inhabitants and other users of schemes that the design principles being used were simply not achieving livable environments. Some users felt that architects were not even concerned about their needs, but were rather pursuing their own aesthetic ends. There were also differences in the perception of the weaknesses of the design principles being used. Anthropologists felt that many design principles and prototypes were culturally inappropriate. Sociologists were dismayed by the low level of intellectual rigor of architects' arguments about the relationship between the designed/built environment and social behavior. It became clear that much architectural wisdom was lacking and that considerably more thought had to be put into the design of cities, suburbs, and other human settlements if the contribution of the built environment (and thus the work of design professionals) to the experiences of its users was to be enhanced. A number of people who began calling themselves urban designers took up the challenge.

There has been a considerable development of urban design as a field of professional practice and as a discipline since the 1950s. In the United States, in particular, it has had a strong pragmatic orientation. Some of its work seems to have been highly successful on many dimensions of human experience, but much still seems to have failed to achieve its full potential and its designers' hopes.

It has become increasingly clear that much of the information used, and being used, as the basis for design was, and is, based on a whole set of prejudices about the world, on casual observation of the environment, on anecdotal information, and on hearsay. There was, and still is, clearly a need for more empirical research on cities, urbanization, and the role of the layout of the world—its architectural and urban design—in human lives. This realization has tangled with the self-image of architects as artists giving expression to their intuitive perceptions of society through urban form.

There is clearly a role for the architect as fine artist in the design of cities and urban places. Some of the most exciting and best-loved places in the world have been created using this mode of considering the world. So have some of the worst. There is, however, a more important role for the architect, certainly as an urban designer, as an applied behavioral scientist. This second role is very much in conflict with the present self-image of architects, partly because it is misunderstood. It was and is often perceived to be the role of social engineer. Indeed architects of the Modern Movement were willing to embrace that role. The results have been less than successful because of the inadequacies of architectural theory in describing and explaining the connections among social intentions, design goals, and design principles. We have learned that the built environment is not simply a stimulus to which people will respond in the way that the designer ordains, although much present architectural ideology still relies on such a view.

One of the failing beliefs of the Modern movement architects was certainly that by changing the physical layout of the world they would cause major changes in the social behavior of the inhabitants of their designs. While more deeply embedded in European Rationalist thinking than in the United States, this belief led architects, often highly politicized, to design models of desired behavior (usually in their own self-image) and then to design buildings, neighborhoods, and cities to achieve this behavior. Their implicit belief was that *function follows form,* an inversion of the slogan *form follows function,* developed for architecture by Gottfried Semper in the nineteenth century.

We realize now that form cannot create function unless there is a strong predisposition of people to behave in the way that the form affords. It is easy to be wise in retrospect. It was easy for Modernists to see correlations between forms and behaviors and to assume a causal link between the two. We know better now. *Form should follow intended function* may well be a useful slogan for urban design today. For it to be so we need to understand the meanings of both *function* and *form* better. Fortunately, the research of the past twenty years helps us achieve externally valid definitions.

A major research field has been developing contemporaneously with the development of urban design. It goes under various names—*environmental psychology, environmental sociology, human-environment studies,* and probably more accurately, *environment and behavior studies.* This contemporaneous development has not been coincidental. Urban design, as an identifiable field, and these areas of study have both been responding to the failings of the Modern movement and Post-Modernism in architecture to come to grips with the nature and lives of people with whom and for whom architects (and other design professionals) were designing. The research has yielded considerable empirical information of direct utility to the work of urban designers. This utility has, however, only partly been exploited because, as yet, no clear method has emerged for making the potential benefits of the research findings effective. The goal of this book is to explore a way of achieving such a method.

During the 1980s, urban design, like many other fields of human endeavor became highly narrowly pragmatic. A major concern was with the financial profitability of proposals—with getting things built and sold (or frequently sold and built). Many urban designers shifted their concerns away from the social and environmental ones of the Modernists because of the political tenor of the times. The field became highly empirical in one way—in response to the marketplace. Urban designs were considered to be simply another commodity. In becoming so market-oriented, not only in action but in *philosophy,* many issues of urban quality were and still are neglected. The assumption that the marketplace is the only and/or the best distributor of resources, and that what can be sold is what should be designed is, given the attitudes presented in this book, unfortunate. What urban design has too frequently lost in its endeavor to be pragmatic is the desire the Modernists possessed to create a better world. This is unfortunate. We need to hang on to the basic goal of the Modernists to create a well-functioning and poetic world. Some urban designers have worked and are still working with these objectives in mind. We can learn from them. We can learn most from those designs that, either by luck or intentionality, have achieved those ends. We need to recognize urban design's full nature and the knowledge required to make it work well. No reductionist philosophy, however attractive, will suffice.

The role of the urban designer in dealing with the social and technological changes taking place in the world (and that will certainly take place in the future) can only be a limited one. It is also an important one. Some of the changes cannot be predicted, but it is clear that the change in the world's population structure, the increasing urbanization of the countries of Africa, Asia, and Latin America, limited resources, and limited political will will result in difficulties in the quest to attain and maintain the quality of life expected by people in the major Western democracies. The profound changes in economic and political structures required to adequately deal with the changes in the world are beyond the immediate scope of concern of the practicing urban designer. Doing urban design well can, nevertheless, make a significant contribution to the achievement of a better world. It can only do so, however, if we substitute knowledge for the personal, often whimsical beliefs many architects have about cities and about people. In striving to do so, we must recognize the essential political nature of city planning, urban design, architecture, and landscape architecture in shaping the future of human settlements.

THE ARGUMENT

This book is an effort to describe and synthesize the work of a number of people concerned with applying the knowledge we have gained about the environment and about people—those for whom we design and ourselves—to the improvement of our efforts to create not only livable, but enjoyable and, where warranted, inspiring built worlds. The book, while striving to present a comprehensive view of urban design in the United States, presents no exhaustive coverage of the subject, but rather develops a framework for asking questions about what it aspires to do and its obligations to individuals and society. It points to the work of others to fill in gaps in the presentation of ideas and methods. As such, this book is a continuation of three earlier efforts of the last twenty years.

The first work resulted from a conference sponsored by a number of institutions in the Philadelphia, Pennsylvania, area and held at the Franklin Institute in 1971. The proceedings of the conference were published by the American Institute of Architects/Philadelphia Chapter under the title *Architecture for Human Behavior* (Charles Burnette, Jon Lang, and David Vachon, editors). It was a time when the architectural profession was searching for a sense of direction. There was much concern with coming to an understanding of the environment and human behavior—a difficult route to travel in the development of architectural and urban design theory. The goal was to help us understand how the environment is experienced and the implications of such an understanding for architectural and urban design. The success of the conference led to the collection of papers being expanded and published in 1974 under the title *Designing for Human Behavior: Architecture and the Behavioral Sciences* (edited by Jon Lang, Charles Burnette, Walter Moleski, and David Vachon, and published by Dowden, Hutchinson, and Ross). The goal of these two endeavors was much more explicitly stated in the third effort, *Creating Architectural Theory: The Role of the Behavioral Sciences in Environmental Design* (Van Nostrand Reinhold, 1987).

Designing for Human Behavior is now regarded as a seminal book, paralleling the work of others, in establishing a more rigorous empiricist approach to design ideology—an approach based on developing and using the knowledge being developed by systematic research—than earlier endeavors. It assumed that the prime goal of design is to enhance and enrich the experience of people who are to inhabit the environment. So the particular concern was with the behavioral sciences. It argued that a paradigmatic shift—a shift in the generally accepted way of modeling problems and solutions—was necessary for architects. This shift had to do with the normative theory, or ideology, of designers and the exemplary forms, or building and urban types, they use in designing. It thus advocated a shift in the constellation of attitudes held by architects.

Creating Architectural Theory is a more mature work because of the recent design research and practice on which it could draw. The reaction to the book has been instructive. Some reviewers stated that every practicing architect should be familiar with it (e.g., Geddes and Dill 1989). Others (e.g., Montgomery 1989; Francescato 1989), while not challenging the premises of the book, simply state that architects have no predisposition to work that way—the effort has no acceptable rewards for them from either their peers or in the marketplace. Their peers are interested in the intellectual aesthetic constructs used and the marketplace in what can be sold easily.

> This paradigm is lost on designers everywhere.
>
> Designers in fact continue to operate on the basis of processes which exclude, by-and-large, the very knowledge, attitudes, and behavior which the paradigm calls for. Perhaps more important, every indication is that they *will continue* to operate in this manner in the foreseeable future (Francescato 1989).

The purpose of this book is, inter alia, to show that this observation is at least partially incorrect and certainly needs to be incorrect especially for the leaders of urban design endeavors—those people establishing new models for the design of the public realm in the public realm. Many designers are moving in an Empiricist direction, and have recognized that much can be learned from both design research and practice that is helpful in designing environments that are psychologically fulfilling for their inhabitants. Indeed the Empiricist tradition is one of long standing in the design professions in the United States.

The urban design endeavor will never be the effortless, intuitive, artistic activity many architects want it to be if it is to create enjoyable worlds for the full spectrum of the population. Many architects would rather reduce their area of concern and continue to operate in a fine arts mode than to tackle tasks that require more than self-expression. Being an artist is an important role in society, and is part of all urban design work, but it should not be the central role for all designers, particularly urban designers, and certainly not the norm. There is a need to distinguish between situations where the artistic mode of thought is appropriate and when urban design as a problem-solving activity serves society best.

ACKNOWLEDGMENTS

There are no original ideas in this book, no original model nor theory. It is a synthesis, in my own terms, of the work of many people. It owes most to my colleagues and students in the Urban Design Program at the University of Pennsylvania, although I suspect they will be disquieted by it. The thoughts of the architects, planners, and landscape architects who teach or taught there during the almost twenty years I spent at Penn have had a great influence on my thinking. Certainly, the intellectual precedents established by the two chairmen of the program whom I succeeded, David Crane and Norman Day, have been important ones. While this book is about urban design in the United States, much of what is said applies to urban design in all democratic societies. Indeed many ideas have criss-crossed the Atlantic Ocean. Many American architects are beguiled by the European experience and have borrowed much from it for good and ill, as this book will show, but they and their international colleagues in looking at the American work need to understand the American experience in its context if the lessons that can be learned from it for future work are to be optimized.

It is neither easy to be comprehensive in one's acknowledgments nor even to recognize the disparate influences on one's thinking. The search for a paradigm for urban design practice and education during the past twenty years parallels the development of the Environmental Design Research Association (EDRA) and the seminal and diverse thinkers who have presented papers at its conferences. Their names parade through this work. The book also reflects the thinking of many other designers who practice in a similar vein. There are many of them.

The major intellectual framework for this book comes from the writings of Abraham Maslow (1943, 1968, 1971, 1987), a humanist psychologist who grappled with models of the human being and human needs. Kevin Lynch as a researcher, theorist, educator, and speculator on the constituents of environmental quality is of fundamental importance in any Empiricist treatise on urban design, as is the work of Christopher Alexander and of Amos Rapoport. Yet there is also the work of many architects, sung and neglected, across the world, who have illuminated the way. They include such well-known figures as Herman Hertzberger, Lucien Kroll, and Balkrishna Doshi, whose work has grown away from that of his mentor, Le Corbusier, in his search for an architecture for India. Less well known architects who are deeply concerned about the quality of the built environment abound outside the spotlight of architectural recognition. Their names crop up in this work too. The focus of attention is not, however, on the creators but on schools of design thought, on completed work and its implications for urban design theory, the basis for practice.

It is easier to identify those who have been directly involved in this work and its antecedents. Charles Burnette was executive director of the American Institute of Architects/Philadelphia chapter and responsible for organizing the Franklin Institute Conference in 1971. Walter Moleski, who has been involved in all the endeavors mentioned above, is executive director of the Environmental Research Group. He puts into everyday practice an Empiricist approach to architectural programming and design. His intellectual and psychological contribution to my work cannot be underestimated. Alix Verge has helped enormously in assembling the illustrations and as a conscientious critic of this work. Jonathan Barnett, Tamas Lukovich, and William Grigsby provided important insights for the improvement of this book. Wendy Lochner, Victoria Craven, and Kelly Francis of Van Nostrand Reinhold provided sound advice and continual support in bringing it to fruition. The illustrations come from many sources as the citations accompanying them and the Credits list at the rear of this book show. Michael Campbell provided invaluable assistance in processing photographs.

It is inevitable that one is influenced by one's own experiences. My life in three major multiethnic, multicultural, and in two cases, multilingual societies has indicated the absurdity of ethnocentric and egocentric approaches to the creation of a design theory. India, South Africa, and the United States have each had, and are having, difficulties in coming to terms with their diversities. The architectural profession has hardly tried.

Inevitably one is influenced by one's own formal education. Educators such as Gilbert Herbert and Wilfred Mallows (author of *Teaching a Technology*, University of Witwatersrand Press, 1972) in Johannesburg and Michael Hugo Brunt, Stewart Stein, Barclay Jones, and James J. Gibson at Cornell University suggested ways of considering the environment, the way we perceive it and the way we design it, that came at opportune times. Colin Rowe's enthusiasm for urban design at Cornell was contagious, although this book represents a very different way of looking at the world than his. Perhaps, however, in the long run, it has been my colleagues when I was a student at Witwatersrand and at Cornell, the students at Penn and Drexel in Philadelphia, and now at the University of New South Wales in Sydney who have been the most demanding critics and, without knowing it, teachers. The intellectual framework for this book was first considered explicitly by a number of them: Mark Cordray (1974), Bruce Swalwell (1976), Nigel Lewis (1977), Jitendra Pathak (1980), and Ann Weiler (1988), among others. Some former students have evolved into professional colleagues and friends. In particular, the friendship, intellectual support, and criticism of George Claflen, professor and formerly head of the School of Architecture at Temple University, has to be acknowledged.

Many people have gone out of their way to show me new worlds. Much of my knowledge of Chicago and the Midwest comes from explorations with Kathy A. Kolnick, of Berlin with Dr. Cornelia Thiels, and Sydney with Alix Verge. The people who have gone out of their way to open my eyes to the relationship of culture to design in India, Brazil, and Continental Europe are too numerous to mention. Their patience with my slowness to comprehend many things goes well beyond reasonable expectations. Paul Reid and my colleagues at the University of New South Wales have provided me with important insights into the nature of Australian cities and thus, inevitably, into the American experience.

Ultimately, one has to recognize the contribution of the Modern Masters, through their writings and work, to the line of thought displayed here even though they would probably be appalled by it. The leaders of the Constructivist and Rationalists movements of Soviet architecture after the Revolution sought a clear Empiricist basis for design. The masters of the Bauhaus, whose thinking was deeply embedded in the Rationalist intellectual tradition, nevertheless intuitively felt such a need, but were unable to implement it. The line of thinking displayed in this book has indeed been dismissed as "the last kick of the Bauhaus." Le Corbusier, surely the architectural giant of the twentieth century, tried to make man the measure of all things. If we cannot do better now, this effort has been in vain.

INTRODUCTION

Pennsylvania Avenue, Washington, DC

The objective of this book is to describe what we have learned from the American experience in urban design. The concern is with urban design both as a product and as a process of communal decision-making. The book contains few detailed descriptions of recent work. Rather, it attempts to come to an understanding of the attitudes underlying these works and, based on (1) the observations and empirical research of the last three decades, and (2) the political positions being taken by a number of urban designers, to present an argument for an Empiricist, or Neo-Modernist, approach to design.

While the concern is with both projects and research developments in the United States, the American experience cannot be understood in isolation from work elsewhere. Throughout this century American attitudes toward urban design have been highly influenced by the nature of European cities, urban designs, and architectural ideals and continue to be so. Indeed, the transfer of generic solutions to urban design problems back and forth across the Atlantic has been a hallmark of the century in much the same manner as for architecture (Senkevitch 1974). More recently, lessons are also being learned from cross-cultural research studies of people and their built environments in Asia, Latin America, and Africa. The observations in this book are thus biased by a set of attitudes toward what has been achieved in urban design and by the studies of the meanings of urban design accomplishments in their users' terms.

The objective of this Introduction is to portray the world view that permeates the book and gives the text its structure. The Introduction begins with a brief commentary (which is further developed in Chapter 2) on the forming of cities and concludes with a description and explanation of the outline of the book. In between is an introduction to the two streams of thought that have guided urban design during the twentieth century: Rationalism and Empiricism.

URBAN DESIGN

From the beginning of time, the building of human settlements has been guided by norms of behavior—rules for how paths of movement and communal spaces should be organized and how one building, and the purposes it serves, should relate to others. Sometimes these rules have been explicitly stated but at other times they have simply been understood, and used by the people involved for fear of ostracism. While much city growth has been piecemeal and apparently uncoordinated, it has always been governed by sets of laws and by the nature of the real estate market. Sometimes the laws have been sufficient to guide individual actions into achieving a desirable environment, but often they have been wanting.

All kinds of people are involved in making decisions about the way cities should be built and in actually constructing them: politicians, lawyers, developers, sanitation engineers, architects, planners, individual businesspeople, householders. Each group sees the built environment in terms of its own attitudes, costs, and benefits but also in terms of its perceptions of the nature of the public interest. Although there has been much that has been meritorious about this piecemeal, largely uncoordinated approach, much has also been lost by it. Individual autonomy in making decisions has been positive in many ways, but the loss to the community has also been substantial. Urban design constantly involves making decisions about individual and communal rights.

The power to make decisions about city form, indeed the whole quality of life of people, is unevenly distributed. Those people in control of resources have the major impact in shaping the future. In capitalist countries, the marketplace rules and the wealthy have a disproportionate power in deciding, largely in terms of their own self-interests, where and how development takes place. The political structure of democracies is designed to place limits on the use of economic power in making decisions about the future social, economic, and physical order of places.

The public sector plays a major role in shaping the city, for much of the urban area is in public ownership. The way municipal governments invest capital resources provides a frame—"a capital web" (Crane 1960)—within which individuals build the "invisible web" of a society's laws (Lai 1988). Urban designers can provide leadership in the intellectual debate about the design of human settlements by proposing interventions in the marketplace and legislative process, by providing ideas, by suggesting potential futures and the policies and procedures to achieve them, as well as in the more familiar role of designing well for the power elite. Urban designers' abilities to do these tasks well will depend on their understanding of people, the multidimensionality of environmental experience, and the processes of decision-making.

The physical city exists in three spatial dimensions but it changes and is changed over time. It thus exists in four dimensions. The necessity for society to have urban design as a professional activity depends on the potential benefits yielded by the coordinated development of the four-dimensional nature of cities, suburbs, neighborhoods, and building complexes—a rethinking of desired ends and the rules for accomplishing them. This coordination can take place in two ways: (1) by setting the design policies and guidelines for such developments, allowing other people to make their own design decisions within them, or (2) by having one set of hands in control of the whole design and development process. In the former case urban design is closer to city planning and in the latter case closer to architecture.

A variety of laws to promote the public welfare and to shape the cities of democratic countries already exists.

Building codes influence the nature of buildings: land-use planning and the use of zoning laws are formal mechanisms for ordering the growth and change of cities in the public interest (Lai 1988; Schultz 1989). They are powerful mechanisms, especially when there is a clear coordination between land use and transportation planning. Few major cities are without a zoning ordinance. Houston, Texas (at the time of writing), is one of them. There the perception is that individuals' rights to do what they want are more important than environmental quality on many dimensions of environmental experience. Even Houston, however, is guided by much planning, in particular in dealing with the major traffic and flooding problems with which it has to cope. We can learn from Houston about the utility and costs of uncoordinated intervention into economically determined city growth patterns (Ghirado 1987).

Traditional land-use planning and zoning ordinances have focused on the creation of a salubrious environment, a logical distribution of land uses (in somebody's terms), and an efficient circulation pattern. They deal primarily with the biological nature of the human being and, occasionally, other animals. Within this framework, developers and architects deal with the design of individual buildings guided by their perceptions of what can be sold or, more likely, by perceptions of whether what they are used to creating can be sold, and by architectural fashions. Much of the richness of cities has resulted from such patterns of development. Where architectural ideas have intervened at a larger scale than the single building, the resulting environments have tended to be very dull because of the emphasis given by architects to the creation of a geometric order illustrating an architectural idea in their designs.

While some attention has been paid to land uses in a city, surprisingly little thought has been given to what makes a good third dimension for cities beyond what are, in most instances, somewhat capricious height and setback regulations of buildings (Attoe 1981). These regulations are capricious since they are based, not on any empirical finding, but on the aesthetic prejudices that exist at a particular time and beliefs about the nature and utility of sunlight. Indeed, building height regulations tend to be easily changed, or disregarded, in response to economic demands except in those places where there is a clear reason for their existence (e.g., San Francisco's height restrictions to avoid the shadowing of specific public places). What is missing in present processes is a concern with the overall urban environment and the purposes it serves for diverse sets of people with needs that change over time. The recognition of this need for a concern with the four-dimensional qualities of the urban environment and what they afford people has led to the development of urban design as a professional field and, increasingly, as a discipline in its own right. Indeed, one of the ques-

tions raised in this book concerns the degree of autonomy urban design should have as a profession in its own right.

Despite its American initiation in the late 1950s as an identifiable area of professional activity and study, twenty years later most architects and city planners in the United States were still asking, "What is urban design?" They also requested, "Show me an urban design scheme." This question and this demand were not surprising as there had been very little built that had formally been called urban design. Projects were seen as large-scale architecture, city planning, and/or possibly, landscape architecture. This situation has changed considerably since 1970.

Urban design is now a recognized area of professional concern born out of the perception that a set of good buildings by major architects can, in themselves, make neither a good city nor a good urban place. Columbus, Indiana, probably has the largest number of buildings by major architects per capita anywhere (Pearson 1990). They are strung together visually, if not behaviorally, by the work of well-known landscape architects. Columbus is a pleasant city, but there still is, as the city now recognizes, an opportunity lost in its development largely because the nature of its streets as a fundamental component of urban design and urban quality was forgotten. The field of urban design was born out of the necessity to recognize the interrelatedness of a city's components, particularly those that constitute the public realm. Urban design was also born out of the recognition that however well land uses are distributed, they will not, by themselves, lead to a good city. Most of all it was born out of the recognition that the sterile urban environments achieved by applying the ideas of the Modern movement to both policymaking and to architectural design at the urban scale were a failure in terms of the lives of the people who inhabited them even though such places might be highly photogenic (when uninhabited) at particular times of day and in particular lights (Jacobs 1961; Brolin 1976; Blake 1977; Huet 1984).

By mid-century there was a need to rethink the whole nature of the architectural and the de facto urban design enterprise. Similarly, city planning and landscape architecture have reconsidered their foci of interest. The result has been the fragmentation of the concerns of the professions originally concerned with the design of cities. Urban design has emerged, largely by default, as a field to fill a professional need. It now has an established history and set of works. It is appropriate to ask what has been achieved by the explicit urban design endeavor of the last forty years and to set a direction for its future as a distinct activity.

The situation is a dynamic one. As an intellectual field of enquiry and as a design activity, urban design is secure. As an emerging profession, much depends on how the traditional design fields develop and on what they focus their professional attentions. Their concerns, in turn, are and will be closely allied to the interests of people and societies increasingly well educated about the nature of the environment and the nature of cities and probably less tolerant of the personal whimsies of individual designers.

THE DEVELOPMENT OF ARCHITECTURAL THEORY

Urban design has traditionally been a specialization within architecture. As such it has both led and been buffeted by shifts in the focus of architecture as a discipline primarily but also architecture as a profession. During the past twenty years, architectural thought has undergone much change. Yet underlying attitudes have remained amazingly consistent. The monotony of Modernism has given way to Post-Modernism (Portoghesi 1979; Bruegmann 1981; Klotz 1988) and more recently to Deconstructionism (Johnson and Wigley 1988; Norris 1988; Betsky 1990) and, possibly, even more recently to a *Weak* or, rather, a *Discrete Architecture* movement (De Solà Morales 1989; P. Buchanan 1990). Strangely lost in the theoretical/ideological debate among the intellectual leaders of the architectural discipline has been a concern with making a more livable, pleasing environment a central issue in design—a concern with how the world is experienced. Rather there has been a set of explorations of various rules for generating form without a clear evaluation of the purpose these rules serve or the results attained by using them.

The concern among leading architectural ideologists today has been with developing analogs of architecture, solving problems in the analogical world, and then applying the results to architecture. This approach has become the subject of debate not because the various analogs may differ in their utility for creating good design, but rather because the aesthetics of the analog have become the main consideration in design (see also Lavin 1990). Not only have the means for generating form justified the forms but the means have become the ends in themselves. Architectural theorists are jockeying to control the intellectual market rather than to improve the quality of the built environment.

Some of the designs generated by these new attitudes and methods have been fascinating, not because of the rules that generated them (except to other professionals) but rather because of experiences they offer and the way they are experienced by the people who use them when they are built. It would be misleading to think that the intellectual construct itself was the cause of the success. The Parc de la Villette in Paris will be a success or failure (except to other designers) based on the experiences it offers, not because of the intellectual cleverness of its geometric systems or its intellectural basis in the work of Jacques Derrida as argued by Bernard Tschumi, its designer (see Norris 1988 and Tschumi, 1988b, 1990). It will succeed or fail because of what these systems offer in terms of experiences. The nature of the human experience of the built environment within different cultural systems needs to be understood as the basis for urban design. The role of analogs in design thinking is also a topic of concern within design methodology. The beauty of the analog per se is of interest only to a few cognoscenti.

Much of the intellectual debate of the past twenty years has bypassed the architectural practitioner. The mainstream of the architectural profession is still concerned with the basic job of designing buildings. Much of an architect's work is certainly good enough for its purpose. The prime consideration has been with solving the circulation problem (a concern with function in its narrowest sense), applying a façade (now often with historical referents), and solving technical problems of air circulation and structure within the budget available. Inherited from the Modern Movement are certain attitudes toward spatial design. Synthesizing these needs into a coordinated whole has been and is becoming an increasingly complex task. Thus the focus of much recent architectural work has been on the individual building. That is enough for most practitioners to worry about. In contrast, urban design, by its very nature, is a public enterprise carried out in the political realm. Urban design might well be regarded as the public interest component of the architecture and also landscape architecture professions.

If a set of buildings built according to any contemporary analog automatically results in a good overall environment, not in terms of literary allusions, but in terms of everyday life, then the urban design theory as developed in this book would be unnecessary. Such a success has not been achieved, nor does it seem to be the case with other architectural theories taken into the realm of urban design. The mainstream of architects today still think about urban design largely in the Rationalist mode, with its focus on a rational world and a rational geometry. All urban designs do have a geometry, but as laypeople as well as those committed to the study of the quality of the city and of urban life know, the pure Rationalist view has been a foolishly limited one.

RATIONALISM AND EMPIRICISM IN URBAN DESIGN

Geoffrey Broadbent (1990) has identified a number of recent ideas about urban design, which he appropriately labels *Emerging Concepts in Urban Space Design*. He divides them into two groups reflecting two ways of thinking about and designing the future: Neo-Rationalism and Neo-Empiricism. The concern of the former group is principally with a well, and simply, ordered social world and "an architecture of abstract geometric purity." Neo-Rationalist work in the United States draws its inspiration largely from Continental Europe, where it is a continuation of the line of thought of French eighteenth-century Rationalists such as Laugier, Ledoux, and Boullée. In political terms they have drawn their inspiration from the marxist philosophy advocating communal living. The

1. Suburban Housing, Sedgwick County, Kansas

2. Crown Hall, Illinois Institute of Technology, Chicago

3. Beth Shalom Synagogue, Elkins Park, Pennsylvania

4. Swan Hotel, Disneyworld, Florida

5. Wexner Center, Ohio State University, Columbus

6. Battery Park City, New York

Figure I-1: Five Twentieth-Century Architectural Movements
While most building in the United States during the twentieth century has been in a vernacular, or neocolonial, style (1), three clearly identifiable attitudes associated with the architectural profession are represented in Modernism: Empiricism (2) and Rationalism (3), Post-Modernism (4), and Deconstructionism (5). Each approach has allied subapproaches, which makes the distinction here a simplistic one but it does represent three major professional attitudes toward people and the world. Better still to look at architecture within the two major intellectual streams represented by *Rationalist* and *Empiricist* thinking. Crown Hall at Illinois Institute of Technology designed by Mies van der Rohe in the 1940s clearly falls into the Rationalism stream with its concern with designing a new world based on idealized models of people and society and with orthogonal geometry. Empiricism drew more heavily from ancient (often exotic) types, past experiences, and models of nature, as in the Beth Shalom Synagogue (3) designed by Frank Lloyd Wright. Post-Modernism, as in the Swan Hotel (4) designed by Michael Graves, and Deconstructionism, as represented in the Wexner Center designed by Peter Eisenman (5), reject Modernism but only at a superficial level. Perhaps a more *Discrete Architecture* is also beginning to appear. Often it is in association with urban design projects (6).

Neo-Rationalists, such as the Tendenza movement in Italy (see Rossi 1982), have been much more highly politically motivated than their counterparts in the United States, and are indeed much concerned with the quality of life of people in their designs, but it is the architect's image of what other people's lives should be, not that of the people involved. The problem has been that these images have been and still are highly reductionist ones. The Neo-Rationalists are dealing with abstract people as much as abstract geometry (Wood, Brower, and Latimer 1966; Stringer 1980; Ellis and Cuff 1989). To the extent these abstract models of people coincide with the people they are considering in design, architects' design ideas are, given the values underpinning this book, legitimate. When the models of people and human needs deviate too much from reality, designs built according to them suffer if evaluated in their users' terms even though their pure geometry of built forms may appeal to designers.

The arguments in this book come out of the Empiricist tradition but they are neither necessarily for nor against the Picturesque design ideologies of the past (e.g., Sitte 1889; Unwin 1909; and Cullen 1961) or the recent work of the Neo-Traditionalists (e.g., Krier 1987 and Duany 1989; see also Handy 1991). Rather they come out of the study of urban realities—of how the environment works and the desires of the people involved. They stand for a user-oriented approach to design—a position most Modernists, both Rationalists and Empiricists, claimed as their own.

Understanding what urban patterns exist, the human purposes they serve, and why they are the way they are does not, however, tell us what to do in the future. *Design is an act of will guided by a set of attitudes.* Any definition of the appropriate attitudes for designers to take is political in nature and based on some world view. The description and explanation of a set of attitudes held by a number of urban designers today are also a fundamental component of this book. The discussion in the book raises many complex questions about the nature of urban design, what urban designers have done and are doing, about the attitudes toward the world urban designers should take, and what the knowledge required as a base for urban design action should be (see also Dalton 1989 and Moudon 1992). The goal is to learn from both our intentions and our actions, from the work of the empirical sciences and quasi-sciences on human needs, how they might be satisfied, inhibited, or supported in and/or through built form. To understand the importance of this aim one has to understand the nature of the environment, how the twentieth-century city has developed, and the successes and failures of the Modern movement in shaping it.

THE MODERN MOVEMENT'S CONCERN WITH URBAN DESIGN

The Modern movement's theories about urban design (i.e., rules/principles for designing cities and their precincts) subsume diverse sets of ideas about what makes a good life and a good environment. During the heyday of the movement, architects, whatever their ideological positions, were generally very much concerned with the city and with creating a better world. They were united in their antipathy to the industrial city—the "Coketowns" described by Charles Dickens—and the living conditions of most workers (Engels 1892; Mumford 1961). They were divided into two main overlapping groups of people: the Decentralists (also known as the Anglo-Americans) and the Centralists (the Continentals). The lines of thinking of each were deeply embedded in their own cultural and intellectual heritages, the former being Empiricist and the latter Rationalist. The first group consisted of those reformers, many not architects, who looked at existing life and found, given their values, the imagined small-town community in a rustic setting or the intricacies of the medieval city to be their models for the future. The second group, who were largely architects, looked to an imagined airy, sunny, highly technological, socialist metropolis for a frame of reference. The goal of the former was to create a picturesque but lively world. The goal of the latter was to create a city in a garden—a city that was a work of art that functioned well, both socially and economically, and used advanced technological means to solve the problems of the industrial city (Sert and C.I.A.M. 1944; Le Corbusier 1973).

It is in the area of housing that the new building and urban types suggested by the two major streams of the Modern movement have had their most clearly separate identities and impacts. The neighborhood unit plan of Clarence Perry, as implemented by Clarence Stein and Henry Wright in Radburn (Stein 1957; see also Fig. 2-8), and the Unité d'habitation of Le Corbusier (Le Corbusier 1953; see also Fig. 2-11), as implemented in Marseilles, might be regarded as the two polar opposite attitudes toward the city. There are other models, such as those proposed by Ludwig Hilbersheimer (Pommer, Spaeth, and Harrington 1988), Bruno Taut, and the Bauhaus (Wingler 1969), that have also been part of the architect's palate during this century (see Sherwood 1978), but Radburn and the Unité (or in the United States, the housing projects of the 1950s) represent the two opposite attitudes toward the future city, even though the problems of the industrial city as perceived by their designers were essentially the same. In their original contexts, both models have worked well for their inhabitants (see Lansing, Marans, and Zehner 1970 on Radburn; Avin 1973 on the Unité), but the adaptations less so.

Regarding the two schools of thought, Empiricism and Rationalism, as Anglo-American and Continental is misleading because the ideas that were propagated from the two lines of thought have been implemented in many places in the world. There is much in the United States and the United Kingdom that comes out of the Rationalist approach to design (e.g., Illinois Institute of Technology in Chicago, the Seagram Building and, perhaps less successfully, Lincoln Center in New York City; and certainly more unfortunately, the South Side of Chicago, Pruitt Igoe in St. Louis, and Roehampton and Thamesmead in London). Much Continental suburban development comes out of the Garden City mold (e.g., much of the housing development in the Scandinavian new towns of the 1950s), and there have been efforts to replicate the intricacies of the medieval city in many places, particularly in Europe (e.g., Port Grimaud in France). The dreams about future possibilities and the design principles of the two lines of thought have frequently been intermingled in practice, although pure types abound. These dreams and their architectural manifestations have fired the imagination of many people throughout the world. They have shaped the thoughts of not only architects but also politicians, property developers, and civic groups about how the built environment should be organized so that it enhances the quality of life of its inhabitants.

Without doubt the living conditions for almost all of us in the so-called developed world are better than for our grandparents. There are many reasons for this improvement. The whole social and political nature of our world has gone through a radical transformation during the twentieth century. Combined with technological developments, these changes have brought a lifestyle to masses of people that only the wealthy could previously afford (Banham 1960). To what extent have the ideas of the architects of the Modern movements contributed to this better world?

If one looks at cities and their suburbs around the world today the impact of one or another school of the Modern movement's design ideologies is clear, if fragmentary. The corporate headquarters building, high-income apartment buildings set in fields of green, the social (public) housing developments of similar pattern, and many urban renewal developments all show elements of the Rationalist thinking about how urban places should be built and/or redeveloped. The suburban superblock of houses centered on a school or shops shows the influence of the Empiricist school, as do the newly created quasi-Italian plazas of city centers. Perhaps, the impact of

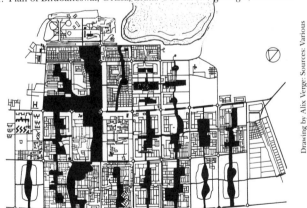

1. Plan of Bhubaneswar, Orissa, India. Otto Koeningsberger, Architect

Sketched from the original plan, Public Works Department, State of Orissa

2. The Secretariat, Bhubaneswar. Julius Vaz, Architect

Photograph by Sanotosh Kumar Misra

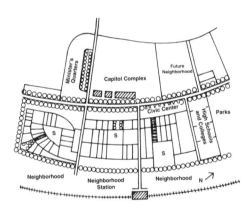

3. Plan of Chandigarh, Punjab, India. Le Corbusier and Others, Architects

Drawing by Alix Verge: Sources: Various

4. The Capitol Complex, Chandigarh, Punjab, India. Le Corbusier, Architect

Figure I-2: Bhubaneswar and Chandigarh
Two new state capitals were necessitated by the reorganization of state boundaries in India during the period immediately before and after Independence. Bhubaneswar (c. 1949), the earliest, was built within the *Empiricist* tradition with the architecture containing many referents to historic architectural styles, partic-

ularly Buddhist. The plan of Chandigarh (1952) is similar, being based on a neighborhood framework, but the neighborhoods (zones) are much larger and have been "rationalized" into an orthogonal geometry. Its architecture is Progressive with little relationship, except coincidentally, to India.

1. Rockefeller Center, New York

2. Penn Center, Philadelphia

Figure I-3: Rockefeller Center and Penn Center
Rockefeller Center, designed in the 1930s to fulfill very clear purposes and largely under the control of a single design team and land ownership pattern, has become the heart of midtown Manhattan, New York (1). Its design was based on a careful interweaving of its elements and its context. Penn Center in Philadelphia was built from the late 1950s onwards. It was designed to be and has been a catalyst for change around it. Its fragmented nature shows that it had to contend with many land ownership patterns (2). The lack of cooperation between many competing interests led to the loss of many opportunities for creating a better design.

both schools has been clearest of all in the new towns built in the post–World War II era across the world.

No census of new towns built since 1945 is available. The number is certainly vast, although there are relatively few in the United States in comparison to many other countries. They include the towns built as a direct result of government interventions in the economy through the policies for the redistribution of industries and/or housing, as well as privately financed developments. The new industrial cities and company towns of countries such as India and the former Soviet Union, the new suburban towns of upstate New York, and the settlements/towns/cities that have resulted from the new towns' policies of many of the countries in Western Europe are all examples. The new towns include a number of new government capitals— Abuja, Bhubaneswar, Brasilia, Chandigarh, Dacca, Islamabad, Gandhinagar—as the demise of colonial empires has occurred and as countries, states, or provinces try to establish their own identities. In the United States there have been thoughts and designs for a new capital that might serve Alaska better than Juneau does.

Two contemporary state capitals of newly independent India exemplify the two strands of Modernist thinking about the city perhaps better than any American or European examples (see Fig. I-2). Bhubaneswar (1949), the new capital for Orissa (Otto Koeningsberger, planner; Julius Vaz, architect), follows Garden City design principles (Vaz 1954; Koeningsberger 1960), while Chandigarh (1952), the capital of Punjab and later of both Punjab and Hariyana (Le Corbusier, architect), follows the Rationalist principles (Evenson 1973; Nilsson 1975; Riboulet 1985). Of these two, Chandigarh, more a work of fine art, is considerably better known, although, rightly or wrongly, Bhubaneswar has the reputation of being the more livable of the two (Katju 1953). However, Indian conditions had little impact on the design of either (see Evenson 1966 and Nilsson 1975 on Chandigarh and Rapoport 1977 on Bhubaneswar). Chandigarh has certainly been the more influential—Gandhinagar (1964), the new capital of Gujarat in India, is its direct descendent. Perhaps more than Chandigarh, Brasilia (Lucio Costa and Oscar Niemeyer, architects) is the exemplar of the Rationalist school of Modernist thinking (Stäubli 1966; Evenson 1973; Gallion and Eisner 1986; Mansfield 1990). It is celebrated as a symbol for Brazil, a work of art (Bacon 1974), although many questions have been asked about its performance on all the other dimensions of human experience (Holston 1989).

Most, if not all, the cities of the world have had major urban renewal projects to meet the changing demands for services required by growing and changing populations and/or changes in their industrial bases. The centers of American cities have been radically transformed, although the streets' patterns endure. Many new building complexes were required to reconstruct the cities of Europe and Japan devastated by bombing during World War II;

many new developments have been built on sites abandoned by owners as the result of the technological obsolescence of their endeavors; and many were due to the changing value of land and rent structures of cities. They have been built in the hearts of American cities, in abandoned railway yards and dockyards, and in the "downtowns" of suburbia (see Fig. 3–2). Much is on the drawing boards or in the process of being built today despite recent economic downturns. Most are based on adaptations by the Rationalist school of the Modern movement's philosophies, for they are dealing with the design of high-density commercial environments, something the Empiricists seldom tackled. Often they are based on economic deterministic thinking—the urban design of fiscal pragmatism.

Some of these new towns, urban renewal projects, and suburban developments built during the course of this century have been highly successful and much loved (e.g., Rockefeller Center, New York). Many have shown the difficulty of achieving environments that are successful both as symbols and as places in which to work and/or live (e.g., La Defense in Paris, the capitol complex in Chandigarh). Others work well enough, but the overall quality achieved was not what the designers had hoped (e.g., Penn Center in Philadelphia). Some design ideas have worked well in some places but not in others because the determinants of success and failure were not intuitively obvious to planners and architects (e.g., the downtown pedestrian malls of cities and suburbs of the United States; see Fig. 20–1). Other designs have proven to be uninhabitable, particularly those based on Rationalist thinking, even though the arguments for them are internally logical and intuitively appealing (Newman 1972; Marmot 1982).

Bold though many of these ventures have been, it is clear that there have been many opportunity costs involved even in the most successful of them; other designs would have worked better. In some cases, taking no concerted action would have been better than the results of carefully orchestrated urban designs. There has indeed been extraordinarily harsh criticism of the Modern movements' endeavors in almost every sphere of architectural design other than custom houses (e.g., J. Jacobs 1961; Kaplan 1973; Brolin 1974; Blake 1977; Wolfe 1981; and Holston 1989). It has been especially harsh in dealing with the impact of the Rationalists' ideas on the city. By the early 1960s, in the face of the criticism, architecture, both as a discipline and a profession, by and large withdrew from dealing with the city to the relative safety of designing individual buildings and the contemplation of new aesthetic ideologies drawing heavily, most recently, on linguistic analogies. The city planning profession, recognizing that thinking deterministically about the impact of the built world on social behavior was foolhardy, became more concerned with social and economic planning than with physical planning. This change in focus of attention

is especially true in academia in the United States. The concern with the physical environment and the design of the public realm has persisted as a professional concern in the United States, but much more strongly in other countries.

If architecture has turned toward the fine arts and critical theory and intuition for its intellectual base, city planning, in contrast, has tried to turn itself into a quasi-science focusing on specific problems: economic development, drug rehabilitation, homeless people. These problems are really symptoms of a deeper malaise that many societies have to confront and are extraordinarily "wicked" (Bazjanac 1974). In attempting to deal with them, city planning's traditional focus on the built environment and on the future, while not completely lost, has been largely dormant in the United States.

Yet populations have continued to expand; there has been a continued investment in infrastructure, suburban development has continued, urban renewal has gone ahead, new towns continue to be built. Some architects and planners are, indeed, concerned about the nature of the physical city, town, or suburb even though the focus of concern of their disciplines has shifted. Although it can be argued that it should not have happened, urban design as a new field of study and professional application has steadily developed over the last thirty years. The field is not unified and it goes under various names in different parts of the world. In this book, I have simply adopted *urban design* because the name is the most widely used in the English-speaking world today.

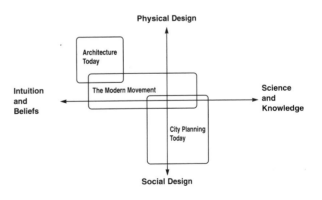

Figure I–4: The Domains of Urban Concern of Architecture and City Planning Today

LEARNING FROM THE AMERICAN URBAN DESIGN EXPERIENCE

There has been much questioning about how best the effort to make better human habitations and/or to preserve the good qualities of existing ones should proceed. During the 1970s and 1980s a number of architects (see Broadbent 1990) and others (e.g., Dantzig and Saaty 1973) developed hypothetical, or exploratory, schemes for the future city. There has also been much highly pragmatic urban design work closely tied into the property development process in the United States and other capitalist societies in contrast to many schemes closely tied into the formal political structure in societies, such as those of Scandinavia, France, and India, which have stronger centralized governments.

There are many streams of thinking about urban design today, and urban design pulls together many lines of thought (Scott Brown 1982, 1990). This book is largely about the current Empiricist stream in the United States, which can be distinguished from other contemporary efforts and from its predecessors by its self-conscious concern about its knowledge base—both substantive and procedural. It is part of a broader attempt to shift urban designers' modus operandi from one relying on personal intuitions, experiences, particularly those of childhood, and preferences as its theoretical base to one based on "verified" knowledge. This effort denies neither the art in science nor the science in art, nor does it deny its heritage in the failing Empiricist thought of the first decades of this century.

All design decisions are based on or imply some assertions about reality—about the world and how it functions, some *positive* theoretical base and attitudes about what is good and bad. In urban design a whole set of issues arises involving the tradeoffs between the achievement of competing goals, between the needs and desires of one group of people and those of another. These issues are *substantive*, dealing with the product of design, and/or *procedural*, dealing with the process by which designs are brought about—the obligations of designers and the rights of the various parties involved, directly or indirectly, in the design process.

There are many *normative* theories, or design ideologies, illustrating the aspirations of urban designers (see, e.g., the positions of Le Corbusier 1934; Sert and C.I.A.M. 1943; Koolhaas 1978; "Charter of Machu Picchu" 1979; Huet 1984; Alexander et al. 1987; King et al. 1989; and Preiser et al. 1991; see also Chapters 2, 3, and 23 of this book). Most of these statements are concerned with the nature of good environments but some focus on the urban design process. Their natures depend on both the sociopolitical stance of their proponents and the society of which they are a part.

An Empiricist approach to urban design implies a set of attitudes toward the design process and the way the information base (the positive theoretical base) for making design decisions is established. It relies on specific procedures for establishing the goals that a design has to fulfill and the substantive knowledge to design the principles to meet them. The designed product results from the goals and the procedures used to achieve them rather than on the preconceived application of typological solutions. What is described in this book is a Neo-Modernist approach to design. As a label "Neo-Modernist" makes as much etymological sense as "Post-Modernist." "Humanist" might be another label, but most design theorists/ideologists would argue that their work is Humanist (Watkin 1977).

THE ADVOCACY DESCRIBED IN THIS BOOK

Can a broader approach to urban design than that advocated by the Rationalists and Empiricists and the mainstream of their intellectual descendants be established? There appear to be a number of existing possibilities. Will they capture the attention of architects whose psychological rewards come largely from the idiosyncratic designs of major public and private buildings and not from, in their minds, the frequently more mundane architecture that makes good cities (Rybczynski 1990)? The advocacy in this book is for a neofunctional approach to design in which the concept of function is broadened to encompass the whole set of human needs identified by Abraham Maslow (1987).

Urban design has to be seen within a cultural frame. In the United States, the design process has to be seen within and as one of the decision-making processes of a competitive, multijurisdictional, capitalist, and participatory democracy. Although much can be learned from the experience elsewhere, American urban designers need to get away from a Eurocentric view of what constitutes a good city, urban place, or suburb in much the same way that urban designers of many other countries need to get away from an Americentric view of urban design. This need is particularly important in a profession that relies heavily on generic solutions, types, and precedents as a basis for design. One can learn much from the study of types, as will be noted in this book, but they must be seen in terms of the problems they address within specific cultural contexts.

Implicit in these positions is the need to shift from a paradigmatic to a programmatic approach to design (see also C. Rowe 1983 and Lang 1985). Types, or paradigms, are important and can and should be applied to solve design problems where appropriate, but they are frequently so adapted for economic reasons to be antiutilitarian (Marmot 1982). The need is to adopt a problem-solving approach to design made possible by the developments in both substantive and procedural knowledge that have resulted from the empirical research of the past three decades.

The argument described in this book for an Empiricist stance is a pragmatic one. Many architects fear that the adoption of such an approach will mean that all designs will be in the same style. This observation is nonsense. Design situations differ and the core of an Empiricist approach is to respond to the situation at hand. Each designer working within this mode of thought and practice will have his or her own predilections. Sometimes that is what is sought by clients. All design situations leave room for something of their designers themselves—designers' own particular styles; a place for the designers to get, as Steven Izenour says, "their own jollies." These styles of design and designing imply different *approaches* to design within an overall understanding of design methodology. These different approaches may result in very different designs, each of which works well. This conclusion is not surprising. For people to be able to act successfully in the everyday world their responses are generalized to a range of social situations and environmental patterns. So, too, many different designs may solve essentially the same design problem. The need is simply to address the problem at hand.

Few living cities are static for long. Urban designers must recognize the changing nature of cities; some are growing economically, others declining, and still others are simply changing their character. Urban designers must recognize that they are working on behalf of the public interest even though the nature of the public interest is difficult to define with precision. Their task will often be to seek discrete, ambiguous settings for the behavioral and aesthetic demands of diverse populations. Sometimes it will indeed be to seek bold architectural solutions. Above all, urban designers have to recognize that their work will evolve over time and must be robust enough to handle unexpected future changes.

Urban design does not occur in a vacuum. While its professional purpose is to change the built environment where it is deemed necessary to serve primarily human ends better, it also exists within a broader environment. The environment of people consists of a complex interrelationship of natural and cultural phenomena and processes of which the built environment is an ever-evolving part and product. Urban design today is an evolving field based on a set of attitudes whose antecedents can be traced back to reactions to the Industrial Revolution. Much has been written on the failure of the Modern movement to address human needs, although its stated goal was to do so. These failures certainly need to be recognized but there is a danger of throwing the baby out with the bathwater. We have learned much from the failures but we can also learn much from the successes. An Empiricist approach to urban design uses the ideologies of the Modern movement as a point of departure in exploring what should be done in the future. The explication and analysis of the implications of this statement is the fundamental focus of this book.

THE GROWTH OF THE SCIENCES AND URBAN DESIGN

There has been an exponential growth in knowledge during the course of the twentieth century even though there is much that remains unknown. There is a tendency for architects to overestimate the quality of their intuitive knowledge, believing what they want also to be what other people want (Michelson 1968). They underestimate the impact of their world views and experience on what they perceive (or rather, what they pay attention to) and thus on what they know. A fetish is still made of intuition by many designers, as Christopher Alexander (1964) recognized almost thirty years ago. Intuition has an important role in designing, but an unwillingness to recognize the depth of scientific and quasi-scientific knowledge available to the designer serves neither the profession nor society well. Sound intuitions are based on a sound background of knowledge.

There have been major developments in every branch of technology associated with buildings from structural systems to comfort systems. Most designers are willing to recognize this growth in knowledge. The design of these systems, as they have become more complex, is now usually under the guidance of professionals other than architects. Structural engineers and other specialists have taken over many aspects of building design. The design of the infrastructure of cities is in many hands and often needs much better coordination than achieved at present. The apparently highly advanced technological urban designs proposed by many architects and engineers (see, e.g., Dahinden 1972; Sky and Stone 1976; Mansfield 1990; P. Cook et al. 1991) show surprisingly little understanding of technological progress when examined closely.

Designers have had considerably more difficulty in embracing the growth of knowledge about the areas central to their work—that is, the provision of better habitats for people. This knowledge is being developed in the social, or behavioral, sciences—psychology, sociology, and anthropology—and is often counter to the conventional wisdom of architects (Mikellides 1980a). It has a direct impact on the issues that architects, whether they are concerned with buildings or the urban environment, have closest to their hearts. This research, its achievements and limitations, has been well documented (e.g., Saarinen 1976; Rapoport 1977; Lang 1987a; and Zube and Moore 1987, 1989, 1991). Some of it is well known to a broad segment of the public (e.g., Newman 1972) and thus architects have to know it and apply it when designing. Other research adds considerable clarity to the debate in which architects engage over such topics as the appropriate approach to aesthetic needs in specific circumstances (Nasar 1988b). There is a utility, in the short run, to avoiding dealing with these issues explicitly in architecture and urban design. They are highly emotional topics that challenge the ego structure of designers. With an increasingly educated public, this avoidance will do the design professions, particularly urban design, no good. If no attention is paid to current research findings and theoretical developments, other design professions will replace the existing ones as they have already done and are doing in the areas of technological knowledge development. If current designers try to simplify the problems facing them rather than handling those problems' complexity and ambiguity, a new set of designers better equipped to handle them will emerge.

We are also learning much more about the nature of the terrestrial environment and its sensitivities to urban change, and we have been made more aware of the impact of our design proposals on their surroundings (McHarg 1969; Hough 1984; Spirn 1984; Goudie 1986; Goldsmith et al. 1990; Lamb 1991). We designers are being asked more frequently to carry out environmental impact statements on major projects. Often we are legally required to do so. We need to be equally aware of the effects of surroundings on our designs, not only in a biological sense but also in a sociological sense. It is true that specialist fields have been developed to deal with many of these issues, but urban designers need to be fully conversant with the issues and how to deal with them. Program design (i.e., problem identification and clarification), for instance, is indeed increasingly being done by experts familiar with social science research, but it is also fundamental to urban designing.

The one traditional design field that is willing to embrace all these changes and to establish a new set of aspirations and their concomitant obligations has been landscape architecture. Sensitized over twenty years ago by such books as Ian McHarg's *Design with Nature* (1969), landscape architecture has broken away from its horticultural background to embrace without much fear both biological and social science research as well as the fine arts mode of thinking. Empiricist approaches to urban design have moved more slowly along similar lines, partly because of their intellectual heritage but also because urban design has had to deal with many complex issues in the layout of the environment. This book is largely about the effort to do so and the lessons learned.

THE OUTLINE OF THIS BOOK

The structure of this book is complex because it attempts to deal in a linear fashion with an interwoven set of ideas.

As a result the outline follows a looping path in which positive assertions are followed by normative positions that, in turn, influence the way the world is observed.

The book is divided into four parts. In the first, *Urban Design in Context,* the dual nature of urban design—as policy design and as architectural design—and the attitudes (beliefs and values) on which it is based are not only described but also evaluated. It is thus partly a set of observations about urban design but also partly a normative statement of what urban designers should be doing, a topic that is dealt with in much greater detail in Part Three. That later segment is based on the assumption that the positive theory presented in Part Two is reasonable. In Part One it is suggested that the consumerism of much recent work needs to be tempered with a much greater concern for the social obligations of designers and the public interest requirements of the public realm. Indeed, urban design needs to be redesigned.

Part Two, Functionalism Redefined, outlines the empirical knowledge that is now at the city planner's, architect's, and landscape architect's disposal and the design issues that it raises. This knowledge has been gleaned from practical experience, the evaluations of the work of others, and from scientific and quasi-scientific research on the environment and on the environment and human behavior. It strives to be a positive statement. The approach views the world through analytical glasses; designers still have to put things together—design is a creative synthetic act.

Part Three; Synthesis—A Neo-Functional Approach to Urban Design, describes what carrying out urban design in an Empiricist manner means. As noted, it draws on the evaluation and prescription outlined in the second half of Part One. The thesis is that a normative procedural theory of architectural and urban design has to be the fundamental basis for urban design rather than any generic model of urban form. Such a theory is described in Chapter 24.

The final part, Conclusion—The Future of Urban Design, clarifies the distinction between urban design as a discipline and as a professional activity if not a profession. It attempts to understand the ambiguous role of urban design today as urban designers strive for their own professional legitimacy. It also asserts: the Modernists really did almost get it right! ∎

PART I

URBAN DESIGN IN CONTEXT

Photograph courtesy of Larry Marks

St. Louis

The built environments of human settlements are continually changing and being changed. Sometimes these changes occur rapidly and at other times the physical patterns of places seem to be static. They never really are static; the natural and artificial environments of cities, suburbs, and villages are always changing. Some of the changes that take place in the built world are due to human interventions, but many are due to the natural processes of the terrestrial environment. These natural processes include the steady erosions, oxidizations, and bleachings resulting from the effects of the sun, wind, and rain, and from the growth of organisms and plants. They also include the more dramatic effects of earthquakes, hurricanes, and other natural phenomena that cause disasters when they impact on human settlements, which are often poorly planned to deal with them. Other changes in the physical structure of settlements result from the wear and tear of everyday usage by their inhabitants. Still other changes are made purposefully by groups of people and individuals in response to changes in their needs. Over time further changes are made in response to these changes because the new patterns have unanticipated effects, both positive and negative. They are also made in response to people's evolving perception of how their own needs can best be met.

People adapt the physical structure of the world for many reasons: to make life easier, more pleasurable, to gain esteem for themselves, and, sometimes certainly, to thwart the attainment of other people's objectives. At different periods in history, the rate of change has varied because societies have had varying levels of economic, technological, and intellectual resources as well as varying perceptions of political necessities.

Nowadays many people are pessimistic about the future. The problems the people of the world face in the coming decades of the twenty-first century are so interwoven and apparently intractable that a concern with the quality of the built environment seems such a marginal one. At a global level the problems people face are essentially economic and social. Unfortunately, it seems that there will be little political will to deal with them until the majority of people in the developed countries are seriously impacted by them. There are changes in the population composition of the world, major population influxes to many of the cities in the countries of the third world, and limited resources available to deal with them effectively. There is the realization that for all the people of the world to live as well as Americans do will result, given our current technologies, in an atmospheric pollution, already high, that will be life threatening. Such observations all raise queries about the importance and utility of urban design. Why should one bother about the subject?

Old buildings will continue to be demolished when they serve no utilitarian function, new ones will be erected, new towns will be built, suburbs will be developed, and villages will be changed. Some economies will expand, leading to high levels of development of the built environment in certain areas of the world; others will contract. Changes in the infrastructure of cities and regions will be made as new technologies are developed and old ones are found to be obsolete or useful in new ways. The way these changes will take place will affect not only the efficiencies of settlement patterns as the infrastructure for modes of production, but also their affordances as ameliorators of potential problems, as providers of developmental opportunities for individuals and groups of people, and as symbols of self-worth. The patterns of places do matter to people for they affect every aspect of their lives.

This book is concerned with professional urban design activities in the United States and the way that they are part of the processes by which Americans change their physical surroundings. Most human settlements in the United States, as in the rest of the world have, however, evolved without the aid of people who call themselves architects, urban designers, or planners. This situation is still true today. Why should one bother to consider the nature of this process? Why should one be an advocate for urban design as a professional activity, as will be done here? Why an Empirical approach? In what way can a concerted and self-conscious concern with urban patterns improve on the unselfconscious processes whereby most settlements have been designed historically?

The objective in Part One of this book is to display our current understanding of urban design in the United States, its purposes, the classes of problems it addresses, and how these have changed over the course of the twentieth century. The goal is to set a basis for the development, in the remainder of the book, of an intellectual framework for carrying urban design theory and practice into the future. To be able to establish such a framework requires not only an understanding of the nature of the environment of people, and of the human enterprise in shaping it, but also an understanding of the attitudes that have promoted the development of urban design as a professional activity, if not a profession.

Part One is divided into two sections: Urban Design Today and An Evaluation and a Conclusion. The titles state the intentions of each. The first section is descriptive and explanatory, and the second analytical and prescriptive. The goal of the first is to provide an understanding of the range of professional activities that fall within the domain of urban design. The second questions the attitudes that drive much urban design work in the United States today and provides a description of an emerging approach to learning from their consequences that should carry us into the twenty-first century with confidence. This approach is described in fuller terms in Part Three of this book with the positive theory that comprises Part Two as its basis. ∎

Mission Bay, San Francisco

URBAN DESIGN TODAY

The physical world, of which the built environment is a part, is locked in an evolving relationship with the social and cultural worlds of people. These worlds also comprise the worlds of other animals and other organisms that, in turn, have an impact on people's lives. Architects and urban designers are primarily concerned with changing the physical world so that it better fits a set of human needs, those of their clients and their own. The way they view their concerns today is largely a legacy of the Modern movement in architecture. The legacy is one of an extraordinary diversity of people, visionaries and practitioners, whose attitudes varied considerably, from Ruskin to Fourier, from Frank Lloyd Wright to Le Corbusier. They all had a belief in common: by changing the physical surroundings of people, new social worlds can be created. It is not, however, as easy as that.

It is still tempting, for architects and politicians alike, to think of the built environment as the major determinant of the quality of life of people. While the quality of the built environment is certainly a major attribute of environmental quality, it is also tempting to go beyond this level of thought to consider the built environment, as the Modernists did, as the independent variable in the relationship between physical and social worlds—social behavior being the dependent variable. We have learned the hard way that the relationship is not as simple as that. Changing the physical world may or may not have an effect on the social world.

Chapter 1, The Nature of the Environment, is an effort to describe the nature of the human environment and of environmental change in a manner useful to architects and others working as urban designers. The goal of the chapter is to provide a model of the environment and of the person-environment relationship that will clarify the role and efforts of the urban designer in striving to create a better world. The models act as the basis for the discussion of urban designs and urban design throughout the book.

All human settlements have a pattern (or design) within which other patterns (or designs) exist. The modern American city and suburb have evolved as the result of many individual decisions. All kinds of people, in their various roles, are involved in this dynamic process of urban change. Architects may design individual buildings and building complexes, landscape architects may design gardens, parks, and plazas, traffic engineers may design the transportation system, sanitation engineers may design a sewerage system, a school board may design the distribution of schools, but all these changes to the public realm tend to be made on a piecemeal, often competitive, and frequently counterproductive basis. The patterns of the built environment produced by these competing forces is the product of an interrelated set of natural forces and shaping actions, economic, social, and legal, by individuals and organizations, formal and communal. Urban designers in the United States today seek to create an order based on their obligations to their sponsors—the clients who pay them—and their own aspirations to be artistic and/or to create a better environment for human lives. Often their interests have been the private ones of their sponsors, but at other times they have sought to make communal decisions based on their perceptions of the public interest. In so doing they have built on the ideas of their predecessors—the Modernists.

The architects of the various streams of the Modern movement recognized the dynamics of private and public interests vying for control in the shaping of cities and the resultant opportunity costs to society. They saw architects being concerned primarily with individual buildings as art works. In contrast, their goal was to put "architecture [particularly in city design] on its real plane, the economic and sociological plane" (Sert and C.I.A.M. 1944). They had difficulty in attaining this goal. It is still, however, worthwhile and should not have been abandoned by so many architects when the difficulty in achieving it became apparent. In retrospect the Modernists were hampered by a lack of knowledge of human lives and the dynamics of urban form-making processes. They relied on their own intuitions and prejudices as a basis for making design decisions. Much recent urban design work has responded to these failings by substituting a financially pragmatic attitude for what was previously a concern for the public interest. Despite some highly regarded urban designs emanating from such an attitude, there continue to be major costs to society. The shortcomings of Modernist theory need to be understood too.

What the Modernists failed to understand was the richness of human needs, the richness of the environment, and the complexity of the relationship between people and environment—that is, the fundamental processes of human behavior. While their intuitive ideas about the people-environment relationship were often sound, the model of the human being that they used as a basis for design was limited. It was, by and large, a biological model acknowledging little in the way of cultural differences in attitudes toward life, the world, and architecture. Their model of the human-environment interaction was a simple Behaviorist one with the built environment being the stimulus and human behavior in terms of activities and aesthetic appreciation being the response. We need to have an ecological model of the human being—of the human being as a part of and a contributor to the biogenic and sociogenic environments. We need to understand the complexities of life, human behavior, and the way the built environment should be constructed to respond to the more elaborate understanding of people and the environment that we now have.

The purpose of Chapter 2, Shaping the Twentieth-Century City, is to place urban design in perspective. It provides the basis for the argument described in the following chapters that urban design is a professional activity beneficial to society and can be made more so. The primary concern in the chapter is with urban design as a self-conscious activity. In the United States and other capitalist countries it is an activity that intervenes in the traditional market and legal structures that guide decision-making. It provides the links between policies and plans in all societies, including those in which central planning is the norm.

Most overall patterns of cities, towns, and suburbs are developed in an unselfconscious manner although their components may be highly self-consciously designed. These patterns have evolved in societies with a low division of labor and those with a high division, in societies with few building types and those with many, and in societies where change has been slow and in those where it has been rapid. These observations do not mean that the development of the built environment has not been and/or is not governed by social norms and rules, but that these norms and rules have evolved over time as pragmatic responses to the need to resolve problems of basic human interrelationships. We can learn much from them, but the concern in this book is with the professional activity of urban design. If self-conscious urban design does not lead to better environments than those that are achieved without it, it is an activity not in the best interests of society.

The twentieth-century American city has been and is being shaped by many interrelated factors. Some of these have to do with the geographical context—the nature of the climate, topography, and geology, and thus the flora and fauna of a particular place. With the technological capacity that people have today, these factors have been largely overridden and are poor predictors of the physical layout of modern cities when compared with the economic and cultural characteristics of the United States, and its state of technological development. In contrast, the traditional vernacular settlements of many parts of the world are very much shaped by local terrestrial conditions. Whatever their geographical location may be, all settlements' patterns have been and are guided by some rules. Sometimes these rules are informal but in many places there are codes of building regulations and zoning ordinances that proscribe certain types of development and prescribe others.

Cities, or parts of them at least, have also been guided by urban design philosophies—design ideologies. A casual glance at most American cities, suburbs, and towns today may lead to the impression that designers' ideas have had little impact on their designs. This conclusion is premature. There are bits and pieces of the City Beautiful movement schemes in a number of cities, and the application of the concepts of the Garden City and of the Radiant City can be found in many places around the country. The failure of many of the designs resulting from these three major philosophies to produce as good a world as was hoped is one motivation for this book. Urban design as we understand it today has emerged from the successes of Modern architecture, but also from the Modernists' failure to recognize many aspects of the basic relationships between people and their environments and the resulting disappointment in the quality of designs that have been implemented. We can do better.

The review of the eras of urban design since World War II that concludes Chapter 2 shows the shift in perceptions of how to accomplish design ends. These shifts accompany perceptions of what makes for high-quality environments and thus good designs. In roughly chronological sequence, they are a concern with guidelines for (1) designing superblocks, (2) designing infrastructure and plugging in the buildings, and more recently, (3) designing the nature of streets and their adjacent buildings.

Since World War II much has been designed that would now be regarded as within the bailiwick of the urban designer at the city or new town level and at the neighborhood or precinct level. These designs can take any of four major forms: (1) the actual design of infrastructure systems and buildings by one designer or team at one time, (2) the design of the individual components of scheme by different designers within an overall framework established by a single designer or team and implemented, largely at one time, under the supervision of that designer or team, (3) the design of infrastructure systems alone, or in combination with (4) the design of guidelines within which other designers create individual buildings or landscape architecture schemes. There are a number of other roles urban designers can play, depending on their concerns. The range of urban design concerns is described in Chapter 3, The Nature of Urban Design Today, and is picked up in the Conclusion of this book. The focus of the chapter is on urban design as a professional activity. The concern with urban design as a discipline comes later in the book. Allied to this distinction between urban design as a profession and urban design as a discipline is the distinction between urban designers as visionaries, looking ahead to dream of potential designs in response to potential problems, and as practitioners, the professionals who deal directly with the present world.

Visionaries open the eyes of societies to possibilities that practitioners and the public would not otherwise have contemplated.

They attempt to deal with the environment in a holistic way, although their claims often fall far short of this goal. Professionals tend to deal with the world in a piecemeal way. Some designers may indeed attempt to prescribe the total physical environment from cities to ashtrays, but there are many inherent dangers in this type of design. It stifles the need for individuals to control their own destinies and grossly overestimates the utility of urban design in American society. More generally, however, professional intervention takes place at one or other of three of the levels mentioned above: (1) large-scale project design, (2) the design of a place's infrastructure—its "capital web," or (3) the design of public policies that guide the myriad individual design decisions that result in the overall pattern of a city's design—its "invisible web."

The problems being addressed by urban designers are only a subset of the major problems facing the citizens of cities and their suburbs in the United States today. Many places seem to be in a total disarray. Crime rates are high, the infrastructure is decayed, and economically they seem to be teetering on the edge of bankruptcy. The quality of life that they afford many of their citizens seems to be low. Yet the metropolitan areas of the United States clearly afford many of the necessities of the good life. People in many parts of the country still flock to them, for the country's metropolitan areas provide the opportunities that people seek, but it is largely a migration to the suburbs. We can learn much from that choice especially as new communications technologies promise to ease the necessity for movement between one place and another. Urban forms are likely to change in response. Urban design will play an increasingly important role in the future as the mainstream of the architectural profession concentrates on the design of individual buildings and city planning professions concentrate on social and economic issues. The success of all these efforts will depend on the coordinating role of the political and administrative frameworks of American society. With this understanding as background, the achievements and limitations of current urban design and the attitudes that form and inform it can be considered. ■

1

THE NATURE OF THE ENVIRONMENT

If urban design is concerned fundamentally with enhancing the quality of human lives, it must be concerned with the qualities of the human environment and, hence, with understanding that environment's nature as the basis for making decisions. Any discussion of the environment must be with reference to an organism. The center of attention in this book, and thus its bias, is the human being, although indirectly all organisms are of concern for they have an impact on human lives. The design ideology described in this book is based on the position that urban design is concerned with the enhancement of human lives and that the human being is diminished by harm to most, but not all, other organisms.

The environment of people is complex for it consists of more than the everyday usage of the word would suggest. It consists not only of the natural world, but also one inhabited by other people, other animals and organisms, and the artificial structures that many of them, but particularly humans, have made for themselves. There are layers of environments of people that are of concern to all designers. The prime concern of urban designers is with the physical structure, or layout, of human settlements that provides the settings for human life. Human settlements are also part of a larger environment, a sociophysical world. Design professionals have some impact on the design of the physical form of human settlements but they have less, but by no means nonexistent, impact on the complex web of relationships that form the larger environment of people. Understanding the interrelationship of the subenvironments of people puts the role of any design professional concerned with environmental quality into perspective, for many people are involved in shaping the overall habitat of people and of other species.

People making decisions about the future environment, particularly those making decisions on the behalf of others, need a conceptual model of "the environment" to organize their thoughts. They also need to have a model of people, and these models must be good ones. A good model is one that is simple yet explains much, if not everything, of possible importance given a particular task. The necessary basis for city planning, urban design, landscape architecture, and architecture is an overall common understanding of the nature of the environment, its structure, and its *affordances* for human life and enjoyment—an *envirotecture* (Thiel forthcoming).

As the urban design concern is with the everyday environment of people, an *ecological* approach to its description and explanation is presented here (see Kaminski 1989 for the strands of intellectual thought behind this position). The physical world of human life important to designers is a world of surfaces organized into settings, or spaces, for behavior, and for aesthetic displays. It is not the world of physics.

THE ENVIRONMENT

The environment can be considered to consist of four interlocking components: the *terrestrial,* the *animate,* the *social,* and the *cultural* (Gibson 1966, 1979; Lang 1987a). The terrestrial environment refers to the nature of the earth, its structure and processes, the animate to the living organisms that occupy it, the social to the relationships among people (and among members of other species), and the cultural to the broader behavioral norms of a society and the artifacts created by it. In this sense the built environment is a cultural artifact, or cipher, that exists within and is part of a particular terrestrial context (Latham 1964).

The distinction between the terrestrial and many aspects of the animate environment is a blurred one so,

1. Rural Pennsylvania

2. Midtown Manhattan, New York

3. The 9th Street—Italian—Market, Philadelphia

Figure 1-1: The Environment
In everyday language the term "environment" has come to mean the biological surroundings of people (1). This meaning is a limited one, for the environment of people consists of their whole surroundings—natural and artificial (2). The artificial environment consists of the elements that form part of people's material culture—their clothes, their tools, and the built environment. The nonmaterial culture consists of language, myths, social conventions, and gestures (3). All these elements are part of the biogenic and sociogenic environment in which urban design takes place and to which urban design contributes.

for design professionals, they can be considered to be one multifaceted *biogenic environment*. Similarly, the distinction between the social and the cultural environment is a blurred one so they can best be considered as one multifaceted *sociogenic environment*. Architecture, city planning, landscape architecture, and urban design all involve the self-conscious reshaping of elements of the biogenic environment to fulfill biological and sociocultural needs. These elements are also part of the sociogenic environment for they are full of potential meanings that shape people's feelings about themselves and the world around them.

The Biogenic Environment

The biogenic environment provides the setting, or physical frame, for human life. It consists of the physical structure of the earth, its atmosphere, and the changes that take place in them due to natural events—changes in the earth's plates and the natural processes of the climate. The nature of the terrain and the climate have historically been of particular importance in creating human settlements, but they, rightly or wrongly, have become less important now. The technology exists to overcome many of the restrictions the biogenic world placed on architectural and urban design historically. People have developed the ability to transform almost every place on earth

to make it habitable. Only the severest climes are uninhabited and even those places have been visited by people. With the increasing population level of the world and the concomitant demand for water and energy supplies as the basis for life, the time is ripe to reconsider the effect of the biogenic environment on human settlements and, just as importantly, vice versa (Goudie 1986).

The nature of the terrain and the climate of a place are the basic elements of the biogenic environment for they affect the nature of the fauna and flora that exist there—those organisms and animals that have found a niche or habitat in a place (Exline, Peters, and Larkin 1982). The nature of the terrain depends on the geological configuration of the surface of the earth. The climate of a place—its seasonal changes, its range of temperatures and rainfall, prevailing wind directions, and humidity—depends partly on its latitude, but also on its altitude and its location in relationship to land masses, ocean currents, and winds. The climate is also affected by the terrain of the place and indeed by the pattern of its physical layout, natural and artificial—by settlement patterns and the patterns of buildings within them.

The nature of the terrain—its slope, its geological composition, and its relationship to sea level—is a basic component of the environment with which people have to work in shaping their settlements. The terrain is also a

1. Beacon Street, Seattle

2. San Francisco

3. North Broad Street, Philadelphia

Figure 1-2: Terrains and City Layouts
The physical geography of a city and its visual appearance are very much affected by the nature of its topography, although in such North American cities as Seattle (1) and San Francisco (2) the grid runs over the hills to the extent it is possible. These layouts illustrate the application of a Rationalist idea to a topography not rationally suitable for it. Much of the loved character of these cities is, however, derived from the relationship of the grids to their topography. Cities built on flat land (3) do not automatically have the vistas characteristic of cities built on rolling or hilly terrain.

major contributor to the aesthetic character of a place. So is its flora and fauna. Designers have long paid attention to the former, seldom to the latter except to reduce vermin. The quality of life of people depends partly on the presence of birds and nondomesticated as well as domesticated animals (Leedy, Maestro, and Franklin 1978; Spirn 1984).

People have so adapted the biogenic character of the world that very little of it is in a virgin state. As they have migrated, so people have transplanted elements of the flora and often the fauna of their native lands (to the extent that such vegetation and animals can survive in their new biogenic environments). Sometimes such exotics have survived so well that they have become highly destructive to native species.

There are many elements of the world that are animate—"endowed with life." Defining what is living is not simple because the definition is culture-bound. Clearly, to me, there are many elements of the biogenic environment that have life but are not animate: vegetation, in particular. Does a lodestone, however, have life? Is it animate? Many peoples of the world believe what others regard as inanimate to be endowed with life—a hill, a stone, a building (E. Martin 1991). Many architects personalize the inanimate environment in thinking about how to design it, but this is different from, say, the Hopi Indians' belief that

their hogans are animate. While I respect the Hopi view and I believe that it has to be a major consideration in the design of Hopi settlements, I, like many other people raised within a Judeo-Christian cultural environment, take a narrower view. The animate environment of humans consists of other human beings and other animals.

The Sociogenic Environment

Individual members of a species provide stimulation and support to others in their quest for survival and for an enrichment of life. The higher the order of species the more elaborate the *social loops* that exist among its members. The life of many species exists within social systems, and animals provide many sources of stimulation for human beings, but the human being is monotypic as a species and our social systems are highly elaborate.

A social system consists of a set of individuals who interact on a regular, although not necessarily a frequent nor a face-to-face, basis in order to achieve specific ends. These ends may or may not be explicitly defined, but one member of a social system has expectations of the behavior of its other members. There are norms of behavior that guide the interactions between people. Almost all people in modern societies are members of a number of social systems based on who they are in terms of their stage in life cycle, socioeconomic status, and the activities in which they engage. They are members of various *organizations*. The nature of their spatial configurations and the physical environmental patterns required to best afford them vary by type of organization.

Shimon Gottschalk (1975) differentiates between *formal* and *communal* organizations. Their similarities and differences are shown in Table 1-1. Organizations may include subsystems of other types. A residential neighborhood, for instance, may include a number of formal organizations but much of the quality of life for people depends on the communal organizations available for them to join and their predisposition to be or not to be part of them. The predispositions of the population depend partly on individual personalities and their competencies and resources but, more broadly, on the culture of which they are a part. The same is true of business organizations. There is a formal structure, but it is often the informal network that enables a corporation to survive and must be taken into consideration when designing (Moleski 1974; Moleski and Lang 1982). Each organization has its own culture.

Culture is an anthropological term that refers to the implicit and explicit rules and meanings shared by a group of people. These rules and meanings cover the basic activities involved in maintaining the necessities of life, working and recreating, the way the genders relate to each other, the way children are socialized into a society, and the ceremonies that bind the family, segments of a community, and the community as a whole into an organization. Cultural norms dictate a whole host of attitudes: toward people, toward the biogenic environment, toward the built environment and, therefore, toward the work of designers. These attitudes themselves fall within a population's broad religious ethos—its attitudes toward life and death, explanations for human existence, and an ethical system.

Organizations exist within a broader societal, cultural, and spatial framework. Some organizations are locally based (i.e., have a clear local territory) and some are not. Marcia Pelly Effrat (1974) identified four types of community: the *compleat territorial community*, the *community of limited liability*, the *community as society*, and the *personal community*. In the compleat territorial community, almost all of people's interactions take place at a local level; they lead parochial lives. In technologically advanced societies most physically and mentally competent adults, if not children, have considerably fewer local ties than in the past due to higher degrees of social and physical mobility, but they have, at least, some obligations to neighbors— they live in communities of limited liability. A personal community consists of the web of common interest relationships a person has at any particular time. Some of these relationships will be parts of formal organizations and others will be parts of communal ones or will depend on kinship systems. Although planners and urban design-

Table 1-1: Similarities and Differences Between Formal and Communal Organizations

Some Similarities Between Formal and Communal Organizations

1. Both are solidary interactional systems.

2. Both are relatively highly institutionalized in that they possess a developed normative structure, a high level of value consensus, and patterned reciprocal expectations.

3. Both may include subsystems of their own as well as of the opposite type.

4. Sentimental collectivity orientations (loyalty, commitment) are a variable.

Differences Between Formal and Communal Organizations

(Each of the dimensions may be considered as representing a continuum.)

Formal Organizations	Communal Organizations
1. Oriented toward a specific defining goal	Not oriented toward a specific defining goal
2. Functional collectivity orientation	No functional collectivity orientation
3. Linked by contract, i.e., by specified and limited cooperation	Linked by generalized cooperation (active and passive)
4. Mechanistic interaction	Structured freewheeling
5. A variety of roles and a formal hierarchy	A variety of roles but no formal hierarchy
6. Normative, utilitarian, and coercive forms of power are legitimate	Only normative power is legitimate
7. Created externally or by its elements	Generated by its elements
8. The inclusive system defines the roles of the subsystems	The inclusive system is defined by the subsystems

Source: Gottschalk (1975)

ers have attempted and often still attempt to localize these places through physical design (Gallion and Eisner 1986; see also Chapter 13), their locations have become increasingly dispersed in space (Keller 1968; Exline, Peters, and Larkin 1982). Many if not most people today are part of "communities without propinquity" (Webber 1963). A society, as a whole, consists of the sum of all these interaction patterns.

1. Minneapolis

2. Los Angeles

3. On Nicolett Mall, Minneapolis

Figure 1-3: The Artificial Environment
The artificial environment is that created by art or artifice. Generally, when we think of it, we think of buildings and other types of shelters (1,2) but much of the rural environment is artificial too. The world that we inhabit today is largely an artificial one of sights, sounds (2,3), and odors. Some of these experiences are orchestrated, others not. Some of the behavior settings in the urban environment are purposefully created by professional planners and other designers, but others are the result of the people perceiving and acting on opportunities (3).

The Artificial Environment

In the design fields we use the term *physical environment* with great frequency. It has already been used a number of times in this book. Its meaning varies from situation to situation. Sometimes we are talking about the terrestrial structure, the nature of the crust of the earth, sometimes we are referring to the artificial environment, the changes people have made to the physical structure of the world. In this book, *physical environment* will be used in the broad sense, whereas *built environment* will comprise the artificial physical environment. This definition is a complex one, for its parts are interwoven.

The built environment is only one component of the artificial world of sights, sounds, smells, and touches that people create for themselves and for others. We have constructed skyscrapers, formed string quartets, written poetry; we play games, invent kinship terms, and organize compassionate systems to aid the weak members of our own species. Much of the physical environment, besides the artificial world of buildings and infrastructure systems, has been organized by the hands of individual people to suit their purposes. The natural elements of the landscape have been rearranged or manicured by people, even where no buildings have been erected. Such landscapes are part of the artificial world of people if not strictly part of the built environment. Very little of the world has not been affected by people and/or other species. Many species of fauna also construct artificial environments (von Frisch 1974), but their overall impact on the total environment of people has been considerably less than the works of people on themselves and on animals.

THE BUILT ENVIRONMENT

Many species construct their own architecture but human beings appear to be the only species to have self-conscious processes for creating the built environment. The built environment can be considered to consist of the artificial arrangement of the surfaces of the world. These surfaces are of different materials and colors, and have different degrees of transparency, rigidity, sonic absorption, or reflectance, they are of different textures and odors, and they relate to changes in temperature in different ways (see also Chapter 9). The patterns and qualities of the surfaces afford different manipulations by people. The results of these manipulations, in turn, afford different human activities and aesthetic displays. We change these patterns and qualities to afford different purposes as our needs change or new patterns are perceived to fulfill existing needs in a better way. The nature of these changes, the perception of the functions they should serve, and the procedures for designing change are at the center of the debates about the appropriate ideological positions design professionals should take in helping societies shape the future.

The changes made by humans to the nature of their environments are vast and become greater every day as populations expand and people strive for a higher quality of life. Land that was forested has been turned into pasture land, pasture lands that are not profitable are returned to woodland, some that were over grazed have become deserts, and cities and roads have been built and are being changed incrementally and purposefully by people and/or through natural actions every moment. Rivers have been diverted, deserts made to flourish, while flourishing pastures and lakes have been turned into deserts by the careless actions of uncomprehending people. New lakes have been created by the building of dams. The earth is riddled with tunnels. The ability to light vast areas has changed the concept of day and night and literally eliminated many "ghosts." We have made machines for all kinds of purposes. In short, we have changed the world available to be sensed and our experiencing of it. All these changes have been made by people on their own behalf and/or on behalf of other people. The way designers consider the nature of the human experiences for which they should be designing depends on the model of people that they have in mind, consciously or subconsciously.

MODELS OF PEOPLE

Human beings are extraordinarily complex. People have various ways of looking at this complexity depending on their purposes. In everyday life, and while self-consciously designing with and/or for people, we make decisions based on models of the human being, but never with a full understanding of people. We are incapable of having that understanding. During the course of the twentieth century we have, however, enhanced our understanding of ourselves and other people and the biological, social, and psychological factors that sustain us. The systematic research has been substantial. We have an overall model, or image, often difficult to articulate, about who we are. Explicit models help us examine our design ideologies and the design process. Moreover, such models are open to examination, elaboration, or contradiction.

The work of city planners and architects in urban design, as in any design, is always biased by the image they have of people and their characteristics (Wood, Brower, and Latimer 1966; Stringer 1980; Ellis and Cuff 1989). The concept of the human being held by societies, by academics such as psychologists, and by professionals such as doctors and architects has varied during the course of history (Neisser 1977). Sometimes we have seen

ourselves as rational beings—economic beings—and sometimes as irrational. There are many models of the human being. By definition, none can be complete.

Compared to the others, the simplest model of the human being is as a biological entity—an *organismic model.* The model is nonetheless a complex one for there are many variables that constitute the human organism. Modern biological and medical research show how much we do and do not understand about the human being as an organism. Luckily not every aspect of the human being as a biological entity is of concern to designers. The organismic model is, nevertheless, the fundamental basis for environmental design because the creation of a salubrious, usable environment is its basic goal. Unfortunately, much design has been and still is based largely on this model alone and, even more unfortunately, on inaccurate versions of it. In terms of social behavior, people are regarded as passive objects. "Organismic architecture defines the built environment as a set of stimuli to guide and contain the human individual, without regard to his own powers or his relations with others" (Stringer 1980). It was the model used by Modern architects as a basis for their concept of "functionalism." It is a necessary model but an insufficient one for urban design today and tomorrow.

Another model is that of human beings in terms of their functions in society—a *role model.* Individuals do have specific roles within a social system and these roles do shape a person's behavior and values because there are norms of expected behavior within every culture and subculture. Looking at individuals purely in terms of the roles they play suggests that the role is the sole determinant of a person's actions independent of the nature of the individual's own personality. Architecture based on the role model focuses on designing for the organizational structure—for example, a house for parents and children, father a worker, mother a housewife, brother, sister; a hospital for doctors, administrators, nurses, orderlies, patients, and visitors (Stringer 1980). This model, like the organismic model, is a necessary one for design but an insufficient one because it deals only with the most basic human needs.

The *relational model* is more complex than the role model. The human being is seen as both a subject and an object, as a succorer as well as a succorent. People are individuals who are the sum of their roles in society and need to be seen in relationship to others. The goal of design, given this model, is to enable people to be what they wish to strive to be within a social and political framework and an ethical, or moral, system. It provides for the self-actualizing person striving to fulfill basic and cognitive needs. To fully understand the implications of this complex model of people for urban designers, we need to understand how human beings experience the environment, and what motivates the way they experience it.

THE NATURE OF ENVIRONMENTAL EXPERIENCE

The environment, biogenic and sociogenic, natural and artificial, is rich in *potential* experiences for people. The basic processes involved in peoples' experiencing of their environment are shown in Fig. 1-4. Information about the environment is obtained through the process of *perception*. This process is guided by *schemata* motivated by *needs*. These schemata also shape our emotional responses to the experiences *(affect)* and our *actions* and, in turn, the schemata are shaped by the results of these responses. Some of the schemata we possess for dealing with the world are innate. Many, however, are learned and are changed, consciously or subconsciously, by the experiences we have (Neisser 1977).

Anthropological, sociological, and psychological research has substantially increased our understanding or these processes, but there is much that remains a mystery. There are also different hypotheses and theories about how these processes work, but there is also general agreement on their fundamental natures (see Lang 1987a).

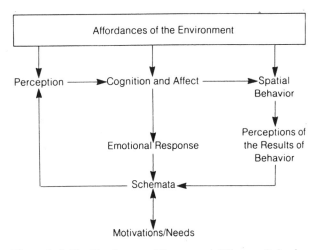

Figure 1-4: The Fundamental Processes of Human Behavior

Motivations and Needs

Needs satisfaction is the driving force behind human behavior. Models of human needs have provided the basis for much architectural theory, particularly Modernist theory (see Banham 1960; Wingler 1969; Conrads 1970; Egelius 1980b). This basis is an appropriate one, as will be argued in Part Two, Functionalism Revisited, of this book. There, however, it will also be argued that we need a richer model of human needs and thus of people than that used in the past, particularly by the architectural profession as the basis for designing buildings and urban areas.

A number of such models exist (e.g., E. Fromm 1941; Maslow 1943, 1987; Leighton 1959; and Cantril 1965; see also P. Peterson 1969 and Mikellides 1980b). Abraham Maslow's *hierarchical model of basic human needs* and of *cognitive needs* is probably the most widely accepted as a working description of human motivations. Maslow suggests that there is a hierarchy of basic needs from the most pressing to the least. These needs are paralleled by cognitive and aesthetic needs. The most pressing needs take precedence over the less pressing but not indefinitely. Once a need is fulfilled to a *satisficing* extent (i.e., well enough), a person's perception of needs shifts to less vitally life-sustaining ones. Although presented as a polemical statement about forty years ago, Maslow's model has stood up to close scrutiny since then, and until it is superseded by a better one, the model can be regarded as a useful point of departure for considering both human behavior and design objectives. Part Two of this book is organized around this model.

The fundamental human need is for *survival*. In order to survive, the basic physiological need for water, food, air, and sufficient warmth has to be fulfilled. The next most basic need is that for *safety* and *security*. This need has both a physiological and a psychological component to it. Physiological safety stems from avoiding harm inflicted, directly or indirectly, by other people and from the biogenic environment; psychological safety and a feeling of security stem from being oriented in space and time, geographically and socially, and being confident of maintaining one's place there. Once safety and security needs have been sufficiently met our perception of our needs tends to focus on *affiliation* needs. People need to feel loved and to be a member of a group. The next level in the hierarchy is the need to be held in *esteem* by oneself and by others. *Actualization* needs represent the need to fulfill one's capacities. Maslow's definition of this need has been misconstrued as the need to be selfish, but Maslow identifies it as the need to be helpful to others as much as the need to achieve one's own potential on one's own (Maslow 1968).

Paralleling these *basic needs* are *cognitive* and *aesthetic needs*: the need to learn and the need for a sense of beauty. These needs serve some instrumental purposes—the need to learn is fundamental to survival—but in many ways fulfillment of cognitive and aesthetic needs is also a perceptual luxury, for these needs refer to learning and the appreciation of the world for their own sakes, not for any instrumental reward. The aesthetic need is also the need to be able to enjoy beauty and/or to examine objects as works of art as a communication by artists of their interpretations of the world and its events, whether the artist is perceived to be a supernatural force or a human being.

Meeting needs results in feelings of well-being, failure in feelings of alienation, isolation, and lack of control.

The degree to which each need has to be fulfilled varies from person to person. Some people have only a minimal requirement for life-sustaining needs in order to focus on the fulfillment of cognitive and aesthetic needs, yet others are willing to give their own lives for others. It depends on what people perceive to be important. Whatever our motivations, they guide our perceptions of the world and our actions within it.

Perception

Perception is the active and purposeful process of obtaining information from the environment. It is guided by our motivations and needs. It is a multimodal process (see Table 1–2). We use our various perceptual systems to explore the environment. We learn to pay attention to its finer and finer details and to classify its phenomena into broader and/or more precise categories (Gibson and Gibson 1955; Gibson 1966, 1979). Of particular importance in the perception of the environment is the role of movement.

Movements of the body to obtain better information from the environment vary from the slight one of turning the head in order to recognize the direction of a sound to the actual movement of the whole body through space at high speed. Movement reduces the ambiguity of the information (particularly visual information) that we obtain from the environment unless its speed is so fast that the environment becomes blurred, or rather our perceptual systems overloaded. Movement does not eliminate ambiguity because stimuli such as sounds reverberate from surface to surface and odors waft in the air.

One of the most important results of movement through the environment is that we perceive the world as a series of vistas, hear different sounds, touch different surfaces (unless we are being transported), and smell different odors in a sequence (Gibson 1950, 1966, 1979). Sequential experience, as many designers have recognized (e.g., Sitte 1889; Cullen 1961; Thiel 1961; forthcoming; Appleyard 1965; Appleyard, Lynch, and Myer 1964; Halprin 1965), is thus the basis not only for perceiving opportunities for survival but also for appreciating the world whether one is on foot or being transported in a vehicle. Much design is, however, still based on how a static observer sees the world, for the most widely used representational technique continues to be frozen graphics.

Cognition and Affect

Cognition is the process of thinking. It involves learning and remembering (or forgetting), generalizing, feel-

Table 1-2: The Senses Considered as Perceptual Systems

Name	Mode of Attention	Receptive Units	Anatomy of the Organ	Activity of the Organ	Stimuli Available	External Information Obtained
Basic orienting system	General orientation	Mechano-receptors	Vestibular organs	Body equilibrium	Forces of gravity and acceleration	Direction of gravity, being pushed
Auditory system	Listening	Mechano-receptors	Cochlear organs with middle ear and auricle	Orienting to sounds	Vibration in the air	Nature and location of vibratory events
Haptic system	Touching	Mechano-receptors and possibly thermo-receptors	Skin (including attachments and openings), joints (including ligaments), muscles (including tendons)	Exploration of many kinds	Deformations of tissues, configuration of joints, stretching of muscle fibers	Contact with the earth, mechanical encounters, object shapes, material states—solidity or viscosity
Taste-smell system	Smelling	Chemo-receptors	Nasal cavity (nose)	Sniffing	Composition of the medium	Nature of volatile sources
	Tasting	Chemo- and mechano-receptors	Oral cavity (mouth)	Savoring	Composition of ingested objects	Nutritive and bio-chemical values
Visual system	Looking	Photo-receptors	Ocular mechanism (eyes, with intrinsic and extrinsic eye muscles, as related to the vestibular organs, the head, and the whole body)	Accommodation, pupillary adjustment, fixation, convergence, exploration	Variables of structure in ambient light	Everything that can be specified by the variables of optical structure (information about objects, animals, motions, events, and places)

Source: Gibson (1966)

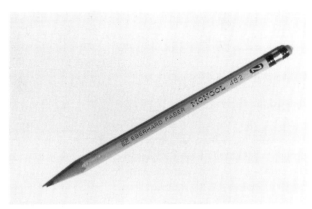

1. Mongol Pencil

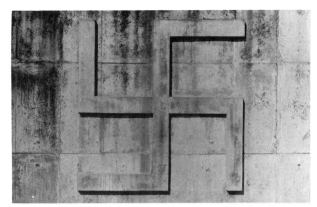

2. Chandigarh, Punjab, India

3. 16th Street Mall, Denver

Figure 1-5: Levels of Meaning
Even something as simple as a pencil (1) has many meanings, some of which (e.g., rigidity—its concrete meaning) are perceivable by a bird or a chimpanzee. Other meanings (e.g., its name and color) are more complex and have to be learned. Meanings vary by context. The swastika (2) in many cultures is a sign of good will and prosperity, as its use in Chandigarh indicates, but this meaning does not hold in Europe today because of its association with Nazism. Urban scenes (3) are complex and full of meanings, some of which are self-consciously developed by designers.

ing and attitude formation, liking and disliking. Human behavior is highly adaptable. We learn to perform better based on formal education, the results of our actions, and from the inner satisfactions we receive from the act of learning itself (Maslow 1987). The ways in which we use the biogenic and sociogenic environments are very much affected by the way we are socialized to use them, but also by their very nature. Much of our behavior is culture-bound, but the way the physical environment, and the built environment, is structured can make fulfilling basic and cognitive needs easier or more difficult. It can provide educational opportunities. We can learn much vicariously simply from an exposure to other people and events. We learn the meanings of patterns of the environment and of the objects it contains.

There are a number of levels of meaning and a number of ways of classifying them. A simple but powerful way is that provided by psychologist James Gibson (1950). If we take a pencil, for example, the simplest level is the *concrete meaning*, the physical characteristics of its pattern—its rigidity (see Fig. 1-5(1)). The second level is the *use meaning*—the pencil's utility for extending one's reach. Many animals recognize this level of utility of a physical object. The third level of meaning is a refined version of the second—that of objects as *machines and instruments*—the pencil as an instrument for making a

mark on a piece of paper, its eraser as a means for eliminating that mark. The fourth level is the *emotional or affective meaning* of an object—whether one likes to write in pencil or not. The fifth level is the object as a *sign;* in this example it is that the yellow color of the pencil is a sign that once the best graphite came from Mongolia, and, at the sixth level, the pencil can be a *symbol*—stand for something else.

Symbolic meanings are the most difficult to comprehend. They are the meanings *associated* with an object or a phenomenon, or classes of objects and phenomena. There are different understandings of what "associated meanings" means. Psychoanalysts postulate an unconscious component of the mind in which memories are deposited to be awakened by the psyche in the form of symbols. Carl Jung suggested that there is a *collective unconscious* in which timeless "nodes of energy" called *archetypes* evoke images, ideas, and behaviors (Jung 1968). The position taken here is that a symbol is something that stands for, denotes, or represents some idea, whether spiritual or laic, that is immaterial or abstract. A pencil could stand for learning, a flag for nationhood, a church for eternity. The symbolic meaning of elements of the environment are learned and are thus, by and large, culture-bound. Some symbolic meanings appear to be based on the universals of human experience and are widely understood.

Other people take the position that a symbol is what it stands for; that the way the "symbol" is used in this book is merely as a sign (Verge 1991). Suffice to say that some city patterns have been based on models of cosmological systems and are symbols for the universal for those people who understand the system. Much religious architecture is similarly designed (Lesser 1957). Other patterns have meanings assigned to them or they acquire meanings through repeated usage. The symbolic aesthetics of the environment are an important concern for designers because they manipulate symbols for many purposes.

The labels that we apply to elements and meanings of the environment can either aid or distort memory, and they affect the way we will pay attention to the environment in the future. We give names not only to individual phenomena but also to classes of phenomena. We categorize things. Categorizing depends on making generalizations about phenomena. There are two basic types of generalization: *response generalization,* in which the same response is given to different stimuli, and *stimulus generalization,* in which different responses are given to the same stimulus at different times. People respond similarly to many situations—different people, natural scenes, buildings, interiors. They can respond differently to the same environment depending on the circumstances in which it is viewed, their expectations/predispositions, purposes, and moods. Human behavior, overt or emotional, cannot be explained simply in terms of the stimuli available. How people respond to the patterns of the environment depends on the people themselves and their attitudes.

Our *attitudes* consist of *beliefs* about the associative (rather than defining) characteristics we perceive in phenomena and a *value* toward those beliefs. Values are related to motivations for they define the attractive and the repulsive elements of the environment and affect our desires to achieve specific ends, to acquire specific objects, or to enter specific social relationships. Because of the process of response generalization we may respond to something, say a work of art, that we perceive to be part of a category we dislike only to find that the categorization has been wrong. In this case, we have to reorganize our beliefs about the work. Much evaluation by architects of buildings depends on their perceptions of the architect and not of the work!

People strive for cognitive consistency in the attitudes they hold about themselves, and about the elements of the biogenic and sociogenic environments. We attempt to eliminate incongruities by changing our beliefs and/or values. The strength with which we hold specific attitudes that are inconsistent with each other will indicate the direction of likely change. Sometimes instead of changing we isolate the attitude, but this places us in a dissonant situation of having to maintain inconsistent attitudes. One of the simplest but most powerful models of the striving for cognitive consistency is that provided some time ago by balance theory (Heider 1954).

Balance theory suggests that if one person has a positive attitude toward another or a set of ideas (the referent), then that person's attitude toward a third set (person, object, set of ideas) will be positive if the referent and that third set are congruent in terms of attitudes. Fig. 1-6 shows the relationship between a person and that person's attitudes toward a referent and an environmental pattern. Fig. 1-6(a,b,c,) shows consistent relationships. Fig. 1-6(d) shows an inconsistent one. Although dissonance theory fails to explain how all inconsistencies are resolved, the balance theory model has withstood challenges to its basic explanations of human nature since it was first introduced to social psychology (Abelson 1968; Newcomb 1968). It thus provides a basis for understanding much about peoples' affective responses to the built environment (Lang 1987a; Nasar 1988a).

Not only do individuals have attitudes, but groups of people (i.e., subcultures) can and do hold common attitudes toward other people, places, and objects. By doing so they maintain a group identity. These attitudes very much affect the way we perceive and think about the world and the actions we execute (for a fuller discussion, see Lang 1987a). It is also clear that architects and laypeople have different attitudes toward the patterns of the built environment and what aspects of it are important. Balance theory suggests that to identify themselves as a group, architects will strive to maintain this difference. Architects have to continue having different tastes from laypeople unless, as a profession, architecture can change its perceptions of itself and the services it provides. Designers need to recognize this discrepancy in taste cultures—the discrepancy between "high style" and popular tastes. Popular tastes are built by the everyday experiences of people, which results in them having an image of a "good world" in their heads. Many architects recognize these issues but find themselves ineffective in resolving the discrepancy (Groat 1982).

Actions

We act on and within our biogenic and sociogenic environments in many ways. We act to sustain ourselves and/or them, we act to change ourselves and/or them depending on our perception of our needs. We carry out a wide array of activities for instrumental and noninstrumental (i.e., for the reward of the activity itself) purposes. We move from one place to another to sustain and enrich our lives. We have developed many kinds of machines and devices to aid this process. We have developed rites of passage to celebrate the transitions in our lives. We educate and entertain each other in many ways. We have developed instruments to wage war. We have altered the world around us for our own gain.

The structure of the physical environment, natural or artificial, when configured in specific ways, of particular materials, meets the needs of specific human ends. It

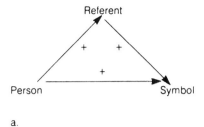

a.

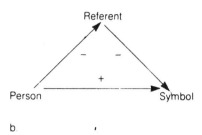

b.

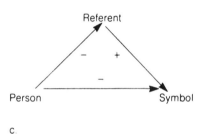

c.

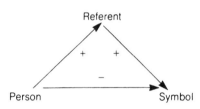

Figure 1-6: Balance Theory and Aesthetic Values

provides for shelter from the elements of the biogenic environment and for the territorial controls required for the human communications necessary for the operation of organizations, formal and/or communal. The built environment creates settings that form part of the activity systems of human life (Barker 1968; Perin 1970; Lang 1987a). The setting and the behavior are part of a unit of the environment—a behavior setting—in which people can choose to participate or not. Sometimes, particularly when the survival of the behavior settings is threatened, they are coerced into participating. These units are bounded one from another by real or symbolic barriers and nested one within the other to form habitats (Barker 1968; Bechtel 1977; Wicker 1979; Kaminski 1989).

The surfaces of the built world can provide not only for the shelter and the control of activities by those involved, but also for opportunities for the nonverbal communication of ideas (Rapoport 1982). If constructed in particular patterns they have a symbolic aesthetic purpose. Humans consciously create displays for each other and even where they have built without such an intent in mind, others will read symbolic meanings into the patterns of buildings and landscapes (Langer 1953).

The act of urban design and building today is frequently a self-conscious process conducted by professional designers and construction contractors. The self-conscious process involves examining needs and/or exploring opportunities, establishing resources, understanding the structural properties of materials in terms of their geometric possibilities, their strengths, and how they may be brought together in order to synthesize designs that meet the needs established in the first place. We learn about the properties of materials in order to make sound structures and the cleverness of the structure can itself be a work of art. We communicate our technological dexterity in this way.

The built environment clearly serves many purposes. It is multifunctional, for it helps us fulfill many needs when it is appropriately configured. As needs change so we strive to change the built environment in order for it to function well.

THE ROLE OF THE BUILT ENVIRONMENT IN HUMAN LIVES

As many architects find, it is tempting to adopt a simple stimulus-response (S-R) model of human behavior as the basis for design thinking, but it is foolish to do so. While it may bolster the self-image of designers to think that changes in the structure of the built environment can deterministically shape behavior, this only works to a limited degree on a limited number of variables. The built environment, depending on its patterns, affords a variety of behaviors (physical and mental activities) to those who are able to perceive the opportunities that the patterns afford. People will use these opportunities, provided they have the competence to do so and are predisposed or are coerced to do so. The built environment itself is only marginally coercive; the sociocultural environment often is powerfully so. The degree of coercion depends on the needs people are seeking to fulfill.

The built environment also changes the biogenic environment by changing the characteristics of the surfaces of the world. How horizontal surfaces are paved changes their permeability and the way water runs off them. Other surfaces change the flow of winds and the heat absorbency of the world. Manufacturing processes and the machines we use create pollutants both in the air we breathe and the waters of rivers and the sea, changing aquatic life. The consequences have been severe and we are only just beginning to fully comprehend them.

The Concept of Affordance

The *affordances* of anything, material or nonmaterial, are what it offers a species in terms of the activities and meanings it allows because of its characteristics (Gibson 1979). The affordances of a particular pattern of the built environment are a property of its layout, of the materials of which it is fabricated, and of the way it is illuminated with reference to a species. The affordances have to be seen both in terms of a species and in terms of its individual members, depending on their individual and collective perceptual, cognitive, and behavioral competencies. The affordances of the built environment cover all the meanings of the built environment described above. They vary from very basic things such as the rigidity of a surface of a table, allowing a person to lean on it, to the symbolic meaning of the material of which it is constructed and the meaning of its size. The more basic affordances are universal for humans. A rigid horizontal surface, for instance, provides support for all people; a wall provides something to lean against.

Some affordances are recognized because of the innate schemata that humans possess while others, such as recognizing the vineyard of origin of a particular wine, require considerable learning. The information is available to be discerned in the wine itself for all people whose perceptual systems are unimpaired, but very few people have the competence to do so. They have not learned the invariant connections between attributes of the wine and its source. Symbolic meanings depend on an individual's own interpretation of a pattern of the environment, but there is often considerable consistency in this interpretation among members of a culture. Some symbols seem to be universal because, as mentioned above, aspects of human existence are universal.

The list of the affordances of the built environment are almost endless, but at a high level of generalization the major purposes it serves are twofold. If properly configured, the built environment affords support and shelter for human activities; it also affords the opportunities to communicate meanings. The set of affordances that exists in any locale constitutes the *potential environment* for human activities and aesthetic appreciations. Not all these affordances are perceived by people, for what people pay attention to depends on their motivations, their knowledge about the environment, and their perceptions of the outcome of actions. The *effective environment* is what people attend to; it is what has meaning for them (Gans 1968).

The built environment can be adapted—its affordances changed—to allow for desired behaviors, or else the people concerned may adapt their behavior to cope with the environment as it is. New settlement patterns can be designed and new social structures can be created. These adaptations may be accompanied by physiological and psychological stress for the people involved. Such stress is particularly likely to occur, as dissonance theory explains, when people are in situations that are not self-selected. However, any departure from what people are used to is likely to be stressful unless they are trying to get away from a highly stressful environment anyway (Festinger 1962). In this case, the overall stress level may be reduced but any uncertainty about outcomes is stressful.

The Concept of Habituation

We become accustomed to particular patterns of the environment. We are socialized to look at and pay attention to certain elements of the environment and they acquire special meanings for us. We get used to using the environment in particular ways, and to particular levels of stimulation. We find it difficult to conceive of life in differently designed environments, although designers must do so. Departures from what we are used to raise our stress levels. This change is motivating and invigorating, but too high a level of stress may fall outside our ability to cope with it (Helson 1964). For this reason, small departures from habituation levels are often liked, but departures too great for us to cope with are disliked.

These observations apply not only to the affordances of the environment for new behavior patterns but also to their aesthetic affects. Some people strive for novelty in experiences and many appreciate the novel. We then become habituated to what was once novel, and strive for something new in an endless cycle. The degree to which people strive for novelty is part of the culture of that people and their competence in handling change.

The world is replete with examples of buildings and other structures that were greeted with hostility because they were so deviant from the norm when proposed and/or when first built only to have become much loved and defended when threatened with demolition. There are also many examples where striving for novelty has resulted in buildings that have never been absorbed into a culture in a positive way. Some have only been absorbed into the professional culture, as balance theory might predict. This is certainly true of much Post-Modern architecture (Groat and Canter 1979; Groat 1982).

People are largely unaware of the constraints imposed on them by their habituation levels. They have expectations of what the layout of the environment should be and the actions they should take in dealing with it and within it. We become acutely aware of having to deal with differences when we travel to different places within different cultural milieus, but usually these situations are temporary changes that we purposefully seek. Some people have a greater ability to adapt to changes than others. They are more competent at it. Those of us less competent want to hang on to what exists.

The Concept of Competence

The biogenic and sociogenic environment in which people are socialized shapes competencies, because what

1. The Eiffel Tower, Paris

2. Habitat, Montreal

3. Chicago

Figure 1-7: Habituation Level and Environmental Attitudes
When first proposed, the Eiffel Tower in Paris was met with considerable hostility, but it has become a much-loved symbol of Paris (1). Habitat in Montreal took time before it became a sought-after place in which to live (2). Chesterbrook, Pennsylva-nia (see Fig. 2–17(2)), has been through a similar experience in the eyes of its neighbors. Many public housing projects in the United States represented a major deviation from people's norms of what good housing areas are. Few have been absorbed into the culture of their inhabitants (3).

we know and what we learn to look at are shaped by what the environment affords us. Everybody has a level of *competence,* ability, skill, or expertise in dealing with the biogenic and sociogenic worlds and thus the built environment. Competence is a term that covers a broad set of our attributes from perceptual abilities, to physiological strength, to mental agility (Lawton 1977). The processes of perception, and cognition and affect, and the actions carried out by an individual are shaped by what the competencies of the individual enable that person to do. The lower the competence level of an individual, the more restrictive the built environment is (i.e., the fewer the affordances it possesses for that person). While it is relatively easy to understand the level of a person's perceptual or motor skills, mental competencies are more difficult to comprehend. Understanding the competence level of different cultures in dealing with their world is even more difficult and open to more controversy. Even raising the question is politically sensitive.

It is quite possible for some people to be able to perceive the affordances of the environment for others

but, because of their own competence levels, not to be able to make use of these affordances themselves. If a person perceives this state as unfair, considerable hostility to those in control of the environment can be generated. This observations applies to perceptions of what the sociogenic environment affords as much as to what the biogenic environment, including the built world, affords.

The greater the competence of an individual, the greater the behavioral freedom that person has in dealing with the built environment. Most designers have a multiplicity of competencies and have difficulty in understanding and empathizing with the needs of those less competent than themselves, especially as acting on this tolerance requires designers to depart from the ways they are habituated to design—their design habits, or style. The hostility of many designers, and their clients, toward having to design barrier-free environments is an example of this attitude.

The level of competence of people that designers should accept as a basis for urban design is a key issue that raises questions throughout this book. Should people be

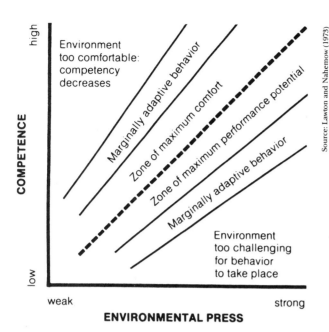

Source: Lawton and Nahemow (1973)

Figure 1-8: The Competence-Environmental Press Model

challenged by the environment or should the designer strive to create environments that are both physiologically and psychologically comfortable? If the environment is too comfortable a person is not challenged. It has been hypothesized that a person's competence level may become lowered to that demanded by the environment. This result is particularly true of institutionalized populations (Goffman 1961; Lawton 1977). In contrast, some people are constantly challenging themselves by seeking adventures that test their competence levels. Automobile accident statistics show that many young male and elderly drivers probably challenge themselves too frequently!

The Concept of Predisposition

Even though the environment affords people particular behaviors and aesthetic appreciations at their competence levels, it does not mean that the behaviors will take place or that the environment will be appreciated. On the other hand, if the affordances are not there, the behavior cannot take place. The human behaviors, both mental and physiological, that actually take place depend on our intentions and habits as well as the affordances of the biogenic and sociogenic environments. Intentions are a complex function of the schemata we possess, the motivations we have, the desirability of particular behavior patterns, and the perceived consequences of carrying them out.

We form *predispositions,* or inclinations, for particular behavior patterns and aesthetic displays based on our motivations, habituation levels, and competencies. We are aware of some of our predispositions and can be articulate about them. We may be totally unaware of other pre-

dispositions until a situation affords a specific behavior, possibly one in which we have never engaged. One of the difficulties designers have is in ascertaining the *latent predispositions* of people. As designers, we tend to overestimate our ability to do so, but people derive much pleasure from the opportunities to engage in many behaviors previously not considered possibilities, so thinking about such possibilities falls within the purview of urban designers.

The Concept of Costs and Rewards

Our perception of the quality of the elements of the built environment depends on our perceptions of the costs and rewards associated with them. Indeed, all activities have costs and rewards associated with them. There are costs and rewards for participating in formal and communal organizations, and for reconfiguring the environment in particular ways. There are costs and rewards associated with the quality of fit between the layouts of the environment and the behaviors and aesthetic displays they were designed to contain. Sometimes these costs and rewards are monetary, but frequently they are social and psychological. Departing from habituation levels has associated costs even if the rewards may be logically high. One of the difficulties designers and laypeople have is in seeing the costs and rewards of potential changes in the built environment. Sometimes only the costs are seen. We are better at examining existing environments than imagined ones and so fail to see the potential of new situations. We are also scarred by seeing potentials where they did not exist.

Some settings may be very stressful but the financial and psychological rewards for being in them are very high so they are tolerated. Others are highly unpleasant and the rewards are low for being there. If there is an alternative, such settings will not be inhabited. If there is no alternative, people will tolerate them for political or financial reasons. There are also situations where the costs are low and the rewards very high. They are the ideal situations (Helmreich 1974).

CONCLUSION: ENVIRONMENTAL DESIGN AS ENVIRONMENTAL ADAPTATION

If one considers people and their environments in the way outlined here, it becomes clear that the processes of design, self-conscious or unselfconscious, involve the continual adaptation of the layout of the environment to meet people's needs. Changing needs, or the perception that needs are changing, are the motivating factors behind the continuing changes we make in and to the built environment. It is thus foolish to think of any design as an end state except in the short run. From the moment the built environment, or a segment of it, is completed it is undergoing change. We change the environment by our

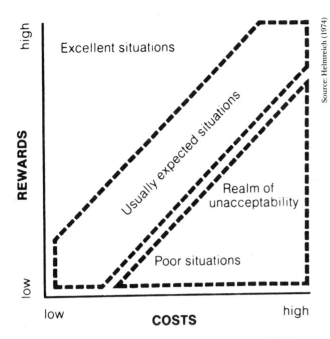

Source: Helmreich (1974)

Figure 1-9: Habituation Levels and Environmental Values

but it seems never to be a self-conscious process. Humans learn faster and we design self-consciously.

We live in extraordinarily diverse places from the south pole to the tropics—from deserts to rain forests. We adapt the world to make it habitable, to survive. We intervene not only for shelter, but to make the environment yield fruits for us, and for symbolic purposes from the trivial to the sublime. Undoubtedly, the refuges of animals have a symbolic content and serve a sociogenic purpose as a communications mechanism as much as they serve a biogenic purpose. Humans are, however, symbol mongers (Langer 1953). Not only do we adapt the layout of the environment to make ourselves more comfortable in carrying out new activities, and invent machines to make life easier, often we change the environment simply to make displays—works of art for their own sake.

In societies where design is a self-conscious process, designers are hired to intervene in the environment on the behalf of other people, but they are also given some license to express themselves. The degree to which they may exercise this license varies from the freedom of expression in creating pure sculptures to fulfilling complex technical needs in designing computer centers. The abuse of this privilege in the past is one of the prime reasons that urban design has emerged as a necessary field of professional design.

MAJOR REFERENCES

Barker, Roger (1968). *Ecological Psychology: Concepts and Methods for Studying Human Behavior.* Stanford, CA: Stanford University Press.

Ellis, Russell, and Dana Cuff, eds. (1989). *Architects' People.* New York: Oxford University Press.

Gibson, James J. (1966). "The Environment as a Source of Stimulation." In *The Senses Considered as Perceptual Systems.* Boston: Houghton Mifflin, pp. 7–30.

Hough, Michael (1984). *City Form and Natural Process: Towards a New Urban Vernacular.* New York: Routledge.

Kaminski, Gerhard (1989). "The Relevance of Ecologically Oriented Theory Building in Environment and Behavior Research." In Ervin H. Zube and Gary T. Moore, eds., *Advances in Environment, Behavior, and Design 2.* New York: Plenum, pp. 3–36.

Lang Jon (1987a). "The Nature of the Environment," "Fundamental Processes of Human Behavior," and "The Built Environment and Human Behavior." In *Creating Architectural Theory: The Role of the Behavioral Sciences in Environmental Design.* New York: Van Nostrand Reinhold, pp. 77–108.

Thiel, Philip (forthcoming). *Notations for an Experiential Envirotecture.* Seattle: University of Washington Press.

very presence. We design and purposefully change both the cultural and built environments. We reorient ourselves in life by designing (consciously or subconsciously) new behavior patterns, new technologies, new social standards, new buildings. Life is always in transition.

Maslow's classification of needs provides a framework for the consideration of the role of the built environment in human lives and the changes we make in both. This framework will be developed much more thoroughly in Part Two, Functionalism Redefined, of this book. Suffice it to state here that the built environment provides for human *physiological needs* such as shelter, for *safety needs* by providing defensive environments and those that provide ease of orientation in place and time, for *belonging needs* through providing channels of communication and through environmental symbolism, for *esteem needs* through the provision of control over the environment as well as the appropriate symbolic aesthetics, for *actualization needs* through the freedom of choice, for *cognitive needs* through the provision of learning opportunities, formal and informal, and for *aesthetic needs* by providing for individual concepts of beauty and/or the intellectual aesthetics of art forms.

Humans are not the only builders. Some of the structures shaped by animals, birds, reptiles, and fish are extraordinarily elaborate and their purpose as environmental adaptation is not always easy to discern; they are not open to logical explanation by humans. It is still unfathomable, for instance, why hamerkops build as elaborate nests as they do. Over the millennia animals have slowly adapted their structures to changing conditions,

2

SHAPING THE TWENTIETH-CENTURY CITY

Most Americans live in some sort of settlement. These settlements vary in size from hamlets to metropolises. Some commentators say that no human settlement is designed (e.g., Kostof 1991), but the position taken here is different. All settlements are designed. True, few are self-consciously designed as a unit by a single design team, but they all have a design, or three-dimensional pattern, whose development, particularly its public realms, has been governed by a set of rules, or norms of behavior. These rules constitute an *invisible web* that forms a people's cultural ethos (Lai 1988; Schultz 1989). The norms reflect the actual culture rather than the idealized image of itself held by a society—its normative model of itself. In many cases, the rules were established by custom and are unencoded, but encoded rules, such as those common in the United States for how components of settlements should relate to each other, go back thousands of years. For instance, the origins of the *Shilpa Shastras*, the ancient canons for town and building design based on the Vedic writings of Hinduism (Rax 1832; Acharaya 1927; Lynch 1984; Maharishi Sthapatya Ved Institute 1991), are largely lost in antiquity. However, in parts of India today the design principles they contain are handed down from mason to mason through the apprenticeship system as unencoded rules for good design based on spiritual explanations. Indeed, the unencoded rules are often more rigidly enforced than the encoded ones today. They are in the hands of the creator rather than the bureaucrat. The present work of urban designers, their aspirations and obligations, and their potential contribution to society have to be understood within the context of the forces that shape and might shape the public realm of cities. This observation is also true of any statement about their future role.

During the last two hundred years, since the time the Industrial Revolution began to have an impact on cities, more and more encoded rules have been established specifying how cities should be laid out and how buildings should be built. Cities in the United States have been very much shaped by the legal doctrines that have been developed since 1800 (Schultz 1989). As the goal of the rules was primarily to create a salubrious and efficient city, they are based on an organismic, biological model of people. The rules have been encoded into zoning ordinances and building bylaws through the concerted and individual actions of sanitation engineers, social reformers, model housing activists, philanthropists, politicians, and for the last hundred years, city planners (Benevolo 1967; J. Peterson 1976; Lai 1988; Schultz 1989). Only during the past thirty years have people calling themselves *urban designers* been actively involved.

American cities may appear to be chaotic and the result of totally irrational decisions. They are not. They are products of the many decisions made by many people in terms of their own self-interests within a market and a legal system and, often, a fragmented political and administrative framework. Much has been positive about the results, but opportunities have also been lost. As our technological abilities have developed, so the variety of possible ways of shaping the city and its components—districts, buildings, and infrastructure—has increased. Visually, the present American city and its suburbs may appear to be more haphazard than their predecessors, but individual freedoms and the quality of life for most of their inhabitants has increased.

The physical layout of all cities is a function of the degree to which individuals and groups of people have sought to adapt the biogenic and sociogenic environments to their purposes or have had to adapt their purposes to the affordances of the biogenic and sociogenic environments. No list of factors shaping the city can be complete, but the factors are those that have to do with the terrestrial nature of the place and the nature of the culture in which it has evolved.

CREATING THE BUILT ENVIRONMENT

Christopher Alexander (1964) distinguished between two types of design processes: *unselfconscious* and *self-conscious*. The adaptations to the environment of human settlements have been and still are largely unselfconscious throughout most of the world, but American cities today are a mixture of the two processes. At the scale of individual decisions there are many self-conscious acts, but the overall design is largely an unselfconscious mixture. Some of these individual decisions have a greater impact on the whole than others. The decision to build the interstate highway network in the United States after World War II, for instance, has more of an impact than an individual householder's decision to plant flowers in a flowerbox.

Unselfconscious design, in a pure sense, is characteristic of societies where there is a low division of labor, few building types, and a narrow range of materials and building techniques. People design for themselves and the process of design is largely preprogrammed. There are few, if any, specialist designers designing for other people. In such societies, almost everybody is a designer, and there is a consistency of appearance of buildings that is much admired by architects today (see Rudofsky 1964). There are indeed rules for siting and constructing buildings, but these are largely unencoded in writing although they are encoded in people's minds and traditional practices. Broadbent has called this process of design *pragmatic design* (1973) because it has evolved over a long period of time in response to the problems faced by a group of people. The nature of the solutions generated change slowly because the problems they solve change slowly. In addition, using traditional methods was not seen as a problem—novelty was not a motivating factor in design as it is in self-conscious design in many cultures today. The term "unselfconscious design" is used here in way akin to Broadbent's definition of *informal planning* (1990). It still stands in contrast to self-conscious design but in a slightly different way than Alexander intended. The city as a whole is the product of many designers, some of whom are professionals.

Self-conscious design processes involve making design decisions before acting. They are characteristic of societies in which there is a high division of labor and people who specialize in designing for others. The division of labor occurs because of the technological and social complexities of modern society. In the United States there is a further division of labor among those concerned with designing the layout of settlements. There are civil engineers, transportation engineers, city planners, landscape architects, architects, signwriters. . . . The list is almost endless. Each profession has its own specialty, each sees the problems of the world in terms of the problems it is capable of solving or gets paid to address. They are often in competition with each other (Gutman 1977; Larson 1979; Blau 1984; Cuff 1991). There are

indeed a number of self-consciously designed, or planned, whole cities in the world if not the United States. Unless these cities and their citizens are strongly controlled administratively, they will tend to turn into unselfconsciously designed ones—they will change from being *planned cities* to *cressive* ones—ones formed by many individual decisions (Gottschalk 1975)—although the basic pattern of their infrastructures may remain largely unchanged.

In U.S. cities as in most around the world a seemingly, but not really, paradoxical situation exists. As entities, they are the result of unselfconscious design, even though their parts—roads, buildings, and plazas—may each be highly self-consciously planned. This observation is as true historically as it is today. The implementation of the design, ultimately under Pope Sixtus V's direction, linking the important churches of Rome was a self-conscious act cutting through a largely unselfconsciously designed medieval city (Bacon 1974; Benevolo 1980). Haussmann's plan for Paris under Napoleon III's direction is similar in character as a design act to Pope Sixtus V's leadership role in Rome (Couperie 1968; Evenson 1979; Benevolo 1980; Olsen 1986). Even though their acts were major ones and give those two cities much of the character we know today, many smaller self-consciously but autonomously designed places contribute much to Paris's and Rome's overall natures. Autocratic power has had an impact on the design of the public realm of cities until the present. President Ceausescu caused not only a political revolution in coming to power in Romania but also an architectural and urban design revolution in Bucharest (Stamp 1988). The power of people such as Governor Nelson Rockefeller in the development of the Empire State Plaza later named after him in Albany, New York, was considerably less.

Public authorities do much self-conscious planning in most countries today. In the United States the nature of such authorities and agencies varies considerably. During the period from the 1930s to the 1950s, Robert Moses, through a web of personal and political connections, had considerable power to shape New York City in his own view (Caro 1974). He was able to integrate the planning of highways, bridges, and public beaches, but much of the public realm remained fragmented and still is. In Scandinavia, public authorities have had much greater power than in the United States to coordinate and set policies for the design of the public realm because citizens have given them that power. In the United States, the power is fragmented into a network of jurisdictions in competition with each other.

All kinds of people are involved in designing cities: lawyers, developers, individual households, and professional designers of various types. Much is designed by people who do not regard themselves as designers, but whose actions nevertheless change the built world. While professional designers are involved in making many decisions about the future of the city, many design acts are made by the citizens of cities on their own behalf. The resulting interlocking sets of social and physical systems are what urban designers see, participate in, and strive to improve today.

UNSELFCONSCIOUS CITY DESIGN

The American city is "designed" within a set of cultural norms, even though some of the norms may be formally regarded as illegal. These norms have to do with the operation of the marketplace and the laws that govern it, and with a broad set of cultural values. The outcome of this operation, the three-dimensional physical layout of cities, can be described in many ways: in terms of the distribution of land uses and activities in space, in terms of its architecture, or in terms of its behavior settings—activities in a physical milieu (see also Chapter 9). The way one looks at it depends on who one is and one's own motivations. Whatever one's bias, it is the biogenic and sociogenic environment of cities that shapes them and gives them their character.

Biogenic Factors

As noted already, the nature of the biogenic environment was a much more important factor in establishing the character of the preindustrial city than that of the American city today. While the climate and native flora of a place have become less important predictors of a city's character, topography is still a major factor in the aesthetic effect of all cities, self-consciously or unselfconsciously designed. San Francisco, Seattle, and Washington Heights, New York City, all get much of their character from the broken and often rugged terrain on which they lie, as do Chicago, Philadelphia, and New Orleans from the flatness of their landscapes (see Fig. 1-2).

The nature of the terrain on which cities are built and the nature of available building materials influence the way buildings are structured and their appearance. There are many examples of this impact in the past. Baltimore, Maryland, with its brick rowhouses differs visually from the cities whose houses are built of timber. Even though building materials are available internationally (e.g., marble from Italy is found in buildings throughout the world), local materials still shape the character of cities and certainly villages in resource-poor areas and, to some extent, in the major metropolises of the United States. A number of critics argue for the continued use of local materials as a way of establishing the regional identity of places (Norberg Schulz 1980; see also Chapter 13).

Although the built environment, because of the availability of climate control mechanisms, may not reflect the climatic differences of cities as much as in the past, the climate is still a major factor in shaping urban form and certainly in shaping the lifestyles of a city's inhabitants. The climate—the nature of the seasons, the diurnal cycle of night and day, the temperature, precipitation, and humidity levels—affect the whole range and cycle of human activities. Economist John Kenneth Galbraith (1985) once noted that the difference between Vermont in summer and winter is greater than the differences among Rio de Janeiro, Sydney, and Cape Town. Recognizing such differences, there are strong advocates for a much more self-conscious concern for designing with biogenic factors in mind in order to reduce energy costs, for aesthetic reasons, and to give a design a sense of place in the world (Olgyay 1963; Spirn 1984; Hough 1984, 1990b; Gordon 1990; Crowther 1992; see also Chapter 11).

In preindustrial, unselfconsciously designed cities, the distribution of buildings in space is very much a response to the comfort needs of their inhabitants. There are major differences between unselfconsciously designed cities located in hot arid or hot humid areas and, say, cold damp ones. Our ability to air condition and/or centrally heat buildings and to enclose open space has reduced the necessity to design with the climate in mind, rather than against it, but the expense involved is high.

The character of a city is also derived from the nature of the flora—the types of trees and vegetation that thrive in that place—and the consequent nature of the fauna. At the extremes of climate this is still a major factor in the appearance and nature of cities, but people have carried their cultural landscapes with them, planting trees in the desert (and thus changing the climate), chopping them down in forested areas and planting flowers from home (Rapoport 1977), as well as bringing their animals and birds (and parasites) with them. Although it might seem to be a trivial factor in the experiencing of places, the appearance of nondomesticated fauna differentiates one city and another. Sparrows and pigeons may seem to be ubiquitous, but the types of songbirds, and such things as the presence of squirrels, raccoons, and/or deer, differentiate cities as does the presence of mosquitoes and butterflies (Spirn 1984).

The cultural landscape is inextricably linked with the affordances of the biogenic environment (Exline, Peters, and Larkin 1982). The presence of the sea or mountains affords many activities that a flat, undifferentiated landscape does not, but there are many other factors involved too: wind, rain, sunshine. We, as societies, shape our cities to provide for our welfare on many dimensions of life. What we do is determined by cultural factors, the operation of the economic and legal systems, and the overall system of values within which people develop their settlements.

Sociogenic Factors

As Plato noted, "the city is the people." It is a set of behavior settings comprised of people and their activities within a physical frame (Bechtel 1977; Wicker 1979). City form must be seen within a cultural frame if it is to be

1. Jaisalmer, Rajasthan, India

2. The Skyway System, Minneapolis

3. Northern North America

Figure 2-1: Climate and Design
Historically, there have been major differences among cities based on their climates. Jaisalmer, India (1), with its flat roofs and narrow streets, clearly ameliorates the harsh conditions of the Thar Desert. Dealing with the climate is still an important factor in urban design, as the skyway system of Minneapolis (2) shows, but technological developments and designing for other ends often blurs the effects of climate on the physical character of cities. The effect of climate on the nature and use of outdoor spaces is still a major factor in the quality of life afforded by a place (3).

understood (Rapoport 1977, 1984; Agnew, Mercer, and Sopher 1984). Some political entities, Japan, for example, may consist of a highly homogeneous population—that is, a population that has a set of behaviors and values that are similar across many, if not all, of the dimensions of human experience. Such a society will have a common religion and style of life and values as well as a set of myths about itself. The built environment in such societies tends to be more homogeneous in "character" (even if it is unified through diversity) because its members share a common culture. Individuals may, however, well belong to different social groupings and have different personalities that are expressed in the "fabric" of the city unless there are strong social taboos against the display of individualism.

Many countries—for example, India, Nigeria, South Africa, the former Soviet Union, as well as the United States—consist of heterogeneous populations with many subcultures. Even in these places, however, if political unity is to survive there must be some shared values. Within such entities the subcultures may be distributed on a regional, city, or neighborhood basis, or they may be spatially integrated. Each area inhabited by a particular population takes on the patina of its residents' values over time because the nature and distribution of behavior settings, and the degree to which people participate in

them, give a place and a city its character. So does the process by which the environment becomes personalized piece by piece over time.

Cultures differ on many dimensions that affect urban form (Rapoport 1977, 1984). There are differences in attitudes toward gender roles, the nature of children, the nature of school, the nature of privacy, and territoriality. More generally, there are differences in what is regarded as appropriate and inappropriate behavior, the degree of tolerance for inappropriate and even antisocial behavior, and differences in approaches to dealing with them. Defense against outside forces was once a major factor in the location and design of cities; in the United States as elsewhere it is now much more a defense against crime from fellow citizens rather than outside forces that is shaping cities on the micro level of the block and house (see Chapter 12). All these factors are reflected in the physical layout of a place, the settings that exist, and the people who participate in them.

American society is not static and the norms of behavior change over time, due to the changes that take place as the result of the entrepreneurial spirit, technological innovation, and the result of "changes in heart," particularly in the concepts of individual and communal rights and of fairness. The marketplace is supposed to distribute goods fairly given the ability of the individual

1. Chinatown, Chicago

2. Southwest Center City, Philadelphia

3. Bella Vista, Philadelphia

Figure 2-2: Ethnic Identity and Neighborhood Personalization
Whatever its original design, any area of a city starts to display the values of its inhabitants over time as they personalize the environment to better meet their needs. The Chinatowns of the United States are obvious examples of this phenomenon (1). Less obviously, but nevertheless very clearly, other groups leave a patina of their values on the urban landscape. Very similar rowhouse neighborhoods in Philadelphia, for instance, have been transformed in noticeably different ways by Irish and Italian immigrants (2,3). The nature of design controls over this process of personalization affects different groups in different ways.

members and their families in a society. Self-conscious planning efforts assume that the market does not do it well enough and that it cannot possibly deal with public goods such as air quality, public facilities, and even the aesthetic appearance of communities. Self-conscious planning intervenes in the market system's way of allocating resources. The failure to recognize the way planning and urban design distort the market has resulted in unexpected and unintended side effects of many planning decisions (P. Hall 1988). If "urban design" is simply a new term for a professional activity that learns nothing from the past—for business as usual—it will have achieved nothing (MacKay 1990).

The Economic Base of Settlement Patterns

Urban design is a purposeful act. All human settlements were created for a purpose, or function, or a set of functions. The fundamental reason for settlements to exist is economic (see also Chapter 8, The Functions of Cities and Urban Places). Economic factors affect the choice of a settlement's location, its internal characteristics, and also its ambience. Its key industries give a city much of its character. University cities such as Ithaca, New York, and East Lansing and Ann Arbor in Michigan differ from

centers of commerce and resort towns. Manufacturing cities, for instance, are "gritty" and often much loved by their inhabitants (Proctor and Matuszeski 1978). Although they have a rugged charm of their own, they are not favored as a *type* by planners and architects, many of whom saw and see either the Radiant City (Le Corbusier 1934) or the Garden City (Howard 1902; C. Stein 1957) as the ideal (White and White 1964; P. Rowe 1991). Economic factors continue to shape attitudes in general, architectural attitudes (Kiernan 1987), and attitudes toward the qualities of the public realm.

The list of purposes for the existence of cities is endless, but purpose and location go hand in hand, and location and character go hand in hand. Few cities in the world are located without reference to water. Almost all major cities are or were ports, or located at fords, or bridgeable points in rivers, or they are resorts in which water plays a major role. Even cities such as Indianapolis, the capital of Indiana, located at the center of the state, have only been able to grow into major industrial and commercial cities because of a sufficient, if not an abundant, water supply to complement their locations within a regional hinterland.

The economic and technological bases of cities are intertwined. The nature of the technology available affects energy resources and transportation costs and consequently the economics of the distribution of people and goods and the location of manufacturing and service industries. The era in which a city is founded and the major means of transportation at that time have had major effects on its land-use distribution and character. The means of transportation dictates such characteristics of a city as its hierarchy of streets and street widths as part of the transportation system, and the location and nature of neighborhoods and suburbs (Stern and Massengale 1981). The differences in the street grids of American cities are the basis for the unique character of each. The civic buildings and spaces—the civic designs—as well as the building types and architecture of the major eras of a city's economic prosperity and development give it much of its character, both visually and in terms of the symbols of identity that are important to differentiate it from other cities (see Chapter 12, Meeting Affiliation Needs). Another factor in establishing a city's character is whether or not its street plan was self-consciously laid out before settlement. Much of the difference between New York City's Wall Street area and midtown Manhattan is simply due to the differences in the pattern of the streets. It also depends on their building types, the functions they serve, and the people who inhabit and/or use them.

The distribution of people by income and activity in a city depends not only on individual actions but on the collective actions of all the people involved operating within their budget constraints. The process can and often is seen as a social class struggle (Castells 1977). In the United States and other capitalist societies, the city evolves out of the competition between individuals, households, businesses, and institutions to maximize their benefits within legally set limits. These limits and the degree of government participation in urban and regional planning and design policy formation vary considerably from country to country depending on the governmental systems that exist and the values they represent (van Vliet and van Weesep 1990).

The distribution of people, land uses, and activities is complemented by the attributes of the built environment. Activity densities, all other things being equal, are highest at the center of the settlement because transportation costs are lower and people's disposable incomes available for purposes other than transportation are higher. Thus most if not all cities have an urban core in the form of a central business district ("there is a there there"), reinforced by decisions of the public sector to locate civic buildings at a place that is convenient to all. Land at the periphery of cities is less expensive so householders can buy more space in a tradeoff for other goods and qualities of urban life that are less important to them than convenient access to public institutions. At the periphery of the city, land becomes urbanized when the financial return to its owners is greater than or the same as the cost of converting land from agricultural use to urban uses. Some

cities are radially constrained by natural features, but others are radially constrained by efforts of planners seeking self-consciously to define a settlement with a green belt (Thrall 1987). Such policies are politically determined.

Open and *closed* cities are two opposite types of jurisdictional forms. Open cities are part of a regional political system. In a closed city, the urban area and the political control are coterminous. Because of the distribution of wealth and the ability to use it in a closed city, the poor reside in the inner city surrounded by the rich. This is the general model in the United States. In an open city, where income and welfare differentials are very high, the richer people live in the center and the poor on the periphery, as in many Latin American countries. More generally, however, the poor are at the periphery in cities where transportation systems for the middle class are poor and building codes are neither strict nor strictly enforced. This situation occurs, for instance, in cities with high immigration rates. If income differentials are high and welfare differentials are small, the population tends to be more mixed and its distribution is due to the sequence in which settlement took place (Exline, Peters, and Larkin 1982; Thrall 1987).

The twentieth-century city has been shaped by a combination of factors—increased wealth due to advances in the technology of transportation and manufacturing, and social and legislative changes. Possibly more than anything, the patterns of distribution of people and activities in a region or city within it depend on the transportation systems built (Attoe 1988a; Cudahy 1988; Cervero 1989). In the nineteenth century the development of the suburban railroad systems and later the subway systems gave opportunities for the middle class to move to the urban periphery. The two decades following World War II saw the full impact of the automobile and the trucking industry on many cities of the world. It is, however, especially noticeable in the United States, particularly in Los Angeles (Bottles 1987). In the United States after World War II, the interstate highway system that transected cities, followed by the construction of ring roads, changed the whole pattern of accessibility in regions and thus their land values. It led to quick commuting of suburbanites to cities by automobile, but also to the location of industries on the periphery of the cities. The postwar highways have allowed the suburbs to develop into more than the dormitory towns that they were when the primary mode of transportation was the railway. Suburbs in the United States have become more like cities with their own downtowns and employment bases (Masotti and Hadden 1973; Muller 1981; Varva 1987; Lang 1987b; Cervero 1989). It can be argued that such new downtowns are developing simply due to population growth, but accessibility by highway and/or a mass transit system is essential (Leinberger and Lockwood 1986; Garreau 1991). American metropolitan areas today often consist of multiple centers. The central business district of the inner city may still be the

1. Glendale, California

2. Bethesda, Maryland

3. Walnut Creek, California

Figure 2-3: The "New" Suburban Downtowns
Glendale (1) has become a major center in the Los Angeles area based on its location in the highway network of Los Angeles County and the initiative of its political leaders. The transformation of Bethesda, Maryland (2), from a low-density to a high-density core has followed its development as a transportation hub on the Washington, DC, Metro system. Walnut Creek (3), California's Golden Triangle area, is related to Walnut Creek being a stop on the (San Francisco) Bay Area Rapid Transit system.

preeminent one psychologically, but its economic preeminence is being challenged by individual suburban centers and has been long surpassed by the set of suburban ones.

Many cities have rapid transit systems. In London and New York the systems are of long standing, but in cities such as Miami, Florida, and Washington, DC, they are more recent. Los Angeles, in contrast, has abandoned over 2,500 kilometers of light rail system since the 1940s, although portions have been and are being reestablished. These systems create nodes of low transportation costs and a density of flow of people at each station. Each node develops into a surrogate central business district unless controlled through legislation. Bethesda, Maryland, and Walnut Creek, California, are examples of traditional low-scale neighborhood centers that have been built into new suburban high-rise downtowns located with reference to a new transit system stop. American urbanized areas thus have a series of nodal points of high-density commercial development. The pattern is of an urban structure with a high peak at the center and smaller peaks at the other points where access is cheaper due to transportation links (see Fig. 2–3(3)).

If a low-cost transportation network is introduced into a closed city, the downtown declines (counterintuitively) in rent and population, the population everywhere

declines in density, rents near the nodes increase, and there are strings of nodes along the transportation lines. Population densities around the nodes will decrease as incomes rise. Government policies to reinforce the centers of U.S. cities have tried to fly in the face of this reality without much success. If low-cost transportation systems are introduced into open-interactive cities, the inner core remains unaffected by the new nodes so created, land rents and population densities increase along the lines of transportation, the urban radius of the city will be extended, and the overall population of the urban region will increase at the expensive of other regions, all other things being equal.

The marketplace, it must be remembered in any urban planning or design effort, is highly deterministic in shaping the city (Dear and Scott 1981). Without enormous welfare subsidies by local governments in the form of improvements to people's quality of life, the standard operation of the marketplace cannot be changed. Indeed, such subsidies simply change the nature of the marketplace. The qualities of new building complexes change the opportunities in the marketplace and the ability of one place to compete with others, but quality has to be based in terms of the welfare it brings to people in *their* terms, not a designer's aesthetic terms. To get major changes in the distribution of people and activities in a city or region to meet some public interest objective requires policies that change the whole sociophysical environment. The changes have to be institutionalized.

The Institutional Base of Settlement Form

One of Mahatma Gandhi's noblest messages is that a "change of heart on the part of men is of more vital importance than mere outward changes in social structure or the political setup." Changing people's hearts and values is not easy. There are two types of institutional mechanisms for doing so: *social* and *legislative* (Thrall 1987). Both are concerned with changing people's welfare, including tastes and preferences; the former by modifying their values and the latter through encoded laws.

Social Tools

People make decisions based on the information at their disposal and their values. They make and will always make decisions based on incomplete, and thus biased, information. It is biased by their own experiences and by direct or indirect manipulation of information by other people. All institutions make decisions about what information they will bring to the attention of the public or, if they are specifically educational institutions, their students.

Commercial and professional organizations attempt to gain a market through direct or indirect advertising of their services in much the same way as manufacturers of products. They are trying to convince people that particular activities should be carried out in particular ways. Retail stores attempt to change people's taste preferences through advertising. Sellers of security equipment want people to see the world as a fearful place and provide people with the information necessary for them to perceive it that way, even when such sellers know that people's own experiences of it differ from what they are being told. Architects vie for recognition in the professional world, and for the sale of services in the marketplace, by the recognizability and quality of work they perform. Urban designers believe that specific design goals are in the public interest and try to persuade people of this (Gutman 1977).

This book, like any text, is a social tool. Its goal is to bring people's, particularly architects', attention to certain aspects of the world and to the opportunities for them to use their skills gainfully, as well as to their responsibilities toward society. The objective of any book on theory is to guide society in making better decisions by enhancing the predictability of the results of action. In this book, the concern is primarily with urban designers and the work we do in reshaping cities. Its goal is to assist the design professions create cities and urban places that are rich in experiences, by bringing their members' attention to what research has informed us of the way people attend (and might attend) to and use the world around them. Another goal is also to bring attention to the mechanisms that are available, and might be available, for urban designers to serve people by helping them in their quest for enriching yet efficient cities while recognizing the cultural frame in which a city operates.

Legislative Tools

The marketplace in the United States is governed by a set of legal codes as well as unencoded norms of behavior. The establishment of legal mechanisms is a self-conscious act to shape the city in particular directions, although the final product depends on individual decisions largely independent of each other, but within the code. These legal codes today are the result of "decades of tug-o'-war battles and short term collusions between special interest groups" (Thrall 1987). They have been established to alter the welfare patterns established by the marketplace by changing the balance of economic power between people. They are established in various ways, autocratic and democratic action being the polar-opposite methods of approach.

There are few, if any, places in the United States without some formal legal base for governing how individuals and organizations make locational decisions and for controlling the nature of buildings they design. *Formal*, in the way it is used here, means a clear and accepted legal code. It may not result in aesthetically formal designs (i.e., where the geometry of the design is itself the focus of concern). Rather the pattern, or design, results from paying attention to other concerns: health, prestige, and so on.

The types of laws that affect the shape and nature of twentieth-century American cities include land taxation laws, laws governing income redistribution, deed restrictions, zoning laws (except Houston, Texas, which has its own peculiar characteristics and problems but does show the limited constructive use of zoning elsewhere; see Ghirardo 1987), and building codes. In countries where land value is the only basis for assessment of property taxes, the incentive is to build on vacant sites, perhaps prematurely. In countries where property taxes are based on a combination of land value and improvements, the incentive to build well is lowered, and one finds more surface parking lots and low-scale development until the demand for land makes those uses economically unfeasible, as it has in Manhattan or as it is becoming in central Los Angeles. The level at which it loses feasibility is higher in such places than where only the unimproved value of land is taxed.

Many kinds of land-use legislation have been enacted to shape cities and regions, but often the shaping legislation has had purposes other than a clear physical image of the city in mind. Cities such as Boulder, Colorado, and more commonly, many European cities, have enacted "green belt" legislation to stop radial growth taking place as a result of market forces that have not considered the full consequences to the city's overall form. The goal has been to give easy access to the countryside for the city's inhabitants and to give identity to a place by preserving or establishing clear boundaries. Such a policy in Ontario, Canada, has, counterintuitively, led to high-rise apartment development on the periphery of cities. In many Canadian cities this type of development was the most profitable for the developers who held land on the urban fringe. This type of development was not the intention of legislators. Similarly, the policy in the United States to build highway networks and, after World War II, to provide low-interest mortgages to former military personnel in order to assist them reestablish themselves in civilian life (and to benefit the building industry) has had the indirect effect of encouraging suburban growth. To be eligible for the mortgage subsidies the buildings had to be detached units and, because little pre-1945 housing qualified, the bill encouraged new construction on available open land. This land was almost entirely in the suburbs, accessible by the new roads but requiring automobiles as a means of transportation. It has had a negative effect on the old cities of the United States by draining them of much of their middle class and potential middle-class people. This was not the intention either. The full impact of the legislation on the marketplace was not understood (Thrall 1987; see also Bottles 1987 and Monkkonen 1988).

In the United States, zoning laws have been widely used by central authorities, usually city governments, to restrict specific uses in particular areas of cities, to specify the distribution of building densities, and to require such things as the amount of on-site parking that must be supplied. For better and for worse, zoning laws have proven to be highly susceptible to abrogation or change. When the demand for a particular land use changes so, almost inevitably, does the zoning.

Zoning laws are based on cultural attitudes about what is in the public interest. Originally, zoning laws were developed to promote public health (Baumeister 1895; Benevolo 1967; J. Peterson 1979; Lai 1988; Schultz 1989). The goal was to create a salubrious environment for human life. The zoning laws that have been enacted tend to segregate areas of a city into homogeneous land and building uses. They are based on an organismic model of people and often clash with behavior patterns that are regarded by people as culturally appropriate, particularly where the laws have been copied cross-culturally by one nation from those of another.

Zoning is now often seen as a vehicle for maintaining property values by preventing what are perceived to be noxious facilities locating near one's property. During the second half of the twentieth century there has been an increasing use of urban design guidelines as an instrument of public policy to restrict some building configurations and uses and to promote others in order to shape the quality of the public realm in the public interest (Barnett 1974, 1982, 1987; Deurksen 1986; C. Ellis 1987; J. Ellis 1987; Fisher 1988; Getzels 1988; Lai 1988; Durgin

1989; Schultz 1989). Often this aspect of city designing is seen as the central component of urban design today (see Chapter 3). It has certainly had, for good and ill, an effect on the distribution of plazas in New York City (Barnett, 1974; Whyte 1980).

The public sector intervenes self-consciously in cities in other, more direct ways. Legislation usually exists giving governments the power to build infrastructure systems—roads, pedestrian ways, plazas, parks, water and sewage systems—individual buildings such as city halls, police stations, and museums, and public facilities such as parks and playgrounds—the *capital web* of cities (Crane 1960). The public sector has built much housing for low-income families. Each one of these activities changes the potential uses of the surrounding land by indirectly changing the rent structure of the city. Building public facilities or improving the existing infrastructure has a multiplier effect. These actions cause both direct and indirect changes (Attoe and Logan 1989). For instance, by building an attractive facility higher-income people may be attracted to an area to live, but lower-income people may be displaced. Population change is the primary effect. Secondary effects result from the services that are built by or for that new population and the impact the displaced populations will have on other areas. Such actions all cause changes in the city by changing land values and thus the attractiveness of land for various uses. The public sector is continuously involved in efforts to enhance the city's image and to change inferior circumstances to superior ones through public programs. Often such programs are viewed as culminations and people are disappointed with each program because it has not solved all problems. These programs need to be seen as an ongoing process of adapting to change.

The twentieth-century unselfconsciously designed city and its parts are fragmented. There is much that ends up being highly desirable, but many problems are associated with the give and take of competition among businesses and among householders. It has proven difficult to provide the services needed to maintain the quality of life of its inhabitants in competition with more recently self-consciously developed areas with newer infrastructure systems. At the same time there is a vitality of life that self-consciously designed cities and/or their precincts do not possess. This result is not because they are self-consciously designed but *how* they are designed. Urban design can and should add to a city's vigor! Unfortunately, this outcome has not always been the case (J. Jacobs 1961; Wolfe 1980; Goldberger 1989).

SELF-CONSCIOUS CITY DESIGN

Self-consciously designed places are those in which the three-dimensional geometry of the layout is specified by professionals or quasi-professionals (i.e., people operating in a professional capacity but not trained as such) in

1. Foxhall Crescent, Washington, DC

2. Battery Park City, New York

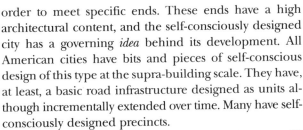

3. Las Colinas, Texas

Figure 2–4: Self-Conscious Urban Design
Most American cities have grown in a piecemeal way with portions designed as units. These units are distinguishable by the uniformity of their designs, either because they were designed by a single architect (1) or controlled by design guidelines (2). In the United States the scale of such designs seldom extends beyond that of a housing project, but there are also many new towns around the world that approximate *total* designs (3) even though their components have been designed by different hands. This kind of design will be called *all-of-a-piece* design later in this book.

order to meet specific ends. These ends have a high architectural content, and the self-consciously designed city has a governing *idea* behind its development. All American cities have bits and pieces of self-conscious design of this type at the supra-building scale. They have, at least, a basic road infrastructure designed as units although incrementally extended over time. Many have self-consciously designed precincts.

Self-consciously designed cities differ from unself-consciously designed cities in a number of ways. In the former, the road pattern is preordained and coordinated with land uses and facilities planning. The building types are ordered geometrically and the land uses tend to be segregated. The overall layout follows a hierarchical geometric order in physical form and in land uses. The basic differences between self-consciously and unselfconsciously designed cities is in the consistency (uniformity) of the design in the former that results from the intervention in the marketplace by the conscious location of facilities and the imposition of an intellectual design aesthetic to fulfill some social agenda. Essentially what happens is that a central authority determines land rent. This is the basic theme in centrally planned nonmarket economies such as those of socialist or Marxist nations. Costs, instead of being borne by the individual or those people who benefit from them, are spread throughout the community. In

the United States, private entrepreneurs have built new towns such as Columbia, Maryland, which is nearing completion, and Las Colinas, Texas, which has been underway for a decade. They are not, however, totally self-conscious designs because much is left for builders and householders to decide. Individualism is important in the United States (see also Chapter 14).

Governments everywhere have bought land, often through the power of eminent domain, to aggregate it into large parcels in a manner that the free market would not allow because of vested interests. Christopher Wren's plan for London after the Great Fire of 1666 failed to be implemented because the government was not prepared to intervene in the marketplace to accumulate land in such a way that the public realm could be redesigned. Once accumulated the government can change land-use patterns from those that would prevail under free-market conditions to that which will benefit some public interest. Throughout the United States, there are examples of government-sponsored construction of housing units in medium- and high-rise slab buildings on a vaster scale than that the free market would allow. Such projects have changed the urban landscape.

The planned cities and planned parts of cities of the twentieth century have seldom lived up to the expectations aroused by their proponents. Few are total failures,

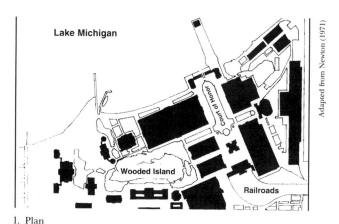

Lake Michigan

Court of Honor

Wooded Island

Railroads

1. Plan

2. Court of Honor

3. View West from Peristyle

Figure 2–5: The World's Columbian Exposition of 1893, Chicago
The basic axial plan (1) and classical architecture of the World's Columbian Exposition made a major impression on the people who visited it. The goal of the Renaissance-style complex was to impart a sense of dignity and beauty as well as convenience to its users. The Court of Honor (2) was everything the contemporary urban environment was not—clean, bold, a unified composition, and functional. The exposition demonstrated the characteristics of what was to become the City Beautiful movement: wide boulevards, vistas, terminal views, and monumental, neoclassical architecture (3).

although there are some rapidly deteriorating into uninhabitability not only in the United States but elsewhere (Montgomery 1966; Marmot 1982; Singh 1984). Too much was promised. They were not built in accordance with the behavioral predispositions of their intended inhabitants, and the limitations of planning were never understood. The well-ordered geometric world in a planner's head did not necessarily work in the real world of real people (Gottschalk 1975). To varying degrees this characterization of the problem designers face is true of the three major movements in planning that have specifically had an impact on the physical layout of cities during this century (Benevolo 1980; Barnett 1986). Their descendants are with us today. An understanding of these ideologies enables their impact on the twentieth-century city to be analyzed with some clarity.

TWENTIETH-CENTURY URBAN DESIGN IDEOLOGIES AND GENERIC TYPES

The three major twentieth-century urban design movements are the *City Beautiful* movement, and two branches of the Modern movement, which are generally called the *Garden City* movement and the *International* movement, but may more appropriately be called the *Empiricists* or *Regressive Utopians* and the *Rationalists* or *Progressive Utopians*, respectively. Each label conjures up a set of design images,

types, or generic solutions. Empiricist design ideas embrace considerably more than the Garden City, Rationalist ideas more than the International Style. All three movements came to fruition during the first quarter of this century. The City Beautiful movement captured the attention of planners, politicians, and architects during the first three decades of the century, but Modernist ideas were only implemented on a large scale from 1945 to 1980. Nonetheless, few will challenge the observation that they form the basis for much urban design work today, perhaps somewhat eclipsed by the recent *Neo-Traditional* movements (Duany 1989; Broadbent 1990). Current architectural ideologies (e.g., *Post-Modernism*, *Neo-Traditionalism*, *Deconstructionism*, and *Discrete Architecture*) have only just begun to affect the urban design of cities. Their ultimate impact will depend on how much they capture the imagination of planners and public officials.

The City Beautiful Movement

The City Beautiful movement developed in the United States at the turn of the century (Newton 1971; J. Peterson 1976; W. Wilson 1989; Schultz 1989; Gilbert 1990). It might well be called the last example of baroque planning, for while its immediate antecedents were the Municipal Arts movement and the World's Columbian Exposition in Chicago in 1893 (Mayer and Wade 1969; J. Peterson

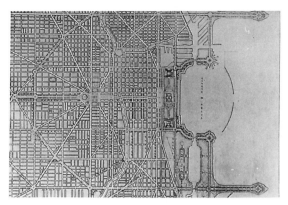

1. The Burnham and Bennett Plan for Chicago (1909)

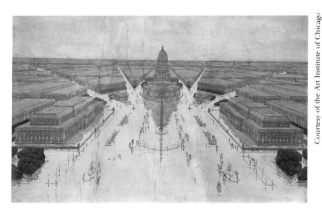

2. The Civic Center Plaza, Chicago (1908)

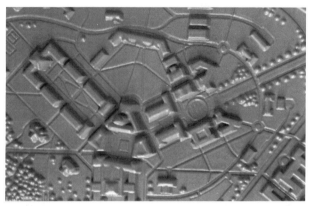

3. University of Washington, Seattle (1915)

Figure 2-6: The City Beautiful
The City Beautiful movement's ideas are exemplified in the plan for Chicago. The axial plan with radiating roads focusing on specific monuments and buildings is characteristic of plans implemented in new towns and on a smaller scale elsewhere (see Figs. 2-17, 2-20, and 2-21). The buildings proposed by Burnham were classical and monumental in character, showing their relationship to their antecedents in the World's Fair of 1893 and earlier baroque planning. One of the major applications of the City Beautiful ideas was in the proposals for university campuses; for example, the University of Washington plan by Charles H. Bebb and Carl F. Gould (3).

1976), its ancestry includes the Baroque city: Pope Sixtus V's Rome (Bacon 1974; Benevolo 1980; Schultz 1989), L'Enfant's design for Washington, DC (Peets 1927; Gallion and Eisner 1986; Reps 1991), and Haussmann's later work in Paris (Couperie 1965; Evenson 1979; Olsen 1986). Indeed, the Columbia Exposition might be regarded as the end of a line of city planning thought as much as the beginning of a new one (Schultz 1989).

The Columbian Exposition was a major planning and design success that captured the imagination of Americans and particularly of civic leaders, who saw it as prototype of what the American city could be. It was sponsored by Chicago businesses as a symbol of the city's commercial and, they hoped, cultural greatness. The planner of the exposition was Frederick Law Olmsted with Daniel Burnham as the architect. The exposition design was a departure from the mainstream of the work of both. Olmsted was better known for his suburban design work in the English Landscape architectural tradition (e.g., Riverside, Illinois), while Burnham's architectural work (e.g., the Rand McNally Building in Chicago, and the John Wanamaker Building in Philadelphia, both with J. W. Root) was a precursor to Modernism.

The City Beautiful movement was an urban design and architecture of display but it also sought a more efficient, hygienic city. The term "civic design" could certainly be applied to it. The goal was to instill civic pride through the grandeur of the built environment. The generic City Beautiful scheme has the basic elements of its baroque antecedents—axial avenues terminating at focal points, grand plazas, wide streets, and large-scale classical buildings enclosing spaces. The inspiration came via the Ecole des Beaux Arts in Paris, which was the leading school of architecture and city design at the beginning of the twentieth century and the inspiration for architects throughout the Western world. Plans for cities had to be large scale, bold and classical in layout and in architecture (Burnham and Bennett 1909; Wrigley 1960; Brownlee 1989; Schultz 1989; W. Wilson 1989).

The chief propagator of the City Beautiful was Daniel Burnham himself. Burnham prepared a number of plans, including one for Manila and another for San Francisco after the fire of 1906, but his best-known plan is for Chicago itself (Wrigley 1960; Burnham and Bennett 1909). The plan is a regional one, but attention was lavished on the development of a symmetrical plan around the city hall. The scheme was grand, embodying the beliefs encapsulated in Burnham's renowned epigram, "Make no small plans; they have no power to seize men's minds." In all senses, Burnham's plan for Chicago is an application of the generic City Beautiful ideas (see Fig. 2-6). Although many other such city plans exist (e.g., San Francisco; Columbus, Ohio; and Philadelphia—see Fig. 2-19), few have been implemented. They were, however, the inspiration for two major capital cities: Canberra in Australia designed by Chicagoan Walter Burley Griffin (National Capital Development Commission 1965; Bacon 1974) and, later, New Delhi in India (Irving 1981) as well as a number of smaller schemes (see also Figs. 2-16, 2-19, and 2-20).

The Modern Movements

In much of this book the Modern movement will be referred to as if it were an entity because of the number of shared theoretical assumptions on which various lines of thinking were based. In Europe and North America, at least, these assumptions were both based on particular interpretations of the concepts of Christian compassion and the Enlightenment tradition—the beliefs that people and environments are perfectible and that making the world free of war and hunger were attainable goals worth achieving. Such ends could be attained by reform or revolution—"Architecture or revolution" according to Le Corbusier.

While there were many shared values among the various schools of thought that comprise the Modernists, there are also, however, major and significant differences. The Modernists can be categorized into two broad streams of thought about city design that are exemplified, but not uniquely, by the *Garden City* as a type, or model, and the *Radiant City* as a type. Both types have had much to commend them but have also been found to be limited approaches to city design (Lesnikowski 1982; Fishman 1987; Broadbent 1990). The two represent very different city design ideologies based on two very different intellectual attitudes. Much of what has been built since World War II is an amalgam of the two in application, and the lines between them are often blurred, but they will be treated as pure types here for such purity abounds.

The *Empiricist* branch of the Modern movement is primarily, but by no means uniquely, Anglo-American in cultural heritage. Its design proposals were based on the assumption that actions should be based on learning from observation of the world. The *Rationalist* branch is predominantly Continental European with its ancestry in the former Soviet Union, Germany, France, and Holland, but has strong adherents in Great Britain, the Americas, and in Asia. In urban design its concern has been with designing idealized future social systems to be housed in an idealized geometrical world. There were bold versions of the Rationalist thinking in Latin America, particularly in Brazil and Venezuela, but the connections to European thinking are clear (Gastal 1982). The ideas and applications of both groups went back and forth across the Atlantic and were carried into colonial empires by expatriate architects and through the return of native architects to their own lands after their education in Europe or the United States.

Despite the visionary work of Americans such as Hugh Ferriss (Ferriss 1929; Leich 1980), Rationalist de-

sign ideals were largely brought to the United States by Europeans. The first major example of a Rationalist architectural application at the building level is the Philadelphia Savings Fund Society (PSFS) Building in Philadelphia by La Casse and Howe in 1932 shortly after La Casse arrived from Europe. The major impact of Rationalist thought on urban design in the United States, however, came with the arrival of expatriate architects and artists from Nazi Germany. Walter Gropius came to Harvard via Black Mountain, North Carolina, Albers to Yale, Hans Peterhaus to Chicago's Art Institute, Mies van der Rohe to the Armour Institute, and Ludwig Hilbersheimer to Chicago to practice (Wingler 1969). Indeed, some of the more pragmatic Rationalist solutions emerged in the United States before they filtered back to the countries of their intellectual origins.

The Empiricists

Empiricism, in its pure form, argues for knowledge based on evidence. In proposing future cities and urban precincts the Empiricists looked at life as lived, but they were highly selective about the experiences they chose to look at. It has been casual Empiricism. When it came to turning observation into design, they favored the picturesque. The label *Regressive Utopian* sometimes applied to the group is unfortunate for the goal of the Empiricists was to create a new world. It is, however, also an accurate label because the groups of people who might be assembled under this rubric looked for solutions to the problems resulting from the Industrial Revolution in imagined idealized pasts rather than in the systematic observation of life, human needs, and human values.

The Empiricists can be divided into two major groups—those concerned with the concept of urbanity, the *Urbanites,* and those concerned with new town design, the *Garden City* movement. The former group is exemplified by the observations and prescriptions of Camillo Sitte (1889) and more recently by those of people such as Paul Zucker (1959), Jane Jacobs (1961), Gordon Cullen (1961), Lawrence Halprin (1963, 1965, 1969, 1974), Philip Thiel (1961, forthcoming), Christopher Alexander (Alexander, Isikawa, and Silverstein 1977), Charles Moore (Johnson 1986), and the recent work of Leon Krier (Broadbent 1990). The latter group is exemplified by the writings and ideology of Ebenezer Howard (1902), Lewis Mumford (1938, 1961), and Clarence Stein (1952).

The urbanists' concern has been with the structure and detailing of the open spaces of cities and urban places, their built frame, and the sequential experience they offer as one moves through them. The street and plaza are their elements of urban design (R. Krier 1979). Their ideal city is, on an aesthetic dimension, the medieval one, the Venices of Europe. This ideal is also reflected in the current proposals of the "city livable" advocates (Lennard and Lennard 1987, 1988, 1990). The group recognizes that many people enjoy cities and urban places

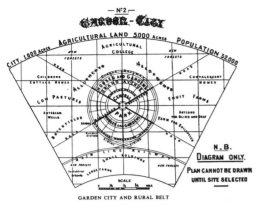

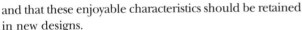

1. Generic Garden City Model (1896)

2. Part of Welwyn Garden City Plan (1920)

3. Verona, Italy

Figure 2-7: The Empiricist City
The generic plan for a Garden City developed by Ebenezer Howard (1) illustrates the attitudes and some basic design principles of the Decentralists among Empiricists. The rural imagery with its regressive architectural imagery is clearly illustrated in many places. The plan for Welwyn Garden City (Louis de Soisson, architect) shows the translation of the generic model to a particular site. (2) In contrast, the Urbanites among Empiricists tended to look back at the dense, often medieval urban fabric for inspiration (3).

and that these enjoyable characteristics should be retained in new designs.

At the core of the second, and more influential, stream of Empiricist design ideology in the United States lies a distaste for urban life and for urbanity. This bias is reflected in a long line of Anglo-American thought from Thomas Jefferson to Frank Lloyd Wright (White and White 1964) and in the suburban design of the late nineteenth century (Darley 1978; Stern with Massengale 1981; Kostof 1985; Stilgoe 1988; P. Rowe 1991). The bias is also often characteristic of Rationalist thinking of the nineteenth century. Similarly, no true Communist could be an urbanist (see Marx and Engels 1848).

The Regressive Utopians, within the Empiricist intellectual tradition in design, had as their ideal model for a human settlement the small green country town, the Vermont village, the Salisburys of England. For them the solution to the problems of the major industrial cities of the world was to decentralize them, reduce their population densities, and create more park land and more space for each household. The vehicle for achieving this end was the creation of magnets for people, new towns, which afforded the best of country and urban life (Howard 1902). Ultimately they were proposing a regional distribution of settlements. Catherine Bauer Wurster, who along with Lewis Mumford (1938, 1961; Miller 1989) was a major figure in the movement on the American side of the Atlantic, even called the group the *Decentralists*.

Their attitudes and goals can clearly be seen in the writings of Ebenezer Howard, whose ideas were first published in *Tomorrow: A Peaceful Path to Real Reform* (1898), which is better known in its reprinted form, *Garden Cities of Tomorrow* (1902). The other major idea, the neighborhood unit, came from the work of Clarence Perry, a sociologist of the Chicago school, and the planning and architectural work of Clarence Stein and Henry Wright (C. Stein 1957; Birch 1980; Parsons 1990; P. Rowe 1991). The line of thinking they represent was taken to its ultimate development in the Broadacre City of Frank Lloyd Wright (1958).

The Garden City

The ideal city promulgated by the architects and town planners associated with the Garden City Movement consisted of about 40,000 people. At its core were the central institutional buildings, surrounded by residential areas and, at the periphery, the industries encircled by a green belt (see Fig. 2-7(1)). It was to have the characteristics of a "green country town" and in the early new towns of Letchworth (1903 onwards) and Welwyn (1920), developed in England by limited dividend com-

Source: New York: Regional Survey (1927)

1. The Neighborhood Unit Concept

2. Radburn, New Jersey, Plan (1929)

3. A View of a Cul-de-Sac

4. The School

5. The Central Park

6. A Main Road Underpass

Figure 2–8: Radburn, New Jersey

The generic plan for a neighborhood unit developed by Clarence Perry, a sociologist of the Chicago school, was perceived to be a solution to the design of residential areas in the motor age (1,2). The application of the generic plan to a particular situation is best exemplified by its first example—Radburn, New Jersey. The plan by Clarence Stein and architecture by Henry Wright clearly show the basic design principles of a bounded, safe,

green residential area. A view up one of the cul-de-sacs shows the pleasant, picturesque environment that was created (3). The elementary school (4) was to be its heart. For children, the walk to school was through the central green area (5) and, where necessary, underpasses were built to segregate pedestrians from busy vehicular traffic (6). Developed in the 1930s, Radburn remains a place well loved by its residents. However, it never became a model for property developers and builders.

panies, the architecture tends to be symbolic of the small village. The roads also followed rural imagery, being

curvilinear sometimes following contour lines and sometimes not. The pattern was as much a symbolic gesture as

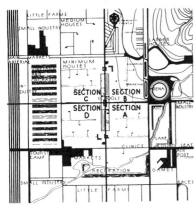

Source: Wright (1958)

1. Plan of the Downtown Area

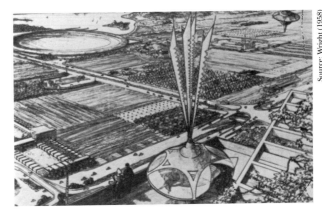

Source: Wright (1958)

2. View

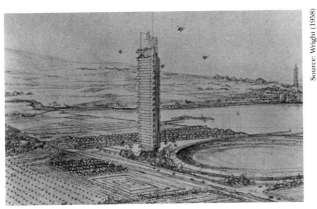

Source: Wright (1958)

3. View

Figure 2-9: Broadacre City
Broadacre city is the logical extension of the Garden City ideal. A fundamental difference between Frank Lloyd Wright's views and those of the British and Australian branch of the movement was his strong belief in individual rather than cooperative action. The plan is considerably more spacious (1) than those proposed by his contemporaries, and the illustrations show the degree to which each element of the design stands as an object in space. In the case of residential areas (2) the open space was for small-scale agriculture. For the major buildings (3) the open space acted as a visual setting. The street was seen as a channel of movement and as a boundary, not a seam.

an ecological necessity and built on the early work of Olmsted and the even earlier Picturesque movement in landscape architecture.

The Garden City, as built after World War II in many parts of the world, also incorporated the *neighborhood unit* concept (Golany 1976). Clarence Perry proposed a generic neighborhood unit type in the 1929 *Regional Survey of New York and Its Environs.* He proposed that cities should be divided into residential areas of about 160 acres each centered on an elementary school so that a child would not have to walk more than a mile to school. Three such areas would form a district large enough to have a high school. About 10 percent of the total area would be allocated to open recreational space; the major roads would be on the periphery, with minor roads serving the houses. It is a conceptually neat model of a well-ordered environment based on a number of middle-class British and American values: individuality and communality, automobile ownership yet acknowledging the worth of walking, safety for children, efficiency in circulation yet openness in spirit, and the school as a community's heart (C. Stein 1957; Gallion and Eisner 1986; P. Rowe 1991). In symbolic aesthetics, the referent was the English landscape garden of the manor. All of these characteristics can be seen in the design of Radburn, New Jersey, the original implementation of the idea (Birch 1980).

Frank Lloyd Wright's generic city plan, *Broadacre City,* stands in strong contrast to the more compact Garden City and even more so to Le Corbusier's *Radiant City* (see below). His conceptual plan clearly represents a political philosophy reflecting his belief in Jeffersonian democracy as well as the importance of land and the automobile in Americans' lives. He wrote: "Ruralism as distinguished from urbanism is American and truly democratic." Also: "When every man, woman and child may be born to put his feet on his own acres, then democracy will have been realized" (Wright 1958; see also White and White 1964). It is clear from his drawings that Wright expected a revolution never achieved in transportation technology (in this sense he was a Progressivist).

Broadacre City is of linear form with industry, commerce, housing and social facilities, and agricultural holdings in a spacious distribution along a railroad and highway arterial. It contains every building type designed by Frank Lloyd Wright. Each family has a minimum of one acre of land so that basic agricultural activities can take place. Although there are neighborhood facilities, no attempt is made to create a neighborhood unit. In many ways, the proposal is the ultimate Anglo-American dream. It provides for a high level of individuality, much open space, and high mobility—all important American values (Zelinsky 1973; Fallows 1989). Stern and

Massengale (1981) note that Wright's "characteristically American pragmatism went with the grain of the Anglo-American tradition" and with the market economy.

The Rationalists

Rationalism is the belief that truth and beauty can be divined from reality by means of pure human reason. The Rationalist, from René Descartes (1596-1650) onward, "argued for a unity of thinking and for a fundamental belief in the facts of existence, without the necessity of confirmation. . . . " (Sharp 1978b). Rationality and Rationalism in architecture are not necessarily allied terms. Rationalism has become a synonym for Functionalism in architecture and the definition of function is seen to be rational (Broadbent 1978). Rationalist urban design has stood for an a priori commitment to Cartesian geometry, monumental simplicity, and deliberate control. Rationalists saw the Garden City and the medieval city as representing a possibly rational past but not the future. Procedurally, Rationalist design relied on a deductive process of establishing a model society, socially and physically. This does not mean that their ideas had no precedents, but rather that they wished to break completely from the present. Rationalists were (and are) intolerant of pluralism, of historic forms, and even of the historic origins of their own forms (Lai 1988).

Rationalist urban design ideas combine a concern with progressive if poorly reasoned political ideas for the social organization of the city with Platonic geometrical shapes for its physical form (L. Krier 1978; Sharp 1978a; Lesnikowski 1982; Boyer 1983). In commenting on the medieval city—the city forms loved by Sitte—Le Corbusier noted: "it is the way of a donkey" (Rowe and Koetter 1979). In rationalizing Albert Mayer's plan for Chandigarh, he turned the curving roads into straight ones without changing the basic format of the city layout (i.e., its neighborhood unit basis). By doing so he achieved a bold, orthogonal, zonal scheme. The idea in urban renewal was to clear the slate and to start again. As Sant'Elia (1973; Caramel and Longatti 1988) noted: "Demolish without pity the venerated city." Taken to its extreme, the Rationalist position on urban planning was expressed by Benito Mussolini in the 1920s:

> Monuments are one thing, ruins are another: yet another is quaintness or so called local color. All such sordid quaintness is sworn to the ax . . . destined to fall in the name of decency, hygiene and, if you will, the beauty of the Capital (quoted in Frampton 1983).

Mussolini's own line of thought is exemplified in the plans and preliminary construction of the E42 area of Rome, which was due to house the Universal Exhibition of 1941 (Mariani 1990). Later it was developed into the EUR, an office and convention complex. The scheme is monumental in scale with broad boulevards, large buildings, and a City Beautiful–like overall organization.

The Rationalists consisted of a more diverse set of people and ideas than the Empiricists because they were dealing with models of an unobservable but imagined, idealized future world more illusory than images of the existing small town life or the medieval city. The Rationalists subsume groups such as the Futurists of Italy (see Caramel and Longatti 1988 on Sant'Elia; Zevi 1978), Italian Rationalists such as Grupp 7 under the leadership of Giuseppe Terragni, the de Stijl group in Holland, architects associated with the Bauhaus in Germany, the Cubists of France, and the Rationalist and Constructivist schools of Soviet architecture in the period 1917 to 1932. It is also possible that Rationalism subsumed an international movement to incorporate occult, theosophy, geomancy, and esoteric imagery as a spiritual heirophany in urban design, but there are also Empiricists who did the same (possibly the architects of the Prairie school in Chicago at the beginning of the twentieth century who were influenced by the Ho-o-den exhibition of the Imperial Japanese government at the 1893 fair). These ideas were perceived to be an alternative to late-nineteenth-century and early-twentieth-century Empiricism as the generator of ideas (Proudfoot 1991). They were highly influential in the United States as they were around the world.

The major proponent of the Rationalist approach to urban design was C.I.A.M., the Congrès Internationaux d'Architecture Moderne (Sert and C.I.A.M. 1944; Le Corbusier 1973; Bakema 1982) and its descendent, Team 10 (Smithson 1968; Smithson and Smithson 1970, 1972). They were highly influential in the United States. Also in the United States, Louis Kahn's proposals for Philadelphia (Ronner and Jhavari 1987) and the work of the Bauhaus masters Walter Gropius (e.g., New Kensington, Pennsylvania), Mies van der Rohe (e.g., Illinois Institute of Technology [ITT] campus), and Ludwig Hilbershemier (1940; Pommer, Spaeth, and Harrington 1988) fall into the Rationalist school.

Although all these different streams of thought exist, there are a number of philosophical positions that the groups have in common. They were unafraid of large cities, of proposing the alteration of the piecemeal ownership of land into large holdings, of radical political theories, of harnessing modern technology, or of developing a new aesthetic. Their designs consist of tall buildings set in open green spaces connected by, but turning their backs on, roads and highways in as orthogonal a pattern as possible. Not only were they simply unafraid to depart from the past, they strongly advocated a new architecture for a new age. They convinced some major patrons that this direction was the correct one for the future (e.g., President Juscelino Kubitschek of Brazil, patron of Brasilia, and Prime Minister Jawarharlal Nehru, patron of Chandigarh). Of all the architects associated with Progressivist ideas, Le Corbusier was probably more concerned about the changing world and urbanism than any of the others, and his models of the future city have been

1. La Cité Industrielle Plan (1904–1917)

2. The Railway Station, La Cité Industrielle

3. Los Angeles, Rush City Reformed (1923–1928)

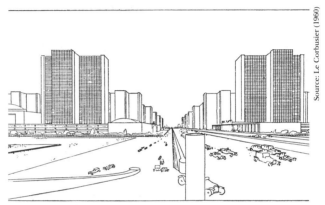

5. Brasilia

6. New York City

Figure 2-10: The Rationalist City

The Rationalists among modern architects were unified by their application of reason to the problems of the day. Their thinking was largely unfettered by the realities of life. Rather it was guided by a distrust of information obtained by the senses. Their focus of attention was on the development of possible future social and physical structures for cities and the buildings within them based on their own imaginations. The schemes include Toni Garnier's *Cité Industrielle* (1,2), developed during the first decade of the century with its forward-looking architecture and the work derived from the Bauhaus. The Bauhaus line of thinking, with its bold rational geometry as exemplified in Rush City Reformed designed by Richard Neutra, has been particularly influential (3). The same thought process, but with considerably richer designs, is shown in Le Corbusier's 1922 proposal for *Une Ville Contemporaine* (4) and the 1933 proposal *La Ville Radieuse*—the *Radiant City*. Their influence is best exemplified in Brasilia (5) and in campus and public housing design in the United States. Although many American cities have Rationalist gridiron plans, they are hardly Rationalist cities (6).

the most influential (Le Corbusier 1934, 1948, 1960, 1973; Evenson 1970; Curtis 1986; H. Brooks 1987).

The Corbusian City

Le Corbusier presented two sets of similar ideas about what the city should be. The first was the *Contemporary City for Three Million* developed for exhibition in 1922, and the second was the more fully developed extension of these ideas in *La Ville Radieuse* (Le Corbusier 1934). In both he was concerned with the geometric order of the city. The ordering system he chose was the straight line and the right angle—a Cartesian order—on a large scale (Eslami 1985, 1988). He was fundamentally concerned with movement through the city at speed. He saw the street as simply a place for moving cars.

The frame of the city would be a large-scale gridiron highway system with superimposed diagonal roads meeting at the center. Access to buildings would be from exits on this grid system but pedestrian routes would be separate. At the center was a railway station and a platform for airplanes as well as the intersection of the highway system. Surrounding the center would be a large park within which sixty-story cross-shaped office skyscrapers were to be located at 250-meter intervals. They would be interspersed with two- and three-story buildings in the form of stepped terraces containing restaurants, cafes, and luxury shops. The civic center would be on one side of the city center. It would house the city hall, museums, and other public facilities. The whole city would be within a park.

The residential areas would be of two types near the center: six-story maisonettes crossing the park lands in ribbons with recreational facilities between them and apartment blocks; and farther out, villas. The maisonettes would be two stories with a balcony so that they would be open to the sunlight and air, and the balconies be large enough for a person to carry out daily calisthenics. The apartment slabs would be in a continuous U-shaped Cartesian configuration with courtyards. His plan for the *Unité d'habitation* was a logical extension of this idea.

The Unité d'habitation

Le Corbusier developed the Unité d'habitation as a concept for neighborhood, which stands in strong contrast to Perry's *neighborhood unit*. The two models can be regarded as exemplars of the contrasting attitudes of the Empiricists and Rationalists. The Unité is another conceptual scheme that has had a powerful influence on architects' thinking about the form of cities, especially as it was actually implemented in a number of places, the best-known of which is in Marseilles (Le Corbusier 1954).

The Unité is a vertical neighborhood—a neighborhood in a building. The building is set on pilotes and consists of shopping on a central floor and areas for a nursery school and other communal facilities on the roof. The apartments are each two floors high, with a balcony

1. The Unité d'habitation, Marseilles

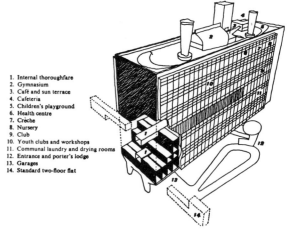

1. Internal thoroughfare
2. Gymnasium
3. Café and sun terrace
4. Cafeteria
5. Children's playground
6. Health centre
7. Crèche
8. Nursery
9. Club
10. Youth clubs and workshops
11. Communal laundry and drying rooms
12. Entrance and porter's lodge
13. Garages
14. Standard two-floor flat

Source: Richards (1940)

2. Cross Section

Figure 2-11: The Unité d'habitation

The Unité d'habitation developed by Le Corbusier during and immediately after World War II (1) stands in strong contrast to Clarence Perry's neighborhood unit scheme and Radburn, New Jersey (see Fig. 2–8). It is a vertical neighborhood. The cross section (2) shows the various components of the scheme: the community facilities on the roof, the shopping strip in the center, the layout of the apartment units, and the skip-stop elevator system employed by it. Its influence has been enormous (see Figs. 4–1(1), 5–3, and 6–6).

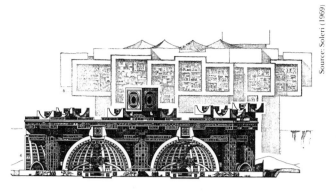

1. Arcosanti (1969–1970). Paolo Soleri, Architect

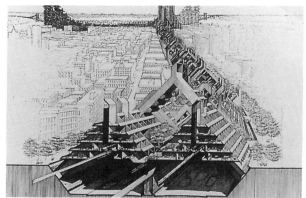

2. Mega-Roadtown (1970). Paul Rudolf, Architect

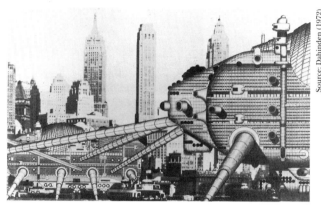

3. Walking City (1964). Ron Herron, Architect

Figure 2–12: Megastructures

There have been many proposals for a city as a building. While no city of this type has been built, Paolo Soleri is making a slow progress on an Arcosanti near Scottsdale, Arizona. It is one of the smallest of his generic designs (population 1,500 to 3,000, with 215 to 400 people per acre). Many of his proposals are over twice the height of the Empire State Building in New York. Le Corbusier's Unité is a neighborhood in a building (see Fig. 2–11). Paul Rudolph's plan for Manhattan, New York (2), and the Archigram group's images of the future city (3) take the idea further.

to provide access to fresh air and sunlight—a primary concern of Le Corbusier. The arrangement of apartments allows for a skip-stop elevator system with elevators stopping on each third floor. The ground floor would be freed for the parking of cars, for circulation, and for recreation. A number of such buildings in a parklike setting would constitute the residential area of a city.

The Megastructure

If Broadacre City is the logical extension of Empiricist thought, the logical extension of the line of thinking of the Rationalists within the Modernist fold was the megastructure (Banham 1976; Barnett 1986). Its forerunners were the City of the Future of Hugh Ferris (Leich 1980), Sant'Elia's Futurist designs (Caramel and Longatti 1988), the Unité, and Le Corbusier's schemes for Algiers and Rio de Janeiro (Le Corbusier 1960). The basic idea is still the "city in a building" as proposed, for instance, in the Arcologies of Paolo Soleri (Soleri 1969, 1981; Wall 1971), the neighborhood in a building, and the university in a building. While many megastructure proposals have been generated (Dahinden 1972; Banham 1976; Sky and Stone 1976), little has really been built at this scale. Some of the proposals have become very well known because of their boldness of design and because they represent the type of thinking very well. One example is the proposal

for Tokyo Bay by Kenzo Tange (Kultermann 1970)—a city built on the Bay. Another is the concept of the plug-in city of the Archigram group (Barnett 1986; Cook et al. 1991). Its basic notion was that the city changes rapidly, so build the infrastructure and then plug in the disposable elements.

Post-Modern Movements

A great deal of recent and current work owes much to the Modernist design principles if less to the spirit of Modernism developed during the first quarter of this century (Portoghesi 1979, 1982). Major projects such as La Défense in Paris or Kenzo Tange's design for a new central business district now under construction in Naples follow the urban design principles of the Modernists, although the individual buildings are clearly more in line with Post-Modernist aesthetic principles, having a higher degree of decoration and historical referents. Post-Modernism of this type is principally European and American in nature. It has hardly penetrated Singapore, Hong Kong, or Jakarta and only barely made an impression on Japan. At best, schemes such as the monumental Neo-Classical work at Antigone, Montpellier, by Ricardo Bofill and the Taller, and the new towns of Marne-la-Vallée and Cergy-Pontoise have moved French urban design away from boredom of the Le Corbusian new towns because of their focus on the space-making qualities of buildings (Torchinsky 1989).

1. Renaissance Center, Detroit

Source: *Architectural Design* 62, no. 5/6: 53

2. Paternoster Square Redevelopment, London

Courtesy SWA Group

3. Harlequin Plaza, Denver

Figure 2-13: Post-Modern Urban Design
With the rejection of the Modern movements' generic types came a new set of urban design approaches. During the 1970s and 1980s schemes ranged from the economic pragmatic (1) to explorations of various historic antecedents in adapted form, as in the work of Hammond, Bebe, and Babka and others at Paternoster Square adjacent to St. Paul's Cathedral, London (2). Some schemes are purely classical, others explore new geometries, such as Harlequin Plaza in Denver (3) by George Hargreaves of the SWA Group. Yet others fall into the mainstream of Neo-Rationalism or Neo-Empiricism (see Fig. 2–14).

Sometimes, the referents seize on idiosyncrasies of past styles to produce an imitation that mocks, or parodies, the original; at others, the referents are used in a somewhat schizophrenic manner as a pastiche. They represent efforts to respond to the criticism of Modernist design and thereby develop new approaches to design, or rather adaptations of traditional approaches. Much of the work, however, misses the point of the criticism. It fails to elevate its residents despite striving for grandeur.

The criticism of the application of Modernist urban design ideas, both Rationalist and Empiricist, has been extensive (J. Jacobs 1961; Gans 1962, 1968, 1975; Brolin 1974; Blake 1977; Newman 1980b; Wiedenhoeft 1981; Wolfe 1981; Herdeg 1983; see also Gosling and Maitland 1984a, 1984b). The response of the design community has been in a number of directions, sometimes simultaneously, and sometimes independently. One attitude has simply been to let the market dictate—what can be sold should be designed. This attitude has seen architecture and urban design become a "commodification" of fashionable images for use by the middle class.

The label "Post-Modernism," like Modernism, generally covers many schools of thought. There have been a number of new movements that can be classified under the general rubric of Post-Modernism (Portoghesi 1979; Bruegmann 1981; Jencks 1986; Davey 1987; Klotz 1989). These movements include those that can be grouped under the titles of *Neo-Rationalism* and *Neo-Empiricism* as

well as a small *Neo-Cosmological* or, perhaps, a *Cosmological Revival* movement and a *Discrete*, or *Weak*, *Architectural* movement and a *Classical Revival* movement. Post-Modernism, in a broad sense, also includes the Metabolists of Japan, with their new urban forms consisting of series of towers linking by highways, and their British counterparts, the Archigram group of the 1960s, the strict Classicism of John Blatteau and Alan Greenberg (Stern with Gastil 1988), and the Expressionists such as Terry Farrell in the United Kingdom (Gosling and Maitland 1984a, 1984b; Farrell 1985; Broadbent 1990).

Two major current philosophies are attracting the attention of both architects and laypeople: (1) *Neo-Traditionalism*, as exemplified by the work of Andres Duany and Elizabeth Plater Zyberk at Seaside, Florida (Duany 1989), the Laguna West Master Plan by Calthorpe Associates (Fromm 1991), in a different vein, Quinlan Terry's work in Richmond in England, and even more startlingly, perhaps, the planning decisions to revive the downtowns of cities by locating facilities (such as Oriole Park—itself a Neo-Traditional structure—at Camden Yards in Baltimore) there; and (2) *Deconstructionism*, as represented by Bernard Tschumi's Parc de la Villette and Corona Park proposal for Flushing, New York (Tschumi 1987, 1988a; Broadbent 1990). Much is being built within the former philosophy, but little in the latter. Most of these Post-Modern movements, however, represent a continuation of the two major philosophical streams of thinking that

1. Solana, Westlake, Southlake, Texas

2. Irvine Town Center, California

3. Kresge College, University of California at Santa Cruz

Figure 2-14: Neo-Rationalism and Neo-Empiricism
The Rationalist spirit in Post-Modern architecture is exemplified in the design of the Solana office campus near Dallas, Texas, by Mitchell/Giurgola (1). The concern is with the design of the environment as geometric art form. Much the same line of thinking but with different geometries is characteristic of recent Deconstructionist work. Neo-Empiricism tends not only to have a different geometry but relies on observations of experiences of the environment as the basis for design (2,3). Recently it has shown a shift away from the reliance on personal observation to the application, consciously or unconsciously, of empirical research in design.

dominate thinking about urban design: Empiricism and Rationalism.

The Neo-Rationalists like their forbears continue to have a major interest in geometries and in what they regard as progressive politics (Broadbent 1990). The basic design principles involves the layering of grids both in plan and in architecture. Much recent work is primarily urban architecture rather than urban design (e.g., the Karlsruhe library by Mattias Ungers in Europe, the Friday Mosque scheme by Derek Walker and Associates, and Peter Eisenman's Visual Arts Center at Ohio State University) but includes such building complexes as the Rauchstrasse housing scheme in Berlin under the direction of Rob Krier, the cemetery at Moderno by Aldo Rossi, and housing schemes by Carlo Anymonimo. In Japan, proposals such as the Nakonshima Point project, a so-called twenty-first-century park by Todao Ando, are a mixture of Neo-Rationalist and Deconstructionist ideas. Deconstruction itself represents a radically different attitude toward the geometrical orders used (Johnson and Wigley 1988; Benjamin 1988; Norris 1988; see also Fig. 4–6).

The Neo-Empiricist stream is comprised of a diverse set of people who have shown a concern with the details of life in their work (Broadbent 1990). They have been called the New Humanists (Fitzhardinge 1990). Probably the most significant designs that have emerged in this line of thought as a response to the failures of the Modern movement are the new university town of Louvain-La-

Neuve, in Belgium, and, as large-scale urban design projects, Battery Park City in New York City and Mission Bay in San Francisco. These designs are on the periphery of the Neo-Traditionalist movement. Architects are looking to the past again to identify patterns of the environment that are pleasing and have some meaning to people (see R. Krier 1979). One major change in urban design ideology hearkens back to the work of Sitte. It is the *Urban Consolidation* movement. The argument is for a return to high-density, relatively low-rise living to promote the use of mass transit and to save agricultural land. It is based on considerable Empirical evidence that such environments can be highly livable but in countries such as Australia and Canada, as well as the United States, people are habituated to regard the suburban environment as the ideal (P. Rowe 1991).

The Neo-Empiricists also include people such as Christopher Alexander and his colleagues (1977), Charles Moore in the United States (Littlejohn 1984; Johnson 1986), and Europeans such as Ralph Erskine (Egelius 1980a, 1980b), Herman Hertzberger (1980), and Lucien Kroll (1972, 1980) as well as the Neo-Traditionalists. Their implemented urban design work is at the building-complex and small town scale.

During the late 1980s and early 1990s, there has been a reaction against designing each new urban design scheme so that it loudly draws attention to itself. A number of architects believe that cities lose much if each new

1. Mission Bay, San Francisco

2. Battery Park City, New York

Collection of Richard Fitzhardinge

3. Les Arcades du Lac, St. Quentin en Yvellines, France

Figure 2-15: "Weak" or "Discrete" Urban Design
A new attitude toward urban design began to appear among a number of architects, particularly in Spain in the post-Franco era. Schemes such as Mission Bay in San Francisco (1) and Battery Park City in New York (2) also fall into this line of thinking. They consist of well-executed buildings that merge into their context and form an accommodating backdrop to life. They are not seen as a set of objects to be contemplated. Such an attitude stands in strong contrast to the work of European Neo-Rationalists such as, say, that of Ricardo Bofill and the Taller (3).

building strives to be a new *center* or foreground building. A movement named *Discrete Architecture* is remarkable because the buildings are not remarkable. It is similar to customary Islamic design in only drawing attention to itself in a discrete fashion—something seen, for instance, in the work of Hassan Fathy. Designers' concern has been with enhancing the overall fabric of the city—of the overall mass of buildings, open spaces, and streets of a place and region. The work is, perhaps not surprisingly, developing primarily in Spain, with the urban and building design work of Jaime Bach and Gabriel Mora, Esteve Bonell Costa, and Antonio Cruz and Antonio Ortiz, but it reflects a more widespread concern about the direction in which urban design has been going (see Chapters 4 and 5). Much of the rebuilding of Barcelona is in this vein. In the United States the concern for regionalism and for architecture that fits into its background is reflected in the work in Battery Park City and in Mission Bay. The work is a continuation of Modernism, a Neo-Modernism, perhaps, but recognizes the importance of history, of the whole, and of the individual expressive talents of architects in creating environments for the future (De Solà Morales 1989; Buchanan 1990).

Despite the concerns with cosmology by Frank Lloyd Wright, Burley Griffin, and other architects of the Prairie school, the effort to draw a correspondence between the

heavens and the geometries of cities and buildings has been largely dormant for some time except in parts of India and China. A small group of architects today have, however, been influenced by the ancient vedas of India. The *Maharishi Sthapatya Ved* is the science of Vedic architecture whose principles, its proponents state, are being verified by modern empirical science. It is an architecture in "accordance with natural law" (Maharishi Sthapatya Ved Institute 1991). Little has been built within the strict principles of Vedic architecture, but a new town is being built near Fairfield, Iowa, and another three or four in Europe, India, and Africa. A number of architects in Asia are also returning to cosmological traditions in architectural design, but the attitude does not seem to have extended to urban design. Indeed, many of those architects (e.g., Itsuko Hasegawa) practicing *Feng-Shui* deliberately shut themselves off from a concern with improving the general nature of human settlements. Still, there are proponents for designing within some sort of cosmological and electromagnetic order (Martin 1991; Swan 1991).

Perhaps the most pragmatic of what might be regarded as urban design ideologies today is the *Community Design* movement. It consists of a number of disparate groups, usually architect-led, that emerged in the 1960s. They are united in (1) being based on the attitude that the people who are to use the environments being designed know best what is good for them, and (2) the desire to enfranchise in planning and design those people who have neither the financial nor political clout to get things done for themselves (J. Stern 1989). The types of projects that have followed such precepts range in type from downtown renewal (e.g., Roanoke, Virginia) to self-help housing, or homesteading. Much of the design falls into the types that mean the most to people—the places where they live (Fig. 4–8; see also Hatch 1984). Beneficial though the work has been, the total output has been low in comparison to the housing needs of the poor in the United States.

The movement also consists of such organizations as church groups who have fought for neighborhood revitalization. Their schemes tend to be modest in size and lack what architects would regard as distinction, but they have become symbols of pride and economic progress for the communities that develop them. In Philadelphia, there are two major examples of such developments of note: Hope Plaza Shopping Center, developed by the Deliverance Evangelistic Church, and Progress Plaza, developed by a corporation affiliated with the Zion Baptist Church of North Philadelphia, an area of public squalor unimaginable to most Europeans today but not atypical in parts of U.S. cities.

THE URBAN CONSEQUENCES OF TWENTIETH-CENTURY CITY DESIGN IDEAS

What impact has this plethora of design ideas had on the twentieth-century city? A quick glance at cities in the United States today yields little evidence of the impact of specific design ideologies at a supra-building level. This observation is both accurate and misleading. It is accurate if one looks at the whole of most existing metropolises, but there have been many building and open-space complexes, new towns, and suburban developments at a supra-building scale designed self-consciously during this century. Many have been mentioned already.

These developments are essentially of two types. The first is the *Administered Community* and the second, the *Designed Community* (Gottschalk 1975). Company towns and public housing projects exemplify the first type. They do not take on a life of their own after they are built. Their inhabitants, or users, have little if any chance to change the environment as they will; the administrators control who enters the community to live and such matters as the behavior and aesthetic tastes of the inhabitants through sets of rules decreeing what can and cannot be done. Designed communities are those self-conscious designs that are turned over to their residents, or users, when completed, as in Columbia, Maryland, and many large-scale suburban developments. Such communities will change over time into the type of design that results from unselfconscious physical planning. Cities such as Brasilia are administered communities in this sense, rather

than designed communities. Designed communities will clearly retain some of the patterns, particularly the street pattern, of their original plans, but the distribution of uses and building types will respond to individual needs and market forces over time. In Levittown, Pennsylvania, for example, it is very difficult to identify the four standard house types now, forty years after they were built.

New Cities and New Towns

New towns are fiat settlements designed to have all the components of existing towns. While few new towns have been self-consciously designed in the United States, many have been built elsewhere during this century. The United Kingdom and other European countries have had major new town programs since World War II; an estimated 1,200, ranging in size from 30,000 to 500,000 people, were built in the Soviet Union between 1926 and 1980 (Gallion and Eisner 1986). India has many new company towns. Possibly as many as 400 have been built since independence in 1947. Israel has used new towns as a way of holding territory. The United States, in contrast, has seen the phenomenal growth of suburbia and suburban designs, sometimes new towns in themselves, during the same time (Stern with Massengale 1981; P. Rowe 1991). As empirical studies of these developments are conducted, so our knowledge about urban design is increased.

Some of the new cities that have been self-consciously designed have been created for administrative purposes; they are not necessarily administered communities, although they tend to be so. Capital cities have been designed for imperial powers and newly independent nations and also as the result the reordering of the internal political jurisdictional patterns within nations. As one of the major objectives in capital city design is to display a people's worth, these cities tend to be tightly administered.

Canberra (National Capital Development Commission 1965) and New Delhi (Nilsson 1975; Irving 1981) were laid out along the design principles of the City Beautiful movement, although the former may have followed certain geomantic principles close to Burley Griffin's heart (Proudfoot forthcoming). Bhubaneswar, the new capital for Orissa in India, may be unique among capitals in following Garden City design principles rather than Rationalist ones (Rapoport 1977; Lang in progress). Chandigarh, the capital of Punjab, and Gandhinagar, the capital for Gujarat, both in India, follow the principles of the Progressivists with their Rationalist geometries and preponderant use of the Internationalist building aesthetic (Evenson 1966; Nilsson 1975; see also Fig. I–2). Brasilia is the prime example of this ideology (Evenson 1973); Islamabad in Pakistan is similar if on a smaller scale (Nilsson 1975). Abuja, the new capital for Nigeria, follows a mixture of design principles.

The new towns in the United States, with a few exceptions (e.g., the Greenbelt cities of the 1930s; see

1. The Mall, Washington DC (1909)

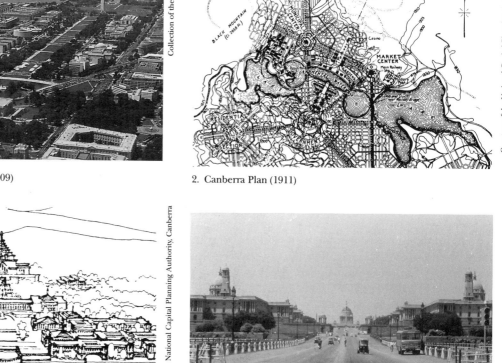

2. Canberra Plan (1911)

4. Raj Path, New Delhi

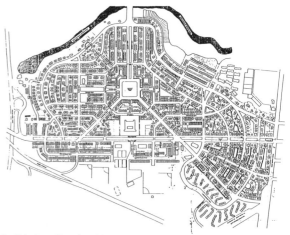

3. Griffin's Proposal for the Capitol Complex, Canberra

5. Fairview, Camden, New Jersey (1917)

Figure 2-16: Implemented City Beautiful Cities

The City Beautiful design principles have never really been implemented for a city as a whole. The extension of the Mall in Washington, DC, as the result of the MacMillan Commission's work is an early example (1). Canberra, the capital of Australia, designed by Chicago architect Walter Burley Griffin, has a City Beautiful plan with a Garden City overlay (2,3). Imperial New Delhi (4) is similar. Designed by Edwin Luytens and Herbert Baker, it is a City Beautiful plan and its capitol complex (4) exem-

plifies the ideas of the movement; however, much of the rest of the New Delhi is a Garden City. On a smaller scale the City Beautiful scheme has been implemented in suburban design. Fairview (formerly Yorkship), in Camden, New Jersey, designed by Electus D. Litchfield for the Emergency Fleet Corporation in 1917, is an example of the City Beautiful ideology on a neighborhood scale (5). While its architecture is not monumental, the planning and spatial enclosure follow the design principles of the movement.

1. Levittown, Pennsylvania (1940s)

2. Chesterbrook, Pennsylvania (1980s)

3. Riverside, Illinois (1870s)

Figure 2-17: Garden City New Towns and Suburbs

An extraordinarily large number of new towns and suburbs (1) have been built across the world since the end of World War II. They include towns built as part of government policies, such as those in Great Britain, and those built largely through private enterprise, as in the United States (2,3), following Garden City principles to some extent. Columbia, Maryland, is a prime example of the Garden City in the United States (see Fig. 13-6). The planning reflects earlier suburban designs in which the single-family detached home is the central building type.

Dreier 1936), have been suburban developments primarily motivated by the desire and the financial necessity to sell land off quickly. These developments (e.g., Levittown, Pennsylvania) thus follow the land subdivision principles needed to optimize land speculation, but they have Garden City overtones. The street system and building plots and some open-space reserves are the only elements of the landscape that are planned. The individual elements of the rest may be self-consciously designed, but the overall settlement is not. There are a number of exceptions to this rule all across the country. They include a number of new towns, but most are large-scale suburban developments. They consist of carefully considered overall plans, but they have to take into account the nature of the market for they are developed privately or by such quasi-governmental authorities as the New York State Development Corporation (Leinberger and Lockwood 1986; Fishman 1987; Stilgoe 1988).

These new towns and new suburbs are *designed communities.* Their developers (e.g., the Rouse Organization in Columbia, Maryland, the Carpenter family in Las Colinas, Texas, and Robert Davis in Seaside, Florida) with their urban designers/consultants have been responsible for designing their overall infrastructure, for providing basic public facilities, and for the control of the quality of the design of individual components of the scheme

through the use of guidelines, controls, and covenants. They hired prominent designers to lead the way. Less well known is that the United States has had many *administered communities* built for industries and defense forces since World War II, but these towns have been poorly documented.

The impact of the Garden City concept on the design of new towns and suburban developments was particularly strong in the three decades after World War II and is influential still (P. Rowe 1991). There was not only the influence in the United Kingdom through the British New Towns Act, but also in the privately developed new towns in the United States such as Columbia, Maryland (R. Brooks 1974), Jonathan, Minnesota (Birch 1980), Woodlands and Flowermound, Texas, and even more recently (1984+), Las Colinas, Texas. The Garden City model was the basis of design of the many new industrial cities elsewhere (e.g., Jameshedpur and Rorkela in India, Elizabeth, in South Australia, and Sasolburg in South Africa, and a number of new developments in Continental Europe as well much of the suburban growth there from Copenhagen to Vienna and European new towns such as the Louvain-la-Neuve, in Belgium). Their success arises from the appeal to many people of a small town life and suburban atmosphere, the ease in using the automobile, and the clarity of their overall organization.

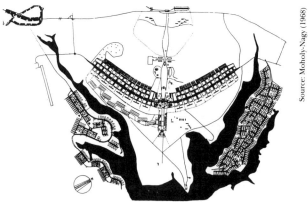

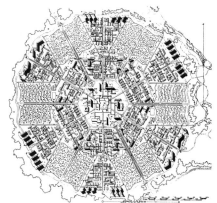

1. Brasilia Plan

2. The Capitol Complex

3. Proposal by Mauricio Roberto, Architect

Figure 2–18: Brasilia

Brasilia was proposed as a capital city for 500,000 people. First settled in 1960, it is a linear city with an expressway as the spine of the plan. The plan (1) by Lucio Costa (see Fig. 21–7(2)) shows the cruciform plan of two main axes. The civic axis of government (2), commercial, and entertainment buildings runs east/west. The residential superblocks are located on the two arms. "The buildings become extensions of expressway structures and are indivisable from it, every part relating to the design of the whole" (Bacon 1974). Other proposals (e.g., 3) show much the same Rationalist spirit.

Le Corbusier's influence on housing project design has been a major one in the United States. The Rationalist influence of town design has been less here than elsewhere, where it has been major. While his only implemented city design is Chandigarh, probably the more Le Corbusian city is Brasilia, the capital of Brazil. In Chandigarh, Le Corbusier was responsible for the overall plan and the design of the capitol complex, but much of the housing design was done by others—Maxwell Fry, Jane Drew, and Le Corbusier's cousin Pierre Jeanneret (Le Corbusier 1960; Evenson 1966; Kalia 1982; Riboulet 1985). Although Le Corbusier was not involved in the design of Brasilia, his basic ideas were faithfully followed (Stäubli 1966; Evenson 1973; Bacon 1974; Gosling and Maitland 1984a). Brasilia's overall design was a competition-winning scheme by Lucio Costa in 1957. Much of the building design is by Oscar Niemeyer.

Brasilia's bold design is based on an architectural idea. The plan consists of two major traffic axes in the sign of a cross. One of the arteries is in the shape of an arc while the other is shorter, with the municipal plaza at one end and the governmental complex—the Plaza of the Three Powers and the Esplanade of the Ministries—at the other. The residential areas are distributed along the other axis.

These areas consist of slab apartment buildings in rows. There is a major lake framing the one side of the composition, which is more like a standard North American suburban subdivision than anything else in Brasilia and is popular with senior officials as a place to live. The primary concern in the design of Brasilia is with the city as symbol—a symbol of independence and modernity—and not with promoting habitability or providing for the type of life lived in Rio de Janeiro. Brasilia is self-consciously not only a planned city but a work of art. It reflects a concern for the city as a piece of sculpture.

New towns and new suburbs have served a number of purposes that will continue into the future. Inevitably, the people of the United States will have to decide how to handle population growth (or decline) while resources decline and land cannot be disposed of simply as the market decides if we are to achieve healthy biogenic and sociogenic environments. The AIA (American Institute of Architects) has taken the position that this can be done by the incremental addition of neighborhoods to the urban periphery (Gallion and Eisner 1986). This extension of metropolitan areas seems inevitable and the question that will be addressed in Part Two of this book is: What issues need to be considered in shaping this development?

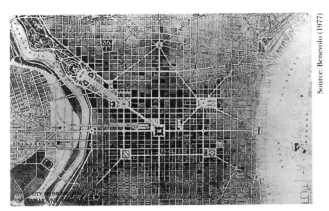

Source: Benevolo (1977)

1. The Gréber Plan (1917)

2. View toward the Philadelphia Museum of Art

Source: Wolf (1975)

3. View of Construction Work (1924)

Figure 2-19: The Benjamin Franklin Parkway, Philadelphia
From the 1880s onward a series of proposals were made in Philadelphia for a boulevard connecting the City Hall (Centre Square of William Penn's plan for the city), Logan Square (another of Penn's original squares), and a proposed public building on a hill terminating the vista. A scheme designed by Auguste Henri Gréber (1) has been partially implemented; the art museum and boulevard were built (2; see also Figs. 14–9(5,6). Schemes of this magnitude (e.g., Lafayette Park, Detroit, Empire State Plaza, Albany, and Southside, Chicago) require considerable political clout to implement for they involve a considerable taking of land (3).

Building Complexes

Many existing American cities have large-scale projects and precincts that are self-consciously designed, exhibiting many of the lines of twentieth-century architectural thought. There are bits and pieces of City Beautiful designs in many cities. There are many new suburbs designed more or less on the lines of the Garden City ideals or like a mini–Broadacre City (P. Rowe 1991). Perhaps the Rationalist influence on urban renewal has been even stronger.

The Benjamin Franklin Parkway in Philadelphia with the City Hall at one end of the axis and the Philadelphia Museum of Art at the other, and with a number of institutional buildings along its sides, is an example of the City Beautiful movement's ideology (Brownlee 1989). There are radial roads built in the twentieth century along City Beautiful principles in a number of other American cities and many more smaller schemes.

While never implemented, Burnham's plan for Chicago (see Fig. 2-6) has been and is the model for government precincts in other places where civic pride is a design goal (e.g., Cardiff in 1897–1906, Berlin in 1938–1943, Los Angeles in 1941, Portsmouth in 1973, Pyonyang in the 1960s, and Bucharest in the 1980s). The application of City Beautiful principles for such a purpose holds even on a smaller scale in suburban design in places such as Yorkship (now Fairview) in Camden, New Jersey (Stern with Massengale 1981), Mariemont, a suburb of Cincinnati, Ohio (Mariemont Co. 1925), and, in plan, even more recently, in Seaside, Florida (Duany and Plater Zyberk 1984; Mohney and Easterling 1991).

Whenever grandeur is sought the attributes of City Beautiful schemes are resurrected. Albert Speer's planning for Berlin in the 1930s and 1940s is a major example (Helmer 1980; L. Krier 1985). The movement's images of the possible city continue to have a powerful pull and can be seen in recent Post-Modern schemes (e.g., Leon Krier's plan for Washington Mall, 1986, the Missassauga City Hall competition winning scheme of Jones and Kirkland, 1987—see Broadbent 1990, and the Carr's Hill Precinct of the University of Virginia).

Perhaps the circumstance in which the City Beautiful ideals has been most widely applied has been in university campus design (P. Turner 1984). Here again, however, strong design ideas have been difficult to implement not, as in the case of city design, because they involved much demolition (see Brownlee 1989 on the

1. Denver (c. 1910)

2. Los Angeles (1942 Plan)

3. Bucharest, Romania (1970s)

Photograph by Ruth Durack

Figure 2-20: The City Beautiful and Governmental Precincts
Many City Beautiful proposals, like many other urban renewal schemes, remain as drawings on paper. On a small scale, the axial planning still adds a sense of grandeur to many state capitol complexes (1) and to city hall precincts as in San Francisco and Los Angeles (2). On grand scale, City Beautiful schemes represent the signature of power as in the 1980s development of the Avenue of the Victory of Socialism in Bucharest under President Ceausescu (3).

Benjamin Franklin Parkway in Philadelphia) but because succeeding university administrations strove to stamp their own identities on the campuses by departing from original plans.

Even more cities have had parts self-consciously redesigned following the precepts of the Rationalists. The images that the drawings of Le Corbusier, his predecessors (Ferriss 1929; Garnier 1932; Sant'Elia 1973), and his contemporaries created of this potential world are extraordinarily powerful ones. There are bits and pieces of neo-Corbusian design in many parts of the world, usually on a whittled-down scale (Marmot 1982). They include universities (e.g., IIT in Chicago designed by Mies van der Rohe and also, but very differently, the campus of the University of Illinois, Chicago, designed by Skidmore, Owings & Merrill), many housing projects (for all income levels from Lakeshore Drive, Chicago, to Kips Bay Plaza, New York City, to Pruitt Igoe, St. Louis, or Roehampton, London, and the housing for La Défense, Paris), and special precincts (e.g., Lincoln Center in New York City and the Government Center in Chicago). These follow Rational design principles but in truncated form due to political and economic realities.

The housing developments have been the most controversial. The basic tenets of Rationalist thought in hous-

ing design have resulted in many developments for middle- and high-income people that have been sought after by families who lead metropolitan lifestyles. Others have been for low-income families. The former have worked out reasonably well in their residents' terms; the latter have proven to be more questionable. Lafayette Park in Detroit (1955–1963) by Mies van der Rohe and Ludwig Hilbersheimer (Spaeth 1985) is an example of a development liked by its residents. It is questioned on policy grounds. It displaced 2,000 low-income, predominantly African-American people (Moholy Nagy 1968).

The Rationalist tenets have, to put it generously, been significantly less successful where people have limited resources, where the developments are people's spatial and behavioral neighborhoods, and so where the affordances of the public realm are fundamental to the quality of life. Robin Hood Lane (1963) in England shows the difficulty that astute architects have had in moving from observation of what makes a good environment to the design of a good environment using Rationalist design principles (Smithson and Smithson 1970).

There are a number of new-towns-in-town, urban renewal schemes, and public housing projects across the world that follow Corbusian principles, usually in a strongly adapted form. La Défense, Paris's new central business dis-

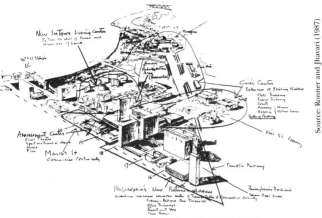

1. North Triangle Area Proposal, Philadelphia (1945–1948)

2. Independence Mall, Philadelphia

3. Charles Center, Baltimore

4. Bunker Hill, Los Angeles

5. Suburban Seattle

6. Southside, Chicago

Figure 2-21: Urban Renewal and the American City

There have been many proposals for the redevelopment of parts of cities in the United States. Among the best known is Louis Kahn's proposals for part of central Philadelphia (1), which shows the Modernist architectural view of what a city might be but is little related to urban life. Many more pragmatic urban design schemes varying considerably in scale have transformed much of the urbanscape of the United States since World War II. Independence Mall (2) turned Independence Hall in Philadelphia from part of a jumbled urban scene into an icon at the end of a greensward. Charles Center in Baltimore, with its elevated walkways and new office buildings, was a major step in the transformation of that city (3). The development of new office buildings in the center of Los Angeles (4) is replacing both the surface parking lots that provided for much of the city's image only twenty years ago as well as the plans for housing that would have fulfilled the intent of the Housing Act of 1949. Extensive housing areas on the periphery of cities have been built, extending metropolitan regions well into the countryside and creating what is disparagingly called suburban sprawl, although it is the type of living environment favored by many people (5). Such developments stand in strong contrast to the high-rise housing that provides for the wealthy quite successfully, but considerably less successfully for the poor (6).

1. Columbia, Maryland

2. Bielefeld University, Germany

3. Stockton State University, New Jersey

Figure 2-22: The Megastructure in Place
While many shopping centers in the United States (1) may be examples of megastructures in size, Bielefeld University in Germany (2) is an example of a building type that represents the ideology more clearly. All the functions of the university apart from the residential and some recreational ones are in one building surrounded by open areas. The climate of Bielefeld makes such an interior world logical, but the design also represents the broader Rationalist view of the world. Stockton State is a commuter university consisting of a series of buildings along a pedestrian spine (3).

trict, lies on an axis from the Louvre to La Concord to the Arc de Triomphe (Etoile) and Porte Mailot to Courbevoie. It follows the design principles of Le Corbusier and is in many ways similar to his 1921 design for it. It, in turn, has become the model for a number of other schemes such as the new downtowns for Bologna and Naples by Kenzo Tange. The new-towns-in-town include such schemes as the Lynbaan in Rotterdam and the work of Dutch architects such as Jacob Bakema (Bakema 1982), the Barbican in London, Roosevelt (formerly Welfare) Island in New York City, in which Le Corbusier's disciple, José Luis Sert, played a major design role, and various designs for the Mission Bay area of San Francisco.

The megastructure, while capturing the interest of many architects and generating many proposals, has been seldom implemented on quite the grand scale that its proponents imagined. Shopping malls, airports, universities, and new town centers are, however, megastructures for all intents and purposes. In Britain, Cumbernauld Town Centre and the central area of Runcorn New Town are in single structures (Gosling and Maitland 1984a, 1984b). A number of universities also provide examples of the line of thinking. They include Stockton State University in New Jersey, the Free University of Berlin, Scarborough

College in Toronto (Taylor and Andrews 1982), and on a much larger scale, Bielefeld University in Germany.

Much recent Post-Modern work is much more pragmatic. The full impact of the thinking of the last twenty years is described in Chapter 3, Urban Design Today. Suffice it to say here, the work is diverse but follows the major Rationalist and Empiricist traditions. For instance, during the last half of the 1980s, a number of housing projects have been developed with a strong Neo-Empiricist bent. They are largely examples of Neo-Traditional urban design and architecture, as in Virginia, where the Randolph neighborhood in Richmond and Middletown Arch and Pinewell by the Sea in Norfolk were designed by UDA Architects of Pittsburgh. The designs consist of a rhythm of single-family houses lining streets; in Randolph each has a porch and the design guidelines for Middletown are based on the design of Williamsburg.

We can learn much from both the earlier and more recent urban design work. The recent work seems to come closer to what their designers were trying to achieve than the work of the Modernists did, but the gap between intentions and implementation still often exists and there are many opportunities lost. The reasons for the emergence of urban design as a field of professional activity thirty years ago was to counter this gap. It has, as yet, only partially succeeded, but it has very much affected the shape and shaping of cities.

IN CONCLUSION—THE TWENTIETH-CENTURY CITY

The building boom of the late 1980s transformed the face of the centers of many American cities. The boom was fed by new investment policies, including the deregulation of banking procedures, and supported by new business technology as well as social and demographic changes. Yet segments of many cities in the developed world lie derelict, and many of the cities of the developing world are physical, if not social, slums. Is there an ideal twentieth-century city in the Weberian sense, a typical model? Probably no single city can be identified as such.

The American city of the twentieth century is a collage of fragments, a mosaic of communities held together by a web of highways, roads, and transit systems (Timms 1977; Rowe and Koetter 1979; Relph 1987; R. Martin 1990). The biogenic and sociogenic qualities of these fragments will vary considerably in quality, depending on the resources the public and private sectors have invested in them and on the way the natural environment has been handled.

The city still has a strong central business area of office buildings, retail shops, theaters, and restaurants. It is not as boisterous as it once was but it is still alive, although quieter in the evenings. Most cities have a number of new and gleaming office buildings designed by the leading architects of today in their central business districts. Yet not as large a proportion of the people of the metropolitan area come downtown to work or for recreation as did thirty years ago. Some are afraid to do so. They have increasingly been brought up in another sociospatial culture. It never occurs to others to do so because the suburbs offer many of the desired amenities that the central areas of cities provide. Other people still love the vibrancy of the center city, the variety of people and the offerings of its shops. Some seek to live in the center, but they are a minority of the metropolitan area's people. Many people live in single-person households, but some nuclear and extended families will seek the high-density, multifunctional, fragmented environment because of its range of offerings for themselves and their children. Other families are horrified by the thought of raising children in such an environment. Some people are trapped in cities.

In many smaller cities and towns, the downtowns have become so deteriorated that many people question whether they are worth saving. Where the downtown is gone, an important sense of identity is lost. Past and existing planning paradigms for dealing with downtowns and the purposes they serve need to be rethought.

There are many examples of planned intervention into the city fabric, particularly in establishing new links between parts of the city and between the city and its hinterland. The most obvious of these links are highways, but there have been many efforts to provide the pedestrian with a more pleasant environment in the hearts of cities and at subcenter nodes. In many small towns and neighborhood shopping areas, streets have been closed to form pedestrian malls with more or less success (Houstoun 1990a). In Houston and Montreal, major pedestrian links at the center of the city are underground; Houston, like Minneapolis, also has a skyway system. European cities more than American ones have been endowed with public plazas and pedestrian ways.

The downtown probably has a circumferential freeway system, connected by a vast freeway system to its suburban surroundings. The major mode of transportation is the automobile, with many of those on the road containing one person. A set of major satellite downtown-like environments around shopping centers—"edge cities"—are located at intersections of the circumferential and radial highways. Washington, DC, has, perhaps, fifteen of them; Houston has eleven (Garreau 1991). Some of these rival or surpass the downtowns of the central city in their total commercial area (e.g., Southfield, Michigan, outstrips Detroit). Tyson's Corner outside Washington, DC, is one of the twenty largest downtowns in the United States. Both the center cities that now have major private indoor shopping developments (e.g., Water Tower Place in Chicago, the Gallery in Philadelphia, Trump Tower in New York City, and the Galleria in Houston) and the suburban shopping malls and areas now have major quasi-public spaces open to people of the "appropriate" type for much of the day, but under the control of private organizations (see Ghirado 1987 on Houston). There is an ongoing privatization of public space.

The city has a number of exclusive residential areas in which the layout was designed by landscape architects of renown, but it also has the remains of industrial neighborhoods, some gentrified and some abandoned, depending on their original housing stock and their location in relation to the central area of the city. The core of the city will be surrounded by low-income areas, some of which will be ethnically homogeneous. The city has urban renewal precincts of offices and residential areas following the ideology of the Continental school of the Modern movement and designed by highly reputable architects. The designs are Rationalist ones and stand in strong contrast to the suburban developments, which would look like minor and less spacious Broadacre Cities. The city planning commission wonders what to do about the housing projects. Their architects do not always include them in the list of projects their firms have done.

There is a sprawling and still much loved park system, but it is not as well kept as older people remember it nor as it appears in photographs of forty years ago. Many of the trees will be badly affected by pollutants and there

1. Orange County, California

Photograph by John Ballinger

2. Phoenix

Photograph by James Blank

Photograph by Deepti Nijhawan

4. Boston

3. Los Angeles County

Collection of the author

5. Boca Raton, Florida

Figure 2–23: The American City at the End of the Twentieth Century

Each American city is unique. Cities such as Los Angeles, Houston, and Phoenix can, however, be regarded as exemplars of the city that has emerged as the result of many apparently independent decisions and with the automobile as the primary mode of transportation (1,2). Originally provided for by an extensive light rail system, Los Angeles is today primarily a city dependent on the automobile as the main source of transportation. Its patterns reflect this reliance. At the end of the twentieth century it, like most major American cities, is a multinucleated (3) "collage" of parts, some working in coordination with others and some not, some self-consciously designed as units and some not. Each part of the American city reflects the era in which it was built, the design ideas and controls that existed at the time, and the efforts made to keep it functioning well (4). To function well the city has to be shaped to accommodate automobile traffic (5). Many cities (e.g., Los Angeles, Baltimore, St. Louis) are now installing light rail systems, but designing without automobile owners in mind seems to be a foolhardy endeavor as far ahead as one can predict accurately.

may be much trash lying around, but the overall effect will be a positive one with lovers strolling along, joggers running by, children playing with kites, and dogs romping. On weekends and public holidays there will be many picnickers. In contrast, many areas of the city are without parks. Children's playgrounds, with one or two exceptions, will consist of two or three pieces of traditional play equipment, such as swings and a sandbox in which to create new worlds, in disrepair but still well used.

The city is rich in institutions: theaters, art galleries, hospitals, and museums, and a tremendous historical investment in an often aging infrastructure. The institutions are its pride and joy, but they are under severe economic pressures. There is an increasing concern with one's own life and less about the public environment. The sense of communal obligation is lower than it once was.

Many cities in the United States and much of the developed world fit this general model, but each also has its unique character because of its geographical location, its age, and the nature of the people who live there, their attitudes toward communal life, the public environment, and to each other. Almost any city that might be regarded as the epitome of twentieth-century development would be a sprawling one except where political and geographic forces coincide to make it denser (e.g., Hong Kong, Monaco, Singapore).

The cities that have had their major growth in the twentieth century—the Los Angeles, Houstons, São Paulos, and Johannesburgs—may be a model of what will come in places that have much land, but almost inevitably cities will have to be denser in the future because of the shortage of land and increasing environmental concerns. The counterforce will be the change in communications technology that will act as a dispersing force. It is in this situation that urban designers of the future will have to act in their attempts to make cities and their parts better places in which to live.

MAJOR REFERENCES

Boyer, M. Christine (1983). *Dreaming the Rationalist City*. Cambridge, MA: MIT Press.

Broadbent, Geoffrey (1990). *Emerging Concepts in Urban Space Design*. New York: Van Nostrand Reinhold.

Dear, Michael, and Allen J. Scott, eds. (1981). *Urbanization and Urban Planning in Capitalist Society*. London: Methuen.

Exline, Christopher H., Gary L. Peters, and Robert P. Larkin (1982). *The City: Patterns and Processes in the Urban Ecosystem*. Boulder, CO: Westview Press.

Frieden, Bernard J., and Lynne B. Sagalyn (1989). *Downtown, Inc: How America Rebuilds Cities*. Cambridge, MA: MIT Press.

Garreau, Joel (1991). *Edge City: Life on the New Frontier*. New York: Doubleday.

Jukes, Peter, ed. (1990). *A Shout in the Street: An Excursion into the Modern City*. New York: Farrar Straus Giroux.

Lesnikowski, Wejciech G. (1982). *Rationalism and Romanticism in Architecture*. New York: McGraw Hill.

Lüchinger, Arnulf (1981). *Structuralism in Architecture and Urban Planning*. Stuttgart: Karl Kramer.

Manieri-Elia, M., and M. Tafuri (1980). *The American City from the Civil War to the New Deal*. London: Granada.

Relph, Edward (1987). *The Modern Urban Landscape*. Baltimore: Johns Hopkins University Press.

Rowe, Peter (1991). *Making a Middle Landscape*. Cambridge, MA: MIT Press.

Schultz, Stanley K. (1989). *Constructing Urban Culture: American Cities and City Planning, 1800–1920*. Philadelphia: Temple University Press.

Sharp. Dennis, ed. (1978). *The Rationalists: Theory and Design in the Modern Movement*. London: Architectural Press.

Thrall, Grant Ian (1987). *Land Use and Urban Form: The Consumption Theory of Land Rent*. New York: Methuen.

3

THE NATURE OF URBAN DESIGN TODAY

It is possible, if one is highly creative, to imagine a situation where the process of growth, bloom, decay, or the regeneration of a human settlement comes to a standstill. The circumstances under which this situation might occur are, indeed, difficult to imagine. We take for granted the continuing adaptations to our environments. The changes aggregate within the broader changes taking place in each society and in the world to make substantial changes in the world around us. The demands placed on the public realm of settlements change accordingly, and thereby, the specific nature of the urban designer's work changes. Inevitably, changes made in the public realm create new opportunities and new problems resulting in the need for future changes. The cycle is endless, so urban design must be seen within the context of competing and allied efforts by individuals to improve their own lives and communal efforts to improve the quality of life for all a settlement's people.

PROBLEMS, URBAN PROBLEMS, AND URBAN DESIGN

Major changes are taking place in the United States today and probably even more dramatic ones in much of the rest of the world. They will undoubtedly have a major impact on human settlement forms. Predicting precisely how these changes will affect a particular place is impossible, but much is clear. We do know that the population of the world will be increasing into the foreseeable future, and that country after country is becoming increasingly urban as a result of population growths and economic dynamics (Monkkonen 1988; Knight and Gappert 1989). Unless some radically new social and economic policies are created, overall population densities in many countries of the world will be increasing substantially. In the

United States the increase will be slower but will require much more thoughtful city planning and urban and architectural design than that required for low-density environments and, possibly, completely new settlement patterns. We do know that family structures are undergoing radical change in many places and that new housing forms are needed (Franck and Ahrentzen 1989). We do know that the technological changes that took place in the first half of this century in countries such as those in Western Europe will be available to more and more people in the poorer countries of the world—the consumer boom is almost everywhere (see Ninan and Singh 1984). The result is a highly fluid situation that will lead to major changes in the world's racial, religious and cultural, and political structures. One hopes it will be a world more tolerant of individual and group differences than it is now. It will probably have to be.

We are consuming the resources of the world at rapidly increasing rates and polluting the environment, and apparently destroying much that is irreplaceable. If the whole world lived at the economic level of Western European countries, which is surely a reasonable goal for us to pursue, the resulting pollution levels will be intolerable, destroying much of our biogenic environment, changing climates (which seem to go through cyclical changes that we do not fully understand anyway), and, ironically, reducing the overall quality of life. The concept of fairness, used so effectively in the striving for independence by former colonial countries, will again be raised forcefully in dealing with the distribution of resources. Urban designers as well as politicians and developers will have to face the issue of the relative importance of their proposals in comparison to other problems needing to be addressed.

Technological changes in the United States have led to major changes in the way life can be lived. Future changes are difficult to predict. While the internationalization of the world through the development of communications media and ease of air travel have opened up many opportunities for people and have changed many attitudes, there appear to have been fewer technological changes that have had the impact on lifestyles and values during the second part of the twentieth century than during the first half. There has been nothing comparable to the electrification of the world and the development of the automobile. The major recent change seems to have been in the array of weapons available to the military forces of the world. We are now said to be in the middle of a communications revolution that will change patterns of life, increasing the striving for privacy and withdrawal from communal life as we know it today (Sennett 1977; Brill 1989; Hitt 1990). Such changes would have a major effect on the requirements made of the public realm, yet there has been remarkably little technologically induced change in the nature of middle-class life in the major industrial countries of the world during the past fifty years. Nevertheless, since World War II many people have had to deal with major social changes, for good and ill, in their cultures and lifestyles, and the nature of the public realm is both a contributor to change and a consequence of it.

Accompanying and contributing to the problems arising in the world are the level of poverty and ignorance of much of its population, racial discrimination and ethnocentric attitudes, and a general lack of caring about others or empathy for their needs by more than a minority of people. Even where people are caring, there is often little understanding of how individual actions shape the world or of how to change one's behavior to attain specific ends. Many problems seem insurmountable.

In 1979, one observer of the urban United States, Kenneth Schneider, made a list of the problems facing the American city that might well have been written today:

> Pervasive deterioration of human environments, physically, functionally, socially, and aesthetically.
>
> A goods intoxication and a forced consumption, based on a social and environmental structure that demands purchases.
>
> A gross misapplication of technology, involving energy, consumer products, housing, construction, transportation, and food preparation.
>
> Exponential depletion of nonrenewable resources, especially energy and metals.
>
> Civic bankruptcy of democratic local government in metropolitan areas, including the nature of participation, control, and services.
>
> Rising health hazards and diseases—ranging from traffic accidents to nervous disorders, heart diseases and cancer—combined with a malfunctioning system of health services.
>
> Misdirected education that emphasizes specialized productive consumptive citizenship while excluding broader humanistic purposes.

1. King's Views of New York

2. 10,000 Years Hence, from *Science and Invention*

Figure 3–1: Past Predictions of the Nature of Future Cities
If one looks at past predictions of what today's cities would look like, one cannot be sanguine about making predictions today of what the future city will be. The 1911 prediction of what New York City would be like by mid-century (1) is fanciful but must be seen with contemporary technologies and technological optimism in mind (see also Fig. 10-1). Current speculations about the possibility of living in space date back to the early years of the century (2, see also Fig. 3-6(1)). The mainstream of urban design thinking has been much more pragmatic and kept its feet on the ground.

A spread of defensive privacy and inability to establish creative intimacy, resulting in a self-deprivation of association, experience, and growth.

A depreciation of the roles, values, and overall validity of family life.

A decline in the meaning of *places* of work, play, and social interaction, the *social continuity and content* of events surrounding the individual, and the *psychological integrity* of the individual.

Deepening social alienation, which calcifies human behavior, promoted by the fractured nature of urban life.

Growth in crime—ironically paralleling the growth of affluence. Surges of drug abuse, mental illness, and suicide (Schneider 1979:11–12).

Even if one does not accept such observations as accurate—because a contrasting list of the joys of life could easily be written—it is clear that the role of urban design is limited in dealing with the major problems and issues confronting the world. It has little to do with solving major social and political problems, although its own goals may change as a result of changes in the sociopolitical culture of the world. Urban design, nevertheless, needs to be seen in the light of the sociocultural fabric of society and the political issues that confront people. It needs to be seen for what it is—a political tool. While architecture and urban design cannot shape the social world to any great extent, they do mirror it. The layout of the environment does affect the affordances of the world, and as such it is inextricably linked with social change. These links need to be understood if social progress is to be made. The goal of this chapter is place urban design and the role of urban designers in their context today.

URBAN DESIGN

Human settlements, it was noted above, are continually changing. Buildings and the urban infrastructure become obsolete as they decay or as the perceived needs of people change. There are a number of typical situations. Indeed the focus of urban design work shifts as economic conditions change. In the 1950s and 1960s the concern was with blighted central cities, and during the 1970s and 1980s much development across the United States from New Orleans, to Davenport, Iowa, Sioux Falls, South Dakota, and along the Hudson River in New York and New Jersey has been on obsolete docks. Recently, we have seen or will be seing the abandonment by the U.S. Department of Defense of land that is located in highly desirable locations (e.g., Charlestown Navy Yard, Boston, and Treasure Island in San Francisco Bay). Some of the land becoming available will require considerable toxic-waste cleanup before it becomes usable. As time passes new opportunities that are not obvious today are likely to become clear. Thus undeveloped land will be built on; built-on land will become fallow.

The twentieth-century city, it was argued in Chapter 2, is largely the unselfconscious result of the competition between individuals and groups of people striving to maximize their own benefits as they perceive them, but there has also been much cooperative action to shape the public realm. There is also a competition between individual architects designing specific buildings for particular clients (as well as individual landscape architects designing open spaces) and needing to display their own dexterities in order to capture a market for their services (Gutman 1977). It is hardly surprising that there are many opportunity costs in terms of duplication of services as well as a loss of an overall design purpose in the unselfconsciously designed city today. Often the design of the spaces between buildings is the last concern. This is particularly true in countries such as the United States, which emphasize private rights over public ones. Can society do better? To begin doing so, some misconceptions about the nature of urban design need to be addressed.

In a sense, any new piece of architecture or landscape architecture is urban design in that it changes the city. The term "urban design" has often come to have this meaning. All the *Progressive Architecture* urban design awards for 1990, for instance, were for little more than individual buildings (see *Progressive Architecture* (1991) 72, no. 1). It is not the meaning used here.

Urban designing involves the planned intervention in the marketplace and in the legal processes of allocating and designing the combination of land and building uses and building configurations that constitute the three-dimensional physical nature of human settlements. Such a planned intervention is based on a model of the human being, an image of an ideal world, a model of the environment, and a set of values. These models and values are seldom clear and almost never stated explicitly.

Urban design is concerned with the built environment of cities (and other human settlements) and the *public welfare*. These two concerns require attitudes toward design based on very different mindsets and bodies of knowledge from those of an architect designing buildings to meet the individual needs of a client/patron. Some architects are able to switch hats from a concern with the individual client and the unique object to a concern with the public interest and environmental quality. Most architects, however, develop a style—a set way of dealing with all problems—and are unable to deviate from it. Many others are unwilling to make this switch because defining the public interest is a highly political process and doing so explicitly exposes them to public censure. Some architects are simply intellectually ill-equipped to do so. Some are politically opposed to doing so—they believe that any public control of architects' efforts, whatever the purpose of the controls, is a personal and an artistic affront. All design, however, is political; urban design is always both a public and a political act.

The Scope of Concern of Urban Design

There are three facets to the work that architects and other design professionals practicing urban design are

3. An Inner-City Neighborhood, Detroit

1. Railroad Yards, Denver

Source: San Francisco (1990)

2. Mission Bay, San Francisco

Figure 3-2: Obsolescent Urban Areas
The physical environment is continuously undergoing change. As populations grow, previously unbuilt-on land on the urban fringe is built up. Areas of cities become obsolete as transportation and manufacturing modes change, setting up lifestyle changes. Railroad yards (1) and existing port and industrial areas (2, see also Fig. 3-7(5)) become available for redevelopment. Housing areas become abandoned as investment priorities change (3). Some people, however, choose to remain in them or are trapped there by poverty. Other areas become gentrified because of the soundness of their housing stock and their location.

attempting to do that are important to understand in thinking about what urban designers might do best. The first, the intellectual domain, concerns the range of considerations and problems that urban designers face; the second, the degree of power, or control, that urban designers have in dictating design outcomes, and the third, the geographical domain, concerns the perceived size and significance of the area being considered. The first two are the essential matters, the third is merely a matter of scale.

The Intellectual Domain of Urban Design

Urban design is concerned with the design of building configurations and the spatial and use relationship between buildings and the spaces created between them. The focus of attention is on organizing the public realm. Thus it is concerned with the way open spaces are framed by buildings that usually have different ownerships, have been designed by different architects, and have been developed at different times (Trancik 1986; Gehl 1987). The concerns thus overlap those of city planners, landscape architects, and architects.

Architects inevitably practice urban design when they design building complexes, city planners when they establish design policies, and landscape architects in the specific design of open spaces. They are all shaping the

public realm. The overall public realm is, however, unlikely to be these designers' main preoccupation unless it is the major interest of their sponsors.

Views differ on what the attitudes and concerns of urban designers should be in these matters. Each view comes out of the particular social and professional context in which its proponents exist, as the range of ideological statements described in Chapter 2 shows. The views are neither mutually exclusive nor independent. A basic distinction can, however, be made among them based on their foci of attention and range of concerns. The overall embracing and apparently polar opposite positions are those of urban design as problem solving and urban design as a pure fine art (see also Scott Brown 1976). Implicit in this distinction is also the question of the range of issues, particularly the social and financial concerns, that should be the purview of the urban designer. The range of concerns engaging urban designers' attention depends on their working environment and on the task they set themselves or, rather, that society allows them to set themselves.

Urban Design as Art and as Problem Solving

The dichotomy between urban design as either art or problem solving is, paradoxically, a false but useful one. It is false because the view of urban design as problem solving does not exclude the question of urban design as art, while the view of urban design as art says that the problem that urban designers should be addressing is that of the city as an art form. The distinction between the two approaches to urban design is, nevertheless, useful because there is a major attitudinal difference between considering urban design as art or as problem solving.

Defining "art" and "problem solving" so that everybody agrees on the terms may be impossible. By art is here meant the external expression, in a variety of media, of an individual's own view of society from within himself or herself. The concern then is with the overall idea that generates the visual qualities of designs and the aesthetic ideology on which the idea is based. By problem solving is meant the primary focus of attention of the urban designer is both on other people's perceptions of issues in the external world and on the attempt to resolve them. There is, however, problem solving in art and art in problem solving, but the artist is concerned with the form of the city per se, as an aesthetic object, and the problem solver sees it as the product of many concerns.

Urban design as art is seen as a service to others, but the mode of service is different from that perceived by those who see urban design as problem solving. The purpose of the art form is to raise the lay population's aesthetic aspirations, or even to shock them—to make them look at the world in a new way. The goal is not directly to advance the social conditions of people by enriching their overall life opportunities. In taking this position, architects have become concerned with the internal validity of urban design ideas in terms of architectural precedents or literary allusions rather than on external evidence. External validity—the effect of urban design policies on the built environment and on people's lives—is simply not a central issue in much recent design. Often it seems that the end product of the design process is the publication of a drawing rather than the construction of a building or building complex.

During the course of this century the primary design concern among the mainstream of architects has shifted from architecture and urban design as art to architecture and urban design as problem solving, and then back again to art. While correct, this generalization blurs the self-image of the masters of the Modern movement as both artists and problem solvers (see Sert and C.I.A.M. 1944; Le Corbusier 1960, 1973; Smithson 1968). If one accepts the view that architectural criticism reflects contemporaneous architectural attitudes then there was, indeed, an expansion of the perimeter of concern of architects during the period 1930 to 1970. There has been a reduction, or a tightening, of the range of concerns of architecture and architects since that period (Belgasem 1987). This change is shown in Fig. 3-3.

The primary, if not sole, concern in architectural criticism is now with individual buildings, ideally set in open space, and the aesthetic theory and philosophy of

Adapted from Belgasem (1987)

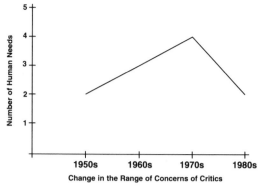

1. Change in Concerns of Critics over Time

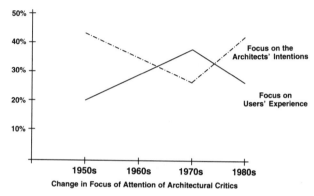

2. Change in Focus of Attention of Critics on the Architect and on Users

Figure 3-3: Changes in the Concerns of Architects, 1930–1985
Ramadan Belgasem (1987) showed a significant shift in critics' foci of attention over time in their evaluations of two major projects designed by Le Corbusier—the Pessac housing and Chandigarh. Generalizing from that study, two conclusions can be drawn. Between the 1930s and the 1960s there was a general broadening followed by a narrowing of their concerns in terms of the functions to be served by architecture (1, see Chapter 7). There was also a shift in their criticism from a focus on the architect's aesthetic principles to the users' experiences and then back to the architect's ideologies (2).

the designer as demonstrated in the building. This concern reflects a change in the focus of architectural criticism over the years, which has shifted from the study of the architect's intentions in the 1930s to the experiencing of the world by its users in the 1950s and 1960s, and back to the concern with the architect's intentions. Despite the development of a number of major urban design schemes during the 1970s and 1980s, a concern for urban design issues among the mainstream of architects in the United States dropped, paralleling public concern. Ironically, the same period saw the intellectual development of the field of urban design as an entity with an Empiricist orientation, particularly within the United States (see, e.g., Ferebee 1982). Today, however, many architects, even when wearing their urban design hats, still focus on urban design as a fine art and as simply large-scale architecture concerned solely with geometric order and visual expression (see Gosling and Maitland 1984a, 1984b; Broadbent 1990). The products of urban design as art are said to be "more powerful." They do, indeed, often capture the imagination.

The view of urban design as problem solving is a much broader view than that of urban design as art. The concern is with the implications of layouts of the physical environment for everyday life and experience. The concern is for enhancing social opportunities as much as for enhancing the aesthetic quality of the public realm in the terms of its users. This view inevitably includes a concern for the aesthetic expression of the architect, but it is seldom the paramount concern. The fundamental concern is with quality of life issues. Many architects oppose this view of urban design because it does not ally itself closely enough with the world of fine arts—the world of sculpture.

The problem-solving attitude raises a number of questions about the competence of architects to deal with the broader social and economic issues that face a society (Gans 1968, 1975; Scott Brown 1976, 1982). As the issues become broader and more intertwined, or rather, as society demands that issues be confronted more comprehensively, so, quite understandably, the mainstream of architects has withdrawn from a concern with urban design. If not architects, who should be concerned? A new group of people willing to tackle the broader issues has emerged during the past thirty years. They are predominantly architects but are drawn from various design disciplines and other professions. They and their activities, for good and ill, are the heart of urban design as a field and as a discipline today.

The Degree of Control

The urban designer is never really in complete control of the decision-making process that initiates a project and brings it to fruition. There are many schemes that deal with new towns, with large-project design, and with the precincts of cities where a single designer or design team may seem to be in control of the whole project, but even with these schemes questions of who decides what arises. This is particularly true in the early stages of urban designing when directions are set.

While social ends are implicit in all designs, the degree to which the urban designers can and should specify them is not clear. With some exceptions (e.g., Goodman and Goodman 1947), the Modernists seldom drew a complete picture of the social objectives their generic designs were supposed to fulfill or the social organizations and political systems required to achieve and/or operate them. The Modernists nevertheless had major social objectives in mind. Indeed, this aspect of their thought has drawn much criticism. *Collage City*, according to Colin Rowe and Fred Koetter (1978), is an alternative to "the disastrous urbanism of social engineering and total design" of the Modernists. Essentially what Rowe and Koetter are saying is that the social plan should be left for others to decide or else it should emerge from the affordances of a design. In other words, architects should support the status quo. They are the "soft cops" enforcing the will of the power elite (Goodman 1971). The power elite are, after all, the paying clients (Mitchell 1974; Zeisel 1974; Larson 1979).

All designs are social statements as well as aesthetic ones. The degree to which a practitioner is perceived to have control over a project is partly a function of the scale of the endeavor and partly a function of the range of variables that the designer wishes to control. However, it is mainly a function of what designers are allowed to control—their scope of involvement. Where urban design merges into straight architecture, the architect is likely to be in control of the translation of the program (or brief) into a physical form, assuming the constraints of the situation are accepted. The design of the program is, however, the truly creative act even though the final physical form is what people see and remember. Urban designers' power comes from their expertise, the public reputation they have, and their individual personalities—their powers of persuasion.

When urban designers are the developers as well as the designers of an overall proposal for changing, say, part of a city, they have considerable power to achieve their own ends. This model is more typical of public works in countries with extensive centralized power, such as in the French public sector. In this case the urban designer, architect, and developer form a single collaborative team with considerable political power. In the United States, the urban designer is seldom part of such a team. The urban designer is one actor and the developer with his or her architect is another often in opposition. The power of the developers is strong and urban designers weak in terms of getting their own way when the location of a scheme is in an economically depressed area and the local political leaders want to see development at any cost. This was largely the case with the design of Renaissance Center in Detroit by architect/developer John C. Portman, on this occasion wearing solely his architect's hat. While dramatically bold, and a help to the city's tax base, the project has largely failed to achieve many of the goals it claimed it would in terms of being an integrated part of Detroit's center. It has, however, had a catalytic effect on property development in adjacent areas.

When urban designers work for a developer they represent the developer's interests, producing conceptual-design diagrams and illustrative site plans. As part of a team they might both produce the program and design the built form. If the development is to be parceled out to subdevelopers, as in Las Colinas, Texas, the major developer takes on a quasi-governmental role and may require the urban designer to produce design guidelines to ensure the overall quality of the scheme. When working for a governmental agency, the urban designer may be required to work on general design policies as well as guidelines that shape the future city, but many design decisions fall outside the scope of design controls that might be established.

In the United States, the usual role of urban designers is as consultants to public agencies or developers, and the degree of control they have is that given them by their sponsors. "Urban designers" with considerable power such as Baron Haussmann in Paris (Benevolo 1967) and Robert Moses in New York (Caro 1974) with their considerable political support do exist, but more often urban designers play and should play a collaborative role in the development and implementation of proposals for the three-dimensional character of the public realm, whatever the scale of a project (see Chapters 23 and 24; Lang 1990; Smith 1991). In private development, the nature of the land market and the nature of land rent have to be fully recognized. Design decisions have to be made within the tolerances of a market economy. The sponsors of the project and the banks that lend money have considerable power over what decisions are made. Lending institutions tend to be financially conservative to ensure their survival. The architecture they support tends to be conservative too.

The Geographical Domain

The question frequently heard about urban design is: How big a chunk of the city does an architect deal with before it becomes urban design? Most urban design involving the actual design of building complexes is at a subcity scale. Occasionally it is at a city scale (e.g., Brasilia, the British new towns). Often it is a street-bound block. At a policy level, urban design may well be for a whole city, which is likely to be divided into precincts for that purpose. It is not, however, the size of an area that is of fundamental concern. It is the question of orchestrating change, of coordinating the work of different clients and different designers to focus on the public realm—the public space within and between buildings, and the façades of buildings and other surfaces that define those spaces—and the activities the public realm affords.

URBAN DESIGN VISIONARIES AND PRACTITIONERS

Today, as in the past, there are two overlapping groups of urban designers, or, perhaps, modes of thinking about urban design—*visionaries* and *practitioners* (see also Reissman 1964). Visionaries are concerned with designing a new world. As artists they are concerned with creating new geometric patterns that are either visually interesting or have an internal logic, or code, of interest, primarily to other architects. As problem solvers they are concerned with the creation of new social, spatial, and architectural

orders. In a sense, all urban design proposals are visions, but the term "visionary" is used in a more limited sense here.

Visionaries prepare manifestos. They design new cities on paper. As such, they have considerable power to create their own worlds. Such designing presents them with the chance to show what their schemes would be like in a way that the social and economic realities do not allow in existing cities because the proposals would require the type of radical surgery that is politically unfeasible. They are Platonists. Practitioners, in contrast, have to deal with the day-to-day problems of design in existing socio-political systems. They tend to be incrementalists. They are Aristotelians (Jones and Sparrow 1980; Peattie 1981a).

The two roles are complementary, even though professionals tends to dismiss visionaries as starry-eyed dreamers in ivory towers, and visionaries are critical of the piecemeal approaches and lack of vision of the practitioners (Buder 1990). The roles are complementary because the visionaries bring possibilities to the attention of the field and sometimes the world, while practitioners bring questions of social reality and economic and political feasibility to the far-reaching and often dramatic ideas of visionaries. They are also the ones who may attempt to translate the generic ideas into specific designs.

The line between visionaries and practitioners is blurred. Frank Lloyd Wright and Le Corbusier were very prolific architects but, like many Modern architects, had highly visionary, if intellectually limited, urban design proposals. Frank Lloyd Wright implemented little at the urban design scale but Le Corbusier was involved in the design of Chandigarh, and his extremely influential ideas were implemented by others in Brasilia, on a mass-housing scale in Venezuela, in places such as Roehampton in England and Pruitt Igoe in St. Louis, and even more prolifically in the Eastern European countries. The ideas of people such as Lewis Mumford (Miller 1989; L. Fried 1990) and the Goodmans (1947) stayed in the conceptual world. Proposals of others (e.g., Leon Krier's plan for Washington, DC) who sought to implement ideas have found their plans remained on paper only. There are fewer visionaries today than in the past, and their work recognizes present political realities and thus tends to be smaller in scale, although their architectural proposals might be regarded as heroic. Today the people we regard as visionaries tend to be the practitioners who can see beyond the immediate day-to-day problems they face to more holistic solutions.

The Visionaries

Visionaries' social and architectural goals, scale of thinking, and perception of the role they are playing in society varies considerably among individuals. The ideas of Le Corbusier for cities were on a grand scale for the whole world. In contrast, James Pratt, a Dallas architect who has initiated a series of "visions" for Dallas, Texas, sees himself as filling in a "void in long term thinking," as practitioners grope with the daily issues. Visions, or images, generated by visionaries can act as models for wide-scale implementation if they capture the minds and hearts of the field as a whole.

In urban design, the visionaries have come from a wide array of professional backgrounds, but they have mainly been architects whose physical design proposals are based on perceptions of a new social order, new formal and communal organizations, and usually, a new aesthetic philosophy. Critics of visionaries such as Le Corbusier say that the social order is simply an end to achieve the desired aesthetic order! While this may sometimes be true, it is a limited observation.

Many visionary architects, as urban designers, want to wipe the slate clean—to demolish the existing city—and to start again. Frequently they are Rationalists who are reluctant to deal with the existing political processes of the world. If they are aware of much of the empirical knowledge available about their worlds, they are reluctant to admit it (see Eaton 1969; P. Turner 1977). Often, the knowledge simply tends to get in the way of what they "want to do" when they are designing. Visionaries are apt to live in an abstract world of abstract people modeled on their own imaginations. Their boldness is much admired and much studied. They are remembered because their works have strong visual images—a drawing or conceptual diagram that captures the imagination.

The proposals of Ebenezer Howard (1902), Tony Garnier (Wiebenson 1969), Le Corbusier (1934), C.I.A.M., Congrès Internationaux d'Architecture Moderne (Sert and C.I.A.M. 1944), the MARS group in London (Gallion and Eisner 1986), Paul and Percival Goodman (1947), Frank Lloyd Wright (1958), and Paolo Soleri (1969, 1981; Wall 1971) all advocated major social changes in society based on their own images of people and good behavior. C.I.A.M., Le Corbusier, and Sert, among others, all advocated major changes in architectural attitudes toward space and building types (Banham 1960; Giedion 1963). During the 1960s, a number of architects were very concerned with the potential of what they perceived to be emerging technologies (see Dahinden 1972). The Archigram group in the United Kingdom and later the Metabolists of Japan explored the possibilities of major new plug-in walking and/or disposable cities (Cook et al. 1991; Banham 1976). They proposed new urban forms with capsules in which to live and work, towers and skylinks. The notion was that the future is unresolved and uncertain, and that cities must be easy to change. The proposals show a fascination with technological possibilities but also a limited understanding of, or even a lack of caring to understand, those technologies or the human purposes they might serve.

There are other schemes and proposals that might be regarded as visionary in nature; they advocate less in

1. Une Ville Contemporaine. Le Corbusier, Architect

A production center for 50,000 workers: 1. Airport 2. Heavy manufacture 3. Light manufacture 4. Industrialized agriculture 5. Housing 6. Sports and social center

2. Part of One of Three Design Paradigms of Paul and Percival Goodman

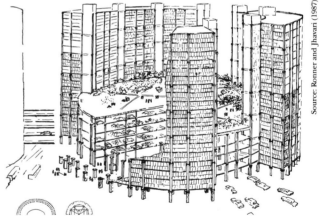

3. Urban Docks. Louis Kahn, Architect

Figure 3–4: Visionaries and Urban Structures
Visionaries look beyond what is being done now to radical future possibilities. Le Corbusier's *Une Ville Contemporaine* (see also Fig. 2–10(4)) not only explicitly argued for physical change but also implied many social changes (1). Paul and Percival Goodman's *Communitas* is more concerned with the design of new social systems and the physical fabric that might house them (2). Louis Kahn perceived the importance of the automobile in people's lives but had difficulty in coming to terms with it (3). While not implemented in their specific forms, visionary designs shape practitioners' and the public's thinking.

1. Fort Worth, Texas—Central Business District Proposal

2. A View of the Urban Texture

3. Streetscape

Figure 3-5: Victor Gruen and *The Heart of Our Cities*
The plan for central Fort Worth developed by Victor Gruen in the early 1960s does not appear to be particularly revolutionary today. His firm proposed a major ring road around the core of the city, off which parking garages would be built (1). The streets would be largely closed to vehicular traffic and enlivened with landscaping, a variety of paving types, and plazas (2,3). Some of the streets would be narrowed, new buildings would be constructed, and various exhibits would be developed. While never implemented, the generic principles involved in the scheme have been applied on a piecemeal basis in many locations, which suggests why the plan does not appear to be revolutionary.

the way of social changes while still implying behavioral changes. Victor Gruen (1964), for instance, proposed sweeping changes in the design of the public realm of the downtowns of existing American cities. These changes, to be implemented, would require substantial changes in the way Americans travel around cities. Other proposals focus on specific issues such as energy-efficient city layouts that would require a Haussmann-like redesign of city layouts (e.g., Messinger and LeRicolais 1972; Danzig and Saaty 1973).

There have been a number of recent statements on urban design that follow the scope of thought of the Modernists, but with a more generous model of people and an understanding of the limits of urban design. They fall within the Empiricist tradition and settle for a "new realism." Their proponents do not regard themselves as visionaries. Preeminent are the works of Christopher Alexander and his colleagues (Alexander, Isikawa, and Silverstein 1977; Alexander et al. 1987) and Kevin Lynch (Lynch 1981; Banerjee and Southworth 1990). Alexander and his colleagues provide a set of design principles (1977) and a set of rules (1987) for the development of cities, while Lynch discusses the overall qualities that should be sought rather than any specific design solutions. While they might regard themselves as practitioners they are visionary in the setting of directions. Along with

people such as Robert Venturi and his colleagues Denise Scott Brown and Stephen Izenour (1977), Lynch and Alexander suggest different but major revisions to the way we look at and design urban forms and places, although they do not share the same values about what should be done in the future. They nevertheless all suggest that urban design must be based on an understanding of people—a greater understanding than in the past.

The people who are regarded as visionaries today tend to be Neo-Rationalists (see Broadbent 1990). Many are Europeans but their ideas are highly influential in the United States, particularly in academia. The visions they present are limited ones, focusing more on novel intellectual aesthetic ideas than on the needs of society as a whole, but they are getting these visions built and so setting directions for other architects to follow. The group consists of a broad array of people with widely different aesthetic tastes. They were introduced in Chapter 2 and are generally classified as Post-Modernists. They include a number of people whose work is classical monumental (e.g., Ricardo Bofill, Leon Krier), Rationalist with its concern for the geometrical grid (e.g., Rossi, Carlo Aymonimo), and expressionist, although this work is more strictly an architecture of buildings (e.g., Hans Hollein). The work of groups such as Coop Himmelblau in their proposal for the Melun Senart area of Paris and Bernard Tschumi's

Future City scheme for Flushing Meadows, New York, which is a mixture of Deconstructionist and Garden City ideas, are on the borderline of implementable proposals but are perceived to be visionary schemes.

There is also a group of architects, many of whose members are Americans, that one can regard as Neo-Modernist. They include Charles Moore (Bloomer and Moore 1977) and Lawrence Halprin (1963, 1965, 1969, 1974), but also the later work of Leon Krier (Broadbent 1990). They are concerned with the nature of human experiencing of the environment, environmental enrichment.

A very different set of visionaries are proposing higher-density living by infilling existing housing areas with additional units—a return to the population densities characteristic of inner-city neighborhoods of the past. Reduced household size and increased wealth make such proposals difficult to attain, but in many countries they are a necessity.

The Practitioners

Practitioners tend to focus on a different set of concerns to visionaries. This is true whether they are in local government or working in the private sector as consultants. Practitioners have to confront the needs of day-to-day professional activity within often severe time, financial, and political constraints. Although some practitioners are well known, many are not because they do not produce grand schemes. They are not Platonists (Jones and Sparrow 1980).

Practitioners can be motivated by a number of concerns—a social conscience, an aesthetic ideology, the need for self-esteem through professional recognition, and/or the need to stay in business. They have to be involved in the daily process of bargaining for design goals in a highly political, and often emotionally charged, atmosphere. In the United States and other capitalist societies they have to deal with property developers (prima donnas as much as architects), bankers, politicians, and a variety of interest groups, each with its own agenda. In dealing with the realities of practice they rely on their own experiences and they tend not to make waves, not to be innovative. There are a number of notable exceptions to this rule, and it is their work that attracts attention either because it brings a successful new way of looking at the city or its components and how they work, or because their ideas fail for the same reason. In such cases it is often the developer as much as the designer who pushes for a particular end (e.g., Robert Davis, the developer of Seaside, Florida; see Dunlop 1989; Mohney and Easterling 1991; and Patton 1991).

The practitioner's work is quite rightly very much influenced by the client—the sponsor of his or her work. Much if not most of it is for governmental bodies whose task it is to represent the public interest. Some of the work is for large-scale developers. Sometimes the client may be

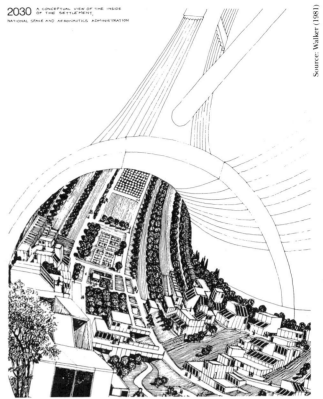

1. Space City (1981)

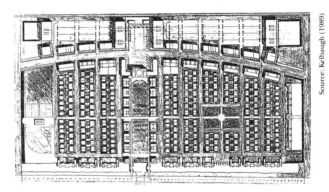

2. A Pedestrian Pocket Proposal (1989)

Figure 3–6: Our Contemporary Visionaries

Our contemporary visionaries are proposing changes in both the substantive and procedural aspects of design. There has been a continuing speculation on what it might mean to build in outer space (1). There have been suggestions not only for the physical form of cities and buildings but for new ways of going about designing them. More typical, however, are suggestions for the end forms of cities and suburbs—the development of generic solutions and types—such as this Neo-Rationalist suburban design by Harrison Fraker and Daniel Solomon (2).

a patron of the arts, but, more usually, urban design is important primarily as a means to achieve financial or political ends. Occasionally the client may be a social-philanthropist, although this role seems to have been more common in the nineteenth century than the twentieth.

Clients hire practitioners, and thus support their ideas. Therefore the architect whose dreams complement the desires of a financier or politician is the one whose ideas get implemented. Sometimes these designers have been thought of as visionaries. The administration of Mayor Dilworth was highly supportive of the work of Edmund Bacon in Philadelphia during the 1950s and 1960s (Bacon 1967, 1969, 1974). More dramatically, in terms of internationally known schemes, Jawarhalal Nehru was highly supportive of the work of Habib Rahman (Ranbindranath Behvan in New Delhi) and Le Corbusier (Chandigarh in Punjab), while Chief Minister Mahatab was responsible for the hiring of Otto Koeningsberger and Julius Vaz (Bhubaneswar in Orissa). The results are shown in Fig. I-2. Giscard d'Estaing's election as president of France and his desire to promote the artistic glory of France has had a major effect on the career of Ricardo Bofill. Bofill was less fortunate with Jacques Chirac. When Chirac was elected mayor of Paris in 1977 he appointed himself as chief architect for Les Halles site, demolished the building under construction designed by Bofill, and proceeded from there (Broadbent 1990).

In the United States, few governmental leaders have had urban design aspirations, but there have been some notable exceptions, such as the sustained concern with urban design quality in Charleston, South Carolina; Portland, Oregon; Pittsburgh, Pennsylvania (where there was considerable corporate leadership as well); and Baltimore, Maryland (see also Smith 1991). Whatever the place of urban designers within the political framework of a society, they are likely to be engaged in similar types of work.

FOUR TYPES OF URBAN DESIGN WORK

In the United States and probably elsewhere too, there are four types of situations in which urban designers find or place themselves. They show varying degrees of participation in public policy formation, in the comprehensiveness of design, and in the degree of control designers exert over the actual design result. The situations are: (1) where a designer or design team carries out the whole design work—its brief and its execution from designing alternatives to the supervision of implementation; (2) where the design is done essentially in one phase under one supervisor who is responsible for the overall design guidelines but with a number of architects and/or developers involved; (3) where the designer simply designs the public infrastructure—the capital web—or the guidelines to achieve it; and (4) where the designers are responsible for the design of infrastructure (or the guidelines to achieve it) and also for the guidelines for the buildings that will follow to frame it, and the scheme is implemented in a number of phases over time. The first, total

design, might simply be regarded as architectural design on an urban scale, the second is analogous to what Rowe and Koetter (1978) call "all-of-a-piece" design, and the last two are analogous to urban design as "the assemblage of fragments" based on some overall design principles. Having the type of design control implicit in total design is the dream of many architects. It is not, however, clear that it results in the most livable environments, although it has generated bold unified schemes. The remaining three types are closer to the heart of genuine urban design work. The identification of types of urban design should, like the identification of any other types, be treated with caution.

The categorization is not a sharp one. The distinction between schemes in the second and third categories if often blurred. Schemes that might originally have set out to be in the first category (i.e., as total designs) have often end up in the second (i.e., as all-of-a-piece designs) and sometimes even in the third (i.e., based on guidelines implemented in a number of phases as a set of semi-independent projects over a number of years). Even more frequently, schemes that might seem to belong in the second end up in the fourth, which is simply an extension of the third.

(1) The Urban Designer as Total Designer

When architects think of complete control over a design—total design—they are thinking of a single designer or design team making decisions about the layout of the environment from the largest to smallest scale—from the city to the ashtrays (Gropius 1962; Rapoport 1967). As one design team recently put it:

> We believe that a designer should be able to design anything, FROM A SPOON TO A CITY because the basic discipline of DESIGN IS ONE, the only thing that changes are the specifics. . . . We strongly believe in the social responsibility of the designer (Vignelli Associates 1990).

More likely, while urban designers (with allied consultants) may be major figures in developing a program for a scheme, they will only have control of the translation of the program into a physical form. The design of the program is, however, the truly creative act even though the final physical form is what people see and remember. Much depends on the type of the project on which the urban designer and architect is engaged.

There are a few occasions when the architect or architectural team has what approximates total control over the design of a whole settlement from site plan down to building design. Radburn, New Jersey, and the green belt towns of the 1930s are examples in which design teams carried out the whole design. Much total new town design occurs only in *administered communities*. The classic example of such a community is the company town.

Centers of existing new towns and governmental, cultural, business, and housing complexes are typical large projects that are done by single firms. The Nelson Rockefeller Empire State Plaza, the capitol complex, in Albany, New York, is an example of a government center that might be regarded as a total urban design in the United States. Lincoln Center in New York City is an example of a cultural center, and there are many instances of housing complexes in all U.S. cities and in suburban areas that are designed as a whole by a single architectural team. Often now, such schemes are purposefully created as all-of-a-piece designs, or even designs based on infrastructure design and guidelines, in order to avoid the monotony of a large-scale design. There will, however, continue to be total design schemes, as large architectural projects are designed and built across the world.

(2) All-of-a-Piece Urban Design

In all-of-a-piece urban design an overall illustrative design is done by one firm, and guidelines are written for developers and architects to follow in the design of buildings (see also "(4) The Urban Designer as Designer of Guidelines for Design" below). The distinction between what is called all-of-a-piece urban design and urban design as infrastructure design and guideline writing is a fine but important one. The basic point is that in the former, i.e., in all-of-a-piece cases, the urban design team acts as the reviewer of each subproposal and implicitly, the elements of the whole project are built within a short period of time of each other, if not simultaneously. The reason that many schemes that were originally perceived to be all-of-a-piece urban designs often become infrastructure designs plus guidelines is simply that the original target time for completion is not met and the administrators of the scheme change.

There are more examples of all-of-a-piece urban design, given this definition, than of total design in the United States. They cut across all scales of development from new towns down to large projects. It is true of new towns such as Columbia, Maryland, developed by the Rouse Company and, more recently, Las Colinas outside Dallas being developed by the Carpenter Organization. Begun in the 1960s, Columbia is only now approaching what might be regarded as completion, but it can still be regarded as an all-of-a-piece design administered by one company. As time passed much learning from what was done took place and directions changed—a truly Empiricist design. Smaller schemes such as Seaside (see Fig. 3-10) and Mashpee Commons on Cape Cod, Massachusetts, are closer to being genuine all-of-a-piece design because they are being built in a short time period.

In urban renewal there have been many coordinated developments consisting of a number of buildings that are all-of-a-piece design schemes. In the United States there have been a number of major center city developments schemes where obsolete areas were rebuilt: Rocke-

feller Center in New York, Penn Center in Philadelphia, Baltimore's Charles Center. The first of these can be regarded as a prototypical all-of-a-piece design. Rockefeller Center, built during the 1930s (Balfour 1978; Krinsky 1978), was the first scheme in which skyscrapers were grouped with self-consciously designed urban spaces to form a unit, although there were many earlier proposals for such schemes (e.g., the Terminal Park project in Chicago; see Fig. 14-2(1)). Reinhardt and Hofmeister were the master planners for Rockefeller Center, which consists of thirteen buildings designed by a number of architects. Although the overall design was changed a number of times, the whole complex was built almost simultaneously (Balfour 1978; Krinsky 1978).

Perhaps what is the best recent Deconstructionist example of an all-of-a-piece urban renewal scheme is a park, Parc de la Villette, designed by Bernard Tschumi (Tschumi 1987, 1988a, 1988b; Papadakis, Cooke, and Benjamin 1989; Broadbent 1990). The design of Parc de la Villette is based on a single architectural idea: that in a multicultural and seemingly chaotic world, architecture should be many-layered and discordant—the Deconstructionist philosophy. The park consists of three superimposed grids—the square, the triangle, and the circle. At each point of intersection is a *folie*. Between and around the folies is a system of paths, which are related to the various grids. The folies consist of 10.8-meter (36-foot) cubes divided into 12-meter cubes forming cages, which are themselves decomposed into subparts or have added features—stairs, ramps, walkways. The structural frame is covered by a bright-red steel envelope. The scheme is not actually entirely the work of one designer since pieces of it have been allocated to other designers—John Hejduk and Peter Eisenmann, for example.

(3) The Urban Designer as the Designer of Infrastructure

As much as half of the built environment of human settlements consists of public space: roads, parks, plazas, and public facilities such as city halls, museums, and schools—the capital web of cities (Crane 1960). Much of the character of a place stems from the layout of these elements in relationship to each other and to the spaces they form among themselves. The effect occurs in two ways: in terms of the pattern itself, and in terms of the opportunities the elements of the infrastructure create among themselves for land uses and building and open-space configurations—the catalytic effect. In this sense, all settlements have an urban design component. The urban designer is the person, or group of people, specifying in advance of its being built, the coordinated layout of the public realm—the capital investment strategy and the design (Buchanan 1988). Cities such as Houston, Texas, which have had no zoning ordinances, have had this level of urban design.

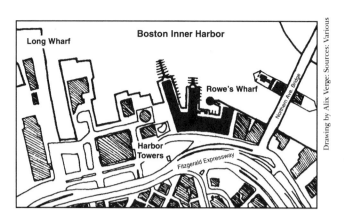
Drawing by Alix Verge; Sources: Various

1. Rowe's Wharf, Boston

Photograph by Deepti Nijhawan

2. Rowe's Wharf: View from the Street with Harbor Towers Adjacent

3. Nelson Rockefeller Empire State Plaza, Albany, New York

4. Levi's Plaza, San Francisco

Source: San Francisco (1990)

5. Mission Bay, San Francisco

Photograph by Ruth Durack

6. Seaside, Florida

Figure 3–7: Total Urban Design and *All-of-a-Piece* Urban Design

Rowe's Wharf in Boston, designed by Skidmore Owings & Merrill, is an example of the type of large building complex that is often called urban design (1,2). The Empire State Plaza in Albany is similar as an urban design project (3). They both certainly include a component of the public realm in their designs. While the plaza of Levi's Plaza and its buildings were designed by different firms, they are one project (4). Such complexes show the scope of total urban design in the United States today. All-of-a-piece designs are closer to the heart of urban design work. Mission Bay in San Francisco (5) and Seaside (6) in Florida (see also Fig. 3–11) are both being guided by a master plan that determines the physical infrastructure, but their buildings are being designed by a number of architects in accordance with strict design guidelines.

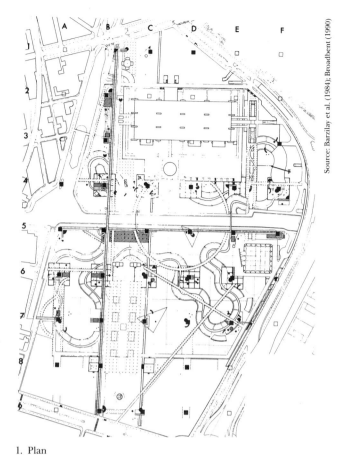

Source: Barzilay et al. (1984); Broadbent (1990)

1. Plan

Photograph by Ruth Durack

2. A *Folie*

Photograph by Ruth Durack

3. A *Folie*

Figure 3–8: Parc de la Villette, Paris

The Parc de la Villette shows some of the design principles that have resulted from Deconstructionist thinking (1). Peeled away from its intellectual foundations in the work of Jacques Derrida, the basic mechanism for achieving a design is the layering of patterns. At the intersection of these grids in the Parc de la Villette are *folies* (2,3) designed by a number of architects. The same design principles have been used for urban renewal proposals. In the United States the line of thought is being explored by Morphosis in their scheme for Hermosa Beach, Florida's central business district.

In much infrastructure design in American cities today, the concern is focused on the highway and road network and sometimes the integration of transportation modes (e.g., Bethesda, Maryland) as well as the location of major facilities. Sometimes it is only the road and service network that is designed. This situation often occurs in suburban development where the site is "improved" with services and the individual lots sold off to purchasers. Similarly, it occurs in sites-and-services schemes where very low income people in countries such as India and Bolivia build their own houses. These houses may be little more than shanties, but the owners have security of tenure and the basic services of water and sewerage. Their inhabitants have the opportunity to incrementally change the environment to meet their needs within the resources they have.

In any city today there is the network of transportation modes segregated or integrated in various patterns: road, rail, and pedestrian ways, at below-ground, ground, and above-ground level (see Okamato and Williams 1969). These transportation modes may be linked into vertical transportation of elevators. The integration of these modes with land uses is a fundamental consideration in the design of cities and their parts. In urban design the concern is with integrating buildings and infrastructure systems into a significant whole not only at a single point in time but also as they evolve. There are a number of basic concerns: (1) ease of movement—maximizing the flow of traffic (which may not necessarily, we have learned, be a good thing); (2) shortening pedestrian routes (e.g., the mid-block pedestrian ways and arcades of a number of cities); (3) protection from the climate (e.g., the skyway system in Minneapolis (see Fig. 2–1(2)), and the *galleria* of Italian cities—Rudofsky 1969; Barnett 1974; Geist 1983; Maitland 1991); and (4) reworking the city to improve the infrastructure and, in particular, retrofitting the highway

1. Central Area Model, Las Colinas, Texas

2. Central Artery Air Rights Scheme, Boston

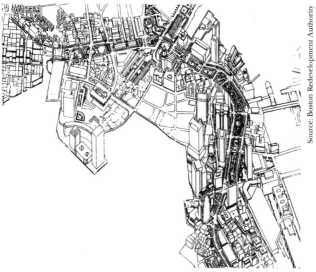

3. The Remains of the Embarcadero Highway, San Francisco

Figure 3-9: Infrastructure Design and Redesign
The design of the infrastructure of a city gives it much of its character. Las Colinas, Texas, is clearly designed for automobile movement (1). The Central Artery air rights development (2) of the Boston Redevelopment Authority is an effort to reintegrate city neighborhoods after a highway has been developed (compare to Fig. 10-4(3)). While this solution may seem radical, the structure of the Embarcadero Highway, which cut off much of San Francisco's waterfront from the city, has been removed (3).

network to make it more conducive to urban life (e.g., the Central Artery air rights development in Boston; see Fig. 3-9(2)). Often the design of the infrastructure is accompanied by guidelines for the design of the buildings.

A special concern of urban designers has been with the appearance of the public realm—with its beautification usually seen in terms of designers' current tastes. The focus has been on improving the landscape through the detailing of the ground and the use of trees and other vegetation as architecture to form spaces and to provide other amenities (see, e.g., Halprin 1963 and Arnold 1980), and with developing coordinated signage guidelines. Public arts programs are allied with this concern.

(4) The Urban Designer as Designer of Guidelines for Design

Design guidelines are the links between public policy statements and the physical design of an area. They are the explicit operational definitions and specification of the principles by which a physical form is to be generated. They set the parameters within which a design is acceptable regardless of other questions. As noted in Chapter 2, informal guidelines date back to the original human settlements. In a sense, guidelines are not unique to humans. The architecture created by animals follows instinctual guidelines—each design is different but follows the same form-generating principles (von Frisch 1974). Human beings are less constrained in their ability to deviate from the norm than other mammals, reptiles, or birds are.

Prescriptive and Performance Guidelines

Guidelines may specify physical forms/patterns or they may specify that whatever physical form is designed must perform in specific ways—it must afford specific behaviors or allow specific conditions to exist or, alternatively, not exist. *Prescriptive guidelines* establish the limit or framework (i.e., the envelope) within which buildings must be built. *Performance guidelines* provide the designer with the criteria whereby the impact of any proposal will be assessed. A simple example of a prescriptive statement is: "the FAR (Floor Area Ratio—the total floor area of a building in relationship to site size) of a particular Block must be under 12." A performance guideline, on the other hand, might say that any design is acceptable provided a particular amount of sunlight falls on a particular piece of ground between certain hours on a certain day (usually the winter solstice), or that infrastructure has the capacity to handle the traffic, or energy loads created, and so on (Shirvani 1985).

The advantage of performance guidelines is that they do not demand a standard form as a solution. The disadvantage is largely administrative—it is easier to simply see whether a building meets a formal prescription than to understand whether it will perform in a particular way. In litigious societies, such as the United States, specificity is essential. Performance guidelines do leave room for greater creativity on the part of the designer. As a result there is a general move toward performance guidelines by urban designers. Where designs have to be highly specific in appearance this approach cannot be adopted. In the design of Brasilia or even the Rue de Rivoli in Paris (1801), where the designs had to be very specific for aesthetic reasons, the guidelines have to be highly prescriptive. The specifications for the façades of the Rue de Rivoli were adopted from the original design by Charles Percier and Pierre Leonard Fontaine. Subsequent designers had to follow the earlier design exactly (Barnett 1987).

There are many examples of the use of design guidelines. A recent New York example is Battery Park City based on a master plan and guidelines by Cooper Ekstut Associates (Fisher 1988). Chicago's current (1992) sector plans follow the same approach, and the city's Department of Planning in conjunction with the Friends of the Chicago River have developed guidelines for that river's front. These guidelines hearken back to City Beautiful images of the treatment of the river's edge. Phoenix, Arizona, even more ambitiously, is developing citywide design guidelines and a design review procedure. In Europe, the ongoing redevelopment of Barcelona is within a master plan but involves many architects working within a set of guidelines to provide for the overall unity of a design idea.

Guidelines have also been applied to suburban and small town design such as Seaside, Florida. The plan itself is a small-scale City Beautiful one. Roads radiate out from a central square where the community facilities are located. The building lots were divided into eight types by building use, and highly prescriptive guidelines were developed to give the design a unified image (Duany, Plater-Zyberk, and Chellman 1987; Dunlop 1989; Patton 1991; Mahony and Easterling 1991). The location of the houses and garages on site, their heights, the nature of the fences, the need for front porches, were all carefully specified. The architects for individual houses had to be selected from an approved group. In the review process, deviations from the norm were encouraged provided the guidelines were adhered to.

For guidelines to make much sense they must be based on an understanding of how the built environment works because they require a prediction of how any patterns a designer has generated will perform when implemented. Well-developed positive design theory can provide the basis for developing strong arguments for guidelines (see Chapter 6). Without it they are unlikely to achieve the ends for which their designers are striving.

The Use of Guidelines

Guidelines may have different purposes. They may be used as mechanisms for:

1. Battery Park City from New Jersey

2. Lower Manhattan Viewed from Brooklyn Heights

Courtesy of *Progressive Architecture*

3. Rector Place

Figure 3–10: Battery Park City, New York
The general development plan being implemented for Battery Park City (1) was designed by Cooper-Ekstut Associates. It specifies the uses, the layout of roads, the development parcels, the general distinguishing features of the public spaces, and the guidelines to be followed by entrepreneurs and their architects in developing individual buildings. The models for residential development included parts of Gramercy Park, Beekman Place, and West End Avenue. The goal was to achieve buildings that are more typically New York City than most being built in Lower Manhattan (2,3; see also Fig. 2–15(3)).

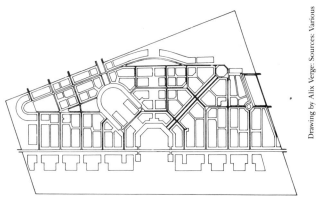

1. Plan

2. Overall View

3. View of a Street

Figure 3-11: Seaside, Florida

While the plan for Seaside, Florida (1), is reminiscent of the City Beautiful, the results are far from it (2,3). The overall plan for the 80–acre site, which came under developer Robert S. Davis's control in 1979, and the guidelines for the development of its individual buildings were created by Andres Duany and Elizabeth Plater-Zyberk. The objective was to attain the spirit of the small towns of southeast United States of thirty years ago—a Neo-Traditional attitude toward design.

    (a) defining and designing the public realm
    (b) specifying and/or restricting certain uses and building forms
    (c) stimulating types of development
    (d) preserving existing urban environments
    (e) specifying the nature and location of public art

(a) Defining and Designing the Public Realm

The public realm, it has been noted, consists of the open spaces among buildings and the surfaces (horizontal, vertical, and inclined) and the objects that define them. Much space is quasi-public in that the public has right of access but people's behavior is under private control. As cities change so the public realm is changed to better meet new needs. Each change needs to fit into the existing environment or initiate a change in it. In either case, to achieve specific ends, guidelines are needed so that each piece, possibly unique in character, fits into the whole.

In much recent design of the infrastructure of cities, particularly the pedestrian infrastructure, each piece is designed by a different authority or private developer. Without guidelines to ensure that the parts fit together, a chaotic environment is likely to result. These guidelines may specify the materials, the nature and spacing of trees and types of vegetation, the nature of street furniture, as well as the more basic necessities to ensure that the parts of the overall layout fit together! We have learned the hard way that all these characteristics need to be specified with exceptional clarity.

Guidelines have been written to ensure that each part of a project has the same territorial hierarchies (see Chapter 13), that rules for accessibility are met, and, where the space is quasi-public, that rights of access to it are guaranteed. Rights of access concern designing for the handicapped as well as when the public has right to access to quasi-public space. The Americans with Disabilities Act of 1990 became effective at the beginning of 1992 and thus must be taken into consideration in writing guidelines for the design of the public realm.

Guidelines often have to be written for the administration of a public place to accompany the design guideline. In interior quasi-public spaces such as the Winter

Garden at Battery Park City or the city center of Milton Keynes, England, the public has the right of access to the space only at certain hours of the day. At Battery Park City, the hours are generous, but central Milton Keynes operates as a shopping mall and is closed when the retail shops are closed. Guidelines for the operation and administration of such places must be written to ensure that public space is open to the public.

(b) Specifying and/or Restricting Certain Uses and Building Forms

(i) Zoning Controls   Zoning controls place a restriction on what a building developer and/or architect can do. Zoning is probably the most widely used tool internationally for controlling land uses. Its purpose is to predesignate the use and character of development within specific geographic areas. Typically the regulations may specify the building envelope—an imaginary volume—within which a development has to take place. In specifying the envelope, the controls may restrict uses permitted in the area, the total floor area of the site, maximum height, the bulk of the building, and setbacks from property lines.

The size of the geographic areas and the purposes served by these guidelines vary. While whole states may be subject to a zoning code, the specific units may be as small as part of a block or even a specific building site.

(ii) Transfer of Development Rights   While the transfer of development rights to a site may be seen as something new, this was advocated by Eliel Saarinen in his book *The City* fifty years ago (Lai 1988). Owners have the right to develop their sites to their own best advantage, but often the public interest is not served by many types of potential developments on sites with special characteristic (e.g., buildings of historical importance or views). In order to preserve such amenities, the owners are allowed to transfer the development rights from one site to another that did not have such rights previously or, alternatively, to sell them to another person at another site. In this way they are able to realize the market value of their own sites. The selling of air rights on a site is a special case. For instance, the sale of 75,000 square feet of air rights over Grand Central Terminal in New York City enabled the terminal to be preserved. It also, for better or worse, enabled the Pan American Building to be built.

(iii) Physical Form and Pattern Guidelines   Guidelines for shaping the structure of cities into particular forms are based on an image of an end product—a design. Guidelines for the physical development of cities may encompass design controls for street and plaza layout, controls for building height, bulk, floor area ratio (FAR), site coverage, street line setbacks (particularly when they are not covered by existing zoning ordinances), and aesthetic issues. The aesthetic guidelines may deal with such things as building envelope and façade design, scale, materials,

textures, and color. The goal is to ensure an "harmonious" relationship between buildings and, often, between new buildings and their contexts (Hedman and Jaszewski 1984). They may specify such items of façade design as the relationship of solid to window area, the nature of bases, cornices, and string courses, and building materials and color (Barnett 1987; J. Ellis 1987).

The essential step in defining what urban patterns should be built is to identify with precision their rationale. One of the clearest examples of this thinking is displayed in San Francisco's *Guiding Downtown Development* (City of San Francisco 1982). This document includes such sections as "Building Size," "Design and Appearance," "Retail Services," "Recreation and Open Space," "Transportation and Circulation," "Housing," and "Preservation and Significant Buildings and Industry" (see Fig. 3-12 and also Shirvani 1985).

The guidelines for urban design in San Francisco are part of the master plan. They are based on a number of objectives (e.g., Objective 3 in Figure 3-12), which are translated into policies and principles (e.g., 1 A, B, and C in Figure 3-12) with commentaries on specific points. The range and specificity of the design guidelines puts San Francisco in the forefront of U.S. cities that are attempting to shape their own futures as a matter of public policy rather than simply following the dictates of the market.

The design variables that are to be controlled by guidelines vary depending on what falls within the perimeter of designers' concerns. Many guidelines are concerned primarily with the city as a work of art. In the creation of Brasilia, the primary concerns of the guidelines were with controlling the distribution of open spaces and ensuring an "aesthetic unity." Other guidelines may focus on the types of experiences people have or with the symbolism of the environment.

Some design guidelines have a clearly educational goal in addition to that of control. For instance, the New York City report "Plazas for People, Streetscape and Residential Plazas" (1976) was meant to educate architects as well as dictate designs. It might be regarded as an indirect set of guidelines.

(iv) Aesthetic Regulation   All zoning regulations and design guidelines are aesthetic in nature (Lai 1988). The basic question here is: "Can aesthetic regulations be imposed on an existing environment to shape its future development?" Specifically such questions as "Are billboards an eyesore?" arise. It is clear that in some places they may be, but in others they add to the pleasure of an experience and very clearly add to the sense of place (e.g., Times Square in New York City).

The overall appearance of the environment comes from many individual acts of self-expression. A negative appearance does affect the quality of life within that environment—it has an adverse psychological effect on our feelings of self-worth (see Chapters 13, 14, and 17). Aesthetic legislation, where it has been introduced, is

OBJECTIVE 3

MODERATION OF MAJOR NEW DEVEL-OPMENT TO COMPLEMENT THE CITY PATTERN, THE RESOURCES TO BE CONSERVED, AND THE NEIGHBORHOOD ENVIRONMENT.

As San Francisco grows and changes, new development can and must be fitted in with established city and neighborhood patterns in a complementary fashion. Harmony with existing development requires careful consideration of the character of the surroundings at each construction site. The scale of each new building must be related to the prevailing height and bulk in the area, and to the wider effects upon the skyline, views and topographic form. Designs for buildings on large sites have the most widespread effects and require the greatest attention.

FUNDAMENTAL PRINCIPLES

These fundamental principles and their illustrations reflect the needs and characteristics with which this Plan is concerned, and describe measurable and critical urban design relationships in major new development.

1. The relationship of a building's size and shape to its visibility in the cityscape, to important natural features and to existing development determines whether it will have a pleasing or a disruptive effect on the image and character of the city.

    A. Tall, slender buildings near the crown on a hill emphasize the form of the hill and preserve views.

    B. Extremely massive buildings on or near hills can overwhelm the natural land forms, block views, and generally disrupt the character of the city.

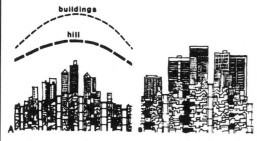

    C. Low, smaller-scale buildings on the slopes of hills, at their base and in the valleys between, complement topographic forms and permit uninterrupted views.

    D. etc.

Figure 3–12: San Francisco Urban Design Guidelines

used as much to maintain property values as to create a sense of identity. It does achieve these ends but it also denies people the freedom of expression to do what they wish. In Coral Gables, Florida, "all buildings should be of Spanish, Italian, or other Mediterranean or similar harmonious type architecture" (Lai 1988). Santa Barbara, California, has to be in the "Monterey Style" (see Fig. 17–7(3)).

In seeking homogeneity of appearance, questions of boredom arise, particularly in Rationalist design. In seeking the opposite, vulgarity often results. In those environments where design guidelines have dictated the nature of the public realm, heterogeneity in design achieved by individual expressive acts results in at least an interesting environment.

Ultimately, wherever there is aesthetic legislation, a design review board is the ultimate arbiter of taste. Such boards, in contrast to boards of zoning adjustment, are generally constituted of design professionals. Clear guidelines and a fair administrative process are essential for review boards to act without prejudice. The guidelines must represent a community's commitment to specific aesthetic ends to be implementable.

*(v) **Restrictive Covenants***   Covenants can control the future directions of development of a property by placing restrictions into the deed. Such covenants have been used to restrict the future use and form of buildings on a site to allow for easements for potential future uses (such as mass transit routes), to maintain such amenities as views (Attoe 1988b), or to restrict the building materials that might be used in an area in order to maintain the economic or historic appearance of an area (e.g., allowing only masonry construction). They are also used to maintain permanent rights of way across portions of sites to give access to areas and activities sites without direct road access.

(b) Mechanisms to Stimulate Particular Types of Development

The goal of controls and guidelines in shaping development in a particular direction that goes against prevailing market forces is to achieve some public good that is not financially feasible in the marketplace (Barnett 1974, 1982; Shirvani 1985). The mechanism for achieving the public good is to tie such a direction into one for which there is financial feasibility (Roddewig 1981; Roddewig and Inghram 1987; Getzels et al. 1988). In using such tools, policymakers recognize that some land uses can outbid others in the marketplace, yet there is a demand and a necessity, in terms of the quality of life, to provide for other activities and places. An incentive system to achieve these purposes is a necessity in capitalist economies where the marketplace would otherwise dictate what the distribution of activities will be (Dear and Scott 1981).

There are two basic ways of stimulating specific types of development. The first focuses on the catalytic impact of specific developments and the second is legislative. The former involves the erection of a building, building complex, or improvement in the public realm so that the character of an area is changed sufficiently to attract desired development (Attoe and Logan 1989), and the second is to create legislation that rewards developers for building certain uses and facilities into the buildings they wish to erect.

One of John D. Rockefeller's aims in developing Rockefeller Center in New York City was to make the blocks around it the city's major shopping area (Krinsky 1978). Rockefeller Center has indeed been a major catalyst for the development of the surrounding areas. Similarly the development of Penn Center in Philadelphia has been a catalyst for the development of an extensive commercial office building area on adjacent sites (Bacon 1974). A number of countries have had policies for public investments in institutions such as museums and other cultural facilities to foster development. The decision to locate the New Jersey State Aquarium on Camden's waterfront is an effort to revitalize a city in extreme economic and psychological distress. At the time of writing it was operating with great success but its catalytic effect was yet to be seen.

The major legislative tool for stimulating types of development is that of zoning incentives; another is tax credits. Through the use of either, developers are directly or indirectly financially rewarded by the public sector for providing facilities that they would not otherwise have built. Incentive zoning provides a conditional exchange between a governmental body and a developer. It allows a developer to contravene an existing zoning ordinance in order that some public good be attained—it involves the giving up of one good for another deemed more important (Barnett 1974; Getzels et al. 1988). Property tax rebates do essentially the same thing. Taxes are reduced or forgiven for a period of time to attain, or retain, a capital investment of public value.

In the United States, San Francisco and New York City were the first to use incentive zoning. New York City's Incentive Zoning Ordinance of 1961 was an effort to improve the quality of the urban environment. It created special zoning districts with specific goals in different parts of Manhattan. The Lower Manhattan Special Zoning District was concerned with designing pleasing pedestrian environments and with establishing view corridors along streets. The Fifth Avenue Special Zoning District was concerned with maintaining retail stores at the street level and having a continuous street façade unbroken by setbacks (Barnett 1982). The city permitted developers in these areas to build larger buildings than allowed by existing zoning ordinances in exchange for such public amenities as plazas, wider sidewalks, or retailing space at the ground level.

Other urban design goals in New York City have been to maintain theaters in the Broadway theater district and to achieve north-south mid-block pedestrian ways reminiscent of the arcades of earlier times—east-west blocks are long in New York City (see Fig. 3–13). In exchange developers received certain bonuses—for instance, total floor area beyond what was specified by zoning regulations, which usually meant additional allowable height to their buildings. Implicit in such an ordinance is that it is worth giving up some quality of light at the ground level for more open space or other amenity. The utility of such an exchange has been much queried. More recently such incentives (sometimes to build at all) have been used to provide for low-cost housing elsewhere in the city, children's creches in office buildings, and so on. For instance, the requirement for developers of buildings in San Francisco's city center to pay "$5 a square foot towards housing improvements related to the downtown, $5 a square foot towards transit, $2 a square foot for downtown parks, and $1 for child-care provisions" was specified in San Francisco's downtown plan, which was part of the city's master plan of 1984 (Barnett 1987). The examples show the essentially negotiatory nature of urban design in the United States (see also Frieden and Sagalyn 1989).

The *planned unit development* is another such zoning incentive used in new suburban residential areas (Barnett 1982). The goal is to provide for communal space, or to preserve open space per se, by allowing, or rather encouraging, the developer to cluster housing in one segment of a development tract. This leaves a significant portion of the tract in a natural state rather than having the whole tract developed at a uniformly low density. The overall density is the same whether the tract is developed with its housing clustered or dispersed. Another goal is to obtain a streetscape more closely related to the natural state of the environment. Such a cultural value is widely held within the Anglo-American ethos, but it is not one universally shared.

The key to successful incentives is to both recognize the nature of the marketplace for land and buildings and to have clearly specified design features as ends, with a clear justification of the public need for them. They have to be based on an unmistakable understanding of how cities and human settlements work. This understanding has to be accompanied by an ability to articulate clearly what the products that are to be developed should be like. Instructional material and design guidelines for architects, developers, and review boards need to be easy to understand, unambiguous, and precise.

(c) Preserving Existing Urban Environments

While traditionally associated with historic preservation, preservation guidelines imply more than a concern with an effort to maintain existing structures of historic significance. Rather, they are concerned with the broad desire to maintain the character of an area (Roddewig 1981; Attoe 1988b). The character is preserved through

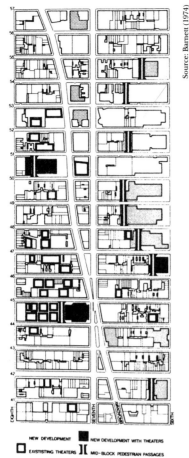

Source: Barnett (1974)

NEW DEVELOPMENT ■ NEW DEVELOPMENT WITH THEATERS

▢ EXISTISTING THEATERS ⫴ MID-BLOCK PEDESTRIAN PASSAGES

1. The Theater District, New York City

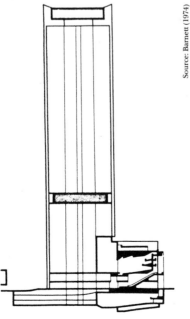

Source: Barnett (1974)

2. Cross Section through One Astor Plaza

the selective retention of elements that contribute to this quality. These elements may be historic buildings, but they may also be curiosity objects and blocks of buildings that, although they are not historically significant, add to the quality of an area simply by their physical character (Jacobs and Jones 1962). In New York City, preservation guidelines have been used in conjunction with special district legislation to protect the character of areas as diverse as Little Italy, the theater district, retailing sections, and Greenwich Village (Shirvani 1981).

The goal of preservation guidelines is to control the process of demolition of the existing environment to obtain a sense of continuity of life and, often, an aesthetic character. The combination of the nature of building economics and cost and the unavailability of many craft skills today means that developers and architects are generally unable to replicate the existing qualities of buildings and neighborhoods.

(d) Specifying the Nature and Location of Public Art

During the past twenty years there have been a number of public art programs. There are two basic types of public art: monuments commemorating people and/or events, and art objects. The goal has been both to provide a forum for artists to display their work and to add interest to the city and to beautify it. The choice and location of the art and the right of artists to express their opinions without interference have been controversial issues. In many places (e.g., Bethesda, Maryland) the selection of works has been the subject of much debate (Shaw-Eagle 1986; Larsen 1987). Part of the problem has been that artists operate without any guidelines and without any understanding for the later context of their works. All too often, art works are used to salvage the quality of poorly designed spaces. They seldom do. Sometimes they make them worse. Richard Serra's *Tilted Arc* sculpture was removed from a New York City plaza because it was deemed by the public, city workers, and ultimately the city administration to detract a great deal from what was already a poor open space. Artists were up in arms over this action and felt it was an infringement on their right of self-expression (Weyergraf-Serra and Buskirk 1990). However, the right to spoil a place in the name of art seems a

Figure 3-13: Incentive Zoning

Incentive zoning provisions have been created to encourage specific types of development that would not be as economically beneficial to entrepreneurs as other types. One example is for the development of new theaters in the Broadway theater district of midtown Manhattan. The buildings shown in black were built under the incentive zoning legislation introduced in New York City in the late sixties (1). Developers were allowed to build up to 20 percent extra floor space in office towers in return for including a theater in their building. The cross section through One Astor Plaza shows how this was done (2).

1. Rural Land Form

2. Planned Unit Development

3. Standard Subdivision

Source: Barnett (1974)

Figure 3-14: Planned Unit Development

Planned unit development zoning is an effort to create higher density residential environments in rural and suburban areas without losing the level of amenities people seek in them. The objective is to obtain a street layout that more closely resembles the rural landscape (1), a large communal open space, and houses tightly clustered together (2). The same overall density in a standard subdivision (3) achieves a much lower level of communal amenities. The idea is similar to the Radburn concept but without the nonresidential components (see Fig. 2-8).

dubious claim. As Michael Sorkin (1991) colorfully notes: "If 'sculpture' behaves like architecture then it gets judged that way. If 'sculpture' makes space in a city, then it takes the rap for its cock-ups as urban design. Calling it art won't do." In Concord, California, *Spirit Poles,* a sculpture, cannot be removed despite strong local opposition because state law prohibits removal of public art without the permission of its creator. *Spirit Poles* does not, however, act as a space-defining element in the same way that *Titled Arc* did.

TYPES OF URBAN DESIGN PROJECTS

It can be concluded from the previous discussion that there are two major types of urban design projects. The first is in new towns design and the second in large-project design. They range across each of the types of urban design work from total design to guideline writing for infrastructure development and building designs.

Infrastructure Design

As noted earlier in this chapter, the capital web of human settlements gives them much if not all of their character (see also Chapters 9 and 10). The design of the highway, road, and pedestrian paths and the placement of key buildings and land uses are the essence of physical city planning, and they are where it and urban design overlap. In addition, the nature of the water reticulation and sewerage system can give a city its basic form. Parks and plazas provide behavioral opportunities, acting as a backdrop and foreground to different components of the physical city and urban life.

Rationalist city design was concerned with getting the capital web into a rectilinear geometry; Empiricists with getting it into more intricate patterns. Much urban design work today involves retooling the existing infrastructure of cities to enhance accessibility and the quality of life. Sometimes it involves rectifying poor earlier urban design and planning decisions. The Embarcadero Highway in San Francisco has been demolished. The Central Artery air rights project in Boston involves the creation of a series of parks and public spaces running the length of the artery tunnel. The historic grid of the city over it will enable adjacent neighborhoods to be reintegrated to some extent. The proposal is similar in concept to the Turia River Gardens designed by Ricardo Bofill in Valencia, Spain. These proposals alter the character of their cities considerably. Certainly the design of infrastructure systems is the basis for almost all urban design because it deals with the links between places.

New Town Design

As has been noted already, most new towns consist of developing a master plan and the guidelines for the

1. Arc de Triomphe, Place de l'Etoile, Paris (1806)

2. Bethesda, Maryland

3. *Tilted Arc*, Federal Plaza, New York. Richard Serra, Artist

Source: Weyergraff-Serra and Buskirk (1990)

development of precincts and buildings. There are a few occasions when the architect, or architectural team, has what approximates total control of the design of a city. It really only occurs in *administered communities*. The classic example of such a community is the company town. From the beginning of the development of company towns, a never altogether achieved goal has been that of control of the lives of their inhabitants by the company. The designs are the result of the collaborative thinking of the company and its designers. This was historically true of the design of such towns as Saltaire, in Yorkshire, the new towns developed by Krupp in Germany, and, more particularly, in Pullman, Illinois (Ely 1885; Benevolo 1967; Gilbert 1990). There were many such developments. Gillian Darley (1978) lists over 400 British examples of "Villages of Vision." Many company towns have been developed since World War II with much the same objective in mind, although the concern is also to attract workers by providing pleasant working conditions.

As previously noted, the best-known example of an administered community is probably Brasilia, where the design team was led by Costa and Niemeyer. Their client was the Brazilian government and, more particularly, President Kubitschek, whose idea it was to implement a longstanding concept to develop the interior of Brazil (Stäubli 1966; Evenson 1973). In such a situation the architect exerts control through the right to review all proposals and the right to veto proposals that fall outside the scope of acceptance he has established. Niemeyer had almost total autocratic power to make design decisions, and the design is essentially as he specified it. He and Costa did, however, have to convince President Kubitschek and his advisors that the design was a good one, as a symbol of Brazil and, implicitly, as a memorial to Kubitschek himself. Even in an administered community such as Brasilia some major design decisions have been changed because they disregarded how such activities as retailing work. The whole layout of the major shopping center in Brasilia has been reversed to make it functional (Brolin 1976).

The administrators of various new town corporations or authorities (such as the New York State Development Corporation) set up to develop specific towns that form part of new towns' policies have the power to deter-

Figure 3-15: Public Art and Urban Design
Public art serves many purposes (see Figs. 13–13 and 17–11). The Arc de Triomphe in Paris commemorates a victory (1). Triumphal arches adorn sites such as Valley Forge in Pennsylvania, the Grand Army Plaza in Brooklyn, and Washington Square in New York. Public art has received government support in a number of ways. Often the results are highly controversial (2,3). After a time, however, people sometimes develop an affection for the work simply because it becomes part of the environment to which they are habituated. This result does not always occur. *Tilted Arc* (3) has now been removed!

mine many aspects of the designs under their jurisdictions. The British and Scandinavian new towns, for instance, are designed as entities, although their components may be the result of many designers. They might be regarded as all-of-a-piece designs. In private developments such as Columbia, Maryland; Las Colinas, Texas; and Jonathan, Minnesota, the nature of the land market and the nature of market returns have to be fully recognized, and thus some aspects of the public good cannot be addressed.

On a smaller scale there have been a number of new towns. Port Grimaud, France, designed by Cabinet Spoerry of Mulhouse is a well-known example of all-of-a-piece waterfront design in Europe (Smithson and Smithson 1972; Broadbent 1990). It was begun in 1966 and continues to be developed. Its image is similar to that of Venice but cars are permitted to enter. Covering 189 acres and with the potential of a little over 2,000 housing units, its design consists of a set of villages on islands in a lagoon. The architecture is unified, consisting of four-story rough stucco-walled houses with barrel-tiled roofs. The villagelike image is enhanced by having a variety of relationships of house to lot lines. Some are set back with trees in front and some are built to the lot line. It might better be regarded as a large-project design rather than a new town. Similar comments can be made about developments such as Seaside (see Fig. 3–11) and Mashee Commons on Cape Cod, Massachusetts, which is only 275 acres in size. The design concern in all three is not only with providing pleasant individual homes, but also with achieving a sense of community and of place. All three are also examples of Neo-Traditional urban design.

Large-Project Design

There are three basic types of large-scale projects that have been built during the twentieth century: (1) the design of precincts within new towns, (2) the urban renewal projects that have occurred as the result of wartime destruction and/or the obsolescence of segments of major cities throughout the world, and (3) suburban development. There are other types that may or may not be subsumed in the first three categories—universities, industrial and commercial campuses, the new suburban downtowns, theme parks, Olympic sports complexes, and vacation resorts. They will be discussed as a group in (4) The Campus. The borders distinguishing one type from another are often blurred.

(1) Precincts of New Towns

The centers and/or neighborhoods of a new town may well be designed as an all-of-a-piece design. Reston, Virginia's central area is now being redeveloped following a conceptual design of RTKL in Baltimore. In the United States such centers are more likely to be built over time, after an infrastructure has been built by the overall de-

velopers and the individual buildings designed according to guidelines, than to be total designs. In other countries there are a number of examples of precincts designed as units. The centers of the British new towns such as Harlow, Cumbernauld, and Milton Keynes are examples (see also Fig. 13–7). They all clearly reflect the eras of their design. Harlow's is a pedestrian precinct, Cumbernauld's is a megastructure, and in Milton Keynes the public space is really private space, so much so that it now closes for security reasons when retail shopping hours are over (Oc 1991).

Since World War II there have been three clear eras of guidelines for large-project designs. Each depends on contemporary design concepts of what a good city is. The first era was based on the Rationalist vision of the good city. The second was based on a vision of the city as consisting of parts that were plugged into an overall framework—a line of thinking associated with the Archigram group. The third era was based not on the dreams of architects, but on a much more empirical approach to urban design—its guidelines were based on how people live and how cities work well. The concept of "working well" still implies a value judgment.

The Post-Modern era in total design is reflected in Arata Isozaki and Associates' design for the center of the academic new town of Tsukuba in Japan (Treib 1985). Tsukuba center is a complex of commercial facilities including a hotel, civic center, concert hall, information center, and retail shops. The client was the Japanese government. The scheme includes many Modernist design principles, such as the vertical segregation of automobile and pedestrian traffic, but it is essentially a Post-Modernist scheme in which "icons are inverted." In particular, Michelangelo's design for the Capitoline Hill in Rome is used as the basis for the design for the central plaza, but the surface of the space at Tsukuba is concave rather than convex, and the colors of the pavement pattern are reversed.

(2) Urban Renewal

There have been three main types of urban renewal projects since World War II, although there are many cases that are a mixture of all three. The first involves rebuilding those cities of the world devastated by bombing and/or artillery attacks (see Diefendorf 1990). The second involves the purchase of buildings and land, the removal of the uses and inhabitants of that land, the demolition and clearance of the land, and the building of the site. It has often gone under the name "slum clearance." The third has simply involved extensive sites abandoned by their inhabitants and made available by their owners for redevelopment.

Rebuilding after warfare (and after internal riots) is still a situation in which a number of cities in the world find themselves at any given time. Much such rebuilding occurs in a haphazard fashion, but there have been a

1. Brasilia, Brazil

2. University of Illinois, Chicago

3. Voorhees, New Jersey

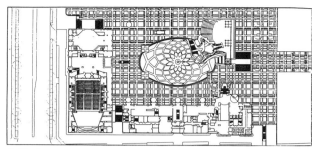

1. Tsukuba Center, Japan, Plan

2. The Campidoglio, Rome (1537)

Figure 3-16: Three Eras of Post–World War II Design Principles and/or Guidelines

Three eras of post–World War II urban design attitudes are reflected in changes in conceptual plans, zoning ordinances, and/or design guidelines. Modernism in the 1950s followed Rationalist ideals as in Lincoln Center, New York (see Fig. 3–19 (6)) or, more dramatically, in Brasilia (1). Motorists and vehicles were horizontally segregated, buildings were set away from streets, and an orthogonal geometry was followed. During the second era the infrastructure with a vertical segregation of pedestrians and vehicles was developed and the buildings plugged into it (2). The most recent development follows the recognition that streets can be seams (3).

Figure 3-17: The Post-Modernist Urban Design Concept

The civic center for the new town of Tsukuba in Japan shows many of the characteristics of the mainstream of Post-Modern design and landscape architecture (1). The center itself is a space and the surrounding buildings are derived from the work of many people, predominantly Rationalists. The surface of the space is, however, derived from Michelangelo's piazza on the Capitoline Hill in Rome (2). The plaza is a metaphoric expression of that piazza. The use of an artificial intellectual aesthetic construct is typical of much recent urban design work.

number of major coordinated efforts at the precinct level. Immediately after World War II, the Lijnbaan was built in Rotterdam along Modernist lines while, in a contrasting manner, central Warsaw was rebuilt to appear externally as it was before World War II. In 1957 a building exhibition, Interbau, was held in Berlin during which several housing schemes following Bauhaus principles were designed in the Hansaviertel. More recently, since the late 1970s, Berlin has explored ways of integrating past, present, and future. The resulting International Bauausstellung (IBA), run under the auspices of a planning association, has seen the design of many residential precincts by internationally known architects as the results of design competitions. The schemes have been in various forms of Post-Modernism from purely Rationalist designs to those emphasizing the habitability of the resultant designs (Broadbent 1990).

The purposeful demolition of parts of cities to house new buildings has occurred through both private and governmental actions, although it is generally associated with the latter. The problem in the former case is to acquire properties without government powers of eminent domain. The rebuilding of the site can also be by a developer, by the governmental agency, or by a collaboration between the two. Designs in the first case are largely market-driven or, at least, highly market-sensitive, while in the second situation the designers have a greater freedom to disregard market forces, especially in the housing area. When a government is involved, the process follows a sequence of steps: an agency buys up obsolete buildings and/or buildings that are regarded as slums (industrial or residential), demolishes them, accumulates the small land parcels into large blocks, and either develops them itself or turns the sites over to private developers, according to pubic goals. The former type of development is more typical of the European experience, while the latter is generally the U.S. procedure, often heavily subsidized by the public sector. The process is essentially that advocated by Le Corbusier to implement his proposals for Paris (Le Corbusier 1960), as was done by Haussmann before him. As a process it always seems to have been controversial (Benevolo 1980).

The third situation has occurred as extensive sites become available for development, largely as the result of the change in manufacturing and transportation technologies during the immediate post–World War II years. Sprawling factories located in dense urban areas have found it to their financial advantage to move to other locations, leaving land in cities open for redevelopment. In addition, large segments of cities that were formerly railroad yards or ports have been and are being abandoned. This is due to the growth of the trucking industry and the relocation of ports to places that have both deep-water access for the larger vessels that now constitute the merchant marine and ease of access for trucks. It has also occurred because the value of land has escalated, often

making even recent developments financially obsolete (e.g., the Paternoster area around St. Paul's Cathedral in London). There are thus a number of typical urban renewal situations: the redevelopment of abandoned industrial areas and railyards, waterfront development, housing projects, and center city (downtown) renewal.

Many waterfront developments are perceived to be total design because of their architectural unity but few are. Indeed, there is a remarkable similarity in basic design and retailing principles among all the waterfront development schemes that have been built in the last two decades in the United States, although they are located in diverse places (Fisher and Dramov 1987; Davey 1989a; Torre 1989). Most are all-of-a-piece designs.

The waterfront urban renewal developments are generally of three types: (1) retail-entertainment centers (which have come to be known as "festival markets"), (2) mixed-use commercial-residential projects, and (3) housing developments. There are also two basic types of waterfronts: those on still water—rivers and harbors where transportation facilities have become obsolete (e.g., Battery Park City, New York, and the west bank of the Hudson River opposite it in New Jersey), and those on the sea where past resorts have become obsolete (e.g., Atlantic City, New Jersey). There are many of the first mentioned type. Baltimore Inner Harbor is the prototype for many that have followed. The Docklands in London consists of much housing, but also mixed-use commercial and high-density commercial complexes. It is under construction at the time of writing and is as much a series of new-towns-in-town as a commercial or housing development (Wilford 1984; Brownhill 1990).

Many housing projects designed in the 1940s, 1950s, and 1960s followed Rationalist design ideas. Others were based on the Garden City model. Many are total designs, sometimes on a vast scale. It is the Rationalist ideas that, when applied to housing design, have resulted in the most dramatic successes and failures. A number of European examples, in particular, are well known to architects: Thamesmead, Roehampton, Byker Wall (Egelius 1980a, 1980b), and, more recently, Les Arcades de Lac and Las Echelles du Baroque. Pruitt Igoe is a notorious American example (Montgomery 1966). A number of recent housing developments are Neo-Traditional ones of houses on streets forming face-block neighborhoods.

We have learned what, with the wisdom of hindsight, is common sense: the design of housing has to be congruent with the lifestyles of the inhabitants of the housing, recognizing the problems that they face. In Philadelphia, the Southwark, Mill Creek, and Society Hill housing developments follow the same design principles. All three projects were designed by internationally renowned architects: Stonerov and Hawes, Louis I. Kahn, and I. M. Pei, respectively. The first is notorious for its failure in terms of people's lives. Few people live there by choice. It was primarily for low-income families facing many social and

1. Southwark Plaza. Stonorov and Hawes, Architects

2. Mill Creek Housing. Louis Kahn, Architect

3. Society Hill. I. M. Pei, Architect

Figure 3-18: Three Philadelphia Housing Projects
The design principles used in the design of the Southwark Plaza (1), Mill Creek (2), and Society Hill Towers (3) developments are essentially the same. The major difference in design is that Society Hill Towers has a major subterranean parking area. It is also administered differently since it is private development and the people who live there have chosen it of their own accord. The importance of matching people, their needs, and the built environment and what it affords is underscored by the success of the Society Hill development in comparison to the other two.

economic difficulties. There are many children and female-headed households living there. There are few families in the high-rise Society Hill towers, while in the rowhouses the families are wealthy enough to use the resources of the city. It is a sought after place in which to live. Mill Creek falls somewhere in between. Most large United States cities have a number of such developments. Many of them lie vacant.

Recent housing developments can still be divided into those based on Rationalist and those based on the Empiricist traditions even though they are usually put together under the rubric of Post-Modernism. The work of Ricardo Bofill and the Taller at Le Lac (Torchinsky 1988; Stern with Gastil 1988), Mario Botta, and much of that of Aldo Rossi falls into the first category, while that of Charles Moore (Littlejohn 1984; Johnson 1986) and many less well known architects falls into the second category. They are less well known because their work is less heroic and focuses on providing a backdrop to life rather than foreground buildings. Both approaches pay considerably more attention to user needs as they actually are than the Modernists did. Little empirical research has, as yet, been done on the outcomes—the complexes in use—so reaching conclusions is difficult. The Rationalists still draw on their own imagined person and the good life while Empiricists try to draw their information more on what is known about human behavior and the built environment. Bofill, for instance, notes, "*For me* a town must be a meeting place . . ." (Torchinsky 1988), whether its inhabitants see it as such or not.

The work of IBA in what was, until 1990, walled West Berlin consists of a series of housing developments and precinct core developments. Although many of the projects have been designed by a single architect, the whole adds up to piecemeal design. This occurred even though the projects were controlled by some guidelines stressing the street and building to the corners of blocks so that the faces of projects relate to each other. The same is true of much of the current housing developments of the Docklands in London. The result is a series of housing developments following different approaches to Post-Modernism, with much attention paid to the private realm and little to the public (Wilford 1984; Buchanan 1988).

Since World War II there has been much rebuilding of the centers of cities. Most developments have taken place on a piecemeal basis—one building replacing one or several others as the size of buildings increase. There have been, however, many coordinated developments consisting of a number of buildings. In the United States all major cities have had major center city development schemes where obsolete areas have been rebuilt. Much of it has been publicly guided and much has been largely publicly financed (see also Chapter 20). Some have been identified already: Penn Center in Philadelphia, Baltimore's Charles Center, and the Empire State Plaza in Albany—the capitol complex for New York State—are

1. Alfred E. Smith Housing, New York

Source: New York City Housing Authority

2. Paternoster Square Development, London (1956)

Source: Architectural Design 62, no. 5/6:12

3. Lijnbaan, Rotterdam

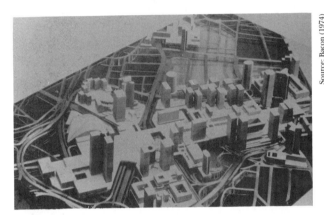

4. La Défense, Paris

Source: Bacon (1974)

5. Empire State Plaza, Albany, New York

6. Lincoln Center, New York

Figure 3-19: Urban Renewal

Urban renewal is a fact of life. Sometimes this rebuilding is on an immediately noticeable scale, as in the examples here, but sometimes it is so incremental that it is hardly discernible. Bit by bit, the city is changed over time. Alfred E. Smith Housing adjacent to the Brooklyn Bridge was built much as the drawing suggests prior to World War II (1). In Europe much rebuilding was necessitated by the damage sustained by cities during World Wars I and II. The area around St. Paul's Cathedral in the City of London was destroyed during World War II, rebuilt, and now, for financial reasons, is ripe for demolition and rebuilding (2).

The present response is very different (see Fig. 2–13(2)). Many European cities suffered the same fate. One of the earliest and most influential rebuilding efforts was the Lijnbaan, Rotterdam, in the 1950s (3). La Défense in Paris (4) has been developed on the periphery of the city's historic core to avoid having to substantially change the core's character from that established by Haussmann under Napoleon III's patronage. It is an all-of-a-piece design. Empire State Plaza, in contrast, was done by one firm of architects (5; see also Fig. 3–7(3)). Most such total urban designs are simply large-scale architecture, such as the design for Lincoln Center, New York (6).

examples. The last mentioned has already been identified as a total design, while the first two, although guided by single organizations, were the work of a number of designers. Few recent center city schemes on close examination are total designs.

There are many urban renewal schemes on the boards of firms around the world. In the United States there are continuing developments in many major cities: The Gateway mall in St. Louis, the CBD in Portland, Oregon (where speedy implementation of proposals has led to a planning award), and the New Orleans waterfront are typical examples. The slowing down of the expansion of the American economy in the early 1990s has given policymakers and urban designers an opportunity to rethink their ideals.

(3) Suburban Development

Most suburban development today, it has been already noted, occurs in a piecemeal fashion and amounts to little more than the subdivision of land and the provision of infrastructure to make sites available for purchase. Zoning controls may exist to govern such things as residential building type, setbacks, and sideyards, but by and large there is no idea apart from ease of sale that is the criterion, or functional base, for the design. This situation is, however, by no means universal.

There has been a long history of design professionals collaborating to produce total or all-of-a-piece designs of suburbs (Unwin 1909; Stern with Massengale 1981; Elazar 1987; Stilgoe 1988; P. Rowe 1991). They include places such as Forest Hills Gardens, a suburb within New York City, developed by the Russell Sage Foundation with the Olmsted brothers as landscape architects and Grosvenor Atterbury as architect in 1912. It has two clear architectural ideas as its base: (1) the journey from railroad station through the suburb is to be seen as a journey from the city to countryside, and (2) the environment is a cozy, domestic one. More recently, the design of Foxhall Crescent, a suburb within Washington, DC, was under the control of a single architect, Arthur Cotton Moore Associates (see Fig. 2–4(1)). It consists of 120 units, in clustered housing form and in a classical revival style. The overall layout is reputed to be based on a model of Bath in England. There are many other conceptual designs that have remained on the drawingboard. An example is a subway suburb in which both the street layout and the houses were designed by Robert Stern in 1976 for exhibition at the Vienna Biennale (Stern with Massengale 1981). The basic plan is a gridiron with a number of ovals creating crescents. The housing type is a simple freestanding cottage based on an image of an early-twentieth-century small town American home. This image is the basis for recent Neo-Traditional design, which is the basis for such designs as the Kentlands in Maryland and Windsor in Florida (Duany 1989; Handy 1991).

There are a number of recent Deconstructionist, or Deconstructivist, proposals for suburban development. Coop Himmelblau's proposal for the Melun Senart area on the southern edge of Paris involves the layering of infrastructure systems and, essentially, a plugged-in set of facilities: a technology business park, golf courses and other recreational facilities, and housing. The result is a complex network of communications, circulation, and cooperation that unifies present-day needs in a design that is claimed to reflect the complexity of everyday life (see also Papadakis, Cooke, and Benjamin 1989). At present it remains a visionary scheme.

One of the emerging new urban design types is the new suburban downtown (Muller 1981; Kricken and Enquist 1986; Lang 1986; Garreau 1991). There appear to be at least four types: (1) the upgrading of traditional street-oriented retail areas into high-rise multifunctional centers (e.g., Bethesda, Maryland, Walnut Creek and Glendale in California, Bellevue in Washington, (2) the transformation of suburban shopping malls into mini-cities (e.g., King of Prussia, Pennsylvania, Newport Center, California, and Galleria–Post Oak, Houston, (3) the central areas of new suburbs (e.g., Reston, Virginia), and (4) the automobile-oriented shopping strip (e.g., the Spennard Commercial district, Alaska, and Olive Boulevard in Creve Coeur, Missouri). The first three all have their European counterparts, but the fourth, while not uniquely North American, is characteristic of many suburban areas in the United States and Canada. The third is a special case of the precincts of new towns as discussed above.

(4) The Campus

While the term "campus" was originally applied to the sets of buildings of universities (P. Turner 1984), it now refers to a variety of uses: office complexes, medical complexes, research parks, summer camps, Olympic villages, zoological gardens, and industrial areas. Implicit in the use of the term is an image of the built environment. A campus consists of a set of separate buildings with plenty of grassed and treed open space surrounding them, with parking lots around them, and a coordinated road-access system. Many are now set in suburbia.

Many office parks and industrial areas have these characteristics. Often they consist of half a dozen buildings designed by one hand, but just as frequently they consist of buildings designed by several firms within a campus-type site plan. The design of industrial and business campuses, or parks, has a long history in the United States and can be traced back to the sanitary reform movements of the nineteenth century. Industrial districts such as the Pershing Road Development in Chicago from the early years of this century show a strong desire to get away from the contemporary "coketowns." They had master plans, restrictive developments, design guidelines, underground utility lines, and landscaping (Beyard et al.

1. Forest Hills Gardens, New York

2. Forest Hills Gardens, New York

3. Vista Verde, San Juan Capistrano, California

4. The Kentlands, Maryland

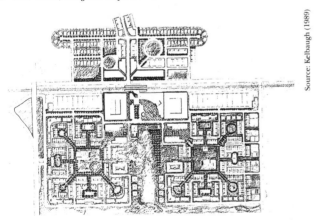

5. Pedestrian Pocket Proposal. Peter Calthorpe and Doug Kelbaugh, Architects

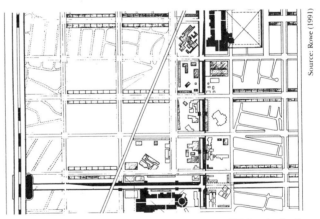

6. Suburban Proposal. Sahel Al-Hiyari (1988), Harvard University Graduate School of Design

Figure 3-20: Suburban Designs

The development of the American suburb parallels the development of the Garden City movement. Forest Hills Gardens, New York, designed by Grosvenor Atterbury and the Olmsted brothers and developed from 1912, clearly represents the Empiricist approach to building new places based on past, presumably enjoyable experiences. The plan, with its curvilinear streets, shows the re-creation of a village-type arrangement (1). Its center, focusing on the railroad station, shows its era. The architecture recreates the past (2). A similar image and set of experiences are presented in any number of more recent suburbs developed during the 1980s and clearly tied to the automobile age (e.g., 3).

Neo-Traditional designs, such as the Kentlands (4), designed by Andres Duany and Elizabeth Plater-Zyberk, show the importance of an enduring image of small town life for many Americans and stands in contrast to designs such as Foxhall Crescent (see Fig. 2-4(1)). The Pedestrian pocket concept (e.g., 5) is a more recent development of many of the Radburn ideals (Kelbaugh 1989), and there is a continuing exploration of other possibilities (6). In the United States very little suburban development is guided directly by architects or even by the coordinated thought of design professionals. It is economically pragmatic. Ease of sale is the main consideration.

1. LaFayette University, Easton, Pennsylvania

2. Hutton Center, Orange County, California

3. Louvain-la-neuve, Belgium

Figure 3–21: Campus Design

The term "campus" has traditionally been used in conjunction with self-contained universities that are segregated as units from their surroundings, ideally in rural settings (1). Nowadays "campus" has been applied to other building complex types such as office parks (2) and even industrial areas that are planned as single entities. The university town of Louvain-la-Neuve takes a very different attitude toward what a university should be as a place. Town and gown are integrated into one system. The main street acts as the unifying element (see also Fig. 13–11(2)). The darker buildings in the model are university buildings (3).

1989). Their descendants abound today (e.g., Riverside Light Industry in Eugene, Oregon, designed by Donald Genasci).

Recent business park designs (e.g. Orchards near Houston, Solana near Dallas, Fair Lakes, Virginia, or the Denver Technology Center) contain a variety of building types and such amenities as lakes and jogging tracks. Until recently the pedestrian was not of concern, but some newer designs are returning to traditional patterns of buildings meeting the street. All of the schemes have master plans, design guidelines for buildings, signs and landscaping, and design review boards to administer the guidelines. The concern for the architectural quality of the buildings is high in economic pragmatic terms, and many renowned architects are involved in their designs (ULI 1988).

A different type of campus is the Paul Newman-sponsored Hole in the Wall Camp in Ashford/Eastford, Connecticut, for children with life-threatening diseases. Designed by Hammond, Beeby, and Babka, it now consists of a unified cluster of buildings, but it will no doubt evolve over time into a scheme designed by a number of firms. Schemes such as the work of Kevin Roche, John Dinkerloo & Associates for Central Park Zoo might better

be regarded as urban renewal. This plan certainly reflects the impact of changing values about the relationship between people and animals and attitudes toward animals.

The traditional university campus might be regarded as the exemplar of the concerns of urban designers. Often based on a master plan and a set of guidelines, universities usually change incrementally over time. There are, however, a number of universities that have been built as total designs or, at least, have had a major component built as an entity at one time. Some are by well-known architects (e.g., Southern Florida College (1938-1950) by Frank Lloyd Wright). Post-World War II examples include the University of Illinois at Chicago (Skidmore Owings & Merrill, architects; see Fig. 3–16(2)), the State University of New York, Albany (Edward Durrell Stone, architect; see Fig. 4–1(2)), Stockton State University in New Jersey (Geddes, Brecher, Qualls, and Cunningham; see Fig. 2–22), and Kresge College, California (Charles Moore, architect; see Figs. 2–14(3), 13–8(5), and 13–8(6)). Often, however, while the basic design of the overall structure is done by a single firm, the individual buildings might be designed by different architects working within general guidelines (e.g., State University of New York at Purchase). They are all-of-a-piece designs. With the growth of college education in many countries during the last thirty years, many universities have been built and others expanded.

The proposals generally follow an amalgam of precedents (P. Turner 1984). During the first decades of this century many university designs were based on the City Beautiful precepts. Most recent designs have been based on the idea of a campus following the precepts of Modernism. They follow various forms: the Garden City, the Radiant City, and the megastructure. One major example deviating from this model is the Catholic University of Louvain-La-Neuve in Belgium, which, if one has to classify it, falls into the Neo-Traditional Empiricist attitude toward urban design. The design of the university is clearly based on (1) the perception that a university as a spatially bounded institution is a poor idea: it rejects the campus model, and (2) the Modernist idea of a university in a park does not easily afford the sense of community and participation in life of the older European universities. Louvain-la-Neuve is both a town and a university. While there is a clear urban design plan to it and great emphasis has been placed on the design of the public domain—much of it was built within a few years—it is not a total design. Indeed it rejects that philosophy.

International Fairs and Expositions, Amusement Parks and Theme Parks

International fairs and theme parks tend to be built all at one time, but they differ in their character. International fairs run for a specific period. Theme parks such as Disneyland and fun fairs such as Hershey Park are operated indefinitely. They change over time as new amusements are invented or developed. The world's fairs as entities tend to remain in place only for the duration of the fair—a year or two. After that they are either demolished or adapted to new uses. The consideration of potential uses after the fair is over may be part of the original planning and thus bias the basic design of the fair buildings and site. This concern for adaptability is particularly true of places such as the stadia and the housing provided for competitors at the Olympic, Asian, or European games. Sometimes these schemes (e.g., the Asiad Village in New Delhi designed by Raj Rawal) are done by one designer, but often the urban design work consists of master plans and a set of guidelines within which individual buildings are designed (e.g., the 1992 Summer Olympics in Barcelona). Indeed their planning and design is often based, as in New Delhi and in Barcelona, on their ultimate use as residential areas with only a basic concern for their interim uses.

World's fairs and athletic games complexes have to be built to strict deadlines and require a coordinated effort of many architects, infrastructure designers, and contractors. They tend to be built in a hurry and all at once. In that sense they are all-of-a-piece designs. The urban design task is to give form to the overall idea of the project and to oversee the design process.

Fairs, amusement parks, and theme parks are designed to be functional on many dimensions of experience of the paying public. They are highly user-oriented. Their goal is to entertain and sometimes educate, but there are many allied functions that have to be fulfilled. They are often not considered to be urban design types but they have all the characteristics of urban design problems. Some have a long history. Coney Island, New York, designed by Frederick Thompson, a Beaux Arts–educated architect, is an example. Tivoli Gardens in Copenhagen is the classic example of an amusement park (see also Cranz 1982). Hershey Park is one of a host of such parks in the United States, while Disneyland in California has spawned many similar theme parks across the world. A recent proposal has been made for Wonderland in Corby, England—a theme park based on nursery rhymes. Some of these parks, particularly the smaller ones, may well be all-of-a-piece designs, but the larger ones involve master planning, infrastructure design, and filling in (plugging individual buildings into the infrastructure).

The world's fairs have often been testing grounds for new urban design ideas. The impact of Paxton's Crystal Palace at London's 1851 exhibition is still being felt (Giedion 1963); Chicago's 1893 exposition, as has already been noted, was a major antecedent of the City Beautiful movement; and recent fairs have explored the problems of enabling people to move around comfortably and rapidly. The Disneylands and Disneyworlds present images of potential new worlds. In doing so they are a blend of regressive thinking (with their village environments) and progressive technologies and imagery. Port Disney, including a theme park, DisneySea, a 350-acre development for Long Beach, California, is currently on the drawingboards.

SUMMING UP

The basic goal of urban design is to ensure a concern for the public interest in the ongoing process of building and rebuilding cities and other human settlements. Urban design involves either the architectural design of cities, neighborhoods, and their subareas or the setting of guidelines for the design of cities by many designers. The focus of attention has been on the public realm.

There are few instances of the architectural design of cities today, but such opportunities do occur. There are many examples of large-scale architectural design projects at the block scale and a number at the neighborhood scale. More frequent still is the need to integrate the work of many designers on behalf of a multitude of clients—sponsors and users—into a coherent whole. Enough has now been built for us to learn from it and from the processes whereby schemes were achieved. The short-term impact is beginning to be understood but many long-term costs and benefits are still open to question.

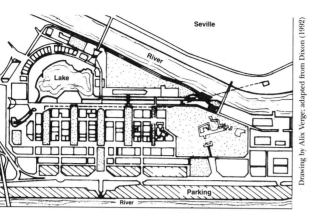

1. Site Plan, Expo '92, Seville, Spain

2. EPCOT Center (Experimental Prototype Community of Tomorrow), Florida, Proposal (1972–1982)

3. Dolphin Hotel Area, Disneyworld, Florida

Figure 3-22: Fairs and Theme Parks

The design and management of change of world's fairs (1) and such places as EPCOT Center and Disneyworld (2,3) have all the characteristics of the work more traditionally thought of as urban design. The design for imagery, modes and clarity of circulation, queueing, the sequential experience of exhibits, and designing for growth and alteration of components of exhibits is fundamental to the quality of the experience of the people who visit these places. Designing for maintenance is a major concern and generally extraordinarily well handled. It has to be to maintain the image they desire the public to have.

What has been built as the result of self-conscious urban design includes many new towns and even more precincts of cities. The number of new towns built around the world since World War II is vast. They include some major capital cities, towns built as the result of national policies, and those built for profit by private developers. Precinct planning includes the rebuilding or transformation of parts of cities as well as suburban developments. Ideas of what constitutes environmental quality have evolved during that time and are reflected in the shift of the focus of attention of design guidelines. The major change has been from a reliance on an architect's own conventional wisdom to a much greater reliance on empirical research. A number of architects find this shift demeaning, but the designs that have resulted from it seem to achieve the goals that architects have claimed to be those of urban design and the need for urban designers' intrusions into the workings of the marketplace. The resulting ambiguity in self-image has placed a conflict in many architects' minds because they see themselves as capable total designers of static end products rather than as people concerned with the ongoing processes of urban change.

Some of these design efforts have been all-of-a-piece designs by one architectural team, but much has resulted from the implementation of guidelines publicly administered. Each effort has been biased by the problems that it was deemed important to solve and must be seen in its political and economic context. Each is based on a set of attitudes. There has been considerable effort made to describe the work of designers but much less in coming to an understanding of the attitudes each design represents.

MAJOR REFERENCES

Attoe, Wayne (1988). "Historic Preservation." In Anthony J. Catenese and James C. Snyder, eds., *Urban Planning.* New York: McGraw Hill, pp. 344–365.

Barnett, Jonathan (1982). *An Introduction to Urban Design.* New York: Harper & Row, 1982.

Broadbent, Geoffrey (1990). *Emerging Concepts of Urban Space Design.* New York: Van Nostrand Reinhold (International).

Del Rio, Vincente (1990). *Introdução ao desneho urbano no processo de planejamento.* São Paulo: Pina.

Lai, Richard Tseng-yu (1988). *Law in Urban Design and Planning: The Invisible Web.* New York: Van Nostrand Reinhold.

Shirvani, Hamid (1985). *The Urban Design Process.* New York: Van Nostrand Reinhold.

Smith, Herbert H. *Planning America's Communities: Paradise Found? Paradise Lost?* Chicago and Washington, DC: Planners Press.

AN EVALUATION AND A PRESCRIPTION

Horton Center, San Diego

Every design, whether it be for a spoon or a city, is based on beliefs and values about the nature of the world—a set of attitudes. Some of the attitudes that shape current urban design work are widely shared, others are unique to schools of thought, and still others are unique to individual designers. Much current professional work in the United States seems to be unified by a financially pragmatic attitude. It is, however, also implicitly divided by two basic attitudes toward the building of knowledge and designing characterized by the Rationalist and Empiricist traditions.

In becoming so financially pragmatic much urban design is in danger of losing its vigor both in its professional work and probably even more so as a discipline. Perhaps it is the very essence of concern with the public interest that has been foregone. Urban design has become "consumerist rather than civic" (Buchanan 1988). Indeed, the very spirit—the desire to create better living, working, recreational, and intellectually stimulating environments for all people—that generated the concern for and growth of urban design in the 1960s seems too often to be dormant in recent thinking. The evolving attitudes of urban designers implicit in current work and the questions they raise are discussed in Chapter 4, Basic Attitudes in Urban Design.

The values of the architectural movements that gave birth to urban design—the antecedents of the field—must not be lost. There is, however, an extraordinarily wide range of attitudes that seem to have motivated those concerned with urban design issues in the past. There has certainly been a strongly reformist and, perhaps, a somewhat patronizing attitude in many of the suggestions about how cities should be shaped. The reformist attitude was deeply rooted in the social and philanthropic movements of the nineteenth century and their goal of creating more salubrious and morally uplifting environments for the people of the industrial cities of Europe and North America. This reformism is reflected in a number of attitudes toward the design of cities. One such attitude was shown in the City Beautiful movement at the beginning of this century. Its concern was for the city as a work of art, a display as a source of civic pride, in response to the grimness of the nineteenth-century industrial city. Historically, this type of urban design has been used even more strongly as a mechanism to demonstrate the power, usually authoritarian, of governing individuals or organizations.

If the social and philanthropic movements of the nineteenth century had an impact on the City Beautiful movement, they had a more profound effect on the Modern movements in architecture. They had an even greater impact on the reorganization of society in Western democracies. The concepts of the welfare state in Western Europe, Australia, and New Zealand and the great society in the United States were direct descendants of the visionary thinking in social terms of the nineteenth-century reformist ideals, as was the Modern movement in design in physical terms.

Current urban design work still shows the duality of thought of how to reform (no pun intended) the city that guided the two major streams of the Modern movement. The Empiricist stream looked back to an earlier world that seemed to work better than their own, while the Rationalists dreamed of a new world based on abstract models of society and people. Both streams of thought were concerned not only with providing more opportunities for a better life but also with the type of urban environment in which such a life should be lived. Many of these design practices and the attitudes they represent have had and still have consequences for urban design practice.

In developing design ideologies and their behavioral correlates in practice, the Modernists drew very heavily on self-referent knowledge. Implicitly, if not explicitly, the assumption guiding designs was what is good for the designer is in the public interest. All the work of the Modernists was indeed based on a body of positive knowledge and beliefs, as well as a set of ideological, or normative, positions, on what a good world is. This reliance by the Modernists on positive theories built on self-referent and imagined information is still with us. It has to be shed as the prime source of urban design attitudes and knowledge. Individual experience is important, but we need to build a theoretical base on the cumulative experience of the profession.

The recognition that the social and physical environments coexist in an integrated system is an important one, as stressed in Chapter 1. The goal of social responsibility of Modern movement designers should be echoed by urban designers today, even if their social engineering goals must be treated with extreme caution. Most architects and schools of architectural thought, recognizing all the contradictions and inadequacies of the Modern movements' thinking, have withdrawn from the political realm concerned with thinking about ideal futures. In the recent search for practicality and ease of implementation, much has indeed been lost in urban design as a discipline and as a professional activity. A sense of direction needs to be rediscovered.

The need for a reconsideration of urban design goals and means is and must remain an ongoing one. As societies change, so the role of the urban designers and the mechanisms for handling those changes will need redesigning. New problems emerge that need redressing. In Chapter 5, Redesigning Urban Design, the strengths and limitations of present attitudes toward urban design and the resultant work are analyzed within the broader context of the decision-making processes of a society: the marketplace, and the legal and political systems. It is assumed that the highest-order goal of a society is that for freedom, with equality of opportunity and justice for all. Urban design has to be considered within some moral order.

In seeking a sense of direction for the future beyond simply getting large projects into place, it is easy for urban designers to overestimate the importance of urban form in the overall social, economic, and aesthetic shaping of a society. Certainly the physical character of a place is a statement on the nature of the culture and the attitudes that prevail within a place at a particular time, but it only shapes society at its margin. In making this observation, it is also easy to underestimate the role of the physical environment in meeting human needs. Much of the humanities and the social sciences, for instance, tend to consider human activities and events in a geographic vacuum. Both the scope and limitations of urban design as a tool in creating new social, economic, and aesthetic orders, and thus the role of urban design in a changing world, need to be understood. Urban design cannot be, or rather must not be, understood simply as large-scale architecture.

The conclusion to the argument of Part One is presented in Chapter 6, A Functionalist, Empiricist Urban Design. The goal of the chapter is to present an attitude toward urban design that both broadens and redefines the field's scope and the knowledge base on which it is to be founded. Self-referent information continues to be an important source of inspiration for the urban designer. It does need to be treated with caution. We shall never have complete knowledge nor is there any evidence that we will ever be completely rational human beings. Fortunately, there now is considerably more experience in designing for cities, and considerably more empirical knowledge at the designer's disposal as the result of systematic research on cities than the Modernists, or even urban designers thirty years ago, had at their disposal. While the body of knowledge is still fragmentary and not as fully developed as we would like it to be, we designers, it is argued here, need to use it. It is easier to state this position than to carry it out, for most designers prefer not to examine the utility of this new knowledge base or to design other than in a mimetic mode (Francescato 1989). In addition, while research can tell us what is, it cannot tell us what design goals to establish and design. Creating design goals, like any other design effort, is a value-laden political act. Rationalist thought processes are needed in imagining a future but such imaginations must be rooted in an empirical base.

If urban design is to have any meaning for society, it must serve a basic set of purposes—it must have a function in much the same way that the built environment serves a set of functions. On the surface this is a clear statement, but the understanding of "function" in architecture is still limited. The concept of "function" that architects have inherited from the Modern movement needs revising as a point of departure in analyzing urban design today and in making prescriptions for future settlement patterns.

If the design process is to be a transparent one, the knowledge base for making decisions, and the attitudes that guide the development of that knowledge base as well as design actions, need to be explicit and clear. Both the knowledge base and design attitudes/philosophies need to be stated within a clear theoretical framework. There is, unfortunately, a continuing and totally *unnecessary confusion in the design professions on the nature of theory and how the theoretical basis for design should and can be built and developed over time. The argument here is for an Empirical approach to the substantiation of claims about how the environment works and also about how design philosophies work. Empiricism in its pure form is now sustaining a challenge from phenomenological approaches to the development of knowledge. Phenomenology, which might be regarded as a form of Empiricism, is, however, more useful in developing hypotheses than in testing them. Poetry serves much the same purpose. Empiricism has its limitations, too, as stated by people such as Britton Harris (1967). Theory has to be built by whatever means are available. As the means improve so they should be adopted. Urban design as a field must be willing not only to act but also to learn.*

The argument here is for what amounts to a neo-Modernist, neo-Empiricist approach to urban design theory building and practice. As a point of departure, it states that the Modernists' intentions were basically sound ones. Similarly, it states that the desire to build a theoretical framework on an Empiricist base is a sound one. There are two basic departures from the Modernist position on urban design: (1) the Empiricism needs to be considerably more rigorous than the Modernists had, and (2) the process of designing is the fundamental concern. Implicit in this position is: (1) that design forms must be seen within a cultural context, and (2) the recognition that all products are generated by, and the design product biased by, some creative process. The Modernists had a highly truncated one. This was partially due to the inherent characteristics of the Cartesian model used by architects such as Le Corbusier, but to a major extent it was simply due to architects' lack of knowledge.

However much architects know about the world, designing processes, and design attitudes, they will always be dealing with uncertainty when designing. There will always be deficiencies in their knowledge base. They are involved with many other people, professionals and laypeople, in creating a future. Recognizing the lack of knowledge is important, but making a fetish of it and regarding it as a desirable characteristic of the field because it is reputed to aid creative thinking is not a viable option if urban design is to serve society well. ■

4

BASIC ATTITUDES IN URBAN DESIGN

Admiring the past ideas and/or work of urban designers and the contribution they have made to society is easy. Finding fault with any urban design, and the attitudes on which it is based, is also easy. Inevitably, planners, landscape architects, and architects have to make tradeoffs between conflicting goals when designing. The variables that have to be considered in any design are too vast to be counted; design problems are what Horst Rittel called *wicked problems* (Bazjanac 1974). Recognizing that design problems are wicked and that no design can be all inclusive helps us understand the tradeoffs that designers make and the attitudes behind their decisions. Much urban design work done since World War II cannot, however, be defended solely on the grounds that compromises have been made (P. Hall 1988).

It became clear a generation ago that the conventional wisdom of the architectural and city planning professions about the design of cities was failing (Montgomery 1966; Mayer 1967). Their thinking was based on a set of fallacious assumptions about people (Wood et al. 1966; Stringer 1980; Ellis and Cuff 1989) and, as a result, on a set of fallacious assumptions about what constitutes a good environment (Blake 1977). Even the strongest proponents of Modernism recognized these failings in their own designs and/or ideological positions. Ludwig Hilbersheimer's reflection on his own 1924 *Metropolis* plan is illustrative: "It was not a metropolis but a necropolis. Its streetscape of concrete and asphalt would have been a most inhumane environment" (Spaeth 1981).

The response to such observations has been an attitudinal shift on the part of those professionals concerned with urban design, but it has been an intellectually superficial response to the problems of Modernist thought. The focus has been on trying to create less visually boring environments by applying historical ele-
ments to the façades of buildings and other elements defining open spaces rather than on rethinking the whole nature of the urban design endeavor (see, e.g., Fig. 4–2(3)). The result has been that many of the basic attitudes of the Modernists that can still serve us well today have been thrown out without being seriously considered while the underlying problems with Modernism's thinking still pervade much urban design thought.

At a building-as-object level of design, this carelessness may matter to only a few cognoscenti, but at an environmental level it matters to society. The evolution of urban design has been hampered by the reluctance of the mainstream of architecture and of architectural education to recognize the specific nature of the shortcomings of Modernist thought so much so that the failure of Modernist ideas can still be presented as a new revelation three decades after they were first recognized (e.g., Goldberger 1989b).

There are a number of ways in which the basic task that urban designers address has been changed by architects themselves in response to the criticism of their work. They have recognized that total design has severe limitations; that architecture cannot shape the social world to any great extent; that there is difficulty in flying in the face of economic realities; that, in a democratic society, the advocacies of urban designers fight for recognition in the political arena with the concerns of other pressure groups. These recognitions are changing the nature of urban design both in the visionaries' statements and in the nature of the practitioners' work. In many ways the resultant changes are intellectually sound, but there are also opportunity costs to society associated with them. This chapter outlines the current attitudes that shape urban design work. It suggests that there is much in past urban design work and the attitudes that shaped it that has been needlessly abandoned.

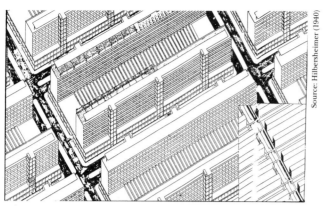

1. Ludwig Hilbersheimer's Metropolis (1924)

2. State University of New York, Albany (1961)

3. Pruitt Igoe, St. Louis, Missouri

Figure 4-1: Rationalist Attitudes in American Urban Design
Ludwig Hilbersheimer's *Metropolis* was a conceptual scheme based largely on a perception of what constitutes a healthy environment—access to open space, light, and air (1; see also Rush City—Fig. 2-10(4)). Many implemented schemes follow the same line of thought (e.g., 2, designed by Edward Durell Stone). The problem with many of them (e.g., 3, Pruitt Igoe in St. Louis) was their singleminded focus on the provision of shelter, rigid geometries, efficiency in circulation, and building construction but little attention was given to the broader concerns of potential user groups (see also Fig. 5-3).

CURRENT ATTITUDES IN URBAN DESIGN

Four attitudes toward the concerns of urban design coexist uncomfortably today.

(1) Financially pragmatic urban design. This type of urban design work results from the perception that because the demands of the marketplace are so severe in the development of urban design schemes, the designs required to meet the profit demands of developers should be the basis for the generation of form. The users of the environment are seen simply as potential purchasers or renters and designs simply as consumer products.

(2) Urban design as art. This attitude is that if urban design can have no social engineering aspect to it then its prime goal should be to be a work of art—the celebration of an architect's idea. While almost all urban design has a component of artistic expression, the Neo-Rationalists and Deconstructionists tend to focus on the aesthetics of geometries of one kind or another as the basic point of departure. In its extreme form the user is simply not considered. At best the user is somebody to be educated and possibly entertained.

(3) Urban design as a problem-solving process. While this approach involves the application of empirical knowledge to design, much of it continues to be based on a naïve nostalgia for the past. The user and users' needs are seen in nostalgic terms.

(4) Urban design as community design. The focus here is on a process whereby decisions are made by the users themselves but that often ends up being pragmatic in the sense that it gives people what they say they want rather than what they would want if they knew that other possibilities existed.

None of these attitudes is inherently right or wrong. Each can serve a purpose in context.

Many schemes are an amalgam of two or more of these approaches to urban design. Seaside, Florida (see Fig. 3-11), for instance, is a mixture of art, empiricism, and economic pragmatism with some architectural deterministic thinking about the impact of the physical design of a place on the social behavior that will take place there. The plan is essentially a small-scale City Beautiful one. It is an economically segregated community based on a need for the buildings to be sold, and its guidelines show that much has been learned, directly or indirectly, from empirical research. It also represents an effort to re-create a way of life and so is based on the assumption that by building in a particular way people will behave in a particular way (Dunlop 1989; Patton 1991). While there has been considerable success in understanding people's predispositions (and it must be remembered that the few people who have moved into Seaside as residents have done so because of their perceptions of what it affords), there were hopes for certain traditional activity patterns to occur that have not occurred. For instance, the porches afford people the ability to sit in semiprivate space and chat to passersby. This behavior does occur to some extent, but not to the level predicted, partly because of the lack of permanent residents in Seaside (Patton 1991) and partly because such behavior is no longer the cultural norm it once was. The porches are more important as an aesthetic symbol of a way of life. Seaside has to be seen as an offering to a public who can afford to live there and chooses to do so.

While there are many examples of such a mixture of attitudes toward urban design today, it is worth looking at the pure types to understand what is happening to the field and the way it is being tugged. The objective of this chapter is to examine the attitudes of current urban design thinking in comparison to the values held by architects during the first part of the twentieth century. It will be acknowledged that much of the criticism of the present approaches to urban designs is valid. We can learn from it. The criticism should, however, lead to a reexamination of the task of urban design, not a withdrawal from its complexities (Mackay 1990). It is time to recognize both the failings of past approaches as well as the utility of many of their underlying philosophical positions.

(1) The New Pragmatism—"The Design of Capitalist Expediency" (Lai 1988)

It is impossible to give all the aspects of a design problem full attention or to consider all stakeholders' interests. In the United States there developed in the 1970s and 1980s, however, a new air of practicality about the task of urban design. The desire for implementability has meant that the consideration of the domain of urban design and the focus of attention of the design task have shifted from those considered by the Modernists and also from those of their critics. Often urban design seems to be concerned with goods not good and seems to confuse symbol with reality. The attitude in much recent thinking reflects a contempt for lower-income groups, a belief in the eternal presence of financial and architectural elites, and certainly a cynical pessimism for the Enlightenment. Urban designs are treated simply as consumer products (Schurch 1991).

Many past ideas, proposals, and schemes failed to be implemented for a number of reasons. Many were hypothetical proposals in response to hypothetical problems and were never intended to be implemented, others dealt with highly simplified visions of the world, and yet others were financially unfeasible. The sponsors and designers of other schemes simply did not have the tenacity of purpose required to get them built. Many design ideas never get built because they are politically unfeasible, or are perceived to be so. The response has now frequently been for urban designers to be more concerned with getting projects built than with achieving good design in other than financial-return terms.

The financial resources available to implement a scheme have always been a constraint on what can be done, but recent urban design shows a new level of fiscal expediency. Philosophically, there is great reliance on the marketplace as an arbiter of both what should be built and of design quality. In taking this position, many architects and urban designers have lost their concern with the public realm and with the externalities—the public goods—of design (Wilford 1984; Ghirardo 1987; Buchanan 1988, 1990; Bird 1990). There have been gains associated with the financial pragmatism of designers but also opportunity costs. The major gain is often that having the scheme in place is better than nothing at all. Indeed, developers have frequently used such an argument to get their schemes built (see also Frieden and Sagalyn 1991).

While there are many American examples (e.g., the Galleria complex in Houston, Texas, and the series of proposals on the west bank of the Hudson River in New Jersey—Hudson Center, Hoboken, Port Imperial, Newport), probably the major example of the new pragmatism is a British project—the Docklands development in London (Brownhill 1990; Williams 1990). The plan was almost infinitely flexible and accommodating, with little concern for the "public realm." The result has been a "free-for-all" set of developer projects without an overall idea behind them (Wilford 1984)—a collage city taken to its extreme. "To ride through the Docklands is to experience a vast Post-Modern Zone in which all notions of neighborhood and urban design have been sacrificed in a frenzy of unregulated construction" (Bird 1990). While such judgments are highly personal statements, even the designers involved with the Docklands are concerned about the lack of consideration for such urban design issues, indeed pragmatic issues, as transportation and working population density linkages (Olin 1991). The financial problems that the Docklands, particularly Canary Wharf, is having at the time of writing (1992) shows the precariousness of the property market. The American examples at least have a greater variety of mixed uses that will enable them to become part of future urban developments around them (when the market picks up again).

In the United States, Houston is perhaps the exemplar of a city in which financial pragmatism and the marketplace as the definers of the public interest have been the urban designers (Ghirardo 1987). The city is replete with recently built skyscrapers designed by America's leading architects, exciting new shopping centers

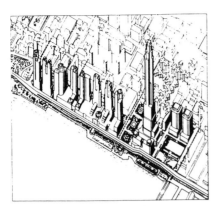

Source: American Institute of Architects (1990)

1. T.V. City, Manhattan, New York, Proposed by Donald Trump, Developer

Photograph by Randolph Griffith

2. Docklands, London

Source: Hanna/Olin Ltd.

3. Canary Wharf Development, Docklands, London

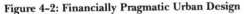

Figure 4-2: Financially Pragmatic Urban Design

T.V. City in New York (1) is an example of an urban design proposal that seems to be based largely on maximizing short-run financial profits to a property developer. Similarly, the Canary Wharf development, part of the London Docklands scheme (2), has been designed largely with economic return in mind, although in 1992 it was in great financial difficulties. The project being built is similar to that shown in an early model (3). While visually more interesting than much Modernist urban design, the infrastructure that is needed, particularly transportation, is predicted to be sorely lacking.

such as the Galleria, and people living in abandoned cars. With no zoning regulations (at the time of writing) and few deed restrictions (which do act as a zoning of sorts), the development community has celebrated itself, striving for profit while the "other America," or, in this case, the "other Houston," has suffered considerable hardship. Much of the city is in a blight of poverty and much in the "blight of dullness." In addition, there has been little design concern for the city's location on swampland or its climate (to say nothing of its susceptibility to hurricanes). Few architects have been willing to speak out publicly on the extent of the city's ills that they recognize in fear of jeopardizing their own careers, nor has there been any political will to change. At the time of writing, however, the reaction to the worst excesses of the 1980s (such as the failures of the savings and loans associations) and the necessity of dealing with the depredation of the natural environment have led to a strong move to introduce zoning legislation—something supported by leading developers such as Gerald Hines and Trammell Crow.

As in Houston, the results of the recent financial pragmatism has increased the general public's awareness of the necessity for a much greater consideration of the public domain in design. Certainly in such schemes as the Cardiff Docks development (designed by Llewelyn-Davies Planning with Eisenman Robertson) there has been much more thought given to social objectives and the design of the public domain than in the London Docklands scheme.

A positive consequence of the new pragmatism of the last twenty years is that it has resulted in a body of work that is open to examination. Even some of the schemes, such as Mission Bay in San Francisco (see Fig. 2-15(1) and elsewhere in this book), that do not treat urban design as a consumer product result from highly economically pragmatic positions. We can learn from them. There are even more designs on the drawingboards. Most of these are concerned not only with being affordable but with maximizing profit. It might be argued that they exemplify the laudable goal of providing settings that fulfill people's image of who they are and what they want to do—a mentally congruent environment. This argument is certainly partially true, but much is also lacking in the schemes. Blaming the private-sector property developers alone for this situation is shortsighted.

The paying client or sponsor of most of the urban design projects in the United States during the 1980s has been the private sector, and naturally enough the fundamental goal of the schemes has been not only to make a profit for the developer but also to reap a tax benefit to the government (and this means, presumably, the citizens) of a location. Tax benefits are accrued not only by an increase in the tax base, but also by having developments that generate no or little need for tax expenditures. There is thus a collaboration between the public and private sectors to avoid a social concern in their thinking. Any social objective other than creating projects that sell well is thus outside their perceived domains of responsibility.

In examining projects and the attitudes on which they are based one must also understand the cultural context in which they are developed. In the United States the ownership of private property is the basic freedom. The American cultural milieu is still rooted in the pre-Revolutionary British philosophies of John Locke, Adam Smith, Jeremy Bentham, and Sir William Blackstone, which were developed when land was cheap. The perception being challenged here, when it is applied to urban design, is the simplistic view that "order and benefit [are] determined through organic, pluralistic experience rather than centralized planning," and that there should be no violation of property rights even for the public good (Lai 1988). Taken to its logical extreme the loss to society of such an attitude is vast.

In a capitalist society, which relies on the market as the major decision maker and in which there is little cooperation between political jurisdictions, the competition for development between jurisdictions leads to a total capitulation to the market. The only situations in which this capitulation does not occur is where the demand for development is very high, where there is strong urban design leadership, and where developers are thus prepared to make many concessions to nonmarket public goods in their projects. There are many examples in the United States of such concessions being made (e.g., Glendale and Walnut Creek in California, Bellevue, Washington, and Bethesda, Maryland; see Lang 1987b and Kay 1991). In all cases, there have been detailed urban design guidelines (and highly dedicated public officials) and a continuing demand for development. Glendale was awarded a *Progressive Architecture* first award for urban design in 1986.

A highly pragmatic attitude toward urban design has many consequences. Most political jurisdictions would prefer to have the profitable projects in their own areas while displacing the additional costs, such as new transportation facilities, on their neighbors. Projects without children are good because the demand for educational facilities is not increased. Such decisions lead to an even more age-group-segregated society in countries such as the United States, where it already exists (Bronfenbrenner 1970). Similarly, projects without low-income people are desirable—indeed, projects without any residents are good. Highly manicured projects are desirable; they yield greater rental income.

One of the ways to ensure that designs are manicured is through the segregation of uses. The monotony of much Modernist design based on use separating design principles has led nowadays to a concern for mixed-use development, but it is a sanitized mixed set of uses that is being provided. The market supports this political conservatism. A prime criterion for the purchase of housing units is their ease of resalability, resulting in conservative building types not responsive to the needs of other than the perceived norm of households. Perhaps in the long term the market will respond to demographic and social changes and to cultural differences in the U.S. population, but it has failed to do so as yet. It needs to be pushed in that direction (see also Hayden 1984 and Franck and Ahrentzen 1989).

This cooption of urban designers by market forces is not surprising because the design fields have always reflected the political tenor of their times. This situation is not unique to the United States. During the past twenty years, many societies have been turning away from the pursuit of collective goals. Despite considerable evidence to the contrary, the perception is that cooperative efforts to deal with collective needs under governmental leadership have succeeded in improving the lives of only a minority of people. In architecture this belief is reflected in the increasingly egocentric nature of much design ideology. This change reflects broader changes in the nature of society—the privatization of public control and control of public space (Sennett 1977; Buchanan 1988; Hitt 1990).

There has been, or appears to have been, an increase in noncompliant behavior sanctioned by controlling governmental bodies (except at election time in order to appear to be for law and order). Noncompliance with existing zoning ordinances and design guidelines seems to be sanctioned if there are many people involved. Such behavior breeds cynicism toward the administration of collective efforts. In the United States there has been a major move of public planning officials from agencies where they set up controls into the private sector where their expertise is useful in avoiding the controls set up by the public sector.

Selling the Sky

Many city governments find themselves in financial difficulties. They are unable to provide many of the new public amenities expected of them or even to maintain existing ones. Developers' personal gains may lead to the public loss of existing facilities, which are unable to compete economically in the marketplace. It is not surprising

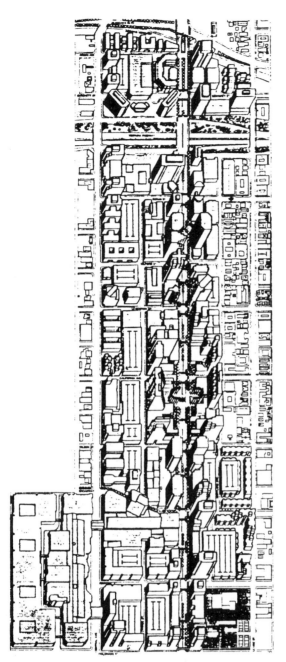

1. Glendale Redevelopment Scheme, Plan

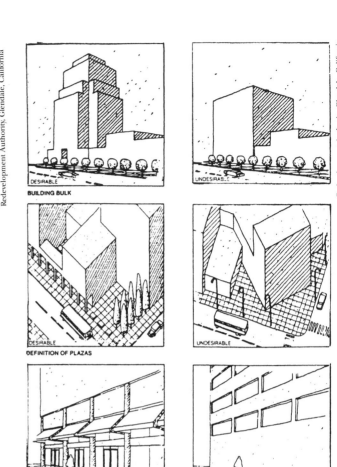

BUILDING BULK

DEFINITION OF PLAZAS

GROUND FLOOR USES

2. Examples of Design Guidelines

Figure 4–3: Glendale, California

The Glendale downtown renewal project consists of three major areas: offices at the north end, mixed use in the center, and retail at the southern end (1). Brandt Boulevard is the main spine, while parking garages are located on adjacent roads. A major design consideration is the integration of major buildings and California bungalow-type residences. The urban design guidelines by ELS Architects of Berkeley, California, were crafted to shape both public and private investment in infrastructure and building development in order to maintain environmental quality standards (2). The results support the utility of detailed urban design guidelines (3).

3. Brandt Boulevard

that urban designers and civic leaders have designed mechanisms (such as the new zoning regulations noted in Chapter 3) to cope with the situation. In doing so, the public sector is now often faced with the dilemma of resolving a conflict between having one good or another.

In much of the *incentive zoning* now being used to encourage specific building types to be developed and/or public infrastructure to be built by the private sector, the incentive is to allow developers to build more floor space than the zoning originally allowed. The marginal cost of building an additional set of floors on a building is comparatively low in relationship to the overall costs of development. The rewards for doing so are high. It is not surprising that developers are prepared to provide certain uses (e.g., theaters in New York's theater district) in return for being allowed to make their buildings taller. The result is less light at the ground level. Incentive zoning is a highly pragmatic response to the development pressures that exist in major American cities. Few city governments have the courage to resist political pressure from the development lobby to make the development process easier nor are they financially capable of doing so given present jurisdictional realities. After all, the developers can take their money elsewhere. Unless broad coordinated development policies are enacted and financial procedures realigned, the process will continue except in those places prepared to put a moratorium on development—a tool used successfully in Bethesda, Maryland, and possibly successfully in San Francisco. Such moratoria are always open to court challenges (e.g., Walnut Creek, California) because they are perceived to infringe on individuals' rights in developing their properties as and when they see fit.

(2) Urban Design as Art: Rational Composition and Deconstruction

With the new pragmatism, the focus of attention of architects has often been on urban design as art. Art, it is felt, is the one unique area of urban designers' contribution to the city. Urban design then focuses on the nature of form per se and the aesthetic idea it represents. This attitude is much more prevalent in Europe than in the United States, particularly within the Rationalist tradition in architecture with its ties to Cubist thought earlier in the twentieth century (Overy 1969; Senkevitch 1974). Following this line of thought, dealing with a multitude of problems and a variety of human needs is fine provided the results do not get in the way of the solution that architects want to generate. Given this attitude, in urban design few of the analyses of problem situations have much to do with the designs that are generated. The design is based on an entirely different and hidden agenda. "Don't let the program get in the way of the solution," budding architects are told. Implicit in this order are the attitudes: "Make up your own problem rather than the

one that requires solution"; "You are doing this for Art"; "The responsibility of Art is to Art and not to the present populations of a place" (see also Weyergraft-Serra and Buskirk 1990).

Urban design as art is not a coordinated movement but is promoted by those architects who want the profession to be most closely associated with the fine arts. If anything, it is most closely associated with the Neo-Rationalists and their concern with an urban design of abstract geometric purity (Broadbent 1990). If urban design can neither achieve a social goal nor express a political ideology in capitalist societies, so the logic goes, then the concern should be with its geometry. While all buildings and urban spaces have to have a purpose, the concern is with the built form for its and/or its creator's own sake in the face of empirical findings, social requirements, or utilitarian purposes.

The basic proposition is simply that if urban design cannot solve social problems then let it give parts of a city a coordinated architectural idea that will inspire people. The view is expressed in recent work hearkening back to both the City Beautiful and Rationalist ideas of the city, with Paris or Vienna as sources of inspiration. Much of this work is also reminiscent of Albert Speer's work for Berlin in the 1930s, although it has neither the same political overtones to it nor is it of such a grandiose scale.

Speer's work has received a strong defense from Leon Krier (1985). Like Wagner's music, classical planning with strong axes and classical architecture have become associated with totalitarian fascism in many people's minds. Krier builds the counterargument that, if anything, Modernism is more closely associated with Hitler's misdeeds than is Classicism. Pure Rationalist design, he notes, displays the same autocratic attitudes. Suffice to say here that classical planning, with or without classical architecture, is still a powerful image maker for urban places (see Chapter 14, Meeting Affiliation Needs). This imagery is clearly shown in the Post-Modern winning entry for the Mississauga (Ontario, Canada) City Hall competition by Jones and Kirkland (Broadbent 1990). In the United States, classical architecture, itself, has strong proponents in John Blatteau, Alan Greenburg, and to some extent, Robert Stern (Stern and Gastil 1989). It has its place in society.

Rationalist schemes, in contrast, continue to be distinguishable by their Platonic geometry and, often their high-tech architecture in its symbolic and architectural form. The built work reflects the earlier Modernist urban designs of people such as Mies van der Rohe (e.g., the Illinois Institute of Technology campus in Chicago), and the conceptual schemes of Ludwig Hilbersheimer (Pommer, Spaeth, and Harrington 1988). They were searching for an expression of artistic purity allied with modern technology. The Rationalist schemes today are self-contained in their simple geometrical unity, and consist of centralized blocks, courtyards, and linear elements (often symmetrical) in exaggerated discontinuity with the remainder

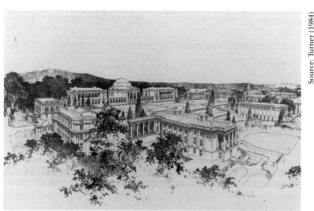

1. Sweet Briar College, Sweet Briar, Virginia (1901)

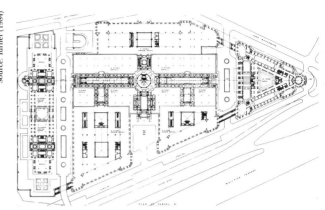

2. Proposed Mixed-Use Development, San Antonio, Texas (1987)

3. Washington Mall. Proposal by Leon Krier (1986)

Figure 4-4: The Attitudes Behind the New Classicism in Urban Design

While Beaux Arts schemes such as the proposal by Cram, Goodhue & Ferguson for Sweet Briar College (1) are no longer the center of attention in urban design, the work of John Blatteau (2) continues classicism in a pure form while schemes such as Leon Krier's for Washington, DC (3), present powerful images of urban possibilities in the classical City Beautiful mode. The basic attitude is that these forms have been around for 3,000 years and are widely understood. While disparaged by Modern architects, they have shown a timeless quality.

of the city (Colquhoun 1975; Broadbent 1990). While there are a few recent American examples, there are many more in Europe. The discontinuities are achieved by placing the geometry of the new buildings at angles to the existing geometry of the city's streets. These attitudes are displayed in Harvard University's Carpenter Center and more recently in such schemes as Carlo Aymonimo's plan for the Gallaratese housing in Milan, some of Leon Krier's work such as his proposals for Luxembourg as the new capital for Europe and Parc de la Villette in Paris, and Ricardo Bofill's work at Les Arcardes du Lac in St. Quentin en Yvellines (Fig. 2-15(3)), and Le Palais d'Abraxas in Marne Le Vallée east of Paris (see Broadbent 1990). Above all, it is exemplified by the Cemetery of San Cataldo in Modena designed by Aldo Rossi—a necropolis. The problems are not in the patterns of geometry themselves; these are neutral. Problems arise when the concern for geometrical niceties precludes the search for the essence of the problem in terms of the people affected by it.

There is also the work of the Deconstructionists in which the design idea, on the surface at least, overrides all other considerations (Benjamin 1988; Norris 1988). This work appeals to the architectural cognoscenti who can appreciate the aesthetic elegance of the ideas behind it. In some instances such as the Parc de la Villette designed

by Bernard Tschumi the work appears to appeal to the public (Tschumi 1988a, 1988b). In this case it is exhibition architecture and its appeal has little do with an appreciation of its design idea. Rather, it appeals to what it is—more like the agricultural shows of many major cities and the state fairs in the United States. The Deconstructionist approach to design has been brought to the United States in a more recent scheme by Tschumi—the Flushing Meadows, Corona Park, scheme for Queens, New York—and in Morphosis's proposal for Hermosa Beach.

During the second half of the 1980s, Zaha Hadid and Daniel Libeskind (Richter and Foster 1988) as well as Bernard Tschumi became most closely associated with Deconstructionism. The work of Frank Gehry, who has long been designing buildings that have been built, has also been added to the list. The attitude behind these schemes is that society is culturally fragmented, and that architecture and urban design as an art form should reflect this reality.

A striking visual unity through diversity, as defined by George Santayana (Santayana 1896), is established in many of these designs. They also show their formal heritage in the Rationalist and Constructivist movements of Soviet architecture after the October Revolution of 1917 (Shvidovsky 1971; Senkevitch 1974; Khan-Magomedov

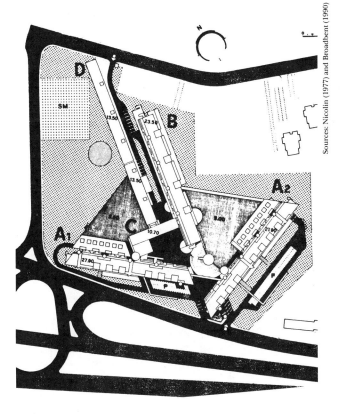

Sources: Nicolin (1977) and Broadbent (1990)

1. Plan of the Gallaretese Housing, Milan, Italy (1967–1969)

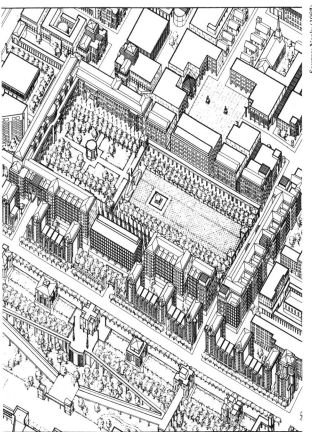

Source: Nealy (1983)

2. Burlington, Vermont. A Student Proposal for an Urbanization Strategy

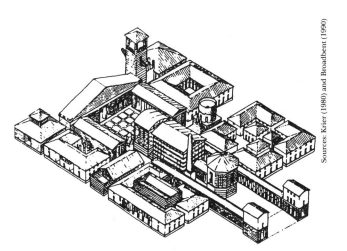

Sources: Krier (1980) and Broadbent (1990)

3. St. Quentin en Yvellines, France (1977–1979)

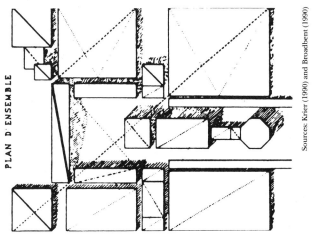

PLAN D'ENSEMBLE

Sources: Krier (1990) and Broadbent (1990)

4. St. Quentin en Yvellines, Geometric Analysis

Figure 4-5: Neo-Rationalist Attitudes and Urban Design

Neo-Rationalism is exemplified by the European work of people such as Aldo Rossi, Ricardo Bofill and the Taller, and Carlo Aymonimo (1). Its concern with geometrical composition reflects earlier Rationalist work but with greater attention to urban spaces. It also shows considerably more concern with the nature of the street and its enclosing elements, as in this Cornell University student project by Craig Nealy (2). The concern for geometrical order is more clearly demonstrated in a large-scale architectural work, the School for St. Quentin en Yvellines, designed by Leon Krier in the late 1970s (3,4).

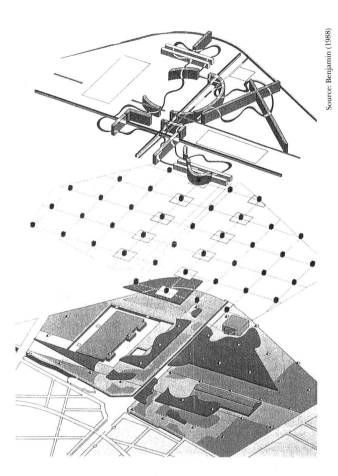

Source: Benjamin (1988)

Figure 4-6: Attitudes behind Deconstructionist Urban Design
The Parc de la Villette designed by Bernard Tschumi (see also Fig. 3-8) is regarded as the exemplar of Deconstructionist design. The conceptual scheme with its multiple layers of solutions to individual environment problems is close intellectually to the morphological analysis proposed by Fritz Zwicky in the 1940s. It is, however, associated by Tschumi with the philosophy of Jacques Derrida. The design goal is to sharpen thinking and possibly the viewer's experience by radicalizing architecture and urban design through the use of patterns that Modernism repressed. Architecture becomes a pure art form, deconstructing metaphors by examining the inherent contradictions in their meanings. The pleasure of the users of such environments, however, depends on their tacit learning of environmental preferences and certainly not on their appreciation of artificial intellectual constructs. Such environments may well be enjoyed by tourists but as everyday environments for life they may well heighten feelings of alienation.

1987). The difficulty is to understand what purposes other than an artistic expression such forms afford. Possibly the goal is to create a more interesting environment and certainly one that may fulfill a set of people's cognitive needs (see Chapter 17). Another interpretation is that by solving the spatial and use requirements of different systems of a city, neighborhood, or building independently and then simply putting them together recreates the diversity of the present city. The focus of attention in architectural criticism on the designer and the designer's ideas continues the trend away from a concern with the users' needs of the environment to designers' expressions in design (see Belgasem 1987 and Fig. 3-3).

(3) Urban Design as Problem Solving— The New Empiricism

The New Empiricism takes two major forms. They were referred to in Chapter 3. The first consists of the work of those architects who rely on the extrapolation of their personal experiences of the environment and, to some extent, the experience of other people as a basis for design. This lies in opposition to the Rationalist approach of dreaming/designing new people and new social systems, and then designing for them. The second group consists of people who have been much more concerned with systematically studying the environment and then using a knowledge-based approach to design.

The first group's attitude toward design tends to be based on the assumption that the patterns of the environment that fulfill human purposes already exist. Design involves the adjustment of these types to the present situation (see also Chapter 6). The second group is comprised more of people doing the research than actually designing. They tend to be critics. Their research has steadily made a significant impact on certain aspects of design, and, particularly, on the programming part of the overall design process.

The rediscovery of typology—the study of building types—has been an important development in architectural thought over the last twenty years (Bandini 1984; R. Krier 1979, 1990; L. Krier 1990; Rapoport 1991), although there are different attitudes about how precedents should be used. The Neo-Traditional movement focuses on replicating much of past urban forms because they are judged to work well on many dimensions of human life. The results tend to continue the picturesque tradition (see also Handy 1991).

The second area of Empiricism has led to an extraordinary output of research on environmental design issues since 1970 (see, e.g., the *Proceedings* of the annual Environmental Design Research Association conferences in the United States and similar organizations across the world). Some of this research is directly applicable to the design but much addresses the issues that concern researchers such as the aesthetics of theory and theory building. While many researchers, particularly historians, complain about the lack of knowledge of designers (e.g., Rykwert 1974), these researchers study issues and/or contexts that yield little of relevance to practitioners striving to design better environments today for tomorrow.

Some empirical research findings have seeped into the practice of almost all architects because those findings are well known outside architectural circles (e.g.,

Source: Cullen (1961)

1. Proposal for Looe, England, by Gordon Cullen (1960)

On local roads, closed to through traffic, plant grass all over the road and set occasional paving stones into the grass to form a surface for the wheels of those cars that need access to the street. Make no distinction between street and sidewalk. Where houses open off the street, put in more paving stones or gravel to let cars turn on their own land.

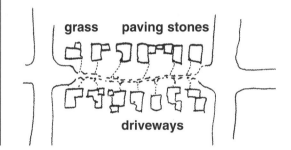

2. A Pattern for "Green Streets" from Alexander, Isikawa, and Silverstein (1977)

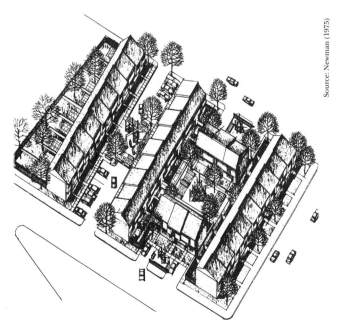

Source: Newman (1975)

3. A Rowhouse Cluster, Designed Defensively. Oscar Newman, Architect

Newman 1972 and Whyte 1980). A content analysis of architects' libraries, however, suggests that the only research of which most of them are aware is that dealing with the technological aspects of design (Nielson 1984). Professionals, like students, have a pragmatic streak in looking at research. If they can get away without knowing it they will (Rittel 1971). There are, however, a number of areas of urban design concern where it is increasingly foolish to avoid keeping abreast of recent research. The difficulty is that, unlike medicine, the design professions have a weak research tradition and the idea of a research-based approach to design is foreign to them.

This second branch of current Empiricism does have ties to the new pragmatism of urban designers. One of the fundamental requirements for any project to sell is that it be safe and be perceived to be so. This objective is increasingly being achieved by the provision of gates, guards, and electrical and electronic surveillance equipment (see also Chapter 13). The creation of safe neighborhoods can also be considerably aided by applying the research findings on *defensible space* of Oscar Newman (1972; Stollard 1991). Similarly, most architects, and certainly those involved in urban design, are aware of Kevin Lynch's research on *imageability* and *legibility* of cities (Lynch 1960), even if they are unfamiliar with more recent work on the subject (e.g., Pocock and Hudson 1978; Passini 1984; and Arthur and Passini 1990; see also Chapter 13). Both Newman's and Lynch's research is clearly and easily translatable into urban design principles.

A number of urban design ideas have emerged from the attitudes toward people associated with this research if not the research itself. It ties the two Empiricist traditions together. When the research is applied, the designs tend to be picturesque ones. This outcome is, in itself, neither good nor bad. The weakness arises when the result is considered to be inevitable and always correct. It is hardly a surprising outcome because most people are habituated to such environments or socialized through the literature they read as children to regard such environments as good. The work of Gordon Cullen (1961), which recognizes the importance of sequential experience in seeing and appreciating the environment (see J.

Figure 4–7: Neo-Empiricist Attitudes and Urban Design
Neo-Empiricists are showing a shift in their design thinking from a reliance on their own personal experiences to a reliance on systematic research findings. The focus on sequential spatial experience by Gordon Cullen (1), while corroborated in the perception theory of James Gibson (1950, 1966), was largely based on his own experiences. The pattern language developed by Christopher Alexander and his colleagues (1977) is based more on empirical research (2). Similarly, the concept of defensible space (3) is based on systematic research (see also Chapter 12). The assumption is that there is much to learn from people's experiencing of the environment.

Gibson 1966, 1979 for the empirical support for this view), is within the picturesque mode. In this sense he is the descendent of Camillo Sitte (Sitte 1889; Collins and Collins 1965). Kevin Lynch's love for Boston (see Banerjee and Southworth 1990) and Christopher Alexander's penchant for small-scale places and individual contributions to the environment (Alexander 1964, 1969, 1972; Alexander et al. 1977, 1987) are reinforced by much of the psychological literature of the past fifty years. Recent schemes such as Leon Krier's plan for Dorchester are, however, based on the reproduction of past urban types rather than on logical deductions from the present research findings about people and their environments (Krier 1987; Broadbent 1990). Design thinking is trapped by the past. Urban designers are not availing themselves of the increase in the knowledge of people and their habitats that recent research is yielding.

The Emergence of a Discrete Architecture Movement

The *Discrete Architecture* in the United States is closely tied to the typological approach to design, without the environments ending up being picturesque ones. The concern is particularly with making urban design contextually appropriate. The attitude that architecture and urban design have to be part of their regions hearkens back to the ideologies of the third generation of Modern architects. The recent concern with the specifics of a site and with defining the urban design problem in relationship to its regional location implies a concern with cultural context. This emerging attitude suggests a shift away from pure Rationalist ideas to a greater empirical concern on one dimension of design at least—the concern with belonging (see also Chapter 13).

While schemes such as Battery Park City in New York and Mission Bay in San Francisco certainly are financially pragmatic, they also exhibit the concern for place, for melding into the city rather than building something that stands apart as an independent entity. The financial success of Battery Park City has enabled other socially necessary facilities to be developed. It is designed based on past experiences but promises to be an integral part of lower Manhattan.

(4) The Community Design Movement

The community design movement, as its name suggests, focuses on a community's participation in making the decisions that affect the lives of its residents. It has been primarily concerned with existing residential communities—the ones that are most important to people. The movement grew out of the activist spirit of the 1960s, which recognized the continuing poverty and denial of rights in the "other America" (Harrington 1963) and in Europe. It persists most strongly in the United Kingdom,

where it has received royal support (Holden 1988), and in Continental Europe, but has endured successfully in a low-key way in the United States (Hatch 1984; J. Stern 1989). British architects such as Ralph Erskine and Vernon Gracie in the Byker area of Newcastle and Rod Hackney in Mackelsfield have made substantial careers in community design, as have Randolph Hester (1975), Robin Moore, and Ronald Schiffman in America at the Pratt Institute for Community and Environmental Development in Brooklyn, New York. With some exceptions (e.g., the Byker Wall Development and Mission Park in the Roxbury Tenants and Harvard Association Area of Boston—John Sharatt, architect), the urban designs produced by community designers tend to be piecemeal and without a strong emphasis on the urban geometries favored by the Rationalists and Deconstructionists. They thus fail to receive the attention of designers in either the mainstream of their fields or among avant-garde aesthetes.

The design process advocated by people associated with the community design movement relies heavily on subjective analysis and designing with the community (i.e., local residents). This cooperation between designer and resident occurs either through the participation of a sample of an area's population in the design process or through the articulation by their leaders or representatives of a position on what the problems are that should be addressed and/or the positions on what should be done. The design professionals create proposals by turning the community's statement of its needs into a design based on their own subjective views and/or empirical knowledge. Those architects working in the United States seem to have relied more on the environment-behavior research of the last two decades and have contributed to it more than their European counterparts.

The Regional/Urban Design Assistance Team (R/UDAT) program sponsored by the American Institute of Architects and begun in 1967 represents a change in attitudes of mainstream professionals in dealing with communities (Batchelor and Lewis 1985). The goal is to listen to communities rather than dictate to them, to work with them on *their problems* not the *designers' problems*. At best, the R/UDATs have been helpful in supplying cities and towns in the United States with the ideas of experts. However, the rapidity with which the teams work (three or four days to understand the situation and design a solution) often results in the promotion of highly reductionist design efforts by the experts, which have raised communities' hopes unrealistically. Still, in times of limited resources for planning ahead and thinking cooperatively in the United States, R/UDATs do focus attention on issues needing resolution.

There are a number of major philosophical statements on the nature of the design process that a cooperative/collaborative approach to design entails (e.g., Halprin 1969, 1974; King, Conley, Latimer, and Ferrault 1989). The involvement of communities, and/or their

1. Mission Park, Boston

Source: Hatch (1984)

Photograph by Joyce George

2. Homesteading Project, Brooklyn, New York

3. Wallace Park, 35th and Wallace Streets, Philadelphia

Figure 4-8: The Community Architecture Movement
The community architecture movement advocates the empow-
erment of specific groups of people in making design decisions.
The resulting environments are seldom noteworthy "architecturally" but meet the needs of people well and afford them a
sense of pride (1), sometimes through their own "sweat equity"
(2; in this case through the Mutual Housing Association of New
York—MHANY). A "give-em-what-they-say-they-want" attitude
on the part of designers, however, often results in underutilized
places (3).

surrogates in the urban design process is essential to the
design process described in the book (see Chapter 24, A
Normative Procedural Model for Urban Design: An Emerging Empirical Consensus). Empirical knowledge helps
the designer focus the discussion on important issues. It
can lead to clear discussions of what might be as well as
what is.

REEXAMINING THE VALUES OF
ANTECEDENT URBAN DESIGN IDEOLOGIES

Current approaches to design are based, without doubt,
on the experience and the work of thoughtful and well-
meaning professionals. Their work is beginning to break
away from the approaches developed during the first
quarter of this century. While some recent urban designs
(and often those that receive the most publicity) might be
regarded as whimsical ego trips, few are. The arguments
that presently exist for a need to integrate the lines of
thinking described so far in this book—to be inclusive

rather than exclusive—are described in Chapter 5. Before
attempting to suggest the direction for this integration,
it is necessary to understand why we are where we are
and what we will give up, rightly or wrongly, in urban
design thinking if we completely reject the work of our
antecedents—the movements that brought urban design
into existence.

The ancestors of present urban designers were reformers with a strong streak of pragmatism in their constitutions.
This observation holds true throughout the history of
what might be regarded as urban design. While urban
design efforts can be traced back to the ancient civilizations of India and China, where a cosmological framework for the layout of cities was developed, and to the
cities of Greece and Italy, it is the political and technological developments of the industrial era that are of concern
here because they have brought us to our present position.

What can we learn from the past? What were the
attitudes of designers and what are the problems with the
results? What were their objectives and what were their

designs? What were the issues of concern to them? The nature of urban design today has evolved from the attitudes built up over the last 200 years. We seem to have gone through cycles of Rationalist and Empiricist thinking as the dominant approach in seeking inspiration for our actions. Except in dealing with aesthetic ideas of the avant-garde, one attitude that we seem to have lost is a reformist one. If one looks around the world today, it seems premature to have done so.

Reformist Attitudes

Reformist attitudes, despite a strong antiurban bias, were very much a basis for urban design thinking and work until the 1970s. Such an attitude is not surprising, for the Modernist ideology was a response to the conditions that prevailed in much of Europe during the first decade of this century—conditions that had been inherited from the technological and social changes of the previous century. The nineteenth century saw the full impact of the Industrial Revolution and the development of the industrial city—the Coketowns of Western Europe. The descriptions of Manchester by Friedrich Engels in 1845, the novels of Charles Dickens, and the photographs of New York City at the century's end by Jacob Riis give a graphic image to it. William Morris and John Ruskin wanted to turn the clock back; Octavia Hill and Jane Adams wanted to deal with the housing and the social problems and, more generally, the lack of opportunities of the urban poor.

In the nineteenth century there was considerable political ferment, and the early reform proposals and urban design ideas came together out of the spirit of revolution. Interestingly, the same collaboration between political and architectural ideologues is reflected in urban design attitudes coming out of post-Franco Spain. Nineteenth-century reformers were utopians considering possible futures outside immediately empirically observable trends (Reiner 1963; Benevolo 1967; Hayden 1976; Darley 1978). They had a strong Rationalist orientation to their thinking. Inevitably they were looking at both the social and physical nature of the world. They considered social goals and then the physical needs required to meet those goals and then the possibilities, in an iterative process. This is essentially the process that Robert Owen followed in planning New Lanark in Scotland, but that he largely lost in the deterministic thinking that led to his design of New Harmony in the United States (Butt 1971). In New Lanark he followed a Aristotelian approach to design, in New Harmony a Platonic. The former worked, but it has a less "photogenic" image, it is thus less well known as a sociophysical model.

The Aristotelian line of thinking was exemplified in Continental Europe by Jean Baptiste Godin (1817–1889) in the design of his *Familistère*, a factory and residential area in a parklike setting, which worked until World War

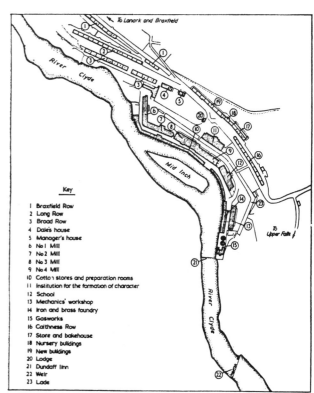

Plan of New Lanark, based on the first edition Ordnance Survey

1. New Lanark, Scotland, Plan

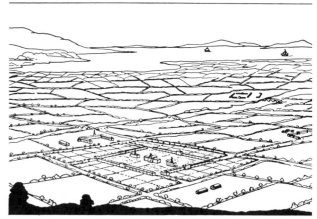

2. Generic Plan for an Industrial Village in the United States (1817)

Figure 4-9: New Lanark and New Harmony

The nineteenth century was characterized by many reform movements aimed at giving people better lives. They were the antecedents for the Modern movement's reformist zeal. Robert Owen, one of the earliest reformers, implemented many employment and social reforms at his mill in New Lanark, Scotland (1). Buoyed with its success he established a plan for a new community in 1817 (2). New Harmony, Indiana, was established but failed to thrive. Such schemes, nevertheless, focused attention on the combination of social and physical environmental problems that masses of people faced.

II. Charles Fourier (1772–1837), in the design of his *Phalanstery,* which was never implemented, followed the Platonic and Rationalist line of thought that had as its descendant Le Corbusier (Benevolo 1967; Gallion and Eisner 1986). The Platonic line attracts attention because of its boldness, but it is the Aristotelian line that has a better record in improving the quality of life. Godin's proposals were based on Fourier's earlier work but were tied to empirical reality.

These ideas spurred the development of a large number of model company towns—administered communities—all of which were based on a social philosophy and a physical design philosophy in tandem. Owen and Godin were among a number of industrialists concerned with enlightened self-interest in the quality of lives of their workers. From the design of Gran-Hornu (1821) in Belgium and Lowell, Massachusetts, into the twentieth century with New Earswick, England (1905), there were many towns built displaying reformist ideals (Darley 1978).

The towns remain of interest today for a number of reasons: the values they represented, for good or ill, in the scope of their planning concerns; the concepts they had of the appropriate lives of workers; the nature of social segregation and integration they sought; the principles of urban design they demonstrated; and the relationship between social organization and physical design they represented. Many of them employed the leading architects of their day: Barry Parker and Raymond Unwin were commissioned by Rowntree to plan and design the housing at New Earswick, the Guëll family employed Antonio Gaudi in Spain. Frederick Law Olmsted was designer of Vandergrift, Pennsylvania (1890), where the winding roads of the English village were the basis for the pattern for Olmsted's later suburban designs. McKim, Mead and White designed Echota, New York (1892), in the manner of a typical American village for the Niagara Power Company. As a result, there was careful attention to the massing and composition in many of the industrial villages. The monotonous rows of houses so characteristic of many of the Coketowns was thus avoided. In addition, much attention was paid to the integration of community facilities and open spaces with the residential parts of the town and to the segregation of the commercial and manufacturing parts from the remainder.

The plans, both social and physical, were highly paternalistic and often conflicted with workers' values. In New Earswick, Parker and Unwin thought the workers' penchant for a front parlor in their houses was a waste of space because it was seldom used. Pullman, Illinois (1881), is probably more notorious for its labor practices than well known as a model design. Though not usually suburbs, the company towns provided the village imagery and progressive social spirit that culminated in the Garden City movement (Stern with Massengale 1981), and their designs were intertwined with ideology in the suburban developments of the second part of the nineteenth century.

1. The Plan of the Familistère at Guise, France

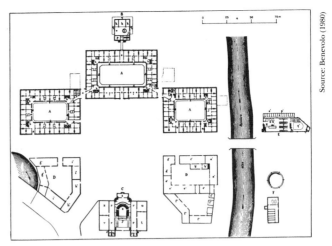

2. A Bird's-Eye View

3. The Children's Nursery

Figure 4-10: Villages and Towns of "Vision"
Many industrialists built new factory towns during the nineteenth century. Jean Baptiste Godin's *Familistère* is one of them. It remained a company town, an administered community, even though run by a workers' cooperative after 1880. Such towns, with their restricted sizes, segregation of uses, and life centered around the central work place and family home, had a major influence on twentieth-century thinking about human habitats. There is much that we can still learn from them. The major lesson is that the model of the human being must be drawn from who we are.

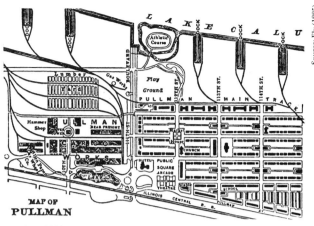

Source: Ely (1885)

1. Plan (1881)

2. Housing, Today

3. Market Square Area, Today

Figure 4-11: Pullman, Illinois
Pullman, Illinois, is an example of a company town in which the plan (1) and architecture are descended from a line of thought that can be traced back to such places as Saltaire (1850), an industrial new town built in a rural setting in England. The goal was to have a reliable workforce. Good housing for families (2) and single workers and places for them to shop and enjoy recreation were provided (3). In Pullman, much of the life of the workers was controlled by the company through the type of facilities provided and the requirements that workers use them.

Paralleling these urban design efforts was the concern for public health needs as the basis for the creation of urban design principles. This can be traced back to the very founding of cities and to treatises on urban design such as the *Shilpa Shastras* and the writings of Vitruvius and Alberti, (but as we know it) to British legislation of the early part of the nineteenth century and the development of zoning in Germany during the latter part of the century (Benevolo 1967; J. Peterson 1979). The nineteenth-century concern was much as it is today, with legislation ensuring sufficient open spaces, defining the nature of streets, lot lines, and building lines, and the provision of adequate sunlight and space for living. It is a necessary but limited concern but does show the reformist zeal of our design ancestors.

Design Principles

Each movement in urban design is clearly identifiable by the generic patterns of form it uses. Our attitudes toward them vary. Each is easy to disparage, but we need to recognize their achievements. Each movement described in this book has provided patterns of urban form that have many affordances and so still have a utility for us. They also missed opportunities. A brief review of their design ideas shows this mixture of success and failure but also their potential for the future.

The City Beautiful and the Grand Idea

Until recently the City Beautiful movement was almost universally scorned. Yet it has produced two memorable capital cities (Canberra and New Delhi) as well as innumerable, if fragmentary, civic design schemes for governmental complexes and university campuses (see P. Turner, 1984). City Beautiful schemes are still being produced. They all have a clear design idea behind them.

There is still much that can be learned from the City Beautiful. One of the major lessons is the one that Le Corbusier learned from Haussmann. Large-scale projects are possible provided there is political support for them. There is also the lesson that people do care about what cities look like, and that architectural ideas that have both simplicity and power, such as the axial composition of the Beaux Arts schemes, are easy to understand and are the ones that capture attention (Bacon 1974). We also learned that they can be very costly, both financially and politically, and when applied to urban renewal, highly disruptive to individuals' lives (Benevolo 1980; Brownlee 1989).

The grand scheme is still a technique for achieving civic pride. It does so in Paris and, with a different architectural idea, in Chandigarh. The City Beautiful, its antecedent movement, the Baroque, and much contemporary Rationalist thought show us that urban design as art is still a potential mechanism for giving an area an identity. A recent study conducted by the City Planning Commission in Philadelphia showed that the Benjamin Franklin Parkway—the only completed piece of a more extensive City Beautiful proposal for the city—is a much loved part of the city. The utility of the grand architectural idea in this regard is one of the sets of design principles explored in Chapter 14, Meeting Esteem Needs.

Empiricism and Rationalism: Looking Back and Looking Forward

While the City Beautiful provides us with a number of design ideas of relevance today, it is the Modern movements that really still show the way. The Modernist had "moral and social ideas of what architecture could do . . ." (Max Abramovitz cited in Goldberger 1989b). The Modernists attempted to deal with what they perceived to be the problems of their times. Their contribution to human development in general and to the intellectual development of architecture and urban design as professional activities and disciplines has been vast. It is clear from any of the manifestos of the Modernists that they were adopting a problem-oriented approach to design rather than a mimetic approach. They were concerned with developing social schemata as well as physical and architectural plans. Their design goals were based on models of human needs. They were concerned with the lifestyles of people and what they might be in the future. They were seeking new spatial patterns that would address the problems of the city with the technological power available to them. These are all, surely, still valid concerns.

The Modernists have provided us with a set of generic solutions, a slogan, three basic attitudes toward planning and design, and a way of looking at the design problem worth retaining. The set of generic solutions consists of two basic models of the city—the Garden City and the Radiant City—and two models of the neighborhood—the neighborhood unit and the Unité d'habitation. The slogan is "form follows function." The attitudes are: that social planning and physical design should go together, that human needs should be the basis for thinking about design, and that design methods had to be changed.

A Set of Generic Solutions— The Design of New Types

The Modernists showed us two very divergent approaches to the design of the city that come out of two very different intellectual traditions. Both of them recognize the important role of transportation in framing the city, and the need to create a salubrious environment, with access to sun, open air, and open space. The generic design of the Empiricists is the Garden City and of the Rationalists the Radiant City. What was unfortunate was that the proponents of neither really recognized the cultural bias of their proposals and presented them as universal solutions. The basic design principles for each proposal are still valid *in context* today. They are powerful generic solutions that can be applied in response to very specific problems provided they are seen in terms of the model of the human being and the culture on which they were based. Architecture has a long history of throwing out ideas and moving to another set without fully evaluating the utility of the first.

Functionalism

One of the major contributions of the Modern movement was its focus on the functions of the built environment as the basis for design. This focus can be seen in both the manifestos and buildings of many of the major architects of the period (see Conrads 1970). The manifesto of C.I.A.M. (Sert and C.I.A.M. 1944), for instance, considers the city in terms of dwelling, recreation, work, and transportation systems. Much of its thinking was based on "the evolution of the means of production [as a] decisive influence upon urban structures" and with the creation of a "functional city" (pp. 228–236). The needs of "man and the city" are seen in these terms. "Form follows function" was indeed their slogan.

Statements ascribing to architecture and urban design a functional goal have a long history. An early written statement is that of Vitruvius, architect to Caesar Augustus. In English his specification of the goals of design are probably better known in the words of Sir Henry Wotton (1624): "Well-building hath three Conditions. *Commoditie, Firmenes,* and *Delight.*" In thinking about urban design, the architects of the Modern movement tended to differentiate between functional and aesthetic goals. Commodity was thought of in terms of efficiency in carrying out the building task and rationality in building construction. The poetics of form and/or the associational meaning of forms was thought of as a separate concern or as a byproduct of meeting the functional goal. This consideration of the aesthetic goal of design as a "nonfunctional" goal of design is still with us today, but aesthetic quality serves many functions, some often more important than the more utilitarian ones.

The separation of the Vitruvian concerns of architecture into functional and aesthetic goals predates the development of Modernism as narrowly defined in this book. Although Etienne-Louis Boulée (1728-1799) is better known for his advocacy of pure geometric forms in architecture, this line of thought can be traced back to him at least. It is, however, more closely associated with the Modernism of the late nineteenth and the twentieth centuries.

Human Needs as a Basis of Functional Design

Although, as will be described later in this book, the Modernist concept of function was a narrow one, it was based on a concept of human needs. In his chapter, "Towards the Functional City," José Sert (Sert and C.I.A.M. 1944) states the position of C.I.A.M. A subsection of his chapter is entitled "Man as the Axis of New Cities: His Needs, the Basis of Their Plans." Unfortunately, neither a clear model of human needs nor a model of the nature of the interaction of human behavior and the environment is specified.

This conclusion is quite clear from an examination of the writings of people such as Hannes Meyer (Meyer 1928; Wingler 1969) and later, C.I.A.M. Their explicit statements of the perceptions of these needs enable us to understand the focus of attention of architects in their proposals and their designs. Their statements clearly show a more limited model than we have today (see Chapters 6 and 7).

The Social Concern

It can be argued that the fundamental social concerns of the Modernists were born of the Industrial Revolution and that those problems are now solved. Certainly rickets and other diseases seem to be a thing of the past in most technologically developed societies, but it's also clear that many planning and, consequently, urban design schemes have exacerbated many social divisions in society. There needs to be a reconsideration of the social basis for design so that, at the very least, we are not making the situation worse through the designs we create.

All physical design proposals assume, explicitly or implicitly, some social organization of the people who are going to inhabit or use the completed project. True, there has been an easy willingness of architects to condemn certain behaviors and their spatial consequences as bad or unnecessary or a waste of space, and to regard other behaviors as desirable and necessary. The perception of what is good and what is bad shifts over time (Blake 1974). Until recently, for instance, most architects considered the use of streets as recreation space as bad. Now some designers urge us to see such behaviors in context (Hester 1975). We have seen pedestrian and vehicles as being in constant conflict; now we think the conflict is a solution to many problems rather than a problem to be resolved. Designers' observations and conclusions and thus attitudes toward behaviors, environments, and design are, like most people's, with reference to their own cultural and behavioral norms. The design professions are judgmental. They have to be. The question is "Whose values should be used as the basis for making comparisons and judgments?"

All designs afford some behaviors more readily than others. All designs preclude some behavioral possibilities in favor of others. The goal should surely be to enhance the positive behavioral possibilities for the people who will use the designs. Architects thus must consider behavioral possibilities in design. The Modernist quite rightly

did this. However, they made many assumptions that even the most ardent Modernists today admit were shortsighted and extremely unfortunate. We now have a much better, if far from complete, understanding of the behavior-environment interface than the architect working in the 1920s. We should use that understanding.

The problems we are addressing today are in many ways substantially different in nature than those being addressed by architects at the beginning of the twentieth century. Yet at heart they are similar—the search for design patterns that are an improvement on the existing layout of cities or future patterns determined solely by market forces. We can certainly learn to be more cautious in our claims about what will and will not work. Any social engineering aspect of a design will be likely to be doomed to failure unless accompanied by a social and administrative plan that will be implemented.

The Father Panic housing in Bridgeport, Connecticut, is a good example of the need to integrate social and physical design. When built in the late 1930s it was a highly successful and much loved housing area and project. It incorporated not only a physical plan but also a social and administrative one. The social plan provided support services for low-income families and the administrative plan a clear management process. As financial problems arose (i.e., as society as a whole became unwilling to support such services) so the social and administrative procedures were cut and largely eliminated. The social infrastructure collapsed and the facilities were reduced. Today the Father Panic project rivals Pruitt Igoe in St. Louis, the housing developments known locally as the "Piggeries" in the Everton part of Liverpool, England (Marmot 1982), and the Venezuelan superblocks (Gastel 1982) in notoriety.

Implicit in any urban design is an image of the lifestyles of its potential occupants even if the assumption is that the occupants will finish or change the design to meet their own needs (e.g., Habraken 1971). It is based on some model of a culture, whether this is a corporate culture or a residential one. The Modernists clearly recognized this relationship and took responsibility for it. The difficulties that the Modernists had in meeting this responsibility is one of the factors in architects' retreat from urban design, from thinking about the social environment they are creating, and their embracing of the new pragmatism in design and a consideration of architecture simply as the creation of individual buildings as objects of art in space.

Design Method

Architects feel comfortable in using a solution-oriented approach to design—a paradigmatic or mimetic approach to design. A solution-oriented approach to design is essentially what computer scientists call a hill-climbing approach. The designer begins with a standard, or generic, solution—a type—to what appears to be the class of problems being addressed and incrementally changes it to meet the present situation. This is fine provided one is on the correct hill to start with. It is fine provided the class of problems to which the type applies is correctly identified. Indeed, it is unnecessary to reinvent the wheel all the time. The need is to recognize types that have a utility in a particular context. There are many examples of types not only being used out of context but that also have had negative consequences in their original setting (Brolin 1976; Wolfe 1981; Herdeg 1983). The zoning and financial incentives in London's Docklands have, rightly or wrongly, become a model for the new pragmatism in many other locations around the world despite the dubiousness of their applicability in their own case (Williams 1990). The way planners and urban designers tend to think about designing needs to be reconsidered.

The Modernists were looking at the world around them. They were trying to understand its problems and to devise solutions to them. With the wisdom of hindsight their perceptions seem to have been limited in scope. The Rationalists looked more at the ills of society than the joys, the Empiricist at what they themselves liked. They both were, nevertheless, looking at contemporary worlds. At times of perceived rapid change, like the present, it is easy to look back to the past and to try to hang on to some of its characteristics that give us a sense of identity. The Post-Modernists are very much trying to do so. The same can be said of the Empiricists among the Modernists. As a basis for their proposals, the Empiricists were indeed looking for built form/urban spatial types where the problems of industrial societies did not seem to occur. The Rationalists were trying to invent new types. In doing so another problem arose not necessarily in the types themselves but in their application. As Alexi Marmot (1982) has shown, it is the adaptation of these types, usually in debased form (i.e., smaller in scale and with reduced facilities), to situations to which they were not appropriate that caused problems (see Fig. 6-6). The design process, particularly the programming or brief-writing part of it, was not well understood.

The Rationalists were indeed attempting to get away from the typological/mimetic approach to design of their predecessors. In his study of Le Corbusier's design method, Manoucher Eslami (1985, 1988) quite clearly shows the influence of the Descartean problem disaggregation-design synthesis algorithm as the basis for Le Corbusier's design method. We know considerably more about the whole process now than the Modernists did. We need to use that knowledge. Indeed, we are beginning to do so and, in so doing, redesigning the design process.

REDISCOVERING A SENSE OF DIRECTION

In conclusion, it can be said that serving the marketplace and thinking of urban design as a work of art are both necessary but insufficient attitudes for urban designers to hold if they wish to make a substantive contribution to the societies of which they are a part. Community involvement is important in many, if not all, situations. Current critics suggest that urban design has to consider the relationship between social and physical planning in a much more holistic way than it has during the decade of the 1980s. The goal is still to create a functional environment, but the concept of functionalism needs redefining. In doing so, our past experience suggests that we cannot rely on our own conventional wisdom and intuitive feelings about other people and the environments that are required and/or sought by them. We need to use the knowledge base potentially at our disposal.

We have learned much about the process of designing during the past three decades. Indeed one of the areas of architectural theory and practice in which the most progress has been made during the past thirty years is in the preparation of the design program. The progress has been based on a highly integrationist attitude and promises much in addressing the problems architects and other design professionals face in urban design today. Urban social and physical change is clearly an ongoing process. Urban design is a process. We need to treat it as such.

MAJOR REFERENCES

Benevolo, Leonardo (1967). *The Origins of Modern Town Planning.* Cambridge, MA: MIT Press.

Collins, George, and Christiana Craseman Collins (1965). *Camillo Sitte and the Birth of Modern City Planning.* New York: Random House.

Gallion, Arthur B., and Simon Eisner (1986). *The Urban Pattern: City Planning and Design.* 5th ed. New York: Van Nostrand Reinhold.

Ghirardo, Diane (1987). "A Taste of Money: Architecture and Criticism in Houston." *Harvard Architecture Review* 6: 88-97.

Goldberger, Paul (1989). "Why Design Can't Transform Cities." *New York Times* (25 June): Section H, 1, 30.

Harrington, Michael (1963). *The Other America.* New York: Macmillan.

Lang, Jon (1987a). "The Legacy of the Modern Movement." In *Creating Architectural Theory: The Role of the Behavioral Sciences in Environmental Design.* New York: Van Nostrand Reinhold, pp. 3-12.

Sert, José Luis, and C.I.A.M. (1944). *Can Our Cities Survive? An ABC of Urban Problems, Their Analysis, Their Solution.* Cambridge, MA: Harvard University Press.

Sharp, Dennis (1978). "Introduction." In Dennis Sharp, ed., *The Rationalists: Theory and Design in the Modern Movement.* London: Architectural Press, pp. 1-5.

Wolfe, Tom (1981). *From Bauhaus to Our House.* New York: Farrar Straus Giroux.

5

REDESIGNING URBAN DESIGN

In recent years, there have been a number of proposals for redesigning the way we go about urban design and/or manifestos on the desirable characteristics of the public realm (e.g., Charter of Machu Picchu 1979; Lynch 1982, 1984; Huet 1984; Alexander et al. 1987; Jacobs and Appleyard 1987; Ostler 1987; Mackay 1990; Preiser, Vischer, and White 1991; and Alexander 1991). These proposals respond to changes in the perception of urban problems, the perceived strengths and weaknesses of the urban design projects of the last two decades, the paradigms that have promoted them, and the development of our knowledge base for making decisions. They also show the need for an emerging professional activity to establish an identity and a sense of direction for urban design. Before considering how urban design should be done, it is necessary to take a position on what the desirable characteristics of any proffered urban design paradigm are. Such a situation needs to be based on some perception of the strengths and weaknesses of past efforts if it is to serve us well in the future.

The perceptions of successes and failures of urban design schemes are highly subjective. Even the abandonment of a housing development by its inhabitants can be seen as a positive action. It is, however, hardly a a hallmark of a good social and physical design. The perceptions of successes and failures in this book are seen primarily from the point of view of the users of the environment not the producers—an *emic* rather than an *etic* approach to design (Moudon 1990a). There is nothing new in the view of architecture and urban design presented here, but it does suggest a rejection of the standard architectural view as the sole arbiter of urban design quality.

THE NEED FOR A PARADIGMATIC SHIFT IN AMERICAN URBAN DESIGN

The arguments for each existing urban design paradigm are compelling. It is easy to read a treatise on, say, Rationalism and be convinced that it is the best approach to urban design, only to pick up one on Empiricism and believe it is the only sensible approach. The problem with any paradigm is that it tends to present a blinkered view of the world that holds until it is unsustainable because the contradictory evidence has become overwhelming. There is considerable evidence that there are limitations, if not major problems, with our present paradigms.

The development of urban design over the last twenty years suggests some stereotypical images of what different architectural and urban design paradigms have brought with them. Like many stereotypes, the images are partially accurate. With the new pragmatism, for instance, have come the ideas that urban design is only concerned with site planning, and then only with enhancing the private realm; that urban design has no social role in society, other than to follow the dictates of the marketplace; that the only important thing is to have an egocentric and original design idea; that there is no developed knowledge base for design, and that one is largely unnecessary. With the new Rationalism has come the idea that what is important is the application of a heroic geometric order to urban design. Empiricism continues to bring a picturesque attitude toward what should be done—an attempt to revive the past, a Neo-Traditionalism. Each group's ideas work from an *emic* perspective in specific circum-

1. Capitol Plaza, Salem, Oregon

2. Portland, Oregon, Rehabilitated Waterfront

3. Lower Manhattan, New York, Battery Park City in the Foreground

4. Suburban Housing, Ann Arbor, Michigan

5. Minneapolis

6. 16th Street Mall, Denver

Figure 5-1: Success and Failure of Urban Design Schemes
All the schemes shown above have been praised and criticized. The same is true of internationally renowned schemes such as Brasilia (see Fig. 2-18). This city has been successful in opening up part of Brazil to settlement. It has grand sculptural quality, which has much meaning for Brazilians, although it is not regarded as a socially rich environment for children. Much of the financially pragmatic urban design of the past two decades in the United States has secured a profit for its developers and increased the tax base of cities but has not enhanced the lives of people displaced. All urban change affects somebody negatively. What are the rights of individuals and of society? In whose terms and on what dimensions should quality be measured?

stances, but their universality of application is wanting.

A closer examination of the agenda of each group shows that each focuses on a different problem, as if it were *the* problem. Each has a narrow concept of the *functions* of the built environment and a narrow model of the human being. Each has its own agenda. Each strives for the internal consistency and validity of its ideas. It is the external validity that is important.

Few major critics of current approaches to urban design are themselves willing to deal with the current

1. Los Angeles

2. Paris, with Recent Office Buildings Located on the Periphery

3. Hong Kong, Housing

Figure 5-2: Culture and Design

Urban development today is dictated by zoning laws, laws that govern the operation of the market, and the tastes within the culture (1). Self-conscious urban designs have to be seen within the cultures that generate them, including their patrons' and designers' values and the latitude that society gives designers to express themselves (2). Many designs that we admire were produced under totalitarian leaders whom we find unacceptable today—Napoleon III, for instance! Large population numbers, political necessity, shortages of resources, and different attitudes make environments intolerable in the United States that are acceptable elsewhere and vice versa (3).

world. They criticize what is being done—the thinking of architects, or more often, because they are architects, the thinking of city planners. It always seems to be another profession that is at fault. The critics also frequently retreat to the past, especially ancient Rome (e.g., Rowe and Koetter 1976 and Rykwert 1988), although sometimes ancient aspects of modern Rome (Abercrombie 1982); or they derive their normative types from cultures other than the one they criticize (e.g., Lennard and Lennard 1987, 1988, 1990 and Rykwert 1988), or in their own work focus on building types other than the ones they criticize (El Wakil 1991). There is a utility to looking at the past and at culturally different situations. They enhance one's knowledge of the realm of design possibilities and, more broadly, the relationship between form and function. Such examinations should not, however, exclude understanding the present-day issues of design within the specific biogenic and sociogenic environments of people and the way those environments are working. Urban design in the United States has to be seen within its own cultural frame, as does urban design anywhere.

The discrepancy between architects' visions of what happens in cities and what diligent observers (phenomenologists, e.g.) see has been recognized as a fundamental problem in design theory for a long time. Architects'

continued fascination with the past isolates them from the problems of contemporary life. Henri Labrouste (1801–1875), winner of the grand prix de Rome at the Académie des Beaux Arts in Paris, saw his five years at the Villa Medici in Rome as an "estrangement from life" even though he studied the ancient monuments of Italy from an engineer-archeologist view rather than a picturesque one (Giedion 1963). A few of our contemporary architects are dismayed by this continued estrangement from life of architects. Robert Venturi (1966) stated forthrightly:

> [An architect] can exclude important considerations only at a risk of separating architecture from life and the needs of society. If some problems prove insoluble he can express this; in an inconclusive rather than an exclusive architecture there is room for the fragment, for contradiction, improvisation, and for the tensions these produce.

The difficulties are to deal with the city and urban design as an open system rather than a closed one and to turn verbal statements of intent into design actions that achieve them.

Each current approach to urban design has yielded schemes of great interest, as shown in the previous chapters. Criticizing or supporting them wholeheartedly is easy. In

1. Pruitt Igoe Housing, St. Louis, Prior to Demolition

2. Pruitt Igoe, Predicted Use of Gallery Space

3. Pruitt Igoe, Actual Appearance of Gallery Space (1965)

Figure 5-3: The Discrepancies between Predictions and Realities
Implicit in any design is a statement of belief about how it will function when implemented. The design can be regarded, given a number of assumptions, as an hypothesis on the part of a designer about the future. The hypothesis is based on the designer's knowledge but also, often, on the designer's hopes— the gambler's fallacy. One of the arguments for a more rigorous positive theoretical basis for urban design is to enhance our ability to predict outcomes of designs well. Too often in the past, predictions (2) have differed substantially from outcomes (3).

analyzing them, however, it has to be recognized that no urban design project of any consequence can meet all the needs of all the people involved equally well. All designs will resolve some problems better than others. All design involves an advocacy for some ideas, and thus for some people over others. Architectural criticism is a criticism of advocacies as much as the means used to achieve or afford them.

The questions arise: "Can a more encompassing approach to urban design be developed?" "If it can be developed conceptually, can it be implemented at all?" "Would it capture the attention of architects who now seem to be more interested in the design of monuments than in urban design?" "Are they willing to deal with everyday life in cities and urban spaces when it is the museums, city halls, and religious buildings that provide vehicles for the aesthetic explorations of interest to architects today?" (see also Rybczynski 1990). To some extent the architects' concerns reflect the concerns of society. Architects as urban designers can, however, be leaders in shaping the public's thinking about the public realm of cities. Some have been in the past (e.g., Edmund Bacon in Philadelphia, Wei Ming Lu in Dallas).

The basic premise of a number of architects, landscape architects, and city planners is that it is worth the

attempt. Urban design as a primarily public act can be redesigned. In its redesign, urban design needs: (1) to be seen within a moral order, (2) to understand its potential contribution in a changing world, (3) to deal with new realities of life rather than the problems of the past, (4) to recognize its political nature, (5) to see itself as a collaborative act, (6) to have a future orientation, (7) to be based on experiential knowledge, and (8) to follow a knowledge-based approach to design. To meet these needs urban design will further need to be based on an *interactionalist* philosophy. It will have to draw on both Rationalist and Empiricist thinking while firmly rooted in the latter approach.

(1) The Need for Urban Design to Be Seen Within a Moral Order

Urban design has to be seen within a broad cultural ethos. The arguments described in this book are presented within a view of such an ethos. It is presumed that the overall goal of a society is to be a good society. A good society is, inter alia, one in which mutually supportive human relationships are fostered and encouraged. It is a society in which freedom of inquiry and expression exist, but also one in which people have a responsibility both to themselves and others. This view may or may not be contrasted with the view that the overall goal of society is to be financially successful.

Abraham Maslow (1987) identified a number of basic freedoms and, implicitly, the preconditions necessary to fulfill other needs:

> freedom to speak, freedom to do what one wishes as long as no harm is done to others, freedom to express oneself, freedom to investigate, and freedom to defend oneself. Justice, fairness, honesty and orderliness in the group are examples of such preconditions for basic needs satisfaction.

Such freedoms must also be considered in the development of a framework defining the nature of a purposeful urban design—a functional urban design. It is thus important for politicians, planners, and urban designers to rediscover Enlightenment thinking—the ability of societies to move ahead toward achieving better social and physical environments.

(2) The Need to Understand Urban Design's Potential Contribution in a Changing World

Urban design as a professional activity can make a number of contributions to the way the overall built environment is unselfconsciously changed as the result of economic, social, and technological changes in society—changes in the manifestation of human needs. The goal of urban designing is to change (through what is essentially political action) the way the traditional market and legal systems shape the physical world. The purpose is to establish the basic parameters of the layout of cities and their precincts. There are two basic reasons for interfering in the marketplace: (1) to ensure that developments on one parcel of land do not, at the very least, reduce the quality of the environment as a whole, and (2) to encourage specific forms of development—the distribution of activities and the nature of the built environment on behalf of the public interest. The first activity is a protectionist one—to protect the existing environment, both biogenic and sociogenic, from damages resulting from change. The second is the creative role of advocating certain types of environments on behalf of specific interest groups. These parties vary from governments themselves, to large corporations building either for themselves or for others, to individual property owners, and, most generally, to the users of the environment who change it by their very use of it.

Historically, the push has been to achieve a more salubrious environment and/or a more artistic environment, but now the goal should be to enhance the quality of life of people and the organisms important to them. The urban designer thus has a dual role to play in the process of environmental change; (1) to *design/set directions* for the configurations and uses of the public realm of cities, their precincts, and specific building sites, and (2) to *mediate* between conflicting needs, desires, and hopes of various parties involved in the development of the physical form of cities, which, in turn shapes the social affordances of cities.

This specification of roles implies that those involved in urban design must have considerable substantive knowledge about cities, about urban forms, and how they are and might be used and enjoyed (i.e., their affordances), and thus about the functions they serve and might serve at both a city and a local scale. It also implies that designers need to have two further sets of knowledge: (1) knowledge of the processes of environmental change, both manmade and natural, and (2) knowledge of the dynamics of the decision-making processes that change cities and, more specifically, knowledge of the nature of the self-conscious design process.

(3) The Need to Deal with Different and Changing Models of Reality

Each school of urban design thought believes it is dealing with reality and with the important issues (see Watkin 1977). There are, however, differing views of reality. The recent financial pragmatism in urban design is a response to the perception of the marketplace as the major location of environmental design decisions. The Neo-Rationalists believe that by relying on their own personal reflections on the world, they can come closer to an objective reality than by any other approach. Empiricists believe that perceptions of reality are individual but are not haphazard and so are shared by groups of like people.

Various events in the world make us look at it in new ways; we attend to specific features of it that we have not focused on before. One recognition triggers another. Increases in population make us look more carefully at high-density environments, especially where there is little available land. The growth of the Mexico Citys, São Paulos, Bangkoks, and Jakartas of the world focuses attention on the vast metropolitan areas of resource-poor countries and forces us to think about resource-poor urban design. Political attitudes in the United States have led to similar situations in many cities, setting up an iterative process of lack of concern with the public environment followed by a deterioration of the private one leading to the further deterioration of the public realm, and so on.

The oil crisis of 1973 brought attention to the need for the design of the future maintenance, operation, and management processes of proposed urban design schemes to be seriously considered as an integral variable in assessing their quality. Although the lesson has been largely lost in the United States, it did bring to focus the issues of conservation and preservation of resources. The economic crises of the late 1980s have focused attention on the role of interest rates in determining what can be built and on the effect of future capital investment opportunities on the phasing of large schemes. The architecture of

1. Bellevue, Washington

Photograph by Lori Leland

2. Suburban Atlanta

3. Los Angeles

4. Lake Elsinore, California

5. McArthur Park Area, Chicago

6. Manchester Avenue, Los Angeles (1992)

Figure 5-4: The New Realities

The world is changing in many ways, so urban designers will have to examine many of the values they hold dear. New communications technologies may lead to radical shifts in lifestyles. Suburbia is urbanizing (1). The convenience of the automobile means that it is the preferred and predominant means of transportation for the majority of Americans, and the suburban strip is a design type of the automobile era (2). Potential energy shortages, pollution, and smog (3) caused by present modes of energy consumption will almost inevitably necessitate a reex- amination of many of our present assumptions about what constitutes a good lifestyle and good design. The single-family detached house is still the desired home for many people (4, see also Fig. I-1 (1)), but family types are changing too. Many parts of deteriorated inner-city neighborhoods are still inhabited. They present a bleak outlook on life and a poor self-image for their residents (5). Frustrations with social deprivations are often vented against the built environment (6). Dealing with them is not an urban design issue per se, but they have major urban design implications.

economic austerity differs from the architecture of plenty (Kiernan 1987).

The normative positions on urban design described in this book are predicated on a number of assumptions/observations about the present and future—a perception of a number of new realities. The positions will almost certainly include these observations: (1) that cities, or rather metropolitan areas, are changing in character; in particular, the distribution and nature of facilities needs to respond to changing lifestyles, (2) that cities have to be dealt with as entities as well as a set of components, (3) that some cities will grow and others decline; urban design needs to be able to deal with consolidation and reduction in the nature of places as well as their growth, (4) that urban design is fundamentally the responsibility of the governmental agencies entrusted with looking after the public interest, (5) that urban design will differ from culture to culture based on differences in perceptions of the importance of the individual and the community, the nature of public goods, and the nature of the public interest, and (6) that the guidelines for urban design should not be regarded as static statements of what should and should not be built but must change as lifestyles and values of the people in whose interests they are written change. Most important of all is (7)—that while total comprehensive planning may be a rational goal, it is impossible to achieve in practice.

(4) The Need to Recognize the Political Nature of Urban Design

All urban design involves an advocacy for certain ends. Some of these ends are universal but others are those of particular groups in society. Urban design has almost always been concerned with the needs of the wealthy and the powerful, and their lives, as any history book will attest (e.g., E. Morris 1974). Urban designers are also very much influenced by their professional peers and the way professional societies reward their members (see Montgomery 1966). Many people, possibly all people, are concerned about the nature of the built environment and the degree of control they have over it, for it provides the physical framework for their lives. It impinges on some lives more than others, and it is of greater professional concern to some fields of design than others.

The future built environment will ultimately result from the decisions made by politicians and the way they place capital investments and frame the laws that regulate the operation of the marketplace—the laws, regulations, and guidelines that control what can be built. In making their decisions, politicians will be seeking advice from design professionals as well as other interest groups as they establish societal goals. Urban designers, as individuals or as part of professions acting as political pressure groups, will be giving unsolicited advice to their colleagues, public/voters/purchasers, civil servants, and politicians. The design process is thus an argumentative one, much of which takes place, and should take place, in the public eye.

If urban designers accept these observations, then they also have to see urban design within the framework of the decision-making processes of any society. This book is primarily concerned with the decision-making process in the United States, but much applies to what the urban designer can bring to the table in the major democratic countries of the world. While there are differences of opinion about the relative importance of the individual and the community among these countries, there are some issues that are universal. For instance, all the democracies in the world take the position that individuals have the freedom to do anything they want unless it infringes on the rights of others. It is clear that "infringement" is interpreted in a number of ways, but if urban designers accept this general statement as a guiding principle then they can start to be advocates for open-ended design and not end-state designs as works of art. The art defense for designs that impinge negatively on the lives of users of the public realm then becomes a difficult one to accept.

Democratic societies also advocate equal opportunity, equal justice, and individual liberties for all their citizens. If urban designers take these statements as operating principles—as an ethical basis for urban design, as statements of the public interest—then they will have to deal with many more variables than they do at present. They will have to be capable of advocating for complex designs because much of the public domain is and will continue to be multifunctional. Urban designers, especially those working in the private sector as consultants, are, however, also businesspeople who have to operate within the norms of business enterprises. A certain degree of economic pragmatism is required to stay in business. A guiding principle, nevertheless, has to be that urban designers should strive to increase human welfare and the behavioral opportunities for diverse sets of people simultaneously.

One of the difficulties in operationalizing the position that urban design needs to be seen within the goals of a society is that there are often major discrepancies between the professed goals, the self-images, and the way a society operates. There are discrepancies between the statements in the U.S. Constitution and the way people in the country behave toward each other. Should the ideal or the reality be the basis for design? The question can be asked of all societies. Should the urban designer in India, for instance, take as a guiding social principle the Indian Constitution, which advocates a casteless, classless, socialist society, when the society itself does not operate in that manner? Whatever stance is taken, it is a political one and is reflected in the mechanisms a society uses to attain its goals.

The results of any urban design process will emerge from the debate among the marketplace, legal and political interests, and design ideas. Urban design as a communal act of public-policy setting by governments is clearly political in nature. As the developers of design guidelines, urban designers are establishing legal instruments that guide development. All-of-a-piece design under the jurisdiction of a developer, either public or private, clearly falls within the competitive framework of the marketplace. Therefore its nature has to vary by the context within which it is carried out, and the results must be seen within that context. This does not mean that the context cannot be criticized. Indeed, a criticism of urban design is largely a criticism of the culture of a society. Nevertheless, urban design's guiding frame of reference has to be the broad interests of society rather than communal or individual interests.

The urban designers of the various schools of thought described in Chapters 2, 3, and 4 clearly have their own agendas. These agendas are obviously political in themselves as they advocate certain ends, and definitely in the marketplace as they attempt to solicit clients for services. They have to be seen as such. The current and potential roles of urban form as part of these processes define the possibilities and limitations of urban design.

(5) The Need to See Urban Design as a Collaborative Act

Many different professions are involved in designing changes to the physical fabric of cities. They are doing urban design or, rather, what results from their work is an urban design—or, more accurately, an evolving urban design. Often the changes made are at cross purposes with each other because they are addressing single problems—for instance, trees are planted to provide shade but will obstruct another plan to enhance automobile movement. Each profession has a specific area of competence and tends to see the environment in terms of its expertise—its members want to do what they know how to do, not necessarily what needs to be done. It is also clear that a wide variety of expertise is necessary to deal with design problems in anything that approximates an holistic way. The technical information on how to construct elements of the public realm, let alone to understand how the technical information affects the goals that can be set, is difficult to assimilate. No wonder so many urban designs emanating from single minds are reductionist in the way they deal with the world. No wonder that so many designs by committee lack coherence. All great urban designs possess a quality of integration and unity. Coherence is achieved when professionals work together in a supportive rather than a competitive way.

Urban design must be a collaborative effort between professionals. What then is the urban designer? While the overall responsibility for monitoring the biogenic (and sociogenic) environment of cities lies in the hands of elected officials, the urban designer is likely to be the designer and manager of specific acts of urban physical change. Within this definition, there are a wide variety of subroles: analyst, designer/packager of solutions, evaluator, mediator. To manage well a person has to fully understand the scope of the problems being considered. Business schools have learned this truth the hard way. Basic management procedures may well be generic, but an ability to manage a process also requires a substantial knowledge of the intellectual area being managed. The urban designer must be someone who understands the overall issues. That person can come from any of the design fields.

(6) The Need for a Future Orientation

Urban design must have an orientation to the future. Understanding history and historical forms and why they were generated either through self-conscious or unselfconscious design processes is essential but must not be a trap. Jawarharlal Nehru's exhortation on the independence of India, "The [idealized] past was well and good when it was with us, it is the future that beckons us now," is a worthwhile political slogan and an urban design slogan as well, despite the resistance to change on the part of many people.

People, including designers, get habituated to certain patterns of the world in their lives and in their work. Change, it was noted in Chapter 1, is stressful and often we are prepared to put up with the malfunctioning present simply to avoid a possibly painful transition to a better situation. There are many examples of schemes that have been bitterly fought by people only to be loved by them later. Unfortunately, there are also many schemes that architects said would be wonderful that turned out to be total failures. While there appears to have been much good fortune involved, the first set is based on the nature of human experience and the second set on models of the human being too deviant from reality to have been useful predictors of people's actual reactions to places when built and inhabited.

(7) The Need for an Experiential Approach to Urban Design

The focus on the aesthetic ideologies, theories, and architectural ideas that enhance the quality of interest of designs adds much intellectual excitement to the discussion among architects about the quality of the analogs or myths that they use to help generate new forms (see Robinson 1990). However, it is a form of avoidance behavior. It avoids dealing with the complex issues involved in enhancing the quality of life of the inhabitants of settlements. Architectural compositions, if organized appropriately, can indeed give coherence to places and enhance their imageability (Lynch 1960; Arthur and Passini 1990). Fulfilling the need for architectural coherence should be regarded as only one small part of the urban designer's task. Urban designers have to be concerned with the broader quality of life and quality of environment issues.

Urban design must be concerned with the experiencing of places and the values people place on them within different cultural frames. It must be concerned with the impact of designs on people's lives and on the sociogenic and biogenic environments that in turn affect people's lives. Urban design must be concerned with the relationship between social and physical space. It must be based on an understanding of how people perceive, understand, and use patterns of the environment. It must be concerned with the affordances of specific patterns of the environment in these terms. Chapter 1 was predicated on this assumption. Urban designs must be functional. For this assertion to be meaningful, *functionalism* needs to be redefined.

The term "function" has come to have a narrow meaning referring to efficiency in circulation systems and building construction processes. To regard the goal of urban design as fulfilling a function with aesthetic considerations added on is foolhardy when one recognizes the fundamental importance of aesthetics in people's lives. The position taken in this book is that the definition of function must be broad. It is that of those scholars who regard aesthetics as a function—the aesthetic characteristics of the built environment serve many purposes. Therefore, aesthetics should be considered a potential function of a design just as physiological comfort or any other purpose that the built environment can help satisfy (see also, e.g., Fitch 1965, 1980). Part Two of this book, Functionalism Redefined, is based on this assumption. Any model of the functions of the environment needs to be based on a *good* model of human needs.

(8) The Need for a Knowledge-Based Urban Design

The Rationalist approach to creating an objective reality has been to reflect on the nature of the world—by imaging, or imagining, the world and its people, their needs and behavior. It has severe limitations in urban design, as it does in other areas of creative design, such as writing novels. Nobel Prize–winners in literature, and even the crime writers held in highest esteem, have been extraordinarily knowledgeable about people, so much so that architects such as Stephen Holl say they find novels a stronger source of knowledge about people than sociology (see also Stringer 1980 on the writings of Thomas Hardy). The failure of Modernism is largely a failure to differentiate situations that require knowledge of people and the environment from situations that require pure imagination. Urban design today requires both.

Using one's imagination to describe and explain the behavior of people and the environment is a limited approach to creating design theory, however much it is favored by designers. It is, nevertheless, necessary to use one's imagination to generate hypotheses about future experience. As the basis for design, imagination is no substitute for systematic observation in drawing conclusions about the nature of human experiences. Observation, on the other hand, cannot create a future. Imagination is the essential component in thinking about ways to create a future given a problem definition. It is an essential part of the design process in generating future possibilities. These imagined possibilities need to be checked against empirical reality extrapolated into the future! Imagination without knowledge, in contrast, has extreme limitations in designing for the future. Urban designers need to have a multifunctional understanding of the relationship between people, places, and events, the process of urban design (i.e., design methodology), the process of communicating ideas, and the ability to engage in debates over ends and means using the knowledge that we have at our disposal (see also Lynch 1982).

THE NEED FOR AN *INTERACTIONALIST* DESIGN PROCESS

Urban design occurs, as Horst Rittel recognized about architecture in general, in a unique combination of context, place, and time (Bazjanac 1974). An *interactionalist* philosophy means that perception—the Empiricist attitude of apprehending the world—and reflection—the Rationalist approach to comprehending the world—need to go hand in hand rather than being separate ways of understanding the world. It will be argued in Chapter 6 that the knowledge base for design has to be empirically derived, but there are limitations in our ability to achieve this end. There are thus certainly limits in our present understanding of cities, places, and people. We have to deal with uncertainty. One of the characteristics of creative people is their ability to deal with uncertainty and ambiguities.

No radical new paradigm emerges from these observations. There is, nevertheless, a need for a shift in the way many urban designers have thought about urban design quality from absolutist positions to relativist ones. Every urban design serves somebody's needs better than other people's. Every urban design is constrained by the resources available.

An interactionalist philosophy must also be the basis for prescribing what the processes of urban designing should be. It implies: (1) that ends and means should be designed through the interactive process of information and ideas exchange among designers and the people involved in sponsoring, operating, and using potential projects, and (2) collaborative work among professionals. The conclusion is that urban design should not be carried out in a black box hidden from nonprofessionals. The process should take place in a glass box, open to scrutiny and debate.

The general interactionalist position is thus that process and product go hand in hand. The products of urban design result from the interaction of the processes of self-conscious design and the legal and market-force framework within which people act. The process of urban designing involves the act of creating a possible future (through the intellectual activities of analysis, synthesis, prediction, and evaluation) and then implementing and managing it. The act of design and the act of implementation need to be integrated.

THE IMPLICATIONS OF REDESIGNING URBAN DESIGN

If one accepts the position that urban design has to deal with contemporary life and its evolution, there needs to be an understanding of what they are and the potential role of the built environment in the future. It means that we have to come to grips with the complexity of life—cultural differences in activities and tastes—and with designing for the future. We also have to see urban design in the broad context of the decision-making processes that democratic societies use in attempting to shape, if not determine, their futures.

The evaluation of urban designs across the world shows that building and urban spatial types that work well in one place do not necessarily work well in another (Nilsson 1973; Brolin 1974; Rapoport 1977; Lowe and Chambers 1989; Holston 1989). Some design ideas have indeed been transferred with success from one culture to another seemingly very different culture. For example, the patterns of public open space and the use of plazas in Italy, which is something that captures the heart of visiting tourists, including architects, have been used with great success as the basis for rethinking the layout of parts of central Copenhagen. There was considerable public skepticism of the possibility. The perception was that Denmark is not Italy and Danes not Italians (Gehl 1987). There are, however, many cases (see, e.g., Nilsson 1974 and Brolin 1976) where the ideas have failed when transferred cross-culturally, so much so that they have been the source for satirical writing on the importation of European models to the United States (e.g., Wolfe 1981). The conclusion is that patterns of the environment, what they afford, and the affordances that form part of people's effective environment must be seen within a cultural context. While the process of design thinking may be universal (although specific design methods may differ from culture to culture), the substantive knowledge of how the world works and the nature of the effective environment have to be framed within cultural contexts. Design has to be theory-based.

Building both substantive and procedural knowledge can take place in many ways. In the same way that there are normative theories of urban design, there are normative theories of research methods. There is, however, considerable agreement on the utility of different research approaches (see Lang 1992). Much of the information used by architects is built through casual observations of the world. Casual observation is a powerful tool but is universally regarded with caution because it is so situation- and person-specific. Making generalizations without repetitive observation has led to many erroneous conclusions about the working of the world. Some of these beliefs are much loved by architects and urban designers, who are reluctant to give them up. An example of this is the continued pursuit of community through design when rigorous research of the last thirty years shows that this end can only be attained in very specific cultural circumstances (see Willmott and Young 1960, Keller 1968, and Gottschalk 1975). There is a continued need for rigorous research and the integration of the research results into design theory. The major approaches to building theory—phenomenology and Empiricism—should be regarded as complementary rather than in opposition. Historical research is important and yields great insights into the relationship between people and the environment provided history is studied in an ecological manner (Rapoport 1990). A knowledge of history raises many questions about what we are doing now, but urban design theorists also need to look at the present world and to look at it with rigor.

Urban design like any other design is a creative statement about the future. The future is unknown. Societies try to shape it. There are differences in opinions among societies about what should be designed communally and what should be left to the myriad decisions made by individuals, corporations, and institutions. Communally, societies attempt to shape the future in particular directions by the laws they write, the socialization processes they use to raise their children and educate their professionals, the economic policies they develop, the system of property rights they adopt, the rules they establish for carrying out trade, the resources they can muster, and in many other ways. Urban design is one of them, but it has little power in shaping the future in comparison to many other processes of society. It is more of a dependent variable than an independent one—it is a resultant rather than the initiator—but the physical patterns of the world are, however, amazingly enduring.

The overall implication of this line of reasoning is that urban design has to be seen in a more multivariate manner than it is now. The result may be that apart from some notable foreground buildings and places, the future city will have a more fine-grained design than most urban design schemes have today. A good urban design may well be one that does not celebrate that it has been the subject of a self-conscious design process. Achieving this end requires a more self-effacing role than the architectural profession has had in the past. The profession generally celebrates the boldness of its designs, but the political power of the urban designers should come from their expertise. We need to have a knowledge-based approach to urban design (see also Jones 1962).

MAJOR REFERENCES

Gottschalk, Simon S. (1975). *Communities and Alternatives: An Exploration of the Limits of Planning*. Cambridge, MA: Schenkman.

Huet, Bernard (1984). "The City as Dwelling Space: Alternatives to the Charter of Athens." *Lotus International* 41: 6-16.

Lynch, Kevin (1982). "City Design: What It Is and How It Might Be Taught." In Ann Ferebee, ed., *Education for Urban Design*. Purchase, NY: Institute for Urban Design, pp. 105-111.

Mackay, David (1990). "Redesigning Urban Design." *Architect's Journal* 192, no. 2: 42-45.

Scott Brown, Denise (1982). "Between Three Stools: A Personal View of Urban Design and Pedagogy. In Ann Ferebee, ed., *Education for Urban Design*. Purchase, NY: Institute for Urban Design, pp. 132-172. Also in Scott Brown (1990), pp. 9-20.

6

A FUNCTIONALIST, EMPIRICIST URBAN DESIGN

No bold paradigmatic shift in the way urban design is considered is described here. No new aesthetic product will be shown. No new physical layout principles will be presented. Rather a position on how we should be thinking about urban design will be described. The position is based on the utility and limitations of the Rationalist and Empiricist approaches to urban design that we have inherited from our predecessors. The utility of Rationalist thinking must be tempered with a strong Empirical understanding of the world and its people if urban design is to make substantive contributions to society and thus make progress as a field of endeavor. Such a proposal may appear to have internal contradictions, but they can be resolved. The direction that urban design thought should take in the future described here represents the attempt by a number of people—visionaries and practitioners—to learn from the successes and failures of the past streams of thought that have informed architecture and urban design. While it recognizes that the "Modernists almost got it right," it represents no nostalgic return to the past.

The observation has been made that urban designers need to sharpen the way they are working (Scott Brown 1982; Ostler 1987; Mackay 1990). We need to enhance our ability to ask more penetrating questions about what ought to be done than we are now. In particular, there is a need for urban designers: (1) to deal with the world in a more multivariate way than they do at present, (2) to understand the cultural framework in which they are working, and thus (3) to generate multivariate and culturally congruent design solutions. It is possible to fruitfully consider how to reorient urban design now because we can learn from the work of the last twenty years. We can also learn from the substantial increase in empirical research of the past few decades on how the environment is experienced and the designing process.

One of the important lessons from the research is that architects and laypeople focus on different variables in looking at the city and thus often possess radically different views of what a good city should be. Designers look ahead to cities and precincts that might exist. These views are biased by their own images of what good people and good lives are. Laypeople tend to look at specific problems in terms of their own lives. Any approach to urban design needs to be able to recognize these differences and the ambiguities they represent. Similarly, architects as observers and architects as designers pay attention to radically different variables. Thus Louis Kahn was able to say that "a street wants to be a room," but in design, to consider streets simply as routes for rapidly moving traffic. The act of designing shifts the definition of the problem to be addressed away from its original definition as designers start to pursue their own interests, particularly their concerns for geometric rationality. There is a need for conceptual clarity in thinking about the nature of the designed environment and about the nature of designing. This clarity can only be achieved if we have a conceptually clear theoretical framework for our work.

THE MEANING OF A THEORETICAL APPROACH TO URBAN DESIGN

All architectural and urban design schemes are based on some theoretical propositions whether or not the designer can be articulate about them. In this sense, a design is the behavioral correlate of a set of views held by a designer to the extent that the broader society allows them to be expressed. The discussion of the interrelationships between the nature of society, the designer's values, and the knowledge base from which the designer is working is not,

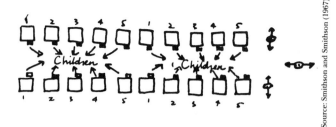

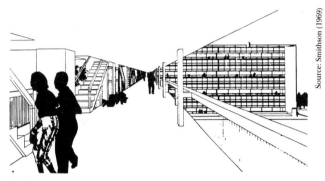

1. The Street as a Catalyst for Life. Drawing by Peter Smithson

2. Streets Equivalent, Deck Housing. Drawing by Peter Smithson (1953)

3. Schematic Plan for Center City, Philadelphia (1956–1957)

Figure 6-1: Observing and Designing
Architects always face the difficulty of turning observations about human life and the built environment into design solutions for the future. The Smithsons (1) and Louis Kahn recognized the importance of the street in human life. The Smithsons' design for the equivalent of streets in deck housing (2), and Kahn's design for central Philadelphia (3), however, show little of the observations carried over into design. The Neo-Traditional movement in urban design has applied existing patterns to design with some success, but how much should urban designers replicate what exists? (See also Fig. 24–5.)

however, what is generally recognized by architects as theory. The view presented here is an emerging one.

In recent years, in the hands of the practitioners held in the highest esteem by the profession, architectural design has, in everyday architectural English, become more theoretical (see Lavin 1990). What is meant by this observation is that recent works of design more frequently portray a clear architectural idea than in the past. Such theories constitute the intellectual aesthetic component of design (see Chapters 16 and 17, respectively, on meeting cognitive and aesthetic needs). Few people, however, are concerned with architects' ideas per se. They are interested in the resulting built forms and the experiences the patterns afford for them. Thus another concern has to be with how the world is experienced by people. In designing, the goal is to achieve a built environment that is congruent with and enhances human experience (see also Rasmussen 1959). A "theoretical approach to urban design" here simply means that both the ideological stance of the designer and the knowledge on which it is based must be open to scrutiny and debate.

The utility of having a clear theoretical framework for urban design practice is threefold (see Boulding 1956; A. Kaplan 1964; Rittel 1971; Lang 1980, 1987a; Eagleton 1990). Good theory: (1) helps us make sense of what is otherwise a chaotic world, (2) enhances our ability to handle multivariate problems in design, and (3) improves our ability to predict the outcomes of our designs with accuracy. Without good theory, we tend to reduce the world to a simple form so that we can provide a conceptual scheme to handle it.

A particular understanding of the word "theory" is implied in the above discussion. Certainly, theory is used in a number of ways and means different things to different people. There is indeed considerable confusion about what is meant by *architectural theory* or *urban design theory*. Designers have generally not used the term in the same way that the academic disciplines have. By *theory* designers generally mean the set of design principles that are used by an individual or school of thought to generate architectural or urban patterns (Gutman 1972). The principles have been described well in the past, but the reasons for their existence have seldom been explicit. Recently, however, sets of very clearly articulated design principles have been developed by academics and practitioners alike. These principles are supported by explicit explanations or arguments for their external validity. Many of them are based on empirical knowledge (e.g., Alexander et al. 1977; Regnier and Pynoos 1989; Preiser, Fischer, and White 1991). At the same time, there continue to be sets of design principles promulgated on the Rationalist position. Geoffrey Broadbent (1990) has recently made a comprehensive effort to categorize the range of these theories/philosophies of urban design. He calls them *concepts* "of urban space design" rather than theories.

In the sciences, and increasingly in the design fields, theory consists of a system of statements that are held to describe and explain a phenomenon or process (see Franck 1987). In a sense, traditional architectural theory does the same—it describes the principles and the design solutions that result from their application—but the concept of theory in the design fields can be enriched. Based on the ideas of a number of researchers, I have argued elsewhere (Lang 1980, 1987a, 1990) that in architecture, and possibly other applied fields, it is useful to distinguish between statements of how and why phenomena and processes work and statements of quality, or goodness.

Borrowing, as others have done, from standard elementary school English grammar, I call the former *positive theory* because it consists of *assertions* of truths and explanations for them. The latter is called *normative theory* because it consists of value-laden positions on what should be done.

Positive theory may not be a good term because many people insist on linking *positive* and *positivism*. However, I have let the term stand because it seems to be the simplest and boldest statement of intent in developing descriptions and explanations of phenomena and processes. The goal is to have a positive theory of architecture and urbanism based on life experiences in order to get away from the autonomous nature of Rationalist theory that has existed in architecture at least since Jacques-Nicolas-Louis Durand's tenure at the Ecole Polytechnique at the beginning of the nineteenth century (Pérez Gómez 1983). The goal is to understand the underlying structure of the world and the way people use it and to get away from simplistic standards of good taste governed by an elite.

It is also possible to distinguish between statements about the environment and statements about the processes of design. The former, for want of a better label, is commonly called *substantive theory* and the latter *procedural theory*. There is thus a two-by-two matrix for the structure of theory for architectural and urban design. This matrix is shown in Fig. 6-2. Filling in this matrix is an eclectic process. It is not the purpose of this book to do so. Rather, the attitudes implicit in an Empiricist approach to building the information that should be contained in the boxes will be described.

Subject Matter of Theory	Philosophical Orientation of Theory	
	Positive	*Normative*
Procedural	Positive Procedural Theory	Professed
		Practiced
Substantive	Positive Substantive Theory	Professed
		Practiced

Figure 6-2: A Model of the Segments of Architectural Theory

BUILDING THE POSITIVE THEORETICAL BASE FOR URBAN DESIGN

If one accepts the model of the structure of architectural and urban design theory presented here, there needs to be an understanding how to fill in the model. All architects have sets of ideas, rules of thumb, experiences, scientific knowledge, and design principles that can be divided, not necessarily easily, into the four basic sets of knowledge explicit in the model. All architects have some knowledge of how the world works, of the values and positions that exist in the field about what constitutes a good city or a good

plaza; all have some models, both positive and normative, of the design process in their heads. They draw on this information all the time and their experiences often change it. If this knowledge is explicit and in a form that can be clearly articulated as a theory or method, it can be examined and evaluated in terms of its relative successes and failures. Much of the information is based on casual observations of the world and on the designer's internalized experience. Much is erroneous. High-density environments are neither better nor worse per se than any other density, public transit is not necessarily better than private, and so on (see also Mikellides 1980).

"How can this knowledge best be built?" "How should it be built?" These are normative, not scientific, questions. Many architects advocate the Rationalist approach of contemplation on the world, others a purely intuitive process. The latter continues to be highly attractive as it supports the self-image of the architect as a fine artist. After all, "the best architects and urban designers were fine artists first!" and "You have to *feel* what is good!" are expressions of opinions that are widely influential in the design fields. Architects have to have feelings. All people do! There are, however, some fundamental problems in relying on this approach to building architectural theory, as there are for any field. The novelist Milan Kundera (1990) has noted:

> [Once these feelings] are considered values in themselves, criteria for truth, justification for certain behavior, they become frightening. When feelings supplant rational thought, they become the basis for the absence of understanding, for intolerance. . . . All over the world people nowadays prefer to judge rather than to understand, to answer rather than to ask.

Much of the knowledge of architects is self-referent, culturally biased, highly ethnocentric, and often close-mindedly justified and universally applied. The fundamental problem is that it is largely obtained casually. The alternative is an Empiricist approach. Arguments for such an approach to design have been made, implicitly or explicitly, in a number of manifestos on urban design (see Chapter 23). Interestingly enough in a major one from the late 1970s, the advocacy for Empiricism applies only to the technological aspects of city building. The human one was to be intuitive and Rationalist ("Charter of Machu Picchu," 1979). It shows our unwillingness to directly deal with the problems we face.

We are born with some knowledge about how to operate in the world. Some intellectual and physiological processes evolve with maturation. Others are learned (E. Gibson 1969). There are, however, only two basic ways of building insights into how the world works: observing and asking. Some people argue that there is also an extrasensory perception. Observation and asking may be direct or may be mediated through the eyes and ears of others: social scientists, novelists, poets, filmmakers. Direct observational techniques vary from the casual observations we carry out as part of everyday life to scientific experimentation. Our beliefs and knowledge of the world come from all these sources. The question is how best to build up our knowledge of the way in which the public realm is experienced and used.

Educators, novelists, and social scientists all bring our attention to elements of the city using their own research methods. Novelists and poets have provided us with strong verbal models of many places: Charles Dickens's Coketown and Theodore Dreiser's Chicago are fixed in the minds of many readers. It is a negative image of what the city affords. Walt Whitman and Kenneth Slessor, in contrast, are among the few poets who provide a more positive image by celebrating the joys of urban life. Filmmakers and cartoonists have provided us with images not only of the present city, good and bad, but also of future ones. In contrast to these fields, which are neither involved in accurately representing the present nor directly involved in creating a future, the professional design fields need to base design theory on a theory of how we experience and learn to experience the world around us.

The process of perceptual learning includes making finer and finer discriminations of the elements of the universe that our perceptual mechanisms enable us to attend to as well as making broader and broader classifications of the phenomena we perceive (J. Gibson 1966; E. Gibson 1969; see also Kolb 1984). There are a number of current approaches to viewing the built environment that might be considered as the basis for building architectural theory. Three of them—hermeneutics, phenomenology, and empiricism—have particularly strong advocates. The hermeneutic interpretation of architectural history may help us formulate some hypotheses about what is happening today and may also provide historical examples of the issues we are now addressing; however, the second two in combination deal more directly with the world today, something few architectural theorists seem willing to do. These three approaches promise much but also have major drawbacks; thus it is important to understand what they offer because much of the substantive theory in this book is drawn from research results based on these three methods.

Hermeneutics

Hermeneutics is a positive theory of understanding and interpretation (Ricoeur 1975; Gadamer 1976; Steiner 1989). It is a systematic method for explicating the interpretative exposition of texts, originally scriptural and classical ones and then ethical and legal ones. Interpretation has a number of meanings: (1) deciphering the meaning of a text, (2) translating one language into another language, and (3) "acting out" material. In the last sense any new work is an analysis and critique of all work done before because it differs from them. Although not intended for that pur-

pose, it has been applied to architectural criticism.

Hermeneutics is an intuitive form of reasoning that has attracted a number of architectural scholars because it is close to the concept of artistic interpretation that architects enjoy. The assumption is that the built environment can be treated as a text. Its meanings are open to interpretation depending on its context. This view is similar to that held by many cultural anthropologists (e.g., Morris 1938).

Hermeneutics uses rhetoric and metaphor to develop understanding. Metaphorically, the built environment is like a text—it is open to interpretation. During the 1970s, Structuralist semiologists, and others with a more practical orientation (e.g., Prak 1968), found it easy to think of architecture as a language (see also Maldonado 1989). The use of metaphor is a prime technique for creating hypotheses, particularly about environmental meanings. The goal of architectural theory in using the hermeneutic approach is to understand tradition and to deal with the future by understanding different ways of looking for sequels to our present situation—scenarios for the future. It is an approach that tends to eschew evidence from the world itself. Indeed there is a great reluctance to test assertions—its positive statements—using means other than logical analysis. It assumes that because Empiricism has not addressed many issues, it cannot. In this way hermeneutics is a development of Rationalism and the mechanism for extrapolating empirical knowledge into the future.

Phenomenology

Phenomenology is a *descriptive* approach to research based on the careful observation and interpretation of what is observed. It is an attempt to understand the world from within the mind of a human being. As such, it is a response to Positivism and has its origins in early-twentieth-century introspectionism. It is perceived as a method of discovery focusing on variations in perceptions that may lead to new empirical formulations (Ihde 1986). It is an approach to research much favored by many recent architects and architectural theorists because it is based on *intuitive insight*. "The phenomenologist hopes that through sincerity, perseverance, and care, he or she will see the phenomenon more fully and deeply" (Seamon 1987). The accuracy of the description is established through the comparison of one phenomenologist's insights to those of other phenomenologists. While a number of methods (see De Rivera 1984) have been identified for carrying out phenomenological research, the basic approach is largely one of thoughtful reflection.

The basic strength of the phenomenological approach is that it attempts to look at phenomena holistically in a largely uncontrolled manner (Vesely 1989). The uneasiness with which many researchers view phenomenology as a theory-building approach stems from the recognition that there have been many counterintuitive discoveries in

1. East Side, New York

2. Southfields, Michigan

3. Taby Centrum, Sweden

Photograph courtesy of Ann Strong

Figure 6–3: Intuitively Obvious Design Solutions

In *Architecture for People,* Byron Mikellides (1980a) presents ten intuitively obvious but nevertheless erroneous beliefs that designers have about people and their environments. It is almost universally believed that high-density environments, with people living in high-rise buildings in mixed-use areas (1), are bad while setting buildings back with lots of open space around them is good (2). These observations can be accurate but the world is replete with examples of the opposite. Designers have often felt that places they visit and admire (e.g., 3) both function well and can be transferred across cultures with impunity.

the social and behavioral sciences and in architecture during the past thirty years (see Mikellides 1980). There is a need for greater confidence in the observations being made than phenomenology yields. Still, the phenomenological approach has enriched much design thinking.

Without doubt, both casual observation and phenomenology have provided many important insights into the nature of the experiencing of the environment and of architecture and urban layouts. These contributions are represented, for instance, by the work of Christian Norberg Schulz (1965, 1980) and Yi-Fu Tuan (1977) on the "sense of place." The reluctance of phenomenologists to have their ideas systematically tested is based on their perception that any testing is likely to be piecemeal and will reduce the wholeness of their findings. Embraced by many architects in response to the failure of the Modern movements to deal with geomancy and other symbolic phenomena, phenomenological research continues to be a major source of hypotheses about the nature of human experiencing of the built world. While this book relies heavily on the increasing body of phenomenological research as well as on the less systemic intuitive observations of many architects, the limitations of both sources of information and openness to cultural bias must also be recognized.

Empiricism

The Empiricist, in contrast, is generally understood to prefer quantitative measures as the basis for drawing conclusions and building theories. This position has been contrasted with that of the theoretician who is attracted to developing generalizations about the world (Reissman 1964). These views of Empiricism are more limited than the one intended here. Research based on the scientific method principles of operational definition, controlled observation, repeated observation, and generalizability of the phenomena being studied is without doubt the methodological goal in architectural research for theory building, but often quasi-scientific methods have to be used. The scientific ideal then becomes a standard, or yardstick, against which the methods used in a study and the degree of confidence in the results can be assessed.

There are two basic Empiricist approaches to building the theoretical basis for urban design: (1) the creation of an urban and/or urban design *typology,* and (2) an *ecological approach.* The former focuses on the classification of urban and suburban forms/geometrical patterns into categories, and the second on the systematic analysis of the forces shaping cities and how the resulting patterns are experienced and evaluated by different people.

Typology

Before the development of self-conscious design processes, all designed artifacts resulted from the application of tradition, habit, and imitation. New types evolved in an evolutionary set of steps, although there were clearly major, possibly serendipitous, new discoveries. The masters of the Modern movement in architecture, in contrast, focused on what they perceived to be the problems at hand, characterizing them as being different from those that architects had been required to address in preindustrial societies. They were visionaries. Most of their followers were practitioners who had neither the scope nor the opportunity to continue designing in the creative way of the early Rationalists and fell back on the process of mimesis—of adapting particular standard solutions to the situation at hand (Marmot 1982). Most architects still work this way and show little inclination to work in any other (Colquhoun 1967; Francescato 1989). Without doubt all architects have a set of patterns of form, and a set of design principles, in their heads. These patterns are developed through their formal education, professional work, and experiences with the world. They rely on types. If this is so then the study of types is a necessary, although incomplete, basis for building urban design theory.

In the design fields, typology involves the study of urban forms, place forms (e.g., R. Krier 1979, 1990), and building forms (e.g., Sherwood 1978 on housing), and their classification into sets based on geometric, use, or symbolic similarities. Existing American cities, it was argued in Chapter 2, have evolved over time as the result of myriad decisions by myriad decision makers, although some major decisions about their infrastructure may well have been developed by a relatively few designers. The observation of typologists is that there are relatively few basic urban form types and that all cities are variants of these forms. Similarly, their components are variants of some basic pattern/use types or models.

The classification of cities and their elements based on their formal (i.e., geometrical) characteristics into types is indeed a useful instrument for description and analysis. Types are, however, also regarded as the basis for the future design of cities and their components. This view has been argued most forcefully by what has been called the "Italian School of Architecture of the 1960s." The work of people such as Piergiorgio Gerosa (1979), Aldo Rossi (1982), and Vittorio Gregotti (1990) has become extremely influential now, almost thirty years later. It has guided the thinking of both architects and urban designers about the nature of the built environment and the nature of design processes in much of the world. As a result there has been a resurgence of the study of types as the basis for architectural and urban design (see also Broadbent 1990).

The argument for typology in architecture is based on the perception that the "new" forms that were developed by the Modernists have not worked, and that we need to go back to traditional patterns that are perceived to be loved by all. The argument is based on an assumption that, on the surface, seems patently absurd but should neither be lightly dismissed nor enthusiastically embraced. The assumption is that, most, if not all, of the patterns of urban form that are required to create cities for the future already exist in present cities, and that solutions to our present-day and future urban problems need not be invented but rather existing patterns need to be reapplied (see Gosling and Maitland 1984a, pp. 134–137). The understanding of the existence of recurrent urban forms that has resulted from the development of typology has, however, yielded a limited understanding of what each type affords different people. An ecological understanding of urban, precinct, and building types and their affordances is essential if specific types are not to be misused in the future (see also Rapoport 1990).

At the same time, population growth, changes in technology—refrigeration, communications media, transportation—and changes in social and political systems have indeed created new urban patterns, particularly in the United States—the shopping center, strip shopping, industrial campuses, mini-cities (or edge cities), the airport city. New types are also being sought by architects. The *pedestrian pocket* is such a concept, although it can be argued that there is a precedent for it in Radburn, New Jersey (Kelbaugh 1989; Calthorpe 1991). One of the problems facing those using a strictly typological approach to designing, as Christopher Alexander and his colleagues (1968) recognized in the development of their pattern language, is that there is a temptation to see present problems in terms of deviations of present patterns from known types. One of the reasons for the continuing use of types in urban design is that defining what the problems are that need to be addressed in other than a typological manner is fraught with conceptual and ideological difficulties. However, the problems need to be faced rather than avoided.

Ecological Approaches

The goal of the ecological approach to building empirical theory is to combine theoretical insights with systematic research. The goal is to come to an understanding of human institutions and groupings, their behaviors within different patterns of physical settings, and with how humans use elements of the physical setting to create aesthetic displays for themselves and each other. This line of thinking has its roots in the Chicago school of sociology of the 1930s and the work of sociologists such as Robert E. Park. Unfortunately, despite their research agenda, they had a limited concern with the layout of the physical environment, and certainly almost none with the architectural environment (Reissman 1964; Michelson 1976).

1. Central Business District (CBD), Columbus, Indiana

CBD District	MAX. FAR	MAX. Height	REMARKS
O-1+	10	450ft	figures are approximate
O-1	8	300ft	
O-2	6	250ft	
OB&R	5	200ft	maximums are attainable only with residential areas
MU	3	100ft	can be encoded if residential use

CBD Height/Bulk Envelope

2. CBD Height and Bulk Ordinance, Bellevue, Washington

Source: Hinshaw (1983)

3. Pioneer Square Area, Seattle

Figure 6-4: Typology

Typology is the study and classification of buildings and urban spaces according to some common characteristic: plan configuration, use, form, material, style, location, meaning, idea, and so on. We give labels to specific types: small town central business district (CBD) (1), "wedding cake" height and bulk ordinance (2), pedestrian mall (3), and so on. The labels conjure up an image and enable us to discuss topics with each other with relative ease, but labels also distort our images of places. Looking at and designing the built environment in terms of types can thus be both useful and misleading.

Ecological theory as conceived here is concerned with understanding human behavior in the everyday architectural and physical world. Its basic concepts were introduced in Chapter 1 of this book, but its roots, as outlined by Gerhard Kaminski (1989), are in the disparate works of Urie Bronfenbrenner (1970, 1979), Eleanor J. Gibson (1969), and James J. Gibson (1966, 1979), and in the work of Roger Barker (1968) as developed by Robert Bechtel (1977), Alan Wicker (1969, 1979), and other of Barker's students. The ecological approach described in this book is a unification of these approaches. It promises to serve the architectural profession well in making decisions about the shaping of the future.

Two attitudes implicit in the ecological approach to theory building for urban design have to be recognized: (1) that research results have to be related to the reality of a multidimensional world (i.e., to the world of human experience, or for other animals, to their world), and not simply the outcome of controlled laboratory conditions, and (2) that research must focus on theory building—it is concerned with explanations, not simply descriptions. It is concerned with developing an understanding.

The world that is of concern to the architect can be described in many ways (see Chapter 9, The Elements of Urban Design). Suffice to say here that it needs to be considered within an ecological framework, as described in Chapter 1, which is the world of surfaces composed of materials with different textures, pigmentations, and illuminated differently. The surfaces are arranged to enclose spaces to a greater or lesser degree. These surfaces and spaces afford different activities and in conjunction with an activity constitute a *behavior setting* (Barker 1968; Bechtel 1977; Wicker 1979; Kaminski 1989). The ability to perceive the *affordances* of a physical setting, or *milieu*, depends on one's physiological and intellectual *competencies* (Lawton 1977). Whether one will use the affordances will depend on one's *predispositions* and one's perception of the *costs and rewards* involved. These settings are related to each other by boundary properties and are nested in an overall social and cultural system. We give names to specific settings and regard them as *places*. We classify them into types.

The research agenda of an ecological approach to building theory for the design field focuses on understanding the use and utility of the different behavior settings that exist in the world and the nature of human displays composed of the elements of the milieu. The goal is to understand these affordances within different cultural frames and for different classes of people. Our knowledge about these differences and similarities is only partially developed. It can never be complete, but we

1. Plaza, 16th and Court Streets, Denver

2. Plaza, 16th and Court Streets, Denver

3. Wichita, Kansas

Courtesy of Marvin S. Krout

Figure 6–5: The Ecological Environment

The ecological environment is the world of everyday life. All behavior takes place in some physical setting, which consists of surfaces that are textured, pigmented, and illuminated in different ways (1). Some of these surfaces are objects and others surround us. Each pattern of these elements possesses properties—its affordances—that enable it to be used and perceived to be meaningful by people in different ways. A hard plaza on a hot day is not very attractive (2). The setting shown in (3) affords shade, viewing, a sense of territorial control, and thus a sense of security for these four people.

understand the variables of concern much better now than the Modernists did, and future research using a wide variety of approaches modeled on the scientific method promises much (see, e.g., Michelson 1975; Marans and Ahrentzen 1987; and Low 1987).

A NORMATIVE STANCE

The approach to urban design that will be described in this book adapts and develops existing approaches. It advocates a reliance on empirical knowledge to the extent that it is available. For want of a better label it is simply called an Empiricist approach. As such, it follows the line of thinking of people such as Kevin Lynch and Christopher Alexander. Adding Functionalist to the label shows its intellectual heritage in Modernism and its goal of creating functional architectural environments.

A Neo-Modernist Approach to Urban Design

Neo-Modernist makes no etymological sense, but it does convey the spirit of an attitude toward design. Urban design should be concerned with the range of issues addressed by the Modernists in addition to the more pragmatic concerns involved in getting projects built.

Building on the arguments of the previous chapters, this stance means that urban designs should, first of all, be functional. This position, in turn, means that urban designers should be concerned with social as well as physical design functions and issues rather than assuming that the social consequences of urban design work are somebody else's problem. In addition, urban designers should be explicitly concerned with the future functions rather than implicitly taking the position that either tomorrow will be the same as today or that tomorrow will take care of itself. While visionaries and practitioners should both be addressing urban design in this way, the concern here is with urban design practice today and in the immediate future.

If the basic advocacy is for a functionalist urban design, then the concept of function needs to be broadened from that held by the Modernists (see Chapter 7, Functionalism). All designs do and should serve a set of purposes. That is their function. All urban design schemes are based on some social schema in terms of activities to be housed and aesthetic displays to be created. In a purely market-oriented approach to urban design, this stance usually means supporting the status quo. Such an approach has strong advocates, but the position taken here is that this stance leads to too many long-run oppor-

1. The Unité d'habitation at Marseilles by Le Corbusier (1946-1952)

2. Alton West Slab Blocks, Roehampton, England (1952)

3. Housing Estate at Crosbie, Everton, Liverpool, England (1962–1966)

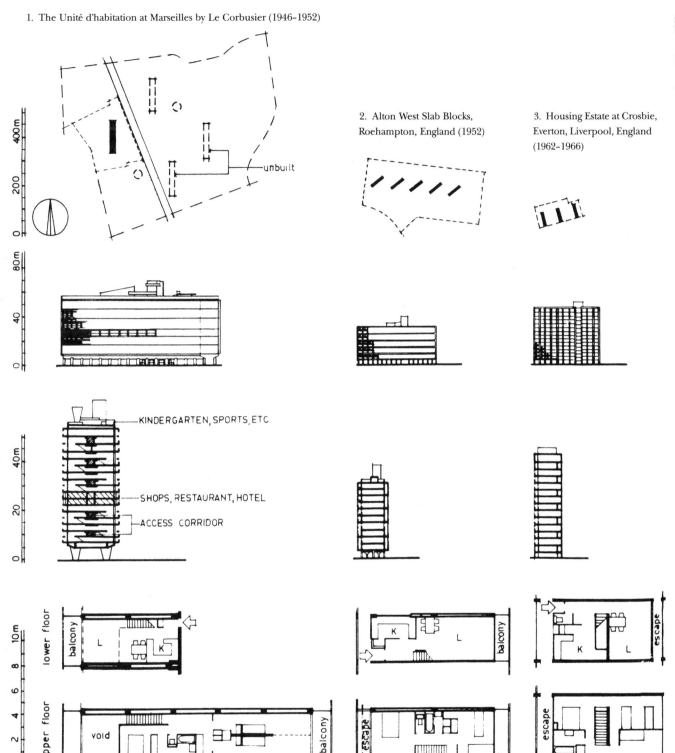

KINDERGARTEN, SPORTS, ETC

SHOPS, RESTAURANT, HOTEL

ACCESS CORRIDOR

Figure 6-6: The Legacy of Le Corbusier

The Unité d'habitation (1; see also Fig. 2-11) has been a model for many subsequent designs, which eroded Le Corbusier's idea (Marmot 1982). Pruitt Igoe, designed by Minoru Yamasaki (see Figs. 4-1(3) and 5(3)), did not have the social amenities of the original type, while the size of the flats and the buildings at Alton West (2), designed by the London County Council architects, are considerably tighter than in the Unité. The scheme, known locally as the "Piggeries," designed by the Liverpool City Architects is even tighter (3). We are now seeing similar adaptations of Bernard Tshmumi's Parc de la Villette.

tunity costs for societies. Urban designers need to understand the social consequences of their work rather than simply stating that social issues fall outside the perimeter of their concern. Stating that they are merely technocrats serving the marketplace is to give urban designers an insufficient role. Sensible though it is in getting projects implemented more easily, it is not acceptable given the problems facing the world and individual societies. All these positions are as political as any already described in this book.

It is, however, unreasonable to expect an urban designer to be also a designer of social systems. That is a politician's role supported by a whole host of social scientists and social planners. The position taken here is that urban designers must know the interrelationship between the physical environment and the nature of social systems. They must understand and be articulate about the social impact of designing one way rather than another (i.e., about what any layout affords and does not afford). They must know what the affordances of different patterns of the environment are for different people. They must design "with man in mind" (Perin 1970), "as if people mattered" (Cooper and Sarkissian 1986). It is unreasonable to blame Minoru Yamasaki for the Pruitt Igoe fiasco (see Figs. 4–1(3) and 5–3 and Montgomery 1966). He was working within the conventional Rationalist architectural wisdom of his times. It would be extremely foolish not to learn from it, particularly about the thought processes that brought Pruitt Igoe to fruition. It is now reasonable to blame architects, in the United States at least, who design major residential complexes without an understanding of the work of Oscar Newman (1972, 1980a) and Cooper and Sarkissian (1986) if their designs fail to be pleasant, livable environments at any population density.

An Empiricist Approach to Urban Design

An Empiricist approach to urban design may seem to be a contradiction in terms. Urban designers *design* the built environment or aspects of it either directly or by the guidelines and other policies they develop for other designers to follow. They deal with the future. They have to look ahead, make predictions. Empiricists build positive theory from evidence, or look for evidence to test hypotheses about theories. In this sense architects are like Empiricists, for every design is an hypothesis—but it is an hypothesis about the future. Buildings are tested in use when built. Urban designers use knowledge—or rather, it is argued here, should use knowledge—as the basis for making design decisions. Empirically derived knowledge is knowledge about the present, or more precisely, the past, because observation precedes conclusion. Designing will always be carried out with a degree of uncertainty about the nature of the future and about the outcome of a design. A knowledge-based approach to design reduces this uncertainty but it cannot eliminate it.

An Empiricist approach to urban design assumes: (1) that the process of urban design involves the building of arguments for a particular future three-dimensional pattern for a city, a neighborhood, or their parts, (2) that the arguments should be built on evidence, and (3) this evidence, to the extent possible, should be based on empirical research rather than on personal intuition or hermeneutic or phenomenological approaches. This statement does not deny the utility of intuition in the design process, especially in generating design ideas. It does, however, assume that relying on one's personal experience is a limited and limiting, but not worthless, approach to building arguments and thus to designing buildings, precincts, and cities for the future. The number of counterintuitive results of our work in the past clearly demonstrates the failure of the intuitive powers of even the greatest architects.

There are still major limitations to our knowledge so we often have to rely on our own beliefs, but this is not the ideal, as urban design after urban design has shown. The act of designing is, however, certainly easier if we can rely on internalized knowledge. This is an argument for architects having a strong theoretical framework within which knowledge can be internalized but also recalled and articulated so that it can be amended and/or communicated to other people as the basis for design. Ultimately we have to recognize that urban design deals with the future. The future cannot be studied empirically—it is created. The failure of the Modern movement was based on its reliance on piecemeal evidence and a largely atheoretical mode of thinking in the terms described here—it eschewed a study of life

Typological and Ecological Approaches

Any urban design ideology has to state a position on two matters: the *process* and the *product*. Most statements on urban design consist of concepts of the product—models of the ideal layout of the city based on a set of criteria. For instance, the Radiant City is a physical model for the future city (see Fig. 2–10(6)). Health, social equality, efficiency in circulation, and rational geometry can be regarded as the basic criteria for its design (Le Corbusier 1934). Similarly, Broadacre City (see Fig. 2–9) is a physical representation of the future based on a concept of Jeffersonian democracy (Wright 1958). Compact City is a more generalized model of the future city based on the need to manage energy more conservatively than in the past (Dantzig and Saaty 1973). Few of these statements on good design say much about the processes of decision making that create the design—the design process—or the rights of people involved in choosing their futures. Few say much about the economics of implementation, although a number do advocate institutional mechanisms such as limited-dividend companies as developers (e.g., Howard 1902 and Stein 1950).

There are many ideas about designs—patterns of the environment—and what they afford that can be explored without a concern for how they might be implemented. The position taken here, however, is that a multivariate, problem-solving process for designing is essential if we are not to be trapped by existing types and short cut the exploration of design possibilities. The general nature of such processes is described more fully in Chapter 21, The Urban Designing Process, and the methodological and ethical issues that it raises in Chapter 22, Procedural Issues in Urban Design, while the normative conclusion is presented in Part Three of the book. It is important, however, to note the implications for the nature of the positive theoretical basis for design here.

Typological and ecological approaches to design are often contrasted (Reissman 1964). A purely typological approach to designing is essentially a hill-climbing approach involving the adjustments of existing types to the situations faced by adjusting the type to the context in which it is applied. The danger is that the hill you are climbing is not only not the tallest hill but simply the wrong hill.

An ecological approach to the development of substantive theory implies a systems approach to design (see Chadwick 1971). It assumes that change is a component of the system. Urban design efforts not only change parts of the city but become a catalyst for change (Attoe and Logan 1989). An ecological approach to urban design is tied into a problem-solving approach to design rather than a typological approach. Yet it seems to be impossible to move through the design process without some image of a solution in mind. This image may change as one moves through the process, but one needs an image to be able to begin. A study of types is a useful basis for forming images, but one must avoid being trapped by the initial types one has in mind and be able to develop solutions for which no precedent exists. One can only do this sensibly if one has a strong substantive theoretical knowledge of the world that enables one to ask good questions. Such a body of theory must start with an understanding of the full nature of Functionalism in design. It must explain the human purposes that can be served by different patterns of the designed environment in a manner akin to the Structuralist approach to description and explanation based originally on the ideas of French anthropologist Claude Lévi-Strauss (Lawrence 1989). It must, however, be seen from the designers' viewpoint.

CONCLUSION

Purists will have misgivings about calling the approach to urban design to be described in this book a Functionalist, Empiricist approach. There are three major worries: ideologies cannot be empirical, the focus on theory is often contrasted with empirical approaches, and the embracing of a variety of research methods to build theory is not strictly an Empiricist position. The legitimacy of the position rests on its advocacy of empirically derived theory as the basis for designing and making predictions about the use and impact of potential design solutions. There are limitations to a science of design as the basis for designing as is generally recognized, but the rejection of the knowledge that empirical and other research has yielded simply because it is not intuitively derived seems foolhardy.

MAJOR REFERENCES

Franck, Karen A. (1987). "Phenomenology, Positivism, and Empiricism as Research Strategies in Environment-Behavior Research." In Ervin H. Zube and Gary T. Moore, eds., *Advances in Environment, Behavior, and Design 1.* New York: Plenum, pp. 59–67.

Kaminski, Gerhard (1989). "The Relevance of Ecologically Oriented Conceptualizations to Theory Building in Environment and Behavior Research." In Ervin H. Zube and Gary T. Moore, eds., *Advances in Environment, Behavior and Design 2.* New York: Plenum, pp. 3–36.

Kolb, D. A. (1984). *Experiential Learning.* Englewood Cliffs, NJ: Prentice-Hall.

Lang, Jon (1987a). "The Nature and Utility of Theory." In *Creating Architectural Theory: The Role of the Behavioral Sciences in Environmental Design.* New York: Van Nostrand Reinhold, pp. 13–20.

Lawrence, Roderick (1989). "Structuralist Theories in Environment-Behavior-Design Research: Applications for Analyses of People and the Built Environment." In Ervin H. Zube and Gary T. Moore, eds., *Advances in Environment, Behavior and Design 2.* New York: Plenum, pp. 37–70.

Maslow, Abraham (1966). "Experiential Knowledge and Spectator Knowledge." In *The Psychology of Science.* New York: Harper & Row.

Rasmussen, Steen Eiler (1959). *Experiencing Architecture.* Cambridge, MA: MIT Press.

Robinson, Julia (1990). "Architectural Research: Incorporating Myth and Science." *Journal of Architectural Education* 44, no. 1:20–32.

Seamon, David (1987). "Phenomenology and Environment-Behavior Research." In Ervin H. Zube and Gary T. Moore, eds., *Advances in Environment, Behavior, and Design 1.* New York: Plenum, pp. 3–27.

Steiner, George (1989). *Real Presences.* Chicago: University of Chicago Press.

PART II

FUNCTIONALISM REDEFINED

Ira C. Keller Fountain, Portland, Oregon

The dictum most closely associated with the Modern movement in architecture and urban design is "Form follows function"—a slogan ascribed to a number of people. Other dicta are Frank Lloyd Wright's "Form and function are one," Ludwig Mies van der Rohe's "Less is more," and Le Corbusier's designation of a house as a "Machine for living." The most enduring of all is indeed "Form follows function" because many designers profess to subscribe to it. Indeed, the functionalist view of architecture is one of long standing.

Often function and aesthetics are regarded as two distinctive and interwoven but often competing goals of design. This distinction can be traced back to Vitruvius, two thousand years ago, but is possibly better known as it was paraphrased by Sir Henry Wotton (1624):

> In *Architecture* as in all other *Operative* Arts
> the *end* must direct the *Operation*.
> The *end* is to build well.
> Well-building hath three Conditions.
> *Commoditie, Firmenes,* and *Delight*

When this is done, the definitions of "commoditie" as function and of functionalism tend to be very limited ones. The failure to fully understand the functions that the built environment can serve, and the functions that people need it to serve, led to the "failure of the Modern movement." In this book aesthetics, "delight," will be regarded as a function.

In writing about buildings, John Ruskin stated: "The first thing to be required of a building is that it shall answer its purposes completely, permanently, and at the smallest expense" (Cook and Wedderburn 1903). Considerable debate about the purpose—the function—of architecture at both a building and an urban level continues. The degree to which architecture should be functional is still a concern to architects. This discussion is largely ill-informed because it fails to come to grips with the nature of the built environment, with models of human needs, and with the relationship between needs fulfillment and the built environment. The objective of the second major component of this book, Part II, Functionalism Redefined, is twofold: (1) to redefine function, and (2) given this definition, to display our current understanding of the nature of functionalism in urban design and the consequences of this understanding for urban designing. The whole discussion is based on the observation that "form follows function" is still a fine slogan for architecture and urban design, and that the desire to make the world a better place is a fine goal for the design professions. It is an outward-looking goal concerned with the interests of society rather than an inward-looking one concerned

with winning arguments within the profession and with being held in high esteem by one's professional peers. We must understand the nature of form and the nature of function better than we have in the past if urban design is to make progress as a professional activity.

Part II is divided into three major components. In the first, Functionalism Revisited, the whole nature of functionalism is explored. The second is the Substantive Issues in Attaining a Functional Environment and the third, the Procedural Issues in Attaining a Functional Environment. The whole examination is based on a model of human needs developed by humanist psychologist Abraham Maslow (1954, 1968, 1987). Maslow never explored the consequences of his model for architecture or urban design. These subjects fell outside the perimeter of his concern. His model does, however, raise a host of issues for urban design. Some of these are substantive issues—those concerned with the nature of the product of design—and some are procedural issues—those concerned with the process whereby designers generate designs.

Each of the three major segments of this part of the book is subdivided into subsections and/or chapters. Much of the argument presented in a linear fashion is much more tightly interwoven than the organization suggests. As a result there are many cross-references in the material covered. Some of it could quite easily have appeared in a different chapter. The eleven chapters assembled under the rubric Substantive Issues in Attaining a Functional Environment not only help define the concerns of the urban designer, presented in Chapter 9, but are also an elaboration of both the model of human needs presented in Chapter 7 and the discussion of the functions of the city presented in Chapter 8. Similarly, the Procedural Issues in Attaining a Functional Environment involve both the methodological issues in designing problems and reaching solutions as well as the ethical problems that arise when choosing one design process over another.

The basic theme throughout Part II is that there are both a set of activities required to sustain and control the communications process between people and a set of symbolic aesthetic issues—both in terms of human behavior itself and in the built environment—at each level of Maslow's hierarchy of human needs. Each chapter title shows its focus of attention, even though the discussion from one may spill over into the next. The complexity and the degree of interweaving of issues may dismay many architects, but there is an increasing societal demand for us in the design professions to recognize what we are doing and to be able to be articulate about it. The "art defense" for our actions carries little intellectual or political weight in discussions about the future. ∎

FUNCTIONALISM REVISITED

Bellevue, Washington

The model of function still most widely accepted by American architects is a narrow one inherited from the Bauhaus. In it, a functional environment is seen as one that is salubrious, efficient in providing for the basic activities of people, and efficient in the way it is built. These functions are certainly important, but there have been strong arguments against the continued use of this model. The view described here is simply that the Modernist's model is too simplistic (Fitch 1965, 1979). There is a need for a richer one.

There are two tasks in redefining functionalism in architecture and urban design. The first involves coming to an understanding of human motivations and needs, and the second, coming to an understanding of those aspects of the processes of needs fulfillment that might possibly be met or affected by the structure and materials of the built environment.

The architects of the Modern movement used models of human needs as the basis of their concept of functionalism (see Wingler 1969), but the American experience, if not the international one, suggests that we need a better model than they had. In Chapter 7, Functionalism, Abraham Maslow's model of human needs (Maslow 1987) is presented as a contrast to that of the Modernists. The model is both conceptually clearer than that used by them and more comprehensive than those of other psychologists (e.g., Leighton 1959) to which architects (e.g., Alexander 1969) have turned since the limitations of the Modernists' views became clear. These other models do, however, offer additional insights into human life and behavior that can inform the task of design (P. Peterson 1969; Mikellides 1980b). The advantage of Maslow's model is that these other models can be mapped onto it. In accepting Maslow's approach, any reductionist philosophy similar to that of the Modernists must be avoided. It is important to understand the variability in needs fulfillment within different cultural contexts and among different individuals.

Understanding the basic concepts of human behavior and needs in the abstract as the basis for a functional urban design is only half of the equation. The other is to understand the purposes served by human settlements and, more particularly, by the structure and details of their built environments. Chapter 8, The

Functions of Cities and Urban Places, takes the model of human needs and asks the question: "What purposes do human settlements serve?" Cities exist for those activities that require cooperative action among large numbers of people. They thus afford a number of primary functions: direct and mediated communication between people, economic activity, and a variety of cognitive and aesthetic ends.

The basic reason for the existence of human settlements may be economic or, perhaps, ceremonial or even recreational. In many ways it is immaterial which is the primary purpose—the functions coexist and they are manifested in the form and character of all places. In addition, any place affords important functions other than the primary one—it serves purposes that are secondary, tertiary, and so on. There are also many byproducts—latent functions—of the manifest functions of a place. Sometimes these are so important that they are instrumental in binding urban and community life together.

Cities and the places within them change as their functions change, and in changing socially and physically they change their functions. Technological innovations afford new ways of building and communicating. Many such developments taking place today suggest that the patterns of human settlements may undergo radical change in the future. At the same time, there are many forces inhibiting change—the investment in the present infrastructure, for instance. The urban designer's task is to aid the process of transformation of urban places to better meet the needs of people today, but also to keep an eye to future populations and their potential needs. ■

7

FUNCTIONALISM

Despite the criticism that Modernism has received over the years, "Form follows function" remains a good slogan for architecture and urban design provided one redefines *function*. Ultimately, what a designer regards as the range of functions of an urban design is a political not an empirical question, but we have an increasingly well developed positive understanding of people and their environments on which to base such positions. Recent research has considerably enhanced our understanding of the functions that the built environment can possibly serve. A powerful way of considering these possibilities is through an understanding of human needs. This is the position that the Modernists took. Our advantage is that the range of human needs can now be established from empirical research and the clinical experience of psychologists, as well as from introspective analyses. Any statement of the human needs served by the built environment will remain fragmentary because our understanding is incomplete. It always will be, but we can now define functionalism more completely than the Modernists did. In order to understand this assertion, it is necessary to first understand the Modernist concept of functionalism. This understanding will put a revised concept into perspective.

THE TRADITIONAL CONCEPT OF FUNCTION IN ARCHITECTURE

Twentieth-century urban design ideas have become closely related to the concept of functionalism of the Bauhaus, the de Stijl movement in Holland, and to the Rationalism of Le Corbusier (Trancik 1986). Functionalism's antecedents can be traced back a considerable time, but the concept as we know it emerged from design attitudes that developed during the nineteenth century.

The nineteenth century saw the major development of industrial production and the rise of engineering. Architects and artists were impressed by the simplicity of many engineering works. European observers were astonished at the 1851 London Exhibition, not only with the Crystal Palace design by Joseph Paxton, but also with the "simplicity, technical correctness and sureness of shapes revealed in American productions" compared to the European counterparts, which were heavily embellished with either applied or attached decoration (Giedion 1963). "All that we see of American domestic equipment breathes the spirit of comfort and fitness for purpose" (Lother Bucher, cited by Giedion, 1963). In 1852 Horatio Greenough, an American sculptor and a "herald of functionalism," wrote:

> Far be it for me to pretend that the style pointed out by our mechanics is what is sometimes miscalled an economical, a cheap style. No! It is the dearest of all styles! It costs the thought of men, much, very much thought, untiring investigation, ceaseless experiment. Its simplicity is that of justness; I had almost said, of justice.
>
> . . .
>
> By beauty, I mean the promise of function.
> By action, I mean the presence of function.
> By character, I mean the record of function.
> (Wynne and Newhall 1939; see also Giedion 1963, p. 214)

Other critics, knowledgeable of contemporary canons of good taste, were, however, dismayed by the lack of ornamentation—the dullness—of American domestic products. This divergence in taste cultures continued through the Modernist era (Eaton 1969) and still persists.

Gottfried Semper, a German exile and founder of the first English school of design in 1851, as well as one of

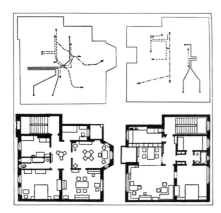

1. Functionalism in Interior Design

Source: Benevolo (1980)

2. Lafayette Park, Detroit (1953)

Source: Arkitekten International

3. Scandinavian Functionalism?

Figure 7-1: Functionalism in Urban Design
Traditional concepts of "functionalism" focus on the biological human being. Circulation was a prime concern both in interior design, as shown in these diagrams by Alexander Klein (1928) (1), and in Rationalist urban designs. The narrow definition led to the types of environments associated with the International style in architecture, and hence urban designs (2). Often it was good enough! The paradox is that the Empiricists considered more functions in their designs, but the results were considered to be less "functional." Too frequently, functionalism simply came to mean an aesthetic style (3).

the formulators of the Modern Movement's concept of functionalism, believed that industry and the physical sciences should provide a model for the arts (Banham 1960; Giedion 1963). The American furniture design that the Europeans admired fulfilled basic ergonomic requirements with a minimum of material.

The concept of functionalism was furthered in the United States by Louis Sullivan and Frank Lloyd Wright at about the time of the 1893 World's Columbian Exposition in Chicago. It was also a time of religious explorations in the United States. Theosophists, Swedenborgians, and Rosicrucians vied for attention and influence. The Chicago school of architects of the time considered form to follow not only function, narrowly defined, but also nature and various symbolic geometrical principles related to the cosmology of Hindus and Chaldeans (van der Plaat 1992). These symbols were only intelligible to the indoctrinated—they followed intellectual aesthetic principles of the past but, as they were not perceived by the uninitiated, they were seen as modern. This line of thought seems to have been displaced in American thinking by narrower concepts of functionalism brought in from Europe.

During the third decade of the twentieth century, Walter Gropius and Le Corbusier argued for an architec-

ture comparable to the functional purity of airplanes, ships, and grain elevators (Le Corbusier 1923; Wingler 1969). Functionalism in architecture came to mean technical efficiency in building construction, with ease and efficiency in the movement of people (i.e., the least movement or fewest actions) as the basis for the internal planning. Functional urban design was thus seen as hygienic, cost efficient, and efficient in the circulation of people and traffic flow while conveniently providing the basic necessities of life (see also Le Corbusier 1948). Sometimes the way climate, but more frequently the way air conditioning and energy consumption as a whole, are handled are items whose performance has to be efficient. The aesthetic quality of the environment, particularly its symbolic aspects, became a byproduct of attaining other ends.

This definition of functional buildings and urban designs is a very limited one, as people like Gropius began to recognize in the 1960s (Gropius 1962), but it is still the basis for much urban design, particularly that based on the speed of vehicular and pedestrian traffic flows. Designs based on purely Modernist functional requirements turn out dull places and, moreover, those that are inefficient in many respects, including their adapt-

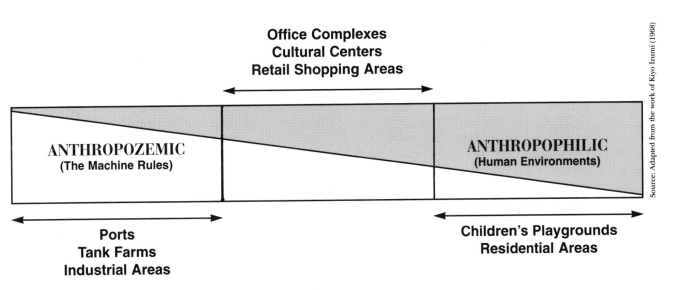

Office Complexes
Cultural Centers
Retail Shopping Areas

ANTHROPOZEMIC
(The Machine Rules)

ANTHROPOPHILIC
(Human Environments)

Ports
Tank Farms
Industrial Areas

Children's Playgrounds
Residential Areas

Source: Adapted from the work of Kiyo Izumi (1968)

Figure 7-2: Anthropozemic and Anthropophilic Environments

ability to change (J. Jacobs 1969). This result is not because traffic engineers and efficiency experts are involved, but because their ends become primary, partly because their studies are understandable, quantifiable, and efficient. As Aldo van Eyck noted:

> Instead of the inconvenience of filth and confusion, we have now the *boredom of hygiene.* The material slum has gone—but what has replaced it? Just mile upon mile of unorganized nowhere, and nobody feeling he is somewhere (Smithson 1969).

There were a number of early groups of critics of the Bauhaus concept of functionalism. One of them was the influential group, Team 10, whose members tried to base their designs on a greater range of human needs than their predecessors (Smithson 1968; Smithson and Smithson 1970). Another was Buckminster Fuller. To him the Bauhaus innovations were mere fashions without a knowledge of science behind them. In Fuller's opinion, the Bauhaus simply

> peeled off yesterday's exterior embellishment and put on instead the formalized novelties of quasi-simplicity permitted by the same hidden structural elements of modern alloys which had permitted the discarded Beaux-Arts garments (quoted in McHale 1961).

Much the same argument is today leveled at the work of architects such as Norman Foster and Richard Rogers. The striving for structural and technological dexterity has become an end in itself without a major understanding of issues of solar heat gain, or of the wearing and weathering of the built environment. Places such as the Beaubourg Centre, Place Pompidou, in Paris, which visually appear to be technologically advanced, illustrate this point (Broadbent 1990). The concern is with the symbolism of functionality, not functionality itself. Despite their criticisms, no new concept of functionalism that can be used as a working base for urban design emerged from the writings of Team 10, Buckminster Fuller, or the recent Neo-Rationalist designers.

Some critics have said the Modern designs are too functional. This point is conceded provided one has a very narrow definition of function. Other critics (e.g., Fitch 1980 and Newman 1980b) say that Modern designs have not been functional enough. This position is the one accepted here. It assumes that the definition of function of the Modernist was simply too narrow. It was based on too narrow a definition of the human being, too simple a model of people and life, and a strong antiurban bias (Wood, Brower, and Latimer 1966; Stringer 1980; Ellis and Cuff 1989).

If urban design is to serve people well, it must be concerned with the needs of people, and thus the mechanisms they use to meet those needs. The term "mechanism" needs to be interpreted broadly. Not only does it mean the patterns of the built environment, it extends to include other people and other animals, the flora of the world, and the machines people have developed to aid themselves in meeting their needs/desires. A functional environment is not simply one that meet people's needs for ease of movement and access to sunlight, but one that meets the broad ranges of needs of many diverse people and the needs of their supportive machinery. All designs involve a tradeoff between the needs of one person and another, between the needs of people per se and the needs of their equipment (Izumi 1968). In some instances the machines required to support human life comfortably, in comparison to humans themselves, have a very low tolerance for variability in the conditions around them. In such situations, paradoxically, to meet human needs, the machines need to be considered more thoroughly than the direct needs of people themselves. Serving the machines indirectly serves humans.

The concept of functionalism that emerges from this line of thought is much more complex than that of the Modernists. It is also clear that defining the functions that an urban design complex or set of urban design policies is to achieve is a *wicked* problem not a *simple* one. A wicked problem is one in which it is impossible to know, given the limits of human rationality and comprehensiveness of knowledge, whether one has defined the problem wholly or not (Rittel 1971, 1984; Bazjanac 1974; Rittel and Webber 1984). Almost certainly it has not been completely defined.

Given the limits of human knowledge and rationality, urban design problems can only be partially defined (see Cartwight 1973). The functions to be served can only be partially defined; the definition is fuller than in the past. *Function* has been thought of in simple terms—in terms of a limited and completely defined set of variables. Kidding ourselves by having a simple model of the human being or by using ourselves as the model of the human being for urban designing is not helpful in attaining rich and satisfying urban designs for the broad range of people likely to use the places we design.

HUMAN NEEDS AS THE BASIS FOR CONCEPTS OF FUNCTIONALISM

Listing all the functions that are to occur in a proposed development by type of activity is one way of organizing one's thoughts for urban designing (see Chapin and Kaiser 1979). It is a very pragmatic way of considering urban design problems and is the basis for the planning and design guidebooks that cut through the process of dealing with recurring problems by presenting design standards. The information in these books (e.g., DeChiara and Koppelman 1975, 1978) enables one to ascertain the spatial needs of many activities, and the configuration of the built environment required to make them possible. These guides enable urban designers to make decisions on matters with which they are unfamiliar and on which they have neither time nor need to do the basic research. The research has already been done. These books deal effectively with such fundamental functional requirements as the turning radii of various automobiles but not effectively with the philosophical issues of what goals should be established. They are not set within an intellectual framework for asking serious questions about life and human problems and desires. Christopher Alexander and his colleagues recognized these limitations in the design of their pattern language (1977), which outlines not only the patterns of solutions but the problems they

solve as well as the empirical and/or other evidence for the connection between problem and solution. The language, however, prematurely assumes that nature of a good world.

If the built environment is to serve human purposes one must have a good model of human needs to use as the basis for asking questions about what should be done—what functions should be served—in a specific circumstance (see Krupat 1985). The Rationalists among Modernists certainly recognized that a model of human needs was necessary to guide their thinking. For instance, in order to focus his thinking about the functions of architecture, Hannes Meyer used such a model (Meyer 1928; Wingler 1969). Meyer, who headed the Bauhaus for a short period in the 1930s until his radical political stance led to his replacement by the more politically conservative Mies van der Rohe, was particularly concerned with improving the residential habitat of people. Meyer identified the following human needs as the basis for design:

- sex life
- sleeping habits
- gardening
- personal hygiene
- protection against the weather
- hygiene in the home
- car maintenance
- cooking
- heating
- insulation
- service

Housing design, in this model, is reduced to the provision of shelter and the provision for a number of activities.

Le Corbusier's Radiant City is based on the human need for light, sunlight, and access to clean open air as well as the provision of a number of services, such as shopping, child care, and recreation (Le Corbusier 1934). Important as these functions are, his is largely an *organismic* model of the human being (see Chapter 1). Issues of territoriality, privacy, security, social action, and symbolic aesthetics, for example, fall outside the scope of such a model. Le Corbusier's design for the Unité d'habitation in Marseilles (Le Corbusier 1953), which came much later in his intellectual development, is based on a considerably more complex model of the human being than his earlier work (see also Curtis 1986). Perhaps this added richness accounts for its success in terms of the lives of its inhabitants (Avin 1973; Schafer 1974).

The model of human needs has to be richer than that used by the Modernists. It also needs to be a model that can be used for asking questions about how human needs are manifested in different cultures. The failure of Modern architecture (and Post-Modern and Deconstructionist architecture, for that matter) to deal with questions

Table 7-1: Models of Human Needs

MASLOW (1987) Human Motivations	LEIGHTON (1959) Essential Striving Sentiments	CANTRIL (1965) Patterns of Human Concerns	GROSS (Lewis 1977)	STEELE (1973)
BASIC NEEDS				
Survival	Physical Security Sexual Satisfaction	Survival		Shelter and security
Safety and Security	Orientation in society	Security, Order		Social contact
Belonging	Securing of love	Identity	Belonging, Participation	Symbolic identification
Esteem	Recognition		Affection Status Respect Power	Growth Pleasure
Self-Actualization		Capacity for choice and freedom	Self-fulfillment	
COGNITIVE NEEDS				
Cognitive	Expressions of love, hostility, spontaneity		Creativity	Growth
Aesthetic			Beauty	Pleasure

Adapted from P. Peterson (1969), Lewis (1977), and Mikellides (1980b)

of culture and design is so well documented now (e.g., Rapoport 1969; Perin 1970; Brolin 1976) and has led to a number of treatises on cultural factors in design (e.g., Rapoport 1977; Low and Chambers 1989) that there is no need to review it here. In contrast, Le Corbusier (1923) observed:

> All men have the same organisms, the same functions. All men have the same needs. The social contract which has evolved through the ages fixes standardized classes, functions and needs producing standardized products. . . . I propose one single building for all nations and all climates.

At a very general level "all men" do, indeed, "have the same needs." However, Le Corbusier was wrong in assuming that the way in which these needs are manifested and can be met is universal. He comprehended neither the full range of human needs nor the individual differences that exist among people within and across cultures or, alternatively, he largely disregarded them in design. Designers need to be sensitive to and argue for environments that fulfill not only "general human needs" but also the specific needs of specific people within specific cultures.

It is clear now that urban design solutions have to be culture-specific. What makes the problem *wicked* is that it is impossible to specify with certainty the important variables of a culture to be used as the basis for design because cultures are always evolving. A general model of human needs has to be one that can be used to ask sensible questions in any culture.

MODELS OF HUMAN NEEDS

There are many reasons why psychologists shy away from the investigation of human needs. Not the least of these is that given by Kurt Lewin. He noted that there are as many needs as there are specific and distinguishable cravings. There are, however, generalizations one can make about groups of needs—categorizations of needs—that can be used as the basis for defining a functional urban design.

A number of models of human needs have been examined by designers (e.g., Alexander 1969; P. Peterson 1969; Mikellides 1980b). There is considerable overlap among the models, but each emphasizes a different aspect of human life. Abraham Maslow's hierarchical model of needs, which is, perhaps, the dominant, all-inclusive model, is presented as a "theory of human motivations" (Maslow 1987). Alexander Leighton (1959) describes needs in terms of "essential striving sentiments." Erik Erikson (1950) analyzes individual identities at each stage in the human life cycle. Hadley Cantril (1965) also focuses on stages in the life cycle as a basic determinant of human needs. All of these psychologists bring important insights to the analysis of human behavior, but ultimately it is Maslow's model that holds up as the best comprehensive view. Indeed, in thinking about design issues, most city planners and architects who are concerned with a user needs approach to design have turned to some adaptation of Maslow's hierarchy of human needs.

In 1954 Abraham Maslow proposed a hypothetical model of human behavior in his book *Motivation and Personality,* which has been recently updated by his colleagues (Maslow 1987). His hierarchical "holistic-dynamic theory" draws on the earlier psychological work of John Dewey and Gestalt theory as well as on the psychoanalytical literature. Maslow identifies five sets of *basic needs* from the most fundamental to the most esoteric in a hierarchy of prepotency. "The most prepotent goal will monopolize consciousness . . . and when a need is fairly well satisfied, the next prepotent [higher] need emerges." His hierarchy of basic needs begins with physiological needs—the need for survival. These are followed by safety and security needs, affiliation needs, esteem needs, and self-actualization needs. Maslow also identified a second set of needs, *cognitive and aesthetic needs,* which guide and shape the processes of attaining the other needs but also have a character of their own.

An examination of individual lives indicates that not everybody, consciously or subconsciously, orders the hierarchy in this way. In some instances people's behavior can still be explained in terms of the model, but in others the values they hold turn the model upside down. Some people hold beliefs that place other ends above the need for survival in the hierarchy. Many people have died for their beliefs. There are also people who seem to lead lives without the need for external approval and indeed thrive on censure. However, while they still perceive themselves as part of a class of people, this kind of life can hardly be ideal.

The consequences of looking at urban designers' tasks as the fulfillment of human needs in this way can only be illustrated by understanding the interrelationships among them. The interrelationships form a complex web that shows the futility of any simplistic model of the concerns of urban design (see Fig. 7-3). The full consequences of a functional urban design based on Maslow's model are developed in Chapters 11 to 17, but in order to understand the functions of cities, they need to be previewed here.

THE BASIC HUMAN NEEDS

Human needs are neither independent of each other nor mutually exclusive. They are, indeed, highly interdependent. Some needs have a biological basis, others are a product of the sociogenic environment, and many have a biological base that is very much culturally molded. Although the nature-nurture controversy is no longer at the center of psychological research, there are many processes that are still poorly understood. The rise of sociobiological research shows that many of the factors that we assumed were purely cultural may well have biological components at their basis after all (Wilson 1978). Suffice to say here that the prerequisite for the attainment of the full set of needs is having freedom of action within a moral order.

Physiological Needs

The basic human need is for survival. To survive one needs life-sustaining inputs of oxygen, food, and water. One also needs to be able to sleep and to move around a territory to obtain the basic necessities of life. If the need for food, say, is unsatisfied, then all the capacities of a person are put into the service of hunger-satisfaction. The architectural need is for shelter from the extremes of heat and cold. Almost no urban design decisions are made only at this most basic level—they deal with higher-order needs that subsume the need for survival.

Extensions of the need for survival are not as fundamental for life but are very much sought after. People have a need to be healthy and to be comfortable. Comfort and health are psychological as well as physiological states. People are often prepared to trade off comfort and health for many other kinds of ends such as prestige, but having a comfortable environment and being healthy are also associated with self-esteem. Thus, in specifying how to design the built environment to meet physiological needs, much depends on individuals' expectations, which are, in turn, based on their habituation levels (see Chapter 1).

There are a number of other needs that might be regarded as semiphysiological—they have biological bases but are very much culturally attuned (P. Peterson 1969). One such need is sexual. Henry Murray (1938) regarded this as a basic physical need, but many people lead fulfilling asexual lives. The next level of needs in Maslow's hierarchy—safety and security needs—can also be seen as semiphysiological.

Safety/Security Needs

There is a need for harm-avoidance among all higher species of animals. This is really a self-protecting device. Sigmund Freud took the extreme position in dealing with harm-avoidance in his definition of the instinct for *self-preservation* (Freud 1949). He believed all human behavior is determined by the principle of avoiding pain and seeking pleasure. The urban design concern here is with the layout of environments that provide safe and secure settings in which people can pursue their lives.

Safety needs combine a diverse set of other needs. The broadest division is into physiological and physical safety needs and psychological needs. The former are concerned with attaining a security of knowing that one is safe from physical harm—from the natural elements, human elements, and from artificially created elements

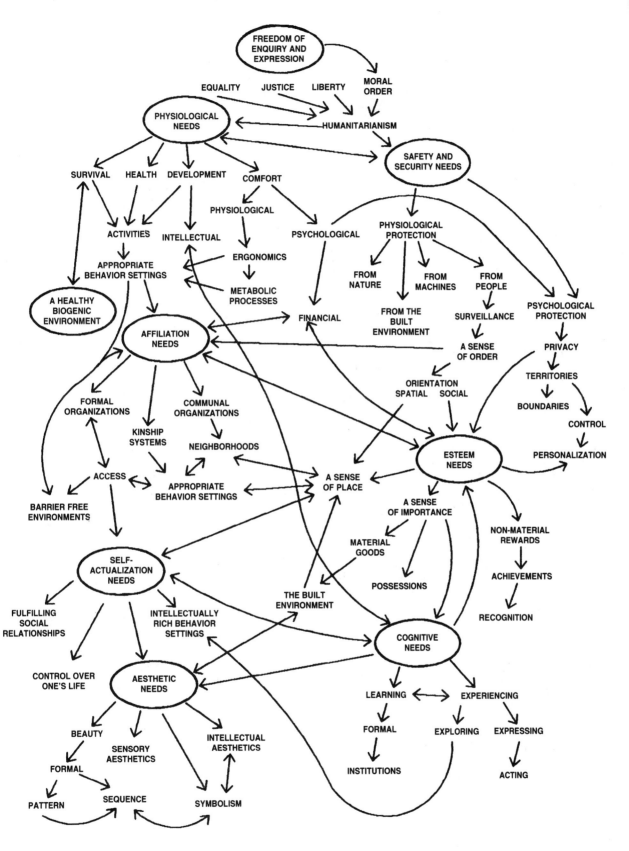

Figure 7-3: The Hierarchy of Human Needs and Design Concerns

1. Self-help Housing, Ahmedabad, India

2. Minneapolis

3. Homeless Man, San Diego

of the environments such as moving cars and structurally unsound buildings. Humans also have the need to be psychologically secure, to have control over the environment, to know where they are in space and in time, to not be socially or physically lost. In addition, there is a need for privacy from censure for carrying out various activities and for developing self-confidence. These needs clearly blur into the next higher set in Maslow's hierarchy, the need for affiliation.

The ways in which safety and security needs are fulfilled have much to do with the nature of the social organization of society, but the layout of the environment also affords or denies the possibility of many kinds of behavior that are necessary for them to be fulfilled. There are many examples that illustrate this observation. The layout of cities for defensive reasons is a major factor in design. Until the nineteenth century the major concern was with defense against outside invasion (A. Morris 1979). Now the concern is more for defense from one's fellow citizens (Newman 1972; Stollard 1991). The layout of the city and its precincts is also a major factor in finding one's way around, in orientating (Lynch 1960; Passini 1984). Fulfilling such needs gives one a feeling of security that results from being in control of situations.

Security is also obtained through being a member of a group—fulfilling the need for belonging. It is obtained through being part of a stable social order. When this stable social order starts to change—often in order to attain other social needs such as self-determination, or if the technological rate of change is so high that people get worried about their abilities to deal with the situation— there is a tendency to hold on to the symbols of the past. Thus there is, or at least appears to be, a correlation between major upheavals in the social order of a society and the degree of concern for the preservation of the existing environment—physical and institutional.

Affiliation Needs

All individuals need to know who they are and to recognize themselves as distinct human beings—as having distinct identities. Identity-formation is a continuous process and has as much to do with the groups of which one is a member as much as one's own uniqueness. Our

Figure 7-4: The Need for Shelter
The need for shelter has always been a prime motivation for building. Some groups of people have sought to have only the level of sheltering necessary for survival (1). Others have sought greater comfort. The modern American city is continually being adapted to provide for higher degrees of personal comfort through the enclosure of previously open public space and with the use of active cooling and heating mechanisms rather than passive ones (2). For many American citizens shelter needs are poorly met (3).

affiliation needs are met by knowing that we are members of a group and of a social and a moral order. These groups are diverse and based on such common characteristics as kinship, locality, and interests. People need to have a sense of belonging, community, and relatedness, as well as to receive affection and approval from other people. This category of needs includes the need to be with others—a desire to please and win affection. The costs of these needs being unmet may well be psychologically high, causing feelings of anxiety and often resulting in a withdrawal from society. Such isolation results in a lack of a feeling of psychological security.

Allied to the need for affiliation is the need for privacy. It serves the need for control of information flows about what one is doing and what others are doing. As such it is also a mechanism for fulfilling security needs, as already noted. Having privacy also helps to meet many other needs such as that of *counteraction* (Murray, 1938). Counteraction involves the active striving to obliterate a humiliation by regrouping and then striving again.

Affiliation needs are complex and interact with all other needs. Thus not only having available groups for us to join is important but also the displaying of symbols that show that we are indeed members. Some of these symbols are highly subtle and are largely unselfconscious; others are self-consciously designed. When we strive to be a member of a group we become very conscious of the symbols of membership, but once we are true members and accepted as such without perceived ambiguity, the symbols of membership are less important. The symbolic aesthetic of the places we inhabit is fundamental to our individual and group identities.

Urban designers tend to think of the consequence of people having a basic need for affiliation in terms of gathering places, of places to watch what is going on—the vicarious participation in the lives of others. It tends to be thought of in the romantic terms of English pubs, French cafes, and Italian plazas (Lennard and Lennard 1989). Similar places in the United States are still important for some people, but all kinds of identity-enhancing events bring people together either in person or through various media such as television. Innovations in communications technology have vastly changed the patterns of behavior related to affiliation needs (Brill 1989; Schmandt et al.

Figure 7-5: Safety and Security Factors in Urban Design
Safety and security issues permeate almost every aspect of urban design. They were prime ones for Modernists, particularly in providing for the protection of pedestrians from clashes with automobiles. It is still a central issue, for both automobiles and pedestrians are users of the public domain (1). The concern is also a broader one due to the need for safety from occurrences such as fires (2) and a variety of hazards in the design of industrial areas (3). Safety from other people used to be characterized by walled cities but now the need is for defense from within—from antisocial behavior.

1. Mission Bay, San Francisco

2. Albanian Islamic Center, Detroit

3. The Liberty Bell, Philadelphia

Figure 7–6: Affiliation Needs and Urban Design
When designers think of affiliation needs they tend to think of opportunities for people to get together, as in Italian plazas or cafes (1). Such places do enrich life, but, more important are considerations of privacy and community in the design of the modern living and working environments, in the institutions that bring like people together (2), and in the symbols of membership (3).

1990). The automobile as a means of bringing people together for a variety of purposes means that propinquity of like-minded people is less important than it once was. The telephone has had a similar impact. Urban designers need to understand these changes and potential changes and to design with them in mind rather than hanging on to a romantic view of life that has too frequently resulted in the creation of places that are unused and unloved (Jacobs 1961; Whyte 1980; Hitt 1990).

Esteem Needs

All people need to have a stable, firmly based, usually high evaluation of themselves. People strive for competence, confidence, independence, and freedom of self-expression. There are two, often interrelated, types of esteem needs—to be in possession of self-esteem and to be held in esteem by others. One gets self-esteem through achievement and through the recognition by others of one's achievements. To get a sense of achievement one needs to be able to master tasks, to be able to manipulate, organize, or own time, physical objects, or ideas, and, maybe, simply to look good—to be regarded as beautiful. John Atkinson and David McClelland (McClelland et al. 1953) identify three types of achievement: unique accomplishment, long-term involvement, and successful compe-

tition with a standard of excellence. Some people have a higher need for achievement than others. They strive harder in order to achieve esteem ends. Much depends on how one is socialized, so much is culturally dependent.

The fulfillment of esteem needs is manifested in many ways. It is shown, for instance, through having control of one's own life, and often over other people's lives, and having the symbols of control to display. The architectural mechanisms are diverse—many have to do with symbolic aesthetics, but they also have to do with territorial control, through real or symbolic barriers, over one's own space. Similarly, architectural and urban layout types and their artistic expression are often associated with specific groups of people. If we wish to be perceived as a member of that group we strive to use the appropriate architectural symbols. If we do not, we avoid those symbols.

Self-Actualizing Needs

Maslow (see 1987) has expressed dismay that the need for self-actualization has been interpreted as the need to be what one can be without regard for others. While there is the need to have freedom of action, to shake off restraints, and to be independent, there is also the need to provide succor to other people.

Once esteem needs have been met, people often

1. Beacon Hill, Boston

Photograph by Deepti Nijhawan

2. Levittown, Pennsylvania

3. Jefferson Memorial, Washington, DC

Figure 7-7: Esteem Needs and Urban Design
People achieve esteem in many ways: by their actions, by having wealth, by having power, by being distinguished by the environments they choose for themselves (1) and/or personalize to their own tastes (2). The display of automobiles is an important part of this picture. Cities are full of memorials to draw attention to successful achievements. The consumption of space is often associated with high status and becomes a symbol of it. Washington, DC, with its wide mall, classical memorials, and baroque layout, is a symbol of power (3).

sense a new discontent and restlessness in themselves unless they can be creative in what is best fitted for them. "A musician must make music, an artist must paint, a poet must write, if he is to be at peace with himself. What a man can be, is what he must be" (Maslow 1987). Carl Jung (1968) has termed this need "individuation," the process of striving toward individuality and self-realization. It may be accompanied by the striving for appropriate architectural symbols (Tyng 1969), but more likely for behavioral control and autonomy. Many people's lives get stuck at striving for esteem and never reach the self-actualizing stage (Maslow 1987). The full implications of these observations for urban design are unclear (see Chapter 16).

COGNITIVE AND AESTHETIC NEEDS

Striving to attain cognitive and aesthetic needs parallels the striving for the attainment of basic needs. The need to be able to learn and the need for beauty are fundamental to human existence and to the attainment of basic needs, as Fig. 7-3 shows.

Cognitive Needs

Acquiring and categorizing knowledge is necessary for survival. One has to have some understanding of the

world in order to survive in it in other than in a purely externally nurtured state. To behave successfully and to understand one has to learn. In any society there is a need for continuing to learn. Many formalized ways exist through the provision of educational institutions, but the opportunities to learn do not have to be organized in a formal way because the everyday world is full of wonder. The whole environment presents a universe to be explored and for testing one's knowledge and skills. It is a storehouse of information, available for use and for attaining understanding and wisdom. People strive to have access to it to the degree necessary for attaining their basic needs. Cognitive needs are thus basic to life. The higher the level of basic needs to be fulfilled, the more learning that is involved. At the highest level such processes are necessary for aesthetic reasons—to learn for the sake of learning. To be a fully self-actualized person there is also the need to understand, to organize, to analyze, to look for relationships and meanings, and to construct a system of values for their own sake and not for any external reward or expression of self.

Aesthetic Needs

People have two sets of aesthetic needs: for beauty and for self-expression. It is clear that the aesthetic quality

1. Philadelphia

2. Quincy Market, Boston

Photograph by Deepu Nijhawan

Figure 7-8: The World Is Full of Wonder
The world is full of opportunities to satisfy one's curiosity—events to watch, elements to examine, places to test one's abilities (1). All cities provide opportunities for exploration and behavior settings in which to participate. Some are considerably richer in the behavior settings they possess than others (2). One of the characteristics of the best-loved places in the world is the opportunities they provide for exploration over a lifetime. One of the major criticisms of many new urban designs is that they have sought neatness rather than opportunities for people to lead rich lives.

of the built and natural environments is an important mechanism in attaining a variety of ends—certainly a sense of belonging and a sense of self-esteem. Aesthetic needs are also, however, manifested more subtly than these needs. At every level of the fulfillment of basic needs there is also the need for beauty as it is defined within cultures. At the highest level, there is also a cognitive need to understand the aesthetic theories of artists for their own sake. Indeed, cognitive and aesthetic needs have, at that level, sometimes been regarded as the same need.

For some people there is a need to understand the creator's objectives in designing a building, in composing a piece of music, in appreciating the culturally defined standards of beauty for their own sake and not for any instrumental purpose they may serve. George Santayana (1896) called this activity the intellectual level of aesthetic appreciation. It is neither basic nor acquired simply through experience, but it is sought after. It is "dealing with moral and aesthetic judgments as phenomena of the mind" (Santayana 1896).

VARIABILITY IN NEEDS FULFILLMENT

While Maslow's model of a hierarchy of needs or motivations for behavior is widely accepted as a general statement about people, it must be recognized that there is considerable variability among individuals in the manifestation of these needs and in the mechanisms for fulfilling them. Some major differences depend on the nature of the individuals, their physiques and personalities, and some depend on their roles as members of a group who share a common characteristic such as their stage in life cycle or their socioeconomic status. There are also broader cultural differences that range from attitudes toward the world as a whole to attitudes toward the relationships between people and between people and objects. These cultural differences are partly a function of the terrestrial environment itself, but people are mobile and their cultures may be, temporarily at least, at odds with the biogenic environment (Vayda 1969). This categorization of individual differences is based on the "functional" sociology of Talcott Parsons (1966). It has been found to be a useful point of departure by a number of designers and by architectural theorists in thinking about how the built environment meets human needs and thus in understanding the utility of specific patterns of the built environment for diverse people (Cranz 1974; Michelson 1976; see also Lang 1987a).

The way we look at the world is motivated by our needs, which, in turn are affected by our competencies. Competence is easiest to understand in physiological terms (see Chapter 1 and Lawton 1977). What we are capable of perceiving, remembering, and doing depends on our physiological and mental abilities. Blind people simply are unable to perceive visual information. Color-blind people are unable to distinguish between certain

1. University of Pennsylvania Campus, Philadelphia

2. Solana, Texas. Richard Legorreta, Architect

3. Santa Monica Arts Center. Frank Gehry, Architect

Figure 7–9: Aesthetic Needs and Urban Design
Beauty has been a concept that has been difficult to define, so aesthetic appreciation is frequently associated with the pleasure that phenomena give us or, rather, that we obtain from them. This pleasure may be sensory, as feeling a surface under one's feet (although not usually in high-heeled shoes (1)), or formal, from appreciating the geometry of the world (2), or symbolic, from the associations a pattern of the environment has for an individual. Intellectual aesthetic experiences of a built form arise from understanding its creator's purposes (2,3).

colors. Mental competence is more difficult to define and understand. Drawing consequential conclusions about the design of public policies and/or the establishment of design goals and design guidelines is fraught with problems.

Personality Type

Individuals differ uniquely in their physiological abilities and also in their personalities Many personality traits/characteristics are stable and enduring, but people do change over time. One dimension of human personality that affects behavior and environmental choices is the degree to which a person is extroverted or introverted. This aspect of personality is complex and has at least two dimensions: the degree of a person's receptivity to outside information, and the degree to which a person is willing, or desires, to act on the environment—sociogenic and biogenic, natural and artificial. The degree to which one needs to express oneself outwardly through one's possessions and their nature depends on one's extroversion on the acting dimension (see Cooper Marcus 1974). Not everybody seeks self-esteem in this manner. While this type of expression is very much culture-bound, different individuals exhibit a greater or lesser need for self-expression within a culture.

We generally think of personality in terms of individuals rather than groups of people or nations, but there seems to be a relationship between the maturity (stage-in-life cycle) of a nation and the manifestation of its needs. After a colonial experience the need for self-esteem seems to be paramount and is architecturally expressed in the symbols of independence (Lang, in progress). In this sense personality and culture are closely related.

Stage-in-Life Cycle

The stage at which people are in their life cycles makes a major difference in establishing their needs and their competence to attain them. The infant's needs for succorance and security are more dominant than an adult's. The need for autonomy seems to be more dominant in adolescence than in adulthood (in the Western world, at least). Our ability to be mobile varies by our competencies and obligations at various stages in our life cycle (Hester 1975). As we age, many of our physiological competencies decrease and, for some elderly, so do mental competencies, but not to the degree that much folklore suggests (Lawton 1977). The decline in mental competence seems to be more related to diseases than to aging itself.

Some psychologists have taken a very strong developmental view of human needs (Erikson 1950; Cantril 1965). According to Erik Erikson (1950) each person goes through eight major life cycle stages, which are closely tied to specific needs. He presents these as a set of polar-opposite psychological states—healthy at one end and unhealthy at the other end. Unless the conflict at each stage is resolved in the healthy way, a person gets stuck at a stage in intellectual development and there is a continuing need to resolve the conflicts. The eight stages are:

Basic Trust	Mistrust	Infant
Autonomy	Shame/Doubt	Infant
Initiative	Guilt	Child
Industry	Inferiority	Child
Identity	Role Confusion	Adolescent
Intimacy	Isolation	Young Adult
Generativity	Stagnation	Adult
Ego Integrity	Despair	Old Age

In *As You Like It,* Shakespeare presents seven stages (no pun intended) of man that are closer to being operational in terms of urban design than are those of Erikson: infant, schoolboy, lover, soldier, justice, elderly person, and finally, the senile one. At each stage in the life cycle, striving for the satisfaction of each basic need in Maslow's hierarchy differs because the focus of attention in one's life differs.

In developing urban design goals for total designs, all-of-a-piece designs, or design guidelines, many public interest questions arise. They are often so complex that it is essential to have a model more directly related to the services one needs today than either Erikson's or Shakespeare's model. William Michelson (1976) identifies the following stages in life cycle as important in raising questions about lifestyles and, more generally, about people's needs: infancy, childhood, adolescence, single adulthood (with roommates or family, but increasingly as a single person), child raising, empty nesters (adulthood after raising children), and old age. The behavioral opportunities, services, and aesthetic requirements to lead a fulfilled life once existed (more or less) at the local level at each stage, but as people's mobility has increased so the need for localization of activities has decreased. The degree to which this dispersion of behavior settings should occur has been a central urban design issue during this century. Neighborhood unit theory derives from it, as do many of Le Corbusier's urban design concerns (Marmot 1982).

Cultural Setting and Human Needs

Expected and accepted behaviors and attitudes vary from culture to culture. A culture, by definition, has a system of beliefs about what behaviors are appropriate in different circumstances; it shares values and symbol systems. Cultures are unique because they have evolved and continue to evolve unselfconsciously in response to the

peculiarities of their histories and of the terrestrial setting (Vayda 1969). Political action is one way of changing a culture self-consciously, but much change continues to result from unselfconsciously responding to changing world views, technological capabilities, and perceptions of how other cultures are evolving.

The attitudes toward both basic and cognitive needs and the degree to which they require fulfilling vary from culture to culture. Indeed, the beliefs about the way some needs should be fulfilled help define a culture. In some cultures, people seem to have a broad need for affiliation and use many symbols to denote their membership in various organizations. This may not be an attribute of all members of that society but may be a strong need for the majority. Similarly, a group of people may have a high need for achievement, and once attaining it they may have a high need for conspicuously consuming to display that achievement (see Reissman 1964). While this behavior is often a personality attribute of an individual, it can also be the personality attribute of a people—a culture.

Social Roles within a Culture

Each individual has a role to play within a culture. This role establishes a routine to a person's life. Needs are seen from the perspective of the role. Identifying them is not easy because roles overlap. The productive roles of individuals may well overlap the roles required at a stage in their life cycles—for instance, being a parent and a wage earner may occur simultaneously. Similarly, being a child in a family or being elderly are not only stages in life cycle but social roles. They are ways of establishing a place in society. In some societies the roles have traditionally been rigidly defined by gender and/or the role of one's parents, for instance. Although there is no place for it in the original Hindu Vedas, the caste system that evolved as a part of Hinduism and Buddhism rigidly assigns people of certain occupations to a specific place in the hierarchy of places in society. Although castism is illegal in both India and Japan, the roles of untouchables (Harijans in India, Eta in Japan) are still rigidly defined in both countries. Crossing social barriers is extremely difficult.

The daily routine of an individual may be a major factor in establishing how the basic necessities of life are met and also in what they wish to do with their spare time. A person isolated at home with children most of the day may have very different needs than a person who works on an assembly line or an executive who has a sedentary occupation. A general rule of thumb for a fulfilling life is that the activities occurring during breaks in the routine must satisfy needs complementary to those served by the routine.

Environmental Setting

Cultures and all artificial physical environments exist within particular terrestrial settings. Each setting has a specific set of affordances. What one knows about the world and thus the perception of needs is shaped by these affordances. The geographic setting is thus part of the culture, shaping it and being shaped by it, and is the repository of the myths and memories of its inhabitants.

HUMAN NEEDS AND THE BUILT ENVIRONMENT

There are continuing attempts to take an empirical, human needs approach to urban design. This is apparent in the writings of Christopher Alexander, particularly his early work (e.g., 1969) and that of Alexander and his colleagues (1977, 1987), the writings of Kevin Lynch (1982, 1984), and the architectural work of architects such as Ralph Erskine (Egelius 1980a, 1980b), Herman Hertzberger (1980), and Charles Moore (Littlejohn 1984; Johnson 1986). It is now possible to give a much clearer portrayal of the relationship between the built environment and human needs fulfillment than the deterministic models of the Modern architects.

The concept of "affordance" introduced in Chapter 1 and borrowed from the work of psychologist James Gibson (1979) is increasingly used among designers because it adds conceptual clarity to the understanding of the link between the built environment, human behavior, and values and needs fulfillment. Any pattern of the built world affords certain activities or aesthetic interpretations. These patterns enlarge or constrain our options for behaviors—physical and mental—depending on the overall configurations and properties of the layout of the built environment.

To meet their needs, people must make behavioral choices. Such choices may be achieved in a number of ways. Individuals can adapt themselves either psychologically or physiologically to a situation; the former may often be difficult and stressful and the latter largely impossible. They can also manipulate the nature of a situation through social or institutional modifications. These changes may, in turn, necessitate making changes in their location in the physical environment or the structure of the built environment. Urban designers' primary focus of concern is on the last choice, relocation, but such changes have to be seen in the context of the first two types of actions.

Relocation

For individuals, the first category of environmental change involves their relocation. The type of relocation varies by scale. At the small scale, it involves *micro-movements* to maintain an acceptable level of comfort in a situation through shifting of the body to another posture or to another place within the setting. At the larger scale, it involves the *macro-movements* of choosing another setting

completely. The first type of relocation is below the scale of concern of an urban designer. The second is the type of change that is of primary importance in urban design. The question is: "What array of possible choices need to be provided in order for people to have an appropriate choice given their needs and potential needs?"

Environmental Change

Changing the environment—that is, reconfiguring the environment—may involve: (1) changing the *micro-climate* by changing the temperature and other qualities of the air, the lighting and acoustical levels, and the nature of odors of a setting; (2) changing the *spatial configuration* of the setting(s) by changing the three-dimensional partitioning of space, and/or the nature of the partitions; (3) changing the *environmental hardware*—the furniture, plants, and other objects that define and control individual areas and the circulation within them; (4) changing those *environmental attributes* such as the materials, illumination, and colors of the elements that constitute the setting and give it its character and mood; and (5) changing the *symbolic attributes* of spatial configurations, materials, objects, and/ or the position of these elements within the setting.

The basic concern in urban design is: (1) to identify/ create and distinguish among possible future built environments, (2) to evaluate them given the resources that a society or an organization has available for building, (3) to consider/design ways of bringing them to fruition; and (4) to oversee their implementation.

USERS' NEEDS, DESIGNERS' NEEDS, AND ARCHITECTURE'S NEEDS

In developing any design there is the requirement to mediate between competing needs of different people and architecture as a self-serving discipline. There is often a competition between the designer's need for recognition and self-esteem and the need to create a pleasant environment in terms of its users' lives (unless the designer's self-esteem comes from creating such an environment). At the high point of the production of the Modern movement's works, Jane Jacobs (1961) doubted that serving the needs of people was the way that many architects saw their role in society. There have been numerous statements to the effect that architects are more concerned about what their peers—the hidden client—think of their work than its utility/functionality for either activities or aesthetic appreciation in terms of the people who will inhabit the environment. These expressions cover the political extremes, socially and architecturally (Montgomery 1966; Holden 1988).

A number of years ago Martin Pawley wrote a book *Architecture versus Housing* (1971). More recently (1986) Clare Cooper Morris and Wendy Sarkissian wrote *Housing as if People Mattered*. In a similar vein, critic Paul

1. Frank W. Thomas House

2. Rose Seidler House

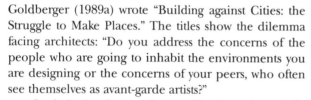

3. Vanna Venturi House

Figure 7-10: Architects and Custom House Design
Much can be learned from the success architects have had in designing custom houses. The lesson comes from understanding the process that generated them and the relationship between clients and professionals. Almost all custom houses are developed through a close relationship between architect and client. The houses designed by Frank Lloyd Wright (1), Harry Seidler (2), and Robert Venturi (3) all unmistakably carry the imprint of their designers, yet they all emerged from a collaborative relationship between client and designer. Can such a relationship be extended into the public realm of urban design?

Goldberger (1989a) wrote "Building against Cities: the Struggle to Make Places." The titles show the dilemma facing architects: "Do you address the concerns of the people who are going to inhabit the environments you are designing or the concerns of your peers, who often see themselves as avant-garde artists?"

In designing houses for specific clients (especially wealthy ones) architects and clients tend to share values, simply because the user-client chooses the architect. Le Corbusier's clients for his early house designs were members of the artistic avant-garde, Frank Lloyd Wright's were largely innovative self-made people, Howard Van Doren Shaw's were drawn from the social elite (Eaton 1969). Each house reflects its client's values as much as those of the architect. In urban design, with its many clients and many architects, this coincidence of values is more difficult to achieve. Urban designers need to be able to think flexibly and to be able to work within value sets other than their own. This does not always come easily, although some architects do have a "give-em-what-they-say-they-want" attitude (Mitchell 1974).

There is often a conflict between the needs of architecture as a discipline striving for internal consistency in terms of its history and the past and the needs of society and the future. Architects often respond to criticism by saying

that a building or an urban design must be seen in architectural terms not in other terms. There is some utility to this view. Many people—the artistic cognoscenti—do look at the environment this way. Their need is aesthetic—not in terms of their own experiences, but in terms of needing to understand an architectural theory. Architecture meets their needs for self-esteem in this manner. The majority of people do not, however, perceive the built environment in this way. Their needs also have to be considered. Urban designs thus have to be ambiguous in the sense that they have to have multiple meanings and uses.

CONSEQUENCES FOR URBAN DESIGN

The concept of functionalism described here arises from an understanding of human needs. If one accepts it then a functional urban design responds to a much broader range of human needs than was traditionally considered under the rubric of functionalism. The most important departure from the past is the recognition that aesthetic display is a fundamental function of the built environment and should be considered as such. It competes with the other functions served by the built environment for the attention of the designer. It is not something added to the list of concerns when other functional requirements have been met. It must be recognized that aesthetic ends and other ends almost always have to be met to some degree for a design to be acceptable. A tradeoff among the requirements to meet each individual's needs in seeking environmental quality almost always exists, as there is never an infinitely elastic money supply with which to meet them. No design is able to totally meet all of everybody's needs simultaneously.

Considering human needs in an hierarchical manner as the basis for design requires great flexibility in the designer's thinking because it raises many questions. Designing by habit is easier. The design process requires creative thinking rather than the adaptation of a set of generic solutions or design principles that can be universally applied without much thought. The intellectual energy required of designers within the financial constraints placed on them is high.

Looking at human needs in the way proposed here as a basis for urban design inquiries and decisions raises questions about how tightly a pattern of the environment should cater to a specific set of behaviors (see also Chapters 20 and 23). How well should the self-consciously designed environment *fit* an activity pattern or an aesthetic value of an individual or a group of people? It must, at least, *afford* the activity or the aesthetic demand. How specific or how tightly should the one fit the other? How *congruent* should the relationship between the pattern of the environment and the behavior be? How does one deal with potential future behavior changes? These are questions much debated when an architect moves away from designing for a specific person using his or her own values with a short-term future in mind to the more general, but fundamental, questions of urban design.

Urban designers like all other designers are always designing for the future. The future is always unknown, although there is much that we can predict with tolerable accuracy. The easiest way to deal with the unknown is to assume that tomorrow will be the same as today. For a short-run future this may be quite accurate. In the long run we know that there are likely to be substantial changes if the history of the past two hundred years is a guide. It is fortunate that history shows that people adapt the environment to their needs—and thus the city evolves. The role of the urban designers is to help shape these evolutionary processes so that problems are avoided and opportunities are not lost.

MAJOR REFERENCES

Banham, Reyner (1960). *Theory and Design in the First Machine Age*. New York: Praeger.

Broadbent, Geoffrey (1978). "The Rational and the Functional." In Dennis Sharp, ed., *The Rationalists: Theory and Design in the Modern Movement*. London: Architectural Press, pp. 142–159.

Cranz, Galen (1974). "Using Parsonian Structural-Functionalism for Environmental Design." In William R. Spillers, ed., *Basic Questions in Design Theory*. New York: American Elsevier, pp. 475–484.

Lang, Jon (1987a). "Fundamental Processes of Human Behavior." In *Creating Architectural Theory*. New York: Van Nostrand Reinhold, pp. 84–100.

Maslow, Abraham H. (1943). "Theory of Human Nature." *Psychological Review* 50: 370–396.

——— (1987). *Motivation and Personality*. 3d ed. Rev. by Robert Frager, James Fadiman, Cynthia Reynolds, and Ruth Cox. New York: Harper & Row.

8

THE FUNCTIONS OF CITIES AND URBAN PLACES

The character of any settlement—metropolis or hamlet—depends on the number and nature of the functions served by the behavior settings that exist there and by the number of people who participate in them (Barker and Schoggen 1973). The quality of any such settlement also depends on the degree of efficiency and comfort with which the milieu (i.e., the physical layout) affords specific behaviors, and on the milieu's utility as the provider of opportunities for the displays that people make, self-consciously or unselfconsciously, to carry messages to each other.

The behavior settings that exist in any settlement serve many different functions for different *agents*, or users. The agents may be firms, institutions, or individuals (Chapin and Kaiser 1979). Different individuals and organizations will have different motivations for participating in specific settings. Behavior settings thus serve different functions for different people, or for the same person at different times. In thinking about urban design, it is essential that in seeking efficiency that the multifunctionality of settings be considered. This task is not easy, for many of the purposes served by a setting are not obvious as Herbert Gans (1962) warned us over thirty years ago in his analysis of the deleterious effects of what appeared to be slum clearance in Boston.

THE MANIFEST AND LATENT FUNCTIONS OF BEHAVIOR SETTINGS

The functions of any component of the city can be divided into two types—*manifest* and *latent* (Gutman 1966). The manifest function is the ostensible function of a place, usually the economic, social, or recreational activities that occur there. The latent function is the byproduct of those activities and may be psychological in character and

may also, but not necessarily, be the "real" reason for a place to exist (Mumford 1961). For instance, a tavern may be a place to get a drink, but the drink may simply be the catalyst needed for human interaction. Historically, a village square may have housed a market, but a market served as more than simply a place to sell and buy gods. It also provided for the dissemination of information on a wide variety of topics. This latent function, in turn, serves further latent functions such as the enhancement of a sense of community. If the market dies the interaction may or may not be replaced by a different set of behavior settings that serve the same latent purposes. Indeed, the emergence of such new settings may be the reason for the market to cease functioning.

Human settlements are full of such places, and the functions they serve are often unrecognized and thus undervalued in planning and design, although they are grieved for when lost (Gans 1962; M. Fried 1963). A tot-lot may be for young children to play in, but it is also a place where parents, or, if it is in a low-income area, the older siblings, of the children will gather to supervise the play. The manifest function is for children to play and the latent function is for them to learn about themselves and the world through the self-testing and exploration of their abilities on the equipment provided. The children, their playing, and need for supervision act as catalysts for the latent function of gathering for their minders. This catalytic function works in much the same way that a new urban development may be a catalyst for another development (Attoe and Logan 1989).

Primary and Secondary Functions

The physical structure of a setting, the milieu, can serve a number of manifest functions depending on what its configuration affords people. There can thus be *primary,*

1. Metropolitan Museum, New York

2. Museum of Contemporary Art, Los Angeles

3. Lafayette Park, Detroit

Figure 8-1: The Manifest and Latent Functions of Cities and Places

Behavior settings provide for two types of functions: manifest and latent. A set of steps may be designed to give access to a building, but they may also have a symbolic function. It may also be a place to have lunch and to watch other people (1). An art gallery may be designed to display art, but it may also boost a city's self-esteem (2); the reverse may also be true! In thinking about urban design we tend to focus on the obvious functions; the latent ones are also important (3).

secondary, tertiary, and so on manifest functions of a physical setting. The primary purpose of a space, its basic function, tends to be the design focus, but efficiency in serving that purpose may have an negative effect on the other purposes it serves. The qualities of urban spaces are too easily evaluated in terms of how well they serve the primary, secondary, and so on functions, and the latent functions they serve tend to be forgotten. For example, the primary manifest function of a street is its design for the movement of vehicular traffic. Often, if not usually, it is the sole design concern. The secondary manifest function of a street may be as a place to clean cars, a play space, or a seam for a face-block neighborhood (Appleyard et al. 1981; R. Moore 1987; Moudon 1987). The latent function may be the development of a sense of community or place (J. Jacobs 1961). In the design of the Dutch *woonerf* (see Fig. 8-2), the secondary use is given as much attention as the primary one (Appleyard et al. 1981; M. Francis 1987a). Whether it was considered purposefully or not the *woonerf* serves many latent purposes such as the possibility of territorial control. The recognition of the primary function and latent functions are as important as the primary functions. Cities, their settings, and their components are multifunctional and should be designed to be

this way, but the primary function must first be served well enough or, as a result, the whole setting collapses.

THE CITY'S PRIMARY FUNCTIONS

Categorizing the city's functions is not easy, for they overlap and are interwoven. Some efforts have been made to classify them (e.g., Chapin and Kaiser 1979), but one activity serves many purposes and has many byproducts. While no general agreement exists on how they should be listed, let alone classified, some fundamental functions— the essence of settlements' existence—can be identified.

Human settlements exist for economic and social necessities, which means that, above all, they serve the fundamental purposes of enhancing the collective actions in which people engage to produce, consume, and express themselves. They provide the physical settings for the functions that require mutual cooperation and interactions between people.

> Cities since the beginning of time have been centres of exchange, both human and commercial . . . the city in its clearest form has been about communality, accommodation, dialogue, protection; a city fostered civic institutions and

1. A *Woonerf*, Delft, The Netherlands

Photograph by Mark Francis

2. Mithun Place, Seattle

3. A Cul-de-Sac, Radburn, New Jersey

Figure 8-2: The *Woonerf*

The *woonerf* was specifically designed to enhance the quality of life of residents of dense inner-city neighborhoods of European cities. The *woonerf* simultaneously affords the needs of pedestrians, provides play space for children, and gives vehicular access to homes. Mithun Place in Seattle provides for many manifest activities: parking, car washing, children's play, and so on, but also for enhanced control of an area by its residents (2). Cul-de-sacs serve fewer but similar purposes as at Radburn, New Jersey (3; see also Fig. 2–8).

taught civility. Civil life and activity within a public realm was directed towards high-minded purposes, the fostering of virtue and beauty, as well as pragmatic ones (Robertson 1985).

The fundamental function might be regarded as the communications one, but this activity is interwoven with the economic one. While these two may be seen as the primary purposes for the existence of human settlements, they also provide settings for learning both formally, in institutions designed specifically for that purpose, and vicariously, as part of everyday life. People also make displays for each other through the expressive acts they perform and through the way they structure the very fabric of the city, as a whole and in the details. If new ways are discovered or invented to serve all these purposes, human settlements' patterns may well undergo radical change.

The Communications Function

Communication involves the transmission or interchange of ideas, messages, or information among people. Many forms and channels of communication are used on an everyday basis. In some of these forms the communication is direct, while in others it is mediated. Direct communication involves person-to-person multisensory interaction (Gibson 1966; Hall 1966), while mediated communication is through some intermediary mechanism. There are many forms of mediated communication: verbal in written form, mathematical symbols, graphic in drawings, visual and sonic in film and art works, but also the patterns of the built environment (Kepes 1966; Rapoport 1982). Direct communication necessitates people coming together, mediated does not. The use of the telephone, radio, television, and a variety of electronic media enables messages to be communicated from one person to another at great distances without face-to-face interaction. In doing so the content of the communication is reduced.

All human settlements have traditionally served the function of reducing the distance between people and thus enabling them to get together to easily exchange messages and ideas, to engage in communal and common activities, and for common actions. Settlement patterns have been shaped by means of communication, and the continuing changes in settlement forms are largely a function of how communications technology changes (Meier 1962) and how goods are exchanged. One of the concerns of urban design is to support and help clarify the needed communication between people and the appropriate media of communication. The goal is to enhance the communications function of cities.

Urban design has been particularly concerned with the communication that takes place in the public realm. Certainly one of the partisan goals of urban design has been to create settings for people that aid the formation of the communications networks that form the basis of communities. The layout of the environment can make a difference in easing processes of communication between people, but the new technologies have gone a long way to reducing the need for face-to-face communication, for good and for bad.

It is clear that in day-to-day life, the communications function of human settlements is highly complex, involving many interacting modes that serve many different purposes. The modes have seldom, if ever, been considered as an overall system because the planning and design of each mode tends to be the responsibility of a separate agent. Urban designers have traditionally focused on transportation as the primary communications device shaping the public realm. Indeed, the Modernists focused on transportation efficiency as the prime shaper of urban space. One of the criticisms of their designs is that they had a very narrow definition of communication (Fitch 1965, 1980). The consequence has been that many modes that are part and parcel of everyday life have been neglected (J. Jacobs 1961; Brolin 1976).

Transportation Costs

Transportation can be thought to include the relaying and carrying of messages, but generally we think of transportation as the carrying of people, materials, and goods from one place to another. Transportation enables raw materials and manufactured goods to be carried long distances. It enables people to reside in preferred locations within their economic means and to work in other locations. Indeed, some people in metropolitan areas such as New York City and Los Angeles are prepared to spend four hours a day commuting for the benefits it brings them (Fulton 1990). The structure of regions and the settlement patterns within them are largely determined by the location and nature of the transportation systems available.

For face-to-face interaction and to engage in common activities people have to get together. To get together they have to transport themselves from one place to another. The fundamental means of transportation for most people is their legs, but many people have difficulty walking and others are wheelchair-bound. Walking is most widely used for short horizontal distances. The definition of *short* varies considerably among the population and depends on the purpose that has necessitated the trip, the amount of interest of the route, and whether destinations are in sight.

Beyond one's legs there are a variety of transportation modes. In the wealthier nations there are relatively fewer types in comparison to many poorer nations, where roads have to cater to a variety of vehicles traveling at different speeds. The modes that have attracted the most attention of the urban designer are the automobile, which provides considerable individual mobility at some social costs, and mass transit systems of various types. Much of the space

1. Nicollet Mall, Minneapolis

2. South Philadelphia

3. Manhattan

Figure 8-3: The Communications Function of Cities
One purpose of human settlements is to overcome the "tyranny of distance" between people to enable cooperative actions—for people to barter, to manufacture products together, to have access to activities of mutual interests, and to communicate with each other for business (1) and social (2) purposes. The dense modern city shows the premium that people have been willing to pay for ease of access to one another (3). The communication has traditionally involved direct access to each other through transportation. Will new technologies reduce the necessity and enable even more spread out settlements than the automobile already affords us?

1. Jaipur, Rajasthan, India

2. Boulder, Colorado

3. Atlanta

Figure 8–4: Transportation Modes
The city is shaped by its transportation systems, New transportation systems change the rent curves of urban space and thus the distribution of activities. There are many modes of road transportation, as this street scene shows (1). One of the design issues concerns the degree of safety and efficiency actually attained by segregating the different modes (2). Many cities were structured by their rail transportation systems, but now it is the functioning of the automobile that is usually the basis for urban design. Some cities have introduced comfortable, elegant subway systems in recent times to help ease street congestion and air pollution (3).

between buildings is devoted to transportation routes. These routes have to serve more than their primary purpose of allowing as free as possible movement of vehicles, but affording the functional needs of the vehicles (and, thus, the needs of the people within them) is the basic design requirement (Appleyard, Lynch, and Meyer 1964).

The history of urban form is largely a history of the effect of changing modes of transportation on land values (see Chapter 2, Shaping the Twentieth-Century City). As transportation modes change so do rent curves. Ease of both horizontal and vertical movement affects the value of land. The development of the safety elevator enabled tall buildings to be built functionally (Giedion 1963). The railway, the streetcar, and the automobile very much dictated the variety of forms suburbs have taken in North American (Stern with Massengale 1981). The trucking industry has enabled industries to be more widely dispersed than the railroad allowed, and this has led to changes in the very nature of metropolitan areas by leading to changes in land-use patterns.

The Economic Function of Cities

The communications/transportation and economic functions of cities are closely intertwined. All cities pro-

vide the behavior settings and infrastructure for some economic activity. This function is a necessary if not a sufficient reason for the existence of urban agglomerations. A city's quality depends on the efficiency with which it facilitates the creation and distribution of wealth. Perhaps even more important is the efficiency with which the infrastructure and buildings of a city can be adapted to the changes necessitated by required changes in the city's economic base (J. Jacobs 1969). There is a question not only of the efficiency and adaptability of the physical frame of a city to afford new economic activities, but also of the efficiency and adaptability of the people involved. If "the city is the people," then their competencies are of major concern in looking ahead. Deciding how to deal with them is a social and educational planning concern.

To some extent, the adaptability of a city to change depends on its multifunctionality. All cities have a multiplicity of economic activities, but in some there is a primary source from which other secondary sources spin off, each conducting its activities with great efficiency. Thus a steel-making center, for example, requires many supporting activities, but if a city relies on such a single industry for its life, then that industry's failure will have major ramifications throughout the community (J. Jacobs 1969). The major cities of the world that have survived and grown

1. New Suburban Development, Denver Metropolitan Area

2. Los Angeles

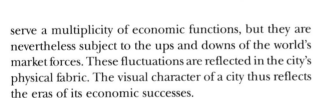
3. Boulder, Colorado

Figure 8-5: The Cognitive Function of Cities
In the United States many people raise their children in suburban environments (1) because the formal opportunities for education and open spaces are perceived to be better there than that in the inner city. The behavior settings that constitute many such environments do not, however, offer many of the informal opportunities to learn about the world that more dense, mixed-use urban environments with their variety of people do. The cognitive function—formal and informal—of everyday environments (2) makes an important contribution to people's learning about the world. We tend to formalize such learning opportunities (3).

serve a multiplicity of economic functions, but they are nevertheless subject to the ups and downs of the world's market forces. These fluctuations are reflected in the city's physical fabric. The visual character of a city thus reflects the eras of its economic successes.

The city and its components are also a means for making wealth in various ways. The manipulation of the land market provides the function of making wealth for some people through speculation on land values. Public policies—investments in the city's capital web—and urban design actions change the relative value of land. Their formulations are thus very much the subject of political pressures in the United States and other capitalist societies. The concern for encouraging appropriate developments and questions of social equity have been paramount issues in urban design. They get lost in a purely consumerist urban design.

The Cognitive Function of Cities

The richness of cities is due as much to the number and variety of the functions served by the behavior settings that exist there as to any other measure one can devise. The quality of life depends on the settings that are

available to fulfill basic human needs, from safety to self-actualization, as well as to fulfill cognitive and aesthetic needs without being overmanned—that is, having too many people per setting so that some people are displaced and become nonparticipants in life (Wicker 1969, 1979; Bechtel 1977).

Cities provide both formal and informal opportunities for learning. The formal opportunities occur through educational institutions of various kinds. The informal occur as the result of everyday life—from the experiencing of the world (Carr and Lynch 1968). Some cities provide a richness of opportunities that afford many vicarious learning opportunities. Others are dull. One of the major problems of the large housing estates based on the Rationalist model was that they did not take into account the cognitive function that the environment provides. There was simply not the variety of informal learning opportunities that even the old slums provided (see Roberts 1971 for a vivid description of slum life). As the change in scale of economic activity occurs and the farther one has to travel to get the variety of experiences historically available at the local level, so the less mobile people in a society (such as children) have difficulty in independently getting access to them (Parr 1967, 1969).

1. Fifth Avenue at 52nd Street, New York

2. Fifth Avenue at Broadway, New York

3. Times Square, New York

Figure 8-6: The City as a Set of Displays
The built environment serves many functions. One of the most important is the display of individual or civic wealth, success, or pride. Sometimes this display arises unselfconsciously as the result of many individual decisions, adding up to a whole greater than its parts, as in Fifth Avenue, New York (1); sometimes it is a fundamental goal of the design of a building (2); and sometimes it is more tawdry than many middle-class people think proper (3). We are constantly making plans to clean up untidy places.

The Function of Cities as Displays

The word "display" often has slightly negative connotations. A display is regarded as something ostentatious. No such value is intended here. To display means to make noticeable, to exhibit. The city is both an exhibition and a set of stages for exhibitions. There are a number of ways in which cities serve as displays: they provide the settings for individual displays of behavior, for group displays of behavior such as parades and festivals, and for displays of status through the character of buildings and streetscapes. In some cases, there is often a self-conscious concern for the city as a work of art (Olsen 1986).

Many cities have been through phases where individual buildings, streets, and whole quarters have been shaped to display civic price or national glory. Washington, DC, Paris, New Delhi, Canberra, and Brasilia are displays of national pride and power. American cities, with the noticeable exception of Washington, DC, and a number of state capitals, such as Denver, Colorado, and Madison, Wisconsin, have been shaped by a series of private displays rather than communal ones—"private values rather than public exhortation" (Olsen 1986). This observation is not unique to the United States, for much the same can be said for many cities around the world. The basic point is that cities are full of displays. Some are intrusive and some have to be sought.

Conscious Displays

Events as well as the built environment can be designed consciously. Cities serve as the location and as a backdrop to almost all the types of events one can imagine and many that do not immediately come to the mind of the designer. The variety of types of display created through built form is too vast to be enumerated. The visual richness of a city is due to its variety of displays. There comes a point when the richness is regarded as chaotic by many people. The Modern movement in architecture had a low tolerance for environmental richness, preferring simplicity of form.

Events

Events may be parades, festivals, athletic competitions, and so on. The urban design concern is for those events that occur on a regular basis—those that constitute standing patterns of behavior (Barker 1968; Sarason 1972; Wicker 1979). Such events are a characteristic of all types of human settlements from villages to metropolises. Indeed, some observers regard them as the fundamental reason for settlements to exist (see Mumford 1961). Events serve a variety of functions: they mark the seasons, signify the history of a place and of a people, and serve many spiritual as well as commercial purposes. They serve the function of uniting people, entertaining them, and giving them a sense of belonging to a place. They may be local, city, regional, or national in character. Some cities provide for them well, and indeed, historically they have been the basis for much urban design work. For instance, the design of Rome under Sixtus the Fifth was at least partially, if not primarily, concerned with designing a city for religious processions linking existing churches (Bacon 1974; Benevolo 1980).

There are three basic approaches to the designing of events and the built environment—specific behavior settings. The first involves designing the event and then the milieu to fit it or designing them simultaneously. The second is to design the event and then to look for milieus that afford that event, and the third is to look at the milieu and ask "What events could take place here?"

The first can be a characteristic of all-of-a-piece urban design, major urban renewal projects, and certainly individual building designs, but the other two types of design involve no change in the structure of the built environment. The first type has primarily been restricted to the design of capital cities because that is where parades are very much part of the ceremonial life. The Rajpath in New Delhi provided a setting for British military parades and now for India's Republic Day parade (Nilsson 1975; Irving 1981; see Fig. 2-16(5)). It was designed with parades as well as dramatic settings in mind and serves them well. Most cities have to make do with existing city streets designed for traffic movement and, perhaps, for vistas. Neither Pennsylvania Avenue in Washington, DC, nor Fifth Avenue in New York are well designed for parades but they function "well enough." Independence Mall in Philadelphia was designed for many public ceremonies as well as to turn Independence Hall into a national shrine by displaying it prominently (see Fig. 2-21(2)).

In existing cities, routes for new parades are chosen for ease of access, for the least disruption of traffic, and for where spectators can gather. They may well link ceremonial places—many patriotic events, ethnic group marches, and sporting events end opposite the Liberty Bell Pavilion in Philadelphia. Sites for localized events such as fairs may be where markets were originally located, but many will be on found spots that usually serve a different purpose—a square, schoolyard, churchyard, a street that is closed off for the day. Some of the places where markets are held are enduring and are very much a characteristic of the city in which they are located.

The Built Environment as Symbol

One of the prime functions of the built environment is that of a symbol. Symbols serve many functions but two are primary: they can provide a sense of identity, and they can enhance self-esteem (see Chapters 14 and 15). In urban design, the goal of the City Beautiful movement was largely to fulfill these functions for a city's citizens (J. Peterson 1976; W. Wilson 1990). Many total urban designs strive to achieve this purpose, but the examples of individual buildings doing so are more numerous.

Cities contain many foreground buildings that have been set apart from the rest of the urban fabric. They may be city halls, libraries, museums, cathedrals. Their presences enrich a city. Lincoln Center in New York (see Fig. 3-19(6)), the Kennedy Center in Washington, DC, and, on a smaller scale, the Guthrie Theater in Minneapolis are themselves displays designed to house other displays in the form of consciously designed performances, but they also act less self-consciously as places for people to display themselves to others. The audience is part of the performance. Both the performances and the buildings have symbolic value as statements of their cities as cultural centers. Each building is also an expression of an age and of an individual architect's talent. Some commercial buildings serve much the same purposes—the Empire State Building in New York, for example. Difficulties arise when the owners and designers of every building strive to make them foreground buildings. The result is a lack of clarity or coherence of form, although a certain unity in diversity is achieved (see Fig. 2-10(6)). One of the debates in urban design is over what kinds of buildings should be the foreground buildings (see Fig. 17-14). Historically, it has been the major civic buildings, but now they have been pushed into the background by office towers.

Not only individual buildings but parts of cities also serve symbolic purposes for particular groups of people. While it is easier to see this function fulfilled in cities of the past than today, it is an implicit if not an explicit goal of any large-scale project. It was clearly the case in Washington, DC (Reps 1991), London, Vienna, and Paris (see Fig. 5-2(2)) from time to time (Olsen 1986), and is still clearly so in the design of government complexes such as the Empire State Plaza in Albany, New York (see Fig. 2-4(7)). It is less clear but nevertheless present in large-scale all-of-a-piece designs such as Battery Park City and, to a lesser extent, in the Roosevelt Island developments, both in New York City.

Unselfconsciously Designed Displays

That a display can be unselfconsciously designed may seem to be a contradiction in terms. Such displays occur as a byproduct of other actions or simply as the result of unmotivated expressions (Maslow 1987). Every design, every built environment, is a potential source of messages. Sometimes the messages may be grand ones but they are often more mundane ones that nevertheless give people a sense of place, positive or negative. As we travel around a city we examine the environment—we recognize the correlations between places, people, events, and time. Any pattern of the built environment consists of what might be regarded as latent messages. These are messages that are perceived as the result of the associations people have with specific patterns and materials of the built environment and the way space is enclosed.

1. Gay Parade, San Francisco (1992)

2. Pennsylvania Avenue, Washington, DC

3. Douglas Street Arts Fair, Wichita, Kansas

Courtesy of Marvin S. Krout

Collection of the author

4. Logan Circle, Philadelphia. Mass Led by the Pope

Figure 8-7: Events
Cities are enlivened by events: boat shows, flower shows, power tractor rodeos, and so on. Civic arenas are specially designed for these types of events. Many events such as parades occur where they can (1). Few streets are specifically designed for parades,

even where that is one of their major functions (2), although some clearly were designed for that (e.g., the Rajpath, New Delhi; see Fig. 2–16(5). Often streets are closed to vehicular traffic to afford gathering (3,4). Such events enrich life.

People draw meanings from their own experiences. We may not make these associational interpretations explicitly or accurately, but we make them nevertheless.

Bit by bit, unless constrained by regulations, people change their habitats until they take on a patina of their own characters. For instance, few Chinatowns, if any, in the United States were designed to be Chinatowns, but their residents have added and deleted elements of the environment to make places that clearly communicate this identity.

THE COMPONENTS OF SETTLEMENTS AS A REFLECTION OF THEIR FUNCTIONS

Human settlements occur in many forms. We differentiate between cities, suburbs, towns, villages, and hamlets in everyday language. Each label conjures up an image of appearances and the range of economic activities housed. Yet defining precisely what we mean is difficult. Urban areas flow into urban areas in many parts of the world.

Today we talk about megalopolis, about BosWash—the urban agglomeration that extends from Boston to Washington, DC. People, however, identify with areas within BosWash, not with the overall urbanized area.

Few if any cities or even villages are seen as homogeneous masses. They are seen as comprising distinctive parts: streets and buildings, neighborhoods and precincts. Each part has evolved to serve a set of functions. They can also be differentiated by their visual characteristics (Lynch 1960). We give them labels too: districts, precincts, or neighborhoods.

The human ecology movement associated with the Chicago school of sociology attempted to divide the city into natural areas—areas that had some geographical boundaries and contained a set of activities and/or people that distinguish them from adjacent areas (Park, Burgess, and Mackenzie 1925; Hawley 1950). This kind of subdivision is considerably easier to do in cities that have clear geographic edge elements, such as a broken topography, than in cities on flat terrain. All cities do, however, have identifiable land-use areas.

1. Beacon Hill, Boston

2. Roosevelt Island, New York; View from Manhattan

3. Roosevelt Island; the Internal Street

Figure 8-8: Meanings and the Built Environment
Whether what they see around them is designed specifically to communicate specific messages or not, people read their own meanings into their environments based on their own experiences. One of the problems urban designers face in suggesting future environments that deviate from the norm is that symbolic meanings are largely derived from past associations (1). The deviance from a norm communicates a symbolic message itself. Roosevelt Island, New York (formerly Welfare Island), is a predominantly Modernist all-of-a-piece urban design (2,3) that has different meanings for different people as it has changed its population composition during its stage-by-stage development.

Districts or precincts can be areas in which particular goods are distributed or services provided or that are physically similar bounded areas. Few product and service market areas are easily conterminous; they do not fit easily into professional city planner's plans (Hester 1975). Yet for urban designers to come to grips with their work, cities (whether new towns or existing ones) are often divided into areas that have particular functions enabling them to be addressed somewhat independently within a broad policy framework established for the overall settlement. Often the areas of concern are defined in terms of land-holding or land-ownership patterns because that is what is available for concerted development. Sometimes it is the visual character that is the basis for dividing a city into parts for design purposes. Kevin Lynch (1960) showed that such areas—he called them districts—form part of people's mental image of cities. Such precincts should, however, be based on broader concepts of geography and character in terms of activities carried out there, rather than simply on their visual appearance.

The term "neighborhood" has had a special attraction to urban designers, because designing to create a sense of community has been a major social concern among urban designers (Keller 1968; R. Brooks 1974). Indeed, the search for community, for affiliation with a group, has been a broad concern for many people in the United States

(Baltzell 1968). While a neighborhood is a physical area, usually, but not necessarily, a residential one, it has social overtones to it. As will be pointed out (see Chapter 14), designing for community is full of difficulties, but planning and design at a precinct or neighborhood level may well be the extent to which an urban designer can effectively operate in all-of-a-piece design.

We differentiate the public realm of cities into functional components: streets, parks, plazas (see Chapter 9). The city also consists of the quasi-public spaces that are either privately owned spaces open to the public or public spaces to which access is controlled. The term "place" refers to open spaces in human settlements. It also implies more—that there is a "there there." Places have an identity because of either their perceptual (usually visual) or social character, or both. The vocabulary we use to describe cities and their components based on the functions they serve, in turn, shapes the way we look at cities. In everything an urban designer does, it must be recognized that the functions served by cities and their components will change in specifics if not generic type.

THE EVOLVING FUNCTIONS OF THE CITY

The developments in communications technology that have taken place during the second half of the twentieth

1. Dallas

2. Boulder, Colorado

3. San Francisco

Figure 8-9: Cities, Precincts, and Neighborhoods
Implicit in the labels we give types of human settlements is a set of activities that they afford and services they provide. Almost inevitably the economic functions that specific patterns of the environment serve have led to a differentiation of the settlement's parts. The central business districts are clearly discernible in aerial photographs of Dallas (1), Boulder (2), and San Francisco (3). The building types and overall textures of space required to afford those functions reasonably well leads to the visual differentiation of parts. The character of a settlement depends on this texture and the degree of integration and segregation of its various activities.

century raise questions about the necessity of the present forms of human settlement patterns (Hepworth 1990; Schmandt et al. 1990). The impact of present urban forms on the biogenic environment raises similar questions. Without doubt the distribution of activities and people in spaces is changing and the way cities function in their natural environments is changing, but cities as we know them will continue to exist into the foreseeable future. The reason is simple: cities and the places within them serve many functions that people seek. The internal organization of cities will, however, continue to change as changing economic conditions, modes of production, values, and technological possibilities affect the way of life of their inhabitants.

Cities are here to stay as the result of growing populations and a limited land supply in many countries of the world. In those countries, particularly some developing ones, the limited land, growing population, and increased efficiency of agricultural production act together to push people from rural areas into cities, while simultaneously opportunities in the cities draw people away from rural areas. Metropolitan areas are here to stay because of political pressures and the availability of buildable land in places where people want to be for positive or negative reasons (i.e., the alternative is worse). They exist for economic necessity and because people are gregarious.

One of the basic questions facing city planners dealing with the overall physical frame of cities is: "To what degree will movement of people be substituted by a change in communications technology?" (Schneider and Francis 1989; Hepworth 1990; Schmandt et al. 1990). The broader question is the normative one: "To what extent should movement be substituted?" In policy planning contexts where such issues are generally avoided, the decision is made in the marketplace. In the future will people have to come together to engage in the activities the way they do today? Will such behaviors persist because of the latent functions they serve even if it is technically unnecessary and/or economically inefficient to retain them? These questions address potential changes in business transactions, and in the nature of recreation and entertainment. Present trends do not, however, suggest a major change in the desire for people to get together to watch sporting events, attend plays, or have business lunches, but radical changes may occur in the future.

Urban design decisions cannot, however, be made on the basis of scenarios of the future much different from today. Change is likely to come in a piecemeal way. The urban design goal is for any infrastructure designed for the future to be adaptable. "Any pattern which the city has to offer, however it is achieved, must be strong enough to survive all its inevitable disorders and their vicissitudes" (Rykwert 1988).

The questions are: "What form will these settlements take in the future and will the overall 'forces' creating change shape the work and thinking of urban designers?"

1. Philadelphia

2. San Diego

Collection of the author

3. Udaipur, Rajasthan, India

"Will the economic function or the needs of people's gregarious behavior be met in other ways in the future?" "Will political and economic pressures lead to the breaking apart of the city?" "Will technological changes in communications processes lead to major changes in the way people live and thus the purposes served by cities?" Such questions have long attracted the attention of architects and planners. Our past success at speculating on such questions has not been high (Mansfield 1990).

There is no doubt that new urban patterns will emerge in the future. It is possible that much of the building stock of existing cities will become obsolete. The new information systems will have a distance-shrinking effect on the distribution of activities, allowing them to be more dispersed. Whether or not these patterns will lead to profoundly new urban forms depends on how the marketplace reacts and how politicians and designers formulate the policies that shape the future. Designers will have to ask questions about the multidimensional experiences afforded in existing cities and whether the same and/or more satisfying arrangements can exist in more dispersed or more concentrated settlement forms of different building types. Existing cities have an infrastructure in place. It consists of facilities for moving goods, people, and institutions. It also consists of various communications modes: telephone, radio, television, and also the emerging technologies of converging computer and telecommunications systems. In addition, it consists of plazas, parks, and public gardens as displays and as locations for public events as well as buildings serving as places for public purposes and civic activities. All these places serve both manifest and latent functions.

URBAN DESIGN AND THE FUNCTIONS OF CITIES

One of the major criticisms of the design professions has been that their attitudes and the consequent policies and designs they generate are highly reductionist in nature. They tend to be variety-reducing procedures. The attitudes are being challenged on two sides—by those who wish to see the city greener with more natural areas (e.g., Gordon 1990), and by those who appreciate the nature

Figure 8-10: Adaptability to Change
Cities are constantly undergoing change (1). The gridiron pattern of the American city is highly enduring under change because it has proven very adaptable to the variety of wheeled transportation forms that have developed in the history of people (2). In contrast, designing to accommodate changes in transportation modes is extremely difficult in the preindustrial cities of the hot, arid regions of the world (3). In designing the future infrastructure of cities the necessity to deal with unforeseen change is an issue of concern.

of high-density living (J. Jacobs 1961), and even gritty cities with the richness of life they afford (Proctor and Matuszeski 1978).

One of the concerns of urban design is surely to raise the density of opportunities available to people. There have been two ways of achieving this end: to localize facilities, and to increase accessibility to facilities. Many of the urban design ideas associated with the Empiricist strand within the Modern movement were associated with the goal of localizing facilities, but transportation planning over the past five decades, particularly in the design of highway networks, has focused on increasing accessibility (or at least maintaining levels of accessibility with a considerably more widely dispersed population). These solutions work for the highly mobile, but not all segments of the population are highly mobile. The broader concern is to increase the total number of appropriately manned settings available to people. Providing settings that are not used, however, does cities considerable psychological harm (J. Jacobs 1961; Whyte 1980).

"All the world's a stage and all the men and women merely players. They have their exits and their entrances." The stage is the milieu and the play the behavior. Some urban designers think of their work as the creation of theater (see Gosling and Maitland 1984a, 1984b). The analogy should not be taken too far, but the creation and evolution of any human settlement does involve the step-by-step adding, altering, and/or abandoning of behavior settings—changing the stage and the players—by many playwrights working simultaneously. Urban design also involves the maintenance of the existing ones of importance or potential importance to people (Jacobs and Jones 1962).

The goal of urban design is to provide either directly through all-of-a-piece design or indirectly through the writing of guidelines the affordances that create a well-functioning adaptable human settlement or set of human settlements. It is a process that may lead society at times and at other times may seem to be more of a process of catching up with society's demands.

CONCLUSION

The city planning and urban design goal is to make the city more functional in meeting what are regarded, within a culture, as the positive motivations of people, and less functional, or totally nonfunctional, in terms of the negative behaviors. The excitement and frustration of urban designing evolve from the effort to deal simultaneously with the multiplicity of functions served by behavior settings. There will be differences of opinion about the functions that particular places should fulfill, differences in tolerance people have for misfits between their existing and desired behaviors and between their existing milieu and that necessary to serve desired functions well. Urban designers are not neutral bystanders in the process of creating opportunities for new behavior patterns or new aesthetic experiences, but any advocacy for change they make needs to be based on an understanding of the basic functions of settlement patterns.

The conclusion is that the overall goal in the design of human settlements must be to create robust places—cities, precincts, open spaces—that endure under change. The goal is to structure the urban experience— the experiencing of the built environment, the activities it houses, and the displays inherent in its structure. The goal is to make the city legible and to fulfill human needs in a multidimensional way. The urban designer has a special role in helping bring these ends to fruition.

MAJOR REFERENCES

Chapin, F. Stuart Jr., and Edward J. Kaiser (1979). *Urban Land Use Planning*. Urbana and Chicago: University of Illinois Press.

Hepworth, Mark E. (1990). "Planning for the Information City: The Challenge and Response." *Urban Studies* 27, no. 4:537–558.

Jacobs, Jane (1961). *The Death and Life of Great American Cities*. New York: Random House.

Meier, Richard L. (1962). *A Communications Theory of Urban Growth*. Cambridge, MA: MIT Press.

Mumford, Lewis (1961). *The City in History: Its Transformations and Its Prospects*. New York: Harcourt, Brace and World.

Olsen, Donald (1986). *The City as a Work of Art*. New Haven, CT: Yale University Press.

Proctor, Mary, and Bill Matuszeski (1978). *Gritty Cities: A Second Look at Bethlehem, Bridgeport, Hoboken, Lancaster, Norwich, Paterson, Reading, Trenton, Troy, Waterbury, Wilmington*. Philadelphia: Temple University Press.

SUBSTANTIVE ISSUES IN ATTAINING A FUNCTIONAL ENVIRONMENT

Chrysler Building, New York City

Substantive theory in urban design is concerned with describing and explaining the qualities of the built environment and what they afford people. The list of individual affordances of all the possible configurations of built form is beyond imagination. The domain of interest of urban designers consists of the elements of built form and the land and building uses that can be controlled by them and/or by urban design policies they create. The domain is limited in a number of ways. First of all, the social and economic planning policies developed by politicians and professional planners set the parameters within which an urban design proposal must function. These social and economic plans will have consequences for urban design, which in turn will affect the nature of those plans in an iterative process. It is thus important for urban designers to be involved in setting social policies for human settlement patterns, not as experts in social issues but as experts in the physical design ramifications of social policies. In addition, except in total design, the urban designer does not deal with all aspects of the built environment, but rather with designing policies that will give direction to individual architects working on building designs, to landscape architects working on open-space designs, and to other professionals working on various aspects of infrastructure design. There are physical limitations to what the urban designer can specify. Not every configuration of built form that seems desirable at an urban design scale can be turned into a viable component of the infrastructure or into a viable building. It is important to understand these limitations.

Chapter 9, The Elements of Urban Design, describes those attributes of the built environment with which an urban designer deals. They are essentially the characteristics of the milieu component of behavior settings—its patterns and the materials of which they are constructed. The milieu and standing patterns of behavior go hand in hand. As a result, urban designers are concerned with the distribution of behavior settings in human settlements and their precincts. Their ultimate concern is, however, with enhancing the quality of life of the people who will inhabit the behavior settings a development affords and the aesthetic qualities it possesses with an eye on future changes as well. It is, however, the elements of the milieu and uses of settings that an urban designer specifies. This specification is made through iterative design steps. Each step is a procedural element of design, and the demands of products at each shapes the way a designer thinks about cities and goes about urban design. Urban designers shape the process.

The elements of the built environment can be combined in so many ways that for all intents and purposes one can regard the possibilities as infinite. The urban designer is, however, concerned with specifying a buildable environment. It is interesting to speculate on future technologies and possible urban configurations, but the patterns an urban designer proposes today are constrained by the possible geometric permutations of the elements of the built environment and the functional requirements of the machines used in the support of human lives and ways of life. Chapter 10, Technological and Geometrical Possibilities, lays out the technical parameters within which urban designers have to work.

Once the elements of concern of the urban designer and the geometric and technological limitations on what is possible have been spelled out, the implications of seeking to design a functional environment can be presented. In the Functional Sociogenic Environment section of this part of the book, the issues involved in shaping the layout of the built environment to meet basic and cognitive human needs are described. The attainment of these ends has to be seen within the goal of attaining a functional biogenic environment (see A Functional Biogenic Environment section of this part) and within the limits of the distribution of decision-making powers in democratic societies. ■

9

THE ELEMENTS OF URBAN DESIGN

The elements of urban design are those aspects of the built environment that are open to manipulation, or shaping, by urban designers in assisting policy makers create futures. In the same way that there are substantive and procedural urban design theories, there are two sets of urban design elements of concern: substantive and procedural. The first deals with the elements of the biogenic and sociogenic world and the latter with the products produced during the decision-making, or design, process. The primary focus in this chapter is on the substantive elements, but as they cannot be discussed sensibly in isolation from the products of each step of the design process, the procedural elements and products of an urban designer's work are also introduced here. They are considered more thoroughly in Chapter 21.

SUBSTANTIVE ELEMENTS

Architects and urban designers have looked at the built environment and thus the elements of design in a number of ways. Le Corbusier (1934) wrote:

> The basic materials of city planning are:
> sun,
> sky,
> trees,
> steel,
> cement,
> in that order of importance.

In specifying this, Le Corbusier brought attention to specific aspects of the environment he believed to be important to all people. There are, however, many other ways of looking at cities and the elements of urban design. Each stresses a particular viewpoint.

Architects have generally looked at cities as geometric patterns. Some designers have looked at the shapes per se in terms of their visual qualities. This approach has been more typical of the Europeans (e.g., R. Krier 1979) than Americans, but a number of American urban designers have looked at cities and urban designs as two-dimensional figure-ground configurations with the built environment as figure and the open space as ground, or vice versa (Copper 1983; Trancik 1986). If one views the environment in these ways, the design problem can easily be seen as a narrow one of the design of pleasing shapes, or interlocking geometries, often in plan form. The elements of design then become spatial configurations per se. In thinking this way there is a danger that we then end up with a design without a program—a physical environment with nothing happening in it (see also C. Rowe 1983). Designing the program (i.e., a statement of the desired behavioral environment) then becomes a process of filling in the built form with what it can accommodate. The process should be the reverse, if anything, but as behavior and space go together, they are increasingly being considered simultaneously.

Another way of looking at the environment that has been more characteristic of Europeans than Americans has been as a collection of types of buildings and open spaces either in terms of activities or spatial configurations per se (R. Krier 1979, 1990; L. Krier 1990). When the types are considered as use types they do indeed combine a form and function, but the function is at a very general level that tends to obscure what actually happens within a space. A *plaza* may conjure up an image of a use—people gathering—but the activities to be housed may be, and usually are, more complex than the image implies (Perin 1970).

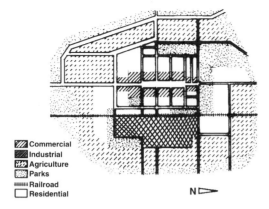

Adapted from a drawing by Jeffrey E. Ollswang (Catanese and Snyder 1988)

Commercial
Industrial
Agriculture
Parks
Railroad
Residential

N ▷

1. Land-Use Map of a Generic Garden City

2. Off Fifth Avenue, New York

Source: *Cornell Journal of Architecture* 2:188

3. Figure/Ground Study, Providence, Rhode Island (1980)

Figure 9-1: Some Ways to Classify Elements of Urban Form
There are many ways of looking at a city. One way closely associated with city planning and zoning is in terms of land uses (1; compare to Fig. 2-7(1)). A richer and more detailed way is in terms of the behavior settings it contains (2). This task is more difficult because the texture is fine-grained. A third way is to look at the plan in terms of solids and voids, positive and negative spaces, figures and grounds (3). Each way biases the way we conceive of a city—what we pay attention to—and thus the way we design it.

Sooner or later the urban designer is indeed concerned with the geometry of the physical environment, its arrangement, and the types of buildings that compose it. Starting out by thinking in this manner, however, truncates the design process. This truncation is both an advantage and a disadvantage. It is certainly a way of designing with which many architects feel comfortable. It is also a process that reduces the need for creative thinking by imposing a "solution" on the situation being considered. This process is unfortunate because it results in a reductionist view of urban design. If we today are to learn from the mistakes of the Modernists, the impact of the limited concerns of many architects and urban designers with urban life, and the subsequent lifeless designs that serve only the needs of the designer, then we need to look at the environment in a fuller manner. The exception occurs in some very specific circumstances when the urban designer's role is simply as a sculptor of urban form. The sculptural role is one seldom given to an urban designer, although many architects would like to claim the role as their own and it is one promulgated in the academy. A richer way of looking at the elements of the environment as units of environmental analysis and design has been sought by a number of people.

A way of analyzing the visual structure of cities has been provided by Kevin Lynch (1960) based on his empirical study of the cognitive images people have of the built environments that they inhabit or use. He identified five elements that form people's mental images of cities and/or their components. The elements are: *paths, edges, districts, nodes,* and *landmarks.* Paths are channels of movement. Edges are boundaries that break or run parallel to the urban texture, which is composed of a texture of individual buildings and of open spaces. A special type of edge is a *port* (Thiel 1961) or *gate* (Norberg Schulz 1971). An edge is a place of transition from one area to another—a place from where a new vista is perceived. Districts are areas of the city that are visually homogeneous in texture and may also be homogeneous in land use. Nodes are places of intensive activity, usually at the intersections of paths. Nodes that are the foci of districts have been called *cores* (Porteous 1977). Landmarks are points of reference based on their visual distinctiveness from their surroundings. Landmarks and nodes often go together.

Lynch's categorization of elements has proven to be useful in designing for imageability and legibility (ease of wayfinding) in cities (see Chapter 12, Meeting Safety and Security Needs) and buildings (Passini 1984; Arthur and

PATHS

EDGES

DISTRICTS

NODES

LANDMARKS

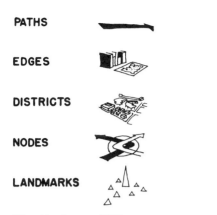

1. The Elements of Cognitive Images of Cities

2. San Francisco

3. University of Minnesota, Minneapolis/St. Paul

4. Horton Center, San Diego

Figure 9-2: The Elements of Cognitive Images of Cities
The form-giving elements of the city (1) that enhance its imageability and legibility are clearly discernible in an aerial photograph of San Francisco (2). Mission Bay itself can be analyzed in terms of these elements. The ease of imaging City

Beautiful schemes, as in this scheme by Cass Gilbert, is due to the clarity of these elements (3). Possibly, the concept of "gates"—points where one crosses an edge—should be added to Lynch's list (4; see also Fig. 17-9(2)). Gates are seldom as literal as in this example.

Passini 1990). The elements when clearly organized are important in giving a visual organization to cities, so in this sense they can be regarded as elements of urban form, but were not intended to be, nor can they be, the basic elements of form for dealing with all urban design issues.

There are other ways of looking at human settlements that are closer to the position described in this book. Ray Studer (1969) proposes that designers consider the environment of their concern to be a behavior-contingent physical system. The task of urban designers in this view is to aid other decision makers in improving the physical component of the environment in response to changing and desired behavioral patterns—behavioral patterns are understood to include both activity patterns and aesthetic patterns or norms. The point of departure for urban design then becomes a model of a proposed behavioral system. The most appropriate unit of analysis and design for urban designing in this case is the *behavior setting* (Le Compte 1974).

Behavior Settings and Architectural Patterns

The behavior setting is a unit of analysis that describes the functional core of urban design concern—the role of the public realm of cities in meeting human needs. As a result it has been already been referred to a number of times in this book (see Chapters 1 and 8). Behavior settings, it was noted, consist of a standing (or recurring) pattern of behavior and a milieu (a physical pattern), which act as a unit for a time period. The same physical pattern may be part of more than one behavior setting at different times or of overlapping settings at one time.

Behavior settings serve human purposes—they serve functions. The activities, or standing patterns, of behavior that form a component of any behavior setting are purposeful. They serve human needs—basic needs and cognitive needs, both instrumental (i.e., to fulfill a task) and expressive (i.e., as a gesture for its own sake). The milieu consists of the patterns of the physical layout of the environment. These patterns afford patterns of behavior;

Source: Alexander et al. (1977)

122 BUILDING FRONTS

1. . . . This pattern helps to shape the paths and buildings simultaneously; and so completes BUILDING COMPLEX (95), WINGS OF LIGHT (107), POSITIVE OUTDOOR SPACE (106), ARCADES (119), PATH SHAPE (121), and also ACTIVITY POCKETS (124).

* * *

2. Building set-backs from the street, originally invented to protect the public welfare by giving every building light and air, have actually helped greatly to destroy the street as a social space.

* * *

3. Therefore:

On no account allow set-backs between streets or paths or public open land and the buildings which front on them. The set-backs do nothing valuable and almost always destroy the value of the open areas between the buildings. Build right up to the paths; change the laws in all communities where absolute by-laws make this impossible. And let the building fronts take on slightly uneven angles as they accommodate to the shape of the street.

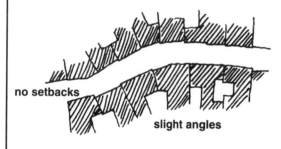

no setbacks

slight angles

4. Detail the fronts of buildings, indeed the whole building perimeter, according to the pattern BUILDING EDGE (160). If some outdoor space is needed at the front of the building, make it part of the street life by making it a PRIVATE TERRACE ON THE STREET (140) or GALLERY SURROUND (166); and give the building many openings onto the street—STAIR SEATS (125), OPEN STAIRS (158), STREET WINDOWS (164), OPENING TO THE STREET (165), FRONT DOOR BENCH (242). . .

* * *

few are highly restrictive. Most patterns of the milieu afford many activities, but some are much more easily and comfortably accommodated than others. When they work well the patterns of behavior and architecture are highly congruent—they fit each other well (Alexander 1964; Michelson 1976). They are said to have a synomorphic relationship (Barker 1968) or, in the words of architect Richard Neutra (1954), they can be said to "be irritant free."

The perceived level of congruence can change for a number of reasons: people's activities, aesthetic tastes, and values may change; the layout may change due to wear and tear or chemical deterioration and aging; and the stringency of the measure applied to ascertain the level of congruence may rise. Indeed, our expectations of the quality of the fit between behavior and environment have increased; we have become more demanding. When the discrepancy reaches a particular level, there is a perceived misfit between environment and behavior and a press for change begins. The level will vary from person to person based on their standards of judgment and their perceptions of the costs and rewards of being in a situation. Often, however, there is considerable similarity among judgments, particularly within stable cultures and among people of similar socioeconomic backgrounds (see also Chapter 1).

When the congruence between behavior (in terms of activities or aesthetic tastes) and milieu is reduced to a point below an acceptable level (i.e., beyond a level of irritation), something has to be changed or a stressful situation will arise. The behavior has to change to something afforded by the architecture, the architecture has to be changed to afford the behavior, or both have to be changed to reach an acceptable level of fit between the two. Alternatively, the behavior can be abandoned. When the milieu serves a purpose that is no longer needed it is abandoned, or its affordances are recognized for another needed purpose and it is reused. Its structure may require some *adaptation* to serve this new purpose and resources are sought to change it. If the resources are not available, the structure will be allowed to deteriorate and possibly be demolished.

Figure 9-3: Pattern Statements and Pattern Language
Christopher Alexander and his colleagues look at the city as a set of patterns, each of which affords a number of activities or experiences. For instance, the observation about "building fronts" (1) forms part of their *Pattern 122* in *A Pattern Language*. The observation forms part of other observations (2) and leads to a design directive (3), which forms part of a further series of design directives (4). Each statement is accompanied by an illustrated argument for its use. (See Fig. 4–7(2) for another example.)

In describing the environment in this way, it must be remembered that the milieu carries meanings beyond any utilitarian use or aesthetic taste. It carries memories of past events, past ideas, past workmanship (Rossi 1982). Buildings and urban patterns are worth saving to remind us of the continuity of life and our place in time and space, but often the marketplace and/or political decisions lead to other conclusions.

The urban designer can be thought of as pattern maker, even though this view is not really acceptable among design professionals. If the concern of design is with optimizing the number and character of behavior settings that exist or should exist within an area, two types of patterns are the elements of urban designing: patterns of behavior and patterns of the layout of the environment. If the urban designer is really responsible for the design of the latter, who is responsible for the former? When urban designers think of use types of urban spatial types, the behavioral program is implicit in the type. A number of designers have attempted to be more explicit.

In a series of reports, papers, and books, Christopher Alexander and his colleagues have developed a "pattern language" for the design of *whole* cities, open spaces, buildings, and rooms (Alexander et al. 1977, in particular). The language consists of pattern statements linking a problem with a solution in the form of a three-dimensional geometric pattern. The pattern is analogous to the milieu of a behavior setting. In Alexander and his colleagues' terms, a pattern that solves a problem (activity or aesthetic) is the element of design. The process of designing is one of synthesizing (not combining) the patterns into solutions to overall problems. The concept of behavior setting extends this idea. It combines behavioral and physical configurations into a single element for analyzing and designing the world. It thus places a considerable responsibility for environmental quality on the urban designer or urban design team.

Human settlements can be seen as systems of behavior settings nested within each other in a complex, interwoven hierarchy. Some of these behavior settings are enduring while others change or disappear fairly rapidly to be replaced by new ones. The layout and use of the four Center City squares in Philadelphia have been remarkably enduring as behavior settings. In 1991 they are essentially the same as Jane Jacobs saw them in 1958 (1961), even though the individuals who have used them have differed over time. Other settings have come and gone and new ones are being designed.

Systems of Behavior Settings

There are two basic types of behavior settings: *places* and *links*. Places are locations where a standing pattern of behavior occurs in a localized area, at a point, whereas in a link the standing pattern of behavior consists of movement between places. Links are analogous to Lynch's

paths. *Nodes* are places where a number of links come together (see also Lynch 1960). Links may contain places where behavior for the moment does not consist of movement between places. In the corridors of buildings or on sidewalks, for instance, many behavior settings may occur at points. They are small ephemeral behavior settings. Indeed, one of the criticisms of the design of such links is that they do not afford places for such behaviors, usually because people have insufficient space to withdraw from the main flow of people or cars (Perin 1970). The concern has been with the primary use—movement—in designing them, and not with the secondary uses—gossiping, playing, and so on. In such situations, the potential functions of the secondary uses aren't fulfilled or are fulfilled in a way that is an irritant to other people.

Enclosing Behavior

Each behavior setting is a territory claimed and defended by its owners and/or by those participating in the standing pattern of behavior (E. Hall 1966; Porteous 1977; El-Sharkawy 1979). The claim may be momentary or enduring. In a conversation by a few people on the sidewalk, or the resolution of a case in the corridor of a courthouse, the territorial claim is momentary. If the momentary ones occur often enough, they become part of the overall standing patterns of behavior of a physical setting.

Behavior settings are always bounded to create a territory. The type of boundary depends on the comfort and privacy requirements for the standing pattern of behavior. All activities have a level of comfort and privacy accorded to them or expected of them whether they are in so-called public areas or private ones. The expectations vary according to cultural norms and the status of the individuals involved (Altman 1975). For instance, men and women differ in terms of the privacy levels they demand in public plazas (Mozingo 1989). One of the objectives of any design is to provide for privacy requirements with the appropriate enclosing or space-defining elements. These elements may vary from a floor and distance to totally enclosed spaces, ones that are walled and roofed. The space-defining surfaces may vary in type from differences in paving patterns to screens to opaque soundproof walls. This is true of spaces in the public and the private realm.

The Public Realm

The public realm is not necessarily conterminous with publicly owned property. It consists of those places and links to which everybody has access, although this access may be controlled at certain times. It is a mistake to think of the public realm as outdoor space only, although certainly much of it is—squares, streets, parks. It also consists of those indoors places in the public domain—the halls of railway stations and public buildings. There

1. Boulder, Colorado

2. Manhattan

3. Union Station, Washington, DC

4. South Street, Philadelphia, Pennsylvania

5. River Walk/Passeo del Rio, San Antonio, Texas

6. Santa Barbara, California

Photograph by Jennifer Taylor

Figure 9-4: Places and Links

An important way for urban designers to look at human settlements is in terms of places and links—aspects of the *capital web* of the public realm. Places are not simply outdoor spaces such as parks and plazas (1,2) but any part of the public realm that constitutes a localized behavior setting. Many large indoor rooms, such as halls of railroad stations (3), the foyers of public buildings such as city halls, and the interiors of shopping malls and parts of major religious facilities, are part of the public or the quasi-public realm of a city. Some places are incidental (4). Many places have a quasi-public character because they are under private control. The links between them consist of streets, pedestrian ways, and transportation routes of a variety of types (5,6). Some of them are both places and links (e.g., 1 and 5) and need to be designed as such.

1. Seattle

2. Interior of World Financial Center, Battery Park City, New York

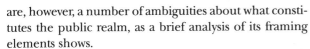

3. Sidewalk Marker, Sunset Boulevard, Los Angeles

Figure 9-5: Public and Private Elements of the Public Realm
Some places are unambiguously public (1). This does not mean that a person has complete freedom of behavior there but that the behavior, allowing for certain tolerances, has to fall within the norms accepted by the public. There are many spaces in cities and suburbs today that are more ambiguous because, although the public has access to them, they are under the control of a private enterprise (2). In highly ambiguous spaces, markers (3) are often necessary to remind us of this legal fact, although many people do not see the markers.

are, however, a number of ambiguities about what constitutes the public realm, as a brief analysis of its framing elements shows.

The public realm is framed by its floor and by the surrounding surfaces of buildings and/or vegetation. Some of these surfaces are exterior walls differentiating between public and private space, but others are the walls and ceilings that frame interior spaces. The ambiguity arises for two reasons: (1) the elements that define the public realm (particularly the walls of buildings) are often privately owned, which raises questions of public versus private rights; and (2) many spaces, both outside and inside buildings, are quasi-public. The jurisdiction over quasi-public spaces, such as the Winter Garden at Battery Park City, is private not public, although the public generally has access to such places for much of the day. There is little confusion over who controls the foyer of a commercial office building, but there is considerable confusion over who controls many open spaces outdoors and also interior spaces such as arcades, shopping malls, sky links between buildings, and underground passages linking other quasi-public spaces in cities such as Minneapolis, Houston, and Dallas. The public has right of access but whether one can loiter or not depends largely on one's appearance and/or time of day.

One of the basic objectives of urban design is to specify what the public realm should be, how it is defined and bounded, what its enclosing elements should be, and how it interacts with the private realm. Increasingly, important questions are being asked not only in the United States but also in other democratic societies about who has the right of access to public spaces and who controls them, particularly in places where much antisocial behavior occurs (A. Francis 1991; Oc 1991).

The Milieu as Display

A display can be the statement of an artist, or it can be a byproduct of meeting other needs/functions, as the early Modernists intended. As a display the milieu serves at least three possible intertwined purposes. It can be (1) a means of communicating information, (2) a vehicle, or medium, for an expressive statement, and (3) a visual experience or, more likely, a sequence of visual experiences as one moves through space (P. Collins 1942; Martienssen 1956; Thiel 1961; Appleyard 1965; Halprin 1965). In the first case the display takes the form of signs—billboards, street signs—and in the second it communicates symbolic messages. In many cases the distinction is blurred because symbols can also be informational and many signs have a high symbolic content. In the third case, one is concerned with the environment as a static geometry to be seen from a single station point or as a sequence of vistas as one moves through it. People's interest is aroused by the complexity of the patterning provided the complexity does not become bewildering (Cullen 1961; Berlyne 1974).

The milieu always carries a number of "to whom it may concern" messages about the activities that take place within it and/or people involved, the period during which it was built, who the people who own it are, their power, and/or the process by which the milieu was achieved (Laswell 1979). These messages serve a number of functions. The prime ones, in addition to being an artistic expression, are as mechanisms: (1) to show people's membership in a group (see Chapter 13, Meeting Affiliation Needs), (2) to promote an individual or a group's self-esteem (see Chapter 14, Meeting Esteem Needs), and/or (3) as an aesthetic experience for the beholder and/or user of a site (see Chapter 16, Meeting Cognitive Needs, and Chapter 17, Meeting Aesthetic Needs).

The purposes served by the milieu as a display may result in patterns that are not those required to best meet the shelter and/or privacy needs of a standing pattern of behavior. This discrepancy occurs partially because at particular periods in art history specific artistic/architectural attitudes exist toward how a space should be enclosed. The classical attitude, for instance, defines space by surfaces, and the baroque uses point elements indicating boundaries (see also Goldfinger 1942). Sometimes affording the behavior well is more important than what a place looks like; at other times the reverse is true.

The Creation of Settings

All human settlements consist of a number of behavior settings—the larger the settlement, the greater the variety of behavior settings that are likely to exist—although often this increase is usually less than proportional to the population numbers of settlements (see Barker and Gump 1964; Barker and Schoggen 1973; Wicker 1979). Creating a future society involves the maintenance, deletion, and creation of behavior settings (Sarason 1972). In democratic societies, many different individuals and organizations will be involved in the design of settings, some in cooperation with each other, others in competition. Many settings will evolve unselfconsciously but others will be purposefully designed. They evolve and are designed to meet aspects of all the basic needs (see Chapters 11 to 15) and cognitive and aesthetic needs (see Chapters 16 and 17) identified by Abraham Maslow.

Great caution should be taken not to think of behavior settings as physical settings, the provision of which will automatically lead to the occurrence of a behavior. One should avoid thinking that *function follows form* (see also Franck 1984). It is not only architects who have an *edifice complex*—the tendency to see the problems of organizations, formal or communal, as problems with the built environment to which the solution is a new building or a new plaza or a new street (Sarason 1972). It is not surprising for designers of the physical environment to think this way, for their professional desire is to design milieus and to have them built to be seen and used. Other people, from politicians to physicians, often also see the world in terms of facilities. Building facilities has self-serving purposes in terms of meeting a need for prestige and/or as tangible evidence of one's concern for others, as politicians know.

The design of the settings of the public realm and specifications for the allied private uses associated with it involve an understanding of what presently exists and the identification and/or design of a desired behavior system to be housed. This design may be done prior to or simultaneously with the design of the physical environment. In designing the public realm or the designing of guidelines for its development, a series of questions arise: "What kind of physical system is required to support the behavioral system?" "Does such a system already exist?" "If it does, how does one educate people to recognize its affordances?" "If not, what kind of changes are required?" and "Do we have the resources to make the change?"

The Creation of Displays

Architects have traditionally been particularly concerned with the city as a display and specifically as a geometric composition. The layout of the environment may be changed not because it fails to meet the needs of an individual or set of people as the encloser of a standing pattern of behavior, but because it fails on aesthetic grounds. This failure may be in one of two types of performance or a combination of them: (1) the layout fails in its function as a communicator of the affiliation or self-esteem, in space or time, of an individual or group of people, and/or (2) the layout may be regarded as experientially boring. Often, however, an artist, or a person acting in an artistic mode, sees an opportunity to reorganize the surfaces of the environment or their character as a means of self-expression. Some of the most cherished and the most disliked urban designs have been generated this way.

Conclusion: The Substantive Elements of Urban Design

What then are the elements of urban design? They are those units of the overall environment over which an architect and/or planner can have, or should have, some control in the public interest. The concern is primarily with the public realm and with the private as well as public development decisions that affect its quality. To attain a good social and physical environment, urban

1. Rittenhouse Square, Philadelphia

2. Central Plaza, Rittenhouse Square

3. Dogs and People, Rittenhouse Square

Figure 9-6: The Elements of the Behavioral Environment
The elements of the behavioral environment are not easy to classify because the urban environment consists of behavior settings nested within others (1). At the smallest scale of urban design one is concerned with the individual actions that people carry out, particularly with reference to the fixed features of the physical environment (2). Beyond this level, urban designers are concerned with the variety of standing patterns of behavior that take place (3), but also with expressive acts and with acts involving the satisfaction of curiosity that do not necessarily occur in a recurrent pattern.

design policies and plans may strive to: (1) encourage certain types of development in particular locations and discourage other types, (2) conserve the good qualities of the present environment (natural and built), (3) relate the new to the existing, and (4) manage the process of change to minimize the damage to desired ongoing standing patterns of behavior.

The Elements of the Behavioral Environment

While not directly concerned with social policy formation, the urban designer's work inevitably is concerned with:

1. The distribution of activities/uses in the city. Very often this concern is at the level of land uses in two-dimensional space, but the life of human settlements is more complex than this; thus the concern is with the layering of uses in space and in time.
2. The byproducts of activities—the sights, sounds, and odors that they generate.
3. The aesthetic attitudes implicit or explicit in public displays.
4. The management of uses of spaces and the byproducts of their uses over time.

There is a variety of ways of considering the elements that constitute these concerns.

In designing activity systems the smallest elements of concern are the *actions* that affect the layout of a behavior setting's milieu. These actions are chained together into *standing patterns of behavior* or *behavior circuits* and given names (see also Perin 1970). The byproducts of the behavior patterns are all the elements of information that a sensing human being can obtain from the environment or have forced on him or her by it (see Chapter 1). The aesthetic values consist of beliefs about the patterns of the environment and the importance of those beliefs. The management policies include a series of actions and their consequences. The positions taken on all these issues very much affect decisions about the milieu and how we organize its elements.

The Elements of the Milieu

As shown earlier in this chapter, there are many ways of looking at urban form. At the most basic level the built environment can be thought to consist of the three-dimensional physical environment of links and places. An itemized list of the elements that comprise them would be lengthy and probably incomplete because they are innumerable, varying from street structure to street furniture to the façades of buildings. Conceptually, the concern is with fewer elements: the surfaces and objects of the environment, the materials of which they are constructed, the way they are illuminated, and their pigments (see also Gerosa 1979). The concern throughout the urban designing process is with what different configurations of those elements afford in terms of activities and as informational and aesthetic displays.

The basic elements of the physical environment are surfaces that have a texture. They consist of specific materials of specific colors and other qualities, such as degree of opacity, hardness, and durability. They are arrayed to achieve specific ends. The urban design concern is with the way the surfaces of the milieu can be used to create the affordances for specific standing patterns of behavior and aesthetic effects. Thus the concern is with the way they create (1) a spatial character, allied with which is (2) an enclosing character, (3) furnishings, and (4) levels of illumination.

1. Spatial Character. The way the surfaces define (a) the volumetric nature of the public realm both within buildings and outside them and (ii) the sequential nature of the volumes of the public realm—in space and time as people move through them over time, and as they are built and changed over time—largely determines the spatial character of the built environment. Much depends on the size of the volumes and their enclosing character.

2. Enclosing Character. The way the surfaces (a) form the horizontal planes of the public realm, (b) form vertical and inclined planes that bound a place, and (c) are penetrated by entrances or *ports* largely determines the overall aesthetic potential of particular places and links.

3. Furnishings. The fixed features, semifixed features, and movable features (Hall 1966; Bechtel 1974; Wicker 1979; Lang 1987a) that constitute the internal differentiation of a behavior setting, and the objects, such as sculptures and even buildings, that sit in a space specify its affordances for activities and, to some extent, its aesthetic character.

4. Illumination. The way the surfaces and furnishings of a setting are lighted (and shadowed) and the way they light or shade the spaces they make over the course of the day and night affect affordances for activities, comfort, and aesthetic appreciation. Implicit in this concern is a concern with the pigmentation of surfaces (i.e., their color).

The elements that constitute the surfaces of milieu can be of artificial or natural materials. The borderline between the two is often blurred. The artificial elements consist of the components of buildings, plazas, streets, furnishings, and lighting that have been manufactured. The natural elements are those components of the milieu that have not been altered by a manufacturing process. Thus the natural elements are those of earth, stone, and vegetation, and the forces of nature—wind and sun. The

border between the natural and artificial is blurred because many materials (such as stone) can be trimmed, which may change the material's appearance without changing its basic chemical structure. Similarly, natural light can be deflected from the leaves of trees or reflected from walls to illuminate places in various artificial ways.

Natural elements can be used to define the boundaries of behavior settings as much as artificial elements. Trees, hedges, and even air movement can be space-enclosing elements as much as walls (Arnold 1980; Spirn 1984). They do, however, have very have different performance characteristics on both instrumental and symbolic dimensions.

PROCEDURAL ELEMENTS

There are specific stages during the overall decision-making process when the thinking of an urban designer (or, more likely, design team) is presented for review by sponsors and, often, users or potential users of any product that is designed. For these reviews urban designers are expected to have specific products in specific forms to inform decision makers about potential designs, the processes by which decisions were reached, and how those designs might be achieved. Based on these reviews, decisions are made. Such a demand shapes the design process. The products required of urban designers at each step of the decision-making process bias what urban designers do and the way they look at the world as much as the way they define the elements of the physical and social environments. For instance, it forces the process into an overall linear frame, but it often also forces backtracking and the reiteration of previously completed steps. The products produced at these review stages are the procedural elements of urban design (see also Shirvani 1985). They may differ in specific actions, but not in essence, if they are concerned with urban design as policy formation or total or all-of-a-piece urban design, whether publicly or privately sponsored.

The Elements of an Urban Design Plan

Except in total urban design (where a specific built environment is the end product), the most usual end product of an urban designer's work consists of a *master plan* (or an *illustrative site plan*) and the mechanisms (such as design guidelines) required to implement it. Increasingly, no specific final form for the built environment is demanded; rather, the way the physical changes in the built environment should be handled is specified—a *policy plan* is formulated. Thus master planning and policy planning are two forms of urban design. There is considerable overlap between them.

The outcome of the master planning process is usually presented in an illustrative design form. The desired product is obtained through the application of a set of

1. Surface Textures and Illumination

2. Rockford, Illinois

3. Minneapolis

Figure 9-7: The Elements of the Milieu
Except in some special circumstances (such as deep in caves and boxes, and for blind people) the basic element of the milieu of human life is an illuminated surface (1). Surfaces are basic. They can be configured in many ways and be composed of a tremendous variety of materials to form enclosures and objects, and thus environments of fixed, semifixed, and movable forms and enclosing planes (2). Each pattern affords certain behaviors and affords being manufactured and colored in specific ways. The patterns of any human settlement are complex (3).

very general building programs (or specification in terms of a type) and design guidelines, which act as policy statements for shaping any possible development that might take place. In policy planning no specific end image is in mind. Instead, the desired characteristics are presented in a series of patterns, and the policies required to achieve them are specified. A number of recent plans have taken this format (e.g., the Center City plan for Philadelphia). In them, no overall end product is presented but rather images of the components of a plan. These components can be organized in any manner provided they fall within the guidelines. Thus design is a building up of parts to achieve a whole and not dividing a whole into parts. The disadvantage of this process is often that no idea gives shape to the overall development. However, this weakness lies in present practice and is not inherent in the process itself because performance criteria for overall ends can also be specified.

There are four basic elements of the *master planning process* for urban design (see also Chapter 20, The Development Process): the *program*, the *master plan*, the *capital improvement plan,* and the *strategic plan*. The program specifies design goals and objectives and the principles required to achieve them. The master plan describes the desired three-dimensional character, facilities, and building uses of a project whatever its scale. It is likely to consist of a

conceptual site plan, or design, that shows at least one possible way in which the goals of design can be implemented. It acts as a demonstration of intentions. The capital improvement plan states where, how, and when the public sector is going to invest in the public realm. The strategic plan is a statement of the phases of the overall development in the foreseeable future. It will describe the nature and sequence of developments, the guidelines, and the time schedule for carrying them out as well as the review procedures at each stage to ensure that the objectives of the master plan are met or, alternatively, changed as new problems arise. There is thus often a major overlap between the master planning process and an urban design policy planning process.

An *urban design policy plan* recognizes (1) that elements of urban development take different amounts of time to implement, and that the actual sequence of development is likely to differ from that envisioned at the outset because of the vagaries of the economic climate; and (2) that public tastes and the norms of good design change over time. General guidelines are developed to achieve specific design qualities (rather than specific designs) and review procedures designed to ensure that the guidelines are followed whenever a new building or other design proposal is made. For example, specifying that all buildings should be built to the property line on street

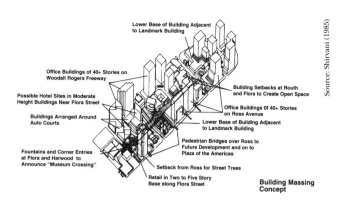

1. Building Massing Concept, Dallas Arts District

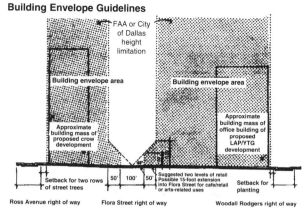

Building Envelope Guidelines

2. Building Envelope Guidelines

3. Tramell Crow Center, Dallas Arts District

Figure 9–8: The Elements of an Urban Design Plan

The ways designers structure the design process and the end products of each phase bias the design effort. The example given here is for the Dallas Arts District developed by Sasaki Associates of Watertown, Massachusetts. The overall project was designed to be carried out by a number of developers with both public and private investments in a number of phases. The building massing concept (1) acts as basis for developing a set of guidelines including specifications for allowable building envelopes (2). The goal is to achieve any end product (3) that meets specific criteria.

frontages ensures a specific quality to a street whatever the design of a building is like. Such guidelines and the accompanying review procedures constitute the end products of the urban design policy planning process (see also Shirvani 1985).

The Elements of the Design Process for Total Urban Designs

The procedural elements of a total urban design are similar to those of a master plan, but they are likely to take on a different form and be administered differently because one design team carries out the process for one sponsor from beginning to end. Similarities arise because a total design is often subject to public review, especially if it does not comply with existing zoning ordinances. The procedural elements are a program, a conceptual site plan, working drawings, specifications, and ultimately the project in place.

If the total design evolves into an all-of-a-piece design where each piece is to be carried out by a subdeveloper, then guidelines would have to be specified for each subdeveloper to follow, as would the specification of the review procedures for ensuring design quality. In this

case, an overall program would guide the whole process. It would consist of statements of the goals and objectives to be met by each component, the design principles to be followed, and the development packages to be implemented.

The procedural elements of urban design may vary in detail from situation to situation but they shape the way urban design is imagined and carried out in every situation. In the United States, the products at each stage will depend on who initiates the process, the private or public sector, and the mechanisms used to represent the public interest.

THE MECHANISMS OF PUBLIC SECTOR CONTROL

There are two broad types of public sector control over how development takes place. One has to do with funding mechanisms and amounts allocated for public infrastructure development, and with the subsidies allocated to encourage various types of development. The other has to do with the control through zoning laws, design guidelines, and the design review process over what is actually built by the private sector.

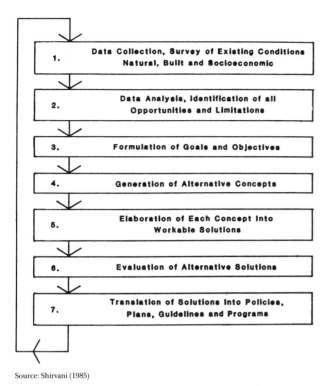

1.	Data Collection, Survey of Existing Conditions Natural, Built and Socioeconomic
2.	Data Analysis, Identification of all Opportunities and Limitations
3.	Formulation of Goals and Objectives
4.	Generation of Alternative Concepts
5.	Elaboration of Each Concept Into Workable Solutions
6.	Evaluation of Alternative Solutions
7.	Translation of Solutions Into Policies, Plans, Guidelines and Programs

Source: Shirvani (1985)

Figure 9-9: Steps in the Synoptic Design Method
Another way of looking at the elements of the design process is in terms of the steps in problem solving. There are a number of ways of structuring the design process, but they all approximate that shown here (see Chapters 20, 21, and 24 for fuller details). The phases can be put together in various ways. In many urban design processes, the first phase involves defining the problem in terms of a set of goals and objectives to be met. Operationally, this action involves the development of a design program. That phase is followed by the design of a conceptual site design—a workable solution. Design guidelines aimed at attaining it are then developed. The implemented design may differ in appearance from the conceptual site plan, but the goal is to attain the same qualities in terms of the performance of the overall design. This phase is followed by an implementation strategy, a capital investment plan, and a strategic plan.

The basic formal mechanisms of control that designers have at their legal disposal have already been introduced. The infrastructure can either be provided by the public sector to subside/encourage the private sector to develop specific types of buildings or the private sector can subsidize the public in order to be able to develop at all. The various types of zoning (prescriptive, performance, and/or incentive) and guidelines described in Chapter 2 can be used to shape the physical configuration of cities. The basic point is simply that the type of product demanded of designers shapes the way they pay attention to the environment.

THE ISSUES OF CONCERN

It is clear that in looking at the elements of urban design in this way that many issues are raised. Some of these issues deal with social design questions and others with physical design questions. The physical design issues are concerned with how best to pattern the environment to meet human needs, the degree of efficiency (or functionality) with which the physical should meet the behavioral objectives in a changing world, and the degree to which design should be context-specific. The social issues have to do with individual rights and group rights, the nature of the public interest, and questions of equity in public investment. These can best be considered after elaborating the definition of how the milieu relates to human needs—the nature of a functional environment—in the ensuing chapters of this book. Much depends on how the physical environment can be configured—the technological and geometric possibilities that exist for urban form.

MAJOR REFERENCES

Gerosa, Piergiorgio (1979). "Architectonic Elements for the Urban Typology." *Lotus International* 24: 121–128.

Krier, Leon (1990). "Urban Components." In Andreas Papadakis and Harriet Watson, eds., *New Classicism: Omnibus Volume*. New York: Rizzoli, pp. 197–203.

Krier, Rob (1990). "Typological Elements of the Concept of Urban Space." In Andreas Papadakis and Harriet Watson, eds., *New Classicism: Omnibus Volume*. New York: Rizzoli, pp. 213–219.

Lang, Jon (1987a). "The Behavior Setting: A Unit for Environmental Analysis and Design" and "Cognitive Maps and Spatial Behavior" in *Creating Architectural Theory: The Role of the Behavioral Sciences in Environmental Design*. New York: Van Nostrand Reinhold, pp. 113–125 and 135–144.

Lynch, Kevin (1960). *The Image of the City*. Cambridge, MA: MIT Press.

Perin, Constance (1970). *With Man in Mind*. Cambridge, MA: MIT Press.

Sarason, Seymour (1972). *The Creation of Settings and the Future Societies*. San Francisco: Jossey-Bass.

Shirvani, Hamid (1985). *The Urban Design Process*. New York: Van Nostrand Reinhold.

Studer, Ray (1969). "The Dynamics of Behavior Contingent Physical Systems." In Anthony Ward and Geoffrey Broadbent, eds., *Design Methods in Architecture*. London: Lund Humphries, pp. 59–70.

Thiel, Philip (forthcoming). *Notes for an Experiential Envirotecture*. Seattle: University of Washington Press.

Wicker, Allan (1979). *An Introduction to Environmental Psychology*. Monterey, CA: Brooks/Cole.

10

TECHNOLOGICAL AND GEOMETRIC POSSIBILITIES

Creating any urban design inevitably involves making tradeoffs among different objectives. A design that is ideal from one viewpoint is unlikely to be ideal from all other viewpoints. One of the major reasons for this discrepancy is that the systems chosen to fulfill one need require a technical and geometric configuration to function well that militates against meeting other human needs. Some functions of the systems required for improving the quality of people's life have rigid technical requirements to work well. Meeting the technical requirements of the milieu of some behavior settings to afford the particular standing patterns of behavior that occur there may result in *anthropozemic* environments while others may result in *anthropophilic* environments (Izumi 1968; see Fig. 7–2).

There are many technical limitations to the design solutions that an urban designer can propose to resolve specific problems. There are issues of financial feasibility, political reality, availability of needed construction skills, and so on. The list may seem almost endless. One of the major concerns is with the technological and thus geometric requirements of the infrastructure that supports the lives of people in cities. Some of these constraints are inherent in a system being considered, but others have to do with the limitations of the mind—we assume things are constraints when they are not (Nader 1970). Our lack of understanding of geometric and technological possibilities in the design of the environment is often a constraint in optimizing designs; we are simply unaware of the possibilities that do exist and are unable to invent new ones because we do not understand geometry. Our naïveté can lead us to propose technical and/or geometric absurdities or, alternatively, to do the opposite, to impose nonexistent limitations on the urban designs we propose.

It is certainly easy to overlook some of the constraints on what can be built when producing illustrative site plans/

designs. For instance, in concentrating on producing a well-functioning public realm defined by buildings, the spaces—building sites—designated for buildings may be functionally/technically inconsistent with the type of uses they are supposed to house. An understanding of building types is essential to avoid such errors. Similarly, a designer may suggest stops on a rapid transit system to produce nodes of activity at intervals that are technically unsound in terms of the efficiency of the operation of the system. For this reason, an understanding of the technical and geometric configurations required for building types and infrastructure systems is essential for the urban designer if multifunctional designs are to be created. The understanding is also essential for creative thinking—it opens up possibilities. To make the urban design task even harder, new technologies are being developed and the geometric possibilities of new urban forms are being better understood as the result of continuing empirical research and speculation. Radical new solutions to the design of urban and suburban forms that are technically functional may not, however, be as functional symbolically. The reverse is also true; symbolically functional designs may not be sensible technically.

TECHNOLOGICAL POSSIBILITIES

Visionary urban designers have tended to focus their attention on creating schemes that stretch the limits of technological feasibility. Usually this means exploring new geometrical patterns or methods of construction, but recently it has also involved a radical advocacy for the return to traditional patterns of urban and building forms and construction techniques for energy consumption, financial, and/or symbolic reasons (El Wakil 1991). The dis-

Drawing by Frank E. Paul, *Amazing Stories Quarterly* (Winter 1928); Source: Mansfield (1990)

1. A Speculation on the Twenty-First Century City (1928)

Collection of the author

2. Habitat, Montreal (1966)

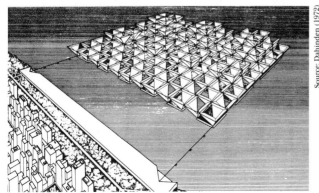

Source: Dahinden (1972)

3. Floating Town with Tetrahedral Residential Units (1963)

play of technological dexterity remains an end in itself not only in the United States (see Sky and Stone 1976; Mansfield 1990) but elsewhere, particularly Japan (see Dahinden 1972). Many of these explorations of potential urban forms have focused on the development of new, high-speed automated transportation systems or new geometries for road systems. Many have looked at cities as megastructures (see Fig. 2-12). Some of Buckminster Fuller's explorations, in contrast, deal with new building technologies and control systems (McHale 1961). His proposal for a skydome over Manhattan (desirable or undesirable; see Fig. 18-1(1)) stretches the very limits of technological feasibility. The practitioner, in contrast, has to deal with the everyday and usually with the immediate future and is seldom technologically innovative (Reissman 1964). Rather than attempting to harness technological innovations, most cities in the United States (with the possible exceptions of Dallas and Minneapolis) have allowed their infrastructure systems to deteriorate and have not explored new ways of redeveloping obsolete ones.

The technical feasibility of soundly and efficiently constructing the geometric patterns that solve specific human problems well may impose limitations on what the urban designer can propose. In Wotton's terms, the necessity of providing for the *firmenes* function of potential elements of the built environment means that otherwise ideal patterns cannot be used. Many bold urban design initiatives are shelved because they are technically, if not politically, infeasible. Sometimes, however, the constraints tend to be self-imposed by the designer or by review agencies—the possibilities are not understood—and potentially sound new design avenues are never entered.

There is much speculation today on the impact of new communications technologies on urban form. The conjecture is that these breakthroughs will afford dramatically new patterns of working, residing, and recreating, and that these changes will, in turn, radically change urban patterns (Schneider and Francis 1989). There is also continued speculation on the nature of new transportation systems and the impact of these technologies on urban form. Our present systems are essentially those that have been in use for the last eighty years, although

Figure 10-1: Explorations of Technological Possibilities
During the course of this century, many architects, engineers, and other visionaries have made suggestions for how new technologies can shape the future city. Some ideas have been more realistic than others. Some images of the future city have been mere speculations (1; see also Fig. 3-1) but others have been serious proposals. Moshe Safdie's exploration of modular building construction came to fruition in Montreal. Stanley Tigerman's generic scheme (3) for the expansion of coastal towns is, however, more typical of many explorations of the 1960s (see Dahinden 1972).

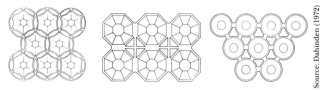

1. Three Patterns of Potential Urban Form

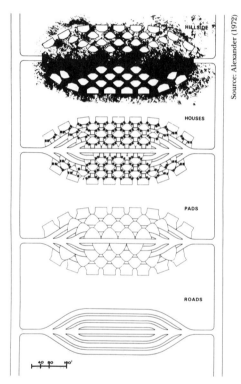

2. Intrapolis, Funnel Town

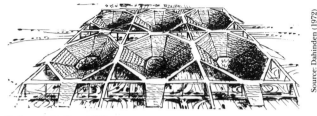

3. Explorations in the Structure of a City "to Sustain Human Contact"

Figure 10-2: Explorations in the Geometry of Urban Forms
Explorations of potential geometries of cities continue. They are of two types: one looks at the potential utility of different forms and the other examines the geometric requirements to solve particular problems. Sometimes they are intertwined. The potential of various patterns to solve the problem of highway congestion and as ordering mechanisms for urban form has been examined by a number of people, including Walter Jonas (1,2). Working from a perceived problem to a solution is the explicit basis for Christopher Alexander's early explorations for the "the city as a mechanism for sustaining human contact" (3).

they are now more technically efficient. While there is little present evidence of radically new systems being implemented in the foreseeable future, the possibility must be considered. More likely, perhaps, is that explorations of ways to operate existing systems more efficiently will open up new geometric possibilities for urban and suburban areas.

GEOMETRIC POSSIBILITIES

Different geometric shapes can be put together efficiently or inefficiently, neatly or untidily. People are habituated to expect specific geometric patterns in the environment. The differences between Rationalist and Empiricist urban designs of the twentieth century are largely due to explorations of two different geometric types—the former seeking an orthogonal geometry and the latter an organic. Often urban designers learn one way of building, or a set of patterns that work well enough, and stick to them rather than to explore new geometric possibilities that might better solve the problems being addressed. Their work is recognized by the patterns they use—their style (Simon 1970). Having a recognizable style has a utility but it also often results in opportunity costs—a better design would have been achieved by using other patterns. Working with a known set of patterns is a failure-avoiding approach to design.

Every urban pattern—neighborhood, street, block, building—has a geometry, a shape and a figure—its quantitative and qualitative dimensions. The urban designer's concern with geometry is twofold: (1) with the possibility of open and enclosed city spaces forming parts of larger shapes in a composition that forms a whole that is both mathematically and structurally possible, and (2) with the meaning of the composition in terms of its affordances for activities and its symbolic messages. The first concern is both technical and intellectual while the second is largely aesthetic (see Chapters 13, 14, and 17).

Geometrical possibilities depend on the feasibility of decomposing a whole into parts according to some mathematical system or, conversely, building up parts into a mathematical whole. A simple example is the "A Format" paper, which is designed for the functional purpose of giving printers a method of dividing large sheets into smaller ones without waste. The proportional system is based on the number $\sqrt{2}$ (Verge 1990). More complex proportional systems were used by Renaissance architects in ecclesiastical and secular architecture as well as urban design (Lawlor 1982). More recently, Le Corbusier based his Modular system on a Rational human body whose proportions coincide with the Fibonacci series. He used it to give order to designs varying in scale from furniture to cities. The scale is fundamental to the relationship of units to wholes in the design of the Unité d'habitation (Le Corbusier 1953, 1954) and the layout of Chandigarh.

There have been studies of more complex relationships between various three-dimensional shapes—polyhedra—and their meanings as shown by Anne Tyng (1969), who along with Robert LeRicolais, were Louis Kahn's geometers (see the shapes in Fig. 6–1(3)). There are only five regular polyhedra—the five platonic solids—but there are an infinite number of mutations of those forms. Pythagoras may have announced that all is arranged according to number, but the difficulty architects have had is to turn abstract geometric patterns into built environments that afford the basic qualities of a good human life. In the United States, despite these explorations, the geometric concern of practitioners tends to be with the functional requirements of the infrastructure systems that shape urban form rather than with abstract intellectual constructs that might lead to radically new urban forms.

INFRASTRUCTURE SYSTEMS DESIGN

The engineering of infrastructure systems is a highly creative act. During the course of this century there have been many novel ideas about what future cities might look like based on suppositions about how their infrastructure systems might be developed and the geometric patterns of cities that might be possible. Most of the proposals have recognized the importance of the infrastructure of a city as its primary form giver but have failed to come up with technologically plausible alternatives to present systems. They tend to focus on single aspects of a system, not the system as a whole.

The overall structure of a city, suburb, indeed, any human settlement at any scale, is highly dependent on the nature of the way its communications and transportation systems are structured. Similarly, the wastewater/sewerage disposal system is an important determinant of form because its requirements for consistent slopes constrain what an urban designer can propose if the form is to work effectively. With the introduction of many pumping stations, this restriction is not as severe as it once was but, as with the use of many energy-consuming devices to solve simple problems, the use of such technologies is being increasingly challenged.

As the technology of each system has changed, so city forms have changed. Each of these systems and its subsystems has requirements of its own to operate well. As a result the qualities of the public realm of a city are very much a product of how its infrastructure is designed. Other systems such as reticulated water systems and cable television and telephone lines that are very much part of life have little impact on the form of cities because they can follow any street or open-space pattern. Often, however, their maintenance requirements leave the open space of cities in a constant state of construction. To avoid this situation, some new manner of channeling them to provide easy access needs to be developed and/or implemented. Yet even they are functionally more efficient laid in straight lines. They are easier to lay and to maintain in that pattern.

There have been a number of explorations that have attempted to design infrastructure systems in Rational (i.e., pure geometric) forms. The gridiron plan based on squares or rectangles is the most common self-consciously planned form for the infrastructure of cities, but the circle (e.g., Circleville, Ohio, before it was changed into a grid plan), the radial, and a variety of other geometric shapes (see Foxhall Crescent, Fig. 2–4(1)) have been used and/or suggested. These patterns include the hexagonal grid, which is the most inclusive space-filling shape, approximating a circle in having a center equidistant from all points on the circumference (e.g., Messinger and LeRicolais 1972). The modern city, however, continues to rely mainly on an orthogonal geometry for the efficiency of its layout. Many architects see this reliance as inhibiting creative urban design, but the three-dimensional layout of many of the world's best-loved places is based on the grid. Much suburban design in the United States, however, follows some organic form, sometimes to resolve biogenic problems but often simply for symbolic reasons.

The Deconstructionist plans for new urban designs (e.g., Flushing Meadows, Corona Park, designed by Bernard Tschumi and others) tend to assume that the infrastructure systems of a city or suburb can have totally independent geometric patterns. When overlapped on plan they create a whole new geometry or urban form for a city. Such systems may work well in low-density environments where access to them is not important, but they will run into difficulties in high-density areas where vehicular transportation and the privacy requirements of individual householders and corporations are the major form-giving determinants of the infrastructure.

Transportation Systems

There are many modes of transportation, and large cities have a variety, each with its own functional requirements from an engineering, financial, and quality of service viewpoint. The basic transportation system for people, it has already been noted, is the pedestrian one, which is highly flexible in its geometric demands. Every other system is designed to enable people to move around the city and region more rapidly and more comfortably than on foot and to enable goods to be moved around with ease and speed. The primary concerns of urban designers are with horizontal movement along the Earth's surface and the vertical movement of people and goods in elevators or via escalators. During the twentieth century a whole new set of urban design and building types has evolved as people have sought ease and comfort of accessibility to services. They include those already mentioned, the shopping mall, strip shopping developments, and the super-church. Some have come and almost gone (the

2. Denver Technological Center

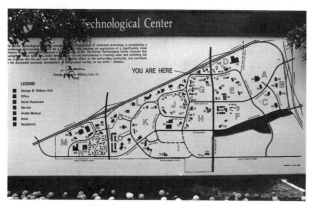

1. Lancaster Avenue, Philadelphia

3. Monorail, Seattle

Figure 10-3: Transportation Systems and Urban Character
The character of present cities tends to be a legacy of past transportation systems as well as present ones (see Fig. 2-23(1)). The ribbon shopping street was a product of the streetcar system. In many of these streets the shops have failed to compete with those stores designed for automobile access (1). Places designed for such access have a very different character (2). There are continuing explorations of new intraurban transportation modes. There has been a particular fascination with monorail systems (3), and more recently with the reintroduction of light rail systems (e.g., Los Angeles, Baltimore, Houston).

drive-in movie theater). The airport is a major new urban design type.

Airports are major urban design problems both in their own layouts and in their impacts on areas adjacent to them. They act as catalysts (or deterrents) for development around them and produce high levels of both sound and air pollution. The location of airports also restricts the height of buildings located around them. In 1987, for instance, the Federal Aviation Administration forced a proposed 52-story building, the PortAmerica Tower, near Washington National Airport to be redesigned into a complex of shorter structures (Draeger 1991). Aircraft, however, have had less of an impact on the other precincts of a city than Le Corbusier (1934) or Frank Lloyd Wright (1958) predicted. They are an integral part of fewer people's everyday lives than the architects of the first three decades of this century predicted and have not become the mode of intraurban transport some architects thought they would.

Of all the infrastructure systems, the transportation system is the one that gives the city its overall character because it establishes the nature of the links between places and of places themselves. Indeed, specific types of transportation have become symbols for a number of cities. Cable cars, for instance, add much to San Francisco's ambience. A settlement pattern based on pedestrian movement differs from one relying on automobiles or mass transit for transportation.

One of the continuing issues in urban design in the United States is the normative question of the degree to which a city should rely on the various modes of transportation to enable people to move around within it. In most new towns and suburbs there is a major reliance on the automobile for transportation. In this way they differ, except for one or two notable exceptions (e.g., Milton Keynes in England (see Fig. 13-7(2)), from recent European designs. The configuration of highways and parking lots, particularly surface parking lots, distinguishes the spatial configuration of the twentieth-century American city from its predecessors. The automobile is increasingly the vehicle used for most trips, although mass transit systems may be very important for local trips in the central business district and the core of cities.

There is a variety of types of mass transit systems, each with its own technical requirements for its channels of movement, its carrying capacity, and the optimal spacing (in terms of its engineering) between its stops. The nature of the stops and their frequency may result in nodes of activity if integrated with other movement links. Where stops are infrequent, nodes of development are likely to occur, as around the stops on the Washington, DC, Metro system, such as in Bethesda, Maryland (see Fig. 2-3(2)). If they are frequent then strip development is likely to occur. The ribbon shopping street of the trolley car era is an example, as is the strip shopping type characteristic of many roads on the outskirts of cities and towns in the automobile era (see Fig. 5-4(2)).

The Road and Parking Network

The road network of any human settlement ties it together. Its elements act as links between parts of a city and as seams for the parts adjacent to them unless they are heavily trafficked and/or very wide. In the latter case they may act as boundaries or edge elements to precincts or *districts* (Lynch 1960). The nature of the hierarchy of elements of the network and the elements themselves are what gives any urban design its character. In the United States, the hierarchy of roads is largely based on their function as channels of movement for people in automobiles. At the high end of the hierarchy in size and traffic volumes carried are freeways, followed by expressways, major arterials, minor arterials, collector streets, local streets, and cul-de-sacs. Each is a behavior setting. Each has its own functions (instrumental and symbolic) and design necessities, capacity requirements and thus widths, spacing requirements depending on population densities served, and frequencies of intersections (De Chiara and Koppelman 1975). Adding parking lots (surface and structured), pedestrian ways (either horizontally or vertically segregated from vehicular traffic) to the list completes the set of facilities for the everyday movement pattern that is largely under an individual's own control. The designs of Radburn, New Jersey (see Fig. 2–8), and Seaside, Florida (see Fig. 2–11), and the pedestrian pocket concept (see Fig. 3–6(2)) are all self-conscious efforts to create environments that are functional both operationally and aesthetically in terms of the road, parking, and pedestrian networks.

The geometry of the road network, the way its elements relate to each other vertically and horizontally, and the manner in which the elements are linked together are all the subject of urban design. Creative urban designs stem from creative solutions to the design of infrastructure networks, which is why so many novel networks are proposed. None of the dramatically new proposals have been technically sound; thus, they remain paper plans (Dahinden 1972; Sky and Stone 1976). In addition, present landholding patterns tend to vitiate the possibility of new systems in the same way as they have in the past.

The increasing popularity of the recreational use of bicycles—and for many young people, their basic transportation use—has led to conflicts between cyclists and automobile drivers on many roads. Some cities (e.g., Boulder, Colorado, and Davis, California, both university towns) and suburban areas have made a considerable effort to cater to the needs of bicyclists with separate networks, but designing with the bicyclist in mind in the United States is not as far advanced as in Europe (see Fig. 8–4(2)).

Pedestrian Networks

The pedestrian network consists of links between the origins and destinations of people's movements and/or the modes of transport that people use for covering long distances. There are many types of pedestrian links: paths,

1. Washington, DC. Detail of L'Enfant's Plan Drawn by Ellicott

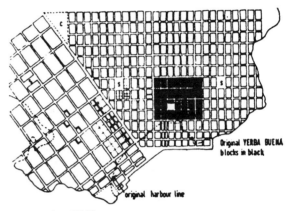

Orignal YERBA BUENA blocks in black

original harbour line

2. San Francisco (1849)

3. Baltimore

Figure 10-4: The Hierarchy of Roads and the Urban Landscape
Streets have been the basic organizer of settlement forms since prehistory. The character of Washington, DC (1), and San Francisco (2) is very much due to their basic plans. The link between the Capitol and the White House proposed by L'Enfant was subsequently blocked by the Treasury Building. The way streets have been organized in urban design schemes is a basic differentiator of one scheme versus another as the plans for Radburn, New Jersey (see Fig. 2–8), and the Rationalist city (see Fig. 2–10) show. Redesigning the American city to provide an easy flow of movement for automobiles is substantially changing its texture (3).

1. Pompei, Italy

2. People Mover Stop, Greektown, Detroit

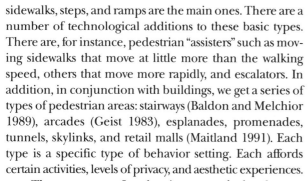
3. Interior, Renaissance Center, Detroit

Figure 10-5: The Geometry of Pedestrian Systems
The way to segregate and/or integrate vehicular and pedestrian traffic has been a major urban design concern for the past two millennia. The standard way has been through the creation of sidewalks, as this Pompeian street shows (1). Since the beginning of this century there has been a concern for as complete as possible a segregation between vehicles and pedestrians through vertical as well as horizontal movement channels (2). The internalization and privatization of public space have led to complex internal pedestrian networks (3).

sidewalks, steps, and ramps are the main ones. There are a number of technological additions to these basic types. There are, for instance, pedestrian "assisters" such as moving sidewalks that move at little more than the walking speed, others that move more rapidly, and escalators. In addition, in conjunction with buildings, we get a series of types of pedestrian areas: stairways (Baldon and Melchior 1989), arcades (Geist 1983), esplanades, promenades, tunnels, skylinks, and retail malls (Maitland 1991). Each type is a specific type of behavior setting. Each affords certain activities, levels of privacy, and aesthetic experiences.

The geometry of pedestrian networks has been a major concern in urban design. The human being on foot is highly maneuverable, so there is little in the way of a geometric constraint on the design of paths except in terms of their slopes, surface materials, and directness of line of travel. The design of pedestrian movement links can thus be based more on the requirements for an overall environmental experience for a person moving through a series of places than on any technological necessity (Cullen 1961; Thiel 1961). In most cities, the pedestrian movement system moves into the third dimension. The integration of horizontal and vertical paths has

been particularly important in those cities with multilayered pedestrian ways. Stairs, ramps and elevators have their own technical requirements if they are to be comfortable and safe for people to use and also be buildable.

Mass Transit Systems

There are a variety of types of mass transit systems for intracity travel: buses, light and heavy rail systems (surface and underground). In many ways, mass transit systems are the most efficient in giving large numbers of people access to various parts of the city, and planners have been strong advocates for them. To function economically and safely each system has its own technical and geometric requirements. Each also has implications for the distribution of activities, densities of people, and their movement patterns in its service area. Today, much urban design in the United States, as in Washington, DC, and now in Los Angeles, involves fitting transit systems to existing urban land use and building patterns. Changes in urban form as the result of the freedom of movement afforded by the use of the automobile as the primary mode of transportation raises questions about the manner in which mass transit and urban development should be related in the future. Unless they are designed together, future transit systems will be economic failures.

As metropolitan areas have grown in size spatially, the traditional movement of people from the periphery of the city to the center has given way to more complex origin and destination flows around the city. It is difficult to design economical transit systems for peripheral movements around the city until there are major nodes to be linked. There is little political impetus in the United States to establish the land-use policies to develop such nodes to make mass transit effective. The pressure continues to be for better highways. This demand is not unique to the United States but is common in countries that still have a considerable amount of open space and emphasize individual freedoms. Yet as highways are built they become more crowded and increasingly clogged. Nevertheless, few people have been enticed to use mass transit systems. They provide neither the privacy nor the control over their own behavior patterns that most people seek for themselves. In the long run, however, much more careful integration of land use and transit systems will surely be in the public interest.

In speculating on the future of the American city, it is often forgotten that a substantial proportion of the population does not drive and is thus severely disadvantaged by the structure of the automobile city. Children, many of the handicapped, and the elderly rely heavily on their legs, bicycles and wheelchairs, and/or public transportation for moving independently around the city and the suburb. Many have been forced to become dependent on those people who do have cars for transportation.

Waste Management Systems

Human activities generate considerable waste products. These products include sewerage and bulkier solid items of garbage and trash, some of which are recyclable and others not given the current state of technology. Sewage is handled in sewerage systems, but bulkier items require removal by trucks and/or barges to be deposited at some distant site or to be incinerated. Places such as hotels and restaurants generate a considerable amount of garbage, and commercial offices generate considerable paper trash despite the development of computer technology. Cities are peppered with service streets that do little more than give access to the rear of buildings. They are often gloomy and dirty. We tolerate them because they remove a noxious activity from the public eye. Urban designers and politicians have been reluctant to deal with issues of waste, particularly trash and garbage removal, in their designs, preferring to focus on the cleaner aspects of city life. The result is often dumpsters loaded with garbage spilling onto the streets and sidewalks of many American cities. Sewerage systems, in contrast, cannot be avoided.

In rural and suburban areas in the United States, sewage disposal is frequently on site in the form of septic tanks. This type of system cannot be used in densely built-up areas if health standards are to be maintained. Even in rural areas they often contaminate water supplies. New systems need to be invented. In rural areas of less affluent countries, the fields serve as latrines. In larger cities, the streets often do so. The lack of public toilets in United States cities turns many alcoves into latrines.

Sewerage systems, sometimes called wastewater systems, are arranged in networks in urban areas. Storm water and sanitary sewerage systems are ideally separate, but in many older American cities they form part of one system. The storm water sewers were often built before sewerage systems were developed. Later, household sanitary sewage pipes were simply connected to the existing storm system. The result is that after heavy rains raw sewage is dumped into rivers because the treatment capacity of sewage treatment plants is too small. There is an ongoing effort in many places to rectify this situation.

The functional concern in urban design is to create urban layouts that allow for gravity falls in sewage lines as much as possible and also for underground pipes. Pipes vary in size from eight inches for laterals to several feet in diameter for major storm water sewers. They are usually located in the center of the street, but sometimes under the sidewalks. Historically these lines fed into larger lines that followed river courses. Indeed, in many cities (e.g., Philadelphia) the stream beds have been enclosed to form sewers. It is only since World War II that this method of locating sewers has been largely stopped. Where topographic changes require major vertical changes in sewage flow, drop manholes or pump lift stations are installed. Manhole covers are often an element of urban art!

In unsewered suburban areas the concern is to have large enough lots for waste to be treated on site and to ensure against seepage of septic tanks into streams and other water courses. Suburban areas are becoming increasingly sewered as densities increase and water pollution concerns rise.

In the design of urban precincts of residential neighborhoods rainwater runoff can be catered for in gutters feeding into natural watercourses. In larger areas, separate underground sewers are a necessity. One of the ecological problems that has to be addressed is that with increasingly paved cities and suburbs, the water tables get lowered and the speed of runoff causes the erosion of stream beds and the pollution of streams beyond the level that they are capable of handling naturally (see Chapter 18, Meeting the Needs of the Biogenic Environment).

Considerable thought is now being given to advancing the technology of waste management. The alternative approach to building infrastructure systems is simply to reduce the amount of waste generated. This approach seems to be the most sensible in the long run, but does require considerable adaptation to current behavior on

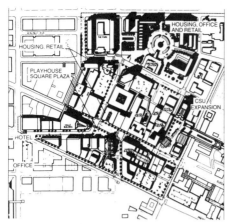

Source: *Planning* 58, no. 1: 9

1. Conceptual Site Plan, Playhouse Square, Cleveland

2. Chicago

3. Philadelphia

Figure 10-6: Service Alleys in Cities

There are certain topics that visionary urban designers seldom include in their design ideas. One of these has to do with the removal of trash and garbage. Often in conceptual site plans used to promote schemes it is, understandably, seldom stressed (1). It is, however, a major design issue. Existing American cities are replete with service alleys often full of overloaded dumpsters (2,3). New designs do not have to be as unattractive. New technologies accompanied by a very different ethic regarding the disposal of the waste products of everyday life may be developed in the future.

the part of people not only in the United States but in the other wealthy countries of the world. The generation of less waste would certainly make the task of designing pleasant urban environments easier.

Energy Supply Systems

Electricity, oil, and gas are the major sources of energy in the commercial and residential buildings of the United States. Solar energy is in its infancy. Wind-generated electricity is seldom supplied to single households except in some rural areas. Gas, water, and electricity supply systems are, at present, similar in their demands on the layout of cities. Gas, as the most demanding, can be taken as an exemplar.

In dense urban areas, a major source of fuel is gas. Once largely synthetically produced from coal, the major source is now natural gas. The distribution network consists of gathering facilities at the source of the gas, transmission lines, and what is of importance in urban design, distribution systems to individual customers at the other end. The networks are similar to those of reticulated water supply systems. Where gas is the primary fuel, efficiency

requirements of the distribution network tend to dictate straight streets leading to a gridiron street pattern, but the technological and geometric demands of the system are not as severe as for sewerage facilities.

The need for much greater efficiency in the consumption of energy may well have a major impact on urban design. There is extraordinarily little concern in American cities with orientation to the sun and, more understandably because of our lack of knowledge, to winds. When and if energy costs rise substantially, there will no doubt be a considerable reworking of building designs. At present there is little foresight in either the design or political world about such considerations.

Public Facilities Systems

Public facilities—part of the capital web of cities—comprise a broad set of elements of urban form and life. They consist of service facilities such as city halls, museums, schools, hospitals, fire stations, libraries, and sometimes cemeteries. The distribution of public facilities is usually assumed to be dependent on the distribution of people and on their accessibility requirements. As a result, the location and nature of public facilities are often dealt with in a typological manner. Any number of guidebooks specify what the distribution of public facilities should be and the amount of land required for them given a particular size and density of population (De Chiara and Koppelman 1975; Chapin and Kaiser 1979). Each should, however, be dealt with in terms of a population's specific needs. An advantage of grouping them with other facilities and retail areas in a hierarchy of service areas is that they form a node, which can serve as the core of an area. Such nodes should be easily accessible and placed toward the point where people enter or leave an area (Porteous 1977). The reason is simple. It is the place that most people pass.

Public facilities can, however, also be perceived to be an independent variable. They can be catalysts for development. Locating facilities such as museums and cultural facilities may lead to a change in the image of an area, leading to further commercial development. Indeed, this is a tactic that is more systematically used in France than in the United States, not only in Paris but in a large number of provincial towns.

BUILDING TECHNOLOGY

Not only do the technology and geometry of the infrastructure system give an urban design its character, so do the nature of the buildings that frame the public realm. There have been a number of technological developments in building construction in recent years, particularly in building skins, the use of steel, and in the fabrication of lightweight structures. The major breakthrough in building technology affecting urban design, however, came at the beginning of the twentieth century with the development of the steel structural framework for buildings and the invention of the safety elevator. In combination, they enabled the first skyscrapers to be built in Chicago (Giedion 1963). New building techniques have been incorporated into such buildings as the Lloyds Bank in London and the Hong Kong Shanghai Bank in Hong Kong, but these technologies have had little effect on the city form, although they change the ambience of urban designs by their visual appearances.

The height of buildings has had a considerable effect on the urban environment and has been a major point of discussion, often heated, among citizens, urban designers, and politicians alike in cities such as San Francisco and Philadelphia. Tall buildings change the micro-climate by channeling winds and casting long shadows. They house many people in a small area of a city and thus become nodes in themselves. A 125–story, 1,950–foot-high building, the Miglin-Beitler Tower, is planned for Chicago at the time of writing (Draeger 1991), and even taller buildings have been proposed for Tokyo. A particular problem such proposals have to face is the extraordinarily high cost of the money required to construct them before any rental returns are received. They also need to

be very carefully designed to create pleasant internal and external environments for people at the ground level (Conway 1977; Lang 1979; see also Chapter 11).

The exploration of the geometric possibilities for buildings has largely focused on the technical possibilities of fitting different geometric shapes together and on the technical aspects of structures. These explorations have often been conducted in the abstract without a consideration of the purposes the configurations may serve. Such explorations open up the eyes of designers to future possibilities and encourage them to look for new ways of fulfilling existing functions more commodiously. It is enticing to attempt to implement the new geometry for its own sake or for the sake of the designer's reputation without consideration for the other human functions it might serve.

TERRESTRIAL AND CULTURAL FACTORS

The biogenic and sociogenic environments in which an urban design has to exist have historically had a major impact on the design of infrastructure systems and alternative geometric schemata. Questions of the "environmental fitness" of these systems have become increasingly important as the side effects of the systems on the biogenic environment become known but also psychologically when new environments depart from cultural norms and people are asked to adapt to them.

The Terrestrial System

Different locations have different climatic and topographic conditions. To develop a functional infrastructure system these condition have to be borne in mind. Some places have to deal with torrential rain, others with tropical sun and humidity, yet others with arctic cold (see Chapter 11). These types of conditions are increasingly well understood—the research and experience is there for the urban designer to use. Other situations are trickier. Often, however, necessity is indeed the mother of invention.

Some cities have very special conditions with which to contend. Venice is sinking. New systems to counteract it have been and are being invented. Other places have to deal with seismic movement of the Earth's crust. The technology for building in areas prone to earthquakes and tidal floods has been developed and is being tested in situations such as San Francisco, London, and coastal Bangladesh, but the only way of dealing with predictable major natural events is not to locate in the areas where they occur (Lagorio 1990). In some places, the cost of using the available technology to reduce damage due to natural events is greater than the cost (financially and psychologically) of sustaining the loss and starting again. Indeed, city after city in the United States has rebuilt damaged

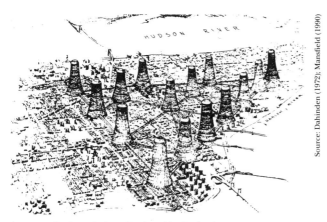

Source: Dahinden (1972); Mansfield (1990)

1. A Plan for East Harlem. Designed by Buckminster Fuller and Shoji Sadao (1965)

Source: Dahinden (1972)

2. Ratinger Area, Berlin. Proposal by Merete Mattern

3. Chicago

Figure 10–7: Tall Buildings and the Urban Environment
Visionary designers have been fascinated by the possibilities of tall buildings. Buckminster Fuller and Shoji Sadao's 1965 plan for East Harlem shows the type of design that results when potential technologies are imposed on a site (1). The concern is not simply an American one. Merete Mattern's late-1950s proposal for Berlin (2) is reminiscent of the much more recent Deconstructionist designs. Such designs do show us future possibilities. Tall buildings are a response to rent values, but also to the need for prestige (3). While they are exciting elements of the urban landscape, they also have many negative effects on cities.

areas on site as before after a major natural catastrophe with the implicit expectation that such calamities will not happen again.

The Cultural System

Some people are highly adaptable to change or even actively seek it; others are more conservative. The same is true of particular cultures. Major changes in our environment tend to be stressful even when they are for the better. These observations seem to be particularly accurate when one is dealing with the introduction of new technologies or geometric patterns into cities. Urban designers, too, often stick with the familiar rather than seek new solutions.

In the United States, one would have expected that since the 1973 oil embargo one of the major urban design explorations would be with energy-efficient new forms and the long-term need to reduce reliance on nonreplaceable resources. There is indeed a greater concern in academia with a number of issues but not to the degree which one might expect. Research in industry and academia has led to an enhanced understanding of the design of façades of buildings to reduce energy loads on heating, cooling, and construction systems, to a rethinking of the possibility of natural ventilation both in buildings and in urban designs, and, more generally, to a consideration of energy-efficient cities (Dantzig and Saaty 1973; Gayden 1979; Arens et al. 1984). Existing landholding patterns and the sacredness of property rights in the United States suggest that new geometries for urban designs to lessen reliance on artificial mechanisms of climate control in buildings, streets, and other open spaces are still some distance in the future.

Specific geometric patterns have special meanings in a number of countries of the world (see Chapters 2 and 3). Particular construction technologies and materials may have significance or are associated with building in particular areas. They give a regional identity. The debate over the appropriate technology to use in specific circumstances will rage on (Brolin 1976; Schumaker 1973; El Wakil 1991). Issues of financial and material resources, the skills of local craftspeople, and the politics of architectural design become entwined.

In the United States the geometric patterns of settlements have a spiritual significance to a number of Indian tribes and to some religious minorities (E. Martin 1991). They do not have the widely accepted spiritual meanings that they do in other countries such as China. There are, nevertheless, expectations as to what these patterns should be. Although much has been written about sacred geometry (Lesser 1957; Tompkins 1973; Lawlor 1982; Swan 1991) and on *basic design*—formal aesthetics—(de Sausmarez 1964; Itten 1965; Arnheim 1965, 1977; Lang 1984, 1987), there has been very little on the meaning of specific geometric patterns (e.g., the gridiron versus the curvilinear) per se in our everyday lives or cross-culturally. There have been

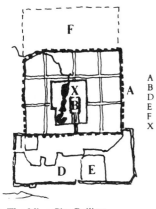

Source: Jellicoe and Jellicoe (1987)

A Mongol city as reduced c. A D 1409
B Imperial Palace
D South extension
E Altar of Heaven
F Abandoned area
X Coal Hill

1. The Ming City, Beijing

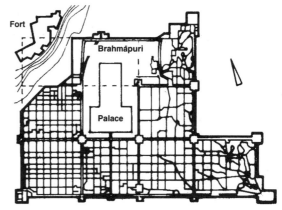

Adapted from Morris (1972), Copper (1982), and Shearer (1983)

2. Jaipur, Rajasthan, India (1727)

Source: Benevolo (1980)

3. Geometric Exploration of Urban Infrastructure Systems

Figure 10-8. Sacred Geometry and Urban Form

Issues of cosmology were important, for instance, in Beijing (1) and in the plan of Indian cities such as Jaipur (2). Jaipur is based on a nine-square mandala, with one square displaced because of topographical difficulties. Geomancy remains an important part of design in China. The layout of Salt Lake City, Utah, has some religious significance, and in the twentieth century, the plan for Canberra by Chicago architect Walter Burley Griffin (see Fig. 2-16(2)) possibly has hidden geomantic meanings. Today it seems more important to understand the mundane geometric possibilities of urban and building forms (3).

a number of cross-cultural studies on the nature of perception, but they have yielded little of utility to the designer.

The major utility of an understanding of geometry is simply in enhancing designers' understanding of the possibilities of form. Joern Utzon's explorations of geometry served him well in the construction of the roofs of the Sydney Opera House, although their lines are not what he originally intended. They had to be adapted to what was technically feasible given contemporary knowledge about shell structures. Considerable adaptation would be required to make many of the explorations in urban form that are being investigated today technically feasible or socially desirable.

URBAN DESIGN CONSEQUENCES

The three-dimensional geometric layout of any urban area is the basis of its visual and aesthetic character and its affordance for activities—its functionality. A major urban design issue is whether the geometry of a design should be regarded as the independent variable shaping behavioral possibilities or the dependent variable resulting from their provision. Does the geometry dictate the design or, rather, is it a byproduct of making other decisions? Ex-

cept in situations where the geometry per se has associational meanings and is therefore very important symbolically in fulfilling a set of human needs, urban designers need to think of geometric possibilities for the public realm of cities in terms of the more mundane problems of everyday life. In the United States they have had to focus on developing patterns that address more basic problems of circulation and context in a way that many European schemes developed in strong centralized governmental contexts have not had to do.

The Infrastructure System—The Public Realm

There are four fundamental design issues regarding the nature of urban infrastructures that will have an impact on future urban designs. They are: (1) the nature of the human needs that they have to fulfill, (2) the nature of and degree of efficiency of the overall infrastructure system desired in relationship to patterns of activities and aesthetic requirements, (3) the technical requirements of the systems, and (4) their symbolic meanings. To this list must always be added the cost, not only of the system itself but the opportunity costs incurred by not spending the money elsewhere. The transportation system can be taken as the major exemplar of these issues because it seems to have the greatest impact of any system on the quality of a city and of urban life, but the issues apply to all infrastructure systems.

The Overall Network

Urban designers in the United States, like their counterparts elsewhere, have traditionally been advocates for mass transit systems and pedestrian networks rather than highways and roads despite the public's inclination to use automobiles whenever possible. Certainly at a precinct level, the nature of the pedestrian network is of fundamental importance in giving a project its character. Planners have argued against the reliance on the automobile as the prime mover of people on a number of logical grounds: the space required for them, both when they are moving and when they are parked; the continual clogging of highways; the consumption of prime agricultural land; the encouragement of urban spatial growth; and, perhaps less overtly, the use of automobiles breaking down a sense of local community. It is also clear that many people simply enjoy driving and the sense of control it gives them. It may, nevertheless, seem worth striving to eliminate unnecessary and undesired driving through design.

It has been recently argued that the major factor in reducing automobile dependency is not new technologies but new urban forms (P. Newman and Kenworth 1989). The argument is that cities need to be reurbanized. There has been little political desire to do so in the United States, at least partly because the major social problems occur in the very core of its metropolitan areas. High densities are associated in many people's minds with inferior living conditions and low status.

The linkage requirements between different modes of transportation and the physical characteristics of each mode—the nature of the vehicles, the right of ways require-ments, and terminal facilities (parking garages, railway or subways stations, etc.)—and the relationship of these modes to the basic pedestrian network have been the subject of considerable urban design exploration both in the heart of cities (e.g., Gruen 1964; see Fig. 3–5), and in suburban areas (Stern with Massengale 1981; Kelbaugh 1989; Calthorpe 1991; P. Rowe 1991). A number of urban design issues arise in dealing with the physical nature of the elements of the overall transportation network: the possible use of air rights over terminal area developments (e.g., Grand Central Terminal, New York City), the development of spaces below elevated rail tracks and over subway systems, the need for automobile storage (i.e., parking) being made available for other activities (e.g., markets and basketball courts) or serving different facilities at different times of the day. All these issues have long been of concern to urban designers. Resolving them will require greater levels of cooperation than is usually seen today between property owners and between developers in the

United States even when people's self-interests are clearly at stake. New administrative and legal mechanisms to encourage cooperation will be necessary if any change is to occur.

The integration of land uses, building types, and transportation modes has been a prime consideration in new town design partly because such all-of-a-piece designs are under a central control even though they may be buffeted by outside pressures. It has also been a major consideration in urban renewal, although the constraints imposed by existing patterns of development and development opportunities place a major constraint on the attainment of efficiency in transportation modes. The United States, like other countries, has yet to see the type of integration displayed in the work of the Rationalists of the Modern movement for whom functionalist design required the integration of modes of transportation with each other and with the building types proposed.

One of the problems in designing efficient public transportation systems in new towns is that population levels and densities have to attain a critical mass before mass transit becomes feasible. The delay between inception of a project and it being "built-out" means that right of ways have to be identified and maintained as the construction phases develop.

Environmental Impacts

The impacts of the various infrastructure systems and their components, particularly transportation modes, on their biogenic and sociogenic environments can be positive or negative. On what is often, but not necessarily, the positive side, transportation facilities are clearly a catalyst for urban development. The building of the interstate highway system after World War II, it has already been noted, radically transformed the nature of metropolitan areas in the United States. Intramode intersections such as exits on freeways and intersections between modes such as road and rail, and air and road, present opportunities for intense development because of the ease of accessibility to them. They can also be designed purposefully to generate specific designs around them or to meet other public policy ends.

The building of transportation facilities has also produced many negative side effects—noise and air pollution, sometimes the reduction of the independent movement of children and the elderly, the destruction of neighborhood territorial groupings, negative aesthetics (by their very presence, however well designed they sometimes are). Some of the negative impacts can be mitigated through design, but others are difficult to consider. Technological modifications are possible in some instances and not in others. Through the use of berms and solid sonic barriers, noise pollution can be reduced; trees help reduce air pollution; parking garages do not have to be eyesores; and, by careful design of the way the ground

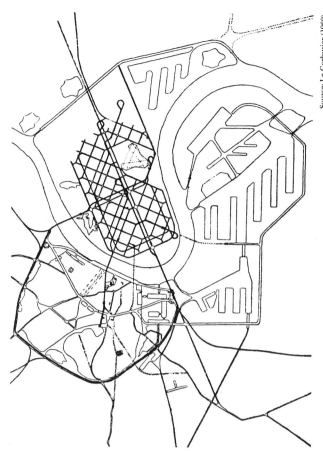

1. Plan for Transportation Systems. Proposal for Antwerp, Le Corbusier (1933)

2. General View of the Proposed Redevelopment

Figure 10-9: The Rational City
The integration of transportation modes based on their performance characteristics is an important geometric form giver in urban design, as Le Corbusier and many other Modernists recognized. Le Corbusier's plan for Antwerp in the 1930s clearly shows this concern, even if many other aspects of the lives of people were neglected. The overall transportation geometry is shown in (1). It is based on interlocking subway, bus and road networks, and pedestrian ways. A general image of what Antwerp would have been like after its demolition and rebuilding if the proposal had been accepted is shown in (2).

floors meet the street to avoid blank façades, their deadening effect on street life can be reduced. All these approaches help meet people's needs for a salubrious and comfortable environment in which to live.

One of the major urban design problems in the past has been that the location of new facilities such as regional hospitals and shopping centers that are out of scale behaviorally with their contexts, particularly residential areas, has generated so much vehicular traffic that the traditional territorial controls in neighboring areas are violated. Over time this violation can lead to urban decay as the negative effects of the traffic affect people's concern with the maintenance of their surroundings. In extreme cases such a situation can lead to opportunities for antisocial activities by people so disposed (Newman 1979). Thus traffic flows can have both a physiological and psychological impact on areas; they change the biogenic and sociogenic environments. Other facilities, such as sewerage disposal works and incinerators, have a purely negative psychological impact on their surroundings in people's minds. Nobody wants to be located near them even if they create no other identifiable negative influences.

FUTURE POSSIBILITIES

We dream of new technological breakthroughs in the design of cities and urban places. We are told that new technologies will transform the city, but there is little concrete evidence of such developments. In comparison to the century between 1850 and 1950 little in the way of new technologies seems to be shaping American cities, suburbs, or small towns. This situation may account for the paucity of new ideas. The century ending in the 1950s saw the transformation of regional settlement patterns, urban forms, and life as a result of the development of electricity, refrigeration, and the major changes in transportation, recreational, and communications technologies. Building technology reshaped the city; the Empire State Building is over sixty years old now. The development of jet aircraft since then has transformed the nature of international trade and tourism, and computer technology is making information processing easier, allowing us to keep pace with information needs. There is little to suggest that major technological developments that will reshape settlements patterns and human lives in a revolutionary way are in the offing. The predictions made twenty-five years ago about the technological status of the world of the 1990s by such informed observers as Isaac Asimov grossly overestimated the amount of change that would occur.

Several new technologies do appear to be on the horizon, but it is impossible to predict their impact on urban design even twenty years ahead with any accuracy. The developments in electronics and microelectronics continue to allow for the separation of information flows from the movement of people and goods. Developments in biotechnology do not appear to have urban design implications nor will new foods or fashions (except in façade design). New developments in transportation, sewage disposal, communication, and the need to maintain a salubrious biogenic environment will almost certainly have an effect. Many activities are becoming spatially dispersed as people seek greater individualism, self-reliance, and privacy. There is an increasing appetite in the United States for new ways of fulfilling human needs that is breaking down civility on the part of people. Will the future world be attuned to self-gratification, sensualism, and sensationalism? If so, urban forms will change. The impact of new technologies on individual life is likely to be great, but on urban form less so. New technologies are likely to have an evolutionary, piecemeal effect, if the past is our guide (Fleischer 1961; Brotchie et al. 1991; Hall 1992). The need to be more careful about the impact of human settlement forms on the biogenic environment may have a substantial effect on future urban and building designs.

There are continuing explorations of different types of transportation innovations accompanied by suggested new types of human settlements. None have reached the development stage, because they failed to give the flexibility and privacy of existing modes. These systems include such things as pedestrian conveyors (used in places such as airports but not as yet on city streets), a variety of suggestions for plug-in automated vehicle movement systems, and the extensive use of monorails. Any of these systems will have an effect on what we do in urban design only at the margin. It is possible that new energy sources will have specific impacts on city form, but these cannot be predicted now on the basis of empirical evidence.

The need is to use what we have effectively, to understand the possibilities of alternative geometries and technological systems, and to seize developments that promise to make the city and the suburbs more functional in terms of the lives of their inhabitants. We need to use what is known already; we need to know what is known already (Rainer 1991). The effect of resource constraints, such as the need for fresh water by burgeoning populations, may have a greater effect on urban form than technological advances.

Cities such as Los Angeles and Baltimore are reintroducing light rail mass transit systems and although these, like Washington, DC's Metro and San Francisco's BART system, may be more comfortable and speedier than the old, they offer little in the way of major technological breakthroughs that will have an effect on urban form or on urban design projects. They do, however, provide better service and access to facilities for a number of people. New communications technologies may reduce the need for personal transportation, but there is more speculation than evidence on the eventual impact that they will have (Schmandt et al. 1990). If they do have an impact they will lead to the decentralization of activities and so counteract centralizing forces and largely maintain the status quo. New structural systems may be developed in the future that will enable the multilayered cities such as those envisaged by the Deconstructionists to be built (see Fig. 4–6). Certainly a developed knowledge of geometric possibilities will be necessary to achieve them. The technology is largely available to do so now. The questions are really: "Do we want to build them?" and "What are the social advantages of doing so?"

MAJOR REFERENCES

Brotchie, John, Michael Batty, Peter Hall, and Peter Newton, eds. (1991). *Cities of the 21st Century: New Technologies and Spatial Systems.* New York: Halsted.

De Chiara, Joseph, and Lee Koppelman (1975). *Urban Planning and Design Criteria.* New York: Van Nostrand Reinhold.

Fleischer, Aaron (1961). "The Influence of Technology on Urban Form." In Lloyd Rodwin, ed., *The Future Metropolis.* New York: George Braziller, pp. 64–79.

Hall, Peter (1992). "Cities in the Informational Economy." *Urban Futures* (Special Issue 5, February):1–12.

Kapproff, Jay (1990). *Connections: The Geometric Bridge between Art and Science.* New York: McGraw Hill.

Lagorio, Henry J. (1990). *Earthquakes: An Architect's Guide to Nonstructural Seismic Hazards.* New York: John Wiley.

Rainer, George (1991). *Understanding Infrastructure: A Guide for Architects and Planners.* New York: John Wiley.

Schmandt, Jurgen, Frederick Williams, Robert H. Wilson, and Sharon Stover, eds. (1990). *The New Urban Infrastructures: Cities and Telecommunications.* New York: Praeger.

A FUNCTIONAL SOCIOGENIC ENVIRONMENT

Photograph by Deepti Nijhawan

Boston

The goal of a Neo-Functionalist and Empiricist approach to urban design is to create the public realms of human settlements that afford the fulfillment of human needs to the extent that they possibly can based on the evidence available to us. The empirically based substantive theoretical foundation for asking questions about the ways in which behavior settings, and, consequently, the built environment, can satisfy human needs is described in this part of the book. The position that has been taken here is that Abraham Maslow's hierarchy of basic needs and his distinction between these needs and cognitive needs is the most comprehensive approach to the study of Functionalism in urban design that is available to us today. No doubt in the future better models will be developed. "Human needs" is, however, an abstract concept and must be translated into activity systems and aesthetic requirements to be made operational for urban design. The goal here is to describe the positive theoretical framework for how this is being done and might be done in the future in the United States. The objective here is to capture our present understanding and to provide a structure into which further developments and the refinement of our knowledge, particularly that on cultural differences, can be slotted. Research is an ongoing process and always will be, so the knowledge base we have is in a state of flux as human circumstances change. The basic propositions are, however, likely to remain stable.

BASIC NEEDS

The most basic human need is that for survival. The most basic concern of urban designers is with the creation of a salubrious environment. Beyond this level it is to ensure that the built environment affords the basic activities—the basic behavioral program—of people as they go about their lives. The task of the designer is really to ensure that the built environment does more than simply afford human physiological needs in terms of anthropometrics and ergonomics. It is to afford them comfortably. How comfortable should the layout of the city make life? There is a certain utility to discomfort, physiological and psychological; it is

211

a motivator of action. Chapter 11, *Meeting Physiological Needs,* deals with the fundamental requirement for shelter that is a prerequisite for many human activities.

The meeting of shelter needs through the affordances of patterns of the built environment is closely interwoven with the meeting of the needs described in Chapter 12, *Meeting Safety and Security Needs.* These two needs have both physical and psychological components to them. The need for security has been a fundamental reason for the existence of cities, their relationships with the outside world, and their internal organizations from the very earliest of human settlements. While we should not exaggerate them, there are many sources of danger from which people need protection in the public realm of cities. Some of these sources are natural and some artificial—from the built environment itself, and from such things as careless driving. The actions of people themselves have been and are unfortunately, also major sources of danger for others in the United States.

In many parts of the world, both urban and rural, much design work is based on the need to protect people from other people. Perhaps we have become paranoid about the need for security in much recent architectural and urban design in the United States, particularly as those industries that produce protective devices keep on telling us how dangerous the world is. The level of concern displayed by people to maintain their personal security against the antisocial behavior of other people does, nevertheless, illustrate how basic a need it is not only in the United States but also in much of the rest of the world today.

Achieving security and a sense of security is a matter of achieving a substantial degree of control over one's environment—biogenic and sociogenic. In design, it essentially involves the achievement of specific levels of privacy and of community through a set of territorial controls—the demarcation of territories through real solid and symbolic boundaries, and through a variety of mechanical devices.

The mechanisms for meeting safety and security needs also have other psychological dimensions. They involve the fulfillment of the need to have a place in society and in a geography. These needs overlap the affiliation need to be part of a group—a member of a society and of a place. This, in turn, leads to a need for easy communication among people and also for the display of their memberships through the use of environmental cues. Thus the designer has to strive to provide simultaneously for shelter and for the displaying of the symbols of affiliation to specific groups and places through the use of patterns of the built environment. The patterns required to fulfill these needs are explored in Chapter 13, *Meeting Affiliation Needs.* Over the course of its existence, C.I.A.M.'s various urban design manifestoes dealt with many of the issues described in Chapters 11 to 13 of this part of the book. C.I.A.M. members never, however, really came to grips with human needs above those based on an organismic model of people. Esteem, actualization, and cognitive and aesthetic needs, at the very best, were only partially considered in either C.I.A.M.'s programs or in the urban designs of its members.

Very few people do not feel, or, rather, do not express, a need for a sense of affiliation with other people or a place. We become highly self-conscious about who we are and to whom and to what place we belong when we are unsure of ourselves as individuals,

groups, or societies. The need to belong is expressed in many symbolic ways. Some of these ways have to do with the activities in which we participate; others have to do with the symbolic aesthetic displays contained in building forms and the elements with which we furnish our milieus. Every work of urban design or architecture carries "to whom it may concern" messages. Sometimes the most important concern of the urban designer in America has been to communicate a sense of prestige and of self-worth to the citizens of a city through its built form. This purpose was central to the concerns of the City Beautiful movement. It remains a major concern of urban designers today, although we do not seem to care to admit it as openly as in the past.

As Maslow (1968) noted, the definition of the need for self-actualization has been misinterpreted as the need to simply do what one wishes to do. Achieving a state of self-actualization is a much more complex process than that suggested by this definition, for it involves the need to help others as well as oneself. In many ways the fulfillment of this need has little to do with the layout of settlements, but much to do with the social organization of society and the interrelationships among people. To some extent the layout does matter in attaining self-actualization needs as it aids communication, but if it affords all the other human needs it will fulfill self-actualization needs too. Chapter 15, *Meeting Self-Actualization Needs,* deals with these issues.

COGNITIVE NEEDS

It is clear that the achievement of all the above needs depends on our ability to learn. There is also the need that many people have to learn about the world for its own rewards and not for any instrumental purpose. Learning takes place in two ways—formally through organized education, and experientially through the successes and failures of our everyday dealings with people and the built environment. Similarly, a beautiful environment adds pleasure to life at all levels of striving to fulfill basic needs, although when one is striving for survival a pleasing environment is hardly at the center of one's attention. With aesthetics, as with basic needs, there is a hierarchy of levels of appreciation of the environment. The most basic concern is with what is beautiful or, more simply, pleasurable to us. A much higher order need is to consider and to evaluate the environment as a work of art. Such a consideration involves the self-conscious learning of analytical techniques. Thus cognitive and aesthetic issues are intertwined.

The design issues concerned with formal learning are briefly reviewed in Chapter 16, Meeting Cognitive Needs, but the chapter focuses more on the environment as a source of learning experiences—with the nature of an educative environment. The concern is twofold: with learning as a means of satisfying basic needs, and with learning for its own sake, to satisfy one's curiosity about the world. An instrumental reward may ensue from such an appreciation, but that payoff is incidental to the internal reward, the pleasure received from the learning experience itself.

While aesthetics is concerned with the nature of the beautiful, Chapter 17, Meeting Aesthetic Needs, brings attention to what Santayana (1896) called the intellectual dimension of aesthetic experience as much as to sensory, formal, and symbolic aesthetics. Intellectual aesthetics stands in strong contrast to the symbolic dimension of aesthetic experience, which is an expression, through form, of the attainment of a set of affiliation needs. An intellectually high level of need is that of understanding an aesthetic theory of an architect or urban designer and its expression in buildings and urban form—as a work of art. This kind of experience is a perceptual luxury. It is, nevertheless, also tied in with a need for some people to belong to an intellectual elite—the taste makers. However, at the highest level of human needs, the pleasure derived from the understanding is a reward in itself rather than a search for self-confidence through the acknowledgment of one's position by others. Few people's lives are conducted at this level of needs fulfillment (Maslow 1987). Few people are fully self-actualized.

The way of looking at the substantive issues in urban design described here is an abstract one that needs to be put into an overall decision-making context. There are many issues that are increasingly of concern to any urban designer, or rather should be of concern to an urban designer, that often fall outside the scope of the professional activity per se. One of these is the need to create, or at least maintain, a functional biogenic environment. Designing for a functional biogenic environment is the subject matter of the following part of this review of the positive theoretical basis for creating a functional environment. Ultimately the urban designer has to balance the need to create an environment that meets the requirements of a set of people and the requirement for a salubrious environment for all people. ■

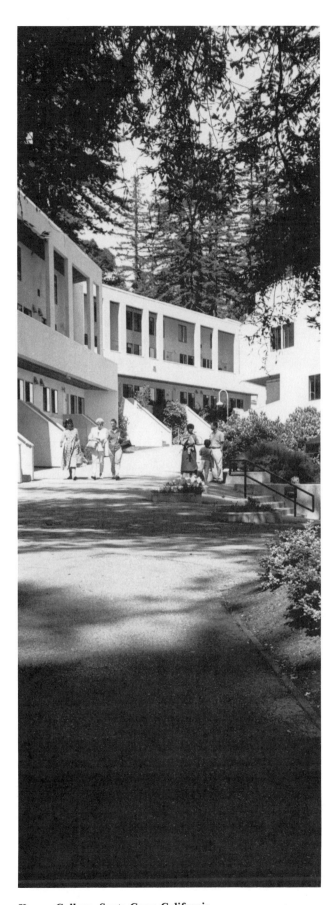

Kresge College, Santa Cruz, California

Meeting Basic Human Needs

11

MEETING PHYSIOLOGICAL NEEDS

Designing to meet the physiological needs of people using the public realm of cities seems so obvious an area of concern for architects and urban designers that we tend to take it for granted. There is, however, little explicit concern for these needs in our contemporary urban design ideologies. They are regarded as given requirements that are easy to meet. Yet there are many examples of environments where the physiological needs of people have been inadequately met or where postconstruction ad hoc solutions to remedy problems that have arisen have led to undesirable social side effects (Oc 1991). At the same time, there is a developing body of empirical knowledge that can be applied to designing salubrious and comfortable environments.

One of the reasons for creating buildings has always been to provide shelter from the extremes of climate (Rudofsky 1964; Greer 1988). Only a handful of cultures in the world has created no artificial shelters, and even in those societies people have sought shelter in caves and other protective patterns of the natural environment. At a more complex level of concern, self-consciously designing to meet health and comfort needs can be traced back to the earliest civilizations on earth such as the Harapa era in the Indus Valley (Mumford 1961; A. Morris 1979). The layout of Mohenjodaro shows a great concern for public sanitation. Vitruvius's locational and design principles for cities were based on criteria, admittedly fanciful, for creating a healthy place (Benevolo 1980). Modern town planning and zoning controls were developed in the United States, following European precedents, to create a more healthy city than those created by the laissez-faire processes that shaped the industrial city—the Coketowns (Benevolo 1967; Darley 1978; J. Peterson 1979). Too often planning, and subsequently urban design, stopped at that level.

In the United States, the necessity of designing a salubrious world is the legal foundation on which zoning ordinances, guidelines for urban design, and urban design policy formulation rest (Lai 1988). It was a fundamental issue shaping the ideology of the City Beautiful and the two streams of the Modern movement (J. Peterson 1976, 1979). The concern at this level of thinking is primarily with people's requirements for survival, health, comfort, and physiological development, but the concept can be extended to two very different concerns that have an impact on the quality of people's lives. They are: (1) the physiological needs of other fauna and flora of the world, and (2) the physical requirements to achieve optimal performance in the range of machines used by people to make their lives easier and more pleasant. The first concern is explored in Chapter 18. The second has already been partly reviewed and is further discussed here. It is also clear that physiological concerns in urban design spill over into other areas of human needs, as Fig. 11-1 shows.

When thinking of providing for human physiological needs and the "physiological" needs of the equipment people use, the focus of an urban designer's thinking is on the aspects of design that fall within the narrow definition of *function* of the Rationalists among the Modernists: a concern for the human being as an organismic entity, and for the efficiency of the various types of circulation systems that enable people to move around the city with ease. For instance, Le Corbusier's generic plans for the "City of Three Million" and La Ville Radieuse, and his plans for, say, Antwerp as shown in Fig. 10-9, clearly show these concerns (Le Corbusier 1934, 1948, 1960). They were also a prime motivation for the generic and implemented plans of the Garden City designers (Benevolo 1967).

Much research has been conducted and sets of guidebooks written showing the architect and/or industrial

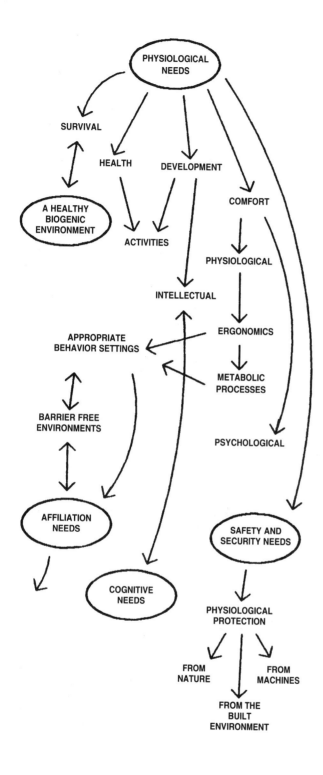

Figure 11-1: Physiological Needs

designer how to meet the physiological needs of people in the built environment (e.g., Kantowitz and Sorkin 1983; Greer 1988; Tillman and Tillman 1990). Much of this research has focused on the indoor environment and particularly on the working environment—on making machines usable and on making the whole person-machine interface safe, efficient, and less fatiguing (Land 1987a). There has been considerably less research on the overall form of cities, neighborhoods, and open spaces and how their patterns affect the comfort levels of people using the outdoor environment. Research, however, progresses and is increasingly forming the basis for urban design policy decisions. Some of the work is recent (e.g., Arens et al. 1984; Arens and Bosslemann 1989), but there are political difficulties in getting the results turned into urban design guidelines because they inevitably interfere with individual property rights (Aynsley 1989; Arens, Bosslemann et al. 1989). As a result, there are places in almost any American city that have highly undesirable effects: gloomy streets or, conversely, sunbaked places, places where downwash vertex winds have made pedestrians' lives miserable, windswept plazas, and open spaces with pockets of polluted air because new buildings have not been designed with the flushing effect of breezes in mind. One of the reasons that vernacular architecture and cities are so admired is that they evolved to respond to adverse climatic conditions with minimal use of high technology and energy-demanding machinery (Rudofsky 1964). Few are, however, comfortable enough to meet our present-day expectations.

THE HIERARCHICAL NATURE OF HUMAN PHYSIOLOGICAL NEEDS

Physiological needs exist in a hierarchy within the hierarchy of basic needs. They vary from survival needs to needs for healthy development to the need for a comfortable environment. The basic survival needs are for air, food, and shelter to stay alive. Beyond this level are the needs for a healthy life and for opportunities to develop well physically. In much of the developed world the urban design concern is with creating salubrious environments that are comfortable rather than ones that simply afford survival. The concern is also with the design of management processes that keep them that way or improve them piecemeal. Comfort is a complex variable because, while primarily a physiological state, it also has strong psychological characteristics.

People vary in their specific physiological needs. The affordances of particular patterns of the built environment depend on the competence level of the people involved and their habituation levels (see Chapter 1). In any group of people there is a hierarchy of abilities. Those people of the lowest levels of physiological competence place the greatest demands on the precision with which the layout of the environment is designed. It has to

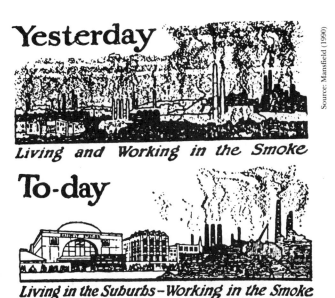

Yesterday

Living and Working in the Smoke

To-day

Living in the Suburbs – Working in the Smoke

To-morrow

Living & Working in the Sun at WELWYN GARDEN CITY

1. Advertisement for Welwyn Garden City

Source: Mansfield (1990)

Adapted from Benevolo (1970)

2. New Kensington, Pennsylvania (1940)

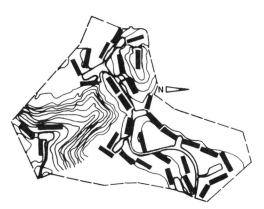

3. Chestnut Street, Philadelphia

fit their needs well in order for them to be able to use it at all. For instance, people who are wheelchair-bound or have great difficulty walking will find stairs a barrier, but those people with sound legs and lungs may not even notice any impediment to their movement. In addition to our capabilities, the expectations we have of the environment depend on what we are accustomed to accept. These levels differ not only because of individual physiological differences but also by social status and cultural background.

Survival Needs

The need to survive is the most basic of human needs. There are millions of people in the world striving for survival. The number of homeless people on the streets of American cities brings this point home. Shelter for survival is what they seek. Urban design, as a professional activity, has little to offer them. Of the basic requirements for survival only access to water and, in most climatic areas, a sheltering public environment fall into the domain of concern of urban designers. The physical design consequences of social policies to provide shelter do, however, have important urban design ramifications. Historically, survival needs have been met by the unselfconscious urban design processes of the people directly concerned. In high-density urban environments this approach becomes more difficult. In resource-poor areas or in the development of certain model life-sustaining communities in places such as Antarctica, outer space, or under the sea, the design of the physical environment is potentially an urban design concern. In resource-poor areas, the goal has been to design the most basic of infrastructure systems, while in the other case the designs of "settlements" have used highly sophisticated materials and support machinery, so much so that they have been primarily the concern of engineers. They have not been true settlements because individuals have spent only short times in them.

For planners in resource-poor countries with high population densities, the goal has been to provide the infrastructure for a settlement and a security of tenure. The design focus has been on the provision of clean

Figure 11-2: Physiological Needs and Modernist Urban Design
A prime goal of Modernist architects was to provide not only a living unit that was uncrowded, sunlit, and well ventilated, but also access to an unpolluted, sunlighted public realm. Their models of the good city were the opposite of the city they knew. The advertisement in (1) shows the environment sought by the Garden City movement. The Rationalists created very different designs, as exemplified in this scheme by Gropius and Breuer (2). We tend to take the same goals for granted now, but many city streets are hardly pleasant places, especially on a winter day (3).

enough water, drainage (actually sometimes forgotten), and the minimal sewerage-disposal procedures to sustain a disease-free life. Sites and services schemes may well represent the basic level of an urban designer's professional concern. In the United States, the urban designer as designer of infrastructure systems is seldom required to design at this level, although it may be an approach applicable in the poorest rural communities of the nation, such as some Indian reservations.

The design of places demanding high technology such as polar stations, undersea habitats, and potential space colonies will only fall into the purview of urban designers when they become places for everyday life rather than simply places for surviving well enough for a short time to conduct scientific studies. Such places, for instance, are the location of empirical environmental psychology studies that are leading to a much greater understanding of what it means to live in close quarters in stressful situations and of the design principles that can make them congenial habitats for people. The quality of life expected in them is low, but the rewards are high enough to satisfy their temporary inhabitants (Helmreich 1974).

Survival and safety needs are closely linked. Buildings need to be sound enough to survive earthquakes and hurricanes. They should be constructed so that elements of their façades hold firmly and do not fall on passersby. Channels of vehicular movement need to provide safety for drivers and for pedestrians. Almost all urban designs are concerned with these issues (see Chapter 12). They often override all other concerns.

Health

In health planning the urban design concern has historically been with the clearing of swamps, the designing of sewerage systems, the provision of clean water, the reduction of crowding, and the provision of services. The urban design concern in creating salubrious environments has been with designing guidelines that ensure sites are designed so that inhabited rooms get sunshine, buildings have cross-ventilation, and there is easy access to open space for their inhabitants and/or users. Often the concerns have been dealt with in a simplistic but nevertheless important fashion, ending up with the provision of open space through the use of building setbacks and site coverage regulations, but there have also been more comprehensive approaches.

At the beginning of the twentieth century in the United States, the Parks movement was primarily concerned with green space as "lungs" for reducing the pollution level of cities (Cranz 1982). A strong Model Housing movement contemporaneously sought to reduce the site coverage of buildings in housing areas in order to open up rooms to sunlight and ventilation (Gallion and Eisner 1986). Le Corbusier saw the Radiant City as being set in a park to give each dwelling unit access to sunlight, air, and greenery (Le Corbusier 1934, 1948). One of the results has been that urban designers, and their clients, almost automatically seek to supply as much open space as they can in a design, assuming it is always in the public interest. We have learned better now. Open spaces have to be carefully located, planned, and designed if they are to serve any public utility (J. Jacobs 1961; Hester 1975; Spirn 1984).

Today, designing to create salubrious environments involves much the same concerns as those of the Modernists except they are now broader in scope and increasingly focused on the health of the biogenic environment itself. Air pollution is still an issue, although the source of the pollution is now the automobile as much as manufacturing industries in both the technologically developed world and in third world countries. Los Angeles has special air pollution problems because of the topography of its surroundings. Conditions in other major cities of the world may be worse: people in Tokyo often wear masks to screen out pollutants, and cities such as Calcutta and Bangkok are notorious for their high levels of pollution from the exhaust of cars and buses. Access to sunlight, especially in areas of dense high-rise buildings, remains an issue, although it is now as often an aesthetic and solar energy access issue as a health issue.

In complex highly developed societies, the city planning concern is also with the provision and distribution of health services and facilities—hospitals, emergency services, and clinics. Medical science and technology have advanced considerably since World War II, and our expectations of health services have increased significantly as costs have risen. The concern is thus more and more with the maintenance of health as much as with the curing of ailments, although the medical model of responding to illness still predominates. The urban designer's concern is partially with the distribution and location of facilities so that people have access to them, but also with how buildings are arrayed in space and with how the nature of open space promotes a healthy environment.

Developmental Needs

A concern for the development and maintenance of a healthy body has become important for many people, particularly in the advanced industrial countries where the provision of medical services is good (especially for the wealthy). The urban design concern is with providing people with opportunities to exercise their bodies and to increase their physiological competence through the self-testing of their abilities. The maintenance of physiological abilities is also a major concern, especially in those societies where occupations demand little more than sedentary lives. The provision of developmental opportunities is usually associated with the needs of young people, and of maintenance opportunities with the needs of seniors, but the need for developmental opportunities applies to all people.

Providing for physiological development abilities is akin to the provision of environments that are educative (see Chapter 16, Meeting Cognitive Needs). Urban design has been more concerned with the formal opportunities for such activities, as the provision for playgrounds, playing fields, and other sports facilities in the Radiant City plans shows (Le Corbusier 1934). There are many guidelines for the distribution and nature of these facilities and their design (e.g., Allen 1968; Dattner 1969; Hester 1975; Rouard and Simon 1977). Some have been written to enhance opportunities for creative play as well as for physiological development and exercising. They provide for cognitive needs. The urban design concern thus also extends to broader issues such as the provision of opportunities for physiological self-testing in the everyday environment for all segments of the population—men and women, children (Pollowy 1977), teenagers (Ladd 1978), and the elderly (Carstens 1990), as will be described in Chapter 16.

Comfort

Comfort, at a minimal level, implies a freedom from pain on all dimensions of environmental experience. Biological comfort has to do with a person's assessment of the level of stimulation to which his or her body is being subjected. The pressure on the skin and joints from the patterns of the physical environment and from wind, the ambient and radiant temperatures, and the air moisture levels of a behavior setting are the major contributing factors to perceptions of comfort. There is considerable individual variation in subjective assessments of comfort for both physiological and psychological reasons. Much depends on habituation levels. Psychological comfort also has to do with the feelings of safety and security, which are the subject of the next chapter.

In devising ways of meeting comfort needs, people have devised a whole set of mechanisms from ceiling fans to automobiles to computers to help them. The basic concern of urban designers as professionals, however, is likely to focus on providing access to services, and a physiologically comfortable public realm—much of it outdoors. At this level of concern the urban designer has to deal with the way the elements of the built environment are to be structured to give access to sunlight, shade, and breezes within specific climatic zones (Olgyay 1963; Chandler 1976; Moll and Ebenzeck 1989), and with the way the furnishings of the public realm meet ergonomic needs so that they can be used safely and comfortably.

PHYSIOLOGICAL NEEDS AND BEHAVIOR SETTINGS DESIGN

In developing the behavior settings required to meet human physiological needs, there are three major areas of concern to the urban designer: (1) the activities—the behavior settings system—required for survival, health, and development, (2) the qualities of the milieu required to afford those activity patterns, and (3) the ambient conditions required to make the carrying out of those activities comfortable. As human needs occur in a hierarchy of prepotencies, once a basic level of comfort is attained, people's perceptions of their needs switch to a higher plane and the demand for environmental quality beyond comfort levels increase. All these concerns need to be seen within cultural contexts.

The Behavior Settings System

In planning for survival, health, and development, the concern of politicians and planners is with the nature of the activities that people can use to meet their needs with the resources available to a society. The urban design concern is to design policies and/or create designs for the layouts of settlements that best afford those basic activities. The goal is to provide the set of behavior settings necessary for survival and/or to create a suitable socioeconomic climate within which people can attain those ends in the way they choose.

The behavior systems required to meet survival needs vary considerably across the United States. In some rural parts of the country the planning concern may be for what are still essentially peasant cultures, where people are directly involved with producing their own food, where settlement designs are concerned with security of tenure and the provision of shelter for people and their animals, and where health concerns are with obtaining clean water and access to medical services. The activity patterns are largely those associated with agriculture but often involve many ritualistic elements. More frequently, in the United States and much of the technologically developed world, the concern has been and will be with getting and maintaining good links between people and job opportunities, with establishing land-use policies that negate the need for extensive energy-consuming transportation, and with social policies to sustain people who do not have the financial resources to obtain the products that will enable them to survive.

Urban designers are seldom directly involved in making policy decisions about the socioeconomic and service requirements for the inhabitants of cities at either a national or local level. The decision-making power in the United States, as in other democratic countries, lies with legislatures and the marketplace. Urban designers can, however, draw on an increasingly well developed empirical knowledge base in drawing legislators' and citizens' attention to the spatial and urban patterns required to promote ease of access to retail and public health services and, more broadly, to opportunities for individual physiological development. They have been strong advocates for recreation facilities, and for open space as lungs for the city in the past. Much of the advocacy, however, has been based largely on aesthetic grounds and on unsubstantiated beliefs about the connection between environmental variables and health, but now there is much scientific and quasi-scientific information available on which arguments for specific designs can be built.

The urban design policy focus in meeting physiological needs in cities today is with: (1) providing access to employment opportunities as well as retail, educational, and other basic services, (2) the nature, distribution, and quality of the behavior settings that provide health services, (3) the recreational activities that promote a healthy life, (4) the developmental opportunities that exist as part of everyday life, and (5) the quality and comfort level of the ambient nature of open spaces and other elements of the public realm. In dealing with these concerns the urban designer will have to work collaboratively with many other professionals.

DESIGNING THE MILIEU

The basic concern of urban designers is with what constitutes a healthy milieu, and the *anthropometrics* and *ergonomics* of urban form—with what has traditionally been called the *functional* purpose of design (Tillman and Tillman 1990). The goal is to enhance the quality of the milieu of the city: (1) as an overall settlement pattern, (2) as a set of places, and (3) as a set of links between places. The concern is with the milieu as an afforder of activities, and as a provider of shelter, physiological stimulation, and comfort.

Designing for Access

While one of the major goals of urban design is to provide channels of access to services, the more particular concern is with the qualities of those links and the qualities of the places that constitute destinations. Most of the links and places will be in the outdoors, highways, roads, pedestrian paths, parks, plazas, and so on, but some will be enclosed. The horizontal surfaces and the enclosing elements will be the units with which the urban designer works. The city can thus be thought of a set of enclosures, some roofed and some not, some in the private realm and some in the public realm.

Transportation Systems

Many of the links between places in cities consist of transportation modes other than pedestrian ways. Transporting sewerage and people and the mechanisms for doing so have been major shapers of urban form as argued earlier in this book. The built environment of cities consists of as much space related to transportation as to buildings—roads, rails, and airports form a major component of the city's infrastructure. The width and surface material of "streets" give a city much of its character: the traditional Islamic city of North Africa was designed for camel-borne transportation and pedestrians, Venice for water-borne transportation, the late-nineteenth-century cities of colonial Africa (e.g., Bulawayo in Zimbabwe) for turning a span of bullocks. The width of the streets of Salt Lake City, Utah, was based on similar propositions. In the late-twentieth-century North American city, designing for automobile traffic has clearly been the prime concern.

The specific design of transportation links has become so complex that these links are in the hands of the engineering professions and will continue to be so. At the same time there are a number of groups that are strong advocates for specific types of transportation. The automobile industry has played a major urban design role in shaping American cities, and there are strong proponents of mass transit, bicycle ways, and pedestrian routes. The urban designer needs to play an active mediating role among special-interest groups.

Urban design in America has shown an increasing concern for the interrelationship of behavior settings (or rather land uses) and an integrated set of transportation modes: pedestrian, automobile, and various types of mass transit. In the United States the responsibility for the design of each mode of transportation falls under such a variety of jurisdictions that coordination is difficult. Where such a coordination has been achieved the payoff is high in terms of urban quality, ease of movement, and attracting people to use mass transit.

One of the major engineering and urban design problems has been the integration of new systems with the existing built environment of cities. Placing new highways and other transit facilities into a city has had a major disrupting effect because they involve the demolition of wide swathes and the building of roads or rails (see Fig. 10–4(3)) in much the same manner as the implementation of City Beautiful ideals at the beginning of the twentieth century did (see Fig. 2–19(3)).

In new towns the problem is different. The transportation system, indeed the whole infrastructure system, can be designed ahead. Recent new town design in the United States (e.g., Las Colinas, Texas), but also places such as Milton Keynes in England, have relied on the automobile as the basic vehicle of movement and thus the structuring element for urban form. This reliance is reflected in the whole relationship between roads and buildings (see Figs. 2–4(3) and 3–9(1)). The difficulty in designing for public transportation is to get a critical mass of people sufficient to make it economically viable. Achieving this end has been a particular problem because most urban designers and their clients in the United States have sought to design relatively low density environments. In such schemes, designers' plans should be based on thinking ahead to provide, at least, the right of ways for potential future transportation links and to avoid future demolition of buildings as the city develops. Needless to

1. O'Hare Airport, Chicago

2. The Loop, Chicago

3. Yamhill Historic District, Portland, Oregon

Figure 11-3: The "Physiology" of Transportation Modes
In urban design there is often a tradeoff between providing for human comfort and for the needs of machines to be able to function well. The various transportation modes that we use may have their own special roadbed requirements. Sometimes special tracks have to be provided (1,2,3). Meeting the technical needs of transportation facilities is a major form giver in urban design (see Chapter 10). When integrated with the overall design, transportation modes can enhance the experience of a place, but often radical surgery is necessary to make their operation feasible.

say, such easements are subject to considerable pressure for development and immediate return on capital invested. In high-density environments, public transit is essential.

There is also considerable pressure to make the centers of cities more comfortable by removing or restricting automobiles from them, widening sidewalks, creating pedestrian malls, and reducing the amount of parking space available as well as improving public transit options. The goal is to make high-density environments more comfortable for pedestrians. While there are many pedestrian malls in the United States, few cities have pursued aggressive policies to achieve automobile-free environments on any large scale in comparison to the European efforts in cities such as Copenhagen (Gehl 1987). One city that has developed an integrated program is Bellevue, Washington (Hinshaw 1983; Bellevue c. 1984), but the design option advocated by Victor Gruen (see Fig. 3–5) has not been taken up.

A Note on Barrier-Free Urban Designs

Physiologically impaired people are demanding that they not be handicapped by the layout of the built en-

vironment, that they be able to use the environment with dignity. Many are demanding to be mainstreamed— that the everyday environment be made accessible to them rather than having special entrances to buildings and special transportation systems designed for them alone. The goal is to allow those with disabilities to be participants in life rather than spectators. The knowledge is now largely available to create successful barrier-free environments (Bednar 1977; Robinette 1985; Welner 1990).

Until recently neither the political will nor the support of architects has existed for building barrier-free cities in the United States. The former perceives the costs as being too high and the latter find the requirements infringe on their artistic freedom. Young architects, however, seem to be more thoughtful about barrier-free design issues than budding physicians. With the introduction of the Americans with Disabilities Act of 1990 the concern for barrier-free environments has been considerably enhanced. The reward for people as a whole is that such environments are good for everybody (Ostroff 1978). When considered as part of all new design work, particularly the design of the public realm, the cost is not high. Retrofitting the environment is costly.

1. In the Loop, Chicago

2. 16th and Moravian Streets, Philadelphia

3. Nicolett Mall, Minneapolis

Figure 11-4: Barrier-Free Environments
While many people are without disabilities and can make do with whatever situation is provided (1), many are not. The political position taken in this book is that the public realm has to be barrier-free for all people. The financial cost has to be borne by society. The design dilemma is that what makes an environment barrier-free for one group may make it more difficult for another. Curbs are good cues for blind people but make wheelchair access impossible (2). The environment should at least give people in wheelchairs access, with dignity, to all public places (3).

One of the requirements in developing a behavioral program for urban design is to specify at what level (i.e., for whom) the layout of the environment should be barrier-free. The standing specifications are: "nonambulatory disabilities"—disabilities that confine people to wheelchairs; "semiambulatory disabilities"—those impairments that result in people walking with crutches; "sight disabilities," including blindness; hearing disabilities; and "disabilities of incoordination." All the regulations being developed at present assume that a person should be able to get around whether on foot, crutches, or wheelchairs. The concern is with paraplegics, the blind, and the deaf.

A set of standards for making facilities accessible to all such people was developed in the United States in 1961 and subsequently amended a decade later (American National Standards Institute 1971). The primary concern is for making the surfaces along which people move satisfactory for wheelchair use. The specifications are for ramp gradients as well as for making toilets, telephones, and elevators accessible. For the blind, wayfinding cues are particularly important. The current specifications deal with signage in Braille or raised letters and with audible warning signals, and with the elimination of hazards such as low-hanging signs, and furnishings on sidewalks where the blind will be walking. The use of the textures on the ground surface can be added to the list of issues to concern the urban designer in thinking about surface materials.

Designing for Activities

The standing patterns of behavior of some behavior settings are governed by a set of formal rules and thus are the basic requirements of the milieu. Games such as baseball and football are examples of these behavior settings. Most other behavior settings are governed by norms of expected behavior within a culture, and the goal is to attain a fit between them and the milieu that enables the behavior to occur at least well enough within culturally determined standards and using the resources available. Many milieus serve a multiplicity of standing patterns of behavior, and one of the issues facing urban designers is the degree to which physical settings should be tailor-made for specific behaviors and the degree to which they should accommodate many behaviors. We have been through an era of multiuse settings, but there seems to be a swing back to designing specific settings for specific activities. For example, Baltimore's new baseball stadium has been designed for baseball alone rather than for baseball and football as many of the stadiums designed in the United States during the 1960s were.

Except in outer space, all human activities are related to the horizontal surfaces of the world. The quality of these surfaces is thus fundamental to their ease of use as the milieu of behavior settings. Different activities require different surfaces, and different surfaces require different levels of maintenance. A particular surface may serve one

1. Plaza, University of Pennsylvania Campus, Philadelphia

2. Shopping Mall, Columbia, Maryland

3. Park Bench

Figure 11-5: Comfort Requirements and the Design of Places
The quality of any public place—outdoor (1) or indoor (2)—is a complex function of how well it provides physiological support for desired activities and its aesthetic character. The fundamental concern is with the nature of the horizontal surface, enclosing elements, furnishings, and the nature of illumination. People's expectations of the quality of these variables vary in interior and exterior spaces, when those layouts are designed to be used in a specific way, whether they are being adapted to a function, and whether the people themselves have the resources for an alternative (3).

physiological requirement very well but not another. For instance, Astroturf—a synthetic grass mat—may serve well for running (provided a person has the appropriate footwear) but it is not thermally comfortable on hot days.

Many activities require enclosure of various types. The enclosure may be required for physiological reasons—to maintain comfort levels but also to meet privacy requirements (see Chapters 12 and 13). In addition, many public open spaces are enclosed by the walls of buildings whether they need such an enclosure or not. The character of a city depends partly on the way the patterns, materials, and furnishings of its places and links afford the range of activities that take place within them.

As already mentioned, the fundamental concern is with the floor of the setting and the way it is provided with fixed and semifixed features (E. Hall 1966). Some surfaces are comfortable to walk on, other are not. Some fixed features (such as benches, steps, and balustrades) are comfortable to sit on, others are not. The way furniture is arranged and lighting provided not only affects the ease and comfort with which activities are carried out but also structures the ambience of a place.

Designing for Shelter and Comfort

The complex geometry of the milieu of cities, the thermal and hydrological properties of buildings, roads, and other paved areas, the heat from the combustion of machines, all change the salubriousness and comfortableness of a place. Two urban design concerns result: (1) the changes, possibly deleterious, in the overall biogenic nature of the place (see Chapter 19), and (2) the effect on the micro-climate of the settings used by people and other organisms (see below). The overall ecology of the city is at stake on both dimensions.

Each new building changes the climate, both inside its walls and outside it. When buildings are aggregated into villages, towns, and cities, they create a distinctive and often "far from pleasant" climate (Chandler 1976; Hough 1984; Spirn 1984). This is not inevitable. We could develop guidelines for urban development that mitigate these effects, but so far we have allowed the market and other urban design concerns to be the sole dictators of urban patterns. The question is: "Whose responsibility is the climatic nature of cities?"

The architect is concerned with the internal environment of buildings and has largely been unconcerned about its effects on the external environment. A number of lawsuits has begun to make the effect of new buildings on their neighbors a design consideration. For example, in the mid-1980s the owners of 22 Cortland Street in lower Manhattan filed a lawsuit in the New York State Supreme Court against the World Trade Center on the grounds that the winds created by the twin towers caused their building to move in an "abnormal rotating fashion" and cost them over $1 million to do structural repairs to it.

The quality of the open spaces adjacent to buildings has had few advocates for it yet in lawsuits, but local governments are increasingly concerned about how buildings shape the ambient quality of life on streets, plazas, and other parts of the public realm of cities.

Designing to make the public realm sheltering and comfortable, particularly in highly dense environments with high-rise buildings, has increasingly become a design concern as the ambient quality of the space between buildings declines. Stringent design guidelines have been and are being established in a number of American cities. The most recent legislation has been addressing the variety of variables, some very difficult to pin down, that make for a physiologically pleasant environment. Not only is sunlight in public places of concern, but also wind effects (e.g., San Francisco, see Arens and Bosslemann 1989; Boston, see Durgin 1989).

Deciding what an appropriate comfort level is depends not only on physiological issues but on cultural ones as well. There are different religious attitudes toward the degree of comfort that a person should have, and there is often clash between designing for comfort and designing for development (see Chapter 20). Americans have an increasingly high demand for physiological comfort. It is now expected that any indoor public space will be very comfortable.

It is also clear that traditional ways of behaving give way to more comfortable ways quite easily. Once the new ways are established it is very difficult for people to return to those less comfortable. Deciding what is culturally appropriate behavior is often a contentious process (see Chapters 21, 22, 23, and 24).

Visual Quality and Comfort

In building cities we have both shaded the public realm and illuminated the night to a higher and higher degree. The patterning of light and lighting in a place gives it much of its aesthetic character, not only through the distribution and nature of light fittings and standards but also through the patterning of light itself. Light, however, serves a number of more basic purposes: making activities possible and visually comfortable (and making antisocial activities more open to view) and aiding orientation, as well as serving both formal and symbolic aesthetic functions.

Visual comfort—the ease of seeing—is very much related to activities and subject to considerable individual variability. There are two major design considerations for sighted people: the ability to see phenomena at various distances in varying light conditions, and freedom from glare. The basic requirement is to have sufficient illumination to see the environment without ambiguities in order to carry out activities, to read signs, to see details of people (see also Carr, Myer/Smith Inc. 1973). The blind have special problems.

People can see under an extraordinarily wide array of levels of illumination (Gibson 1966, 1979). The finer the work in which we are engaged, the higher the level of illumination required; the older we are, the more illumination we require. Levels of illumination must not be so high as to dazzle either through contrast levels of one surface adjacent to another in place or time or through absolute levels of illumination (Kantowitz and Sorkin 1983; Tillman and Tillman 1990).

New materials have had a number of unanticipated effects on visual comfort. With the development of curtain wall and reflective glass buildings, for instance, the concern with avoiding glare in people's eyes, particularly those of automobile drivers, has become an issue in urban design. It has seldom been specifically addressed.

The Sonic Environment and Sonic Comfort

Sonic comfort depends not only on the decibel level of sound, but also on its pitch, the nature of its source, and perceptions people have of the degree to which others have control over that source. Undesired sounds (i.e., noise) can be an invasion of one's privacy as well as disturbing to the activities in which one is engaged. People adapt to extraordinarily noisy environments, but there is now an increasing concern with the sonic pollution of the urban environment, particularly in the centers of major American cities such as New York (and probably even more so in European cities such as Rome and London and Asian ones such as Jakarta). Noise from traffic and machines such as air conditioners reverberates among buildings, reaching decibel levels that people find unacceptable. Similarly, the noise generated in the flight paths of aircraft, especially those across residential areas adjacent to airports, is a problem that planners and designers will have to deal with as the number of flights into and out of airports continues to increase.

Buildings themselves can generate noise from exhaust fans of various types. Somewhat unusually, in a recent case in New York City, the building configuration itself was the generator of noise. The owners of the 720-foot-high Cityspire Building were fined because the louvers on its dome caused a high-pitched whistle that its neighbors found annoying.

The everyday sonic quality of the environment has seldom been of major concern to urban designers, partly because it cannot be drawn—our modes of representation focus on the visual aspect of the environment not its other perceptual qualities. The sound of a place can be orchestrated in much the same way as its visual qualities by the choice of materials used for the surfaces of the environment and the nature of objects within it. The concern is not simply with removing the negative but, in specific settings, with increasing the positive—the sounds of birds, of children's voices, the crunching of leaves underfoot during the autumn (see Chapter 17). There are

1. Las Vegas, Nevada

Source: Venturi, Scott Brown and Associates

2. Kennedy Boulevard, Philadelphia

Courtesy of Ann Strong

3. Shopping Center

Figure 11-6: Visual Factors in Urban Design

Generally urban designers think about visual quality in terms of aesthetics, but the ease of seeing elements of the environment clearly is more basic. There is, for instance, a relationship between clutter and size of lettering, speed of movement, and the appropriate distance at which to see signs or views (1). In addition, there is the need to avoid "rogue reflections"—from buildings that blind drivers. This issue has become more of a concern as curtain wall and reflective glass buildings become an architectural feature (2). Artificial illumination has enabled us to extend the use of cities considerably (3, see also Fig. 14–12).

many positive sounds that make cities and specific settings attractive places (Southworth 1969). Sometimes a positive sound can be made to mask the negative ones in order to create a sonically comfortable environment.

There are relatively few techniques that designers can use to reduce the impact of noise-generating sources on their surroundings. One way is to reduce the level of noise at its source by modifying its design. The other is to use solid materials between the noise source and the setting under consideration. Buildings, walls, and berms, banks of earth, are the major techniques we use to absorb noises. It is important to do so because high levels of noise have a deleterious effect on life. In adapting to noise people tend to tune out other important aspects of sonic communication. This type of adaptation has a negative effect on such things as family life and the intellectual development of children.

Olfactory Comfort

The odors resulting from the biological environment and the activities taking place in a city are a major source of both pleasant and unpleasant experiences (Gibson

1967). We seek the former and avoid the latter where possible. Human settlements are full of negative odors from the machines we use and the manufacturing processes that occur there. People do adapt to negative odors to an extraordinary degree. For instance, they seem to live without apparent discomfort adjacent to factories producing strong sulfurous odors.

Zoning laws were at least partially developed to segregate noxious uses from everyday life and are still the main technique. In everyday urban design we have been less considerate of the effects of the invasion of people's privacy and the resultant psychological consequences as a result of olfactory pollution.

Places can be designed to contain pleasant odors through the nature of the trees, shrubs, and flowers planted and through the selection of enterprises that produce positive odors in context (e.g., bakeries in shopping areas). It must be remembered that what is regarded as a positive or a negative odor is not simply a physiological factor; it is also culture-bound, dependent on habituation levels and on the meanings associated with the odor. The smell of oil may be expected and be part of the positive experience when visiting an automobile service station but not

1. Denver

2. Riverwalk, San Antonio, Texas

3. State Street, Chicago

Figure 11-7: The Sonic Environment of Cities
Noise is unwanted sound. Protection from regular sources of noise can be achieved through the use of solid barriers such as buildings, walls, and berms or by masking the noise with another sound such as falling water, as in Paley Plaza, New York City (see Fig. 17-3(3)). Noise barriers are becoming standard along busy highways, but they also destroy the visual experience of the environment for drivers (1). Sonically pleasant places in busy areas can afford great joy (2), but removing the bustle of cars coming and going can also reduce the life of a place (3).

at home. Americans, in general, have the reputation of seeking a largely odorless environment.

Metabolic Comfort

The *metabolic* comfort of a person outdoors depends on the level of activity of that individual and on the air temperature, humidity, radiation, air movement, and clothing worn. The degree of acclimatization and adaption of the individual is an intervening variable in subjective views of comfort. All these factors are affected by the layout of the environment.

The negative effect of much of the built environment, particularly that component recently built, on human comfort outdoors has led to a number of major studies of urban places over the last thirty years (Olgyay 1963; Givoni 1973). Historically, cities that evolved over considerable periods of time in one set of cultural hands were very much shaped to their climates. Hot, arid cities consist of closely packed houses, with interior courts to act as mechanisms to draw air through the house and narrow alleyways to increase the shading offered. The buildings in hot, humid cities were, in contrast, spread out allowing the breezes to flow through them. Although American cities vary considerably in their climatic locale, only a few architectural cues show these differences. Many recent urban designs have paid scant attention to the direction of the sun in the sky or to prevailing wind directions. The result is that streets are often climatically unpleasant places in which to be and plazas are often located on the sides of buildings where they are climatically inappropriate (e.g., W. R. Grace Plaza, New York City; see also Whyte 1980).

Temperature

Americans have increasing demands for thermal comfort in moving about the city. The concern is one of long standing as the developers of arcades and, more recently, shopping malls and skylinks have demonstrated. There has been considerable empirical validation of the necessity to design for people's thermal comfort in outdoor spaces.

Those center cities in the northern United States that rely very heavily on pedestrian traffic for retail success have a significant drop in the flow of people when the temperature falls below freezing or goes above 80°F and when it rains or snows. In such cities, designers have sought ways of increasing the comfort level of pedestrians. The result has been the development of shopping malls, of a snow-melting system under the sidewalks of central Holland, Michigan (annual snow fall of 75 to 100 inches), of skyway pedestrian systems in cities such as Minneapolis or Duluth, Minnesota. Dallas, for different reasons, has extensive below-ground movement channels. The purpose in such designs has been to enhance retail activity. This has been done with success in places where the designs provide people with convenient and easy access, security, and amenities.

1. First Federal Bank Plaza, Minneapolis

2. Pioneer Square Area, Seattle

3. Rockefeller Center, New York

Figure 11-8: Urban Design and Metabolic Comfort
Many places in American cities today are unpleasant and thus deserted at potentially high-use times (1)—"a stage set for a play that never happens" (Cooper Marcus and Francis 1990). Attention needs to be paid to the everyday outdoor environment of cities through the use of appropriate planting, such as deciduous trees in temperate areas (2), and capturing the sunshine in outdoor areas likely to be used on cool days. More and more, we rely on artificially temperature-controlled environments (3). Often we have to do so!

As technology has been advanced, heating and cooling systems have been improved. With this improvement has come a rise in people's expectations of the comfort level of the ambient environment. Indoor comfort levels have improved, particularly with the development of central heating and air conditioning. The improving quality of the indoor environment has led to major changes in the location and nature of semiprivate, semipublic, and public open spaces in cities. The porches and verandas that were once used as cool areas in houses during the summer are less used as a place for sitting out because the internal environment is now air conditioned. In Seaside, Florida, the design guidelines stipulate that each house have a porch of a particular size facing the street, but this seems to have been done for social reasons as much as for climatic ones (Langdon 1988; Patton 1991).

In the outdoor environment, the comfort level depends not only on the ambient temperature but also on the degree of radiant heating and cooling from the ground surface and walls of a place, the humidity level, and the air movement there. It also depends on the patterns of sun and shade. Desirable conditions will vary by the season and by the activities that take place. The problem in most American cities is that open spaces are increasingly overshadowed by tall buildings, thus urban design guidelines for cities in temperate zones of the United States have been more concerned with making sure that spaces receive sunlight rather than whether they receive the appropriate shade in summer.

In places where heat from sunshine is a problem, people using open spaces need shade and breezes. The shade can be obtained from trees, awnings, and buildings. The advantage of trees is that they set up convection currents below them, thus aiding the cooling process and, if deciduous, they allow the sun to penetrate in winter (Arnold 1980). Trees can be used on a broader scale in helping cities as a whole and the people within them to keep cool (Moll and Ebenzeck 1989).

In the more frigid climes of the northern United States, as in Canada and northern Europe, the indoor living period can extend for as much as 70 percent of the year. There are two contrasting philosophical positions on what urban designers should do: not protect people from nature much above minimal survival levels, or keep the world at about 70°F (21°C). Young active people feel less affected by winter climes, but people such as the frail elderly need protection. The logical solution is to give people a choice (Pressman 1987; Mänty and Pressman 1989; Carper 1991).

There has been a reaction by many environmentalists and also some architects to the heavy reliance on air conditioning in cooling. The design mechanisms that have been used to reduce this reliance include projecting surfaces, screens, vegetation, and other low-technology means of maintaining comfort levels in hot areas or times of the year. Similarly, there has been more thought given

1. Fifth Avenue, New York

2. Greenway System, Society Hill, Philadelphia

3. Allentown, Pennsylvania

Figure 11-9: Physiological Needs and Urban Pedestrian Links
In the public realm, the nature of the horizontal surfaces, its material and slopes, are the basic factors of concern in designing links between areas, whether they are broad sidewalks (1) or separate pedestrian ways (2). Different materials have long been used to differentiate one behavior setting from another. Providing for shelter from rain and snow through the use of awnings and canopies (3) and internal links protected from the weather has increasingly become a part of urban design considerations (see, e.g, Figs. 7-4(2), 11-3(2), 11-4(1), 11-5(3), and 11-8(3)). Often such links also provide for feelings of safety and security as well (see Chapter 12).

to the orientation of buildings, to open places to catch the sun in cool areas, and to designing for shade in hot areas.

Humidity

Relative humidity levels of 40 to 50 percent feel comfortable in both cool weather and heated environments, while slightly higher levels are acceptable in hot weather. High levels of humidity and of temperature are found to be uncomfortable by almost everyone. There are differences in opinion as to what constitutes high temperature, but at 40 percent humidity few people find temperatures over 80°F (28°C) comfortable.

Fountains, trees, and other vegetation have long been used with great success to change humidity levels in the design of urban plazas, courtyards, and avenues, particularly in hot, arid climates to make the ambient temperature of such places more comfortable. The lack of careful thought behind the use of water and vegetation has also resulted in the opposite effect. In places such as the retirement and resort communities of Arizona, the introduction of lakes, trees, lawns (especially golf courses), and flowers requiring watering has raised the humidity level

of the air to unpleasant levels in summertime, abrogating the very reason for the choice of location in the first place. In addition, the layout patterns in these communities are based on the patterns familiar to people in the areas from which they are drawn—the northern cities.

Air Movement

The movement of air is caused by atmospheric pressure gradients. There are three basic types of winds that affect cities: prevailing winds, mesoscale winds (thunderstorms, tornadoes), and local winds. The last mentioned can take several forms: land-sea breezes, Foehm winds, where flow of air over mountains can cause major temperature changes, and katabatic and anabatic winds, which occur from the change of solar heating on valley floors.

Designing for mesoscale conditions is certainly an imperative for survival in areas that are susceptible to cyclones and flooding (see Chapter 12). Prevailing winds and local winds have more of an effect on comfort level. Air movement through cities serves many purposes: keeping a place cool, flushing out pollutants, and simply ventilating a city. The increased wind effect caused by the

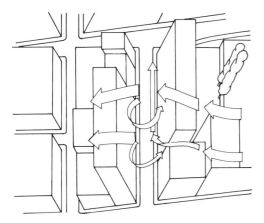

1. Pressure Connections

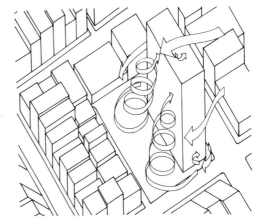

2. Vortex Effect

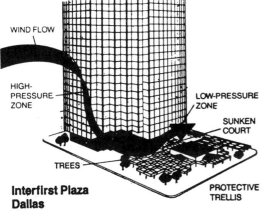

WIND FLOW

HIGH-
PRESSURE
ZONE

LOW-PRESSURE
ZONE

SUNKEN
COURT

TREES

**Interfirst Plaza
Dallas**

PROTECTIVE
TRELLIS

3. Wind-Mitigating Elements. Interfirst Plaza, Dallas

Figure 11-10: Wind Effects of the Urban Fabric
While the effect of winds on buildings, especially on tall buildings, has been a major factor in design, the effect of building configurations on wind flows and hence on the quality of open spaces has seldom been a consideration in urban design. Our understanding of the effects of building forms on the channeling of winds on city sidewalks (1) and plazas in front of tall buildings (2) is being considerably enhanced by recent research (Arens and Bosslemann 1989). Urban design guidelines are beginning to be formulated to inform building developers and architects of their obligations to the public (3).

configurations of buildings and open spaces in cities is created by two factors: (1) three quarters of the wind striking the face of a building pours in a straight downdraft to the ground where it sets up a rolling motion (thus the taller the building the greater the strength of the wind), and (2) differences in wind pressure between the windward and leeward sides of buildings cause high local wind speeds as air rushes from the area of high pressure to low. The negative effect of winds can be reduced substantially in cities only by lowering the heights of buildings to less than six stories. Such an action would, however, cause other problems. The negative effects of winds in cities can, however, be mitigated by the design of buildings in relationship to each other (Aynsley, Melbourne, and Vickery 1977).

Wind speeds of 50 mph (23 meters/second) can bowl over a person. The configuration of buildings very much affects the speed of winds through streets and across open spaces (Durgin 1989). If winds go above 11 mph in pedestrian areas and 7 mph in seating areas, people complain. While most American cities have areas where the wind effects on certain days are notorious, there are cities in other countries where the problems are even more serious.

In Tokyo, for instance, on windy days ropes are strung along some streets to help people keep their footing. For some people this is fun, but for others it is a very trying experience. The basic urban design goal is to strive for comfort and to avoid danger (e.g., people being blown over or blown into the paths of vehicles, pieces of buildings being torn away, and billboards and trees being blown over).

One of the problems facing urban designers in establishing general policies and guidelines to deal with such matters is that prevailing winds are not good predictors of wind movements in particular areas of cities. Often the only way to predict the effects of winds prior to buildings being built is to test models in wind tunnels. General progress is, nevertheless, being made on our understanding of winds and cities, and design principles are being developed based on this understanding.

Among the design principles are: (1) the creation of "barriers" of tall buildings around edges of urban areas should be avoided—the abrupt height change increases speeds in open spaces windward of them, but prevents the flushing of polluted air; (2) the provision of height zone transitions to alleviate problems (e.g., height changes should not occur along streets where pedestrians walk, but should be drawn in the center of blocks); and (3) the specification for the heights of buildings in areas defining the spacing between buildings so that they are far enough apart for sun and close enough to each other to avoid downwash effects.

URBAN DESIGN CONSEQUENCES

As the deleterious effects of neglect and the side effects of design decisions become apparent, so have urban designers become more self-consciously concerned with basic survival or comfort needs of the users of the outdoor public realm of cities. Yet the health and, to a lesser degree, comfort of a city's inhabitants have been major considerations in both the unselfconscious and the self-conscious design of human settlements from the beginning of history. Early humans sought refuge in caves and created underground as well as above-ground dwellings in their search for survival and comfort (and security).

The development of zoning and the engineering of reticulated water systems and sewerage systems resulted from the concern with designing the city salubrious (J. Peterson 1979). A series of urban design questions arises today: "What are the appropriate levels of comfort for various activities?" "How does one trade off comfort for other design considerations?" One of the questions repeated in this book is: "How comfortable should the environment be made?" There are also the allied questions: "How efficient should it be?" and "How stress-free should it be?"

In total urban design, these concerns are very much under the control of the architect, but in all-of-a-piece design as the scale of development and the complexity of variables with which designers have to deal increase, so is there a tradeoff among physiological needs, the resources available, and the need to fulfill other design goals. There is now a considerably enhanced understanding of the principles for the design of salubrious and comfortable built environments in comparison to what the Modernists knew. This development of knowledge has made the design of design guidelines both a more complex and easier task. It is more complex because we are considering the environment in an increasingly multivariate manner; it is easier because the empirical knowledge is now available to guide us. Designing for climate is becoming an increasingly professional task in itself, particularly if we are also concerned with energy efficiency.

Urban designers need to pay special attention to the relationship between indoor and outdoor spaces, the protection of pedestrians from rain, snow, and the hot sun through the use of colonnades and arcades (Geist 1983; Bednar 1989; Maitland 1991), and the seasonal use of outdoor spaces. There is a particular need in winter cities to integrate activities and celebrations, such as the Carnaval

de Quebec, into life if winter is not to be seen as an enemy but as a friend. Similarly, access to outdoor activities such as skating and skiing makes life not only tolerable but fun for many people.

Designing Guidelines for Human Physiological Needs in Cities

Many zoning requirements and design guidelines have to do with meeting the health and comfort needs of people. Zoning laws have dealt with the location of noxious facilities, the distribution and size of areas devoted to different land uses, the bulk of buildings, and indirectly with population density. The overall quality of the spaces between buildings was largely neglected until recently. A number of examples, already noted in this chapter, show that a change is taking place.

One of the major zoning requirements that has shaped the public realm of many cities in almost all countries has been to provide for sunlight at the base of buildings for at least an hour at the winter solstice. Other zoning ordinances have been concerned with ventilation and the required amount of open space to be left on a site. More recently, the concern has been for the amount of sunlight in public open spaces. One of the leaders in this area has been the city of San Francisco.

The San Francisco regulations have resulted in new height and bulk controls on buildings, and in the creation of solar access standards to assure direct sunlight. The acceptable height limits have been lowered and also varied to simulate the natural hills of San Francisco. Zones for taller buildings are clustered in the financial core, with gradual tapering of building heights down to the bay. Bulk controls have also been revised to state that the taller a building the less its bulk should be (San Francisco, Department of City Planning 1983). Much the same set of guidelines has been adopted in other places (e.g., Bellevue, Washington; see Bellevue c. 1984). Even more recent are the examples of wind control in places such as Boston and San Francisco (Arens, Bosslemann et al. 1984; Durgin 1989). There has also been increasing thought given to dealing with comfort issues in ways not so demanding of energy consumption as those prevailing today.

Instead of simply separating people from snow in northern climates through the use of skywalks and internal malls, urban design guidelines are being developed to angle streets to the sun and to provide shelter from winds. Similarly, prescriptions for the use of warm colors (such as in the Guthrie Theater in Minneapolis) and materials and warm spectrum lights are being proposed. The goal is to get away from the simplistic solutions of the past to consider alternative ways of achieving similar ends (Carper 1991). Such proposals do, however, also assume that people are willing to give up a degree of comfort to enhance their experiencing of the environment!

1. Drexel University Campus, Philadelphia

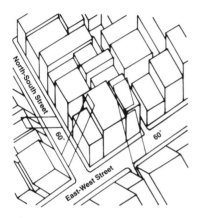

2. Solar Cutoff Angles in Dense Environments

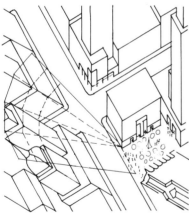

3. Solar Fans

Figure 11-11: Design Guidelines for Open Spaces
The comfortableness of any urban open space depends on the nature of the light it receives (1). Zoning controls have long been concerned with the penetration of sunlight to the street level by defining solar cutoff angles for east-west and north-south streets of gridiron city plans (2). Policy 3 of the "Recreation and Open Space Element" of the *San Francisco Master Plan* states: "preserve sunlight in public open spaces." The concern is focused very specifically on particular locations, particularly small open spaces, to ensure sunlight on winter days at lunchtime. The concern then is with defining "solar fans" (3).

Collection of the author

Courtesy of the Department of City Planning, San Francisco

Meeting human physiological needs is clearly a multidimensional concern. It is also clear that designing for physiological needs as the sole focus of concern will have negative impacts on the overall quality of the built environment, as the criticism of the work of Modernists has shown. Maslow's model of human needs shows that we are prepared to give up on many dimensions of comfort to attain other needs.

MAJOR REFERENCES

Arens, E., P. et al. (1984). "Sun, Wind and Comfort." University of California at Berkeley, College of Environmental Design, Institute of Urban and Regional Development, Environmental Simulation Laboratory.

Chandler, T. J. (1976). *Urban Climatology and Its Relevance to Urban Design*. Geneva: World Meteorological Organization (Technical Note 149).

Cooper Marcus, Clare, and Carolyn Francis, eds. (1990). *People Places: Design Guidelines for Urban Open Space*. New York: Van Nostrand Reinhold.

Greer, Norma Richter (1988). *The Creation of Shelter*. Washington, DC: American Institute of Architects.

Lang, Jon (1987a). "Anthropometrics and Ergonomics." In *Creating Architectural Theory: The Role of the Behavioral Sciences in Environmental Design*. New York: Van Nostrand Reinhold, pp. 126–134.

Mänty, Jorma, and Norman Pressman, eds. (1989). *Cities Designed for Winter*. Helsinki: Building Book.

Moll, Gary, and Sara Ebenzeck, eds. (1989). *Shading Our Cities: A Resource Guide for Urban and Community Forests*. Covelo, CA: Island Press.

Robinette, Gary O., ed. (1985). *Barrier-Free Exterior Design: Anyone Can Go Anywhere*. New York: Van Nostand Reinhold.

Spirn, Ann Whiston (1984). "Dirt and Discomfort" and "Improving Air Quality." In *The Granite Garden: Urban Nature and Human Design*. New York: Basic Books, pp. 41–87.

Tillman, Peggy, and Barry Tillman (1990). *Human Factors Essentials: An Ergonomic Guide For Designers, Scientists, and Managers*. New York: McGraw Hill.

Welner, Alan H. (1990). "Environmental Accessibility for Physically Disabled People." In F. J. Kottke and J. F. Lehman, eds., *Krusen's Handbook of Physical Medicine and Rehabilitation*. New York: W. B. Saunders, pp. 1273–1290.

12

MEETING SAFETY AND SECURITY NEEDS

Once their survival needs and basic comfort requirements are reasonably well satisfied, people's concerns shift up the scale to focus on the fulfillment of other ends, particularly safety and security needs. While the lives of some people are dominated by such needs, for most physically and psychologically healthy people safety and security needs are reasonably well satisfied in the United States. Sadly, there are many areas in the country where there are still many people in vulnerable situations. The fear of antisocial behavior results in safety and security issues taking precedence over many others in urban design. Indeed, in many situations the reality of life results in the concern being one for survival, so that takes precedence over concerns for comfort.

Despite a general lack of fear of wild animals in most Americans' everyday lives (although rats are still a menace in a number of low-income neighborhoods) and a generally smooth-running society, many of the social mechanisms that provided for relatively high levels of safety and security during the first half of the twentieth century in North America and Europe have broken down. In many American inner cities, in particular, the boarded homes, empty lots, and barred liquor stores attest to a sense of fear. Safety and security needs, while not necessarily dominant in all the United States, are the focus of considerable attention of many people. The partial fulfillment of these needs remains a prerequisite for being motivated to seek the fulfillment of higher-order needs.

There are two basic types of safety and security needs that have an impact on the work of the urban designer: (1) physiological—to have freedom from bodily harm, and (2) psychological—to have a sense of place, geographically and socially in a society. To achieve the former, people need to feel safe from wild animals, criminal assault, and various types of accidents: household, vehicular, and so

on. To achieve the latter, there is a desire to avoid the unexpected, to be in *control,* to know where one is in one's social and physical surroundings, and not to be afraid of other people and social situations.

It is clear that in the same circumstances there are varied demands for safety from different people—personality differences are involved. Some people tend to see the world as hostile and disorganized, while others are able to organize their thoughts more rationally to identify the dangers that do exist. At the extreme, obsessive-compulsive people try "frantically to order and stabilize the world so that every possible contingency may be provided for . . . so that anything unexpected cannot occur" (Maslow 1987). There are also some groups of people—for instance, the frail elderly, particularly in cities but even in rural areas of the United States where social networks are still strong—who are especially susceptible to dangers. These dangers are from the natural elements and events of the biogenic environment, accidents of various types, and antisocial human behavior. Such groups of people are especially in danger because their physiological competence levels are low.

SOURCES OF INSECURITY

Sources of people's insecure feelings vary considerably. There is still a fear of nuclear disasters and the effects of the continuing pollution of the earth in many minds, particularly those of the young, many of whom have a highly pessimistic view of the future. There is a fear of antisocial behavior, even when walking around one's own neighborhood in much of urban America. There are other fears, such as losing one's job or, for some people, being caught committing a crime. Dealing with many of these issues falls outside the scope of concern of design-

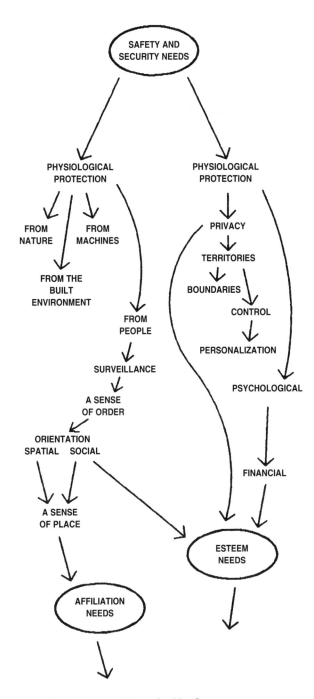

Figure 12-1: Safety and Security Needs

Physiological Insecurity

There are four basic sources of danger to one's physiological condition in the environment: (1) harmful bacteria and pollutants, (2) natural events of the biogenic world, (3) elements of the artificial environment—the built environment and the machines we use, and (4) the antisocial behavior of segments of the population. Fears of any of the four may also cause feelings of psychological insecurity. The ability of individuals to cope with these dangers depends on their level of competence. Addressing any of the sources of problems has implications for urban design.

Harmful Bacteria and Pollutants

The urban design concern here overlaps that of regional and city planners and sanitation engineers. Harmful bacteria come from many sources: poor waste disposal, stagnant water, bites from insects, and so on. Pollutants too come from many sources: mining and industry, automobile usage, and even from various plants. Many of the specific urban design issues have already been mentioned; others will be addressed in Chapter 19. The urban design concern is with the provision of good sanitation and the location of the noxious facilities that are at present needed to maintain our living standards.

Natural Disasters

The natural elements of the environment are sources of potential danger in many ways. People have built settlements in a wide variety of places for economic, defensive, or climatic reasons sometimes without knowing the potential dangers that exist in a location, but sometimes knowing them full well. There are cities on seismic faults, in cyclone/typhoon areas, susceptible to choking dust storms or torrential downpours, and on sand dunes (McHarg 1969). People are clearly willing to tolerate the potential dangers in order to achieve other satisfactions, but many costs are incurred in not using our present knowledge to establish the controls that minimize the dangers. The 1989 earthquake in the San Francisco Bay area in California showed the utility of such controls and our ability to design well in earthquake-susceptible areas (Lagorio 1990). Buildings designed according to earthquake codes and the BART system tunnels, built with the necessity to avoid damage by earthquake, were largely unharmed. Building codes, zoning ordinances, and engineering design principles have been developed to minimize the effects of such disasters and the more everyday ones such as fires. No doubt these codes will be further developed as more empirical data become available through experience and systematic research. Such efforts will still not, however, avert major catastrophes.

ers as professionals. They are social problems. Urban design can only deal with the symptoms, not the problem. It is possible to design layouts of the environment that provide various types of safety and personal defense mechanisms, but they do not address the social and economic roots of antisocial behavior. Sets of both physiological and psychological safety concerns do, however, have major implications for the design of the public realm.

Patterns and Materials of the Built Environment

The utility of specific patterns and materials of the environment to make the milieu safe is largely well known. The concern is twofold: (1) for horizontal and other surfaces to support behavior patterns safely, and (2) for elements of the built environment to be structurally sound—not to catch fire or collapse or have sections break off and hurt people (e.g., decorative moldings from buildings). Lawsuits and the fear of legal actions are making architects much more concerned with such problems. The courts regard the meeting of safety needs as fundamental. A lawsuit against the city of Baltimore and the designers of Inner Harbor by the survivors of an allegedly intoxicated man in a wheelchair who drowned when he went over the unguarded edge of the quayside is in litigation. For aesthetic reasons, a guardrail did not exist there, nor has it been put in because it would mar the experience for other people. We are willing to forego much in the way of safety levels to meet aesthetic needs. Future lawsuits (or fear of them), however, may make urban designers seek even higher levels of safety. One of the questions society and we designers will have to address is: "How far should designers have to go in making the built environment safe against irrational behavior?" There are, however, areas of design and construction for which we do have to accept the ultimate responsibility.

Building materials deteriorate, clamps holding panels on the façades of buildings erode as the result of chemical interaction with other materials, wind forces make windows pop out of buildings. Certain surfaces are slippery when wet. Such matters are increasingly well understood, and the major problem is one of technology transfer—getting the information out to practitioners. New materials with seemingly high potential are made available on the market prior to our understanding their impact. It took us a long time to understand the impact of asbestos fibers on health. The sick building syndrome—where the gases from materials and machines in hermetically sealed, air-conditioned buildings make people nauseous—is recent and not fully understood. These issues are largely biogenic ones and can be scientifically studied. They have great implications for building design, but few for urban design beyond issues of façade design controls.

One of the major causes of accidental death and injury in the United States continues to be fires initiated through human error, mechanical failure of some building systems, lightning, or purposeful instigation by people for their own financial benefit or amusement. The knowledge of how to prevent fires and how to build to reduce their possibilities is well known today. One of the earliest purposes of building codes was to reduce threats to human safety from fires by specifying the nature of escape routes, building techniques, and fire-retardant materials. Fire-fighting equipment has been repeatedly upgraded. Still, their use in specific circumstances such as fires in high-rise buildings has been very difficult.

Machines

Machines of all sorts, from stepladders to construction cranes, are a source not only of potential assistance to people in their endeavors but also of potential danger. The city planning and engineering concern in urban design has been with the design of safe highways and public transit systems—intersection configurations, lane widths, road cambers for various speeds of movement, and so on. The urban design concern in the United States has been overwhelmingly with the relationship of people on foot, pedestrians, to people in cars, drivers, so much so that we have created what, in retrospect, are needless levels of segregation between modes of transport. At the same time, as already noted, the needs of pedestrians and bicyclists are frequently neglected because of a lack of concern for their welfare in the United States in comparison to Europe (C. Buchanan 1963; Benevolo 1980; Appleyard et al. 1981; Moudon 1987).

Much of the concern with safety issues in urban design has been highly prejudiced by architects' subjective values (usually negative) toward the use of automobiles (particularly by people other than themselves), and designs have been in response to designers' intuitive feelings rather than empirical knowledge. There are many examples of what seem to have been rational segregation patterns between automobiles and people that have had highly negative economic effects and reduced the liveliness of cities and neighborhood shopping areas, thereby increasing safety problems by removing "eyes on the street" (see also Chapter 20). The gap between the role of the automobile in people's lives and designer's normative positions on what it should be has been substantial. Automotive and automobile-person safety issues are, nevertheless, a fundamental concern in the design of the public realm, much of which consists of the streets and paths of people's movement.

The Sociogenic Environment

In many American cities, antisocial behavior seems to have reached a point where there is a regression from a concern with higher-order needs to concerns for safety and security from criminal behavior. Whenever a chaotic state arises, or a threat of such a state or nihilistic attitudes occur, safety and security needs become preponent, and designing social programs and physical environments to deal with them becomes the focus of much attention. Certainly designing for internal security from criminal threat rather than external warfare has become an important enough consideration to often replace other livability criteria in the design not only of individual buildings and total and all-of-a-piece urban designs, particularly housing developments, but also in the broader public realm of urban design concern. Indeed, it remains a prerequisite for people, especially women, children, and the elderly, to use public spaces at all (M. Francis 1987b).

1. San Diego

2. Arch Street, Philadelphia

3. Market Street, Philadelphia

4. Suburban Housing, Ann Arbor, Michigan

5. Atlanta

6. Paley Plaza, New York

Figure 12-2: Expressions of the Need for Security

Evidence of the necessity to provide a shield against antisocial behavior is everywhere in cities in the United States and many other countries today (1). Often it is unsightly. It is also psychologically depressing to recognize the necessity for it. Increasingly, shopowners in North American cities are protecting their shopfronts from looting. With some mechanisms it is still possible to see the merchandise on display (2), but in others window shopping is impossible during nonshopping hours (3). The spiral of fear often begins this way. There are no protective eyes on the street. The same situation prevails in suburban housing areas (4), especially in wealthy residential areas where resort to private guards may be necessary (5). Even much loved quasi-public spaces have guards and need to be secured at night (6).

For instance, places such as Bryant Park in New York City were simply not used by the general public because people felt insecure in them. The people who did use them were perceived to be largely "derelicts" and drug users "hanging out" (Nager and Wentworth 1976; Schroeder and Anderson 1984). The recent redesign and refurbishment of Bryant Park have changed both its image and the use of space (see Fig. 13–15(6)). Such observations raise many questions about the nature of society and our attitudes to different people.

One of the most intractable and emotionally charged issues with which the urban designer has to contend is both the actuality of high levels of criminal behavior in many places and the fear of it in people's minds. Crime is a social problem, but we can see the physical design responses to it increasingly in cities, with individual business proprietors putting up riot screens on shop windows and householders barring their windows and doors. Riot screens may deter shopbreaking, but they also deter the presence of eyes on the street. Boring streetfronts are avoided by pedestrians and the riot screens are symbols of impending danger. Although crimes of violence are a reality in many American cities, they should not be considered an inevitable urban problem; there are many cities in the world largely devoid of such crimes. In those cities, adults and children alike have greater personal freedom in the choice of the behavior settings of which they wish to be a part.

Psychological Security

Psychological security is attained through having control over one's life—with peace of mind. At one end of the scale it is closely related to survival needs and physical security, but at the other end it has to do with meeting affiliation, self-esteem, and self-actualizing needs (see Fig. 12–1). Peace of mind can also have spiritual characteristics. Some people feel the need to be part of a cosmological order. Certainly this need has been exemplified in much religious architecture but also in the design of cities (such as Jaipur and Madurai in India, Beijing in China) that follow a cosmological order. If one does not understand the cosmological order the geometry of the city is largely meaningless as a symbol. As mentioned in Chapter 2, the only group concerned with such urban design issues in the United States today seems to be the Maharishi Sthapatya Ved Institute (1991), although it is clear that much Native American design has a cosmological basis, and as such it remains an urban design concern in some situations in the country today (R. Martin 1991).

The ways of achieving a sense of security depend on the type of security one seeks. *Static security* can be achieved by closing oneself off from one's surroundings, but the goal of improving the quality of life of people is surely through having them achieve a *dynamic security* where they are secure as individuals, possessing skills and being ultimately self-actualized (see Maslow 1987). Providing mechanisms for attaining such needs falls outside the urban designer's purview, but the type of security that stems from control over one's activities and the access other people have to them is a central issue in both architectural and urban design.

One of the mechanisms for attaining control is privacy. A well-functioning built environment provides appropriate levels of privacy for activities. People need to be able to carry out activities, particularly idiosyncratic behaviors, free from censure, and to have opportunities to withdraw from people and the activities of the world.

A well-functioning environment also provides people with the ability to know where they are in space and time—"to be able to organize the universe and people in it into some meaningful whole" (Maslow 1987). The need is for them to be able to orient themselves and to find their way around cities and other places. It has to do with the world being a stable, predictable, and usable place. It does not achieve much purpose to design places to include the behavior settings that would enrich people's, especially newcomers', lives if the settings do not form part of those people's cognitive images of the environment they inhabit. If places are not part of such cognitive images, they will be unused.

People have many other security needs. Financial security is one of them. The concern in this book is primarily with users of the environment, but householders and sponsors of urban design schemes almost invariably wish to have financial security. The result is that urban design work tends to be highly conservative in nature—it does not explore new ways of doing things but relies on types that have been successful enough financially in the past (see also Chapter 20).

THE BEHAVIORAL PROGRAM

Meeting physiological and psychological safety and security needs raises two broad areas of urban design concern. Designing for physiological security involves recognizing, or designing, the behaviors that are likely to take place in different settings under different conditions (e.g., walking along a sidewalk when it is dry and when it is icy) and dealing with many of the criteria that meet the comfort needs of people (see Chapter 11). Psychological needs are more subtle.

There are five interrelated concerns in developing the behavioral program to provide for people's safety and security needs: (1) the degree of segregation of incompatible uses, (2) the degree of surveillance—natural and artificial—of everyday life, (3) the mechanisms for attaining the appropriate level of privacy for the behaviors in which we engage, (4) the attainment of a sense of orientation in place and time, and (5) a sense of place—social and geographical. Much of this concern for enhancing a sense of security is a concern for reducing uncertainties, or unpredictabilities, in the environment. Exposure to people who are culturally different, the disorder, friction, and creativity displayed in particular places, all cause uncertainty. Some people embrace it, but most avoid it.

The Segregation of Incompatible Uses

The same milieu may contain different standing patterns of behavior. Sometimes these behaviors coexist well, at other times they may be in conflict (Bechtel 1977). This observation holds at city, neighborhood, and building or room scale. One of the criticisms of Modernist urban design has been that it tended to unnecessarily segregate uses, with the result that many new towns and new urban precincts and projects are very dull places in which to be (J. Jacobs 1961; Blake 1977). The reaction of many urban designers has been to strive to create highly mixed-use environments. Such environments are seen as a desirable attribute of the unselfconscious urban designs of the past. When incompatible uses clash, however, the situation can be stressful, but so can the opposite—when compatible uses are segregated. Mixed-used areas provide the possibility of having people around to provide a sense of security for others (J. Jacobs 1961). There are eyes on the street to be concerned with what is happening and to exert a protective stance over an area. Such areas are also experientially rich. Not all uses, however, are compatible with each other.

Some uses are perceived as being dangerous because of perceptions of impending natural disasters, and some, such as manufacturing, are perceived to be undesirable as a type. Some of these perceptions are part of a historical legacy (e.g., factories generate dirt), but others are still a reality today. While many modern factories need not be segregated for any biogenic reason, they may still be causes of psychological stress to people forced to live nearby because of the negative impact of such places on those people's self-esteem.

The Nature of Surveillance

There are many areas of American cities where people, including their own inhabitants, fear to go without the protection of third parties—police and security guards. The downtown areas of many cities are perceived to be unsafe. Unkempt areas, poorly served by police, are avoided. The behavioral response in such situations has been to bolster the visual presence of security personnel. In Portland, Oregon, for instance, 80 percent of the budget of the central city's Association for Portland's Progress is spent on attaining cleanliness and safety. There have been strong advocates for developing the responsibility of the general public for such activities (J. Jacobs 1961; Newman 1972).

Natural surveillance involves the everyday looking after the activities and the people involved in them as part of one's own life. Literally, it has to do with actually watching out for people. Figuratively, it means offering succor to others. Artificial surveillance involves the use of television cameras to watch what is going on in a place. The watchers are usually law enforcement officials. Natural surveillance involves being able to see other people as you and they engage in the everyday activities of life.

Natural surveillance—in this sense, looking out for one's neighbors—for good or bad, has been part of the folk culture of villages. Many people have emigrated from such villages. Ease of natural surveillance was also a goal of the proponents of neighborhood unit design principles. The basic thesis is that the environment can be designed to provide for eyes on the street. In a way, this end also reduces one's privacy. Not everybody likes to have such a lowered level of privacy, despite its other advantages (Kuper et al. 1953). The use of artificial surveillance mechanisms in places such as subway stations does provide people who use them with a sense of security, but a broader question is: "To what degree does such surveillance infringe on privacy rights?"

The Role of Privacy and Community in Attaining Security

Every behavior in which we engage has a level of expected privacy associated with it (Westin 1967; Altman 1975). Attaining privacy involves two processes: (1) the control of information about a behavior given to, or obtainable by, people outside the setting, and (2) the intrusion of unwanted information into a setting (Rapoport 1977). The flow of information is multimodal so the invasion of privacy can be visual, sonic, olfactory. Less frequently perhaps, it can be haptic as the result of vibratory events such as the shaking of buildings by passing heavy trucks, and to some extent the recurrent earth tremors. The types of events such as earth tremors that are perceived to be outside the control of other people are more easily tolerated than those over which outside agents are perceived to have control. They may still be perceived as a threat to safety and security; but they are not an issue of privacy. The behavioral program on which to base urban design decisions needs to establish the appropriate levels of privacy for the behavior settings to be included in a design. If people do not have the privacy appropriate to the setting, they will strive to attain it through behavioral changes or through the structural adaptation of the milieu. If they fail to achieve what they need, they can move to another milieu. If they are trapped by the setting, they will feel crowded and stressed.

The level of privacy expected for a standing pattern of behavior varies from culture to culture and also by the attributes of people within that culture—their social status, roles in society, and age. People with different personality types demand different levels of privacy. In many cultures, women are accorded and expect a greater degree of privacy and thus control over the flow of information

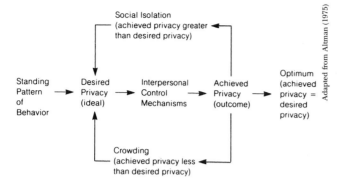

Adapted from Altman (1975)

Figure 12-3: A Dynamic Model of Privacy

about themselves and their activities than men; young people are accorded less privacy control than their elders, and socioeconomically higher status people more than the lower status ones. There are also groups of people to whom more privacy is accorded than they themselves desire—the handicapped, for instance, are often shunned by the able-bodied, as evidenced by many planning and architectural design decisions. Facilities for their use are provided out of sight of the able-bodied.

Expected privacy levels for an activity vary depending on the context of the behavior—whether it is indoors or out or, behaviorally, whether it is in a city square or on a beach. It is important to recognize these conventions in designing, so that the appropriate level of privacy can be achieved by the people concerned. The conventions are seldom obvious when one is designing outside one's own cultural context. Even within it, problems arise because one is trying to deal explicitly with one's own unselfconscious behavior. Privacy demands have thus often been counter to the intuition of many architects. In designing for the future it is also important to recognize that some of these conventions will change. There are, however, some stable concerns in the actual design of the layout of the environment about which questions can be asked in program development and design.

Mechanisms for Attaining Privacy

Privacy can be attained in a number of ways. Behavioral mechanisms such as withdrawal, either through reserve when one is in company, or physically distancing oneself from people, seeking solitude, are two ways. Another is through the use of physical elements of the environment to screen, visually or sonically, a standing pattern of behavior from nonparticipants (Westin 1967). Often it is obtained through a combination of factors represented in territorial behavior.

Territories have three characteristics: they are bounded, marked or personalized, and defended (E. Hall 1966; Newman 1972; El-Sharkawy 1979; Lang 1987a). The bound-

aries may be real ones such as walls and fences that do not allow physical penetration by a person, or they may be symbolic ones such as the change in a surface material to denote a boundary. Well-behaved people pay attention to symbolic barriers but, as they present no real barrier to actions, they do not severely inhibit people with antisocial behavioral tendencies (Brower, Dockett, and Taylor 1983). The personalization of spaces may take many forms, including moving one's possessions into them, decorating the surfaces of the environment in various ways (including graffiti), and placing ethnic names, signs, and symbols in neighborhoods. Similarly, defensive behavior may take several forms, ranging from active antagonism to strangers in the public spaces of a neighborhood to simply keeping an eye on the street.

The whole physical environment is divided into territories, or jurisdictions, from the national level to the personal space level. Who has territorial control over many demarcated spaces is very clear, but problems may arise when the nature of a jurisdiction is ambiguous. In cities, territories occur at various levels of scale: the city as a whole, neighborhoods, and specific behavior settings (Skaburskis 1974). Historically, territories may have served primarily a defensive function, and they still do so in many ways, but territories not only provide for control, they can also give people a sense of place and belonging at the national, regional, or local level, depending on how their boundaries are configured.

Territories occur in a hierarchy of control exerted by the person or people holding the territory, depending on the degree of privacy the territories afford visually and behaviorally. There are various ways of categorizing the levels in the hierarchy (see, e.g., Porteous 1977 and El-Sharkawy 1979). One of the simplest yet generally applicable for the analysis and design of the public realm in the United States is from public to semipublic to semiprivate to private (Newman 1972, 1980a). In public territories a wide variety of behaviors is tolerated and little control is exerted over the space. Semipublic territories consist of places to which the public has access, but local people will exert control over the behaviors that take place there. Semiprivate territories are those under the jurisdiction of a person or group, but there is no visual privacy for those holding them. In private territories there is complete visual privacy, and the occupier has complete rights of control. Such a categorization is by no means universal, and there are many places in the world that have much finer gradations of privacy.

The Meaning of Orientation in Space and Time

In order to have a sense of security many people need to know where they are geographically, to be able to find their way around a place, and to be able to develop an image of the overall environmental layout and its opportunities in their minds. We feel more secure, more

1. Defensible Personal Space

2. World Financial Center, Battery Park City, New York

Collection of the author

3. Public Housing, East Harlem, New York

Figure 12-4: The Hierarchy of Control over Urban Space
Within the mainstream of North American culture, territories vary across a hierarchy from public space over which public authorities have control but individuals can colonize for a while, sometimes strongly (1) and sometimes weakly, to private space at the other end. In much of the public realm, the controlling authority is not clear, but people feel secure there because the spaces are clearly controlled by some management (2). Yet other spaces are ambiguous because nobody seems to have control over them. Where the public realm is divided into clear territorial hierarchies and is well managed, it survives well (3).

in control of our lives, if we know where we are spatially. Similarly, there is a feeling of greater security or control over one's life if one knows what time of day it is, what time of year, not simply by one's watch or the calendar but through reminders from the surrounding milieu. It is also clear that these needs are often highly personal and culture-specific.

There are times when we want to be lost, especially if we know fully that we are not really out of control (Passini 1984; Arthur and Passini 1990). We enter mazes and strange surroundings in order to explore them (see Chapter 16, Meeting Cognitive Needs). In contrast, in stressful situations (e.g., if we are in a hurry to reach a destination, especially under emergency conditions) wayfinding becomes particularly important. While different people have different competencies in finding their way around the built environment, the layout of the physical environment is itself the major contributor to the degree of its imageability and legibility for people (Pocock and Hudson 1978).

The psychological implications of perceiving or not perceiving oneself as part of a continuity of life, of history, are poorly understood. Nevertheless, achieving such an understanding of oneself not only enhances a sense of security but helps fulfill spiritual ends in people who seek such meanings for life. It also contributes to the fulfillment of cognitive needs for many people by providing opportunities for them to satisfy their curiosity about the universe.

Achieving Security through a Sense of Place

One aspect of fulfilling safety and security needs is to have a stable world of which one is a part—where one has some cognitive control over the physical world around one. Possessing a sense of place—being associated with a geographic area and/or a role in society—is a major contributor to the fulfilling of affiliation needs, but it also enhances a sense of territorial control (see Chapter 13).

THE DESIGN PROGRAM

There are many aspects of attaining safety and security needs that have little to do with the layout of human settlements, but there are also many ways in which the built environment can directly aid the social and cognitive processes that make the patterns of the public realm better meet people's striving for a feeling of safety and security.

Physical Form and Physiological Safety Needs

It has already been noted that designing the surface materials of the environment to prevent accidents, designing for the technological and structural safety of buildings both in everyday use and in emergencies (e.g., during cyclones or fires), and designing to prevent accidents between people in moving vehicles, and between people in motor vehicles and pedestrians, are of major concern in urban design (see also Chapter 11). Our very survival depends on such designing being done well.

There has been considerable research on designing buildings to withstand natural disasters such as earthquakes, high winds, and floods. There has been considerably less on urban design. The main considerations have been largely the engineering ones of channeling water and building levees to deal with floods and structurally designing buildings to withstand high winds and the terrors of earthquakes (Lagorio 1990). There have also been zoning regulations prohibiting building in floodplains or to raise ground floors above, for instance, 100-year flood levels, building codes specifying what materials can be used for building construction, and such measures as sufficient means of egress to ensure a modicum of access to safety during fires.

The main mechanisms for achieving road safety have been driver education, the improvement of the quality of roads and highways, such as clearer sight lines, appropriate lane widths, and road banking on curves, and increasing the segregation of people in motor vehicles from those on bicycles and on foot. The first two concerns are primarily those of road safety organizations and traffic engineers, but the last is also that of the urban designer.

There are two types of segregation of modes of transportation—horizontal and vertical. In horizontal segregation the paths of movement of vehicles, bicycles, and pedestrians are separated in the horizontal plane. There may still be some perceived problem—sources of conflict—where these paths cross. The solution has been to reduce the number of crossing points. Alternatively, the crossing points can be eliminated by having the channels of movement on separate planes vertically. Multilevel vertical segregation of movement routes was characteristic of much Rationalist design both in concept and practice. It has been less successful as a mechanism to achieve an overall environmental safety than it has been as a mechanism to speed up traffic flow—until the capacity of the roads is reached and they become clogged.

The problem with grade-segregated crossings is that pedestrians are reluctant to go up or down steps or a ramp to cross a street. They would rather cross at grade level unless it is much easier to do so in the grade-separated crossing. Clarence Stein and Henry Wright achieved this ease in Radburn, New Jersey (C. Stein 1950), and it is also a characteristic of the green belt towns of the 1930s and the post–World War II rebuilding of towns in Europe (C. Stein 1950; C. Buchanan 1963; Parsons 1990). One of the side effects has simply been that grade-segregated pedestrians ways result in less interesting places in which to be. The major horizontal segregation of vehicles and pedestrians has often had the same effect. Once the liveliness of cars and drivers coming and going is removed from places

they become dull unless there is a compensatory density of activities. Many competent people also prefer to deal with the bustle of busy streets, full of activities and even danger from automobiles, than have the additional safety provided by the segregation. Removing cars from traveling and parking on streets also removes eyes from the street, thus reducing the natural surveillance of the streetscape (A. Francis 1991; Oc 1991).

Many people feel that they have greater control in dealing with cars than with dangerous people. In addition, dangerous situations under one's control contribute to fulfilling the cognitive need to test oneself (see Chapter 16). People may contradict this observation about themselves in interviews—a case of the difference between what people believe/say they will do and what they will actually do when a design is built. For the designer this potential discrepancy often creates the dilemma of choosing between striving for a mentally congruent or a behaviorally congruent environment (see Chapters 21 and 22).

There have been many proposals to create safe streets from a traffic and from a territorial viewpoint. The basic goal has been to create a hierarchy of densities and speeds of traffic flow, with residential streets having the lowest level. Other design types that have been implemented in recent years are the pedestrian shopping mall on Main Street (see also Chapter 20) and the woonerf in Europe. The urban design necessity is to identify the appropriate hierarchy of streets, pedestrian paths, and other transportation routes and the range of functions they serve in addition to being movement corridors, and then to design for them (Appleyard et al. 1984). Streets are often seams joining the two sides into a territorial unit. For such a territory to be formed those streets should have low vehicular-traffic flows. They should not be closed to vehicles unless they have substantial pedestrian traffic flows or have facilities that can attract or generate such activities or can cater to people, such as children, with low competences. Nor should they be pedestrianized if they are too wide to act as a seam tying the sides together into a territory.

Physical Form, Privacy, and Territorial Behavior in the Public Realm

The specification of the requirements for the elements of physical form to create a sense of privacy at various scales of life needs to be part of the design program for urban design at all scales—city, precinct, or urban place (such as plaza) level.

In the design of many aspects of the public realm the provision of the mechanisms that afford the creation of territories is often neglected. Territories need boundaries. Historically, cities were often walled to provide for defense. The walls, however, not only served this purpose but also to delimit an area—the enclosure gave a psychological security, a sense of belonging to a place. In cities where

1. Los Angeles

2. Fresno, California

3. Freeway Park, Seattle

Figure 12–5: Grade-Separated Transportation Routes
Some transportation routes cross at grade-separated bridges if the traffic volumes warrant it (1). There have been many attempts to provide grade-separated pedestrian–motor vehicular crossings to enhance human safety (2; see also Fig. 2–8). They work effectively if they are easier to use than continuing to cross at grade. Some of the efforts to segregate pedestrians and vehicles have been made for economic and/or aesthetic reasons (3).

the walls have been demolished (e.g., Vienna, Paris, and Brussels) and replaced by buildings, highways, or parks, the new elements still serve as a boundary between districts. In a similar vein, there have been many attempts to establish green belts to define the borders of a city—to stop the blurring of one city into another or into the countryside without any differentiation (and also to give people easy access to parklands). Such green belts also give a strong sense of belonging to those who live within them in much the same way that islands do to their inhabitants.

The same design principles have been used on a smaller scale. The city can be subdivided into districts with which people can identify by giving areas of built form the similar elements of physical and textural attributes identified by Lynch (1960) and clear boundaries. These boundary-making elements can be streets or open spaces created by parks, commons, rivers, or hills. Some cities or areas are rich in natural characteristics of topography that have been or can be consciously or subconsciously used to form *edges* of districts. Urban designers in cities without such advantages have to resort to artificial mechanisms.

The behavior settings that constitute the public realm have various levels of privacy accorded to them depending on the activities that take place there. Each one is a territory. The public realm consists not only of a hierarchy of publicness of territories, but also a hierarchy in the degree to which they can be colonized by individuals or groups of people for varying lengths of time. Large urban spaces such as parks and plazas can be designed to be spatially indivisible or to consist of internal differentiations that make it possible to use parts of them as units. At the small scale, there are elements such as the individual seat—an individual territory for as long as it is occupied. In an undifferentiated public space, people may form their own territories for a conversation simply by the way they stand in relation to each other (E. Hall 1966). The territory lasts for as long as the conversation takes place.

The objective in the design of open spaces is to identify the expected and/or desirable behaviors that are likely or desired to take place there and then to design their fixed features—steps, benches, trees, walls, and ground surfaces—so as to enhance the quality of potential interactions between people or the solitude of an individual.

1. Battery Park City Promenade, New York

Photograph by Felice Frankel

2. Fittler Square, Philadelphia

3. Penn's Landing Square Housing, Society Hill, Philadelphia

Figure 12-6: The Public Realm and Personal Security
The public realm of the street and the plaza is one in which people usually know others only by categories. In North American cities it is an increasingly hostile place for many people. A higher degree of security can be achieved by having clear territorial demarcations for specific activities (1) and having places overlooked by neighbors (2). Streets with blank walls or buildings that, in seeking security, turn in on themselves are not only boring but also reduce the feeling of security for passersby (3).

A feeling of safety and control is essential for this purpose. The promenade at Battery Park City in New York City clearly shows the assignment of spaces for specific purposes—walking, sitting, watching passersby—with little ambiguity (see Fig. 12-6(1)).

Some spaces are designed for major public presentations by individuals or groups. Their structure needs to give the performers a public distance from their audiences; other places are for dyads or small group gatherings; and yet others for festivals. The research on proxemic behavior—how people relate to each other in space—shows the kinds of variables that must be considered in design in order to fulfill the need for people to feel secure in public spaces within different cultures (see E. Hall 1966; Sommer 1974; Lang 1987a). William H. Whyte's research (1980) provides the designer with specific principles for designing places that are likely to sustain social life and thus indirectly give their users a sense of security. More recent work has shown strong gender differences in the characteristics of the spaces men and women use in a public place largely on account of the degree of privacy and control (and thus security) that they perceive that they will have (R. Peterson 1987; Mozingo 1989).

The design goal is to provide a variety and thus freedom of choice to sit on one's own or in a group pattern where eye contact is easy. Clearly demarcated territories give a feeling of safety and security. Women in many countries simply do not use plazas at all. In the United States they use spaces that provide comfort, safety, and security. Women prefer to sit on physiologically comfortable benches (i.e., at normal sitting height rather than standard steps) where they are not on public display. For men, although not uniquely so, watching others is a primary activity—they have less need to be anxious about their personal security.

Defensible Space

A controversial empirical study done primarily in New York by Oscar Newman (1972, 1975, 1980a) showed that using a number of design principles enhances the degree of control people exert over their "own" environments by changing the concept of *own* through using territorial markers in an area. Follow-up work has generally supported Newman's findings (Stollard 1991), and his urban design principles have been applied to both project and neighborhood designs (Gardiner 1978). The results of Newman's research support earlier phenomenological observations of people such as Jane Jacobs (1961) on the design of neighborhoods and streets as well as earlier quantitative research (e.g., Angel 1968). Where territorial demarcations are clear people take control over an area.

Newman found that crime rates were lower in areas with the following qualities: (1) a clear set of territorial markers—real or symbolic barriers–differentiating public spaces from semipublic from semiprivate from private spaces; (2) little open space under nobody's clear jurisdiction; (3) opportunities for natural surveillance—the affordances for people to watch out for other people as part of everyday life through the placement of halls, windows, and seating where people are and that overlook other areas; (4) the use of building and landscaping forms and materials that communicate a positive image of the residents of an area to outsiders rather than saying that the population is a vulnerable one; and (5) locating new developments for vulnerable populations in safe areas—areas of low antisocial behavior (see Newman 1972, 1975; De Chiara and Koppelman 1978; and Stollard 1991).

Defensible space principles have been applied with some success in a number of cities across America: Fort Lauderdale, Miami Shores, Miami Beach, and Hollywood Plantation, all in Florida, are examples. In each case both a psychological and an actual sense of security were created. Dayton, Ohio, and Bridgeport, Connecticut, are cities that have recently followed suit, but it is still too early for the results to be measured. Perhaps the greatest success has been in St. Louis, where the closure and "privatizing" of specific streets resulted in the stabilization of communities and property values (Newman 1980a).

Allied to the achievement of a sense of security through defensible space is the idea of reducing uncertainties about what lies ahead. Although this thought can be applied to life as a whole, it has a much more pragmatic application to the creation of safe environments. Good lighting reduces opportunities for miscreants to hide and enables people to scan the environment. Certainly the development of good lighting has reduced the number of ghosts; it is also reputed to reduce thefts in an area.

A major design issue that emerges from this research and practice has already been mentioned: "Who should control what are behaviorally public spaces?" (M. Francis 1987b; P. Buchanan 1988). These spaces may be indoors or outside. With the increase in the number of urban open spaces that are open to the public yet under the control of private corporations, there has been an increase in design guidelines (San Francisco, Department of City Planning 1985) and public policy statements on who has the right to be where. The requests for development proposals for the Winter Garden of the World Financial Center at Battery Park City specified that it had to be open to the public for eighteen hours a day. It is. There is,

however, no reason for the public to be there for much of that time, so the place is empty a great proportion of the day. The situation in Milton Keynes illustrates the dilemma more severely. Downtown Milton Keynes closes when the shops are closed, for security reasons (A. Francis 1991).

The Physical Form of the Public Realm and Orientation

The three- and four-dimensional character of the built environment affects three aspects of orientation in cities: (1) where people see themselves as part of a cosmological system (assuming people see themselves as part of such an order), (2) where one is geographically, and (3) where one is in time. The first is achieved through the geometry of the built environment and through elements of the natural landscape, such as trees or flowers, having specific symbolic referents that are meaningful to people; the second, by having an imageable and legible physical environment (i.e., a clear cognitive map of one's surroundings enhanced by good wayfinding signs); and the third, by elements that give a sense of continuity in time. It is possible to have all three characteristics present, although the first, it has been noted a few times already, seems of little importance to most people in the United States. Perhaps it should be!

Orientation in a Cosmological System

Historically, one mechanism that was important in helping people attain a sense of security, particularly in the achievement of a sense of immortality, was through environmental symbolism (Lawlor 1982). In the Western world this was important up to the early 1800s through the use of geometry and mathematics in the design of urban and building layouts. However, the influence of religious beliefs on human imagination has diminished to the extent that Martin Heidegger (1971) was able to announce the end of metaphysics, signaling the dissolution of many timeless and mythical truths about ourselves and our existence.

In some parts of the world the importance of building within cosmological rules is still high. In South India (Tamil Nadu and Kerala), for instance, the *Shilpa Shastras* are still a guideline for much housing architecture. In some parts of the world, including the United States, with populations of a Chinese cultural heritage, geomancy is important. However, in the United States at least it is reflected nowadays more in building design than in urban design and more by recent migrants than American citizens. As mentioned earlier, the Maharishi Sthapatya Ved Institute (1991), based in the United States (Fairfield, Iowa) and the Netherlands, proposes to build villages according to the ancient Vedic science in a number of countries in order to demonstrate how stress- and disease-free societies can be created and the urban designs which are

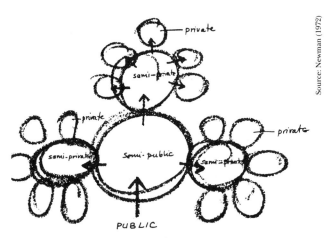

Source: Newman (1972)

1. The Required Territorial Hierarchy on the Horizontal Plane

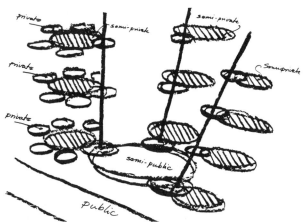

Source: Newman (1972)

2. The Required Territorial Hierarchy in High-Rise Buildings

Source: Newman (1972)

3. Natural Surveillance Requirements

Courtesy of Ann Strong

4. Territorial Hierarchies in Suburban Areas

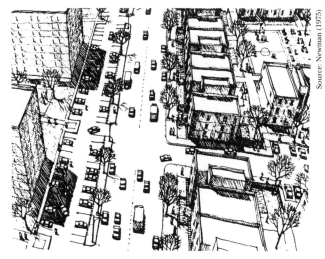

Source: Newman (1975)

5. Territorial Hierarchies in High-Rise Housing

Source: Newman (1975)

6. Retrofitting High-Rise Housing

Figure 12-7: Defensible Space

Oscar Newman (1972) uses three diagrams (1,2,3) to illustrate his hypotheses that defensible space is that space that is clearly under the control of local people, and that this control can be enhanced through physical design mechanisms. The design objective is to create spaces that are clearly defined territories under natural surveillance in a culturally appropriate hierarchy.

Such environments are easy to obtain in single-family detached-home neighborhoods (4) but more difficult in high-rise building environments where projects such as the one on the left turn in on themselves (5). Many design mechanisms can, however, be used to afford the appropriate hierarchical organization in such places (6).

necessary to provide supportive environments. Their success in achieving their ends will presumably be open to empirical verification.

Orientation in Geographic Space

The study of *cognitive mapping* is well advanced (Lynch 1960; Downs and Stea 1973; G. Moore 1979; Passini 1984; Arthur and Passini 1990). Kevin Lynch provided the designer with a set of design principles that enhance people's ability to organize the city into a cognitive whole in their heads and thus to find their way around in it with some ease. More recent studies have done little to change Lynch's findings (Pocock and Hudson 1978). The principles can be applied at the city, neighborhood, or building interior scale (Passini 1984; Arthur and Passini 1990) and have their theoretical roots in the Gestalt laws of visual organization (see Wertheimer 1938). Lynch's study focused on the visual world, but the same principles seem to hold for blind people, although the cues are different for them.

As already outlined in Chapters 1 and 10, Lynch found that the clarity of five elements in cities gives them imageability and legibility. Two are elements of continuity (paths and edges), two tend to be point elements (landmarks and nodes), and the fifth is a spatial element well bounded and having a visual texture of its own distinct from that of surrounding areas (the district). By texture is meant similarity in street widths, the height and mass of buildings, and the way the buildings meet the streets.

The most important element in aiding orientation is the path, simply because paths are the points from which we see the city, whether we are tourists or habitués, on foot or in vehicles. Indeed, newcomers to a place may organize a place only in terms of paths (Appleyard 1970; G. Moore 1979). Paths are literally the routes of movement through a place. Edges can be wide paths that are difficult to cross and/or see across with clarity (otherwise, if they do not have traffic volumes, they are likely to be seams holding two sides together), natural features such as hills and rivers, or designed features such as parks. Open space was used as the dividing element in the design in the first generation of British new towns after World War II, in Columbia, Maryland, and more recently in Las Colinas, Texas, among many other places. Both Chandigarh, designed in the Rationalist tradition, and Milton Keynes in England, in the Empiricist, have highway systems that act as the overall structuring pattern both as paths and as edges separating districts.

Landmarks can be of many types. Their defining characteristic is that they are different from their surroundings and easily discernible from particular station points. In terms of the Gestalt theory of visual perception, they are figures against a background. They may literally be buildings that are different from their surroundings, but they may well be an element of the urban scene such

1. Central Park, New York

2. Cox Park, Philadelphia

3. Seattle

Figure 12-8: Children's Playgrounds and Defensible Space
The playgrounds in (1) and (2), although different in content, have the same characteristics that give young children a sense of security when playing there. Each is a territory in itself, which can be easily seen by passersby, and has comfortable seating for parents, older siblings, or other minders within easy visual and auditory reach of the children. The same minding behavior also occurs in (3), but the design does not afford it as comfortably.

1. Central Philadelphia (1973)

3. Rittenhouse Square, Philadelphia

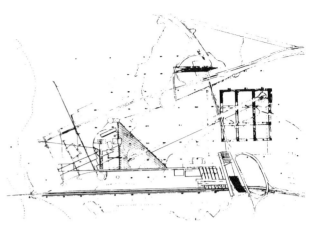

2. Student Proposal for the Redevelopment of the Framingham-Natick Commercial Area (1986)

Figure 12-9: Designing for Imageability and Legibility
The gridiron street pattern of most American cities affords easy orientation (1). Deconstructionist schemes remain largely on paper (e.g., 2 by Guy Perry at Harvard University), but their more complex geometry can still afford easy orientation provided there is an order to it in terms of Lynch's principles (see Fig. 9-2). Where security through creation of a sense of orientation is the design goal, habitations, whether cities or particular places (3), should have clear paths, districts, landmarks, and nodes. Edges seem to be less important than Lynch thought.

as a park in a densely built up area, a curiosity object such as an old clock tower, or a place where some special event occurs or occurred—something deviant from the norm (see also Appleyard 1969).

Ease of orientation is not automatically a design goal. Although many places have such characteristics through the simplicity of their geometric forms, other places, such as Venice, were purposely designed to make orientation difficult for outsiders for defensive purposes. Lynch's design principles were applied in reverse! Over time all people without brain malfunctions can learn to find their way around the most contorted layouts, but strangers cannot immediately form a cognitive map of such areas. They soon learn paths through even the most complex urban street patterns even if overall spatial schemata are elusive.

Bold architectural ideas (see Bacon 1974) can give a sense of coherence to a scheme, but to do so they have to follow the principles identified by Lynch. The designs of the City Beautiful movement and the Rationalists often have highly simplified geometries that enhance the formation of cognitive maps and thus the imageability and legibility of cities and neighborhoods. Proposals for anchoring urban design proposals into meridians and parallels

have the purpose of linking a design to the world (Corner 1990b). In a way this reference gives people a cosmological sense of orientation provided they recognize the reference. Deconstructionist design often seems to have the opposite intention.

Orientation in Time

Time occurs at various scales: day, year, year as part of an era. Ascertaining the first is relatively easy for people, although with the increased use of interior space as public space (Chidister 1989), often the only way of telling the time is by looking at a clock. No natural light penetrates. In some places, such as casinos, clocks are purposely absent in order for people to lose track of time (and money)! People who work in places that have no access to natural light report feeling disoriented in time despite having watches. They work in environments with levels of illumination that are constant in both intensity and the direction of the source. Their image of the outside world is gray.

In places other than some of the equatorial regions of the world there are naturally occurring seasonal cycles—wet and dry, summer and winter, monsoons—and in temperate climates there are four seasons. Even in dense cities with extensive indoor circulation systems and behavior settings, one cannot get completely away from the impact of these daily and seasonal changes, but it is possible to feel removed from them. The need is to mitigate their most discomforting impacts but also to enhance people's feeling for seasonal changes. This end can be achieved through having trees and other vegetation that change over the year, walls that reflect light in different patterns, and events that celebrate the time of year or are season-specific (see also the commentary on winter cities in Chapter 11). Exposure to the elements also provides such a reminder, but may counteract a desire for comfort.

The built environment is very much a statement of continuity and change (Lynch 1972). Old buildings give us a sense of history and a sense of permanence; new ones remind us of the cycle of life. It is clear that major social changes are often accompanied by strong movements to retain the old, because old buildings give a feeling of stability to life. For many people, change is difficult to deal with; they want to have a sense of permanence. In some situations, however, there is a desire to eradicate the past, to obliterate memories of the past inhabitants of an area (e.g., the Bronx, New York, where recent immigrants have shown a hostility to the symbols of past Jewish residents) or those who were in control of it. Newly independent colonial societies go to great lengths to remove the memorials and signs of previous regimes.

Change is stress-inducing for all people. Some peo-r'e can cope with such stress, and others even seek it because they handle it with high competence. Stress is not necessarily negative; it is also motivating provided the stress levels are not too high—that is, not beyond the coping capacity of people. Some people, however, simply want the expected. They want the social and built worlds to which they are habituated. Hotels that are part of international chains are designed with this end in mind and make it part of their advertising to stress that guests will not have to deal with the unexpected. In democratic societies, the built environment reflects the tussle between the competing desires for stability and for change. The stress of dealing with physical changes in the city may well contribute to feelings of alienation from society, but such feelings are much more likely to result from other life events.

Physical Form and a Sense of Place

There has been criticism of much recent urban design because it has little relationship to its architectural or terrestrial context (Brolin 1974, 1980). It is true that, say, many festival markets associated with waterfronts seem to be similar in character whether they are in Baltimore or Miami (or Europe or Australia) but, in reality, every urban design has a sense of place. The sense may not be what

2. The Mall, Washington, DC, in January

1. Las Vegas, Nevada

3. Central Los Angeles

Figure 12-10: Orientation in Time
Having a clear orientation in time means many things. The strength and angle of light from the sky tells us the time of day as do clocks (1). The change in the seasons can be told by the change in the nature of vegetation in temperate climates (2) or by rainfall in many warmer ones. Orientation in historical time can be partially achieved by perceiving the artifacts (including buildings) around oneself, the eras they reflect, and their changing uses (3). In highly artificial environments awareness of the changing environment can be severely reduced.

Source: Venturi, Scott Brown and Associates

1. Wilson Park, Philadelphia

2. Clason Point Housing, New York, before Rehabilitation

3. Clason Point Housing, after Rehabilitation

Figure 12-11: Rehabilitating Housing to Enhance Residents' Security

Designing for a sense of security is relatively easy, but the roots of the problem are more intractable. The cumulative impact of applying Oscar Newman's principles to the design of residential environments is, however, high. The landscape design and exterior appearance of both Wilson Park in Philadelphia (1) and Clason Point housing in New York (2,3) were changed to enhance a sense of territoriality, to provide ease of orientation, and to establish a sense of pride (3). Accompanied by new management attitudes, the results at least demonstrate a sense of caring about what the housing is like.

architects think of as good and it may not be obviously tied into its local environment. The strip development, the decayed urban area, the tank farm—places deplored by many people—all have as much a sense of place as a Currier and Ives New England village. What is generally understood by design professionals by "a sense of place" is that this place is different from that place—it has unique qualities and is not simply a generic type. The goal of every physical setting having a character unique to its surroundings seems to be more of an aesthetic issue for well-traveled people or architects than for those people who live in a place, although they may feel their identities and self-esteem threatened by "foreign designs" or designs foreign to them. They may also, as mentioned above, feel threatened by change as represented in a new architecture appearing in their midst. Contextual design in that case will be important. The mechanisms for achieving it are described in Chapter 13.

A CAUTIONARY CONCLUSION

It may be felt that in existing cities of the United States whose designs have resulted from individual entrepreneurial activities and piecemeal development that meet-

ing the safety and security needs of diverse people with varied interests can only be achieved in a haphazard way. In all urban design projects and in the development of guidelines for design, on a local or metropolitan basis, the research work of those involved in developing design principles for structurally safe (e.g., Lagorio 1990), psychologically secure in terms of ease of legibility (e.g., Lynch 1960), and defensible environments (e.g., Newman 1972, 1975, 1980a) can be applied immediately. Some of the design principles are certainly more difficult to apply in retrofitting the existing city than in new work, and the tradeoff required in meeting other needs may not make it worthwhile.

In existing cities it is difficult, for instance, to achieve a precinct with strong clear boundaries, or even a district in which the building texture is similar where it does not already exist. It is difficult to retool the environment to meet territorial criteria, although the example of changing the Clason Point housing project in New York shows how much can be done in a small-scale urban design (see Fig. 12-11). It is difficult to argue in the political arena for such retooling of the environment except where the social costs for not doing so are clearly very high, because the political rewards for rebuilding rather than doing something new seem to be low. Nevertheless, design guidelines applied consistently over a long period of time can shape the city to better meet the safety and security needs of its inhabitants in the long run.

It is clear, even obvious, but it must be remembered that the quality of people's lives depends on the social organization of society—its legal framework, health delivery systems, and educational opportunities. In a society where there is no crime, Newman's defensible space principles are unimportant, although they may still act very well in meeting aesthetic needs.

The application of the design principles for defensible space or for aiding orientation in space, for instance, helps people to organize their environments in their heads, to understand the behavior expected of them within their cultural frames, and to deal with issues of control of space without ambiguity. Their application will not, however, solve social problems.

MAJOR REFERENCES

Appleyard, Donald, with M. Sue Gerson and Mark Lintell (1981). *Livable Streets*. Berkeley and Los Angeles: University of California Press.

Arthur, Paul, and Romedi Passini (1990). *Wayfinding: People, Signs and Architecture*. New York: McGraw Hill.

Cooper Marcus, Clare, and Carolyn Francis, eds. (1990). *People Places: Design Guidelines for Urban Open Space*. New York: Van Nostrand Reinhold.

Francis, Alan (1991). "Private Nights in the City Centre." *Town and Country Planning* 60, no. 10: 302–303.

Francis, Mark (1987b). "Urban Open Spaces." In Ervin H. Zube and Gary T. Moore, eds., *Advances in Environment, Behavior, and Design 1*. New York: Plenum, pp. 71–106.

Gardiner, Richard A. (1978). *Design for Safe Neighborhoods*. Washington, DC: U.S. Government Printing Office.

Lang, Jon (1987a). "Cognitive Maps and Orientation" and "Privacy, Territoriality and Personal Space—Proxemic Theory." In *Creating Architectural Theory: The Role of the Behavioral Sciences in Environmental Design*. New York: Van Nostrand Reinhold, pp. 135–165.

Lynch, Kevin (1960). *The Image of the City*. Cambridge, MA: MIT Press.

Newman, Oscar (1980a). *Community of Interest*. New York: Anchor.

Oc, Tanner (1991). "Planning Natural Surveillance Back into City Centres." *Town and Country Planning* 60, no. 8: 237–239.

Skaburskis, Jacqueline (1974). "Territoriality and Its Relevance to Neighborhood Design: A Review." *Architectural Research and Teaching* 3, no. 1: 39–44.

Stollard, P., ed. (1991). *Crime Prevention through Housing Design*. London: Chapman and Hall.

13

MEETING AFFILIATION NEEDS

Participation in a supportive social system is necessary for an individual's survival with a modicum of psychological comfort. This is particularly so in an urban world. Once their need for survival is met reasonably well, people feel most keenly the need for membership in a group or, more likely in the modern world, a set of groups. These groups consist of individuals and settings that provide individuals or other groups with affection, support, and identity. A person "may forget that once, when he was hungry, he sneered at love" but once basic physiological, safety, and security needs are met, affiliation needs become preponent (Maslow 1987). Often, however, at least a partial fulfillment of affiliation needs is a prerequisite for survival, safety, and security!

For both individuals and groups of people, there are differences in the manifestation of the need for affiliation with others and/or identification with a place. It is, however, a need that requires fulfilling to avoid "the commonly found core [of alienation] in cases of maladjustment and more severe psychopathology" (Maslow 1943, 1987). If one accepts these observations as valid, one of the functions of an urban design is to enhance people's abilities to fulfill their needs for affiliation to the extent it can. At the same time, designers must not assume that the layout of the public realm can dictate specific social patterns, social organization formations, or that it is the sole determinant of the symbols of identity. The built environment, as has been noted already, can play only a supportive role in this aspect of people's lives.

The systematic research of the past three decades has considerably enhanced our knowledge about the interrelationships among social organizational patterns, individual and group identity, and the patterns of the milieu. It has brought our attention to the nature of organizations and the role of symbolism in establishing a sense of identity. This increase in our information base does not mean that we have a completely integrated positive theory of the nature of American society, its subcultures and their trends, or the design implications of this knowledge. The whole programming and design process can, however, be carried out more thoroughly and thoughtfully than much of it has been in the past. The goal of this chapter is to demonstrate this point. The first objective is to describe the levels and types of organizations with which people seek affiliation and the nature of the activity patterns and symbols that establish membership in them. Based on these observations, it will be possible to comment on the behavioral program that public officials, social and city planners, and urban designers can develop in order to enhance people's abilities to fulfill their affiliation needs.

All such discussions are guided, explicitly or implicitly, by models of a *good society*. In the United States, with its focus on individual initiatives and the marketplace as mechanisms for people to meet their own needs, it is important to recognize that design decisions can affect the possibility of community formation. This chapter thus ends with an outline of our knowledge of how the design of the physical environment can foster social ends.

BELONGING

People's need for belonging is fulfilled by having supportive relationships and an identity as a participating member of a set of groups. The uniqueness of each person's patterns of membership also gives each individual a personal identity and a sense of self-worth (see Chapter 14, Meeting Esteem Needs). There are a number of often highly interrelated groups that people are either

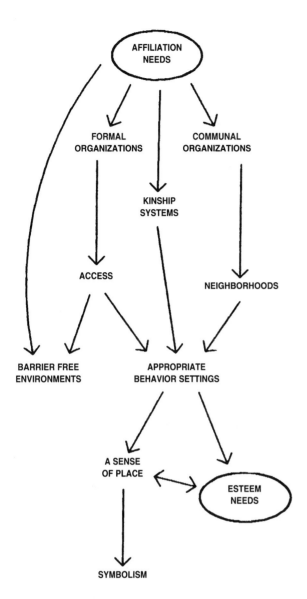

Figure 13-1: Affiliation Needs

The mechanisms for having membership in a group are either biological (in the case of kinship systems) or sociological in nature. Developing the links between people has only indirect implications for urban design. Yet these implications are important to understand if urban design is to fulfill its potential role in society. More directly related to urban design is that many people also feel a need to belong to a place—to have roots somewhere. Even here, however, it is only the placelessness of the symbolic content of the built environment of many physical environments that urban designers can remedy. The price for individual mobility in the United States is often a sense of loss of a "home."

Belonging to a Family and a Kinship System

One is born into a family and thus into some sort of kinship system. These systems vary from the nuclear family to horizontally and vertically extended systems. Sometimes, particularly in preindustrial societies, these systems are clearly reflected in the physical layout of human settlements. Kinship systems in this case are conterminous with physical environment patterns. In the *pols* of the Old City of Ahmedabad, India, for instance, there is a close tie between kinship (caste), occupation, and a clearly bounded residential territory (Doshi 1974; Lang 1989a; see also Fig. 13–2 below). Such an integration does not occur in the American city today. Extended kinship systems are important in subpopulations in the United States, but due to the high social and spatial mobility of most Americans, it is the nuclear family unit that is important. Generally the broader kinship pattern is not locally based. This situation has had its urban design manifestation in the single-family detached suburban or rural house throughout the country and the urban rowhouse of the older East Coast cities.

Membership in a kinship system, like any other organization, carries with it a set of obligations to other people and a set of expectations of their behavior toward oneself. These behaviors provide support in day-to-day activities, affection, and a sense of identity through not only the blood relationship but also the celebrations of rites of passage and other communal occasions such as Thanksgiving Day. In the United States, as in Europe, there have been major changes in the family structure as traditional ties have loosened. The ties provided by kinship are either replaced by other organizational ties or done without. Some of these new ties are through quasi-kinship systems held together by formal organizational structures and habitats such as those represented in the co-housing movement (Franck and Ahrentzen 1989).

All urban design ideologies assume some model of the family. Both the Rationalists and Empiricists among Modernists assumed the nuclear family as the basis for their proposals. The city (except for the department store) was the male domain and the suburb the female. This

born into or have to join in order to fulfill their needs. Some groups or organizations are more important than others to individuals, depending on the nature of the culture within which they exist.

In order to meet the need for affiliation a person can be a member of a kinship system, a set of organizations, a people, and often a nation. Most people in the United States have affiliations with each type of group, but observers of current affairs cast doubts as to whether the ties that bind are strong enough. There are many Americans who feel alienated from their sociogenic and biogenic environments, so that one finds a continuing search for supportive communities by many segments of the population (Baltzell 1968; Gottschalk 1975; Hayden 1984; Franck 1989).

model has been challenged by a number of recent theorists because in the United States fewer people choose or are able to live in a nuclear family (e.g., Hayden 1984; Franck and Ahrentzen 1989). Changing gender roles and the diversity of individual interests have resulted in the search for new models of potential urban and suburban design.

Belonging to Nonkinship Organizations

In industrial and postindustrial societies, such as the United States, people belong to a number of organizations of various types—business organizations and organizations of common interest. At the most global level is a society itself. The intensity of commitment of an individual to an organization depends on that person's needs, but it is also a function of the broader culture of which he or she is a part. Whatever the type of organization, there are some things they all hold in common. These characteristics were introduced in Chapter 1, The Nature of the Environment. The purpose here is to elaborate on those aspects that have urban design implications.

All organizations consist of a group of people held together by a common bond and purpose. Some of these provide the mechanisms whereby people can meet survival needs; others provide more directly for affiliation needs per se. All institutional memberships—religious or secular—achieve this end to some extent. The rules that govern entry into the behavior settings and govern the activities that take place within an organization may be contractual (as in the workplace) or simply generally understood by the group members. These differences reflect the two basic types of organizations: *formal* and *communal* (Gottschalk 1975).

Formal and Communal Organizations

The distinction between *formal* and *communal* organizations was presented in Table 1-1. Formal organizations are those in which there is a very specific goal that defines the organization. The function may be the provision of a service, such as those of a nonprofit institution, or the attainment of a return on an investment in profit-making organizations such as commercial businesses. An institution such as a hospital may do both. To be employed in the United States means to be a member of a formal organization.

A formal organization is functionally oriented to achieve its basic purpose and its members are linked by contract to do so. For the organization to function efficiently each of its members will have specific tasks. The contract defines the roles and obligations of individuals, the links between them, and their relationship to each other in some sort of hierarchy. In return, the organization provides the means for an individual to meet a variety of goals, including affiliation ends. From a design

viewpoint the important fact is that formal organizations can be self-consciously designed by an individual or a group of people. Thus the maintenance procedures of a new neighborhood can be designed to be administered by a new formal organization to which all households have to belong. Such a conterminous organizational and physical structure in a neighborhood would immediately give householders an affiliation with an organization on the local level. Whether or not this membership achieves any other ends depends on the predispositions of the people involved.

Communal organizations do not have the instrumental orientation of formal organizations. They are linked by generally understood rules for cooperation and have a freewheeling structure in which the members play a variety of roles. Perhaps the most important aspect of communal organizations for urban designers to understand is that they cannot be designed from the outside; they have to generate themselves. All an urban design can do is to provide the opportunities and affordances in its physical structure for communal organizations to develop. They *cannot* be developed by coercion. The urban designer can recognize, say, the local behavior patterns that promote a sense of community and create a milieu that affords them easily, but that does not ensure that neighboring will occur (Gans 1968; Keller 1968; Lang 1987a). Such a design, would, however, certainly increase the probability that it will. It depends largely on the degree of homogeneity of the population (in terms of perceived values—see Lee 1970) and their need for mutual support.

Within any formal organization there are likely to be communal organizations. These organizations are important because they cut corners in the official hierarchical operational structure of the organization to make it operate effectively. While formal organizations are relatively easy to identify, the communal ones that exist are not, especially as many operate in a quasi-clandestine fashion. Creating urban design programs based solely on a formal organizational chart may lead to considerable difficulties for people who form the organization, if the interior design of buildings is any indication (Moleski and Lang 1982). In Harlem, in New York City, for instance, it was found that for neighborhood playgrounds not to be vandalized the communal organizations had to have cooperated in their planning.

Formal organizations, whether a firm, neighborhood, or city, differ from each other in many ways. They have their own personalities and degree of communal organizations that exist within them. There are differences in the way higher- and lower-status members relate to each other, in the degree to which individuals within them are able to express their own personalities through the personalization of the environment—that is, the degree to which they have an individual identity rather than one simply associated with a role—and in the way they link with the outside world. In the United States, much urban design work, because it deals with the public realm, involves communal organizations, but it is the formal organizations who are the sponsors and/or implementers of urban design policies. They often have their own ends in mind.

Belonging to a People

The concept of belonging to a people, say an ethnic group, in addition to depending on its social linkages between individuals also means having a shared history, usually language, symbolic aesthetic values, and the types of symbols that are needed to be displayed by individuals to be members of the group. Some of these symbols are formal (e.g., flags), but others are communal (e.g., dress codes or images of home). The communal symbols are particularly important where groups of people are striving to maintain a self-identity through territorial control.

Any area of a city, whether a total or an all-of-a-piece urban design—particularly the face its buildings present to the public realm—is personalized over time (if personalization is administratively allowed and often even if it is not—see also Fig. 2-2). The rapidity with which the personalization takes place will vary depending on the resources of the people and organizations that occupy an area, their sense of permanency, and their need to make displays. These displays serve two purposes: to establish membership in a group and to establish a sense of personal esteem. The two frequently go hand in hand.

Personalization takes many forms, but it is essentially a mechanism for defining territory, of laying claim to an area. It may involve the adaptation of an area to make it fit the behavior patterns of a particular group or the display of signs and symbols associated with it. For cultures that bury their dead it may be having a local cemetery. Certainly the urban designs of cemeteries—their layouts—are very much statements of the cultures to which they belong (Jackson and Vergara 1989; see also Fig. 16–7(4)).

Belonging to Regional Jurisdictions and Nations

Nations consist of people tied together in a formal organization in a geographic space. This combination in itself does not create a sense of nationhood, as recent experiences in the Balkans indicate. Indeed, largely aspatial cognitive and symbolic regions based on ethnicity or social status may transcend national boundaries in providing both sources of affiliation and self-esteem for people. Similarly, geographic subareas of a country may be more important to an individual as entities than the whole. This feeling can be reinforced by the formation of regional jurisdictions by binding them together with a coordinated infrastructure system and a set of regional symbols. Attempts have been made to create a sense of nationhood through the creation of national networks and symbols, but these design efforts will not necessarily create a sense of identity. Many newly independent countries have found themselves in this situation. Their boundaries were defined by struggles between colonial powers rather than any sense of community among their people.

The symbols of nationhood take on many forms. Some are obvious because they were created as symbolic gestures. These symbols vary from flags to national capitals to languages to shared histories. Washington, DC, New Delhi, Canberra, Brasilia, Chandigarh, are as much unifying symbols for diverse sets of people as legislative and administrative centers. In the United States the flag is venerated as in no other country except, perhaps, the Dominican Republic. Other symbols are less obvious—such as the landscape and the way it has been tended by people or represented in art forms.

Belonging to a Place

One aspect of fulfilling the need for security as well as affiliation is to know, be familiar, or have strong associations with a specific geographical area—urban or rural. The rebuilding of totally destroyed European cities (e.g., Warsaw) so that they appear to be almost exactly as they were before World War II is a symptom of this need (Diefendorf 1990). The reverse is also frequently manifested in the need of newcomers to an area to eradicate the traces of previous inhabitants (e.g., the Bronx, New York) so that they can claim it as their own.

Many writers have been successful in evoking a sense of place. Perhaps they have been more successful than architects, because the readers can provide their own images of the physical form. Isak Dinesen's *Out of Africa* begins: "I had a farm in Africa, at the foot of the Ngong Hills." It evokes an image.

The search for a character in the built environment—an architecture—that enables a people to identify with a region or a country—and the writing of guidelines to achieve it—has been a difficult one, particularly as there is often a clash between wanting the built environment to signify both a past and a future. The concern for a regional identity in the United States (e.g., for New Mexico, see Markovich, Preiser, and Strum 1990) and national identities elsewhere has been a topic of architectural debate all this century. The discussion was largely obscured by the Internationalism of the Rationalists but has emerged again during the last two decades with the failure of Modern urban designs to give a clear symbol of identity (other than being part of the International movement) to those people who inhabit them. The emergence of Post-Modernism has been a major response.

One of the major urban design concerns has been to maintain the character of an area of a city as it changes. The Vieux Carre in New Orleans has retained its character over the last century despite changes but it is now in danger of becoming a theme park rather than a lived-in and lively area of a city. Many cities have such areas that are almost a symbol of the city (e.g., Beacon Hill in

Boston; see Figs. 7-7(1) and 17-13(5)). More generally the concern is with a city retaining its uniqueness as it changes.

COMMUNAL LIFE, THE PUBLIC REALM, AND A SENSE OF BELONGING

In order to understand the role of urban design in providing the settings that afford diverse people the opportunities for fulfilling their need for affiliation, one has to understand the nature of the activities that bind people together and also the symbols that give them a sense of belonging. The concern here is not with the development of kinship systems, although this may well be important in some cultures, but rather with understanding everyday activities and what they mean in terms of potential urban design actions. The focus here is thus on communal systems.

Social Networks, Activities, and Events

All people who are not socially isolated are members of communities. As many commentators have noted, urban designers (e.g., Le Corbusier, Clarence Stein, Christopher Alexander) have long sought to enhance a sense of community through a physical design and the location of facilities that provide for social opportunities (C. Stein 1957; Gutman 1966; Gans 1968; Keller 1968; M. Kaplan 1973; Hester 1975; Michelson 1976; Saarinen 1976; Newman 1980a; Lang 1980b, 1987a; Brill 1989). In doing so urban designers have tended to rely on the notion that the creation of institutions and public places—the enhancement of the qualities of the public realm—will bring people together. The belief has been that by providing specific buildings and open spaces people will get together. While intuitively appealing, this notion needs considerable investigation. It should, however, neither be lightly dismissed, as some sociological critics are wont to do, nor should designing for community formation be seen as the sole reason for bothering about the enhancement of the public realm. Before any design conclusions can be drawn or design patterns promoted, there needs to be a clear understanding of the nature and interrelationship of organizational design and spatial arrangements, the nature of communities and neighborhoods, and the relationship between family organizations and neighborhood layouts. These conclusions are likely to be culture-specific. The research reported here either comes from the American experience or is applicable to the United States.

Social Organization Design and Participation

All urban designs projects and policies at least imply that a social organizational model has been used as the basis for designing. Willy-nilly the urban designer is involved in the creation of settings. In purely financially pragmatic

urban design (see Chapters 2 and 4), the behavioral basis for deciding what should be built depends on what can be sold easily. Given the ideological position advocated in this book, urban designers need to be fully aware of the potential social consequences of their work. If one accepts this position, then the scale of the social and physical organization of both the social and physical environments, and the nature and distribution of settings, become important. The question is: "How can such settings, if they can at all, best afford participation in the organizations that form a human settlement in order for their users to meet their affiliation needs?"

Human scale is an attribute of the built environment. It is also an attribute of the social environment and the link between social and physical worlds. Much confusion exists about whether specific environments—social and physical—are in or out of human scale because people often attribute feelings of alienation to the physical world that should really be attributed to the social. This attribution probably arises because the physical component is more immediately tangible than the social.

Anecdotal evidence suggests that attributing a quality of scale to the environment is closely related to an individual's mood at the time; evaluations of the quality of the physical settings certainly are (Gutman and Westergaard 1974). In architecture, human scale is poorly defined so it often ends up being a synonym for a statement of affection. Lower Manhattan is in human scale for those people who like it; it is not in human scale for those who do not. The same can be said for the highway systems of Los Angeles or Houston. The empirical research of the past three decades clarifies much of this confusion, particularly with regard to the size of social institutions and participation in them. While most of this research has been carried out in the United States, it can probably be transferred cross-culturally in essence if not in detail.

Based on his own research and that of other *ecological psychologists* (e.g., Wicker 1969; Barker and Schoggen 1973; Srivistava 1975), Robert Bechtel (1977) presents a theory of human scale that relates population numbers to the number of behavior settings in which an individual can participate. The basic thesis is that when the ratio of settings to population is high, people are "coerced," or feel obligated, to participate in the maintenance of a system. As a result they belong to a number of organizations. For instance, in a small school, a student is likely to be coerced to participate in many behavior settings—the school play, the football team, the chemistry club—so that the settings needed for the school to really be a school can function (Barker and Gump 1964). The same is true of a neighborhood unit or small town (Barker and Schoggen 1973). A small town has proportionately more behavior settings per person than a large one. The advantages of the large city or a large institution are the opposite of a small one. They allow more opportunities for specialization; they also offer more chances for withdrawal or to be pushed aside—to not be members. They also afford a degree of anonymity that small organizations do not. In a large city some people are likely to fall by the wayside; they will be nonparticipants. Such nonparticipation is sought by some people for both positive and negative reasons. In David Popenoe's study of suburbia, adolescents who did not like living in Levittown, Pennsylvania, were those who were essentially nonparticipants in the behavior settings of their schools (Popenoe 1977). They felt socially isolated. Many people, however, lead satisfying but isolated lives.

It is not inevitable that large institutions or cities have proportionately fewer behavior settings than small institutions and cities. They have evolved unselfconsciously in that way. Market forces and apparently individual preferences for noninvolvement have pushed them in that direction. Economies of scale in production and marketing over the course of the twentieth century have led to larger and larger institutions and the depersonalization of many interactions between people, not only in the United States but in the other major industrialized countries of the world (see also Parr 1967, 1969). The degree of face-to-face interaction is similarly declining. Urban designers have generally regarded this decline as a bad thing, but Michael Brill (1989) suggests that people are simply substituting new interaction mechanisms, particularly those relying on electronic media, for old and that urban designers, along with other public policymakers, should recognize this change.

The Nature of Community and Neighborhood

In the everyday language of urban designers and developers alike, *community* and *neighborhood* are often used synonymously. This usage is unfortunate because the two words really have different meanings. A neighborhood is a physical entity and a community a social one. Urban designers can design neighborhoods and they can locate institutions and design the public realm within them, but whether or not a neighborhood is also a community depends on the type of social organization and organizations that evolve there. As mentioned earlier in this chapter, it is possible to design formal organizations that are conterminous with neighborhood boundaries, but only the potential settings for communal organizations can be provided. Whether communal networks do grow from the grass roots depends on the predispositions of the people who live there or, in the case of nonresidential neighborhoods, work there, and their perceptions of the opportunities for such developments.

Much design thinking is based on the image of a neighborhood that Marcia Pely Effrat (1974) calls the *compleat territorial community* and Gerald Suttles (1972) the *defended neighborhood*. In such a community many activities—living, shopping, recreating, working—take place at a local level within a bounded area. Effrat contrasts this with the *community of limited liability* (see also Suttles 1972), or what David Thorns (1976) calls the *partial community*, which is a neighborhood where people have some obligations to each other because they live in close proximity, but these obligations and the number of shared activities on the local level are few in number.

The prototypical neighborhood plans that have been generated by designers tend to assume that people will create a compleat territorial community if local facilities are provided so that their service areas coincide with neighborhood boundaries. There are two difficulties with this assumption: different services have different trading areas (Hester 1975); and in a highly mobile society there are few groups that rely on local services—they prefer to travel more widely to get services closer to their own values (Lansing, Marans, and Zehner 1970; Lee 1970; R. Brooks 1974; Cooper 1975; Hester 1975; Cooper and Sarkissian 1986).

Planners' neighborhoods are not local communities in many instances. Even in highly successful neighborhood design (i.e., those much loved subjectively by their inhabitants) the communities are ones of limited liability (e.g., Radburn, New Jersey; see Lansing, Marans, and Zehner 1970). The sense of belonging is, however, reinforced by the formal organizations that exist conterminously with the neighborhood's boundaries. Local facilities are used by the less mobile segments of the population—children, young families, and the frailer and/or poorer elderly—when these fit into their ways of life, but the spinoff in terms of the development of a stronger sense of communal identity appears to be low. The design and layout of neighborhoods do, however, matter.

The compleat territorial community and neighborhood should not be dismissed as a possible model for urban designers. While they cannot be created from the outside, they do exist. In addition, there are situations in many poorer countries where the mutual support systems provided by neighbors are vital to not only a sense of belonging but also to survival. The compleat territorial community, or a close approximation to it, often exists when there is an homogeneous population and the following conditions: an area is occupied by a clan or an ethnic group that is distinct from others around it, income and/or mobility are low, and people choose a parochial lifestyle. In pre-1960 American industrial cities such a type was not uncommon, but as industries have moved out of neighborhoods, they have frequently disintegrated socially and physically.

Newcomers to the United States have historically clustered together: the Irish in parts of Boston, Jews and Italians in New York City, and Germans in Milwaukee, for instance. By choice, necessity, or external prejudices, ethnic neighborhoods still abound in American cities. Black populations are probably more clustered in cities and suburbs than they have ever been. Many cities have Chinatowns and recent Asian migrants to the United

1. A Traditional "Neighborhood" in a North Indian Walled City (1984)

2. Interior View, *Pol*, Ahmedabad, Gujarat, India

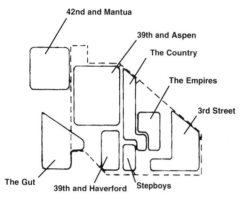

3. Gang Turfs, Mantua, Philadelphia (1970)

Figure 13-2: The "Compleat" Territorial Community

There are examples of "compleat" territorial communities around the world, but there are none in the United States except for some self-contained religious communities. The *mohallas* and *pols* in North Indian walled cities were once very much so and remain so in many ways. They consist of a clan or caste group linked by formal and communal norms of behavior in a gated territory (1,2). For teenage boys, gang turfs remain a feature of many American cities (3). They do indeed provide for a sense of community and identity, but the social consequences are severe.

States continue to live in ethnic enclaves. Vietnamese refugees, many traumatized by their experiences, alienated from the mainstream of American life, and with a strong need for mutual support have formed a Little Saigon, with a population of 70,000, in Orange County, California. Such areas do have conterminous neighborhoods and communities, although the borders are likely to be overlapping and not neatly aligned.

Apparently benign planning efforts can inadvertently destroy the existing social and architectural affordances of such neighborhoods so that the social infrastructure that provides considerable support to the neighborhood's inhabitants fails. The worst case is when a neighborhood is seen as physically blighted because it does not have the architectural character that fits a decision maker's image of what a good neighborhood is. Such neighborhoods can be socially sound. In these instances (e.g., North Boston in the late 1950s), the razing of the neighborhood for urban renewal disperses people and destroys a functioning social network (Gans 1962). Such a destruction of traditional and locally based affiliation networks is accompanied by a great sense of loss and stress (Fried 1963).

In thinking about social organizations and the design of the public realm, whether for new towns or neighborhoods, the design of intra- and interneighborhood social and physical links is important. New town and neighborhood plans should depend on: (a) the nature of the needed links to the outside world, (b) the links between their subcomponent organizations, and (c) the nature of the relationship between their inhabitants. Gottschalk (1975) differentiates between four types of communities based on the nature of these links.

1. The *crescive community*—the local community which has grown up over time—is essentially the same as Effrat's compleat territorial community. All three levels of relationships are communal ones.
2. The *administered community* may have communal organizations at the family level but the other two links are formal ones.
3. The *designed community* is one where there is a formal organization at the family level (in terms of its having a high goal orientation) and at the level of links between the community and outside, but the local links between elements of the organization are communal.
4. The *intentional community* has communal links to the outside world but formal ones at the local and family levels.

The folk village is probably the best example of a crescive organization. It grows up over time in an unselfconscious manner. The other three communities can be

Table 13-1: A Classification of Community and Anti-Community Types

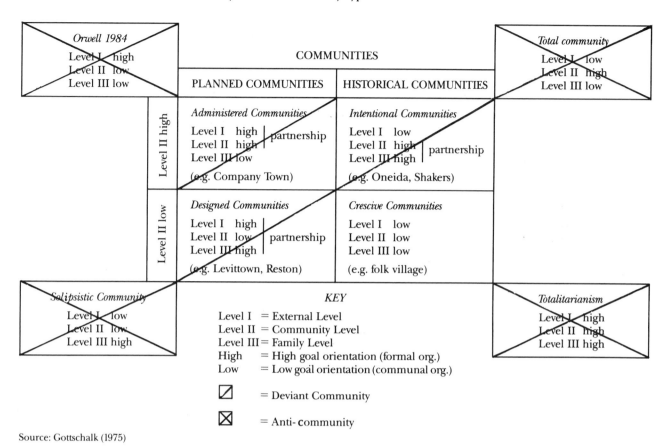

		COMMUNITIES	
Orwell 1984 Level I high Level II low Level III low			*Total community* Level I low Level II high Level III low
		PLANNED COMMUNITIES	HISTORICAL COMMUNITIES
Level II high		*Administered Communities* Level I high Level II high │ partnership Level III low (e.g. Company Town)	*Intentional Communities* Level I low Level II high Level III high │ partnership (e.g. Oneida, Shakers)
Level II low		*Designed Communities* Level I high │ Level II low │ partnership Level III high │ (e.g. Levittown, Reston)	*Crescive Communities* Level I low Level II low Level III low (e.g. folk village)
Solipsistic Community Level I low Level II low Level III high		KEY	*Totalitarianism* Level I high Level II high Level III high

KEY

Level I = External Level
Level II = Community Level
Level III = Family Level
High = High goal orientation (formal org.)
Low = Low goal orientation (communal org.)

◪ = Deviant Community

⊠ = Anti-community

Source: Gottschalk (1975)

designed to some extent. At least, their formal attributes can. Company towns are examples of administered communities. Urban designers today tend to think of company towns as nineteenth-century U.S. phenomenon—for instance, Lowell, Pullman—but there are a number of post–World War II examples in the United States and many in other countries. They are prime examples of total designs (see Chapter 4, Urban Design Today). As such their designs reflect the attitudes of their sponsors, for they are designed in a close collaboration between the urban designer and the sponsoring organization, the company.

Designed communities, really neighborhoods, as their very name suggests, are the focus of much urban design work (e.g., Mission Bay in San Francisco). They range in type from housing projects (which are actually often administered communities), but also include places such as Roosevelt (formerly Welfare) Island, New York (see Fig. 8-8 (2,3)), and new suburban developments such as the neighborhoods of new towns like Columbia, Maryland, or Las Colinas, Texas. They are, by and large, communities of limited liability, although they may evolve into something half way between such a community and a

crescive community, but they are unlikely, in modern situations, to become more than that, even with the potential of more people working at home if the development of the electronic cottage really takes place.

People in designed neighborhoods have at least one thing in common—that is, they are homogeneous on at least one dimension—they have chosen to live in them. They are also likely to be approximately of the same socioeconomic status because of marketing processes—the urban design of pragmatism. Their residents also tend to perceive themselves as more homogeneous than they are (see also Lee 1970), and this acts as a springboard for informal communication between them.

The Bruderhof and places such as Shaker villages and the Oneida communities are historical examples of intentional communities (Gottschalk 1975; Hayden 1976). The links at the family and local level are highly formalized—governed by rules. Probably the closest examples in recent times are the kibbutzes of Israel, communes, and collective housing complexes in the United States and elsewhere, but the local level of organization in all of these organizations is likely to be more communal and the external more formal than pure intentional communities.

1. Subway Suburb; Robert A. M. Stern, Project (1976)

1. Parking
2. Common house
3. Community plaza
4. Sandbox

2. Trudeslund Community, Birkerod, Denmark

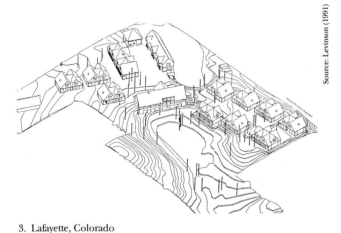

3. Lafayette, Colorado

Figure 13-3: Gender Roles, Identity, and Urban Design
The traditional neighborhood unit concept (see Fig. 2-8(1)) and suburban patterns assume specific identifies for men and women, with the house as haven for men and as workplace for women (Hayden 1984). It could be adapted to provide a more mutually supportive environment (1). The emergence of the Co-housing movement in Scandinavia in the 1970s (2) and, much more recently in the United States (3), illustrates shifting gender roles and the consequences for a more mutually supportive social and physical environment, particularly at the child-raising stage in the life cycle. The design goal is to provide both for privacy and community.

Family Organization and Neighborhood Design

The design concepts of the neighborhood unit and the traditional suburban layout of single family homes assumes particular roles for the household members. The husband is seen as the breadwinner and the wife as the sustainer of the household (Saegert 1981; Hayden 1984). Family types are evolving and new social organizations are becoming necessary (Franck and Ahrentzen 1989). In particular the nuclear family is no longer the norm in the United States.

Much of the recent thinking about urban design has focused on the changing role of women, and thus of men, in the family and society. The concern is exemplified by the research on women in suburbia (e.g., Saegert 1981), and their use of public open spaces (Cooper Marcus and Francis 1990) and suggestions about potential futures (Hayden 1984; Franck and Ahrentzen 1989). David Popenoe (1977) showed that for women who wanted or had to work outside the home for professional reasons and/or financial reasons, the set of facilities and the layout of the Swedish post–World War II suburb of Valingby outside Stockholm was considerably better than its contemporary American example of Levittown, Pennsylvania, a suburb of Philadelphia. The former has considerably more shared facilities and social infrastructure than the latter. People in Levittown have to rely more on their individual initiatives in accordance with the prevailing American ethos. More recently there has been a growth in a variety of communal living arrangements, particularly in Europe especially Scandinavia (McCamant and Durett 1988, 1989; Woodward 1989), but there are a number of American precedents (Hayden 1976; McCamant and Durett 1988; Franck and Ahrentzen 1989; Franck 1989) and recent examples (e.g., Lafayette, Colorado; Levinson 1991).

Dolores Hayden in *Redesigning the American Dream* (1984) advocates new ways of balancing family privacy with collective arrangements. She suggests that the work of Hans Wirz, a Swiss architect, provides an example of what is possible. She advocates higher densities of housing and turning the center of suburban blocks into communal green areas, possibly with child care and other communal facilities.

There has been a long history of explorations of alternative types of households and their implications for design. This was also the concern behind the design of many *intentional communities*, particularly utopian ones

(Gottschalk 1975; Hayward 1984). The concern recently has not been for such a radical reorganization of society but to recognize that the nuclear family is no longer the norm in the United States or in many other countries where it is still assumed to be, particularly by politicians and the development community (Franck and Ahrentzen 1989).

Activities and the Public Realm

Many European cities are full of plazas where people gather in a ritual of promenading, or hanging out, on a regular basis. They form behavior settings of importance in relationship to their surrounding land uses. Places such as Rittenhouse Square in Philadelphia with a diverse set of land uses around them serve much the same purpose (J. Jacobs 1961). We designers look at such places with nostalgia and want to create them in new developments or in remodeling the existing city on the assumption that public life will occur there and that people will develop a sense of belonging to a citizenry and to a place. Such hopes should be treated with extreme caution. They can be achieved provided they fit in with the social and physical ecology of a place, as Jan Gehl (1987, 1989) argues in his analysis of Copenhagen, but they have proven a failure in many places in the United States. Plazas, squares, and pedestrian ways have to be located where people are or want to be or else they will be deserted. They serve many purposes, but it is presumptuous to assume that the interactions that might occur there will more than marginally aid in the development of a sense of community. They may be more important as symbols of community.

In the United States the experience of designing public spaces has been very mixed. The intuitive belief that any open space is good has proven to be an unfortunate one. Almost all American cities have spaces designed by leading architects that are underused at best and forlorn at worst. The AT&T Building in New York City (now the Sony Building) is having its base reconfigured to make it more usable.

Much has been learned during the last twenty years about the design of public places—what makes them work and what does not. Their location in terms of their surrounding is fundamental. Plaza d'Italia in New Orleans might have worked well as a plaza of interest more than simply to touring architects if the developments proposed for around it had been built (see Fig. 13–13(3)). As it is, the plaza is not part of a larger place. We have also learned how to make places pleasant and attractive to people (e.g., Paley Plaza, New York; see Fig. 12–2(6)). The observations of Jane Jacobs (1961) on neighborhood parks and city squares, the research of Christopher Alexander and his colleagues (Alexander et al. 1977), and the work of William Whyte (1980), Jan Gehl (1987, 1989), Dolores Hayden (1984), Louise Mozingo (1989), and Clare Cooper Marcus and Carolyn Francis (1990) provide urban designers with the design principles for making good places in

North America and, possibly, many other areas of the world. People will use well-located, safe places that afford them appropriate levels of privacy and of interest, but expecting the public life of urban areas to be what we want to remember it as having been is expecting too much. City squares, neighborhood parks, good promenades, and good "city rooms" give a place an identity. They can be designed to be well loved and well used if well located.

Events

There are many events and situations that bring strangers together in ways that establish a sense of group identity. Sometimes these events are recurrent and sometimes infrequent if not unique. Regular and frequent events include such occurrences as athletic events. Indeed the regalia of the teams is worn by fans and, for prestige reasons, U.S. cities vie to have major league teams in their cities. The hallmark of a city's membership in the group of major American cities is to have major league teams in baseball, basketball, football, and, to a lesser extent, ice hockey.

Less frequently recurrent events are also important. New Year's arrival is celebrated in Times Square, New York City, Lent with Mardi Gras in New Orleans and, in very different mood, the Mummer's parade on South Broad Street in Philadelphia on New Year's Day (weather willing) all give a sense of belonging to a city. The Pope's Easter public audience and other papal ceremonies in St. Peter's Square (Benevolo 1980) and the running of the bulls in Pamplona, Spain, have come to have international significance, while the Anzac Day parades in Australian cities are a statement of national identity.

Almost all American cities have such events that bring people together for entertainment, but latent functions of their uniqueness to a city are a reaffirmation by its citizens of who they are and to give a sense of participation by its citizens in the place's life. Such events vary considerably in nature. They can be citywide, such as the Rose Bowl parade in Pasadena, California, local markets, or ethnic parades on St. Patrick's Day or Steuben Day. The life of the city would be poorer without them. Some cities are richer in such events than others. Some of the places that are used for them are well fitted to their purposes and others require that the activities be adapted to the affordances of the physical surroundings. Frank Lloyd Wright recognized the importance of such events in American life in the design of Broadacre City by providing an arena for them (Wright 1958).

The Symbols of Belonging

People consciously or unconsciously use symbols that identify them with groups of people. Hairstyles, clothes, possessions, and where they live all contain symbolic messages about people that they send to others. Their

Photograph courtesy of Hanna/Olin, Ltd.

1. Westlake Plaza, Seattle

Photograph by Michael McKinley.
Source: Cooper Marcus and Francis (1990)

3. Crocker Plaza, San Francisco

Collection of the author

2. Piazza San Marco, Venice

4. Sproule Plaza, University of California, Berkeley

5. Sixth Avenue, New York

Figure 13-4: Affiliation Needs, Public Life, and Plazas

Plazas serve many purposes: letting light into dense urban areas, giving a node to an neighborhood, providing a gathering place, or simply allowing a person to be anonymously alone in the sunshine (1). The image of the European city square or plaza as the center of a city's activities and as a source of identity for the city as a whole is a powerful one (2). The European plaza's function as a major center of social intercourse is not easily exportable to the United States. Plazas can only function as such when people know each other, as in the small town or neighborhood in which an extrovert, often gender-separated, parochial lifestyle exists. Most Americans need catalysts (such as children) to engage in conversations with strangers (see Fig. 12–8). Small urban spaces (3) can serve as settings for people to meet with friends and acquaintances (see Whyte 1980, 1988; see also Paley Park shown in Fig. 12–1(6)). They can provide psychological hearts to neighborhoods and both activity and psychological hearts to universities, especially if accompanied by symbols with which an institution identifies (4). Urban designers need to avoid feeling nostalgic about the role of open spaces as gathering places in designing for the future. The American city is replete with forlorn plazas achieved as the result of public policies (5). They add little to urban life.

1. Chestnut Hill, Philadelphia

2. Village Homes, Davis, California

3. Fifth Avenue, New York

Figure 13-5: Belonging to a Taste Culture and Urban Design
The environments people choose for themselves reflect a number of decisions. Some of these decisions are narrowly instrumental ones, but others have to do with broader functional needs related to people's desires to display their values, or to belong to a particular taste culture or to a particular group of people. The greater the social and physical mobility people have, the greater their set of opportunities to display an identity. The three places shown here are inhabited by people with considerable ranges of housing choices but belonging to very different taste cultures (1,2,3). All three housing types are very different from, say, those shown in Fig. I-1(6) or 2-4(1). Often the choices are made unselfconsciously. Sometimes people seek anonymity. Often it is forced on them.

home environments and housing units act as symbols of self (Cooper 1974). So do the attributes of the neighborhoods in which they live and the buildings in which they work. The design of any urban environment implicitly, if not explicitly, is an act of symbol creation.

Historically, the sharing of a view of the cosmos created symbolic settings wherein "a culture would communalize and comprehend its history. The built environment was a way of knowing one's place in the world" (Corner 1990a). Not only the buildings but also town plans and the landscape environment were used symbolically. The landscape was particularly important, possibly because cities were considered to be evil places (Jellicoe and Jellicoe 1982). Mathematically rationalized geometric systems were self-consciously used in the layout of towns and buildings, but such systems were superseded from the nineteenth century by the use of mathematics to describe the existing world rather than to specify the ideal, and the tradition was largely lost (see also Figs. 10–8 (1,2)).

If one of the functions of a design is to support the identity of a group, then designers have to recognize the group's symbols of identity and how they may be used or transformed to continue to provide that support. In designing for those ends, designers are likely to run into a clash between their wishes to express their own attitudes and the attitudes of the people they are supposed to be supporting. The architectural attitudes get in the way of achieving an environment congruent with attitudes of the people who will inhabit or use it.

The built environment also acts as a symbol of the tastes of people—their aesthetic values. The environment one chooses is a statement about oneself and the taste culture to which one belongs. To some extent taste cultures indicate membership in a particular socioeconomic and/or cultural group. They may also signify membership in an intellectual group. Deviations from the norm are often very self-consciously selected. This is one means by which architects, for example, can show they belong to the avant-garde.

THE BEHAVIORAL PROGRAM

Unless one supports a purely laissez-faire process for developing future societies, it is clear that much public policy concerned with providing an environment in which people can meet their affiliation needs must first deal with social planning issues. In the United States and other democratic countries, social policy decisions will be made by politicians based on their own needs and experiences, and on the advice they are given or seek from social and city planners. The decisions will largely depend on what populations are willing to support through votes and taxes. Many social planning decisions will inevitably have urban design implications because they involve the need to distribute or redistribute facilities and develop the layout of the public realm.

Institutions and Activity Patterns Required to Sustain Human Contact

What is a good society? It is clearly one that provides opportunities for the development of human contacts through both the formal and communal organizations that provide for a variety of instrumental and social ends. Face-to-face contact remains a prime mode of human contact, although sustained contact by various other media is an increasingly important aspect of life, even though it is often decried by critics (Brill 1989). The social design goals should be to foster all types of positive human contacts.

Human contacts occur in formal and communal organizations and also haphazardly as people meet as part of their daily lives. To feel one is part of a broader society one has to know what is going on in it. This observation leads to the argument for people to have many opportunities to meet each other and to be able to, at least vicariously, participate in the lives of others, thus attaining a sense of affiliation with them (see also Chapter 16, Meeting Cognitive Needs). Therefore, the argument is for an environment rich in behavior settings.

The research on the scale of organizations and participation rates suggests that not only should there be many settings but that the settings should be relatively small in size. Institutions should be small enough to provide opportunities for participation so that people are not pushed aside, yet large enough to provide a variety of opportunities for specialization in what one is good at doing. Defining the best size for any institution or even a neighborhood is fraught with political conflicts. Among them is the conflict between the efficiency of operation of an overall social system and the degree of participation in the various settings that comprise it. The functional goal of helping people meet their affiliation needs stresses the importance of opportunities for participation and thus the provision of a multiplicity of behavior settings. Such a provision would tend to coerce people to participate in the behavior settings. It also suggests that inefficiencies in the overall performance of the economic system will have to be tolerated. In a highly competitive and individualistic society such as the United States this is a difficult position to advocate. In many ways, the United States is a highly participatory society, but it is also true that many people, including the poor and many minorities, feel alienated from it. They are not participants, not members of it. The institutions clearly need to be designed to bring all who care into the mainstream of life.

Homogeneity or Heterogeneity of Populations

Groups that are homogeneous in terms of age, ethnicity, and socioeconomic status are clearly more cohesive, and their members can provide considerable mutual support for each other. In general, urban designers have been advocates for integration on many dimensions of human life—for example, the stage in life cycle, economic status, and race of residents of new towns, and, more recently, for land uses. Ideas about how to do so have been proposed by many authorities (Gans 1972; Alexander et al. 1977—see Pattern 8), but the achievement of this integration by designing physical enclaves and mixing building types in order to create a "mosaic of subcultures" has been more elusive. There are a number of existing residential neighborhoods in cities in the United States that do have a diversity of people on a micro-neighborhood level (i.e., house by house), but the institutions that are located there are used by homogeneous groups of people so that the degree of genuine social interaction among neighbors is minimal. This kind of integration may well be the socially desirable end.

The argument for growing up in culturally homogeneous areas is that it enables a child to develop confidence, to understand that he or she belongs to a community of values, and to develop a feeling of self. The argument against it is that it reduces the diversity of experiences that also can enhance the development of self in a self-confident and warm household. Quoting Joseph T. Klapper, Christopher Alexander and his colleagues suggest that "a nondescript mixture of values leads to nondescript people." The design principles of both Herbert Gans (1972) and Christopher Alexander and his colleagues are based on these observations—one should strive for micro-homogeneity and macro-heterogeneity. Implementing such an idea self-consciously in the United States, where one has freedom of choice, is only possible to the extent that a particular combination of building types can suggest to the purchasing public how to organize themselves. People (individuals and organizations) do, however, observe the populations that live in an area and make locational choices based on that perception. The social problem arises when people are trapped by a lack of choices. Many Americans are.

Heterogeneity in terms of stage in life cycle is comparatively easy to achieve by providing the facilities that will attract a diversity of ages. Not everybody chooses to live this way. The number of residential developments in the United States that preclude young people, and particularly children, as residents indicates that homogeneity removes certain stresses that many people wish to avoid. The flight of middle-class people from U.S. inner cities is indicative of this need to avoid stress and to seek security.

The plight of the remaining population can only be marginally improved through urban design. Their problems are largely social in nature.

An Egalitarian or Socially Hierarchical Society

The United States is a highly socioeconomically hierarchical society. There is an extraordinary range of incomes in the population and thus of disposable income. While some people choose to live a humble life, others are trapped by poverty and lack of opportunities. The social mores of the country, as reflected in the income tax system, illustrate the general acceptance of this situation. It does not redistribute wealth. The voting patterns of the people mired in poverty (when they actually vote) suggest a very different view of society. The stated goal of many social programs in the United States is to provide equality of opportunity for people to attain their own ends within the socially acceptable norms of behavior defined by the country's legal system. The gap between social goals and public policies in many other countries is often larger. There are a number of countries in which the goal is stated to be the achievement of a classless society, but their economic and social programs do not seem to have been geared to actually achieving this end.

In the United States a number of nineteenth-century communities were based on a philosophy of egalitarianism (Hayden 1976). The philosophy was behind the development of communes in the 1960s and 1970s, and to some extent it underpins the co-housing movement today. In none of these instances has there been a broad effort to create an egalitarian country. From time to time there have, however, been efforts to create equality of opportunity, although there has been little evidence of it during the last decade. It requires a sustained and long-term effort to achieve. If the effort is successful, people will have the opportunity to achieve many of their affiliation as well as other needs more easily than they can now.

Allied to these questions is the question of the display of social status through design. It is clear that one of the goals of the Rationalist Modern urban design was to obliterate indicators of social status in housing. In Brasilia and many French new towns this was a social goal that was official policy and was translated into a design goal. Possibly it was the other way around! In the United States some people certainly choose not to display their wealth through their possessions, but this behavior does not seem to be the norm, and social status (in terms of assets and/or income) is very much reflected in the neighborhood and building choices people and organizations make.

The position taken here is the traditional liberal one in the United States (see also Lang 1987a). An egalitarian society is one where there is equality of opportunity. Not everybody is equally endowed with either the ability or the motivation to seize on opportunities. Equality of opportunity is worth striving for and, although urban design is by no means the leading contributor to achieving this end, it is often the level at which social decisions are made regarding the distribution of services and the formal institutions of which one can be a member.

THE DESIGN PROGRAM: CREATING THE MILIEU

If one accepts the observation that the behavioral program should be defined before the design program can be, then the role of the urban designer is to bring to the attention of decision makers the urban design opportunities and issues that might impinge on the behavioral program. Four sets of design issues affect the social environment: (1) the way sets of behavior settings are bounded to form identifiable units with which people can identify and affiliate, (2) the sets and locations of institutions and facilities that are provided, (3) the design of links and places, and (4) the way the milieu and the objects it contains provide for symbols of affiliation. In everyday life a prerequisite for the development of a sense of community is the sense of security achieved by having a safe and secure environment and enough privacy. Often, however, the need for security makes people band together. Such a banding does not, however, necessarily have spatial implications except for the less mobile in society.

Nodes and Boundaries and the Creation of a Sense of Place

The way urban designers have traditionally thought about the design of the built environment to meet affiliation needs is to divide the city into bounded districts, which are further subdivided into neighborhoods. The goal is to provide a hierarchy of well-defined areas, each with the appropriate facilities located at its core (a *there* there) and a number of people with which an individual and/or families can identify. The idea of people identifying with a well-bordered area has its theoretical support in the Gestalt theory of visual organization. In two-dimensional pattern perception, areas with good contours are seen as units more readily than those without. This observation was taken into the third dimension in the work of Kevin Lynch (1960) on the elements of urban form and corroborated by subsequent research (see Chapter 12 and Pocock and Hudson 1978). The bordering elements can be natural features of the landscape such as hills and rivers, artificial elements such as parks, roads, and rail lines, or a mixture of elements that have a linear form.

The Loop in Chicago (see Fig. 11-4(2)) is defined by elevated rail tracks; this is not a very clear definition, but it gives a name to an area of the city within which many businesses and shops are located. The Fort Worth proposal of Victor Gruen gave the downtown a clear identity by creating a loop road around it (see Fig. 3-5). Boulder, Colorado, has a green belt, a common enough idea, but

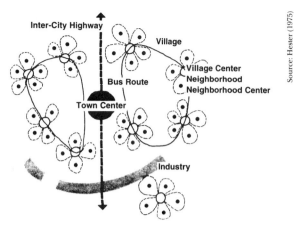

1. Conceptual Plan

2. City Center

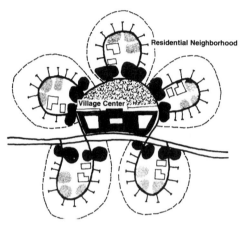

3. Conceptual Plan for the Villages

4. A Village Center

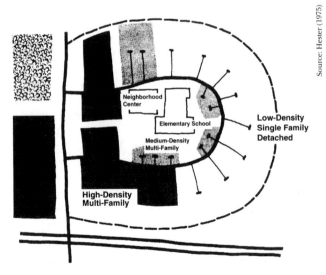

5. Conceptual Plan for the Neighborhoods

6. A Neighborhood Center

Figure 13-6: Columbia, Maryland

The overall organization of Columbia, Maryland, designed in the 1960s, is similar to the first generation of British new towns. The city is served by one major center, which is really a regional center (1,2), and a set of village centers (3,4), each of which con-tains a number of neighborhoods (5,6). While people identify with their neighborhoods, it is the village centers that serve their local needs. They afford a greater range of choices. It is also easier to develop a cognitive map of Columbia's village than its neighborhoods.

few cities have been able to withstand pressures from developers to make the land available for development. In Columbia, Maryland, a mixture of roads and open space is used to define a hierarchy of loosely defined territories.

Columbia, developed and designed by the Rouse Organization and now approaching completion, is divided into villages, which are divided into neighborhoods, each providing a set of services (R. Brooks 1974; Tennenbaum 1990). In many ways it is a Neo-Traditional scheme designed thirty years before the term came into use with the work of Andres Duany and Elizabeth Plater-Zyberk. It is an implementation of a generic new town schema based on British new towns of the immediate post-World War II era and the earlier work of Clarence Perry and Clarence Stein (C. Stein 1957) in Radburn, New Jersey. Columbia is similar in concept to a number of other American new towns developed in the 1960s and 1970s (Golany 1976; Birch 1980). The clarity of the village concept with its centers does lead people to identify with them, but their residents' broader sense of affiliation is with groups that have little to do with neighborhood, village, or town boundaries.

Downtowns

Traditionally the central business district of a metropolitan area has been a core both in terms of activities and as a symbolic heart. With the relative decline of the importance of downtowns in terms of their economic role in their regions, questions arise about the necessity of such places in the future urban realm, especially as many suburban areas work well enough without such cores. In addition, many Americans heartily dislike, indeed fear, the busyness, disorder, and the density of people who inhabit existing downtowns as places to work, shop, or recreate. Yet for other people the mixture of activities and people still holds the essence of life. Interestingly enough a number of suburban areas are seeking to build downtowns. Indeed, the development of urban galleria and the Neo-Traditional suburbs of America is an effort to create a sense of place.

Southfield, Michigan, is a major location for offices and retail outlets in the Detroit metropolitan area. It has, however, not had a "place" that public and commercial interests can think of as a focus. In contrast to other new suburban downtowns that have developed around shopping malls, the proposal in Southfield is to extend its present civic center complex with the addition of new commercial facilities, pedestrian connections, and public spaces. It may well develop into a new type—neither suburban mall nor existing downtown. Similarly, the same type of thinking is occurring in the Bronx, New York. What is essentially a new downtown is being built there to help the Bronx's overall development by giving a focus to the area's services and to provide a psychological sense of place.

This sense of place still appears to be important to many Americans. A recent survey in Amarillo, Texas, a city whose downtown is in considerable economic trouble, showed that its citizens still overwhelmingly regard the area as an important symbol. The current thinking is that such downtowns need to be thought of as special neighborhoods and not simply as areas of skyscraper corporate buildings. Mixed uses, including residential, are needed to get the vitality that attracts people to downtowns and makes them survive economically. They have to be pleasant and safe places in order for the power of attraction to work. They need to have easy accessibility by automobile.

Institutions and Facilities: Their Locations and Scale

One of the concerns in urban design is with the appropriate specification for the location of institutions and facilities in relationship to the public realm, and of the places in the public realm where people might gather to meet friends and acquaintances and to participate vicariously in the lives of strangers. The basic thesis is that when people have the opportunity to meet or simply see each other, then their identity will be reinforced.

The neighborhood unit concept was at least partially based on this idea. At its center was an elementary school and recreational facilities. In Columbia, the neighborhoods have an elementary school, local shops, and recreational facilities at their center. In the next step of the hierarchy, the villages, a broader array of facilities exists. The thesis was that if people use common and local facilities they will set up a web of relationships. Residents will get to know shopkeepers and schoolteachers, children will get to know classmates who live nearby, and their parents will get to know each other through their children. The research results on the success of such designs in meeting designer's goals is equivocal. While much neighboring does occur in Columbia, and it is a well-loved place, James Rouse expected too much of the physical environment as a shaper of the social environment (R. Brooks 1974; Tennenbaum 1990).

British research sheds some light on the matter. The findings of Peter Willmott and Michael Young (1960, 1973) show the dilemma designers face in responding to studies of how people actually live. First they found that the concept of neighborhood unit had little meaning for people residing in them, then they found (in Cumbernauld) that people tended to impose neighborhood constructs on local areas, and finally they found that increasingly people live metropolitan not parochial lives and enjoy it. Milton Keynes reflects this opinion. The conclusion is that local facilities and neighborhoods are important as service areas but not too much should be expected socially as a consequence. Propinquity is not necessary for community for those people who are mobile (Webber 1963). However, not everybody is.

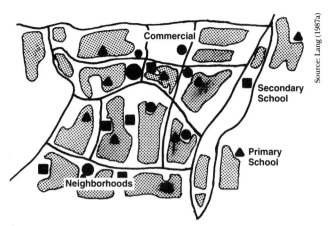

1. Harlow, England

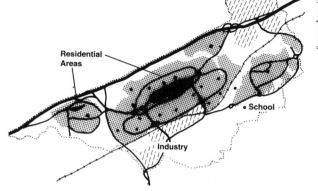

2. Cumbernauld, Scotland

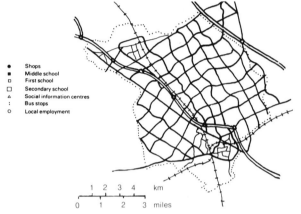

Shops
Middle school
First school
Secondary school
Social information centres
Bus stops
Local employment

1 2 3 4   km
0   1   2   3   miles

3. Milton Keynes, England

Figure 13-7: Neighborhoods in British New Town Design
The postwar new towns in the United Kingdom show the change in generally accepted design principles over time. The new towns of the first generation built after World War II (e.g., (1) Harlow) were divided into neighborhoods (as was Columbia, Maryland), the second abandoned the idea because neither people's lifestyles nor their sense of affiliation coincided with neighborhood boundaries. The design of Cumbernauld focuses on a single center for the town (2). Now the assumption is that people have high automobile mobility, so Milton Keynes is designed to facilitate it (3), as in the United States at Las Colinas.

In Columbia and in Radburn the recreational facilities are used and nearness to them is a major factor in explaining who uses them. They do bring people with a common interest together and provide a source of affiliation (Lansing, Marans, and Zehner 1970; R. Brooks 1974; Tennenbaum 1990). Local shopping areas, provided the ownership of the stores and the people who work in them are stable over time and that their number is not excessive, do give people a focus of attention and act as a source of identity (ERG 1990). It is also clear that such facilities are likely to work best as catalysts for local affiliations in areas with homogeneous populations. When the populations are highly heterogeneous, the institutions that subgroups will join, the shopping areas that they will use, and the schools to which they will send their children will be based on common values rather than propinquity. The urban design task is to ensure that such facilities exist and that access to them is easy enough for people to use them and thereby avoid feeling isolated. The design concern on the local level thus needs to focus on the needs of people of low mobility.

In designing local facilities it must be recognized who the true "localites" are (Hester 1975). They are chil-

dren (and their parents when the children are young) and the elderly. Children living in a neighborhood, using the streets and other neighborhood open spaces to play, and attending the local neighborhood school are much more likely to know each other than their parents are likely to know other adults well. They are, indeed, likely to be catalysts for adult interaction. The school must be attractive to the parents because they are the ones who make decisions about where to educate their children. Such facilities and their associated activities are more likely to work in bringing people together where common values exist than where values differ. In multiethnic countries or heterogeneous areas of the United States (except where people are poor), the local school as a mechanism for getting people together has had very limited success (Brolin 1976). In poor heterogeneous areas, only the children will know each other as a result of going to a common school, although their parents may because of the need for mutual support.

The facilities that children use—playgrounds, swimming pools, good streets in which to play (recognizing where children do play, see Hester 1975; Ward 1990)—all enable children of similar ages to get together provided

Table 13-2: Stage in Life Cycle and Mobility

LIFE CYCLE CLASSIFICATION	MOBILITY	Extremely Low	Low	Moderate	High	Extremely High
Preschool Child		●				
Elementary School Child			●[1]			
Teenager				●[1]		
College Student						●
Unmarried Adult						●[2]
Young Marrieds					●[2]	
Family with Young Children		●[1]				
Family with Older Children				●[2]		
Middle Aged					●[2]	
Elderly		●				

[1]Significant sex differences in mobility, females generally being lower.
[2]Most significant class differences in mobility, lower income being generally lower.

Source: Hester (1975)

their parents allow them to do so. Parents, especially mothers at present, with young children will rely heavily on child-minding facilities and tot-lots. These facilities may act as catalysts for generating some contact between adults who have something in common—children. In lower-income families, the older siblings of the young children are likely to be the child minders. Space for them to get together needs to be adjacent to those where young children play. Where adults are the minders, there need to be seats close to where children play. The seats should be organized so that eye contact between adults and children is easy to maintain (see Cooper Marcus and Francis 1990).

Children are also users of incidental spaces—front-door steps, open lots, buildings under construction, fields, and, in general, nooks and crannies. In today's highly manicured, financially pragmatic designs, these places tend to be eliminated simply because they fall outside the scope of developers' and designers' concerns. Such patterns can still be elements of design but require considerable self-conscious attention to the detailing of the environment (Ward 1990).

The elderly are not an homogeneous group, but they tend to become localites as their mobility reduces with age. If not employed they may also have leisure time and be in need of mutual support. Facilities that serve them provide opportunities for friendship and group solidarity. Although there has been a growth in retirement home communities, these serve only a very small proportion of the elderly (possibly 4 percent) in the United States and none in countries where the third generation is still regarded as part of the residential family. Designing retirement villages raises the same general questions that designing any neighborhood does. Whether such segregation of people is in the public interest or not is an important social question. Certainly a minority of the wealthy elderly who have a complete freedom of choice do choose age-segregated retirement villages as places in which to live. The homogeneity of concerns and the need for mutual support make such villages as close to "compleat" territorial communities as can be achieved by neighborhood design in the United States today.

Recognizing the limitations of these schemes, conceptual plans have been devised based on the mechanisms used today to sustain human contact in cities. Some are very different from what we plan in cities today (e.g., Alexander 1972), but others such as the pedestrian pocket model are really adaptations of the neighborhood unit schema (Kelbaugh 1989; Calthorpe 1991). It has not been a conceptually easy task to devise patterns that might better afford a sense of community than standard suburban subdivisions. The reason is that the effort flies in the face of the tendency for people to strive for greater privacy rather than a sense of community when their economic status gives them a high degree of physical mobility.

Some ideas are insightful about what an urban designer might advocate, but they are based on an outdated model of human relationships (see also Brill 1989). In his generic plan for a community that affords contact between people, Christopher Alexander (1972) grappled with the issue, but ended up proposing some basic behavioral changes in people that are necessary for his community to work. He assumes that there is indeed a high degree of desire for face-to-face interaction between friends at home and proposes that a quasi-formal mechanism be established to attain it.

Alexander recognizes the importance of children in establishing a sense of community, and his generic scheme is based on a population, and thus a building density, that would allow children to find friends of a similar age within it. Also recognizing that American families prefer to live in single-family detached homes, he suggested that each home have two living rooms so that people can use one that is visible from the road when they are at home to visitors and the other when they want privacy. Friends driving by in their cars will recognize when they are welcome to visit or when not to do so.

The most important part of residential area design today becomes the street—the face-block neighborhood with the street as a seam tying together opposite rows of houses. This configuration is particularly important in areas of high-density housing where the street serves many purposes, such as a playground for children and a

1. Germantown Avenue, Chestnut Hill, Philadelphia

2. Fairmount, Philadelphia

3. Brooklyn Heights, New York

4. Little League Baseball, Coronado, California

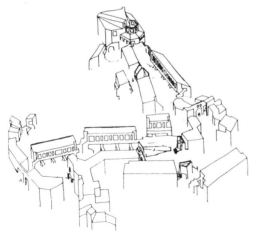

5. Kresge College, University of California at Santa Cruz

6. Kresge College, View of the Internal Court

Figure 13-8: Designing to Afford Easy Human Contact

Forming a sense of local community through physical design is difficult. The environment can create opportunities for people to see each other and get together if they so desire (see also Fig. 10–2(3)). Some people do lead parochial lifestyles. Localizing of facilities such as shopping areas where one deals with the same people on a recurrent basis helps (1). Children tend to be the true localites (2) and also the catalysts for parents to get to know each other. The elderly and people with few resources also use local areas (3). More importantly, there is a need to create behavior settings that afford the opportunity for like-minded people to get together (4). Colleges and other institutions, as total or all-of-a-piece urban designs, can be designed to afford the easy casual meeting of people and thus the building of a sense of community (5,6).

place where people meet and chat (Hester 1975). The need is for it to have a clear territorial demarcation and low volumes of traffic to afford easy contact between the two sides of the road (Appleyard with Gerson and Lintell 1981). Alison Smithson and Peter Smithson (1967) recognized the importance of this arrangement in Great Britain many years ago. In Radburn, the cul-de-sacs are often playgrounds. The difficulty has been to translate these observations into design principles in other than low-rise housing areas (Smithson 1969).

Dealing with Change

One of the human realities that developers and urban designers have failed to recognize in past designs of new towns and neighborhoods has been that people age. They have designed Peter Pan suburbs. New suburbs and neighborhoods have attracted and still attract people at the early child-rearing stage in the life cycle because of the emphasis placed on single-family homes and the nuclear family in their design. The assumption was that parents would move when their children left home and new young families would replace them. Instead, the parents have aged in place and total population numbers in such areas have dropped. The result has been that the facilities designed for the young, especially schools, often stand empty. In addition, the changing structure of the American family is putting pressure on the suburbs. Developers have been slow to respond. The need is therefore to design for a population structure that reflects more closely the age structure of the population as a whole, and to design for flexibility and robustness so that the infrastructure survives under changing conditions.

The Design of the Links and Places of the Public Realm

In the core areas of cities and in residential areas, market squares and plazas, clubs, bars, cultural facilities, all provide the affordances for people with at least some common interest to get together. Clubs, bars, and restaurants provide catalysts for assembly, but they are part of the private realm. A warmth and camaraderie does exist in many such places. Urban design, taxation, and land-use policies can encourage their development. The development of public spaces, indoors or outdoors, can be through direct public investment or incentive zoning programs (Barnett 1982).

The design of urban open spaces has long been of a major concern to urban designers (Sitte 1889; Zucker 1959; R. Krier 1980; Lennard and Lennard 1987; Gehl 1987, 1989; Cooper Marcus and Francis 1990). For architects, urban design is epitomized by the creation of urban spaces like the central piazzas of Italian cities (Brill 1989; Reid 1990). The Italian piazza is as hypnotic an image for urban designers as the neighborhood unit plan. There

1. South Philadelphia, Philadelphia

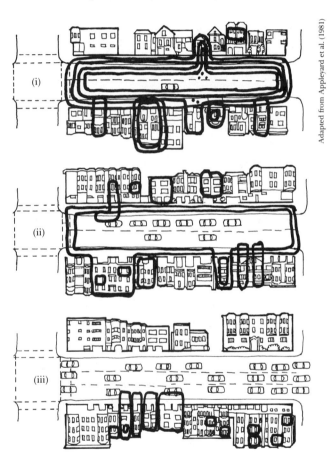

Adapted from Appleyard et al. (1981)

2. Territoriality and Traffic Flow

Figure 13–9: The Face-Block Neighborhood

The face-block neighborhood consists of the houses facing each other across a street (1). It can be a through street, a cul-de-sac, or a woonerf. Such a design becomes a semipublic territory with the semiprivate territories spilling out onto the street. It is the one area in which people in the American city will be likely to know each other. The Smithsons (1967) used the diagram shown in Fig. 6–1(1) to show its importance as a place for children. For such a pattern to function as a territory the traffic flow through it must be low (2i), otherwise the two sides become separated (2ii and 2iii).

1. Rittenhouse Square, Philadelphia

2. Grand Central Terminal, New York

3. Trump Plaza, Fifth Avenue, New York

Figure 13-10: The "Great Urban Rooms"

Most cities have "great urban rooms" that give them a sense of identity. Such spaces have to be seen within their context. Rittenhouse Square, Philadelphia (1), is surrounded by an intensity of uses that have changed over time but that are still varied. Grand Central Terminal's great room is an internal one but has many of the same characteristics (2). It is also a place where many homeless people spend the night. New spaces of that type tend to be privately controlled ones (3). All three examples here give opportunities for participation in life and a sense of belonging to the whole.

has been a tendency on the part of architects and landscape architects to argue for public open spaces in the form of plazas, squares, and parks on the grounds that they establish a sense of community. While this belief should be treated with caution, public places can certainly give an identity to an area by acting as landmarks and symbols, and they can provide opportunities for people who are friends (or strangers) to gather and share the experience of being in a place. The people may be office workers at lunchtime, people waiting to meet other people, or individuals simply enjoying the open area in the sunshine. Indirectly, such places may give people a feeling of belonging to, or at least being part of, a larger group. Unfortunately, there are also many examples of places where nobody wants to go.

Some cities still have "great urban rooms" of the past that give identity to the whole city or large portions of them. Rittenhouse Square in Philadelphia and Grand Central Terminal in New York City act much as Piazza San Marco in Venice, Trafalgar Square in London, Connaught Place in New Delhi, or Circular Quay in Sydney. These examples show the diversity of ways in which the public realm can be configured. The attribute that they have in common is that they are surrounded by lively diverse areas and act as nodes and landmarks within these areas (Lynch 1960; J. Jacobs 1961). They also act as symbols for the city. Some major urban squares, such as Pershing Square in Los Angeles, fail to act in this manner as well as they could if refurbished. At the time of writing it was beginning to be rebuilt to make it a more congenial place.

The quality of urban open spaces—streets, sidewalks, arcades, plazas—very much affects the pleasantness of being in a bustling environment among strangers. One can get vicarious pleasure from the lives of other people in such situations. The achievement of design quality in such places does not have to be accidental. Oscar Newman (1972, 1980a), William H. Whyte, in *The Social Life of Small Urban Places* (1980), and Clare Cooper Marcus and Carolyn Francis (1990) provide overlapping sets of observations of the attributes of places that will be lively and well liked by their users. Our empirical knowledge has been increased substantially based on studies of success and failure of past designs. Some of the research has focused on the general population and some on the needs of special groups of people (e.g., the elderly; see Cranz 1987; Regnier and Pynoos 1987). The knowledge is almost directly translatable into design guidelines. Popular gathering places are those that offer comfortable seating, good light, people watching, and some catalyst for people being there; food is a major catalyst (see also Alexander et al. 1977; Whyte 1980, 1988). They are also connected well to streets.

Designing places so that women enjoy being there can only enhance the overall environmental quality. In some societies, such as traditional Islamic ones, women simply do not use plazas at all. Such open spaces are men's territory. Louise Mozingo (1989) suggests that Whyte's research is also primarily a study of men's use of open space. She suggests that women are more susceptible to urban annoyances such as dirt and noise, are less desirous of being on exhibit, need to feel safe both physically and psychologically, and need to have seats at standard height. They are less likely to use stairs as seats than are men. Women tend to find downtowns grimmer places than men do.

There are a number of other spaces where people gather in cities to be part of a group. Some of these places are intended to be used as gathering places and others not. The gallerias of Italian cities serve not only as pedestrian shortcuts but as places to meet (Geist 1983). The modern galleria in the United States is the suburban or center city shopping mall, which, where management allows, is a gathering place for teenagers and, often, the elderly (Bednar 1989; Maitland 1991).

One of the major issues in the design of public places is how to deal with seasonal changes. Many of the traditionally outdoor spaces in cities have gone indoors to areas that can be air conditioned in summer and heated in winter to provide greater comfort. They also tend to be under private control and do give a sense of security to their users. That is a very basic need. The consequence is that other people, the undesirables, are kept out. With the increasing crime rates in many parts of the United States and the world, the privatization of what was previously public open space is being carried out for other than comfort reasons. This privatization has been accompanied by, causes, and responds to a general decline in the quality and maintenance of the public realm. This decline can be reversed, but it will require major social programs and a long-term commitment to reverse the decline in social order and provide equal opportunities for all before such changes can be envisioned.

The interior, privately owned plazas of New York City are part of this trend of the development of privatized "public" spaces to serve the public. IBM Plaza on Madison Avenue is open to the public under the surveillance of the company. The Winter Garden at Battery Park City is similar. People do use such places and at lunchtime they are often crowded. They provide a place for people to get together with friends or relax watching people, but the space is not part of what has historically been the "true" public realm (Chidister 1989; Goldberger 1989a).

Parks and recreation facilities have also been advocated as places to provide people with the opportunity to get together. There have been four eras of park design in the United States: the pleasure playground, the reform park, the recreational facility, and now the open-space system (Cranz 1982). Play lots, open spaces such as the central area at Radburn, all provide opportunities for people to recreate together, especially the young. Recreational facilities such as swimming pools have proven highly desirable for subgroups of the population (R. Brooks 1974). They serve many purposes; opportunities for getting together is merely one of them.

Promenading

Promenading is a behavior that gives people an opportunity to see and be seen, to nod at acquaintances, and to meet friends. With the increasing privacy of life, one might suspect that such a behavior had disappeared in American cities, but it still exists, although the middle-aged and middle class engage in it much less frequently than in the past. It still exists in specific locations, such as on the Boardwalk in Atlantic City (see Fig. 13–11(3)), and/or at specific times of the day or year. Until the late 1960s places such as the Grand Concourse in the Bronx were major places for taking the air and seeing friends and acquaintances, but with changing populations such behavior has ceased, although the Grand Concourse still affords it well. In smaller urban cities promenading tended to occur on Main Street; now it takes place in the suburban mall, especially for teenagers, where it can clash with other expected behaviors (see also Sasuki 1976). No streets have been specifically designed for good "cruising" in automobiles by American teenagers, a type of promenading not generally regarded as "good."

Much of the character of cities comes from the opportunities they provide for promenading. Again, a catalyst seems necessary for people to choose a place for doing so. The catalyst may be a good view, a set of shopfronts for window shopping, or centrality of location. Promenading also needs a good sidewalk for parading, one that is wide enough to walk leisurely and to stop and talk with people without holding others up. Many cities with waterfronts have good esplanades or public promenades. Their use for promenading seems to depend on their connectivity to the core of the city. Baltimore's Inner Harbor and the edges of Manhattan provide such a place, while Atlantic City's Boardwalk is connected on one side to the hotels, casinos, and shops and on the other to the beach and sea. People have to have a sense of security for the behavior to develop at all.

Natural Surveillance

Natural surveillance has already been discussed as a mechanism for aiding people in attaining a sense of security in an area. It can also be a mechanism for sustaining human interaction. People used to talk over back fences and to passersby as they sat out on their porches. Cul-de-sacs provide an enclave where people can see others come and go (Kuper 1950). It is easy to have a sense of nostalgia for such patterns of the environment and what they afford. They may still, nevertheless, have utility today.

Jane Jacobs (1961) advocated short blocks, mixed land uses, and eyes on the street as mechanisms for

1. Locust Walk, University of Pennsylvania Campus, Philadelphia

2. Louvain-la-Neuve, Belgium

3. The Boardwalk, Atlantic City, New Jersey

Figure 13–11: Links, a Sense of Place, and Urban Design
In many cities it is the links between places (or the links as places) rather than the places themselves that are often the mechanisms for helping to provide a sense of community. Sometimes it is their symbolic value that is the important factor (1); at other times it is the nature of activities along the link (2). It is the informal gatherings and opportunities to see others and be seen that are important. Many promenades are along waterfronts (3), where people watching and the possibility of meeting acquaintances is as important as the view or "taking the air."

providing not only a sense of security on the street but also the fine-grained interactions that form the basis for the development of interlocking webs of friendships and acquaintances at the local level. If sustained over time such webs are the basis for the development of a deep sense of community and a commitment of people to each other. Following her design principles would result in a Neo-Traditional design.

In the design of Seaside, Florida, the guidelines stipulate that all houses have to have porches facing the pedestrian ways or streets. While this requirement is highly successful in giving the town a homogeneity of appearance—it gives a clear sense of place—it is only partially successful as a mechanism for sustaining contact between people. Seaside is a community of "limited lability." Indeed, it is not as yet a residential community. Too few of its houses are occupied by permanent residents. The porches are pleasant places on which to sit, and they do afford easy contact with passersby, but whether the contact will occur depends on the predispositions of people to actually engage in that type of behavior. Some casual contacts have occurred but not as many as some people expected (Langdon 1988).

The Symbols of Affiliation

It has been suggested in this book that the structure of the public realm and the elements that enclose it are also displays. As such, they communicate meaning. One of the major functions of the symbolic aesthetic of the environment is to provide a sense of identity. These symbols can be formal, such as coats of arms, or informal, such as the architecture of a place or the patina of alterations and signs that designate a specific area as belonging to a particular group of people (see Fig. 2–2). Specific patterns are associated with specific values. In urban design there is a twofold consideration: providing an overall identity for an area by providing the symbols of association of the people who use or dwell in it, and providing opportunities for people to personalize the environment so that they can get a feeling of ownership.

In providing for the first, either directly through design in a total urban design or through design guidelines, the goal is almost inevitably to have a unified design in which the building configurations, materials, color, and decoration systems are consistent within specific limits. In meeting the second, one is creating a soft architecture—one that can be easily adapted. In residential areas, if everybody adapts the environment in similar ways a unity through similarity can be achieved. If everybody personalizes the environment in different ways, a unity through diversity is achieved. In between, one ends up with an environment that is simply untidy. That, in itself, is a symbol of affiliation, but probably not one displaying self-esteem at the community level.

2. Close-up of the List of the Names of the American War Dead

1. Vietnam War Memorial, Washington, DC

3. Vietnam War Memorial, Washington, DC

Figure 13–12: Memorials and Affiliation Needs
Memorials can provide a sense of affiliation of people with each other through specific historic events (1). The Vietnam War was an unhappy episode, and the design of a memorial has been a controversial one because it was not in the form of many people's images of what constitutes a memorial, nor does it heighten self-esteem, a major function of memorials. Yet its list of names is a moving sight to behold (2). A later, more typical, memorial has been created and stands nearby (3). It fails to hold people's attention in the way the first does.

A Note on Public Art

Public art, it was suggested in Chapter 3 (see also Fig. 3–15), has been used extensively as a symbolic cipher to lay claims over areas of the city: parks, plazas, neighborhoods. It has achieved this end by celebrating the heroes of the group of people of concern, by using symbols that denote the group to outsiders, and by simply being a mode of expression for local groups. As such, the art work lays a claim to an area and becomes a symbol with which the people for whom the work is important can identify. The intensity of arguments over the nature of public art illustrates the emotional value it possesses (see Chapter 2).

The Affiliation of Place with Its Surroundings: Contextualism

Many new urban designs have been criticized because they do not "belong" to the place in which they are located—they are foreign to it. They are said to be out of context. Phoenix, Arizona's Design Review Manual addresses the issue in its guidelines:

Each project should reflect the broader environmental context of Phoenix as a desert city and respect the value of our scarce resources, the abundance of sunshine and the richness of our natural resources and amenities.

The New York City Planning Commission has worked to develop a new zoning ordinance for its low-rise neighborhoods to protect their character.

The study of contextualism has been pursued widely in the last three decades particularly from a phenomenological orientation (Tuan 1977; Lynch 1972, 1976; Brolin 1980; Norberg Schulz 1980) but also experimentally by people such as Linda Groat (1988). The design question is: "How does one get a new total design or an all-of-piece design to look as if it belongs to (or is part of) its surrounding context?" This question becomes more important as cities vie to simultaneously achieve economic supremacy and maintain their own characters.

There are three basic variables of built form that seem to be fundamentally important in achieving this end. All are related to one of the laws of visual organization of Gestalt theory, the law of similarity. To appear to be

1. San Francisco

2. Philadelphia

3. Plaza d'Italia, New Orleans (1975-1978)

Photograph by Ruth Durack

Figure 13-13: Public Art and Affiliation Needs

Public art can be used to personalize and lay claim over an area. There is no mistaking the ethnic identity of the areas in which the murals shown in (1) and (2) are. They are also expressions of pride and self-esteem (see Chapter 14). The Plaza d'Italia (3) designed by Charles Moore and others was designed to reinforce the identity of an area. It was also hoped that it would act as a catalyst for development around it. It has failed to achieve that end (see Chapter 20). Its more abstract nature than of the murals in (1) and (2) clearly indicates its professional origin.

in context with its surroundings a new development needs to meet the street in the same fashion as its surroundings, have essentially the same mass as its surroundings, and have, if not the same type of architectural style as its surroundings, at least the same colors and materials. Another principle related to the Gestalt law of visual continuity is that the new development should have its horizontal lines in line with existing development (see also Groat 1988). An additional hypothesis is that the new development should have the same symbolic content as its surroundings even if the style is different.

A sense of contextual fit can be obtained by using formal elements of the vernacular tradition or, in places where no such tradition exists, by creating one (Claflen 1992). These elements may be the general form of the buildings, their materials, the structural system and/or the materials of which they are constructed, or their detailing and decoration type. Post-Modernists suggest that an abstraction of these elements would still lead to buildings being seen in context. Recent studies show that while such a connection might be made intellectually, the similarities are not something subconsciously recognized unless the symbols are completely blatant—really signs.

During the twentieth century in the United States there have been a number of efforts to fit projects into a

context or to create a future context. In New Mexico, for instance, an effort has been made time and again to adopt (and adapt) the adobe form and appearance for use in a number of buildings built out of concrete and masonry (Markovich, Preiser, and Strum 1990). Santa Barbara, California (see Fig. 17–7(3)), has design controls that promote a Spanish colonial architectural style (Lai 1988).

In the case of the residential buildings of Battery Park City (see Fig. 3–10), which, from critics' reports, is seen as in context within New York, careful guidelines were developed based on the nature of an existing New York building type—the early-twentieth-century apartment buildings of New York's Upper East and Upper West sides. "These buildings are masonry-clad structures with punched windows and stone bases, mid-height belt courses, and stepped-back penthouses" (Fisher 1988). Presumably another distinctive type could have been chosen just as well, but the type chosen is residential and it also has connotations of upper socioeconomic status.

The Deconstructionist Alternative

Past urban design efforts have tried to integrate facilities, boundaries, and symbols into unified wholes. This observation applies to the design of places such as

BUILDING APPEARANCE

OBJECTIVES AND POLICIES

OBJECTIVE 15

TO CREATE A BUILDING FORM THAT IS VISUALLY INTERESTING AND HARMONIZES WITH SURROUNDING BUILDINGS.

POLICY 1

Ensure that new facade relate harmoniously with nearby facade patterns.

When designing the facade pattern for new buildings, the pattern of large nearby existing facades should be considered to avoid unpleasant juxtapositions. Incongruous materials, proportions, and sense of mass should be avoided.

As a general rule, facades composed of both vertical and horizontal elements fit better with older as well as most new facades.

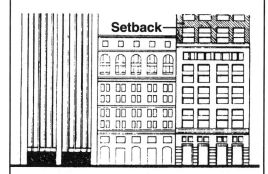

The all vertical pattern of this building has little in common with the center structure

Strong verticals and horizontals strong base and similar street wall height help give building a positive relationship to center building

POLICY 2

Assure that new buildings contribute to the visual unity of the city

•
•
•

Figure 13-14: New Buildings and Existing Urban Contexts
Defining aesthetic criteria for making buildings belong to their context has not been easy. It is, however, an objective in much urban design today in the United States and also across the world. This example forms part of the Downtown Area Plan of the City of San Francisco. Architects are generally opposed to such guidelines because they want to have freedom of expression.

neighborhoods, industrial precincts, and central business districts. The alternative is not to worry about this integration because it means little to current lives of people but to follow the morphological analysis and design method (Zwicky 1948) as implicit in recent Deconstructionist thinking (Corner 1990b). In this approach each problem is dealt with independently and the overall solution is simply the combination of the independent solutions superimposed on each other. Such an approach would inevitably lead to major conflicts between partial solutions, but conceptually at least these could be ironed out. The result would be a highly diverse environment with a sense of the whole relying on an area having clear boundaries.

CONCLUSION

Many of the research findings and speculations on the way the built environment can reinforce feelings of community and identity are equivocal. It might seem that there is little that the urban designer can really do to help meet or provide the affordances for people to meet their needs. Item by item, little seems to be of great importance. Cumulatively, however, design actions can have an effect and result in a very different environment than if the designer pays no heed to recent research. It is important to recognize the changes taking place in society and, however much some of us might regret it, the changes in how affiliation is achieved. It is also important to recognize the new places in the United States where acquaintances and strangers meet and to design with both community and privacy in mind. Such places include airports (especially transit airports—or hubs) and the enclosed semipublic places of cities.

The empirical knowledge of the mechanisms whereby people's affiliation needs are met also raises a number of concerns for urban designers at all scales of urban design activity—total design, all-of-a-piece design, and at a design policy and guideline writing level. The reason is that some of the mechanisms that might help people fulfill their affiliation needs also detract from the fulfillment of other needs. Some of these issues are substantive ones (see also Chapter 19) and some are procedural (see also Chapter 22). The procedural questions concern methods for choosing what meanings to implement, and the substantive ones have to do with the linking of goal statements to a design via a set of principles and/or guidelines. These questions are partly political but also partly empirical. The basic point is that the studies of types of design patterns that might be implemented must tie the spatial qualities and the qualities of the surfaces that constitute them into a broader study of how and when they are to be used. Relying on existing types, particularly types derived from other cultures, is likely to mislead the architect in designing the city for the future. For urban designers working in the United States there is

1. Central Business District, Los Angeles

2. Rural West Virginia

3. Museum of Art, Tempe, Arizona

4. Quincy Market, Boston

5. San Francisco

6. Bryant Park, New York

Figure 13-15: Creating a Sense of Place

Every place has a sense of place, but when critics say an urban design has no sense of place they mean that the built form has no character unique to its region. Certainly much architecture pays little heed to local climate or to the architectural history of a place established in the days before air conditioning. The new buildings of downtown Los Angeles could be found almost anywhere, although those in the foreground are clearly part of the region (1). Soil, climate, natural vegetation, and the subtle qualities of light are unique to a place (2). Artificial factors such as the character of a place's streets, building types, and the materials with which they are constructed all help give a place a particular identity (3). It is not, however, simply the milieu that gives a place a character. It is also the nature of people, their activities, and even the modes of transport they use that make a place unique (4,5). The nature of a place can be radically changed to create a new sense of place. Recent renovations of Bryant Park in New York City (6) have changed its affordances considerably. As a result a new group of people feel comfortable in using it.

now a considerable body of empirical evidence on which they can rely in helping people to fulfill their affiliation needs.

The Future

The planned city of Las Colinas in Texas (see Fig. 3–9 (1)), like others in the United States and Milton Keynes in England (see Fig. 13–7(3)), is designed with the automobile as the primary mode of transport, although a monorail is planned for Las Colinas's downtown area and may eventually link Dallas with Dallas–Fort Worth Airport. Such towns are a response to a new sort of community. For many adult middle-class Americans, privacy is important and community and a sense of belonging are no longer based on face-to-face contact at a local level. Many people look back with warmth on their army or college days when such a sense of community existed, but their lives now, for better or worse, no longer reflect this need. Ease of access to facilities by automobile has become important.

The future mode of personal transportation will remain the car, of communication, the telephone, the television, the radio, the facsimile. A sense of community comes from similarity in possessions and/or experiences. In this world children and the less mobile lose their independence. There are fewer local behavior settings in which to participate.

There are growing signs today of dispiritedness, alienation, and a rising violence among American youth, including middle-class suburban youth. They have been attributed to various social sources: broken families, ease of access to drugs and handguns, the increasing competitiveness of society. Maybe adolescents have just been shoved aside in the planning for the future of the United States, and age-group segregation has increased. It should be geometrically possible to weave together the transportation systems for "cosmopolites" and localities in new town design. Is it politically possible to think about the needs of the whole population and the behavior settings necessary to meet those needs?

MAJOR REFERENCES

Alexander, Christopher (1972). "The City as a Mechanism for Sustaining Human Contact." In Robert Gutman, ed., *People and Buildings.* New York: Basic Books: pp. 406–434.

Brill, Michael (1989). "An Ontology for Exploring Urban Public Life Today." *Places* 6, no. 1: 24–29.

Claflen, George (1992). "Simulated Stimulation/Stimulated Simulation: Regionalism and Urban Design." Paper presented at the Association of Collegiate Schools of Architecture Conference. Photocopied.

Cooper Marcus, Clare, and Carolyn Francis, eds. (1990). *People Places: Design Guidelines for Urban Open Space.* New York: Van Nostrand Reinhold.

Effrat, Marcia Pelly, ed. (1974). *The Community: Approaches and Applications.* New York: Free Press.

Gottschalk, Shimon S. (1975). *Communities and Alternatives: An Exploration into the Limits of Planning.* Cambridge, MA: Schenkman.

Hayden, Dolores (1984). *Redesigning the American Dream: The Future of Housing, Work, and Family Life.* New York: Norton.

Keller, Suzanne (1968). *The Urban Neighborhood: A Sociological Perspective.* New York: Random House.

Lang, Jon (1987a). "Social Organization and the Built Environment." In *Creating Architectural Theory.* New York: Van Nostrand Reinhold, pp. 166–177.

McCamant, Kathryn, and Charles Durrett (1988). *Cohousing: A Contemporary Approach to Housing Ourselves.* Berkeley, CA: Habitat Press/Ten Speed Press.

Steele, Fred I. (1973). *Physical Settings and Organizational Development.* Reading, MA: Addison-Wesley.

Suttles, Gerald D. (1972). *The Social Construction of Communities.* Chicago: University of Chicago Press.

Whyte, William H. (1980). *The Social Life of Small Urban Spaces.* New York and Washington, DC: Conservation Foundation.

14

MEETING ESTEEM NEEDS

Almost all people have a need for self-respect or self-esteem. Maslow (1987) regards those who do not as "pathological exceptions." The need to be held in high esteem is a characteristic not only of individuals but also of groups of people: business organizations, religious organizations, institutions, ethnic groups, nations. An ideal society would be one where all people have a high degree of self-esteem without achieving it at the expense of others. In the United States, a highly competitive society, this end is difficult to meet.

There are two interwoven sets of esteem needs: the need to hold oneself in high esteem, and the need to be held in esteem by others—to have prestige or reputation—and to perceive this esteem. The satisfaction of both is necessary to have a feeling of self-worth and self-confidence. Both are prerequisites for the fulfillment of self-actualization needs. The failure to hold oneself in high esteem leads to feelings of inferiority and weakness.

The need to hold oneself in high esteem can be met in a number of ways: through the development of a mastery of knowledge and competence in its use, through control over one's own life, and through the possessions one has. Perceiving that one is held in high esteem by others is achieved through external rewards—the support and praise that one receives—and the reliance other people place on one. It is possible to perceive one is held in high esteem when one is not, but this is hardly a desirable situation. For few people is the satisfaction of one of these two sets of esteem needs sufficient.

Some people allow the search for fulfillment of esteem needs through the rewards and/or respect one receives from other people to dominate their lives rather than allowing for self-respect to develop through the *deserved* respect of others based on displays of competence. In doing so they often espouse positions that they do not hold or adopt the symbols of status that they do not like.

The lower one's perception of status and self-esteem, the more one is likely to behave in that way (see Menzel 1957). In contrast, some people are satisfied by simply knowing their own competence without the need for any external accolades.

Not everybody strives for prestige to the same degree; some people have a high need for achievement and others not (McClelland et al. 1953; Maslow 1987). To some extent the strength of the need for achievement is based on the degree to which affiliation needs have been fulfilled, but much depends on the individual's socialization process and the cultural frame in which it took place. Some societies are highly achievement-oriented; others are not. The same society may well change its character over time. People differ too; for some the need for prestige seems to bypass the need for affiliation, although it is difficult to conceive of prestige without at least a self-perception of belonging to a group—even if it is simply a group sharing a set of tastes rather than a social network.

People use various ways of achieving prestige: victory in the battlefield or on the athletic field, capturing markets, producing work held in high esteem by critics, achieving high educational standards, having and displaying material possessions, sending one's children to the right schools, living in the right areas, and so on. Even the name chosen for a building or an urban design development has a symbolic value (Michelson 1976; Lang 1987a). In a "good" society, people strive to fulfill their need for esteem through socially acceptable channels, but too often antisocial mechanisms, such as deceitful or criminal means, are used.

In looking at the fulfillment of esteem needs in this way it is clear that the mechanisms are closely related to the fulfillment of cognitive needs (see Chapter 16) and aesthetic needs (see Chapter 17), as well as to the fulfillment of affiliation needs (see Chapter 13). The reasons are clear. To fulfill the need for competence and mastery

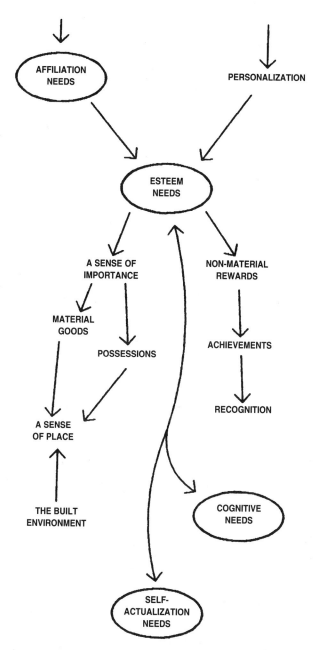

Figure 14–1: Esteem Needs

ASSOCIATIONAL MEANINGS AND AFFECTIVE VALUES

Every environment is a potential source of meaning to be read into it by an observer. These meanings may be acquired through one's formal education, they may be the result of the associations between patterns of the built environment and meanings that are acquired through everyday experiences. The meaning of the pyramid and eye on the United States dollar bill is based on an intellectual construct. People are unlikely to know what the two elements signify unless they are told of the meanings. Few Americans, on the other hand, will mistake a wealthy for a poor residential area in the United States, although they might when visiting another country where the environmental cues are different.

It is clear that some associational meanings of the built environment have to do with beliefs about specific patterns of its architectural layout and the values attached to those beliefs. Balance theory (see Chapter 1) explains the formation of attitudes and their affective dimension. It is a model that has stood up very well to continued analysis. Our beliefs are built up as we perceive correlates between the patterns of the built environment, the types of people using places, and the behavior in which they are engaging. We gain this knowledge as we look around and use different parts of the city, as a result of what we are told casually by others, and as part of our formal education. The values we associate with the correlates are also a product of our socialization process. This observation applies to the built environment as much as to any other aspect of life (Lukashok and Lynch 1956).

All architects go through a socialization process and are taught over the drawingboard through intermittent reinforcement—a very powerful device—about what are good and bad urban patterns without realizing the cultural bias of what they are learning. As Oscar Newman (1976) notes, architecture students say that prior to their going to architecture school they were unaware of their parents' poor tastes. Architects such as Robert Venturi are concerned with urban designers' ability to shed themselves of their own design predispositions enough to deal with the world as it is (Venturi, Scott Brown, and Izenour 1977). He and his colleagues note that many architects do indeed recognize the symbolism of the environments preferred by the mainstream of middle-class Americans (e.g., Las Vegas, Nevada, and the Levittowns). They note that at the same time, these architects find that taste culture distasteful because it falls outside their own realm of expression and what they have been taught is good taste (see also Rybczynski 1990). Urban designers need to be able to recognize what these types of environments afford their residents or users on all the dimensions of human experience and how such places reinforce the subjective sense of self-esteem of those people. Property developers and builders have been better at doing so than most architects.

of skills requires opportunities for learning, testing, and self-testing. While it is self-rewarding to have the skills, almost all people also need opportunities to display them to themselves and, in seeking prestige from other people, to others.

In considering the fulfillment of esteem needs as one of the functional goals of urban design, the urban designer is concerned with the provision of opportunities for various activities that meet cognitive needs. In addition, the designer is concerned with the symbolism of the built environment itself—the messages it conveys about people and, implicitly, their achievements. Inevitably, questions of the nature of public interest and fairness arise.

THE BEHAVIORAL PROGRAM

The behavioral program to fulfill esteem needs must cover three areas: (1) the provision of learning opportunities for the development of abilities, (2) the provision of opportunities to display skills, and (3) the display of the symbols of success to oneself and to others. The first points out the importance of the social and physical environments being educative and, more generally, the importance of the fulfillment of *cognitive needs* in people's lives. The second focuses on the importance of being able to perform, being a participant, not merely a spectator in life. The third raises many questions about the degree to which designers should strive for community and privacy, and about whose meanings and values should be incorporated in the aesthetic qualities of the environments they design (Rapoport 1967). Many of the issues raised in attempting to deal with esteem needs fall outside the scope of concern of urban designers because they deal with the social and economic organization of society. However, an examination of these issues shows that they have implications for the design of the physical environment because the behavioral mechanisms that are required to fulfill them have urban design consequences and vice versa.

The Development of Competence

Competence, both physical and intellectual, is developed in many ways that fall into two groups: formal learning and informal learning. The first occurs through formal organizations; it involves being taught and having supervised opportunities for practicing skills and demonstrating what has been learned. The second is concerned with learning about the world through one's everyday experiences, through the information one picks up as the result of talking with others, through watching television, and through exploring the world as a byproduct of other activities and for the pleasure it brings.

The behavioral program for providing formal education and the opportunities for informal learning clearly have many urban design implications. They range from a concern for the nature of playgrounds and the learning experience of children to the nature of universities, to the nature of open spaces, and to the textures of experiences that should be offered in high-density environments.

Much of what we learn is from contacts with other people, seeing what they do and listening to what they say, from reading books, and from the byproducts of recreational activities. The layout, content, and accessibility of the behavior settings of human settlements—the activities and their locations in the buildings and the open spaces—can play an important if not the major role in human development. Such places do not act deterministically, as their utility depends on individual predispositions to explore and use them. These issues are dealt with more thoroughly in Chapter 16, Meeting Cognitive Needs. It

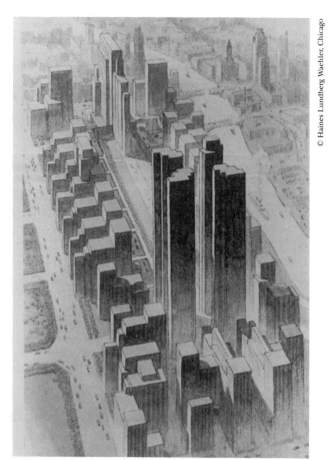

1. Terminal Park Project, Chicago (1929)

2. Mission Bay, San Francisco (in progress)

Figure 14-2: Status, Architecture, and Urban Design
People's affiliation and esteem needs are closely related. The symbolic aesthetics of the environment are a major communicator of esteem. Urban design during the course of this century has been closely associated with the search for prestige by cities and the designers themselves. Proposals for Chicago (1) and, on a much smaller scale, for San Francisco (2) show some of the variables associated with prestige in the United States: scale of development, materials, spaciousness, unity of architecture. The types of environments held in esteem by architects are not necessarily those held in high esteem by other people.

1. Classroom

2. Philadelphia Museum of Art

3. Walter Moleski, Architect

Figure 14-3: Displaying Skills

Self-esteem is achieved not only through having skills but also through displaying them. There are many ways in which skills are displayed, from schoolroom (1), to the display of physical skills (2), to mental dexterity (3). Older cities are usually full of informal opportunities to display skills; new cities often have fewer informal ones, although they may be replete with formal ones because designers seldom think about the informal. Urban design policy and design principles need to be geared to providing opportunities for a wide-ranging display of skills in both formal and informal settings.

suffices to say here that cognitive needs fulfillment is closely related to the achievement of esteem—an observation that reinforces the importance of environmental opportunities to explore and be curious about life (see Fig. 14-1). Many implemented urban designs provide few such opportunities. They are boring, especially for children.

Displaying Skills

The displaying of skills is an important way in which esteem needs are met. For some people, the public display of skills is a basic way of achieving esteem, but to others the opportunities to display their own skills to themselves is sufficient. These observations seem to hold true across the stages in the life cycle and across all cultures, although the manifestations vary considerably from context to context.

All social and physical environments provide some opportunity to display skills. A rich environment, however, is one that provides many opportunities, both formal and informal, for people to display skills. One of the ways in which people test themselves with success is in driving an automobile. This is a partial explanation for the importance of automobiles in people's lives. Sometimes people push beyond their driving skill levels with disastrous results. This outcome is particularly prevalent among adolescent males and the elderly—two groups of Americans who have a strong need for high esteem but are not generally accorded it by the remainder of society.

The design implications of providing settings for such activities can be divided into the same two types as for the development of knowledge and skills: formal and informal. The distinction between them is very much blurred because informal displays can take place in formal settings and vice versa, but formal settings are designed specifically for displays. A variety of opportunities is needed in the everyday world so that individuals have a chance to display their own abilities.

Formal settings include such places as classrooms, offices, theaters, athletic fields, and other recreational locations. Such settings provide not only for the display of skills by performers but also for the potential aesthetic appreciation and learning on the part of those watching. Informal settings are not specifically designed for performance but may involve them—kitchens, parks, playgrounds, laundromats. Almost anyplace has the potential for the display of skills, although not necessarily the skills people want to display or, if they do, not in a socially acceptable manner.

Sometimes the skills themselves are antisocial even if they do fulfill a person's esteem needs through opportunities for display. In this case, society is better off if opportunities for such displays are limited. It is impossible to eliminate them although the built environment can be "deopportunized" (Wise 1982). Logically it would seem easier to deal with the problem through the provision of alternative possibilities, but this is not necessarily easy in the United States because these alternatives are expensive. There are also disagreements about what constitutes legitimate displays. Attitudes toward such displays as graffiti differ considerably, partially depending on their context. Graffiti is socially acceptable if properly channeled through formal institutions but generally not as individual acts of frustration or of territorial control.

The lack of opportunity to display skills seems to be a particular problem during adolescence. In the United States male adolescents seem to be increasingly turning to antisocial behavior, including violence toward weaker members of society, to secure a feeling of self-esteem through the admiration of their peers. Kevin Lynch (1977) showed that young adolescents in many countries have few opportunities for testing their abilities in unstructured ways. Florence Ladd (1978) and Colin Ward (1990) point out the difficulties that many city children in the United States and the United Kingdom have in finding outlets for legitimate informal adventure, self-testing, and the display of skills. Suburban American children are often even worse off (see Lynch 1977; Popenoe 1977). The environment simply does not contain the appropriate behavior settings. The result is often illegal or illegitimate behavior. There are two possible solutions: to channel behavior into other activities through social programs, and to change the environment—social and physical. Neither is easy to achieve.

Displaying Status

Status is displayed in a number of ways: through one's socioeconomic achievements, through the amount of privacy one is afforded, through the way one talks, through membership in institutions, through the activities in which one engages, through the objects one owns, and through the environment one occupies. Not only are the built environment's characteristics important but also the nature of its creation—who the designer was and the nature of the design process. As a result, the urban designer's concern is with how the built environment communicates status, the normative question of the degree to which status differences should be displayed, and who controls the aesthetic qualities of the environment, either through its actual design or through the guidelines that are used to shape it.

Privacy, Community, and People's Esteem Needs

One way of enhancing people's self-esteem is through providing them with the privacy they seek or enabling them to attain it. A sure way to reduce their self-esteem is to remove opportunities for privacy. Being part of a community held in high esteem also contributes to one's own feelings of esteem. Having sufficient privacy may be a necessary prerequisite for reaching out to communal organizations (Altman 1975; Michelson 1976; Rapoport 1977).

Photograph by Ruth Durack

1. Street Performer

2. Los Angeles

Figure 14–4: Legitimate and Illegitimate Displays
What are regarded as legitimate and illegitimate displays of behavior in public spaces vary from culture to culture and even within a culture. Many public displays of behavior or performances enrich the lives of others (1). The displays we create for each other help individuals fulfill their self-esteem needs. Some are regarded as legitimate but others not (2). Committing a crime might raise the self-esteem of the perpetrator, but society benefits when there are opportunities for legitimate adventure (Ladd 1978). Providing such opportunities is largely a social planning task, but it has many urban design ramifications.

The amount of privacy one desires for specific activities is very much culture-bound (see also Chapters 12 and 13). It varies considerably among the populations of the United States. In addition, the amount of privacy accorded to a person or a group is closely associated with social status. The higher the status the more privacy is accorded people. The architectural mechanisms for attaining privacy are well known (see Chapter 12). The major issue is that the more control one has the more one's esteem is boosted. Such control also contributes to the achievement of more basic needs such as the need for security.

Behavior Settings, Land Uses, and Self-Esteem

The values associated with a particular place are a function not only of the quality of its milieu but also of the activities that take place there, and of the people who engage in them. Our response is to the bundle of variables (Rapoport 1977). Thus the attitudes people have toward areas of the city are associated with the land uses, behavior settings, and people (Perin 1977). Low-status areas in new towns tend to be located near industrial areas. There is some legitimacy in doing this in terms of giving access to jobs, but the location establishes a negative image of the area in many people's minds. In nonmanufacturing new towns such as Columbia, Maryland, or Las Colinas, Texas, the population is generally middle class and the residential areas are not socially differentiated, although components of their neighborhoods may be of different residential building types.

The status of a residential area depends on the type of homes, the types of shops and other facilities, the way the vegetation is handled, and the nature of the locale with its *panoramic,* or *contemplative,* views (Berleant 1988). The status of a precinct of a downtown area or the whole downtown is dependent on the types of buildings and on the social status of the companies located there, the land-use mix, the spaciousness of the sidewalks, and the nature of the skyline. Indeed, cities vie with each other to have dramatic skylines to show their status and so to boost their self-esteem, their self-images.

In New York City, the lower Manhattan area, with Wall Street and its international firms, is more prestigious than the mixed-use area of midtown Manhattan. Fifth Avenue has its own reputation because of the prestige of the retail stores (along with Rockefeller Center, St. Patrick's Cathedral, and Central Park) that are located along it. Its wide sidewalks and cosmopolitan crowd add to its distinction. All major cities have such distinctive areas that give them a variety and excitement that homogeneous new towns lack. The urban design task is to help create such a variety without infringing on the self-esteem of the people associated with other areas of the city.

Many urban designers in the United States today are strong advocates for mixed-use developments as a reaction to the boredom of the work of the Modernists. There needs to be considerable caution in mixing uses in developing or maintaining the specific qualities of specific areas of the city. Mixed-use areas offer much for many people, but the nature of the mix is important. Mixed uses should not be seen in reaction to urban design efforts of the past but in terms of the needs they might fulfill today and tomorrow. The city planning and urban design movements favoring segregated land-use areas were originally responses to the insalubrious conditions in which many people lived. Now segregated land use is often a mechanism for maintaining the prestige of an area. People are prepared and desire to trade the benefit of mixed uses, especially for helping to meet the cognitive needs of children, for an environment that meets their self-esteem needs.

The fight to exclude certain building types from areas is often based on neither the building nor the use but on the perception of the nature of the people who will be using them. A proposed church may be fine on an empty lot in a residential area in suburban America, but neither a mosque nor a Hindu temple would be developed. The reverse may be true in India. The overt argument against such a development may well be presented in terms of the traffic such a facility will generate. Indeed, oversized facilities and the traffic they generate can easily lead to neighborhood deterioration (Gardiner 1978), but the fear is often of people different from oneself—a fear of the unknown impinging on one's need for security.

Status, Culture, and Environmental Display

The built environment is an important communicator of status because it is rich in symbolic meanings based on the associations between its specific patterns and the people who inhabit it, or did inhabit it. People read meanings about status and personalities into these linkages in surprisingly consistent ways within a culture, both in terms of housing (Nasar 1988a) and neighborhoods (Cherulnik 1982).

The residential environment that one chooses to inhabit is selected not only for instrumental reasons (nearness to work, to kin, etc.) but also for status reasons. Some people choose environments below their full purchasing power, others overextend themselves. Both groups are communicating a message about how they want their relative statuses to be perceived and, implicitly, the importance of the built environment as a symbol of who they are.

The attitude to the display of status through the patterns of the built environment varies considerably from culture to culture, within multicultural countries such as the United States, and from subculture to subculture. There are also personality differences involved; extroverts and introverts have very different attitudes toward the display of status (Cooper Marcus 1974). Indeed, the definition of these two personality types is partly based on this distinction (Jung 1968). It must be remembered that

1. Philadelphia

2. Philadelphia

3. Philadelphia

Figure 14–5: The Prestige of Residential Areas
Different areas of a city have different prestige levels not because of their architectural quality per se, although it contributes to the prestige, but because of the overall ambience that exists in each. The ambience depends on the mix and nature of the activities that take place there and the prestige of those people involved in them as well as the nature of the built environment. These three rowhouse areas of Philadelphia (1, 2, and 3) have essentially the same building type, but the streets, paving, quality of trees, and mix of uses differ. They are perceived as having different levels of prestige by both design professionals and laypeople.

Status Differentiation Through Design

The behavioral program implicit in the generic design proposals of the Rationalist branch of the Modern movement was generally to obscure the status differences between groups of people. If one examines Toni Garnier's *La Cité Industrielle* (Figs. 2–10(1,2)), Richard Neutra's proposal for Los Angeles (Fig. 2–10(3)), or Le Corbusier's scheme for the City for 3 Million (Fig. 2–10(4)) or *La Ville Radieuse,* there is little in the symbolic aesthetics of the environment to differentiate between the residential areas inhabited by people of different socioeconomic status. The same is true of the original plan for Brasilia, although status differences have emerged over time as the result of differences in the quality of the maintenance of buildings, the development of suburban areas for high officials, and the growth of squatter settlements on the periphery of the federal capital. In contrast, the behavioral program for the design of Chandigarh led to a clear differentiation

between people by status. Knowing the zone in which a person lives immediately tells other people who know Chandigarh that person's social status. Distance from the capitol complex, size of housing, and the space allocated to people are immediate cues. The transfer of Rationalist design principles to the United States resulted in high-status office complexes and low-status residential ones—a major environmental Freudian slip (Verge 1992; see also Wolfe 1981).

In much Post-Modernist design in the United States, the concern has not been with social equality, but rather with providing for the esteem needs of specific people and corporations by having highly renowned architects produce building designs with high-status connotations. Indeed, the architect's name is often part of the advertising used to rent space in new office buildings. The buildings are even called "signature buildings." The search for prestige through architecture, landscape architecture, and urban design is part of the history of each field. Historically, there are many examples of the display of power through design—the Rome of Pope Sixtus the Fifth, the Paris of the Medicci queens, the Paris of Napoleon III and Hauss-

1. Hopkinson House, Philadelphia (1950s). Stonorov and Hawes, Architects

2. Heurtley House, Oak Park, Illinois (1902). Frank Lloyd Wright, Architect

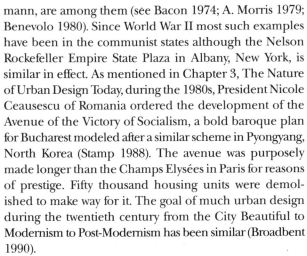

3. Tegeler Hafen, Berlin (1980). Moore, Ruble, Yudell, Architects

Figure 14–6: Individual Displays in Residential Environments
An objective of Rationalist Modern architecture was to eliminate personal displays of social status in cities (Figs. 2–10(5), 3–4(1), and 10–9(2)). In parts of the world and among some groups in the United States, this anonymity is desired (1), although the buildings they chose are statements of status. Other groups seek the opportunity to display their status. This is easier in a single-family home when a prestigious architect was the designer (2). Much Post-Modern design seeks to provide heterogeneity in design (3), but Neo-Rationalist design continues to frown on any display of individualism other than the architect's.

mann, are among them (see Bacon 1974; A. Morris 1979; Benevolo 1980). Since World War II most such examples have been in the communist states although the Nelson Rockefeller Empire State Plaza in Albany, New York, is similar in effect. As mentioned in Chapter 3, The Nature of Urban Design Today, during the 1980s, President Nicole Ceausescu of Romania ordered the development of the Avenue of the Victory of Socialism, a bold baroque plan for Bucharest modeled after a similar scheme in Pyongyang, North Korea (Stamp 1988). The avenue was purposely made longer than the Champs Elysées in Paris for reasons of prestige. Fifty thousand housing units were demolished to make way for it. The goal of much urban design during the twentieth century from the City Beautiful to Modernism to Post-Modernism has been similar (Broadbent 1990).

Urban designers need to be able to perceive the potential prestige of a design proposal through the eyes of future inhabitants, not architectural critics. The 1963 East Harlem project carefully designed to meet user's needs was rejected by its potential users because it was not prestigious enough (see Fig. 2–1). Les Echelles du Baroque,

a housing project in Montparnesse in the heart of Paris, and Les Arcades du Lac in St. Quentin en Yvellines (see Fig. 2–15(3)), both designed by Ricardo Bofill and the Taller, for instance, use the classical orders as a direct referent and a large scale of elements of built form to establish a sense of prestige. They have become well-known architectural icons. To people who live in them they are supposed to be home and a home environment. The complexes are prestigious because they are monumental and because they are the work of a prestigious architect. The degree to which they are prestigious places to live depends on sociological variables and on the more mundane concerns of everyday life.

The same concerns are raised in the design of non-residential areas such as office complexes or the insertion of a new building into an existing high-density area. Corporations are willing to spend substantial sums for prestige reasons and to possess the symbols of power (Lasswell 1979). Cities have similar concerns when promoting their self-image. An urban design with prestigious buildings and prominent works of art is often the vehicle for promoting that image as much as or even more than the nature

1. State Capitol, St. Paul

2. World Financial Center, Battery Park City, New York

3. "Red Square," University of Washington, Seattle

Figure 14-7: Monumental Urban Designs

Monumentality generally refers to the spaciousness, large scale, and solidity of the built environment. The search for the monumental was something sought by the City Beautiful movement (1). In recent large-scale urban designs the search has been a characteristic of much European Neo-Rational architecture (e.g., Fig. 2–15(3)). In the United States it is represented in the search for prestige in the design of such places as Albany's Empire State Plaza (Fig. 3–7(4)) and Battery Park City's World Financial Center (2). Such places, while impressive, can also be dull except when packed with people (3).

of the activities that take place within it or the physiological comfort the environment so created (Strauss 1961).

Maintenance Level and the Prestige of Areas of the City

One of the major factors in establishing environmental quality is the quality of maintenance of a place. Relatively poor but well looked after places exhibit the sense of self-esteem and care of the people and organizations that inhabit them. Maintenance level is not only a mark of territorial claim but also a contributor to the perception of order (and orderliness) of a place. Many American cities have substantial areas that show considerable neglect. There are boarded-up houses, trash-strewn streets littered with debris, and abandoned motor vehicles. They not only fail to provide a positive educative environment, they also condemn all but the strongest people to a feeling of self-doubt. Is it surprising that the achievement of prestige in such areas is often through antisocial behavior?

It is not, however, just such areas that have problems. A number of well-known and prestigious places have been allowed to deteriorate to a point of tawdriness. This deterioration is most noticeable in cities but applies to many suburbs and small towns across the country. The problem is not uniquely American, though the lack of action may well be. Plans were recently announced to revamp the Champs Elysées in Paris, perhaps the world's most famous boulevard, by closing two traffic lanes to make sitting on the sidewalks more pleasant and by planting trees to restore a sense of order to the street. The boulevard's decline has been a slow one and has had much to do with the effect of land rents on occupancy. The decline of the Plaza d'Italia in New Orleans has been more rapid. Its materials require a high level of maintenance, which it has not received. Consequently it is badly deteriorated. While architects still regard it as having prestige, the New Orleans City Council recently (1991) removed its status as a public place. Its experience is not unique. There are many languishing fountains in the public squares of the United States. With the decline of public services, private groups have created their own organizations for maintaining the public realm (e.g., the Association for Portland's Progress in Oregon).

Controlling Designs and the Design Process

There are two areas of concern that affect how urban design is carried out in order to afford people an opportunity to develop a degree of self-esteem. The first has to do with participation in the design process before a design is created, and the second has to do with the degree of control an individual or a group has in operating and/or personalizing a design once it has been completed. Attaining self-esteem through the exertion of control over one's own life is what unites the two issues intellectually. Such control displays one's skills and one's status.

The Design Process

All urban design products reflect the way decisions have been made and the power distribution among those involved in making them. They act as symbols of the process. Having an internationally renowned architect design a scheme, as Le Corbusier did Chandigarh, may be a prestigious action however well or poorly the development works when built. There are, however, a number of psychologically complex effects on perceptions of the quality of a design, depending on how the decision-making and design process is conducted and on people's expectations of their roles in making decisions. In the United States there is considerable public expectation of participation in making design decisions about the public realm.

For people to maintain their self-esteem, they often fail to recognize that the decisions that they have made are not in their own self-interest. The consequence is that if people have made decisions of their own free will about the environments in which they choose to work or live, they will evaluate those environments highly even if the environments are not good ones given objective measures in those people's own terms. Individuals (and groups of people) tend to avoid being in a situation of *cognitive dissonance* that affects their self-esteem (see Festinger 1962). Similarly, if they are involved in the design process, they will have a degree of self-esteem because their opinions are being heeded. The impact is that the resultant environment will be closer to their needs than if they had not been involved. They will also tend to regard the decisions that they have made highly, whatever the outcome. In contrast, if people are forced to live in environments because they have no choice, they will have a relatively low self-esteem (in that respect) and will be unlikely to evaluate those environments highly, however good they may objectively be seen to be. Thus, the roles of participation, choice, and allied feelings of self-esteem are important variables to consider in postoccupancy evaluation studies, and also in the way that one goes about the program writing and designing process. Similarly, if the developers are involved in writing urban design guidelines that will affect their own work, they will be more likely to follow them partly because they will understand their logic and partly because they have been involved in their creation.

A number of commentators (e.g., R. Goodman 1971) regard the urban renewal efforts in the United States during the 1950s and 1960s as a symbol of the effort of middle-class society, the building industry, and the architectural profession to keep the poor in their place. This observation leaves the urban designer in a quandary. On one hand, designers are obligated to do their best in creating a good future. On the other hand, if they pursue what they perceive to be the best design at odds with what the community with whom they are designing says they want, they are unlikely to attain a good solution because of the affront to the self-esteem of the community. This situation holds even if what the community says it wants is not logically in their own self-interest. However, this observation may apply more to low-status communities than to high ones, whose people are able to acknowledge they were wrong without losing face. This dilemma is one of a number of procedural issues that have to be resolved in designing for the future (see Chapter 22, Procedural Issues in Urban Design). To make the situation even more complex, an urban design originally held in low esteem may acquire high esteem through its history over subsequent generations. The reverse is also true.

Personalizing Designs

Some architects have recognized the importance of people being able to shape their own environments to meet their own activity and aesthetic needs in building their self-esteem. Indeed, Le Corbusier showed considerably less dismay than other architects over the multiple changes made by the residents of the Pessac housing he designed (Boudon 1972). Many artists and architects are too much concerned with their own self-esteem to be tolerant of their designs being examined and changed by others. The lasting furor over the removal of the *Tilted Arc* sculpture from the Federal Plaza in New York City exemplifies this feeling (see Fig. 3–15(3); Weyergraff-Serra and Buskirk 1990).

Much concern has been expressed in the United States for low-income people and the inability of the public sector to provide good living conditions for them within the resources that are available except in "hard architecture" buildings—buildings where personalization causes damage (Sommer 1974). The result is myriad rules specifying forbidden behaviors. The impact of these rules is to reduce the esteem of the people living in those environments. High-income people work out their needs very well either through careful selection of environments in which to live or through designing for themselves with their own architects. They have considerable choice—an esteem-boosting factor in itself.

In urban design, issues of the personalization of the environment relate primarily to the exteriors of buildings rather than to their interiors. When a section of a city has a uniform character that gives it its status, should people be allowed to alter the exterior of their own homes or places of business as they will? The argument for them being able to do so is that cities are always changing and reflect the individual aspirations of their inhabitants. The argument against allowing them to do so is that making such changes infringes on the processes whereby esteem and/or aesthetic needs of other people are met.

THE DESIGN PROGRAM: CREATING THE MILIEU

In developing a design agenda, and/or a design response to a behavioral program, a number of questions arise: "How does one design for individuals' development and display of competence?" "How does one deal with the symbolism of status?"

The Development and Display of Competence

In thinking about the design implications of providing settings for the development and display of competence, there is a need to distinguish once again between formal and informal settings. The role of formal education was a central concern in many of the generic plans and utopian proposals of the nineteenth and early twentieth centuries. The relationship of school to home has been previously described in this book as a major organizing concept for the neighborhood unit plan. The distribution of schools in relationship to residential areas has been a basic consideration in the new towns built throughout the world. Similarly, many planning texts (e.g., Chapin and Kaiser 1979) give guidelines and methods for working out the distribution of schools and their spatial requirements in urban areas. The debate over the nature and distribution of formal educational opportunities is, however, a highly political one that seldom focuses on a comprehensive view of education.

The design implications of considering the whole environment as an educative one are explored in Chapter 16. Suffice to say here that the structure of the environment not only provides learning opportunities but can also be regarded as a testing ground for people's competence in carrying out various activities. People who learn and can demonstrate that learning effectively will have a feeling of self-esteem; those people who find either difficult will have a lowered self-esteem. This observation applies to such behaviors as task completion, wayfinding, being able to use the environment without impediments, social or physical, and not being socially isolated because one cannot legitimately gain access to the behavior settings in which one wishes to participate. To help people attain a feeling of self-esteem the environment must have

sufficient behavior settings to not be overpopulated—that is, not have too many people for them to operate well (Srivastava 1975; Bechtel 1977)—and the layout must be otherwise usable to the people who inhabit it.

The Symbolic Aesthetics of Status

Given a behavioral program specifying the nature of the self-esteem that people need to be able or are striving to attain in a proposed development, there is much that an urban designer can do. One of the goals of urban design is to create environments containing the patterns that communicate meaning (ideas, messages) of importance in establishing a sense of self-esteem for the groups of concern through the associations they carry with other places, people, ideas. There is an increasing body of empirical knowledge on this most slippery issue in the purview of urban design (Broadbent, Bunt, and Jencks 1980; Rapoport 1982; Lang 1987a). The designer must, however, first understand the variables involved if sensible questions are to be asked.

The overall configuration of buildings, their spatial distribution, the character of the open space, the materials of both the artificial and natural components of the built environment, the way they are illuminated, by day and by night, their colors, and the character of the nonvisual environment (its odors, touches, temperatures, sounds) all carry symbolic meanings. While there have been a number of advances in the analytical methods designers can use to predict user responses to the environment (Hershberger and Cass 1988), designers do not have a good categorization of the correlations/linkages between specific patterns of the environment and the statuses they communicate at their disposal, nor do designers have a clear method of ascertaining them. Much is still left to the designer's subjective judgment, but understanding the basic variables of concern allows sensible questions to be asked about the linkages between environmental patterns and the meanings they communicate to specific groups of people.

The Spatial Configuration of Cities and Their Precincts

Some spatial characteristics of a city afford their users a greater feeling of self-esteem than others. As balance theory would suggest, the basic hypothesis is that people's feelings of self-esteem are heightened when they use environments that they like, that they associate with prestigious people, and that they have control over (Heider 1958; see also Chapter 1).

The Geometry of the Built Environment

Sooner or later an urban designer has to make a decision about the geometry of the environment. The

1. Fifth Avenue, New York

2. Washington, DC

3. Metropark, New Jersey

Figure 14–8: Spaciousness and Prestige in Urban Design
Spaciousness is often linked with luxury in the way that many consumption items are. Broad streets, wide sidewalks (1), and broad vistas (2) have long been associated with power and wealth. Such characteristics tend to be associated with planned capital cities—as seen in Washington, DC (2), New Delhi, and Canberra—but there are many portions of existing cities that have this character. It is also sought after in many office campuses, or parks, today (3). Places with such characteristics can also be dull public realms if there are insufficient behavior settings to sustain them.

layout can be designed to meet a multitude of functions, but the geometry has a function as a geometry regardless of the other purposes it fulfills. People respond to its order, or coherence, and its complexity—its formal characteristics per se (Kaplan and Kaplan 1982; Heath 1988). They also respond to the symbolism of the geometry.

While questions of order and disorder, simplicity and complexity, have attracted the attention of architects such as Robert Venturi (1966) and behavioral scientists (e.g., Arnheim 1977), they have not been applied to the urban environment in any systematic way. An ordered urban environment is one in which some fundamental principle or set of principles is perceived to dictate the arrangement of its components. In this sense it is related to the concept of *legibility* developed by Kevin Lynch (1960) to discuss wayfinding in cities. Stephen and Rachel Kaplan (1982) explain legibility as the "characteristic of an environment that looks as if one could explore extensively without getting lost"—without losing one's self-esteem for the moment, at least.

A complex urban structure is one with a large number of components and/or a large number of ordering principles involved. When the principles support each other, the environment may be both complex and ordered; when they do not, the environment appears to be disordered (Berlyne 1974). Social significance is usually associated with the formality of the order, the clarity of the form. It is also related to the symbolic meanings of the environment, acquired social meanings, and how interesting they are—the degree of ordered complexity they possess (Heath 1988).

Most of the empirical research on pattern perception focuses on the two-dimensional world of diagrams on paper. It is the four-dimensional world of urban patterns that is important to urban design. The experiencing of the geometry of a city is really one of sequentially experiencing its three-dimensional layout over time and the degree of order and degree of complexity it possesses as it is perceived over time (Gibson 1950, 1966, 1979; Cullen 1961; Thiel 1961, forthcoming; Halprin 1965; see also Chapter 17, Meeting Aesthetic Needs).

The Character of Open Space

The prestige of an area of a city is frequently associated with the amount of well-kept open space that it possesses. In suburban areas, it is generally more prestigious for a householder to have a large lot rather than a small one, although the design of some prestigious areas is based on the observation that some people are prepared to trade size of plot for convenience of location. The single-family detached home is the preferred and, to many people, the socially acceptable type of housing in the United States and many other countries (Lansing, Marans, and Zehner 1970; Michelson 1976; Audirac, Shermeyen, and Smith 1990). It is not always financially accessible to people. People may still have the goal of owning such a house one day, and their self-esteem is partially dependent on striving for that goal, however, illusory it might be (Thorne, Hall, and Munro-Clark 1982).

The nature of streets, the amount of traffic, the nature of the sidewalks, if any, the nature of the buildings enclosing the space, and the nature of the vegetation, and the way water is used in the open spaces are all variables that contribute to the degree of prestige of a locale. The configuration, the degree of its formality, the degree of compliance to a landscape design ideology, and the degree of control over nature that a design displays all communicate meaning (Nohl 1988). Open space also provides for the opportunities of vistas of a panoramic nature or of a more enclosed type. The control or ownership of views is prestigious and can be bought and sold on the real estate market.

Architectural Character

The architectural character of the built environment can be assessed in terms of the variables that contribute to its texture—the massing of its buildings, the way they relate to the street, and their detailing at a smaller scale. In between, one is dealing with the nature of the articulation of buildings themselves and how they enclose space. Certainly the size of a building or public space is linked to its social significance, and the endeavor to build the world's tallest building is closely linked to the search for self-esteem of a city, organization, or architect (Heath 1988).

Often almost directly opposed to spaciousness (although it need not necessarily be) is the height of the skyline of a city. Tall buildings have the signature of power (Lasswell 1979). Chicago continues to vie with New York City to have tall buildings. The 1,012-foot StratoSphere owned by the Vegas World Hotel and Casino is under construction in Las Vegas. Philadelphia, with its abandonment of the gentleman's agreement not to build above William Penn's eyeline atop City Hall, has joined the throng. The cluster of new tall buildings has engendered considerable pride on the part of the city's citizens, although it seems to have done little for the its overall economy (see Fig. 14-9(5,6)). Hong Kong's Central Plaza now being built in 1993 will be the tallest building in Asia—for a year or so, at least. Almost inevitably, a city with many tall buildings gives up certain street-level qualities to attain an impressive skyline, or, as John Kaliski notes about Houston, "It is great from afar, far from great" (Ghirardo 1987). As the verse states:

THE
SKY-
SCRAPER
T A L L
IS   A
WONDER
TO ALL
A THING
TO ADMIRE
BEYOND
QUESTION
Butoh!downbelowwherepedestriansgo
itcertainlyaddstocongestion
(Source unknown)

Washington, DC, and San Francisco are two of the few cities in the United States that have consciously restricted the height of buildings. In Washington, DC, there is a height line for all buildings that has the effect of emphasizing the Capitol building and, also, affects the configuration of use types of buildings—they tend not to follow standard American slab patterns and sizes. San Francisco is paying considerable attention to the amount of building in its central business district and to the effect of the buildings' heights on the quality of light in street-level public spaces. Some cities have zoning ordinances aimed to shape the skyline, recognizing that the prestige gained by the height of buildings has to be weighed against other concerns. In Bellevue, Washington, for instance, the goal is to have the tallest buildings in the center of its business district, with building heights diminishing toward the periphery to meet standard suburban development heights in a wedding-cake–like manner (see Fig. 6-4(3)).

The formality of the architecture of a place, whatever style it is in, is closely linked to its prestige value. For some people (e.g., the clients of the avant-garde architects), however, being part of the artistic world is highly prestigious. For other people, being in the mainstream of correct style is more rewarding and shows that they belong to a social world acceptable to them. Most such observations and corroborative research have been done on individual buildings (Eaton 1969; Nasar 1988a) rather than on urban designs, but the same principles probably hold true at the larger scale. Leonard Eaton (1969) has shown that Howard Van Doren Shaw's house designs and those of his contemporary Frank Lloyd Wright appealed to two very distinct groups of clients, both of whom had a high degree of self-esteem. Shaw's clients derived their esteem through their inheritances and their roles in the social life of Chicago, Wright's derived theirs from their achievements in manufacturing—they were self-made people. Certain styles are associated with certain taste cultures, which in turn are associated with particular people and/or views of the world.

1. Lower Manhattan

2. San Francisco

3. Pittsburgh

4. Dallas

5. Philadelphia (1985)

6. Philadelphia (1992)

Figure 14-9: City Skylines

New York City is famous for its skyline. The Wall Street area is one of the world's most prestigious locations for major business corporations (1). San Francisco is one of the few American cities concerned about restricting the burgeoning height of its buildings as a matter of public policy (2). Other cities vie for self-esteem by the number and height of their tall buildings (3,4). Chicago's John Hancock and Sear's Tower buildings lead that city's striving for height (see Fig. 10-7(1)), and a proposed tower there will, if built, be the world's tallest building. The price paid in terms of comfort at the street level can be high. Washington, DC's decision to limit the height of its buildings results in an environment of a very different character (see Fig. 8-7(2)) from New York's and Chicago's. Philadelphia, until 1984, had a gentlemen's agreement that the height of its buildings not be above the eyes of William Penn on City Hall (i.e., 491 feet (5)). The substantial increase in the height of its tallest buildings (6) has boosted its self-image and does enable its central business district to be seen from substantial distances—but in doing so it lost a powerful myth.

The Materials of the Built Environment

Some materials, and the quality of workmanship they require to be used effectively, have a positive association in people's minds, while others have a negative value. These values are not necessarily related to the performance of the material on another dimension of functionality—their susceptibility to wear, for instance. It is the characteristic that Rudolf Arnheim (1966) refers to as "high definition." It is not simply the visual quality of the materials but also their haptic, sonic, and increasingly olfactory natures that provide the basis for the associations they evoke. Natural materials are generally held in higher esteem than artificial ones. The use of artificial materials to simulate the natural at a lower cost is, by and large, to attain a heightened esteem value. There are taste culture factors involved in whether the artificial in this case is really perceived to be higher in value because some people maintain that materials should be true to their own natures.

Certainly the quality of materials enclosing the open spaces of a city is an important contributor to the esteem in which a place is held. Tom Heath (1988) notes:

> One thinks of the Erectheion or the Barcelona Pavilion by Mies van der Rohe; in the same way, the quality of paving [visually, haptically, and sonically], of street furniture (such as railings, lamps, and fountains) and of the surrounding buildings has often been used to mark the importance of public spaces.

The public has considerable difficulty in coming to grips with cheap material being used for an intellectual aesthetic effect (e.g., Frank Gehry's use of chainlink fence and corrugated iron in his own home).

The Nature of the Illumination

There are two types of illumination of concern to the urban designer and to any other designer: natural and artificial. The concern is with the appearance of the city and its precincts and their elements during the day and at night. Bright, sunny, and colorful environments generally lift one's spirits during the day. Unfortunately, many places in cities dominated by high-rise buildings do not achieve this result because of the tradeoff made between the quality of light at the ground level for other perceived benefits. The quality of artificial light at night in urban places, other than providing for task and security reasons, has only been considered in very few American cities.

The selling of natural light, particularly sunlight, by allowing buildings to cast shadows over streets and plazas throughout much of the day in return for some other public benefit has become a major factor in urban design since the beginning of the 1970s, as already mentioned (see also Barnett 1974, 1982, 1987). The demand by developers to build taller buildings for prestige and financial

1. Philadelphia

2. Xerox Building, Las Colinas, Texas

3. Independence Hall and Square, Philadelphia

Figure 14-10: The Nature of Prestigious Buildings
The term "signature building" has come into common usage to refer to a building by a famous architect. The building becomes prestigious because of its association with the architect. Philadelphia's Center City (1) now has buildings by I. M. Pei, Helmut Jahn, and Kohn Pederson and Fox. Glass towers (e.g., 2) may be prestigious to some but not usually to those concerned with urban design issues. Some buildings are prestigious and contribute to people's self-esteem not because of their architecture or architects but because of their association with famous events or people (3).

return has led cities having fiscal crises to seek the private sector to pay for public services either directly through linkage programs or indirectly through increased taxes. The carrot has been to allow developers to build taller buildings. Dark urban streets do not, however, enhance the pedestrian's feelings of comfort, security, or self-esteem; as a result, the shadowing effect of buildings has become a major issue in urban design politics.

Urban places are also seen at night, and so the way areas of the city are illuminated, the patterns, degree of illumination, type of light, and light sources are all contributing factors to the aesthetic effect of a city or its part (Watson 1990). Well-lit places contribute not only to people's feelings of security but also to their sense of well-being. The aesthetic effect of lighting is seldom given the attention it deserves in either architectural or urban design. Not only are plazas and street lighting of concern but also the use of lighting in advertising. Places such as Times Square in New York and Piccadilly Circus in London owe much of their character to lighted advertising. The urban designer's problem is how to establish design principles and guidelines to make such places less tawdry during the day.

One of the few American cities to have a self-consciously designed lighting scheme is Milwaukee, Wisconsin (Davidson 1991). The design prescribes selective illumination of streets based on Kevin Lynch's principles of making cities legible (Lynch 1960). The goal is to give coherence to a district and its subsettings. For example, low-level street lighting is contrasted with high-pressure sodium lamps in cannister fixtures for illuminating recent architecture of note and monumental processional avenues. Such a concern is primarily aesthetic but it also serves purposes of prestige.

Pigmentation

The psychology of color has long been the subject of architects' attention, and the use of color is reputed to have behavioral implications (Birren 1965, 1982; Porter and Mikellides 1976). In Western societies at least, colors are divided into warm and cool. The warm colors, from yellows to red, are supposed to be arousing and exciting; the cool colors, greens, blues, violets, are reputed to be soothing. The research on color is highly contradictory; much has no empirical base and is simply an advocacy for more colorful environments within the taste preference of the writer.

The colors of the built environment can carry symbolic meanings. Some of these meanings are by explicit social conventions, but other meanings are associated with taste cultures within a society. Both sets of meanings are symbols of membership in a group and/or status. In the United States at present, good taste tends to favor pastel colors. Bright colors tend to be associated with lower status. The reverse view is, however, held by some

1. Washington, DC

2. 16th Street Mall, Denver

3. Hutton Center, Orange County, California

Figure 14–11: Detailing the Public Realm and Prestige

While Washington, DC, has considerable prestige as the capital of the United States and through its overall design and spaciousness, there is much that is poorly detailed and unkempt (1). Considerable effort has been made in many places in the country to pay attention to the detailing of the public environment and to maintaining it in good condition once it has been established (see also Chapter 17). Although they are very different places, both the 16th Street Mall in Denver (2) and Hutton Center in Southern California (3) have these characteristics. The first is public territory and the second really only semipublic.

Photograph by Alix Verge

1. Chicago

Photograph by Steve King

2. San Francisco

Collection of the author

3. New York City

Figure 14–12: Lighting and the Urban Environment
The lighting of the public realm of cities serves many purposes. It provides sufficient illumination for activities, it entertains, it gives visual order to a city, it gives identity to places, it brings our attention to their specific features, it advertises. The quality of lighting, and of signs and signage, also serves aesthetic purposes and can enhance our sense of pride if well executed.

subcultures within the U.S. population. Color usage in the United States is very much subject to the vagaries of fashion and the search for novelty in design. Some societies, in contrast, have explicit color conventions for buildings. For instance, in parts of India today (e.g., Jodhpur) only Brahmins may paint their houses blue, while in imperial China brighter colors were associated with high status. They were reserved for palaces, temples, and other important buildings, while lower-status buildings were made less colorful, often artificially.

There is indeed a ladder of taste in most Western countries. In the United States it parallels but is not uniquely associated with socioeconomic status. Each group aspires to have what they perceive, rightly or wrongly, are the possessions and symbols of the group above it. Oscar Newman's modification of the design of a low-income housing project at Clason Point, New York (see Fig. 12–11(2,3)), based on his analysis of higher-income-group preferences, including those for color, has been a great success among the residents, raising their self-esteem considerably (Newman 1976). The changes to the building façades are more highly evaluated than the new lighting fixtures, benches, or the reorganization of the open space to create clearer territorial differentiation (Kohn, Franck, Fox 1975).

Deviations from the accepted range of colors used in a society also carry messages, but it is more the act of deviation than the actual color used that seems to be important. One of the impacts of Post-Modernism has been the introduction of colors deviant from the norm as an effort to attract attention and show status by doing so. The goal was also to get away from the grays of raw concrete so loved by the Modernists but never embraced by the majority of the lay population in the United States other than the artistic avant-garde. The nouveau riche were never self-assured enough to accept it either. The use of color to enliven a place and to show concern for people also raises their self-esteem, provided the colors chosen are not too deviant from habituation levels.

Land Uses, Activity Patterns, and Status

Almost all societies are structured into social hierarchies. A person can achieve self-esteem at any level in the hierarchy. The nature of the physical environment, artificial and natural, inhabited by a person says much about that person's status in society and the lifestyles associated with it. The city is structured into districts with different characteristics in terms of the built environment, the activities they house, and the people who inhabit them.

Many people in modern society have a high degree of mobility. They choose from among the city's offerings those behavior settings that are congenial to them and reinforce their self-esteem. Other people are trapped because of poverty or racial or social discrimination in areas where the streets are poorly designed, treeless, ill-kept, and have a mix of uses that are unpleasant to them. A good society surely tries to raise the quality of such places in the terms of their inhabitants' views.

There is a certain financial utility to having old, poorly maintained areas of the city. Rents are low, so businesses can start up there and artists can find studio accommodation. The present urban design task is to develop policies that enable such places to exist without reducing the perceived quality of the whole environment. The goal would be to ensure that such areas are at least not decrepit.

Designing for Good Maintenance

Poorly kept environments do nothing to help one's self-esteem as one moves through them except by providing a yardstick of comparison to one's own environment if it is better kept. People simply do not like to be in poorly maintained places and will seek other places if they have a choice. Those who have to endure poorly maintained and serviced areas can only have their self-esteem damaged. Many people in the United States do not, however, see the maintenance of the quality of the public realm as a high priority as long as their private realms are prestigious.

Much recent urban design work has involved setting policies and guidelines for the creation of components of the public environment by the private sector. When these components are completed, they are turned over to the public sector for operation and maintenance. Many such schemes provided excessive amounts of hard-to-maintain public spaces. With the fiscal difficulties many municipal governments face, the results have been disastrous. This concern for maintenance is not simply for the quality of public space, it is also a major consideration in the design of private developments. The costs of maintaining a place adequately have risen, partly as a result of the energy crisis, but also as a function of the increase in labor costs as custodial staff seek self-esteem through earning a reasonable salary.

The response has been that management plans are now being asked for as part of urban design proposals. Thinking about or designing how a space or building complex, or even a precinct of a city, will be maintained or managed thus now falls very much into the domain of concern of an urban designer. The need for ease of maintenance has an impact on the spatial configuration of buildings in relationship to each other, the amount of space allocated to public purposes, the materials chosen, and, increasingly, the amount of time a place is open to the public. The design of urban design complexes or guidelines thus goes hand in hand with a design for operating

the resulting built environment, or at least the public and quasi-public parts of it.

URBAN DESIGN CONSEQUENCES

There are three basic concerns with which urban designers have to deal in helping people fulfill their need for esteem: (1) the need for people who are going to use places to be participants in the designing process, (2) the need to ensure that the behavioral opportunities for exploration and learning are provided in future designs, and (3) the need for the symbolic aesthetics of the future environments to fulfill people's needs for self-esteem in their own terms. The design process, total and all-of-a-piece designs, and the formulation of design guidelines all need to be aimed at meeting these ends. To do so means that design policies have to create ambiguous environments—ones that have different opportunities and meanings for different people (Rapoport and Kantor 1967). The design programs written by or on behalf of the public sector soliciting development proposals for cities need to specify the nature of the mixed experiences that should be included in those proposals. Urban design guidelines can then be written specifying the physical characteristics required of places to achieve these ends.

Many groups of professionals and laypeople are concerned with promoting specific ends that impinge on the work of urban designers. The consideration of formal educational opportunities falls within the domain of concern of educators and social policy formulators. Urban designers are concerned with the way educational facilities are used as a basic infrastructural component of human settlements to give an organizational structure to the layout of new towns and residential areas. The symbolic aesthetics of prestige are of concern to developers because it has an economic value in terms of rental and sales returns. The creation of informal learning settings is of concern to advocates of children's interests in the environment, but it is unlikely to be a major consideration in most residential area designs unless promoted by urban designers. Designs based on such needs are likely to be opposed to the self-esteem needs of adults seeking well-kept environments. Careful and creative designs may result in environments where the apparently conflicting needs and the resulting designs complement each other. Resource constraints will always limit the range of possible designs.

MAJOR REFERENCES

Cooper Marcus, Clare (1974). "The House as Image of the Self." In Jon Lang et al., eds., *Designing for Human Behavior: Architecture and the Behavioral Sciences.* Stroudsburg, PA: Dowden, Hutchinson, and Ross, pp. 130–146.

Duncan, James, ed. (1982). *Housing and Identity: Cross Cultural Perspectives.* New York: Holmes and Meier.

Lang, Jon (1987a). "Symbolic Aesthetics." In *Creating Architecture Theory: The Role of the Behavioral Sciences in Environmental Design.* New York: Van Nostrand Reinhold, pp. 203–215. See also "Symbolic Aesthetics in Architecture," in Jack Nasar, *Environmental Aesthetics,* pp. 11–26.

Lasswell, Harold D. (1979). *The Signature of Power: Buildings, Communications, and Policy.* New Brunswick, NJ: Transaction Books.

Nasar, Jack, ed. (1988b). *Environmental Aesthetics: Theory, Research, and Applications.* New York: Cambridge University Press.

Perin, Constance (1977). *Everything in Its Place: Social Order and Land Use in America.* Princeton, NJ: Princeton University Press.

15

MEETING SELF-ACTUALIZATION NEEDS

The psychological concept of self-actualization has been developed largely in the United States so any commentary here is likely to be culture-bound, although the essence of being a self-actualized person applies everywhere. The pursuit of self-actualization is seldom done self-consciously. Fully *self-actualized* people have become everything that they are capable of becoming. They feel a sense of fulfillment and they are content with their philosophy and outlook on life. They are fully functioning beings (Rogers 1980). According to Maslow (1971), few individuals fully reach this stage of psychological maturation. They remain at the level of striving for greater self-esteem.

Self-actualized people are those who concentrate more on the problems at hand rather than with boosting their own egos—they are problem-centered rather than self-centered. They are autonomous and independent, have a strong identification with humankind, a strong social interest in people and in democratic values and attitudes. They have an ability to transcend the difficulties of their social and physical environments rather than simply coping with them. They have the ability to turn frustrating situations to their advantage. They possess a high degree of self-acceptance and are accepting of other people as they are and the natural world as it is. They may have a need for much privacy in their personal lives. They tend to have strong intimate relationships with a few people rather than superficial relationships with many people.

The pursuit of self-actualization has high civic and social consequences. People with a high degree of self-esteem tend to love others. They get involved with life. In apparent contradiction to all these attributes, self-actualized people also exhibit more idiosyncratic behaviors. They are, nevertheless, considerate of the feelings of other people while following their own inward longings. They

are creative in some sphere of action. Self-actualization is not a characteristic of young people. Children, adolescents, and young adults are striving, within the predominant North American cultural frames at least, to achieve a sense of identity or autonomy, and have a need to work out their own system of values. They tend to be highly self-centered.

It might erroneously be thought that self-actualized people are content with everything in their lives, but "human beings seem almost never to be permanently satisfied or content . . . even the highest pleasures may grow stale and lose their newness. It may be *necessary* to experience loss of their blessings to appreciate them again" (Maslow 1987).

THE BEHAVIORAL PROGRAM

What should one assume about the lifestyles and aesthetic values of self-actualizing people? What are the characteristics of the behavior settings such people will inhabit? Can such settings be designed?

A habitat rich in opportunities for learning and aesthetic appreciation for their own sakes, and not for any instrumental rewards, is what self-actualized people will seek. Almost any environment provides these opportunities, but self-actualized people, while capable of making themselves at home anywhere, will seek places that meet their own criteria of beauty, not to boost their self-esteem, but for the sheer pleasure those places give them. Similarly, environments rich in the provision of cognitive needs will best enrich the lives of self-actualized people (see Chapter 16, Meeting Cognitive Needs, and Chapter 17, Meeting Aesthetic Needs).

They will be concerned with how well the urban layout meets the needs of others, and will push for change

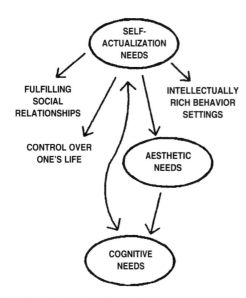

Figure 15–1: Self-Actualization Needs

when they perceive it is necessary. Opportunities or outlets for them to pursue these needs and contribute to the improvement of the world are what they will seek. They will participate in community organizations to seek these ends. If such organizations do not exist they may well initiate them.

THE DESIGN PROGRAM

As self-actualized people are inner-directed in their behavior, there is little unique in terms of the layout of the environment that is required to meet their needs. If an existing milieu or a new urban design (whether total, all-of-a-piece, or guidelines for design) provides for people's cognitive and aesthetic needs as well as the lower-order basic needs, self-actualizing people will find their own rewards.

An environment rich in aesthetic experiences and cognitive needs—both in terms of experience and opportunities for expression—will meet the needs of self-actualized and also self-actualizing people. One difficulty urban designers face is simply to build such attributes into a self-consciously created, new built environment because many meanings can only be acquired over time as a place becomes inhabited, events occur, additions are made to its elements, and the environment gets worn (see Chapters 16 and 17). An urban design that affords all of people's basic needs from physiological to self-esteem may still lack the historical associations that enrich the environment by enabling people to get vicarious pleasure from the lives of those of the past. Even in those environments, however, self-actualized people will find their own rewards.

URBAN DESIGN CONSEQUENCES

Self-actualizing and self-actualized people will be the ones pushing for civic reforms and for the betterment of conditions for others. They are the ones who are likely to best appreciate the work of urban designers and thus be supportive or critical of designers' efforts. The consequences for urban designers are procedural, not substantive; both self-actualized and self-actualizing people need to be involved in the decision-making process on behalf of others if not themselves.

MAJOR REFERENCES

Maslow Abraham (1971). *The Farther Reaches of Human Nature.* New York: Viking.
————(1987). "Self-Actualization." In *Motivation and Personality.* 3d ed. Rev. by Robert Frager, James Fadiman, Cynthia McReynolds, and Ruth Cox. New York: Harper & Row, pp. 53–57.

Philadelphia

Meeting Cognitive and Aesthetic Needs

16

MEETING COGNITIVE NEEDS

For people to meet their basic needs, from survival to esteem, requires a continuing process of learning to deal with their biogenic and sociogenic environments. The need to learn is a necessary part of any definition of *cognitive needs* but it is by itself insufficient. People also have a need to gratify their curiosity about how the world works for its own sake rather than any instrumental ends. This varies, depending on where they are in their stage of life cycle and the degree to which basic needs are satisfied. While this attribute of people is particularly one of self-actualized people and not of people struggling for survival, it is a hallmark of human nature.

Freedom of inquiry and freedom of expression, as discussed in Chapter 5, Redesigning Urban Design, are prerequisites for people to strive, consciously or subconsciously, to meet their needs. They are basic requirements for a good life (see also Maslow 1987). To these two can be added the freedom to create as a requirement for learning and acting. The United States has a proud record in this regard, but many people find themselves hampered by economic exigencies that make it difficult for them to fulfill the American dream. The urban design concern is that the built environment possess the affordances for the fulfillment of both people's cognitive needs and the linkages among cognitive needs and basic needs.

From this introductory statement, it can be deduced that people have three interrelated sets of cognitive needs: (1) those that are necessary for achieving instrumental ends—doing a job, and so on, (2) those concerned with the need to learn for its own sake and not for any instrumental reward, and (3) those involving expressive actions. The first set is concerned with the development and/or maintenance of competence—with acquiring knowledge and developing skills—in dealing with the world; the second with the need to satisfy one's curiosity about

places, people, and ideas; and the third with rewards obtained through the experience of performing enjoyable acts—with the experience itself being the reward.

Acquiring knowledge and developing skills are mechanisms for perceiving the dangers of the world, the affordances for participation in the activities that exist or developing new ones, for wayfinding, and for recognizing the symbols that denote status. Learning is a process of perceived finer and finer differences in the world and broader and broader categories of phenomena (Gibson and Gibson 1955; E. Gibson 1969; Santrock 1989). It enhances our competence in dealing with the world and subsequently enriches our experiencing of it.

There are two categories of competence that individuals strive to develop: physiological and mental. The former involves the development of strength and motor skills, and the latter the processes of acquiring knowledge, memory, convergent and divergent production of ideas, and the transformation of knowledge to bring it to bear on the problems people face and the opportunities available to them. Physiological competence develops through the early stages of the human life cycle, peaks, and then gradually declines with aging. Some aspects of intellectual competence seem to follow the same curve, but others (e.g., vocabulary growth) continue to develop throughout people's lives as long as they are healthy (Lawton 1977; Santrock 1989).

A number of theories explain why we are curious about the world and like to explore it and to engage in expressive acts. One explains them in terms of Darwinian theories of evolution, the need for the survival of species. A variant of this theory is that the satisfaction of one's curiosity is a sublimated act that is an aspect of the drives to pursue basic needs (Csikszentmihalyi 1975). Certainly, however, we carry out many acts that are self-

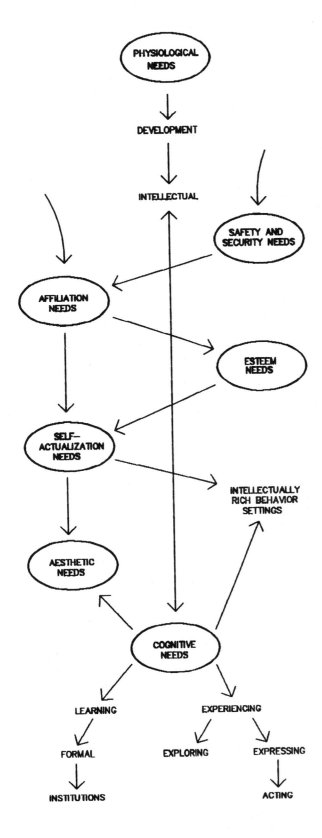

Figure 16-1: Cognitive Needs

initiated and for the sheer joy of experiencing the act itself (Maslow 1987).

Curiosity seems to be universal and not restricted to human beings. Other animals have a sense of curiosity about the world, but human beings are shaped by what they find out. This observation is akin to the Greek concept of *paidea,* with people being considered to be works of art formed by their life experiences. Learning more and more about music, or flowers, or jackhammers for one's own satisfaction is something of concern for many people whatever their age or socioeconomic status. For some people such a devotion to learning about a subject justifies their existence.

Almost all environments, social and physical, present people with opportunities to continue learning, but some places are richer than others. There is simply more going on in them and they possess a greater variety of places to explore. One of the major criticisms of recent urban designs is that they afford few opportunities for exploration and performance. They have "a stifling immanence where all is exposed and nothing left to the imagination." There is no mystery to them (Kaplan and Kaplan 1982).

These observations apply to all stages of the human life cycle, but they are perhaps most critical for children between the ages of five and twelve. They need to have access to places "they can conquer and shape themselves" (Mark Francis, quoted in Devereaux 1991). There is a need for unstructured time and space for children to develop an intuitive understanding of many of the abstract concepts they will learn later in life. Often the very environments designed with children in mind (or sold to their parents as such) preclude such opportunities. They are based on a limited model of a child. Europeans have been aware of this situation for many years, Americans more recently.

THE BEHAVIORAL PROGRAM

An educative environment is one rich in learning opportunities for personal growth and for performing expressive acts. There are a number of concerns in devising a generic behavioral program that affords people the opportunities to fulfill their cognitive needs. The concerns, potentially, have design implications. The concern is with supporting and/or devising activity patterns associated with four highly interrelated behaviors: learning or exploring life tasks, exploring for its own sake, testing oneself, and expressing oneself. Often the same behavior pattern affords all four experiences simultaneously. The first and third behaviors are clearly aspects of competence development whether for instrumental ends or not; the second and fourth are somewhat different. Exploratory and expressive acts may serve developmental ends but they may also serve no end other than self-expression—they may be purely expressive acts—and can be self-testing (Maslow

1987). As has been argued earlier in the book, all these activities are closely associated with the fulfillment not only of basic needs (see Chapters 11 to 15) but also of aesthetic needs (see Chapter 17).

The Development of Competence

Both physiological and psychological competence can be developed through formal education, but much human development occurs as a byproduct of the informal activities of everyday life and the vicarious participation in the lives of others—learning from observing what other people do or have done. Formal education is institutionalized, but even in formal learning situations much learning occurs informally. Informal education occurs in many ways, as a byproduct of playing (including videogames), conversations with people, watching television programs, reading novels, participating in a variety of settings, watching people working and playing.

Much learning also occurs through observing, acting, and testing ourselves. Children climbing trees or playing word games or running races are testing themselves, sometimes against themselves and sometimes against others. The child learns from the results of the act. Acting and testing also help maintain one's skills (Lawton 1977).

Formal Learning

Formal learning and formal testing take place primarily through direct instruction and examination by a teacher in a classroom or, if the subject is something like rock climbing or flying an airplane, on location. The communication may be mediated through radio, television, computer, or self-instructional text. A person can also set out to become an expert in some activity through directly practicing skills. The classroom experience may be the most formal educational type and the self-teaching the least, but the objective in all is to purposively learn.

Formal learning is organized and formal learning experiences can be designed. While the design of the means of instruction is well outside the scope of this book, several issues do fall within the domain of the urban designer's consideration because they concern the nature and distribution of facilities and people's ease of access to them. For example, the location of the primary school as the center of a neighborhood has long been a basic urban design principle for residential areas (C. Stein 1957; Gallion and Eisner 1986). It is a principle that makes many assumptions about the nature of education.

One of the purposes of education is to have informed citizens as well as competent ones. In the design of educational policies this goal has to be translated into a set of operational objectives in terms of the nature of institutions, the degree to which they are specialized by age group, the courses they offer, and their sizes. The link between social and physical planning has to do with the scale of operations,

as was discussed in Chapter 13 and again in Chapter 14.

The basic point is that large institutions tend to have fewer behavior settings per capita than smaller institutions, although they present the student with a wider array of choice and are not as coercive in getting students to participate in as many different activities as smaller institutions are (Barker and Gump 1964; Wicker 1969, 1979; Bechtel 1977). Smaller institutions are, however, more intimate. The standard way of dealing with these observations is to have small schools at the primary level and larger institutions as one goes up the scale to tertiary institutions. The larger institutions are also more efficient economically. There tend to be fewer supportive behavior settings and thus less social and physical space per student.

Large institutions do not have to be impersonal. They can be designed to provide a greater sense of intimacy, but the organizational structure required to achieve this end has neither the simplicity nor economies of scale that economic Rationalists like. Such experts in the United States still have by and large the narrow Modernist concept of function in mind. The opportunity costs that result from this line of thinking appear to be high but do not enter into most calculations.

Developments in communications technology in the future may shape the way formal education is organized. There have been suspicions that a breakthrough in the way education is delivered to people will lead to a radical change in the nature of schools and universities. Such a change has not yet taken place, and all such suggestions remain speculative. The same can be said for current thought on the nature of semiformal education and its implications for urban design, but not for informal learning and its implications.

Semiformal Learning and Exploration

While schools and educational institutions are specifically designed to teach people about a particular topic and also to provide opportunities to explore the universe in a structured way, places such as libraries and museums have a high educational mission but do not usually instruct people directly. Libraries provide resources for entertainment, education, and the exploration of ideas in general. Museums of science and technology, natural history, and art serve a similar purpose. Their primary purpose is to display our understanding of ourselves and our intellectual heritage. They give us an identity and boost our self-esteem by showing us the breadth of our cumulative knowledge. Indeed, museums are often used to boost civic self-esteem (see Chapter 14). Their primary purpose is, nevertheless, as educational institutions. In the past, it was education through looking and pondering, but more and more frequently today it is education through doing and indirectly through entertainment. Although many if not all museums offer specific classes on specific topics in a formal mode, their primary role is to expose

1. Classroom

2. Central Park, New York

3. Quincy Market, Boston

Figure 16-2: Formal, Semiformal, and Informal Opportunities for Learning

The environment consists of many situations in which a person is taught how to carry out activities in places specially designed for the purpose (1). Much learning in such situations also happens vicariously by observing other people, such as the photographer of the classroom in the illustration. Learning skills can be a byproduct of recreational activities (2) and/or can be acquired simply through the observation of everyday life (3).

people of all ages to the variety of phenomena that exist and the way they function. Their goal is to enhance and to satisfy people's curiosity about the natural world, other people, and about the material artifacts of culture.

Other cultural institutions such as theaters not only set out purposely to entertain, but also to provide opportunities for learning. Theater and film offer it through vicarious participation by people in the lives of people in situations in which the audience is not involved. They also offer opportunities to explore the use of language, new values, new lifestyles, and new places. Some people may attend plays and concerts and see films specifically to learn something instrumental to their lives, but they are in the minority. Most people go to be entertained (and, if the setting is prestigious, perhaps to display their presence to boost their self-esteem), and any learning is a byproduct of their attendance.

The Nature of Educative Environments

Educative environments provide for informal learning. Cities with abundant libraries, museums, theaters, fun fairs, and educational institutions are intellectually rich, but the everyday environment provides many opportuni-

ties for fulfilling some cognitive needs. Informal learning occurs as the byproduct of the interactions with the people and places of everyday life, the observations of the biogenic and sociogenic environment around one, and the changes that take place in them. Much knowledge about the world and many skills come from doing things. Activities such as driving a car, shopping, and simply playing may develop both knowledge and skills. Apparently passive pastimes such as reading and watching television broaden one's knowledge about the world and the opportunities it contains. Such opportunities abound, but the types of environment that best meet cognitive needs are *participatory landscapes* (or cityscapes). Newly designed environments seldom possess such qualities because they have not been considered in the programming process. Participatory environments are ones that "draw" us in to explore and act. They can be contrasted to *panoramas,* which are sweeping views, something simply to look at and wonder about (Berleant 1988).

Educative environments are ones in which there are many opportunities for learning through experiencing (see also Kolb 1984). They are rich in a variety of accessible behavior settings. Such environments possess a wide variety of potential experiences for people from child-

1. Portland, Oregon

2. Chinatown, San Francisco

3. Ira C. Keller Fountain, Portland, Oregon (1969)

Figure 16-3: Panoramic and Participatory Landscapes
Panoramas provide opportunities for aesthetic pleasure simply through the enjoyment of their splendor (1). Often the creation of panoramas has been an important aspect of urban design (see, e.g., Figs. 3–4(1) and 10–9(2)). Participatory environments offer opportunities for active engagement and self-testing, physically and/or socially, in the way a panorama does not. They come in many forms: busy urban areas (2) and more tranquil ones (3). The first of these two examples is a byproduct of the marketplace and the second is designed by Lawrence Halprin.

hood to old age. They also present many opportunities for seeing and doing new things. For a child such activities may be watching workers on a building under construction, playing in a stream, building a hut, or making a fire without infringing on the rights of others. Children who have the opportunity and are allowed to independently roam, play, and explore have been shown to have better developed intellectual and social skills than their peers (Weinstein and David 1987). Some urban and suburban environments have become so designed that such opportunities are lost. Other environments have become so hostile and unsafe for children that access to such opportunities is severely reduced. There is indeed a richness of life in the poorest parts of American cities, but the role models for children are severely restricted, and most of those on television are a poor alternative.

Any environment affords possibilities for exploration by curious people. Even the most barren landscape is a source of wonder. Some environments, are, however, much richer in the ease of access they provide to the natural world and to a variety of opportunities, formal and informal, in the built environment. Certainly, environments that are educative also provide opportunities for us to satisfy our need to be curious.

Educative environments provide not only opportunities to explore the world but also opportunities to explore and understand ourselves, however much this may be done subconsciously. They give us opportunities to understand who we are in relationship to others and in so doing provide us with opportunities to establish our own identities as individuals and as part of a society. The process of learning to understand who we are is also enhanced if we can see ourselves in relationship to the past, through the use of plaques and signs reminding us of events that occurred in a place, and through elements of the built environment associated with people, events, and eras that act as symbols of the past (Attoe 1988b; Hayden 1989).

Not all educative behavior settings have to be permanent attributes of a place. Traveling fairs and circuses, which cannot be economically supported on a permanent basis, open a person's eyes on the world. Agricultural shows proclaim the seasons. What is needed are sites that may serve other purposes at other times of the year but are available for such occasional displays.

In thinking about the affordances of the physical world in this way, and perceiving correlations between environmental opportunities and the learning process,

1. Baltimore Inner Harbor, Maryland

2. Savannah, Georgia

3. Detroit

Figure 16–4: The Material Culture as a Source of Learning
The material culture of a society holds memories about past incidents and values. The nature of buildings, artifacts, such as ships, and open spaces both give a sense of continuity with the past and teach us about it (1,2). Sometimes a place is important because of its association with a famous person or event; this may not be obvious from the appearance of the place and our attention needs to be brought to it. Sometimes a place is important for more mundane reasons (3). Monuments can serve much the same purpose.

one must again be careful not to assume a simple deterministic relationship between environment and behavior. Much depends on the social circumstances in which we find ourselves. The social environment is paramount in the informal education of people. The extra intellectual development of children in environments that afford much exploration over their peers, as noted by Carol Weinstein and Thomas David (1987), may simply be due to the enriched social environment of the home. However, the correlation between the nature of the behavior settings of the broader environment and intellectual development should not be dismissed too easily. Much learning comes from the sheer joy of doing things, from exploring the world, because the exploration is internally rewarding.

The Child and the City

Opportunities for children to explore tend to be more easily found in the countryside and small towns than in the large modern city, with its segregated land uses and people clustered according to stage in life cycle and socioeconomic status. Many older cities do possess a fine-grained texture of behavior settings and thus experiences that provide a rich set of opportunities for children to explore independently. Such environments tend to have learning opportunities involving the nature of people, the nature of adult activities, and the nature of places.

Albert E. Parr's (1967, 1969) evocative description of life as a young boy, the responsibilities that it was possible for him to have, and the variety of behavior settings that he participated in directly or vicariously as he went to market for his parents in a small city in Norway early in this century tell us much about the characteristics of educative environments. It was an environment full of diverse experiences from seeing submarines, trains, and fish markets, to water and hills, town halls, and people working. The experiences were densely packed into a relatively small space and one in which a small child could feel secure. Parr admits he had special parents, who allowed him to travel independently to market when he was a four-year-old, but it is also accurate to note that the layout of the physical environment made it possible, as it still does in many countries today. Such opportunities have been severely reduced in American cities during the past forty years, not simply because of alterations in the physical environment due to changes in the scale of activities and the homogeneity of much tract housing development but also because of the increasing hostility of the social environment.

Robert Roberts's (1971) portrayal of growing up in the slums of the northern English city of Salford during the first decades of this century shows both the richness and poverty of experience at the disposal of an active and intelligent young boy. Girls were seldom allowed to avail themselves of the opportunities that existed in such places, at least not independently (Ward 1990). In today's suburbia, the advent of the automobile and the freedom of movement it provides for adults have made a day-to-day independent living environment accessible to children only through adults. Similarly, the mobility of families means that the environment of childhood is increasingly an environment of strangers.

Television programs are now a major source of information and entertainment for both children and adults alike. They require little in the way of active participation, although the development of interactive programs may lead to changes. The full impact of television on people's lives and on the development of our cognitive processes has still to be documented. Suffice to say here that anecdotal evidence suggests that the outdoor world beyond children's home environments is used less by them today than in the past. While a whole new process of vicarious education may be developing, the local environment, if properly designed, can be an important part of it.

Many places that afford a richness of experiences for children have evolved unselfconsciously (in terms of any overall plan) over time and are full of nooks and crannies for their imaginative play. They tend to be unmanicured sites and scenes of change. They contain the shops and places of business where children are exposed to the adult world. With the increasing scale of economic activity and the need for adults to have an environment that supports their desire for self-esteem, such mixed-use areas to which children have independent access tend to be disappearing. Where they still exist they tend to be under the jurisdiction of strangers. The result is that learning experiences as a byproduct of play and the use of the local built environment have become formalized with the introduction of places such as adventure playgrounds that do allow for the manipulation of the environment in much the same way that the rural environment once did (Cooper Marcus 1978). In adventure playgrounds, children can build structures from junk material, make fires, and play games, but under the supervision of adults (Allen 1968). Similarly, playgrounds can be designed to present children with a challenge and yet be robust enough to survive with little maintenance (Dattner 1969; Rouard and Simon 1977; Cooper Marcus and Francis 1990).

One factor that ameliorates the problem of designing appropriate environments for children's play is that children can play almost anywhere with almost any objects. Of particular concern in designing for children is the nature of transitional space in areas of the city where people live. These spaces include "access yards, courtyards, and streets adjoining the home" (Chawla 1991; see also Ward 1990). One of the major play spaces for children in the city is the sidewalk, especially for traditional games that girls play. The sidewalk is also the place from which the passing scene is perceived, not only by children but also by adults. In dense residential areas the nature of the sidewalks and streets is a major consideration (see Appleyard et al. 1981; R. Moore 1987; Moudon 1987), but more generally, the character of the home-based territory is important for children growing up in any environment whether the single-family homes in the suburbs or the high-density housing environments in the inner city.

In new suburban areas, the affordances for such vicarious participations in the life of a child's surroundings are very difficult to achieve, but these areas often, but by no means invariably, provide for a child's more basic need—a safer world. Adult lives in the suburbs tend to be more segregated from those of children than in the older mixed-use neighborhoods of cities, and the parents' role in shepherding children is a major one. The use of any environment outside the home is, however, a "negotiation between caretakers, child, and [the characteristics of the] environment" (Chawla 1991). High-rise environments, for instance, make the supervision of children more complicated when families live on high floors. The solution is the patchwork one of providing facilities on site and thus reducing the orbit of a child's life.

In thinking about the child and the affordances the designed environment should possess, a chicken and egg situation exists. Unless human settlements can be secure places, socially, psychologically, and physically, children will not have the freedom of movement to take advantage of potentially highly educative environments. Lower-order needs have to be met first, but paradoxically, informal education contributes much to the development that leads to them being met. The urban design task is to devise patterns of the environment that give children access to exploration and play opportunities "without danger but ones which provide unpredictability [i.e., risk] which is the basis of adventure" (Hart 1978, 1979; Chawla 1991). Latchkey children living in high-crime areas in the United States have particular problems, as they are told to lock themselves in when they get home. The solution to this problem is a formal one (unless the social environment is radically changed). Social facilities for children's use between class time and their parents' (or, very often, one parent's) return home from work have to be provided if their worlds are to be kept open. At present, the American taxpayer is, however, largely unwilling to pay for such facilities and the social programs they represent.

The Particular Needs of Adolescents

Adolescence is a difficult period in many people's lives. The social and physical environment of suburbs (Popenoe 1977) and center city areas (Ladd 1978) afford few amenities for adolescents of low-income families. Those whose lives are school-centered do not feel so deprived, but with the preponderance of large schools containing few behavior settings per capita, many teenagers become alienated—they are shoved aside. They have difficulty in getting access to a wide variety of places independently if they live in the suburbs, and when they do, typical American adolescent behaviors such as "hanging-out" become a problem in many of the places that they

Collection of the author

1. Rittenhouse Square, Philadelphia

Photograph by Clare Cooper Marcus

2. Pulleys, Sand, and Trapdoors

Figure 16-5: Children and the Designed Environment
The types of behavior shown here (1,2) while enjoyed by children everywhere are often planned out of the environment and/or prohibited by administrative decree. The change in scale of economic activities, roads and highways, and fear of antisocial behavior reduce children's opportunities for *independent* use and exploration of the world. Playgrounds are important substitutes and, if designed for active involvement, afford much learning (2). Similarly, watching the environment being changed and people at work provides opportunities for learning.

choose (e.g., shopping malls, streetcorners, parking lots, parks, ERG 1990).

While the home environment is still an important factor in the lives of teenagers, the peer group becomes a dominant behavior-shaping force. High-density environments rich in behavior settings that afford an involvement in life still seem to offer the most to teenagers. They do need to be pleasant places in which to live and many street patterns have traffic volumes that detract from the quality of life. Studies of the European woonerven show them to be congenial places for both young children and teenagers (Eubank-Ahrens 1987), and a number of suggestions have been made about how to adapt their pattern to the American context. The pedestrian pocket concept is a step in this direction (Kelbaugh 1989). In all these places the built environment is complete. Undeveloped land as refuge and as a place to carry out activities where damages can be repaired by nature is important during teenage years, as it is for younger children (Popenoe 1977; Hart 1979; R. Moore 1987, 1991). Such spaces are difficult but not impossible to create purposefully.

There has been a substantial growth in antisocial behavior on the part of American teenagers. This growth reflects many changes in society, including the lengthening period of education and dependency on adults, the simultaneously increasing segregation of the population by stage in life cycle, and the decrease in the active participation of generations in each other's lives. The last mentioned trend may now be reversing. Some things can be done through physical planning and design to enrich the lives of teenagers, but most of the concerns are social ones. Formal efforts such as the teen centers in Columbia, Maryland, have not proven to be a great success (Tennenbaum 1990). There is a need for more opportunities for teenagers to participate actively in life, to explore, and to self-test without harming others (Ladd 1978). The characteristics of the good environment described by Jane Jacobs (1961) over thirty years ago would, if applied, help fulfill many of teenagers' cognitive needs. Better schools would too.

The Environment of Adulthood

In thinking about the nature of educative environments for adults, much the same argument as for children exists. Adults, on the other hand, are more mobile and can seek out opportunities for formal learning and recreation throughout the urban fabric. Indeed, it has already been noted that many adults are metropolitan people (Willmott and Young 1973). Many adults do, however, choose to lead routine lives, segregated from many aspects of life and contact with people unlike themselves. They feel secure in their lives and do not seek challenges out of the norm. They are content and are most interested in maintaining their own security—their place in society. They are neither self-actualized people nor striving for self-actualization. They are who they are and choose to remain that way. Other people, however, choose places in which to live that are rich in diversity, but for them safety and security needs are still the prime environmental concerns. The renewed flight to the suburbs in the 1990s of many middle-class people who had chosen the inner areas of cities such as Washington, DC, as places to live for their density and variety of behavioral opportunities reflects this necessity.

Many elderly people also wish to be exposed to various settings. Studies show that they like to be able to view neighborhood activities (Cranz 1987). At the same time, they prefer to be able to live apart from environments with young children, although they enjoy being able to see them. As life expectancy and accompanying health levels increase so many elderly seek new experiences. The growth in the "experience industry" includes the growth of tourism. It reflects the desire for exposure to new experiences while simultaneously feeling secure.

For all people, but for the elderly in particular, security is a basic concern, as Maslow's model of human needs predicts. Any consideration of the sociophysical design of educative environments must go hand in hand with considerations of secure environments. Without a feeling of security the elderly choose to be cut off from the surrounding hostile environment. The United States requires a host of well-crafted social programs to create a safe environment for all people (see Chapter 12).

The Maintenance of Competence

The maintenance of competence involves the continual testing of one's abilities. The desire to maintain competencies varies from person to person depending on how necessary they are for instrumental ends and the degree to which they contribute to a person's self-esteem or to which a self-actualized person wishes to retain competencies for their own sake.

If the biogenic and sociogenic environments are less demanding of an individual than their competencies are capable of dealing with, then the competencies tend to atrophy (Lawton 1977). While competencies can be maintained through self-consciously selected exercises—mental and physical—our abilities are also tested in a less formal way through the carrying out of day-to-day instrumental tasks (see Fig. 1-8). Some environments are so comfortable, physiologically and psychologically, that very little is demanded of an individual. This observation is an argument for environments that are not altogether unstressful. Politically, this is a difficult goal for which to argue. It tends to be a more acceptable issue in designing for institutionalized populations (Goffman 1961) than the everyday environment of most people, but the conceptual question still remains. How easy or pleasant should be environment be? The everyday environment of many people contains so many potentially stressful situations that they avoid that it hardly seems necessary to consider retaining them through self-conscious design. We choose to participate in some stressful situations to test ourselves but we are forced to participate others.

Opportunities for Expression

People express themselves in many ways: verbally, through drawings, and through physical actions including body language. The concern here is not with such expressive gestures as a reflection of a person's state of mind, but through the use of actions to express feelings. Some actions, such as drawing graffiti on a wall, may serve territorial and self-esteem functions as well as expressive needs. As already noted, doing something that is not socially acceptable by the broader society might be highly regarded by a teenager's peers, but its overall impact on society is negative. Drawing a picture in the sand on a beach only for it to be soon washed away is more likely to be a purely expressive act that harms no one and might give pleasure to some people.

Much art work and dance, or even running for the joy of it, are acts of expression. It is difficult to design for expression. Expressive acts can be carried out anywhere. Kicking fallen autumn leaves to see them fly or to hear them crunch underfoot is an act of expression that requires autumn leaves. Highly manicured environments tend to reduce the opportunities for expressive acts because they clash with management policies favoring hard surfaces and the mundane (Sommer 1974; Nohl 1988).

THE DESIGN PROGRAM: CREATING THE MILIEU

The urban design program is concerned with providing the physical environment for formal, semiformal, and informal education, self-testing, and expressive behavior. It is concerned with identifying and including in designs the characteristics of places that are educative, and with providing opportunities for exploration. Such environments tend to be more disordered than those that are normally the goal of design (Sennett 1970). They are more complex ones with a quality of mystery (Kaplan and Kaplan 1982).

Educative environments will contain formal, semiformal, and informal learning opportunities. They will be rich in cultural centers, educational and athletic facilities for people to use, and places where performances of various types can be watched. Rationalist thought in urban design during the first part of this century was clearly very much concerned with the physiological development of the human being—with the human being as a biological entity. The generic urban designs produced by the Rationalists were full of opportunities for people to have an easy access to the outdoors to participate in athletic activities. Le Corbusier's Radiant City provides opportunities for

1. Clarke Park, Philadelphia

Photograph by David Allison

2. Dallas Arts District, Dallas

Figure 16-6: Expressive Acts and the Urban Environment
Some expressive acts can be very simple and unselfconscious
(1). Others require some artificial catalyst, such as music by
which to dance (2). One of the difficulties in urban design is to
incorporate opportunities for expressive acts in self-consciously
thought-out design. If we do not think about them explicitly,
however, we can end up with overdesigned, manicured environments in which such acts are administratively prohibited.

walking, jogging, swimming, and soccer (Le Corbusier
1934, 1960). The same concern is reflected in the wave of
European new towns built after World War II following
Rationalist or Empiricist principles but less so in the
United States (Golany 1976; Popenoe 1977). In the United
States the concern has been more with enhancing the
ease of sale of houses, apartments, and commercial buildings through the images of the recreational opportunities
their landscapes offer. Often this action does, however,
serve the same ends.

It was noted in Chapters 13 and 14 that in new town
design, as in the neighborhood unit concept, there was
also a concern for the distribution of educational facilities,
particularly schools and technical schools. These concerns are tangible and many planning guidebooks specify
the principles for the location of such institutions, the
facilities that each type requires, and the amount of land
each type needs (De Chiara and Koppelman 1975, 1978;
Chapin and Kaiser 1979). Applying such principles assumes
that the institutional types are given as well as an unstated
philosophical approach to education. There are, however,
a number of philosophical questions on education the
answers to which have a major impact on policies for the
nature and distribution of facilities.

An informal educative environment should have the
following characteristics to afford a variety of behavioral
opportunities, the vicarious participation in the lives of
others, and opportunities for expressive acts:

1. A variety of housing types to meet the housing
   needs of populations at all stages in the life cycle
   (Ritzdorf 1987), perhaps clustered into small
   groups (Gans 1972; Alexander et al. 1977).
2. Street and block patterns that afford a variety of
   behavior settings (J. Jacobs 1961).
3. Mixed uses in close juxtaposition with each other
   (J. Jacobs 1961; Parr 1969; Alexander et al. 1977).
4. A richness of formal institutions—schools, libraries, museums, and so on—accessible to children
   independently.
5. Buildings of different eras (in existing built
   environments).
6. Accessible unmanicured open space (Hart 1979;
   Olwig 1986; Nohl 1988; R. Moore 1991), both
   within the built environment but also in adjacent natural areas.
7. Broad sidewalks (J. Jacobs 1961; Ward 1990) and
   good streets in which to play games (R. Moore
   1987).
8. Formal places for playing and for games that
   provide testing environments (Dattner 1969;
   Rouard and Simon 1977; Cohen et al. 1979;
   Wilkinson 1980; Eriksen 1985; Cooper Marcus
   and Francis 1990).
9. Adventure playgrounds (Allen 1968).
10. A wide variety of sensory experiences—an edu-

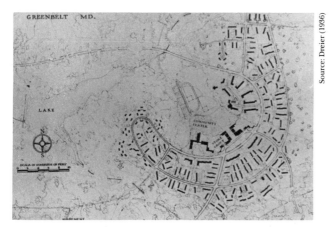

1. Greenbelt, Maryland

2. Bethesda, Maryland (1992)

3. Generic "Pedestrian Pocket" Proposal

4. Graceland, Chicago

Figure 16-7: New Towns and the Design of Cognitive Affordances
Designers of both European and American new towns during the Modernist era purposely sought to provide much open space (e.g., 1). The difficulty in the design of new towns is to create self-consciously what has developed over time in the dense environments of existing cities (2; see also Fig. 4–7(1)). Some recent designs have attempted to achieve this end (3). Creating instant histories is, however, impossible, and architects seek visual order in their designs so new towns often end up being dull places in which to be. Some places about which we have ambiguous feelings (4) we tend to avoid considering in new town design.

cative environment should have sources of sensory experience that are natural elements of the landscape and also those that are from artificial sources (Olds 1987).

11. Deciduous trees in temperate climates.
12. Posters and plaques explaining important buildings, events, and experiences (e.g., Hayden 1989).
13. The ability to watch neighborhood activity from safe areas (Cranz 1987).
14. Sites for occasional activities such as fairs and circuses.

These general design goals must be seen within cultural and climatic contexts. The way one achieves them (i.e., the patterns the urban designer strives to actually implement) will depend on the biogenic and socio-genic environment in which they are located. Some places are fortunate because the nature of the terrain and the way it is vegetated afford many experiences. Other places are flat and featureless. They demand considerable creative thought on the part of the designer to achieve the characteristics in the built environment listed above. There are no universal design prototypes, but the basic design objectives remain constant.

URBAN DESIGN CONSEQUENCES

One of the traditional urban design goals has been to provide a well-ordered, geometrically neat, and well-manicured environment. It is important to achieve this goal in many parts of the city where the need for the display of organizational and civic status is desired. The view of the goal of urban design is, however, a limited one.

1. CambridgeSide Plaza, Cambridge, Massachusetts

2. Traveling Exhibition

3. The Setting for County Fairs and Pageants in Broadacre City

Figure 16–8: Open Spaces and Cognitive Opportunities
Open spaces in cities and suburbs provide the foreground for buildings (1). There are, however, often aspects of life that enrich it but that are forgotten in design. Luckily many such activities and events can take place on any found space. The traveling show (2) can locate on any reasonably accessible open space. Many events, however, require some forethought. Frank Lloyd Wright recognized the importance of places for the annual events, such as state fairs, that enrich life and mark the seasons (3).

The problem is not static but dynamic. A certain amount of change and novelty is an essential prerequisite for the enjoyment of the days and years of our lives. The task of environmental design is not to provide a terminal retirement home for our civilization, but to guide the evolution of our surroundings in such a manner that we may find delight and assurance both in the process and in the stages it takes us through (Parr 1969).

We need to think more broadly about design goals than simply to create a well-manicured, timeless world. Museums, plazas, and well-ordered streets are essential parts of cities but so are unkempt spaces. There is a "cult amongst adults" (and designers too) to turn scrap spaces to economic advantage (R. Moore 1991). We need to think differently about the nature of open spaces and the range of activities they should afford. Unkempt places offer many opportunities for "children and adults to leave their marks without guilt" (Nohl 1988). Such uses of open space are often at odds not only with official planners, but also with efforts to green the environment for purely ecological reasons (see Chapter 18, Meeting the Needs of the Biogenic Environment). These observations do not deny the utility of carefully designed exploratory playscapes, but what is often needed is "planning abstention" (Lozano 1988) or, rather, planning for unplanned spaces (Olwig 1986)!

The consequences of urban design decisions are especially important for children. The city is the nursery for much of the world's future population. The Jesuit maxim, "Give me a child until he is seven and I will show you the man," should be heeded for girls and boys alike. While much of the character and competence of a person is genetically determined, the sociogenic and biogenic environment in which children are socialized plays a major role in shaping their future. Parr (1967) points out that the orbits of children and adults were once largely the same but have become highly segregated since the beginning of the century in the United States. Adults are increasingly independent and have greater spatial mobility. For children independent mobility has been severely reduced, and they are exposed to considerably less in their day-to-day lives as active participants rather than passive recipients. Although they do have access to new worlds through electronic media and opportunities for interaction with other people, it is largely a passive experience.

Playgrounds are important components of childhood environments as places in which to play and develop motor skills, but the preferred playground of children is the sidewalk and street. Few urban designers and public officials can accept this observation as a basis for planning. Their goal is to get children off the street and into playgrounds, although the empirical studies show that these designed playgrounds, while enjoyed, are not the play spaces of children's choice (Hester 1975; R. Moore 1987; Chawla 1991).

The concern for geometric order has been particularly strong among architects with a Rationalist orientation. In contrast, the concern for more "responsive environments" has come largely from Neo-Empiricist urban designers, many of whom are landscape architects rather than architects by profession. They advocate small-scale, intricate environments (Bentley et al. 1985). These characteristics can also be seen in Christopher Alexander's proposals for the University of Oregon (Alexander et al. 1975) and more generally in the pattern language he and his colleagues have developed (Alexander et al. 1977). The same line of thinking is displayed in the proposals Leon Krier has made for Poundbury (Krier 1987; see Fig. 23-3(2)) and even Atlantis (Broadbent 1990), although both of these schemes are highly manicured environments. Similarly, other Neo-Traditional designs such as the town of Seaside, Florida, show the search for diversity within uniformity in a highly manicured environment (see Fig. 3-11).

At the same time, urban designers concerned with designing educative environments need to avoid being trapped by a nostalgia for the past and by their own experiences. The home-territory–based environmental experiences described by Parr are difficult to reconstruct. The utility of the automobile has changed that world. Its use affords the segregation of living environments from commercial and cultural ones. This segregation has been embraced by many people without much thought for its full consequences. The design need today is to consider ways in which the environment can continue to be educative. The particular concern is to provide opportunities for people to be actively involved in the social environment and to have a rich set of behavior settings at their disposal. The need seems to be for people, if they are to move toward self-actualization, to be active users of the world rather than passive recipients of information. Providing opportunities will not, however, cause people to use them.

Some of the recent proposals of the Deconstructionists, such as Daniel Leibeskind's proposal for the City Edge competition in Berlin or Peter Eisenman's Biozentrum project, potentially could provide opportunities for exploration and vicarious learning, as does Bernard Tschumi's Parc de la Villette (see Fig. 3-8), but this type of experience is purportedly coincidental to these architects' main explorations of geometries and objects in space. The opportunities they provide are happy happenstances if the professed ideologies on which they say their work is based are accurate.

Educative environments are difficult to achieve in the present economic era in the United States and indeed in any developer-driven total or all-of-a-piece urban design with or without public subsidies. Educative environments will only emerge on a large scale from public policy inputs in the form of design guidelines, or from very persuasive urban designers working with politically progressive private-sector developers. In addition, a concern for educative environments has so far been demonstrated by only a handful of designers. Fewer still have implemented anything.

Educative environments can also be more stressful ones in which to live. They require a tolerance of other people uncharacteristic of most of us. Most Americans prefer to live in low- to medium-density environments with a homogeneous character, both in people and building types. They are safer, less challenging, and less stressful than diverse ones. In the search for higher amenity levels, and with increasing population pressures in many places, the design of denser environments may be necessary in the American future. The suburban environment is indeed becoming denser. The types of environmental characteristics implied in this chapter can be built at any density but are easier where some clustering of units is part of the design, otherwise distances become too large for children to travel independently.

MAJOR REFERENCES

Bronfenbrenner, Urie (1979). *The Ecology of Human Development.* Cambridge, MA: Harvard University Press.

Chawla, Louise (1991). "Homes for Children in a Changing Society." In Ervin Zube and Gary T. Moore, eds., *Advances in Environment, Behavior and Design 3.* New York: Plenum, pp. 187–228.

Csikszentmihalyi, Mihaly (1975). *Beyond Boredom and Anxiety.* San Francisco: Jossey-Bass.

de Monchaux, Suzanne (1981). "Planning with Children in Mind: A Notebook for Local Planners and Policy Makers on Children in the City Environment." Sydney: New South Wales Department of Environment and Planning.

Hart, Roger (1979). *Children's Experience of Places.* New York: Irvington.

Jacobs, Jane (1961). *The Death and Life of Great American Cities.* New York: Random House.

Kolb, David A. (1984). *Experiential Learning: Experience as the Source of Learning and Development.* Englewood Cliffs, NJ: Prentice-Hall.

Lynch, Kevin, ed. (1977). *Growing Up in Cities: Studies of the Spatial Environments of Adolescents in Cracow, Melbourne, Mexico City, Salta, Toluca, and Warszawa.* Cambridge, MA: MIT Press.

Moore, Robin C. (1991). *Childhood's Domain: Play and Place in Child Development.* Berkeley, CA: MIG Communications.

Nohl, Werner (1988). "Open Spaces in Cities: In Search of a New Aesthetic." In Jack Nasar, ed., *Environmental Aesthetics: Theory, Research, and Applications.* New York: Cambridge University Press, pp. 74–97.

Santrock, John W. (1989). *Life Span Development.* 3d ed. Dubuque, IA: Wm. C. Brown.

Ward, Colin (1990). *The Child in the City.* Rev. ed. London: Bedford Square.

Weinstein, Carol Simon, and Thomas G. David, eds. (1987). *Spaces for Children: The Built Environment and Child Development.* New York: Plenum.

17

MEETING AESTHETIC NEEDS

To fulfill their aesthetic needs people need the opportunity to contemplate beauty. This act involves their appreciation of the characteristics of the world for their own sake—for their beauty—and not for any instrumental reward. The reward is internal (Maslow 1987). In that sense, aesthetic needs parallel cognitive needs. It is also clear that aesthetic needs are closely related to affiliation and esteem needs. While the concern here is for the aesthetic appreciation of the environment for itself and not to achieve other ends, it is difficult to disaggregate our aesthetic experiences. We experience the environment as a totality.

Some people crave beautiful settings. "[This craving] is seen in every culture and in every age group" (Maslow 1987), but the definition of beautiful is very much culture-dependent and often highly individual. Some cities in the United States are generally regarded as beautiful and some not, based on whether they are manufacturing cities or not, on the character of their natural settings, on the number of trees they possess, and on the perceived speed of life. The overall visual orderliness of the built environment plays a major part in people's perception of the beautiful, so the elements and layout of the public realm, if properly arrayed, do make a substantial contribution to the aesthetic effect of all human settlements (Lozano 1988). The focus of designers' attention in the United States has been largely on the private realm. In urban design the concern has been with such visual factors as view corridors, the preservation of natural elements of the environment, and the unity and orderliness of the architecture of a place.

While the need for aesthetic experiences crosses all cultures, it is clear that some cultures place greater emphasis on them than others. Some cultures are more materialistic than others and esteem needs rule. Within cultures, some individuals place greater emphasis on aesthetic experiences and the aesthetic quality of the environment than others. The way the need is manifested may differ in terms of such aspects of life as one's stage in the life cycle—older people have different perceptions of what is beautiful than younger—but the evidence nevertheless points to aesthetic needs being present at all ages. What people regard as beautiful is certainly likely to differ based on their life experiences. Aesthetic preferences thus change for individuals (including design professionals) over their lifetimes.

There have been a number of problems in meeting people's aesthetic needs in self-consciously designed environments. Much that is admired by architects is regarded as boring by laypeople. There is thus a need to reconcile the gap between professional and lay taste cultures by coming to an understanding of these differences and why they exist. Designers have also found it difficult to recognize that laypeople respond to the behavior settings of the world rather than simply to the physical environment, whereas architects focus professionally on built form. As a result little attention has been paid to the full set of dimensions of the aesthetic experience of the world.

THE CONCEPT OF BEAUTY

"Beauty is in the eye of the beholder" may be true but it is not an observation that provides much guidance to the designer. We seldom talk about designing beautiful cities anymore. We do talk about giving a city visual order or neatness, but this does not take us very far. Speculative philosophers (e.g., Santayana 1896; Dewey 1934) and psychologists (e.g., Eisenmann 1966; Pickford 1972; Berlyne 1974) alike have found it useful to consider beauty in hedonic terms—as the intrinsic qualities of an object, person, or event that give us pleasure or at least hold our interest (see also Lang 1987a). Aesthetic pleasure arises not from the value of such experiences in establishing

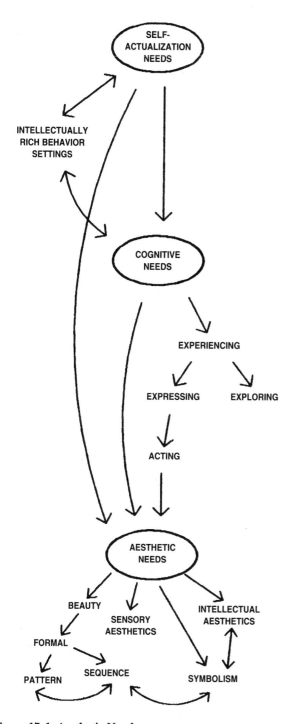

Figure 17-1: Aesthetic Needs

We apply the term "beautiful" to people, places, and events. The primary concern of the urban design is with places—behavior settings—but, it must be remembered, settings consist of people and activities as well as the milieu. We can and do stop to examine the milieu without paying attention to the behaviors that are going on in it and can get pleasure from that experience. This act involves a mode of attention that differs from our everyday behavior. Architectural photography focuses on built form almost entirely in this manner—devoid of people. In everyday life, however, we also get pleasure from the act of participating in the settings without any instrumental purpose being involved. In this sense we can stop to purposely examine behavior settings as works of art—as if they are Breugel paintings. We can look at the activity and the milieu as a unit and enjoy its aesthetic qualities.

From the above observations it can be seen that there are two modes of looking at behavior settings. We can look at them as observers from the outside or we can be part of them and respond to them as participants. In both cases our responses are highly subjective unless we self-consciously apply a structured intellectual model to the analysis. Urban design is, however, a self-conscious act and needs an intellectual structure to guide designers' work. There is a growing body of empirical knowledge on environmental aesthetics that helps the designer formulate questions about the goals of design and the ways of fulfilling those goals in specific cultural and social contexts.

THE NATURE OF ENVIRONMENTAL AESTHETICS

The list of places and objects and their attributes that are considered to be beautiful, or pleasurable, can be endless. The objective here is to review our present understanding of environmental aesthetics and what it means to meet the aesthetic needs of people through urban design. In so doing it is necessary to draw on several sources.

There are a number of books that bring attention to what their authors regard as pleasing scenes in cities (e.g., Rasmussen 1959; Arnold 1980; Ashihara 1983) and to pleasing details of the environment (e.g., Halprin 1963). Their views coincide considerably. It is clear that almost everything covered in the discussion of the constituents of a *functional urban design* so far in this book contributes to the aesthetic effect of cities. There is an aesthetics of function (Fitch 1965, 1972). For example, the nature of territorial demarcations of cities that are appropriate within a culture are visually pleasing to people of that culture because they feel psychologically comfortable in seeing them and in being in such an environment (Ashihara 1983). However, this experience is different from having a pleasurable environment to contemplate. We are also socialized to regard some types of places as pleasing and others not, but these views are further shaped by our positive and negative life experiences with places and peo-

identity or status but from the experience resulting from the examination or use of an object or environment for itself. "The mystic experience, the experience of awe, of delight, of wonder, of mystery, and of admiration are all subjectively rich experiences . . . they are end experiences rather than instrumental" (Maslow 1987). They are not related to the fulfillment of *basic needs*.

Collection of Ann Strong

1. Rural Pennsylvania

2. San Francisco

Figure 17-2: Beautiful Places

For many Americans, the concept of environmental beauty is associated with the natural environment (1), the small town with its trees, tranquility, and perceived slow pace of life, or with places such as villages on Aegean islands (see Fig. 17-7(2)). Complex behavior settings are seldom called beautiful. We may enjoy participating in them and talking about how interesting they are, but we seldom discuss their beauty. Yet in much recent discussion of aesthetics the term "beautiful" has been replaced by "interesting" and "pleasurable." San Francisco (2) and Charleston, South Carolina, are among the few American cities that are described as "beautiful" with any regularity.

ple. We get used to specific environments and feel uneasy about strong deviations from what we are habituated to seeing, but change itself holds our interest!

The socialization process is a complex one. Each of us has grown up with certain images of the good world in children's books, by what our parents tell us, and in the films and paintings we see. The way European paintings, for instance, are composed, with foregrounds and distance views, affects what those of us reared in such an ethos regard as aesthetically pleasing intellectually. The types of landscapes that hold our attention and that we actually enjoy are often denigrated because they do not fit into these historically and culturally appropriate molds. For this reason, we need to understand the factors underpinning aesthetic experience better. Otherwise we will be using constructs that have little meaning to people as the basis for design, as the Rationalists among the Modernists did.

There have been a number of theoretical approaches to the development of an understanding of the aesthetic experiencing of the environment (see Pepper 1949, Cole 1960, and Lang 1987a for reviews). Recently, they include hermeneutics, phenomenology, existentialism, and political science methods as well as theories derived from the more rigorous empirical aesthetics. The approach described here is the ecological one introduced at the outset of this book; it deals with the everyday world of human experience (Barker 1968; J. Gibson 1979; Kaminski 1989). It draws on phenomenology (Norberg Schulz 1971, 1980; Tuan 1977; Ashihara 1983) and on empirical studies within psychology (Berlyne 1974; Arnheim 1977; Nasar 1988b), but it also owes a major intellectual debt to the speculative philosophers (e.g., Santayana 1896; Dewey 1934; Bosanquet 1931) and the highly speculative artistic ideologies related to the Gestalt theory of perception (e.g., Kandinsky 1926; Klee 1953; Albers 1963; De Sausmarez 1964; Isaac 1971; Arnheim 1977). It is, however, rooted in the continuing study on what the underlying processes of experiencing the world are. We have learned much during the past forty years.

The research supports much of what we have been lead to believe from introspective analyses. It sharpens some ideas and contradicts some beliefs. We know, for instance, that people, given their motivations and their actions, pay different degrees of attention to the environment. Perception depends on our motivations. Motivations, in turn, are "driven" by our needs. Philip Thiel (1964) differentiates between *tourists* and *habitués* as two polar modes of paying attention to the environment. The former give the environment closer scrutiny than the latter, both for the experiences it evokes and for finding their ways. The latter tend to be preoccupied with other thoughts. A third and special category of users is the *cognoscenti*, who explore the environment to understand it in terms of the reasons for it being the way it is. There are thus two related modes of paying attention to the environment: as

1. Villa Rotunda, Outside Vicenza, Italy

2. Mission Bay and Central San Francisco

3. Gateway Mall, St. Louis

Figure 17–3: Urban Designs as Objects and as Environments
Much normative architectural theory is concerned with the Palladian ideal—the building as object in space, as a jewel (1). We can stop and stare at components of the city in this way and certainly we can look at aerial views of the city or any specific urban design in this manner (2,3). Usually, however, we experience the world as an environment—as a set of behavior settings—and the aesthetic pleasure that we derive from a city and city life (or from rural life) is as a set of behavior settings (see, e.g., Figs. 12-3(6) and 13-5(4)).

an object to be examined for the sake of assessing its aesthetic qualities, and as a byproduct of one's purposeful and/or expressive activities (see Chapter 1).

We can examine people and their behaviors and appreciate them from an aesthetic viewpoint. The actions of ballet dancers and actors are seen from the outside as performance, but the expressive behaviors of people involved in carrying out the everyday events of life with flourish—hawkers, pedestrians, playing children—are evaluated as part of the environment, for we are participants in their behavior settings too. Similarly, we can look at cities as objects to appreciate their structure, although this experience requires being in an airplane or atop a tall building. Indeed, many of our drawings of urban design projects are in aerial axonometric form. In everyday life, however, it is the environment as a set of behavior settings that forms the basis of our aesthetic appreciation of the world around us. Nevertheless, almost everybody must, at least every now and then, look at the milieu for the sake of looking at the milieu, and in examining its character must recognize their own feelings about it. The purpose is not an instrumental one, but the joy of the examination itself. The examination is in this sense a

perceptual luxury (J. Gibson 1966). The design qualities of the public realm are fundamental to this experience. The implication is that urban designers must be concerned simultaneously with a number of ways of looking at the aesthetics of the environment.

It is clear that some people, and not only the cognoscenti, carry out this kind of examination more than others. For some people it is part of their daily lives, but for many it is something they do only occasionally. Some people are aesthetes, others are not. When fighting for survival, people's concerns in general are not with fulfilling aesthetic needs. Folklore is nevertheless full of examples of people dying of hunger or thirst while focusing on some aesthetic experience—for instance, the beauty of water in a gourd, which might involve the anticipation of the beauty of its thirst-quenching quality and the sensory experience of drinking it. The moral varies. Sometimes that behavior is held in high regard, but more frequently it is regarded as stupid.

To understand our aesthetic responses to the environment we need to understand how we experience it. There are three types of experiencing of the elements of the environment that give us pleasure: the *sensory*, the

1. Pioneer Square Area, Seattle

2. Sears Tower, Chicago

3. Eisenhower Expressway, Chicago; Sears Tower in the Rear

Figure 17–4: The Ground Floor of the Public Realm
The public realm is usually seen by people at a human-eye level above the ground. Panoramic views are important and cities rich in them are well endowed. It is the richness of the ground plane and its enclosing elements that make for pleasing environments in which to be (1). Blank walls do not enrich the experience of either the pedestrian (2) or the driver. Luckily the building in (3) has had the "evidence of life" painted on to it in the form of murals. Many urban design guidelines now prohibit blanks walls on the ground floor of buildings.

formal, and the *symbolic* (Cole 1960; see also Lang 1987a). Sensory experiences derive from the pleasures of pure sensation, the formal from the pleasures of the three- and four-dimensional geometric character of the environment, and the symbolic from the associations those patterns arouse in us or that we assign to them. We can also appreciate the layout of the environment in terms of specific intellectual constructs of what is good and bad—in terms of its sensory, formal, and symbolic qualities. This appreciation is the *intellectual aesthetic* aspect of environmental experience.

Sensory Aesthetics

The experiencing of the environment is a multimodal perceptual process (J. Gibson 1966); consequently so is the aesthetic appreciation of it (Rasmussen 1959). Unless we have some problems with our perceptual systems, we can see how the world around us is structured, provided it is illuminated. We can examine the surfaces of places, their textures, temperatures, and colors; we can hear the sounds (or feel vibratory events) generated by the occurrences around us; we can smell odors. We can feel the

wind move through the hair on our heads and arms and press against our skins. Sometimes we actively seek out pleasures of this kind; such experiences always impinge on us but we do not necessarily heed them.

There are many situations in which sensory experiences are pleasurably heightened: feeling the radiant heat from a brick wall on a cold winter day, enjoying the moisture of a waterfall on one's skin, half closing one's eyes to experience a sunny world as patches of color, listening to the laughter of children at play, or feeling the texture of a gravel walk or autumn leaves under one's feet. Not all such experiences are pleasurable. There is a range of stimulation within which experiences are very pleasant, below that we do not heed them, and beyond that range they can be so pressing as to be negative. The flickering effect of succeeding bright and dark patches of light as we drive down an avenue of trees is nauseating for many people, although walking through the avenue at a more leisurely pace may be pleasurable.

Much sensory experience is subconscious but we can consciously attend to it. We usually attribute our feelings to the object (e.g., it is a hard seat, it is a beautiful sunrise). Sometimes these experiences are so heightened

1. Atlantic City, New Jersey

2. Oceanside, Oregon

Collection of the author

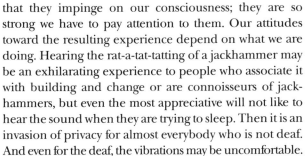

3. University of Pennsylvania Campus, Philadelphia

Figure 17-5: Sensory Aesthetic Experience
The sensory experiencing of the environment is, perhaps, the most basic level of aesthetic pleasure or dislike (1). There are times when we are very much aware of pleasurable sensations of heat, light, the touch of the winds, and the odors around us (2; see also Fig. 16-3(3)). In some cases these experiences may be so overwhelming, especially when they are strange to us, that we suffer from sensory overload and the experience is negative. At other times they engender a sense of tranquility even though they may not be places in which we wish to be for other reasons (3).

that they impinge on our consciousness; they are so strong we have to pay attention to them. Our attitudes toward the resulting experience depend on what we are doing. Hearing the rat-a-tat-tatting of a jackhammer may be an exhilarating experience to people who associate it with building and change or are connoisseurs of jackhammers, but even the most appreciative will not like to hear the sound when they are trying to sleep. Then it is an invasion of privacy for almost everybody who is not deaf. And even for the deaf, the vibrations may be uncomfortable.

There are major individual differences in our attitudes toward various sensory experiences of the world. There has been very little effort to come to an understanding of them. Much has to do with the experiences of childhood and our whole socialization processes. Childhood experiences of the environment shape our aesthetic preferences for good or ill (Lukashok and Lynch 1956). While most designers think of good sensory experiences in terms of the scents of flowers and trees, there are many people for whom the sensory experiencing of *gritty cities* is a delight—they thrive on it (Proctor and Matuszeski 1978). Similarly, there are people who enjoy the dramatic seasonal changes of continental climates and the

sensory experiences and activity opportunities that accompany them (Galbraith 1985). They enjoy the sensual pleasure of the changes in the panorama and the change in the sounds and odors of a place. They enjoy the sensory experience of the rustle of fall leaves and the glow of a snow-filled landscape, and they are exhilarated by the slush of a cold rain. Others get no joy from such experiences. They look at the environment in a different way. They desire comfort not arousal.

Much depends on what we know—on the invariant relationships between form and experience that we have been taught or have discovered. It becomes an intellectual exercise. Associating a scent with a flower is something that is learned. Understanding why that species of flower has different strengths of odors is a fine detail that may be instrumentally important to horticulturists, but to another person it may simply be a joyful experience—it fulfills both *cognitive* and *aesthetic needs.*

Formal Aesthetics

Every environment has a geometry. It consists of patterns. There are many geometric patterns that serve essentially the same purposes—they possess the affordances required of the environment to meet a number of pressing needs simultaneously. Sooner or later a designer imposes a pattern, a geometry, on the layout of the environment to give some order to it or as an act of personal expression. Indeed, some urban designers regard this focus of concern as the major if not the sole purpose of urban design (Sitte 1889; Schubert 1965; Bacon 1974; R. Krier 1979).

The composition of the geometric pattern of the milieu can be analyzed in terms of its proportions, rhythms, balance points, and expressions (Kepes 1944; Prak 1968; Hesselgren 1975; Arnheim 1977; Lang 1984, 1987a). The positive theoretical basis for this analysis remains the Gestalt theory of perception despite its flaws (J. Gibson 1950; Lang 1984).

Assuming the Gestalt laws of visual organization are correct, formal aesthetic pleasure derives from our subconscious responses to the degree of order, and the mechanisms for attaining order, in the geometry of built form (Kaplan and Kaplan 1982; Lang 1987a). Some ordering principles are relatively simple (e.g., bilateral symmetry); others are more complex (e.g., broken symmetries and helical and spiral forms). Different people have different tolerances for the complexity of forms. Anne Tyng's hypothesis is that we have an empathy for different forms given our level of psychological development. Our response is not based on an intellectual exercise but is an immediate subjective response to the environment.

Anne Tyng (1969, 1975) draws on Jungian concepts of the process of *individuation* by which an individual (or a people) is able to integrate greater and greater amounts of the unconscious into his or her (or their) conscious life. Psychological growth and change is accompanied by an empathy for particular geometric forms. The sequence of empathy begins with forms of a bilateral, twofold or fourfold symmetry, followed by more complex rotational, helical, and spiral forms, and then back to the simple symmetrical forms. Loosely interpreted, her sequence coincides with the urban design movements of this century: City Beautiful, Modernism, Post-Modernism, and Deconstructionism. Now there appears to be a full circle back to more obvious ordering systems, with the emergence of Weak, or Discrete, Architecture as a design ideology (De Solà Morales 1989; Buchanan 1990).

An ordered environment is one where the parts form a whole given some principle or set of principles that may well fall outside our realm of awareness. These principles are usually based on some proportional system. In a simple order, the proportional system may be an ababa relationship, something more complex with overlapping proportional systems, or some other ordering mechanism. The Golden Section is a proportional system that is said to be pleasing because of synchronistic processes in the brain. The proportion of the "ratio between bigger and smaller measurable qualities is equal to the

1. Las Colinas, Texas

2. Kresge College, University of California at Santa Cruz

Figure 17-6: The Formal Aesthetics of the Built Environment
Formal aesthetics is concerned with the pleasure derived from the geometry of the environment per se. Much recent American architecture and urban design continues to draw from the Rationalist tradition (1; see also Solana, Texas, in Figs. 2–14(1) and 7–9(2)) with its concern for orthogonal geometries. The Kresge College layout is based on the geometry of sequential experience (2; see also Fig. 2–14(3)). Post-Modern urban design plays with shapes in a new manner. The thesis is that the geometry itself and not the intellectual logic behind it gives us pleasure.

1. New York

2. Mykonos, Greece

3. Santa Barbara, California

4. Mission Bay, San Francisco

Source: San Francisco (1990)

5. Salem, Oregon

6. Pasadena, California

Figure 17-7: Ordered and Disordered Built Environments

There is a general feeling among architects that the modern urban landscape has no order—that it is chaotic. At a glance, it certainly seems that way (1). The orderliness of many European environments is much admired (e.g., 2). Urban designers have been very concerned with developing an ordered environment based on the similarity of its components, and, particularly if they are Rationalists, on a proportional system. In Santa Barbara (3) an historic referent is used as a unifying element, while in Mission Bay (4; see also Fig. 2–15(1)) it is a complex set of urban design guidelines. On many streets it is the tree line that gives a visual order (5), and in the Plaza Las Fuentes in Pasadena (6) it is the sequence of spaces and the use of water that integrates the scheme. More complex orders, as in some recent Deconstructionist schemes, are based on intellectual constructs that are only understood if one understands the construct. They are not based on visual perception theory.

ratio between the sum of the two and the bigger one" (De Sausmarez 1964). Built environments in which the planes are organized according to this proportional system are said to be visually pleasing to all people, but there are doubts as to whether it is universal rather than a culture-dependent phenomenon.

More complex patterns both hold one's attention and arouse greater pleasure at the moment. There does seem to be a point of optimal input to the brain beyond which the patterns of the environment become too complex and are simply not enjoyed (Pickford 1972; Berlyne 1974; Rapoport 1977). The difficulty is to operationally define *complexity* in measurable terms. In addition, the research focuses on the static viewer. We may see distant panoramic views from single station points, but usually we perceive the environment from a continuous sequence of station points as we move through it.

Highly complex environments with a number of ordering systems at work may still be subjectively seen as ordered. Environments based on such a principle stand in contrast to disordered environments. The results of Deconstructionist designs may be seen as ordered intellectually by those who understand the ordering principles used by their designers and disordered by those who do not. Such schemes, to be seen as ordered both intellectually and subjectively, have to incorporate those principles that are genetically based or have been inculcated within a culture over time. We understand little about them at present, for there has been little if any research on them.

Kevin Lynch's research on the imageability of the city (see Chapters 1 and 12) also provides principles for creating an ordered physical environment or, if applied in reverse, a disordered one (Lynch 1960; Arthur and Passini 1991). Ultimately, he suggests that the attractiveness of Boston has to do with the richness of the elements of visual order that it contains—a variety of clear paths, nodes, landmarks, districts, and edges of form. It is an alternative to the gridiron plan as the basis for giving geometric order to the American city plan, to its neighborhoods, and to more recent types of urban form such as the strip developments along so many highways of the country (Banerjee and Southworth 1990).

The Sequential Experiencing of the Environment

Most architectural photography focuses on the individual building or urban design complex from the ideal station point and in the ideal light to throw the ideal shadows on the façades of the surrounding buildings. Often the foreground is hosed down in order to get a reflection of the building in the photograph as well. This type of representation has its place as photography, but it reduces architecture and urban design to a picture. The experiencing of the geometry of the environment is not like that. Probably the most important of all formal aesthetic concerns is the *sequential experience* that results from

moving through the environment (Martienssen 1956; Thiel 1961; Cullen 1961; Appleyard, Lynch, and Myer 1964; Halprin 1965).

As we move through the environment we see it as a series of vistas. Some of these vistas will be *participatory landscapes* that offer the moving person (on foot or in a vehicle) opportunities for engaging in some activity, and some will be *panoramas* to be contemplated from a station point (Passini 1984; Berleant 1988). People get pleasure from both types of experiences. Picturesque landscape architecture and urban design ideologies argue for more of the former as a goal of urban design (e.g., Sitte 1889; Cullen 1961; Alexander et al. 1977). Japanese landscape gardens incorporate a series of participatory landscapes, although each view in a sequence can also be regarded as a small-scale panorama—something to be seen and to be intellectually contemplated but not touched physically. Rational architecture and urban design has focused more on a simple, pure, Platonic geometry with panoramic views (e.g., Le Corbusier 1934).

The layout of the environment holds our unselfconscious attention when it is stylistically deviant or complex. Whether it is liked or not depends on the nature of its ordering, or compositional scheme, but above all on the character of the spaces and the transitions between them that we pass through as we progress from one place to another—the *ports* (Thiel 1961) or *gates* (Norberg Schulz 1971). Cities with many such transitions seem to be highly loved by people because their structure cannot be easily perceived at once; they require time to learn through the successive unveiling of places; they have to be explored to learn one's way around them so that their structures can be understood and their affordances known. This exploration serves the need for *psychological security* through being able to orient within the structure of the city, but also it serves a *cognitive need*. Cities such as Venice and many medieval European cities are full of opportunities for exploration because the layouts afford many "ports" that control the sequential opening up and closing of vistas and spaces. The topography of San Francisco gives many such opportunities in the horizontal plane as one travels over crests of hills. The new vistas "invite" exploration; their physical structure has a mystery to them when they are first revealed (Kaplan and Kaplan 1982). We see and enjoy Beacon Hill in Boston, Greenwich Village in New York, and Disneyland in that way as pedestrians—at the speed of movement. Those environments seen at high speeds (if it were even physically possible) would be chaotic.

Much of the conceptual work for designing for the sequential experience of the environment has already been developed (Thiel 1961, forthcoming; Cullen 1961; Halprin 1965). One of the difficulties facing designers is to design sequential experiences for people moving through the same environment at different speeds. In particular, the concern is for designing the experiences of people on foot and in automobiles (Westerman 1990). Designing for

1. Forest Hills Gardens, New York

2. San Juan Capistrano, California

3. Illinois Institute of Technology, Chicago

Figure 17-8: The Aesthetics of Sequential Experience
We comprehend the world by moving through it. Much of the fascination of a place arises from the sequential experiences as vistas open up as we go through gates or ports (1; see also, e.g., Nicollet Mall in Fig. 2-1(2) and Riverwalk in Fig. 9-4(5)). The curving street not only has symbolic significance but also our views shift as we drive or walk along it (2; see also, e.g., Fig. 2-17(1)). The same kind of experience can occur as one moves through the gridiron planned city or a Rationalist urban design (3), provided the vistas change.

environmental perception at different speeds is easier when the movement systems are segregated in space. When one is dealing with both automobile and pedestrian speeds simultaneously, more is demanded of the designer. Much of the research has indeed been focused on the pedestrian, but Donald Appleyard, Kevin Lynch, and John Meyer (1964) developed a notation for designing the sequential experience of vistas seen by automobile drivers and their passengers on highways. Similarly, Lawrence Halprin (1963, 1965) was concerned with the sequential experience of moving down Nicollet Mall in Minneapolis on foot and in buses.

The Expressive Meaning of Line and Form

Gestalt psychology postulated that lines and forms can communicate meaning directly without any intervening intellectual process. This connection implies a simple stimulus-response model of human behavior. The form (i.e., the geometry of the built environment) is the stimulus and the emotion the response. Borrowing from Cubist art theories, this belief became a tenet of the Expressionists among the Rationalists of the Modern movement in architecture (Gray 1953; Overy 1969).

There is indeed some empirical support for this position. Most of the research, however, has been conducted on perceptions of two-dimensional line drawings, and the results extrapolated to the three-dimensional built world by a number of theoreticians (Isaac 1971; Levi 1974; Arnheim 1977). The conclusions have been applied to the analysis of the aesthetic effect of individual buildings rather than to building complexes or urban environments.

The conclusions of Gestalt theory are based on the assumption that an *isomorphism* exists between patterns in the visual field and the neural mechanisms of the brain. While such a process cannot be discounted, it now seems more likely that the patterns and associations are learned and are thus culture-specific rather than innate and universal. The patterns act as symbols. Thus, within much of European-derived cultural patterns the conclusions drawn from Gestalt theory, such as those of Rudolf Arnheim (1977), seem to hold true.

Symbolic Aesthetics

The symbolic aesthetic value of the built environment is a fundamental component of the human experi-

1. Lincoln Center, New York City

2. Entrance to Little Village, Chicago

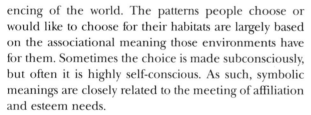

3. Portland, Oregon

Figure 17-9: Symbolic Aesthetics and Urban Design
Different environments communicate different meanings to us. Symbolic aesthetic concerns are central to establishing identity and feelings of self-esteem (see Chapters 13 and 14). One can also appreciate the symbols for themselves. Lincoln Center (1) has clear classical referents associated with high-style architecture. The Little Village gateway (2) is a symbol as a gate, but the materials and tiling also suggest it belongs to a Hispanic culture (see also Santa Barbara in Fig. 17-7(3)). It is not only the fixed features of the environment that communicate symbolic meaning but also the people and artifacts that it contains (3).

encing of the world. The patterns people choose or would like to choose for their habitats are largely based on the associational meaning those environments have for them. Sometimes the choice is made subconsciously, but often it is highly self-conscious. As such, symbolic meanings are closely related to the meeting of affiliation and esteem needs.

Our perception of symbolic meanings is so immediate and our aesthetic reaction so spontaneous that some aestheticians believe that at least some of our responses are based on innate mechanisms in the brain (Berleant 1988; Bourassa 1990). We can certainly get pleasure from recognizing the symbolic meanings of the environment without any psychological implications other than that we see them as pleasurable. It is also clear that we can examine the symbols of the environment for their own sake, as we can the environment's geometry. This examination is, however, an intellectual activity.

Intellectual Aesthetics

One of the ways in which people appreciate the environment is in terms of their understanding of *why* it is the way it is. It is a highly self-conscious process. This kind of appreciation seems to be of two types: in terms of the way the environment fits its instrumental purposes (Fitch 1965), and in terms of the normative theory of the creator of the pattern—that is, the consideration of the environment as a work of human art (Santayana 1896; Olsen 1986).

The Fit between the Built Environment and Task Functions

Few people pay attention to how the environment works except when it does not. They are aware of the misfits more easily than the fits. People who care do look at the environment critically and appreciate it in traditional *functional terms*—how well it fits its instrumental purposes, that is, its tasks (Steele 1973). This kind of analysis deals with the congruence of function and form (Michelson 1976) or, as others put it, the synomorphy between standing patterns of behavior and milieu (Barker 1968; Wicker 1979). Architects as a group seldom do such studies in any depth, although individual ones such as Herman Hertzberger are constantly recording in sketchbooks the patterns of the environment and how their affordances are put to use. Hertzberger calls it a recording

1. City Hall, Columbus, Indiana

2. Horton Center, San Diego

Figure 17-10: Intellectual Aesthetics
Most people simply respond to the built environment and its components as they experience them and not based on the designer's reason for them being the way they are. A building (1), a total urban design (2), and even a city can, however, be seen as a work of art (Olsen 1986). Any artifact or environment can be perceived in this way. Such an examination involves understanding the ideology of the designers and seeing the work as an expressive act. Such a concern is, however, largely that of the cognoscenti.

of the environmental *mechanisms*—that is, the affordances of various patterns of built form (Rietfeld 1983).

The same type of experience arises from the contemplation of historical cities and places and the analysis of why they are the way they are (Attoe 1988b). Indeed, they may well be easier to understand than our contemporary ones. This kind of understanding probably serves primarily cognitive purposes—the need to know. The act of modeling such relationships may be a process that is rewarding in itself; it involves the aesthetics of theory building.

Santayana (1896) believed that the highest aesthetic effect was achieved when the purpose was served with efficiency of form. However, this position seems to have simply been a statement of the prevailing avant-garde cultural taste at the end of the Victorian era. It was the position of the Modernists too.

There is another aspect of function that is important in this type of intellectual aesthetic assessment. It is the *firmenes* objective of architectural and landscape architectural design. This concern focuses on the structural soundness of the built environment and the utility of the materials chosen. For the aesthete the concern is with the overall cleverness and/or novelty of the structure at a broad scale and in its detailing. "God is in the detail" is an aphorism attributed to Mies van der Rohe.

The Environment as a Work of Art

The environment can be regarded as a work of art in two intellectual aesthetic ways: as a medium of architectural expression for its own sake, and as a medium for conveying an architect's message to others. The first is not a deliberate act of communication, although one who observes the results may assign a meaning to the expression; the second is deliberate. In a sense all works of urban design end up being works of art. They are expressions of the culture of a city or a community, and they are the expressions of what an urban designer or urban design team thinks is good. A work of art implies that an individual wishes to express his or her view of society using elements, in this case of urban design, as a palette. The Empire State Plaza in Albany, New York, is an expression of Nelson Rockefeller (after whom it is now named) as interpreted by Harrison and Abramowitz; nineteenth-century Paris of Napoleon III as implemented by Baron Haussmann; and the new Bucharest, Romania, capitol complex of President Ceausescu as designed by Anca Petrescu.

Works of art are artificial displays. They can enrich our experience of the world, both pleasurably and negatively. Richard Serra's *Tilted Arc* across Federal Plaza in New York City was his personal statement, an expression of his view of the world (see Fig. 3–15(3)). It was little understood and spoiled an already dull plaza even further. It has now been removed despite strong protests from the art community that the rights of artists to express themselves were being infringed (Weyergraff-Serra and Buskirk 1990). Few people in New York City regarded it as an aesthetic (i.e., a pleasing) object. It was an intellectual aesthetic statement that provoked thought on the part of a number of people, enough thought certainly for them to lobby for its removal.

The Environment as a Container of Works of Art

In many places artists have been asked to adorn walls with murals, reliefs, or billboards. Sometimes the pavement is designed as a work of art. In these cases there is a blurring of the environment as a work of art and as a container of art. More specifically, squares, boulevards, parks, internal public spaces, and other urban places have sculptures and fountains. In these cases the art works are clearly seen as objects in space.

The purposes of public art are at least fourfold: (1) to beautify a place (often, after the fact, to enliven it), (2) to raise the identity and self-esteem of people through the display of heroes and heroic behavior, and to commemorate important events, (3) to enable artists to exhibit work—to give them "rooms" for self-expression, and (4) to educate the public (see also Gallion and Eisner 1986).

The development of public art programs during the last three decades in the United States and elsewhere has led to a concern for the integration of art objects in an artistic environment. Much of the abstract art that has been placed has been highly controversial because it does not relate to popular taste cultures. That which is realistic is often criticized because it has the wrong symbolic messages. Public art nevertheless has succeeded in raising interest in art forms.

Urban Design Ideologies

In looking at the environment as a work of art, the intellectual aesthetic concern is with the normative theory of the designer(s) and the appreciation of the environment that comes from understanding that theory. Many normative theories are obscure and thus not easy to understand. Others deal with a multiplicity of variables, many of which are not explicitly stated but are implied by the work (Lang 1987a, 1988). What is explicitly stated may well have a single focus and thus be easier to comprehend (see Gosling and Maitland 1984a, 1984b). The view of urban design as theater, for instance, is at least understandable, even if it is a very limited view.

In examining the environment in terms of the intellectual aesthetics theories that form its logical basis, the concern is with designers' intentions, the patterns they have used, and the linkage between intention and design. The concern is with a designer's normative theory. For the cognoscenti who care, an understanding of the relationship between normative theory and design patterns heightens their appreciation of the environment. However, whether one responds warmly to the environment as a result of the understanding or not depends on one's attitudes toward specific designers and their intentions and on one's own feelings about the environment itself. Some extraordinarily poor work is held in high esteem by professionals because it was done by a famous architect. The opposite is also true; some good designs are held in low esteem because they were done by practitioners perceived to be run-of-the-mill. Balance theory explains these relationships well (see Chapter 1).

Few people other than architects and the cognoscenti pay much attention to the ideas of designers and their aesthetic intentions per se. If one accepts that many different forms can meet the same need and that the same form can meet many needs (i.e., the processes of response and stimulus generalization apply to people in their use of the built environment), then urban designers have some latitude, or freedom, to impose an idea on the geometry of the layouts that they design and yet to achieve a functional environment in terms of the basic and cognitive needs of its inhabitants or users. Designers can get their own "jollies"—make their own expressive acts. The question is: "How much can urban design be an autonomous expression of the designer's own values and still be a service to others?" It is a frequently repeated observation that the failure of much urban design, particularly that admired by professional designers, has been due to such expressions that have not considered user's values (Norberg Schulz 1965).

There are a number of coexisting urban design ideologies today (see Chapter 3). Understanding Neo-Rationalism, Neo-Empiricism, Neo-Traditionalism, Weak/Discrete Architecture, and so on, and considering a design in terms of the ideology on which it is based, demand a high degree of intellectual knowledge and caring about design ideologies. Few architects have this ability and probably even fewer laypeople care about urban design ideologies. We respond to what the environment affords us in our own terms. The number of people who are concerned with the ideologies behind the production of paintings and sculpture is much higher. The examination of fine arts ideologies is part of the formal liberal arts education of many more people than is the examination of urban design ideologies.

Some architects, particularly those out of the Empirical school, regard many present ideologies as frivolous because they have very little to do with enhancing the experiencing of the environment. Christopher Alexander (1990), in a letter to *Progressive Architecture*, comments:

> I think the time has come to take the gloves off, and to acknowledge publicly that the cabalistic confraternity of architects in the United States, as in England, has been perpetuating a gigantic scam on the almost unsuspecting public for 50 years.

1. Daley Plaza, Chicago

Photograph by Alix Verge

2. 1984 World's Trade Fair, New Orleans

Figure 17-11: The Aesthetics of Public Art

Public art is used to educate the public to appreciate an artistic taste culture, to heighten a group's self-esteem by memorializing successes in their histories, or to provide artists with an opportunity to express their views of society. From an urban design viewpoint, works of art, particularly sculpture, are used to give a focal point to an otherwise uninspiring place (1), to neaten the world, perhaps to amuse us (2; see Fig. 17–4(1)), and sometimes, with murals or reliefs, to reduce the boredom of a blank façade (see Fig. 17–4(3)). Frequently public art serves many purposes simultaneously.

The designers that Alexander attacks evaluate the environment in terms of their own motivations and associations—their own Rationalist art theories unrelated to human experience. In the United States, as in the countries of Western Europe and Latin America, and in Australia, there are no universally understood codes that are used to explain the layout of a city or place in the way there were in ancient Rome (Rykwert 1988). People cannot compare the layout of their own built environments to the ideal form suggested by such codes. There is no intellectual aesthetic of this type. We can analyze historical cities based on the codes contemporary to their development and get pleasure from that understanding. For instance, understanding Madurai or Jaipur (Shearer 1983) in terms of the Hindu *mandala* heightens our understanding of the symbolic purposes the layout served.

It is possible to sustain contradictory feelings about the environment—to like the environment for the experiences it affords but not for the ideas that generated it. We can sustain the contradiction because the feelings are about different things—the design product and the design process. We can also appreciate the way a design meets a stated or implied goal of designers and their clients while disagreeing with the goals set up in the first place. An example of this contradiction appears in our appreciation of Baroque urban design. One may disparage the intention of arrogant display but admire the results because the places created are fine ones in which to be. In the same way one might ridicule the ideas and the professed methodological logic of Bernard Tschumi in the design of Parc de la Villette but admire the results for their playfulness or see that he has, apparently unknowingly, used the *morphological analysis* approach to the generation of new design forms. In reverse, one might recognize the utility and the logic of the unselfconscious design of the Las Vegas Strip, as many architects do, and yet hate its vulgarity. Admiring Las Vegas's ingenuity is one thing; liking it requires a greater sympathy for middle American culture than most leading architects possess.

Both the professional architect and the architectural cognoscenti become habituated to existing urban design theories. Sometimes a new ideology is sought not because it provides for a more livable environment, but rather for itself, because it is new. It is a new avant-garde idea. Such an ideology might be absorbed into the field if influential critics deem it to be the right thing to do, or else it is shelved because it does not capture the hearts of major decision makers or potential new leaders in the design fields (Prak 1984).

AESTHETIC EXPRESSION

Expressive behaviors used to entertain other people are instrumental and not the type of behavior being considered here. Many genuine aesthetic expressions occur within the built environment. Individuals plant trees, grow flowers in boxes, paint their houses, and so on. Such expressions are unmotivated artistic ones when the pleasure derived from them is intrapersonal rather than interpersonal. Such works may have side effects if somebody else regards them as motivated art—assigns a communicative value to them. There is, for instance, considerable debate over graffiti. The intention of pure expressive acts is not, however, to communicate meaning to others. They are done for their own pleasure. As such they stand in contrast to works of public art.

Expressive acts are difficult to identify and prohibitions against them are more likely to stem from the social controls a society exerts rather than the lack of affordances of the built environment. The behavioral program needs to identify the expressive acts that have urban design implications—a difficult task.

THE BEHAVIORAL PROGRAM

If it is to meet people's aesthetic needs, any behavioral program to be used as a basis for urban design must recognize the following: (1) the aesthetic character of the environment is very much due to the behavior settings that exist in the public realm—the places that a city, or a precinct within it, possesses; (2) people's aesthetic experience of these places is multimodal; (3) expressive behavior is part of the aesthetic experience of many people; (4) while the fundamental nature of an aesthetic experience is universal, what are regarded as pleasurable characteristics of a behavior setting or simply its milieu will vary by personality, stage in life cycle, socioeconomic status and, above all, culture; and (5) intellectual aesthetic constructs are only of interest to a very few people. There are constant reminders of these factors in novels as well as the research literature.

> Is it the mindlessness of childhood that opens up the world? Today nothing happens in a gas station. I'm eager to leave.... But at thirteen, sitting with my back against a wall, it was a marvelous place to be. The delicious smell of gasoline, the cars coming and going, the fresh air hose, the half-heard voices buzzing in the background—these things hung musically in the air, filling me with a sense of well being (Conroy, source unknown).

The feelings people have about a city or its precincts depend on their attitudes toward the sequence of behavior settings they encounter and the people participating in them. As a result the aesthetic goals of any urban design program should define:

1. The range and nature of the major behavior settings to be provided in the public realm based on the potential behaviors and attitudes of the range of people of concern.

2. The required orchestration of behavior settings along the links between these major settings based on the set of likely movement patterns that people will follow in seeing places.

The difficulty in making precise specifications is that, as always, we are designing for the future based on our present knowledge plus some predictions about what might be required then. One of the obligations of urban designers is certainly to bring future possibilities to people's attention (see Chapter 23, Fundamental Attitudes for Urban Design).

To meet the diverse population's aesthetic needs in the public realm the above two sets of specifications need to be elaborated to deal with:

1. The feelings of pleasure that the designers should be expected to create so that users derive a full multimodal and sensory experience (a) from their interactions in and with the environment as a set of behavior settings, (b) from the geometric composition of the public realm's milieus, especially as users move through them and the links between them, and (c) from the symbolic or associational meanings that both the behaviors and the milieu have for them.

2. The results people should get from the conscious analysis that they might make of the environment as a purposefully orchestrated and designed environment—as a work of art. The concern is with the orchestration of sensory, formal, and symbolic experiences within an artistic attitude. This concern may or may not duplicate the first. It depends on the attitudes of designers and what society allows them to do.

Ultimately urban designers focus their attention on the milieu and its design or the guidelines for its design by other people. In doing so it is easier for them to deal with designing for the affordances of environmental experience and contemplation of the environment than with designing the affordances for expressive behavior. Unless the expressive behaviors form part of a formal organization and can be designed from the outside, all the urban designer can do is to create a *potential environment* for them or to write design guidelines for their creation. Whether or not the behaviors actually take place depends, as stated previously, on the predispositions of the people concerned.

One of the major design goals that has to be established in the behavioral programming process concerns the degree to which individuals have latitude in carrying out expressive acts that actually change the milieu of the public realm. What should be designed formally and what should be left for people to do themselves? Resolving such issues is the heart of behavioral programming for urban design (see also Chapters 19 and 22).

THE DESIGN PROGRAM

Translating a generic set of aesthetic goals into a specific and universal set of design actions and patterns is impossible. At a broad policy level, however, it can be stated that the urban designer's task is to create or write guidelines for the creation of: (1) a set of milieus for events and activities so that, as behavior settings, they afford the sensory, formal, and symbolic experiences that make places pleasant to inhabit; (2) a sequence of pleasurable experiences, or pattern of places; and (3) places having a clear intellectual idea that is the basis for the geometry of places and the links between them. The first two tasks are rather like the design task James Joyce set himself in writing *Ulysses*—designing for simultaneously occurring events in space. The third is something over which we have direct control.

Behavior Settings

The ultimate aesthetic goal of urban design is to create pleasurable places—behavior settings—in the public realm. The specific urban design task is to specify the milieu that should exist. Any programming effort, whoever carries it out, is a specification for the desired and possible sets of actions that should occur in places and along the links between them (see Chapter 10).

The urban designer's domain of concern, in conjunction with, or for, other decision makers, includes the design of the behavior settings of the public realm. Such a concern is manifested in decisions regarding land and building uses as well as the use of places and the links between them. It is seldom that an urban designer thinks holistically about the sequence of behavior settings for their potential contribution to meeting people's aesthetic needs. The work of some architects such as Charles Moore and Herman Hertzberger and, especially, landscape architects such as Lawrence Halprin shows considerable concern for these matters. It is easier to consider the overall aesthetic effect of places in total urban design than in the redevelopment of existing cities. In the latter case, the focus tends to be on specific places, be they plazas, city blocks, or streets. The overall relationships that exist have been largely unselfconsciously developed in the United States. Over time they can be orchestrated into a system along with appropriate new places and links by applying design policies with persistence.

The Milieu

The design of a multifunctional milieu is difficult. This difficulty partly explains why designers select only a few issues to address. The layout of the public realm has to keep people comfortable, provide the appropriate privacy for their activities through screening and through territorial markers, symbolically help them attain a feeling of self-esteem, and provide opportunities for continued learning about the environment. It would be possible to stop there and to claim that by solving all those issues a new aesthetic would be developed. There is, however, also the aesthetic factor per se to consider. Providing well for other human needs will make a substantial contribution to the overall aesthetic quality of the environment, but whether that environment impinges on us and gives a feeling that it is beautiful, or we examine it to see how well it meets our own aesthetic criteria or recognize its underlying "artist's" aesthetic ideology, depends on additional aesthetic concerns. For this reason urban designers must consider the aesthetic effect of what they do in a multidimensional way that parallels the way we experience the world.

Sensory Aesthetics

Designers can orchestrate the sensory aesthetic experience of single places, but we seldom do. Dealing with the sensory experience through a sequence of places has hardly been addressed as a design issue. A landscape designer may pay special attention to the sequence of odors generated by plants or to the sequential visual experience as people move through a garden. The traditional Japanese garden has much to teach us about this character. In these gardens, but not in the modern Japanese city, there is an aesthetic code that can be learned so that the aesthetic experience is both sensory and intellectual.

It is perhaps easier to design for sensory aesthetic pleasure using elements of the natural world than the other elements of the human environment. Using natural elements also contributes to meeting a number of basic needs—the need for a belonging through obtaining a sense of place in the environment and an orientation in it, for instance (see Chapters 11 and 12). Flowering trees, annuals, and perennials can be planted in parks and plazas, the odor and sounds of the sea can be brought into a waterfront design, but such things as the odors of baking are more difficult to plan for specifically. Indeed, the capriciousness with which such sensations impinge on our senses contributes to the aesthetic effects of cities; they surprise us. It is perhaps easier to identify the negative sensory experiences—the noise and odor pollution—and attempt to eliminate them. The intellectual aesthetic appreciation of how this is done is beyond the scope of all but a few people, but the subconscious sensory experience is part of the pleasure almost all people derive from the environment.

The design concern is also with channeling breezes by the configuration of the built environment not only to make the public realm physiologically comfortable (see Chapter 11) but also for their aesthetic pleasure. Much the same point can be made about the textures of the surfaces of the environment (particularly the ground surfaces) and the pleasure they may yield to the sense of touch, about the colors of the environment, and about the whole array of sounds (an argument for making the environment hospitable for songbirds). The basic point is that urban designers can make the public realm much more pleasing sensually than they do at present. Nowadays the sensory aesthetic quality of the public realm is largely accidental.

Formal Aesthetics

The patterns of the city serve many purposes and functions. Each individual function requires a specific geometry of the milieu to operate ideally, although for many activities precision in form is not required. Each geometry also has an aesthetic value of its own. The design goal to meet aesthetic needs is to create geometries in the environment that are complex enough to hold one's attention and yet not so complex that they are unintelligible and appear to be a haphazard mess. They need to be interesting in themselves and yet not be so complex that other, more basic design goals, such as the need to have an environment that helps wayfinding, are abrogated. The need is to identify where on the simplicity-complex continuum a target population's tastes are now and to design for some temporal distance ahead. If this action is taken the environment will be deemed to be satisfactory now and will retain that feeling for a while. After that it will be regarded, for good or ill, as the product of an era by those who understand the change intellectually, and as something for which they have little empathy by those who do not. The design goal should be to strive for ambiguous designs, those that can be seen as simple or complex depending on one's attitudes! In addition, the goal would be to have a variety of formal compositions so that there are a number of places for which people have an empathy (Lozano 1988). These tasks are demanding.

It is difficult to formulate detailed urban design guidelines to achieve specific aesthetic ends in the absence of a detailed empirical theory. The constituents of what makes a complex design will have to remain largely intuitive, but current understandings of what is ordered and what is disordered, and what is simple and what is complex, can aid us considerably (see Kepes 1944; De Sausmarez 1964; Arnheim 1965, 1977; Venturi 1966; Isaac 1971). Proportional systems, the repetition of patterns and units, and the continuity of line have long been used to give an order to the patterns of the environment (Rasmussen 1959). The number of elements that can be seen at particular distances can also be orchestrated to give a sense of order or disorder to the environment (Schubert 1965).

The more intriguing design task is to take these observations into the fourth dimension and to design for the sequential experiencing of the world. The type of sequence one should strive to achieve will be situation-specific, depending on the activities in which people are

1. Southern California

2. Boulder, Colorado

3. Pike Market Place, Seattle

Figure 17–12: The Motion of Objects in the Visual Field
The moving and apparently moving elements of our physical environments such as the waves of the sea and people themselves attract our attention and form part of the milieu of places (1). The movement of cars and people not only generates activities but can make an important contribution to the aesthetic effect of cities (2). The movement of people, cars, tree limbs, and flags and the stroboscopic effect of advertising lights should all be considered in urban design, for they are part of the milieu of everyday life (3).

engaged and on people's speed of movement through the environment. For pedestrians, a dense sequence of spaces is desirable to hold their attention. The definition of "dense" will vary depending on the situations to which people are habituated (Balint 1955). Those people who are used to the wide open spaces of the prairies will require much lower density of transitions than those used to denser urban environments, but the same design principle holds. Where immediate wayfinding is necessary, the layout of the environment should be clear from specific station points along a route. Similarly, in the design of settings to be seen from moving vehicles, the nature of the traffic flow is an important determinant of the nature of the sequential experience desired. Designing a limited access highway differs from designing a city street, but it is clear that in both cases the aesthetic quality of the environment depends largely on the sequential experience people derive from it.

The design task is to create occluding surfaces that obscure vistas. As one passes them one will see a new vista opening up. The goal is to provide a variety of vistas, short and long, busy and quiet, again ensuring that the diversity is not bewildering (Lozano 1988). Some locations have natural features, such as hills or valleys, to which vistas can be opened up. In others, it is the sequence of places within the built environment itself that offers the predominant vistas along paths of movement. Not only do we see the environment through our own movement, but there are many elements in the environment that move and attract our attention. They need to be seen as elements of design too.

City Beautiful designs provide not only for *esteem needs* but for open vistas that act as a contrast to the denser urban environment that is adjacent. Much of the charm of Paris or the Benjamin Franklin Parkway in Philadelphia comes from this type of contrasting experience. Ultimately, however, the symbolic values of the built environment are more important than the formal, although they are so closely intertwined that it is difficult to separate them.

Symbolic Aesthetics

Designing the symbolism of the environment is generally associated with meeting people's needs for affiliation and esteem (see Chapters 14 and 15). At a high level in the hierarchy of human needs, mathematics and geometry have a transcendental value for many people. Where this value still exists it is important to design within the canons that specify good form. Failure to do so will make people uneasy.

Designing built environments or the guidelines that shape them to provide the symbolic meanings that amount to an aesthetic experience per se requires an understanding of the values people within a culture hold. This understanding can only come from analyzing the choices people make. It is clear that for many Americans the symbolic landscapes that they enjoy consist of elements of the natural world—trees and open space—in the English landscape tradition, but many have a Continental European ancestry and the formal garden type of landscape is attractive. If the mainstream of children's literature is any indicator, Americans continue to be socialized to regard urban environments that are well manicured, treed, and ordered as visually pleasurable. If urban designers can design environments that meet people's expectations in terms of their affiliation and esteem needs, their aesthetic needs are likely to be fulfilled as well.

Intellectual Aesthetics

Given the dynamics of the marketplace in the United States, and that different people are simultaneously striving for their own esteem through design, there will almost inevitably be different design ideologies being used simultaneously to shape the city. Sometimes these ideologies will complement each other and sometimes be in conflict. Different projects will be designed for different markets and by different architects. Their availability for different interpretations will enrich the experiencing of the overall city provided they do not add up to a chaotic environment. The goal of urban design policy is to provide the framework for achieving unity in diversity.

Urban residents throughout the world are habituated to cities that are not agglomerations of object buildings in space but are a densely woven fabric of streets, sidewalks, built forms, and natural forms. The Modernists tried to get away from this pattern, and where they have done so the results have been appreciated mainly by other architects supporting the same ideology, not by broader populations. At the same time it must be recognized that new urban forms are emerging related to the automobile as a primary means of personal transportation and the truck as the primary means of transporting goods. Superimposing an artificial aesthetic structure, such as Deconstructionism, on cities helps little unless the resulting forms have meaning for more people than just the artistic elite.

It is possible to make the intellectual constructs that architects use when designing better known in the same way that historical buildings are marked. Signboards could bring people's attention to the pattern of the environment and inform them of the design ideas that generated it. For example, signboards could tell people visiting Battery Park City about the guidelines that shaped its development and their basis. Such devices would serve cognitive as well as aesthetic functions and may well also make wayfinding easier.

Expressive Aesthetics

Expressive acts, it has been noted, can and do take place everywhere—on sidewalks and in parks, in private

1. New York City

2. Bunker Hill, Los Angeles

3. Brandt Boulevard, Glendale, California

4. 16th Street Mall, Denver

Photograph courtesy of Hanna/Olin, Ltd.

5. Beacon Hill, Boston

Photograph by Deepti Nijhawan

6. Trenton Commons, Trenton, New Jersey

Collection of the author

Figure 17-13: The Aesthetics of Detailing

The details of the environment and their level of maintenance contribute to its sense of orderliness and to its symbolic qualities. The public realm of the U.S. city, with few exceptions such as downtown Portland, Oregon (see, e.g., Figs. 11–4(3) and 16–3(3)), is detailed on a purely ad hoc basis with attention being paid only to bits and pieces of it. Much is economically "satisficing"— that is, good enough (1). There are, however, many examples of efforts to do better with both surface materials and street furniture (2,3,4,5; see also Figs. 13–11(1), 14–7(2), 14–11(2), 16–4(1) and 17–7(3) for other instances). Not only do surfaces have to support behavior patterns under different conditions, including rain (4) and snow, but they need to be visually pleasing for both cognoscenti and the laypeople who care. This end is not always easy to achieve because of the symbolic qualities of different ways of detailing. The furniture of the Trenton Commons (6) has long since been removed because it was seen as foreign to the city. In addition, many environments should not be too highly manicured because minor damages through heavy use lead to an air of neglect.

1. Santa Barbara, California

2. Lower Manhattan, New York

3. Seattle

Photograph by Steve King

and in public. Expressions in art form are usually carried out as drawings or sculptures using different media. Graffiti has been mentioned as an expressive act that is generally not condoned and that may be an act of striving to meet an esteem need rather than an expressive need per se. One can design walls that do not take graffiti well in order to reduce the problem, but ultimately it is the social planning of society and the opportunities for legitimate expression that must be sought.

One of the difficulties in urban design is to design simultaneously to achieve a communal order in built form and to include the myriad individual expressive aesthetic displays. On the one hand, the goal would be to encourage architects to give individuals freedom of expression; on the other hand, it would be to ensure that such acts do not detract from the whole. In total designs such as the Illinois Institute of Technology (see Figs. I-1(2) and 17-8(3)), future architects have little freedom to express their views without creating a major change in the complex's present aesthetic qualities.

The present urban design goal must be to give an overall structure to a scheme that is powerful enough to persist as an ordering device when future architects make changes to it based on their own aesthetic expressions. Le Corbusier proposed such a scheme for Algiers (Le Corbusier 1960). In the United States the way this end is actually achieved in practice is usually to impose controls over the public realm yet allow designers a complete freedom of choice (given the need to meet basic survival needs) in the private realm. Such moves are, however, still seen as infringing on both people's property rights and their freedom of expression.

The display of expressive art works needs to be integrated into the design of behavior settings rather than simply being added to the milieu at will. Often, however, the desire is to find a place to display art or to commemorate an event. In this case, the problem is to find "niches" where the displays can be made to their best effect without disturbing the quality of a setting.

URBAN DESIGN CONSEQUENCES

Total and all-of-a-piece urban designs are likely to have their own aesthetic character based on architects' norma-

Figure 17-14: Foreground and Background Buildings
In the traditional city, and often in smaller American cities today, it was the religious and civic buildings that differed from the others and were special places (1; see also Fig. 17-2(2)). They also possessed the symbols of their status in their architecture and siting. In the modern city (2), all buildings seem to be striving to make a statement, although in the case of Seattle it is the deviant type—the Sky Needle—that has become its symbol (3).

tive positions and the guidelines within which they work. These guidelines in the United States are likely to be very responsive to the marketplace. While the marketplace does tend to work toward a unity of character of buildings, architects will still tend to design them as objects in space to the extent that they can do so. The question thus still is: "Will the pieces add up to a collage that means something as a whole—will the city have some character—or will the city end up being a hodgepodge of ideas (which is, in its own way, a character)?"

The city is likely to be a collage of unrelated projects, but if contextual issues are considered in the design of each—if each project is seen as part of a whole, a city and a region—as a true functional urban design should, then the parts, despite their differences, should add up to a whole. A system of guidelines can be worked out at the city level that allows for some coordinating aesthetic framework within which the disparate architectural and landscape designs sit. The focus in writing these guidelines should be on the connecting elements—the streets and sidewalks and other longitudinal elements of the environment such as parks. The design should be concerned with enhancing the sensory, the formal aesthetic, the symbolic aesthetic experiences, and possibly with fulfilling the expressive needs of specific populations; the intellectual aesthetic effects will follow automatically.

Most cities have found that they have to deal with more pressing needs than aesthetic ones, yet in so doing municipal governments are making many decisions that shape the city's aesthetic character. With some forethought and persistence in application, an overall aesthetic strategy can be formulated to enhance the city's aesthetic qualities while simultaneously dealing with the basic needs of its inhabitants. San Francisco (1988) has formulated such a strategy in a series of urban design plans and amendments for the city and for precincts within it (e.g., Van Ness area, the Northeastern Waterfront, the Rincon Hill) as part of its Master Plan dating from 1971 to 1990 (see also A. Jacobs 1980). The urban design plans specify the overall objectives and policies required to achieve them. The results are still open to debate because "beauty is still in the eye of the beholder!" Nevertheless, San Francisco retains its reputation as one of the most beautiful cities in the United States, partly because of the topography, but also in large measure because of the way people have handled the continuing development of the city.

Considering aesthetics in the way suggested here is a complex task. Many designers thus prefer to use apparently successful existing places as the basis for their own design rather than to use a full-scale analysis of what should be done in a particular situation. They use a typological approach to design. It would enhance their creative abilities if they came to an understanding of what makes such places (e.g., the Great Mosque of Shah, Isfahan, Iran) so esteemed. To do so they would have to look at the attributes described here.

MAJOR REFERENCES

Ashihara, Yoshinobu (1983). *The Aesthetic Townscape.* Translated from the Japanese by Lynne E. Riggs. Cambridge, MA: MIT Press.

Broadbent, Geoffrey (1990). *Emerging Concepts in Urban Space Design.* New York: Van Nostrand Reinhold International.

Gosling, David, and Barry Maitland (1984b). "Urbanism." *Architectural Design Profile* 51. London: Architectural Design Publications.

Lang, Jon (1987a). "Aesthetic Values and the Built Environment," and "Normative Environmental Design Theory." In *Creating Architectural Theory: The Role of the Behavioral Sciences in Environmental Design.* New York: Van Nostrand Reinhold, pp. 170–241.

Lozano, Eduardo E. (1988). "Visual Needs in Urban Environments and in Physical Planning." In Jack Nasar, ed., *Environmental Aesthetics: Theory, Research, and Applications.* New York: Cambridge University Press, pp. 395–421.

Maslow, Abraham (1971). *The Farther Reaches of Human Nature.* New York: Viking.

Nasar, Jack, ed. (1988b). *Environmental Aesthetics: Theory, Research, and Applications.* New York: Cambridge University Press.

Rasmussen, Steen Eiler (1959). *Experiencing Architecture.* Cambridge, MA: MIT Press.

Relph, Edward (1987). *The Modern Urban Landscape.* Baltimore: Johns Hopkins University Press.

San Francisco, City of (1988). *Urban Design: An Element of the Master Plan of the City and County of San Francisco.* San Francisco: City and County of San Francisco.

Santayana, George (1896). *The Sense of Beauty.* Reprint. New York: Dover, 1955.

A FUNCTIONAL
BIOGENIC ENVIRONMENT

Ithaca, New York

The terrestrial environment has evolved over eons and continues to evolve. Even within more recent historical times there have been significant shifts in climate and a reconfiguration of the topography of the Earth due to natural processes and events. These modifications have led to alterations in the flora and fauna of places. Since these developments and their causes do not occur in neat, easy-to-predict cycles, they are difficult to understand. The changes resulting from human activities make accurate predictions of the future state of the biogenic environment even more difficult as we strain to understand the chain of their effects. Thirty years ago a new ice age was predicted; now there is a very real fear of a global warming resulting from human actions in the foreseeable future, with a concomitant rise in the level of the sea. Little attention is being paid to this possibility by urban designers and public officials. Such changes seem remote from us and we see little evidence of them now. The focus is on the more immediate situation. Urban designers, however, need to do more than simply comply with building ordinances and zoning codes. They need to be part of the process of "turning the planet into a house we can live in" and in which we can continue to live (Gapp 1990).

Historically, settlements were shaped by their inhabitants with a significant consideration for the nature of the biogenic environment. As with the act of designing, it was a largely unselfconscious process. People had to be considerate because they had little power over nature. Changes in the biogenic environment were almost entirely due to its own internal processes. There were substantially fewer people on Earth to cause changes in its nature. The process of design was a biologically pragmatic one standing in contrast to the financially pragmatic one that predominates today. The results were a vernacular architecture and a set of urban forms very much in keeping with the processes of the biogenic environment. Human settlements were developed in a way that demanded low technology and low energy in comparison to the high-technology and high-energy demands of the hermetic interior environments of U.S. cities and much of the technologically developed world today. Traditional vernacular environments are much admired by architects today (see Rudofsky 1964), although few people would choose such places in which to live. They are simply not comfortable enough to meet most modern standards. People have become habituated to greater comfort, and in seeking it they have made radical changes to the environment. As the population of the world increases, with the concomitant growth in urban agglomerations, so the changes become even greater.

In the development of the modern city scant attention has been paid to the possible effects of physical changes on the characteristics of the biogenic environment. The concern has been with ameliorating the effects of the biogenic environment on the city. The climate has been controlled through the artificial mechanisms of heating and cooling, rivers have been channeled to serve as underground sewers, water runoff patterns have been changed, building densities and configurations have formed heat islands, towns have been built in swamps and floodplains, migrating birds fly into tall buildings. In the United States little notice has been taken of the topography of a site except where it has been too steep to build on or where it helped the natural fall required by sewer lines. Vast natural resources have been consumed, some of which are replaceable and others not. Human settlements have been developed in accordance with the cultural needs of people rather than the biogenic needs of the environment around us. In the long run, changes in the biogenic environment will affect the affordances of the natural world for human life.

Unlike preindustrial societies we have the technology to make major changes in our world. Its use has resulted in the cities that are loved by their inhabitants—San Francisco, New York, Venice, London, Paris, Sydney, even Calcutta, despite the appalling living conditions for some of their inhabitants. Contrary to popular myths the list of loved metropolises in the United States is a long one and urbanization has benefited many lives. The side effects of urbanization have, however, been vast. In building cities serious questions are now being raised about the impact of humans and their artifacts on the biogenic world. It is in the human self-interest to do so. As populations increase in size and as the amount of garbage and pollutants generated increases as mass consumerism reaches down into the ranks of the previously poor, the patterning of human settlements needs to be reconsidered. The reconsideration is needed not simply to make cities more salubrious places in which to live but rather to create a healthy biogenic environment. The depletion of resources consumed in development and the effect of cities and human activities on the quality of the air, wetlands, rivers, and sea all need to be understood.

The expressed concerns about cities and urban design have been, quite rightly, twofold. We need to understand and to take action on the deleterious nature of the effect of humans and cities on the operation of the natural world per se, and vice versa. We are beginning to understand the variables of importance in describing these relationships as a result of the empirical research carried out by social and natural scientists. Some of this research has focused on the biogenic environment in general (e.g., Hough 1984; Spirn 1984) and some on particular cities (e.g., Goldstein

and Izeman 1990 on New York; Cronon 1991 on Chicago and the West). The goal is to create a paradigmatic shift in the nature of the design fields—regional planning, landscape architecture, and urban design in particular—from seeing people as controllers of nature to husbanders of nature.

One of the major paradigmatic shifts that has already occurred in the normative theory of the design fields is landscape architecture's shift from a nineteenth- and twentieth-century anthropocentric view of human dominance over nature to a form of "ecological integration between human systems and environment" during the second half of the twentieth century (Corner 1991). There has been a growing courtship of nature by landscape architects. Accompanying this change has been a strong advocacy for designers to learn from preindustrial settlement how to reduce energy consumption at three levels of design decision: urban patterns, building patterns, and the devices used to heat and cool buildings. In preindustrial environments these patterns were developed over time as a pragmatic response to the need to use the forces of nature to their advantage given the limits of their technology. Much of the argument for an increasing concern with the quality of the biogenic environment, however, seems to be as much an advocacy for a particular landscape aesthetic—the picturesque—on the part of biological ecologists and designers as an advocacy for a biologically sound environment.

This advocacy seems particularly true among those designers who have come out of the Empiricism of the Anglo-American tradition with its regressive utopianism and its antiurban bias. The goal is to create green cities and particularly cities with wilderness areas in contrast to manicured parks (see also Chapter 16, Meeting Cognitive Needs). Perceptions of ecological soundness are used as a defense. Thus there is not only an art defense used to justify some urban design aesthetic decisions, but also a green defense used to justify designers' own aesthetic goals. Finding that such aesthetic attitudes are based on a taste culture (which in itself is legitimate) rather than on ecological soundness tends to defeat the basic design goal. The concern should rather be with the biogenic environment as a system that if harmed harms us all.

The ecological issues that need to be addressed by urban designers are major ones. They are important in shaping human futures, let alone the future of other organisms. The goal is to develop human settlements based on biologically sound design principles so that the biogenic environment is not harmed. This position does not mean that the biogenic environment needs to be kept in a static state. It can be changed for the better—in terms of its own functioning. Sometimes we may have to allow damage to the natural environment to occur. Almost inevitably we may have to sacrifice the quality of the biogenic environment for other public interest benefits. The outline of design attitudes and actions that such a set of observations implies is presented in Chapter 18, Meeting the Needs of the Biogenic Environment. The details have been well articulated by others (e.g., Hough 1984; Spirn 1984). ■

18

MEETING THE NEEDS OF
THE BIOGENIC ENVIRONMENT

The biogenic environment consists of many interrelated components (see Chapter 1). They are those that constitute the *edaphic* environment—the topography, geology, and climate of a place; and the *bionic* environment—its flora and fauna. The two are inextricably linked in an evolving system as changes in one component affect the other. Some changes are minor, but a succession of minor changes can result in major modifications to the working of the overall system. In addition, some relatively minor changes can have major effects. Human settlement patterns are very much part of this biogenic system—they are adaptations to it and are changed by it over time.

Our ability to develop ecosystem models that include the essential feedback loop between changes in settlement forms and changes in the condition of the biogenic environment, while substantially furthered by recent empirical research, is still limited (Goldsmith 1990). Much still has to be accepted with uncertainty. One of the reasons for this lack of knowledge is simply that, until recently, ecological studies have focused on the countryside. There has been little consideration of the nature of the natural systems that operate in a city. During the course of the twentieth century in the United States the design goal has been to provide more open space—more parks—for the health of people rather than the health of the biogenic environment (J. Peterson 1979). This bias reflects the attitudes of the planning professions at the beginning of the twentieth century (Laurie 1979).

In much urban development during the course of this century, dealing with the environment has been seen as an engineering problem in much the same way that dealing with traffic has been; the goal has been to solve problems of the speed of flow. Indeed, the existence and growth of cities such as Houston and New Orleans (95 percent below sea level) are engineering feats in overcoming natural obstacles to development. Natural systems in both cities are now fighting back. The time has come to take designing with nature rather than against it seriously (see McHarg 1969).

A primary concern in city planning and urban design has been and still is with creating a salubrious environment for people (see Chapter 11). While this objective overlaps the need for creating an environment that is healthy in itself, the two are by no means synonymous. To create a healthy environment for people, Buckminster Fuller proposed doming over entire cities (McHale 1961; Dahinden 1972; Sky and Stone 1976), while architects such as Kenzo Tange and Paolo Soleri (1969, 1981) made proposals that put thousands of people under single roofs (Dahinden 1972). They were advocating hermetically sealed cities (see Fig. 18–1). Absent from their proposals is any major consideration of the cognitive and aesthetic qualities of lives sealed off from changes in the seasons, weather, and atmospheric phenomena occurring outside the seal. The side effects of such a scheme on the sociogenic and biogenic environments would be major. Such cities would require vast amounts of energy to be generated, almost inevitably by polluting power stations. Nuclear power is indeed relatively clean but the magnitude of possible catastrophes is high. Solar and wind power as yet only make sense in relatively few places.

The difficulty that urban designers face in making politically and economically astute proposals for either new towns or urban renewal projects is that, in designing to meet people's sociogenic needs as they are expressed today, they will be creating serious environmental problems. Often the problems will only arise at some future time, so they can be avoided politically now. At that time they may ultimately affect the attaining of people's most basic needs—the physiological needs that are the basis for survival.

Source: Dahinden (1972)

1. Proposed Dome over Manhattan, New York

2. State of Illinois Building, Chicago

3. 30th Street Station, Philadelphia

Figure 18-1: Hermetically Sealing the City
Many urban designs recognize the desire of people in technologically advanced countries for a comfortable, clean environment. Some proposals, such as that of Buckminster Fuller, suggest that portions of cities be domed so that the weather is controlled (1). The closest we have come to implementing such an idea is in the design of building complexes in harsh climates. The Minneapolis system of interlocking buildings with sealed links is a minor example. Indeed, many buildings are sealed from the outside (2) to create major indoor worlds (3). Visionaries today suggest that the windows be openable!

Many of the issues in designing both salubrious environments for people and a healthy biogenic environment are well beyond the usual geographical scale of urban design work. They occur at the metropolitan, regional, and planetary planning level. Dealing with the issues, nevertheless, has ramifications for urban design because piecemeal urban design decisions can build up to cause regional problems, particularly if economic pragmatism continues to be the primary determinant of urban form.

Many planning and urban design decisions have had predictable but unheeded effects on the quality of the biogenic environment. Suburban developments led by highway construction and the neglect of urban mass transit systems have created serious air pollution problems, exacerbated by the location of some cities, such as Los Angeles, in valleys in which polluted air can easily be trapped by temperature inversions. The Middle East oil crisis of 1973 made many people throughout the world aware of the wastefulness of much urban development and the buildings and roads that constitute it, but the cultural, economic, and political forces that generated those patterns are powerful ones and persist.

Similarly, the growing populations of many parts of the world and the increase in wealth as the result of manufacturing developments have led to voracious consumption. These, in turn, have led to the byproducts and wastes of human life and manufacturing processes, polluting the waters and the air of the world. Such outcomes are particularly noticeable in densely populated areas. Traditionally, the earth, the air, the waterways, and the sea surrounding highly populated areas have been convenient dumping grounds for human and industrial wastes. The question is how much longer can they absorb such abuse and recover. Bodies of water such as Lake Erie, the North Sea, and the Mediterranean Sea are highly polluted, although Lake Erie has never been as polluted as popular myths have suggested. The catching on fire of the Cuyahoga River in Cleveland, Ohio, in the 1960s brought to widespread attention the condition of many other rivers in the world, such as the Rhine, which are heavily polluted with chemical wastes. Major restoration efforts have brought much life back to Lake Erie and to rivers such as England's Thames, but the major oceans of the world are still becoming increasingly more polluted. There continue to be many major efforts to benefit people that have had unintended side effects that are devastating to the health of the biogenic environment and are thus a threat to human life.

The side effects of the efforts of the Tennessee Valley Authority and other river basin plans throughout the world have brought into question many major planning schemes developed during this century. The massive Soviet engineering works irrigating farmlands with water diverted from the Aral Sea is an example of a planning decision gone awry. The sea is drying up, destroying the fishing industry, leaving vessels stranded in a sea of sand and former fishing towns miles away from the water's edge. In addition, the overdose of agrochemicals has turned much of the adjacent arable areas into a wasteland (Selyunin 1990). There are a number of such "planning disasters" resulting from planners' and policymakers' failure to understand how the ecological system of a place works (P. Hall 1980). It is easy to pass the blame for them on to other people. The intention here is not to point the finger at any particular profession, but simply to state that such results stem from sets of attitudes that must change.

The factors that inhibit the biogenic environment from functioning well have resulted largely from the effects of people's inhabitation of the Earth, particularly since the Industrial Revolution. The Industrial Revolution has had the simultaneous effect of raising the quality of life for many people while increasing environmental despoliation. It increased human abilities to change the world purposefully in response to specific ends. Seldom considered, the byproducts and side effects of these activities have come home to roost.

Reactions to environmental despoliation will no doubt result in some major changes in environment design, from regional planning to architecture. The design professions, as a whole, have been reluctant to recognize the need for change even though there have been expressions of concern over the last two centuries (Mumford 1961; Boardman 1978). During the last three decades, landscape architecture quite naturally has led the way (McHarg 1969; Hough 1984; Spirn 1984).

In many ways, the Modern movement in architecture and urban design was very much concerned with the creation of a salubrious environment. Almost universally Modernists recognized the importance of the location of industries and open space in their generic plans. Many of their ideas were based on a simple analysis of the relationship between open space and human habitation and on the assumption that open space is good whatever its nature and wherever it is located. Some of their proposals would have had counterintuitive results if implemented on the scale proposed. For instance, most Modernist generic city plans such as the *linear city* located industrial uses on a town's leeward side as defined by the prevailing wind (Garnier 1917; ASCORAL 1945; Gallion and Eisner 1986). Recent empirical research has shown that such intuitively obvious solutions should be treated with caution. Prevailing winds are often associated with highly turbulent airflows, which bring the pollution back over the built-up areas. In addition, the worse pollution conditions often occur at times of low winds rather than from the direction of the prevailing winds. Location would be

better determined in relationship to these lesser winds (Chandler 1976).

A Well-Functioning Biogenic Environment

A well-functioning biogenic environment is self-correcting, self-sustaining, unpolluted, and unpolluting. It is able to withstand stress. In cities, as in the countryside, it is one that has considerable diversity—a mixture of ecological communities. Such a community fosters healthy species of flora and fauna and inhibits undesirable species such as rats and pigeons (Hough 1990). Sometimes this diversity is visually obvious—woods, streams, and marshes may exist in a place—but in other settings, such as deserts or grassland plains, it is not. Diversity is not static—it is an ever-changing equilibrium over time.

ENVIRONMENTAL DESIGN ISSUES

A number of intertwined changes brought about by human actions have to be considered in designing for human habitations while simultaneously designing a well-functioning biogenic environment. These changes include: (1) alterations to land forms, and thus (2) changes in the hydrology of cities, (3) changes due to the effects of pollution through the production of garbage and other wastes, (4) changes in the habitat for birds and animals, and (5) the consumption of irreplaceable resources. The design goal is to have a biogenic environment in which the natural forces of the world create a regenerative system while affording people the opportunities to meet their basic and cognitive needs. It is to have a healthy environment that is fulfilling to people.

Changes in Land Forms

During human history there have been many changes in the structure of the land forms of the world due to natural occurrences: volcanic eruptions, floods, and earthquakes. The human hand has made major changes too. Dams have been built, rivers diverted, floodplains filled, and highways constructed across the land. Major effects on landforms have taken place at a local level. Stone is quarried removing hills, lowlands are filled and hillsides and hilltops flattened to create building sites. Land has been cleared of natural vegetation, allowing wind and water to carry away the topsoil and clog delicate waterways with silt. As these changes have occurred, so the local climate is changed because wind and rain patterns are changed. The consequences are that the vegetation is changed from natural to human-organized and often from native to exotic and the habitats of native animals and birds are destroyed and opened to new species or none at all.

The built environment itself creates, and behaves like, a landform. Skyscrapers soar up to 500 meters into

1. Southern California

2. Los Angeles

3. Ballona Creek, California

Figure 18-2: Biogenic Environmental Concerns
Population growth and the accompanying need for housing and an infrastructure (1) that affords a high quality of life for people has directly or indirectly had negative side effects on the environment and thus on people. The quality of air is poor in many places (2). Other negative impacts result from the amount of waste we produce and from the runoff of water from large paved areas into streams, sometimes now channeled into concrete-lined beds (3). These negative side effects of urban development are not inevitable.

the air, changing patterns of light and shade on the ground and creating new patterns of wind flow. The mass of buildings creates a new physical pattern that in turn creates heat islands where the temperature may be as much as 20°F higher in the city than in the surrounding countryside. The side effects are to change rainfall patterns (although apparently not snowfall patterns), and the hard surfaces of roofs, streets, and plazas change the hydrology of cities.

There are numerous examples of places that exist in areas with major problems for people: cities in geological fault zones and in cyclonic paths, towns on barrier islands susceptible to storm damage, and cities in the flood zones of river valleys. Poor site location has led to the destruction of parts of U.S. cities and elsewhere. Often the damaged parts are rebuilt almost as they were, as were the towns of the Wyoming Valley in Pennsylvania after Hurricane Agnes in the early 1970s, and houses in Harvey Cedars, New Jersey, after they were destroyed when Long Beach Island was severed in a storm a decade earlier (McHarg 1969).

Changes in the Hydrology of Cities

Luna Leopold (1968) has identified three major effects of urban areas on hydrology: changes in total runoff, changes in peak flow characteristics, and changes

in water quality (see Chandler 1976; Hough 1984). As cities grow in size and more and more surfaces are paved, there is a growing concern for the channeling of water, the effect of runoffs on watercourses, and the lack of penetration of water into the ground to replenish water tables. The speed of runoff causes problems of erosion in water courses and oil from parking lots raises the pollution levels of water, which in turn affects aquatic life.

The actual effects vary from city to city, but the overall impact of the high degree of hard surfaces in cities is to increase flood discharges by as much as 50 percent in areas with highly pervious surfaces, and up to 400 percent in cities with 80 percent impervious surfaces and whose areas are 80 percent storm-sewered (Chandler 1976). Not only does the total discharge increase, but so does the speed of runoff, leading to erosion and the scouring of riverbeds. The changes to patterns of vegetation and aquatic life diminish the ability of rivers to cleanse themselves naturally over time, causing the loss of aquatic and riverbank habitats and their native plants and wildlife populations.

Pollution and Its Effects

The growth of populations, the development of an industrialized world, and the consequent growth of urban agglomerations have generated waste products in various

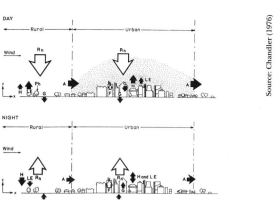

1. Two-Dimensional Scheme of Heat Exchanges in Rural and Urban Areas

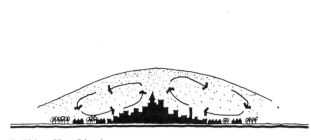

2. Urban Heat Island

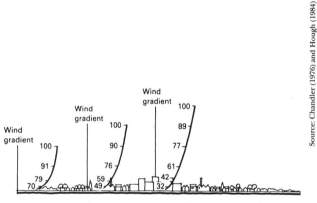

3. Typical Wind Profiles over Built-up and Urban Fringe Areas

Figure 18-3: Urban Patterns and Climatic Change

Our models of the effects of specific patterns of the urban environment are crude. We know that some cause heat islands changing humidity levels and wind patterns by changing the pattern of heat balances between rural and urban areas. (1) shows the flow of heat during the day and night (R_n = radiation, H = sensible heat, LE = latent heat, Ph = photosynthesis, G = heat storage in buildings and ground, A = advection); (2) the configuration of a heat island over a city; and (3) how wind velocities are reduced in urban areas by the aerodynamic roughness of the texture of the built environment.

forms. In the United States waste products are disposed of in the sky and waterways or buried in the land. Each has an impact on the functioning of the biogenic environment. In our search for individual mobility, the automobile was regarded as and has been a godsend. It was perceived to be less polluting than the horse, and certainly has made streets cleaner, but it, in turn, is now seen as a major polluter of the environment. Similarly, industries that provide many benefits we now take for granted have been another polluter. In many places the cyclical cleansing functioning of the natural environment has been well exceeded and the pollutants continue to build up.

Pollution has many consequences. Air pollution reduces the radiation levels of the sun at ground level, temperature patterns are changed, and the particulate matter in the atmosphere is increased. At the same time it causes changes in ozone levels, increasing radiation in parts of the world. Pollution is a health hazard for humans, destroys trees on city streets and in parks, transforms the countryside, destroys the habitat of animals, and causes climatic change. We as a society are having trouble checking these impacts.

The accelerated rate of global warming as a result of the increasing concentration of greenhouse gases in the atmosphere (or possibly the increase in the sun's brightness) may result in the increase in sea level by as much as 2 feet by the year 2050 if climatologists are correct. Accord-

ing to a 1990 Geneva report of the Intergovernmental Panel on Climate Change the sea level will be rising from between 2 and 10 centimeters (i.e., up to 4 inches) a decade unless the growth of carbon dioxide levels in the atmosphere is reduced. It is predicted that if these levels are not curbed, then these changes will cause problems in all coastal areas, but particularly in those areas where warm waters will cause a shift in the location of tropical cyclones and hurricanes. Rainfall patterns will almost certainly change, causing lands that are presently arable or pastures to become deserts and bringing deluges to other areas. People can either accommodate themselves to these changes or try to ameliorate them by reducing pollution levels. There may be other effects—for instance, climatic changes over time due to human actions that are poorly understood and appear to go back for millennia.

The Fauna and Flora of the World

The flora and fauna of the world have developed together over the ages in specific niches. As human habitations have expanded so the natural flora has been decimated and the habitat for animals reduced. This effect has resulted not only from the process of clearing and settling land, but also from changes in the climate and air quality in and around urbanized areas, the filling in of wetlands, the channeling and diverting of rivers and other bodies of water, and the creation of dams. The situation has become such that the existence of many species of fauna is threatened. During the past five hundred years many species have indeed disappeared. The deliberate actions of people have also reorganized the distribution of both the world's flora and fauna.

As they have migrated, people have brought both commodities of their native lands and the symbols of home with them. Crop types have been transported and planted across the world. The symbols include not only building types but also the flora and fauna of their native lands. In addition, travelers have brought exotic species back from their journeys. Architects and landscape architects have incorporated specific types of vegetation in their designs to achieve special effects. All these changes have, in turn, set up a chain of consequences. For instance, as already noted, the introduction of many exotic trees into desert climates in the retirement towns of Arizona and the need to water them has raised the humidity level of areas of the state, changing the climate. A more common experience has been that exotic species have overrun the native ones, as they have no natural enemies to control them. This observation can be made about both flora and fauna. European sparrows are ubiquitous in the United States; the Australian eucalyptus is causing problems with water runoffs and endangering native species in Florida; Australia is overrun with rabbits and foxes introduced from Europe for sport.

Much of human history has been concerned with making human habitats safe from animals and pests. This concern still exists in many places, as urban pests such as rats need to be controlled. There are, however, more positive urban policy objectives that have implications for design. The first objective is to enhance the quality of the urban world with the presence of local wildlife that both enriches human aesthetic experiences and acts as a weathervane for environmental quality. The second is to make a good environment for the pets that provide companionship to humans without simultaneously making the environment detrimental to other animals. The third is, in some places, to use fauna, especially pigs and birds, as scavengers to maintain sanitary conditions.

The Consumption of Biogenic Resources

There has been a growing concern that we are using up the resources of the world without replacing them. In urban design the concerns are twofold: the consumption of irreplaceable natural materials in building, and the consumption of fuel in construction and in heating and cooling. If this process continues the resources will be unavailable for human use in the future. Some resources could be replenished if they were consumed with less avarice than we now display: hardwood timbers used in buildings are an example. Hardwood forests, particularly tropical forests, are difficult to replace, but they could be

if the rate of consumption of such timber was substantially reduced. Some resources are clearly nonreplaceable: oil, which is used as an energy source, and quarried stone, which is used as a building material, are examples. The latter can at least be recycled and the quarries used as sites for the disposal of wastes. There may, however, be many negative side effects of such uses, particularly the effects of seepage on groundwater quality.

Conclusion—The Consequences

It is clear that to ensure that the biogenic environment is restored to health, there is going to have to be a broad-scale change in public attitudes toward a whole set of behaviors. Some of these behaviors are the everyday ways of carrying out the basic activities of life. Some will require national and international planning and programs to be addressed adequately, yet others can be dealt with at a local level. The last mentioned involves a reconsideration of the nature of the urban patterns we build. Urban designs need to work in cooperation with the natural processes of the biogenic environment. In competitive societies such as the United States this cooperation will only occur if the consequences of avoiding it are clearly obvious, and if broad-scale legislation and detailed design guidelines are established. The latter measures will only be implemented when public support for them increases.

THE BEHAVIORAL PROGRAM

To create a functional biogenic environment significant behavioral changes will be required at two geographic scales. One level is the supralocal, and the other is the local level. At both scales programs and policies are necessary to change people's attitudes as well as to specify the actions to be taken by individuals and industries. The specific actions that can and should be taken to tackle the problems of the biogenic environment include urban design actions.

Attitudinal Changes

For biogenic health to be universally attained it is clear that a number of deeply rooted attitudes held by people throughout the world will have to change. Many people in the United States with a European intellectual heritage have inherited the Judeo-Christian attitude that the environment is something to be exploited in the service of people. This attitude is by no means unique to the Judeo-Christian tradition. Indeed, as soon as people anywhere have achieved the power to exploit nature they seem to have done so. We all have to recognize that the environment has to be husbanded and not simply consumed.

Individuals' rights in the United States to exploit land and buildings as they see fit have already been

1. Gary, Indiana

2. New Jersey

3. Almost Any City

Photograph by Ruth Durack

Figure 18-4: The Flora and Fauna of Cities
Without doubt the nature and health of the flora and fauna of a city enhance the quality of life of many people. Parts of cities (and rural areas) are now in a state where the flora has difficulty surviving (1). Certainly promoting the types of vegetation that support the local species that give us pleasure (2) is an important issue in urban design. There are species that give us pleasure in context but may also be regarded as public nuisances in other contexts. Pigeons are an example (3).

curbed by a number of laws and ordinances in terms of the public health, but it is clear that many widely held attitudes have yet to change. There is, however, considerable reluctance in the country to interfere with the rights of individuals to do what they wish with their properties. Value changes are difficult to instigate.

In the United States, the behavioral emphasis has been on getting things done in haste, on changing the world, and on individual mobility. According to Wilbur Zelinsky, the landscape of cities in the country reflects four attitudes toward the world and people that derive from these emphases: "(1) an intense, almost anarchistic individualism, (2) a high value placed on mobility and change, (3) a mechanistic vision of the world, an (4) a messianic perfectionism" (Zelinsky 1973; cited also in Saarinen 1976; see also Relph 1987). As a result it is difficult to instigate communal actions for the general welfare of all. There are, however, many indications that a concern for environmental issues is possible and that new polices are implementable, but it will require a fundamental shift in present attitudes to get more than a marginal change. In some ways this necessity is surprising.

Until the mid-1930s considerations of human health were paramount in dealing with many environmental issues. As medical and technological progress has eliminated many health problems, many recent urban design decisions are now based on an economic pragmatism and on a desire to maintain individual property rights, all in the name of progress. The major city planner in the United States has indeed been the tax assessor. The result is what we see around us today (Relph 1987).

Now there is a need to have *regional* land-use, land development, and taxation policies if the health of the biogenic environment is to be improved. Probably the most important attitudinal shift that will be required in the United States is to accept government restructuring. At present, local autonomy is prized and a distrust of central government is part of the country's political heritage. The need is, however, to delegate authority over land development to larger-scale jurisdictional control at the state, regional, and often international level. Such a shift can only happen if there is a shift in attitudes toward life in general and in the attitudes that Zelinsky identifies.

The broadest modification required will be to revise the mechanistic view of the world. A fundamental change in attitudes toward the consumption of resources and products and the disposal of waste would ensue. This change is primarily required in the wealthier nations now, but it is a universal necessity. Societies must become less "consume and throw-away" ones. Accepting this change would mean that the means of production and waste disposal would have to change. In many parts of the United States there are now increasing problems in finding ways to safely and aesthetically dispose of household wastes, let alone toxic wastes such as nuclear products and poisonous gases. Simply identifying new sites for the disposal of household garbage and trash has become a major problem in the metropolitan areas of developed nations. There are now few easily accessible sites available to America's major cities.

Equally difficult to accept will be new urban forms that fall outside the aesthetic vocabulary of both laypeople and professional designers but are necessitated by the need to conserve energy resources and perhaps to be more dependent on solar energy. There undoubtedly needs to be a change in urban forms, in building configurations and their spacing requirements, and in the heating and cooling devices used. These changes will be demanded by a change in focus in cost-benefit studies from short-run economic benefits to broader considerations of the long-term environmental effects of the built environment. There will undoubtedly have to be changes in attitudes toward the visual appearance of the environment. For instance, much that is presently highly manicured (such as the grass verges of highways and parts of the grass surface of urban parks) can best be left partly unmown (Hough 1984; Spirn 1984).

New urban forms may well involve more compact living arrangements in some of what are now spread-out areas and vice versa in other places to save on energy consumption (Steadman 1975; R. Stein 1977; Robinette 1977; Gayden 1979). It may require the abandonment of the single-family detached house as a symbol of home in parts of the United States. Yet the urban design goal must still remain the fulfillment of the full range of the basic and cognitive needs of people. In urban design there will almost inevitably be clashes between opposing design objectives. For instance, the need to reduce energy consumption and the need to create a biogenically well-functioning environment do not necessarily go hand in hand. Settlement layouts that are sensible for reducing the need to cool buildings in hot humid areas clash with the design of energy-efficient transportation systems. Energy-efficient mass transportation modes require high-density compact cities (Dantzig and Saaty 1973; Steadman 1975). Such forms may be excellent contributors to maintaining the biogenic quality of the environment in hot arid zones and even in the temperate climatic zone of the United States, where the tightly textured city captures the warmth of the sun. However, buildings in hot humid areas need to be dispersed to allow breezes to pass through and among them (Olgyay 1963; Givoni 1974). Similarly, designs of the public realm that are now culturally appropriate may result in buildings that are inefficient consumers of energy because they are poorly oriented to the sun. Creative urban design solutions may be able to resolve some of these clashes; others will require us to modify our behaviors considerably.

At the same time, there are pushes for attitudinal changes that need to be considered with caution. The Ecological City movement is an increasingly powerful political one that has the goal of changing cultures to fit in with its image of the good life (Register 1987; Hough 1990a; Ingersoll 1991). It has highly puritan overtones not unlike those behind much of Le Corbusier's thinking (Le Corbusier 1934, 1973). It also has the strong antiurban bias and regressive utopianism of the early Empiricist designers such as Patrick Geddes (Boardman 1978) and Ebenezer Howard (1902). In addition, it advocates greater community participation in local activities involving communal gardening, recreation in "natural areas" instead of manicured parks, and, following Fritz Schumacher (1973), thinking small. Many people do enjoy gardening and many more might if given the opportunity, but few wish to be urban farmers. The ecology movement's focus on cultural change to attain ways of life it believes to be appropriate should not obscure the importance of designing to minimize environmental harm and to retrofit cities to do less damage to the biogenic world. Behavioral changes will indeed be necessary to achieve those ends.

Many of the people involved in the ecology movement also have as deep-seated a set of environmental deterministic beliefs as the Modernist architects had in architectural determinism. If only there were more green spaces in cities there would be "more freedom, peace, solitude ... spiritual refreshment." Such beliefs should be treated with extreme caution. It is clear some people are predisposed to have such experiences, whereas others find the same experiences in hard architectural environments, many of which are among the best-loved places in the world. The important design concern is to create biogenically well-functioning environments and not simply to foist on to people what a minority believes is good for them. One of the roles of the designer is to bring people's attention to the consequences of designing in particular ways and the costs, including opportunity costs, and benefits of doing so. Certainly one of the advocacies of designers should be for the attainment of a biogenically healthy environment and the development of policies and designs to achieve it.

Policy Planning

Policies and legislation will have to be developed at the international, national, and regional as well as local levels if a biogenically functional environment is to be achieved. At the international level, cooperation will be needed to attack sources of environmental damage, including building damage, such as acid rain, and to promote such ends as economic development and education to curb population growth rates in developing nations. Such policies are already being developed.

During 1990 national governments from around the world set an ambitious target of reducing the emission of greenhouse gases by 20 percent by the year 2005. Attaining this goal will involve a range of actions from legislation affecting the technology of automobiles to the greater integration of land-use and transportation planning to reduce the reliance on the car as the primary mode of transportation for many purposes. Broad-scale land-use and urbanization policies are likely to be required. Decentralization policies have been pursued without much success in a number of countries throughout the world with the goal of attaining smaller urban agglomerations. There are still strong advocates for such policies (e.g., Leff 1990). Policies will be required for preserving open spaces that are biologically sensitive and restoring other places to a biogenically well-functioning state.

There is also the need to be able to pay for major conservation and retooling efforts in cities. Governments need to have the ability to capture the windfall profits made as the result of planning decisions so that people who have had their rights removed can be compensated for them. Such policies have been implemented in a number of countries, such as the United Kingdom, with socialist leanings (Gallion and Eisner 1986). Many of the problems are, however, global in nature and compensation systems need to be developed through international cooperation. Implementing such measures has proven to be extremely difficult.

THE URBAN DESIGN PROGRAM

In dealing with the biogenic environment the concern in architectural design has been with making the interiors of buildings more comfortable places in which to be. Much of the focus in urban design has been on ameliorating the effect of climates by developing guidelines for the building of skywalks or tunnels linking buildings and for creating internal plazas and squares. Recently there has been a greater concern with making the public environment outdoors more pleasant too (see Chapter 11). There has been considerably less interest in the creation of a well-functioning biogenic environment. That has been assumed to be somebody else's problem.

Much of the discussion on making the urban environment less harmful to the biogenic one tends to assume that cities can be completely redone, that there are infinite financial resources to work on them, and that no other human ends are important. This means the discussion assumes that there are no possible tradeoffs between meeting other human needs and the purity of the functioning of the biogenic environment. Like all design decisions, there are tradeoffs involved between the attainment of one goal and another (see Chapter 21). The urban design obligation is, however, to progressively mod-ify the built environment to ensure the future health of the biogenic environment. As all built environments alter the biogenic environment, guidelines need to be established that will shape environmental change so that not only is no further biogenic harm done but also so that future urban developments, piece by piece, have a restorative impact.

Human Needs and the Biogenic Environment

With some exceptions (e.g., swamps) a healthy biogenic environment usually results in a healthy human environment. The character and purposeful design of many aspects of the natural world help meet human needs on many dimensions. Designing with climate in mind and growing native species of plants (or no plants in desert areas) aid in meeting the need for a sense of place (Hough 1990b). Designing to make people aware of weather changes will also meet this need, but it may not meet people's need for physiological comfort. A tradeoff is required in design. In the United States at least, comfort is generally a more basic need than having a sense of place, although as Maslow (1987) points out, we do not seek to have comfort needs met infinitely before our needs shift up the scale.

There are strong arguments that urban designers be much more concerned with the nature of the biogenic environment in the future than they have been in the past (Lamb 1991). There are many reasons. In the first place, the future health of the planet is of concern. In addition, many environmentalists perceive a major "rift between people and nature." They see this rift as a bad thing in its own right and wish to see people's lives integrated into nature. The kind of life such an integration implies is indeed sought after by a number of people, and maybe in the future there will be the types of cultural changes in the United States that are being advocated by environmentalists (e.g., Ward and Dubos 1972; Gordon 1990; Goldsmith 1990), and thus a greater demand for participatory natural environments along the lines they imagine. Such environments may well provide for some people's cognitive and aesthetic needs.

Since the early 1970s, an Empiricist approach to urban design that can be traced back to Patrick Geddes and Lewis Mumford has begun to emerge among landscape architects. Places such as Woodlands, Texas, and perhaps more dramatically, Village Homes in Davis, California (see Fig. 18–8), give a sense of direction. However, as our knowledge of the interaction between artificial and natural environments increases, so the invisible web of laws and design principles that govern the layout of human settlements will undergo change. These changes are likely to be led by an informed public as much as an informed profession. At present, most efforts are going into the preservation of existing wildlife areas and into fighting the location of noxious facilities rather than thinking about the nature of urban environments as a whole.

A Pragmatic Principle for Urban Design

Many conservationists take the position that any development is inherently destructive, but new landscapes can be created that are healthy even though they differ from the existing ones (Hough 1984). A pragmatic approach for urban designers to take in dealing with the biogenic environment is to ask what is in the human self-interest in the long run. The urban design objective is then to avoid creating patterns of built form that *might* ultimately harm people by leading to a deterioration in the quality of life. Given this position and recognizing that the future needs of people are partly unpredictable, a conservative design ethic seems wise in dealing with the biogenic environment. It is possible that humans may not find technological ways out of the present bind. Necessity may be the mother of invention, but the invention that may well be necessary is for urban designers to have a conservation ethic. There are two other arguments for being conservative: it leaves a greater set of options available in the future, and it is psychologically wise. Many children see a grim future for the planet based on what they see and hear around them.

Leaving a greater set of options open for future generations recognizes the dynamics of urban change. Such a position is also in line with the principle that urban design decisions made today should preclude as few positive possibilities for the future as possible. The second argument is trickier. Many children are fearful about the future because of the doom and gloom prophesies that capture their imaginations easily and that are abundant in the marketplace of ideas. If children grow up cynical, creative design responses to the problems at hand will be difficult to attain in the future.

In making biologically sound design decisions, urban designers need to get away from age-old, often intuitively sensible attitudes that have simply not served people well. There has, for instance, long been the general goal of striving to maintain green belts around cities. The argument has been and still is to give people easy access to the countryside while giving a city a clear boundary in order to enhance people's sense of belonging to a unit. There is little evidence that these design decisions meet their stated aims at the city level, although at the neighborhood scale they can do so (see Chapter 13). In addition, national and city governments have found it extraordinarily difficult to maintain green belts, and they have had counterintuitive effects on urban development patterns in capitalist societies (see Chapter 2). Boulder, Colorado, is one city in the United States which has been successful in developing a green belt, but the result is an exclusionary, largely middle-class city. It seems more sensible today to think in terms of green fingers and/or zones that serve many human purposes as part of the types of urban patterns in the urban designer's vocabulary. However, we designers are reluctant to give up on the concept of the green belt because it is so intuitively appealing.

Design Actions and Design Principles

Today urban designers in the United States usually find themselves creating proposals for developments that consume land already in use—whether for agricultural or for urbanization. There may be a third environmental context—designing projects on virgin land. This situation may occur in rugged terrain or arctic and desert areas where new mineral resources are being developed, but almost everywhere else that urban development could take place has already been touched by human hands. Developments on virgin or agricultural land are those most likely to be opposed by environmentalists. Unless population growth is reduced to zero, an urban design objective will almost certainly be to build new towns, new suburbs, and urban renewal projects in the service of people. Most of the actions required to design biogenically sensitive new towns and suburbs also apply to the redevelopment of cities. In urban renewal the existing urban fabric limits biogenic considerations to piecemeal ones, whereas in new town development comprehensive approaches can be implemented. However sensitively these approaches are carried out, the biogenic nature of the environment will be changed. The goal should be to change it for the better! The definition of "better" will be politically charged.

New Towns and Suburban Development

The basic issues in designing for a healthy biogenic environment in new towns may be universal, but each place has to be addressed uniquely. One of the aspirations of urban design must surely be to create a biologically self-correcting system of built and open areas. Consequently, several concerns become apparent. There is always a need to consider how local conditions of inputs of energy and outputs of waste are to be handled, how best to deal with the atmospheric pollution that any settlement generates, how to avoid the creation of heat islands and down drafts, how to organize and build drainage systems using natural wastewater renovation systems and conservation cycles that use evapotranspiration beds, and how to avoid hydrological imbalances. The design principles to achieve these ends have been developed during the last two decades. In many ways they recapture age-old techniques of preindustrial times (Rudofsky 1964; Steadman 1975; Robinette 1977; Hough 1984; Spirn 1984). City planners, urban designers, and landscape architects must learn to think of the components of urban form in a multivariate manner. For instance, golf courses can be designed to be not only recreation areas but also wildlife preserves, natural hydrological areas, and so on. Many city streets in predominantly residential areas can be thought of as places for traffic, recreation, urban farming, and so on.

Many of the requirements to achieve a biogenically healthy environment while building new developments

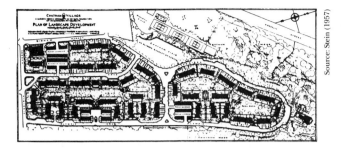

Source: Stein (1957)

1. Chatham Village, Pittsburgh, Pennsylvania (1930)

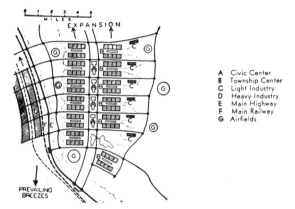

Source: Gallion and Eisner (1986)

A Civic Center
B Township Center
C Light Industry
D Heavy Industry
E Main Highway
F Main Railway
G Airfields

2. Generic Plan for a City of About 1 Million People, by José Sert

3. Davis, California

Figure 18-5: Designing New Towns and Suburbs
The Empiricist tradition in urban design has historically paid considerable attention to the nature of the natural environment in cities, partly for biogenic reasons but largely in pursuit of a picturesque aesthetic (1). Rationalist design paid scant heed to the biogenic environment except to automatically place industrial areas of cities on the downwind side (2). With the growth of empirical research on biogenic factors in urban design, the principles behind urban design policies and plans are being reconsidered. Some recent suburban designs, but more especially what their residents have done, show this concern (3; see also Fig. 18-8).

will also provide a means of supporting many other human purposes: (1) physiological needs through providing weather-ameliorating devices and avoiding the development of heat islands, (2) affiliation needs by creating a sense of place, (3) cognitive needs by offering a diversity of learning opportunities, and (4) aesthetic needs through making the milieu interesting.

Most of the future policies that will undoubtedly affect what an urban designer does will be developed at the overall urban level. Some of these policies can be readily predicted. In the first place, no developments should take place on environmentally sensitive land. These lands, their flora and fauna, are both providers of the natural mechanisms for cleansing air and, more generally, supporting the health of the bionic environment, and are indicators of that environment's edaphic health. In the second place, urban design policies and design guidelines are needed to ensure that built forms are created that shape wind flows that will enable the air to be cleansed and will avoid the development of heat islands. European countries have made significant advances in developing such design controls, but the United States will assuredly follow in due course as the problems that result from not doing so become more apparent.

Avoiding the Creation of Heat Islands through Urban Design

One of the goals of new town and suburban design in the future will surely be to avoid the development of heat islands. The actual patterns of built forms to be employed by the designer will vary by climatic zone. In hot areas of the United States, the goal will be particularly to avoid the build-up of temperatures at street level. This goal can be achieved through the spacing of parks, creating an aerodynamically rough urban surface by varying building heights and masses, having a street pattern that channels prevailing winds (e.g., Stuttgart, Germany), and the use of appropriate building materials—those with a high albedo, low thermal capacity, and a low thermal conductivity (Bach 1971; Givoni 1974; Chandler 1976; Spirn 1984). In the coastal towns of the United States, high buildings along the seafront will have to be avoided in order to allow sea breezes to flow inland to the center of potential heat islands. Urban design guidelines to achieve this end already exist in some cities (e.g., Haifa, Israel). Street trees and canopies of trees in parks (rather than isolated specimens) all help to reduce heat build-up in urban areas.

Open spaces close to highly developed, high-density areas will also have to be provided. This pattern establishes a cellular system of cool areas adjacent to hot ones and sets up air flows that ventilate the city. Some existing cities are fortunate to have such patterns. Lake Michigan cools Chicago to a depth of two kilometers from the waterfront and "warms" it in wintertime (Chandler 1976). In

1. Central Park, New York

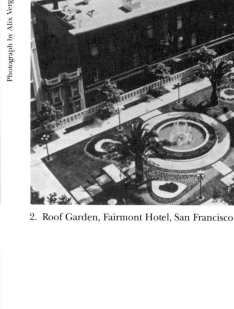

Source: Halprin (1963)

2. Roof Garden, Fairmont Hotel, San Francisco

3. Copacabana, Rio de Janeiro, Brazil

Figure 18–6: Designing to Avoid Creating Heat Islands
Any reduction in the heat island effect of cities will help meet environmental goals. Spacing parks to serve cooling as well as recreational purposes, creating a canopy of trees (1), changing roofscapes (2), and varying building heights to help channel prevailing winds will all help attain this goal. Guidelines to achieve these ends in a piecemeal away over time are difficult to implement in the face of financial exigencies and political demands (3). For instance, tall buildings along seafronts reduce air flow through the city, but stopping their erection is difficult everywhere.

New York the summer temperatures in central Manhattan are much ameliorated by the presence of Central Park.

Reducing Pollution through Urban Design

There is no single, unique urban design solution to air pollution problems. Policies can be developed to reduce the emission of pollutants, but the goal of a pollution-free atmosphere is impossible to achieve in urban areas. Some actions to reduce the build-up of pollutants can, nevertheless, be taken. Most importantly will be the coordinated development of land-use and transportation polices making mass transportation more efficient to operate and easier to use, and the location of parks (which act as emission-free zones and if vegetated with the appropriate trees, as filters). Open space can also be used as a *cordon sanitaire* between industrial and residential areas. This urban design principle is one of long standing and common to the urban design ideologies of this century.

In establishing land-use policies, polluting industries should not be located in low-lying areas that have light winds and are subject to temperature inversions. Exposed hilltop sites are preferable, although the choice

of these sites may clash with fulfilling aesthetic needs. Cooperative production of systems of heating and cooling are less polluting than individually operated systems, and guidelines can be developed for chimneys so that plumes are dissipated.

Water and Urban Design

Water has been used in many ways in urban design: as a decorative element, as a space-defining element, and as a temperature-modifying element. Water elements will continue to be part of the architect's, landscape architect's, and urban designer's palette for creating interesting and pleasant places. Similarly, cities on natural waterways or on the sea have a special character that those cities without significant bodies of water lack. In the United States as elsewhere, these bodies of water are often highly polluted. Pollution sometimes has a preservative effect by denying oxygen to wooden piles (e.g., the wharves of many American port cities); however, in the design of new towns, the concern is with having clean water from the beginning. In older cities the impact of clean water may well have more positive effects than worrying about problems created by the need to maintain old piles. Other policies will have to deal with them.

1. Third Street, San Francisco

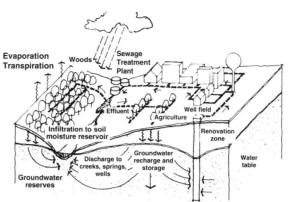

2. The Wastewater Regeneration and Conservation Cycle

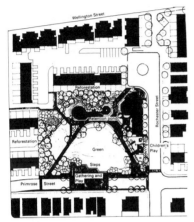

3. Lebreton Park, Ottawa, Canada

Figure 18-7: Groundwater and Urban Design

Water has long been used as a decorative feature, space defining, and as a sound- and temperature-modulating element in urban design (see, e.g., Figs. 12–2(6), 16–3(3), 17–7(6), and 17–13(2)). There are many other problems that need to be dealt with today. For instance, there is a need to deal with water runoff from large paved areas (e.g., 1). There have been suggestions for development of wastewater regeneration and conservation cycles (2) that will have considerable effect on urban form. Increasingly retention ponds to hold rainwater are incorporated in new suburban developments (3).

There are three concerns in creating urban design principles for the overall structure of new towns and suburbs: (1) to reduce stormwater runoff as a result of the increased proportion of hard surfaces—roads and surface parking lots—in the environment, (2) to avoid the transmission of pollutants into waterways, and (3) to ensure that proper sewerage-handling systems are built. The focus of attention can be on recharging groundwaters and forming retention ponds in parks. In many places it will be possible to devise rainwater and wastewater disposal systems that rely on the natural processes of the Earth and aquatic plants as filters, and on evapotranspiration beds. Where this can be done it should be the goal to do so.

The Role of Flora in Urban Areas

One of the major urban design concerns is with the relationships between built-up and open spaces, between manicured open space and wilderness areas, and between fragile and robust environments—and with all of these elements in relationship to each other (Spirn 1984; Nohl 1988). The urban design objective should be to provide habitats for the flora and fauna that enhance ecological cycles and ameliorate negative conditions, and that do well in urban environments, without harming people, other flora or fauna, or themselves. The environments that are good for them will by and large also be salubrious ones for people, and their presence will be an indicator of a healthy biogenic environment.

In urban design the concern is with the flora as an integral and functional part of a design and not simply something added on to it for aesthetic reasons. Trees, for instance, in addition to being space-defining elements in the creation of urban environments (Arnold 1980), can also be biological filters (Hough 1984: Spirn 1984; Gordon 1990). The concern is with the type of vegetation that does the job best, that will survive in particular micro-climates and that will be supportive of particular sets of human behaviors. In many places there is a particular concern with planting native species not only to provide a sense of place by their presence but also to act as a habitat for native birds and insects. In other places exotics may be the most beneficial. After all, human beings are an exotic species in many environments.

Trees and other flora also have an effect on humidity levels in cities. The circulation patterns that link the cool moist air over parks with the hot dry air of densely built-up areas at times of light air flow during summer result in the edges of the built-up areas having not only lower air pollution levels but also moister air flows. Trees also build up moisture in any area, but the changes they bring are especially noticeable in dry climates. This increased humidity is not always a good thing for either people or the biogenic environment. A particular design problem arises when designing in desert environments. Trees and other flora need to be introduced with caution. The objective will often be to design possibly treeless environments that are full of life and to use indigenous plants judiciously to give a sense of place without increasing humidity levels and possibly upsetting the usually delicate arid ecosystem. Vegetation thus plays a number of roles in the design of cities.

Fauna and Urban Design

Animals that do well in urban places vary from locale to locale. They may be raccoons, squirrels, and even deer in North America, monkeys in parts of Asia and Africa, and possums in Australia. There are other species that find the urban environment hostile but are important elements of the biogenic environment. Butterflies and birds, whose presence enriches human lives, also act as indicators of the biogenic health of the city. Some of these species are desired by many people, others are regarded as pests. The urban design concern is to identify and create the type of habitats in which the desired fauna thrive and to set up the procedures for maintaining niches for them (Leedy, Maestro, and Franklin 1978; Hough 1984; Spirn 1984). In the past these issues were considered too trivial for urban designers to consider, but times are changing.

Existing Cities and Urban Places

Much thought has been given to making cities healthier places for people (see Chapter 11) and an increasing amount of thought to making cities, if not good for the biogenic environment, at least less harmful (Lamb 1991). In places such as Manhattan or Los Angeles or Bangkok (one of the most polluted of all cities) the task of ameliorating the negative effects of urban development and the activities of the city on the biogenic environment is a mammoth one. In such cities, and also in small towns and existing suburbs, the urban design actions that can be taken are essentially remedial in nature: regenerating natural systems, modifying winds and air flows, planting native trees to attract native birds (or eliminating trees where they are not helpful to the functioning of the biogenic environment), and controlling feral animals and pests. The goal is to retrofit the city, piece by piece, over time so that the principles for new town design also are the principles that dictate the shape of the reformed city.

Regenerating natural systems may involve the return of waterways to their natural state by diverting sewerage into new sewer systems and opening up enclosed creeks and rivers to form river channels. The design response to the problem of excessive rain runoff from paved areas has led to varied solutions, from planting grass on concrete rooftops to absorb the initial spate of water (and also reduce the build-up of heat) to having water-pervious materials in the parking lots of regional shopping centers. Wetlands can be recreated to form natural habitats for birds and other organisms. Such places have already been developed. The Tifft Farm Wetland Nature Reserve on what was an abandoned hazardous-waste dump on the outskirts of Buffalo, New York (Gall 1990), and in a larger metropolitan area, the Camley Street Natural Park in London (Johnston 1990) are examples.

There has been considerable concern with the design of buildings to withstand earthquakes. This was true historically in much of China and Japan, for instance. Guidelines for development of buildings in earthquake zones were given a severe and successful test in San Francisco during 1989 (Lagorio 1990). It is not clear, however, whether the location and design of cities have an effect on earthquakes!

URBAN DESIGN CONSEQUENCES

The argument for a change in stance of urban design professionals regarding the biogenic environment has been described in this chapter. This stance differs from that advocated by most current urban designers (see Chapter 3), but it stems, as noted earlier in this chapter, from the recent ideological positions of landscape architects who are also interested in urban design (e.g., McHarg 1969; Hough 1984; Spirn 1984, 1989). This stance implies a change not only in the culture of designers but also in the broader society. The environmental lobby demands an even greater change in the culture of societies across the world to achieve the ends it advocates.

Much that is being done today to make the biogenic environment of cities function better is on a limited and piecemeal basis There is a need to coordinate and extend these efforts based on a thorough understanding of the nature of ecological systems and the problems that exist in a place or might exist there if current trends persist (Spirn 1984). Urban designers can argue that they work within the policies, codes, and regulations set by other professionals and legislatures, and that the issues of designing to create a biogenically healthy world fall outside their direct scope of concern. This view is shortsighted. It is clear that the layout of the urban environment, the way its streets and buildings are configured, and the types of vegetation that exist or do not exist all contribute significantly not only to human physiological and psychological comfort, but also to the natural ecological processes required to cleanse and restore the biogenic environment of the world to health.

Many of the arguments for designing with nature in mind have to do with fulfilling the human need for a

1. Aerial View

2. Solar Architecture

3. Typical Common Area

Figure 18-8: Village Homes, Davis, California

On the surface, Village Homes may seem to be a typical suburban neighborhood (1). Over time, however, it has been considerably adapted to be ecologically sensitive. Housing orientation has been important to enable solar-energy-generating mechanisms to be used (2), berms have been created and common areas planted to yield fruit and vegetables (3). Few Americans are as yet willing to expend this type of energy on their environments, but in the future fundamental changes may be required in the thinking of people, including designers, about suburban design.

physiologically sound environment that has a unique sense of place and that fulfills cognitive and aesthetic needs. The world consists of niches in which unique combinations of topography, geology, and climate provide a habitat for native flora and fauna. Celebrating the differences among places rather than diminishing them with exotic species of plants and animals can potentially enhance the quality of life of all people. Some people will be predisposed to avail themselves of the opportunities for experiencing such differences. Other people will be indirectly affected by them.

The major change required in the thinking of urban designers and many laypeople alike will be to reorganize their attitudes to the symbolic meaning of the natural elements of the city—the associational meanings of its topography, water, flora, and fauna. The linkage between these elements and the natural life processes of the biogenic environment must become part of the symbolic aesthetic attitude of both professionals and laypeople. Without such attitudes, it will be difficult to create a more salubrious environment for people and for its own sake—for its own aesthetic logic (Hough 1984; Spirn 1989).

Competing arguments have been presented in this book—the need for more dense environments to reduce infrastructure costs, the necessity of creating a biogenically healthy environment, and the necessity of fulfilling a variety of basic and cognitive needs. Reconciling all these objectives may result in urban environments that are very different from those to which many of use are habituated. Arguments have been made for the conservation of more natural landscape and vegetation however dense cities should become, for worrying about the nature of roofscapes, and for arranging streets and buildings to channel air. Perhaps more than a new aesthetic, a new environmental awareness is needed.

MAJOR REFERENCES

Arnold, Henry F. (1980). *Trees in Urban Design*. New York: Van Nostrand Reinhold.

Chandler, T. J. (1976). *Urban Climatology and Its Relevance to Urban Design*. Geneva: World Meteorological Organization.

Gayden, Ernst L. (1979). "Design Model for the Energy Efficient City." In Rocco A. Fazzolare and Craig B. Smith, eds., *Changing Energy Use Futures*. New York: Pergamon Press.

Givoni, Baruch (1974). "Architectural and Urban Planning in Relation to Weather and Climate." In S. W. Tromp and J. J. Boama, eds., *Progress in Bioclimatology*. Amsterdam: Swats and Zeitlinger, pp. 183–193.

Goldsmith, Edward, et al. (1990). *Imperiled Planet: Restoring Our Endangered Ecosystems*. Cambridge, MA: MIT Press.

Gordon, David, ed. (1990). *Green Cities: Ecologically Sound Approaches to Urban Space*. Montreal: Black Rose Books.

Hough, Michael (1984). *City Form and Natural Processes: Towards a New Urban Vernacular*. London: Routledge.

Ingersoll, Richard (1991). "Unpacking the Green Man's Burden." *Design Book Review* 20:19–26.

Lamb, Richard (1991). "The Challenge of Ecology to the Design Professions: 1. Invention and Intervention." *Exedra* 3, no. 1:16–24.

McHarg, Ian L. (1969). *Design with Nature*. Garden City, NY: Natural History Press.

Olgyay, Victor (1963). *Design with Climate: Bioclimatic Approach to Architectural Regionalism*. Princeton, NJ: Princeton University Press.

Rodger, Allan, and Roger Fay (1991). "Sustainable Suburbia." *Exedra* 3, no. 1:4–15.

Spirn, Anne Whiston (1984). *The Granite Garden: Urban Nature and Human Design*. New York: Basic Books.

Stein, Richard (1977). *Architecture and Energy*. Garden City, NY: Anchor.

Ward, Barbara, and René Dubos (1972). *Only One Earth: The Care and Maintenance of a Small Planet*. New York: Norton.

CONCLUSION

Wilshire Boulevard, Los Angeles

During the past twenty years there have been a number of expressions of a belief that the use of a strong body of positive theory as the basis for environmental design will automatically lead to specific design solutions in specific situations—that all one has to do is to press a button and the right design will pop out, and that by creating the right pattern of the environment the desired behavior will occur (Rusch 1969). No Empiricist can possibly hold these views. Life is much more complex than that.

Architects and urban designers prefer to use a typological approach to design. This approach involves the adaptation of generic solutions to particular situations. Patternbooks were popular in house design in the nineteenth century; the generic neighborhood solutions developed by Clarence Perry and by Le Corbusier have been applied in adapted form across the world regardless of their applicability to local cultures. Both solutions seem to work much better in their original application (the neighborhood unit in Radburn and the Unité d'habitation in Marseilles) than in adapted forms. The same observation can also probably be made about Seaside, Florida, and Parc de la Villette as generic patterns.

Empiricists in recent times have been reluctant to generate such generic "solutions." There are a variety of possible explanations for this position. One is that such processes have been abused in the past. Another is almost certainly because of a lack of confidence that such generic solutions are possible. There is possibly a third observation. Few of the people involved in environmental design research are themselves designers. For good or ill, the Empiricist approach to urban design—particularly of those people working within an ecological framework—involves addressing the problems of everyday life and making conjectures about the particular patterns of the built environment that will likely solve those problems based on the evidence that we now have available to us.

There has also been the fear that Empiricism will lead to a reductionist approach to design. The opposite is true. If designers were totally rational and had comprehensive knowledge then a pushbutton approach to problem identification and design would be possible (see Chapter 21, The Urban Design Designing Process). Empirical knowledge in the design fields has not simplified the problems of design but has rather given us sets of tools to start dealing with their complexity. It has also provided designers with exciting new knowledge and the potential opportunity to be much more aware of the issues they confront and to be articulate about them. This is particularly true in recognizing the differences in the way the environment is used by people and the diversity of the aesthetic attitudes that exist in the population as a whole. This knowledge enables urban designers to move from "black box" to "glass box" approaches to design—from a situation where all issues are clouded in mystery to one where issues are openly discussed. It also makes them acutely aware of the limitations of knowledge. Design will always be carried out under uncertainty.

Urban design will never be a pushbutton process except possibly in dealing with some repetitive technical components of the environment in which no functional advance is being made. The nature of the public realm and how it should be designed will always be open to debate. It is clear that much urban design deals with highly controversial issues. The definition of functionality described in this book helps to add some rationality to the discussion by providing a framework for asking questions and suggesting directions in which to explore for solutions. A series of issues, however, will always need to be confronted. Questions of whose needs should be addressed, the nature of the public interest, and how tightly a proposed design should fit a problem remain. They are all questions of values. In addition, while the previous chapters have outlined how designing to meet individual human needs might be considered in future urban designs, the mechanisms for doing so are often in conflict. The purpose of Chapter 19, Substantive Issues in Urban Design, is to outline the dilemmas an urban designer faces in making proposals for the future. With that as a foundation, some of the conclusions that are being drawn today about future urban design practice in the United States can be presented in Part Three of this book. ■

19

SUBSTANTIVE ISSUES IN URBAN DESIGN

There are people who assume that the goal of environmental design research is to produce a technical, mechanistic process of design that combines the elements of built form into a totally rational solution that solves all problems (Rusch 1969). No Empiricist can believe this. Design is and always will be an argumentative process. There are limits to our understanding of phenomena and in the United States as in many other countries, we deal with a multicultural world filled with people with varying aspirations.

We understand much about the general nature of how activity patterns and aesthetic preferences are related to human needs. We understand much about the affordances of different patterns of the built environment for different activity patterns and the meanings they hold for different people. We understand much about the geometry of enduring, robust types of urban places. There is much, however, about which we know less. The same Empirical research has generated considerably less understanding, for instance, about the details of how affordances of the patterns of the built world are perceived by different people and their attitudes toward them. We know even less about how preferences evolve.

Our positive theoretical knowledge of the environment, of people and the interactions among them, and between people and the built environment, is substantially stronger than that at the disposal of the Modernists. We understand much more about the multidimensional utility of the built environment in people's lives. The act of applying our knowledge, of moving from a positive observation to a normative statement—the act of designing—is still a value-laden political act and always will be. It is also a process that involves making many decisions under uncertainty. There is much room for debate over which positive theories are the most accurate, about the nature of a "good" society, about which design objectives are important, about which mechanisms should be used in attaining them, and about the degree of fit that should be sought between behavior, aesthetic values, and the built environment. Much of the fascination and excitement of urban design stems from this debate. Empirical information adds some rationality to the debate, but there will always remain issues to resolve where rational debate will be difficult. The urban designer will almost always have to deal with competing design objectives. Weighing their merits is difficult.

THE LIMITATIONS OF POSITIVE THEORIES

All design decisions that are not totally capricious are based on some positive view of the world—correct or incorrect. They are based on some observations or assumptions about how the world works and some position about how it should work. However well developed our positive knowledge of the world is (whether it is developed through scientific, phenomenological, or historiographic techniques), there will almost inevitably be contradictions in the explanations offered by competing positive theories, which lead to different predictions of the outcomes of a design, and a lack of research on many topics of architectural and urban design concern. Resolving these contradictions and filling in the gaps are goals of both the natural and social sciences.

There are competing positive theories, particularly in the explanations of many phenomena with which urban designers deal. For instance, there are a number of theories of perception, two sets of which (sensation-based and information-based—see Chapter 1; Lang 1984, 1987a) offer radically different views of the nature of expression in architectural and urban forms. In this book the ecological-based theory has been accepted, but making predictions on the basis of it still leaves uncertainty about design outcomes. The outcomes themselves are difficult to evaluate, so the theory-building feedback through *action research* (Wisner, Stea, and Kruks 1991) has not yet been achieved. Similarly, there are competing theories on the nature of community in sociology. The Functionalist theory of Talcott Parsons has been the one accepted here as having the greatest external validity in dealing with the problems of design from an ecological viewpoint. In dealing with meaning there are phenomenological, semiological, and hermeneutic approaches as well as the empirical approaches associated with environmental psychology. In this book the approach which presently yields the greatest understanding of the development of associational meanings has been adopted. It is based on an ecological model of perception and cognition (J. Gibson 1966, 1979; Neisser 1977; Kaminski 1989).

Urban designers are always dealing with the future. Positive theories tell us what is and possibly what trends exist, but the future is unknown. While a number of researchers (e.g., Tyng 1969; Franck and Ahrentzen 1989) have attempted to understand how behaviors and aesthetic values change, the process of change itself is not well understood. We know that there have been radical changes in the family organization in many societies, and we can predict well from them what short-range futures will be, but the social organization of the family in the middle- to long-term future cannot be predicted with any sense of confidence. Social policies can be designed to shape the nature of the future family, but in the United States it is more likely to evolve unselfconsciously. Similarly, we know that there have been changes in form empathy—preferences for specific shapes and patterns. These changes have taken place in a cyclical fashion. Will the cycle of form empathy continue in the same way as in the past? We believe it is likely to do so based on our current understanding, but we cannot conclude that with the certainty with which we can predict the cycle of seasons. Even in dealing with the biogenic environment, we are uncertain whether the present climates of regions of the world will remain the same during the next half century. Designers deal with today's problems, but their solutions have to exist into the future. We are constantly making assumptions about what the future will be. There are many assumptions about which we are uncertain. We guess. The results will sometimes be successful and sometimes not.

There will always be a difficulty in devising new ways of meeting basic needs well, but much of the excitement in urban designing comes from resolving such problems. The experience with Post-Modern design, where mechanisms were used to give laypeople a sense of esteem and belonging and also to fulfill their aesthetic needs, has been illustrative of the problems that urban designers face. The built environment devices and symbols created by architects in order to achieve these ends were supposed to communicate specific meanings to people but have been less than successful in doing so (Groat and

Canter 1979; Groat 1982). The meanings that architects thought would be communicated are not recognized by laypeople to any large extent. While the design intention may have been sincere, the means used to achieve that intention failed. They were based on what have proven to be intuitively appealing but erroneous positive theories. Reading meaning into the environment is a highly individualistic activity, and the degree to which architects can depart from standard conventions is limited if they wish to communicate meanings effectively. While future research will help us make better predictions, it cannot eliminate potential problems.

COMPETING NORMATIVE THEORIES— CONCEPTS OF A GOOD WORLD

Maslow's model of human motivations is based on who we are. It is a positive model, not a normative one, although it is highly suggestive about the nature of a "good" person and a "good" world. We perceive a set of necessities for ourselves to have a good life. The questions are: "How necessary is the fulfillment of some of the 'needs' for us to achieve a satisfying, happy life?" "Should we take ourselves as we are or do we accept some ideal model?" "Do we accept the culture of which we are a part as it is, or do we accept a model of how we state we want it to be, as the basis for design?"

Defining the relative importance of the various human needs and identifying the appropriate way to consider the elements of urban design ultimately depend on a world view. All designing, and indeed all research, is guided by a normative position on the nature of the present world, the future world, and the behaviors that do and should take place within its physical fabric. Designing for children, for instance, is based on an image of what a child should be and on what being a child means. This image has varied considerably in history (Ariès 1962). Is a child to be seen but not heard? Is a child to be encouraged to be independent? Or to conform? Should urban designers adopt a child's view of the environment? Different societies and different advocates within them have varying views on these issues (Bronfenbrenner 1970; Tobin, Wu, and Davidson 1989). They take different positions, often subconsciously, on what is good and bad and on what the future should be.

Concepts of a City

Urban design is inevitably guided by designers' and decision makers' concepts of what a good city or any other settlement is. The same positive theories give rise to competing concepts of what a good environment is, because different designers draw inferences from them based on their own values. Implicit if not explicit in all normative urban design theories, however, is some concept of human needs and how these needs are reflected in human aspirations and in the built environment.

In late-nineteenth-century Western Europe the mercantile city was seen as a treasure trove, a museum, of human history and civic aspirations. Architects designed buildings with a sense of decorum. There was an understanding among the power elite of the place of each building type in a hierarchy of importance and the appropriate architectural treatment at each level. There was a generally accepted aesthetic order. A contrasting image of the nineteenth-century city was that of the Coketown, the industrial city. Today we have been through a period of economic rationalism where the nature of the city has been seen in terms of rent theory. The city is the place of competition for profit. In following this line of thought, the "idea of a town" has been lost (Rykwert 1988). The town becomes the byproduct of economic processes. At the same time, many architects are still guided by the image of town derived from medieval Europe.

All designers' actions are guided by their own image of what a good world looks like, an image of its visual attributes. Their models are created based on different value systems. Frank Lloyd Wright's Broadacre City is substantially different from Le Corbusier's Radiant City, Paolo Soleri's Arcosanti, and Leon Krier's Poundbury (see Chapters 2 and 3). Kevin Lynch (1984), rather than providing a visual image of the good city, prescribes its performance characteristics. Lynch listed five basic dimensions of performance that a good city form must afford: (1) *Vitality*—the city must support the biological functions of people; it must provide for the need for survival; (2) *Sense*—the city's form must be clearly perceivable; it must afford people the development of clear cognitive images; (3) *Fit*—the city must provide for the behaviors people engage in and want to engage in; the behavior settings must be adequate; (4) *Access*—the city must provide people with access to places and to information; and (5) *Control*—the city must provide appropriate levels of control for people over places and over the processes by which the city is changed. To this list Lynch adds two fundamental criteria for meeting the above requirements. They must be fulfilled with (6) *Efficiency* in cost and time, and (7) *Justice* in the distribution of power and resources. This model has clearly very much influenced this book.

The model of the physical city presented here consists of a linked set of behavior settings serving civic and civil purposes. In this model there is a variety of milieus that ideally should be organized under a clear overall idea. In potential contradiction to this ideal is that of individual rights and expressions as the basis for design decisions in a competitive manner. Individuals have rights, but so does the community. How does one define these rights?

If a society as a whole is not to suffer from major opportunity costs there is also the need to consider the city as an open system of linked entities, each with its own attributes. Any total or all-of-a-piece urban design scheme or implemented design policy changes the system because it changes the entities within it, the links among them,

and the financial values associated with the entities and with the links (Attoe and Logan 1989). Urban design projects in the United States today tend to be presented as closed systems within the larger urban system. They are considered to be independent units, but all schemes of any consequence will have an effect on the outside world and be affected by it. While it makes economic sense to consider the impact of the outside world on a project, there are few economic rewards for the sponsors of schemes or for urban designers themselves to consider the impact of their proposals on the outside world unless the impact on their own schemes will be negative. Sometimes they are legally required to do so. Implicit in all these observations is a cultural bias.

Concepts of the Cultural Basis for Design

Different issues arise in assessing design quality in different cultures, but they all derive from people's self-image and their cultures and, consequently, their idea of what constitutes a good life, and *the* good life. People within cultures have *mental constructs* of who they are, the appropriate tastes for people to hold, and the appropriate patterns of behavior. There is both a general societal ethos and a professional culture guiding design decisions. These normative views may well deviate from the choices people actually make and the behavior in which they engage. The image Americans have of themselves seems to be derived largely from the portrayal in movies of the 1930s and not from their own history or current behavior. The issue is whether to design for the normative model—a mental construct—or for the positive one—the way people behave. Designing for the mental construct will result in a *mentally congruent* rather than a *behaviorally congruent* environment (Michelson 1976). Urban designers are thus confronted with having to decide the extent to which they accept the present behavior, the normative model, or some other statement of desired behavior as the basis for design.

Explicitly establishing the cultural model to be used as the basis for design is fraught with difficulties. Relying on what people say about themselves and their hopes and aspirations is frequently unlikely to lead to the best environment for them in the future. Often we respond in a culturally acceptable way to what is desirable or undesirable. We do not necessarily behave in the way we say we will, so that busy sidewalks and mixed-use areas are stated to be bad even if people seem to go out of their way to use them. The images of the good world to which we have been socialized make it difficult for us, laypeople and professional designers alike, to consider other possibilities (Wolschke-Bulmahn 1992).

While creating and propounding models of the future may seem to be largely the concern of visionaries, different models of the future still shape the work of practicing urban designers. Practitioners have the reputation of being less articulate and less concerned about how a good world should perform than theoreticians. Nevertheless, their actions are implicitly based on some sense of "better" unless those actions are perverse (Lynch 1984). Their focus is on producing individual products, but as references throughout this book indicate, there are also many urban designers who think of the environment more holistically. One of the major issues in developing working models of future cultures to be used as the basis for design is over the degree of rights that a community has and the degree of rights that are the prerogative of the individual.

Views of community and individual prerogatives differ among societies. The United States, Australia, the United Kingdom, and the Netherlands emphasize individuality and individual expression. In such countries it is difficult to get the uniformity of expression that architects generally seek in determining urban design quality.

One of the major conflicts between a widely held view of the good world of architects, planners, and urban designers and the reality of everyday life has to do with the concept of community and of life in public spaces. Many architects' images of a good city are full of plazas where people gather—the medieval one (see also Chapter 13). Yet in many societies such plazas are not used. Sometimes when they are introduced they will be used if judiciously placed (i.e., in busy locations well connected to the flows of people among the areas of the city). This was the result in Copenhagen (Gehl 1988), but often open spaces remain forlorn—they are not part of the behavior patterns of people. With the availability of new communications technology and an increasing emphasis on privacy and individuality of life (something generally deplored by architects even though their own lifestyles tend to follow standard norms), such places will not be used.

In the United States, there is an increasing privatization of public spaces in response to the cost of maintaining and policing them and the decline in the ability of the public sector to pay for them. Many of us deplore this action. Do we go along with the trend or strive to develop designs that allow public space to remain public space? Urban designers are constantly facing such decisions. To what extent should urban designers try to lead society and to what extent should they follow? It has been pointed out already that the ability to change social patterns through physical design is limited unless the user clients themselves are predisposed to change (Gans 1968; see also Chapter 1).

The Model of the Human Being

The places urban designers design are used by many different people. Like the designer of automobiles, the urban designer has to have a model of the human being in mind as the basis for making decisions. Even in culturally homogeneous societies people will differ physiologically and psychologically, and thus in competence. Does

one design for the modal person or attempt to fulfill the requirements of the full range of people likely to use a place? The latter choice usually means that one designs only for the least competent, but this does not have to be the case. One can design different parts of a plaza, for instance, to be used by different people. The question is: "Should one?" If the answer is "Yes," then the question becomes: "How far should one take designing different facilities for different people?" Men and women use public plazas differently and feel comfortable in different types of settings (Mozingo 1989). Does one design all plazas so that all women and all men are both physiologically and psychologically comfortable in them or design some places for some people and some for others? Urban designers, implicitly if not explicitly, take stands on all these issues in designing the public realm or designing guidelines for its development. In answering these questions, substantive and procedural issues merge (see Chapter 22, Procedural Issues in Urban Design).

The answers to some of these types of questions are relatively clear. Children's playgrounds have clear user client groups. Should one, however, mainstream the handicapped, or provide separate, say transportation, facilities for them? These questions raise social design issues that have urban, architectural, and industrial design ramifications even with apparently straightforward issues. Clearly, special toilet facilities are necessary for the use and comfort of people in wheelchairs, but how separate should they be? Should every toilet be designed for the handicapped? Who should pay? What is in the public interest?

Concepts of the Public Interest

One of the major claims of city planners, urban designers, landscape architects, and to a lesser extent architects is that we design as much for the public interest as we do for the demands of the paying client and for the present users of a proposed development (Conrads 1970; Watkin 1977; Jacobs and Appleyard 1987). Yet one of the major conflicts urban designers face is in identifying short-term and long-term consequences of their designs and in taking positions on issues in the face of the fiscal demands of the sponsors of projects. Presumably for urban design to be a worthwhile activity, designers are designing for the good of the public, both in the present and the future. In assuming this attitude, we are taking a position on a number of substantive matters.

Among these positions is the one that fulfilling present needs should not preclude future possibilities. In taking this stand urban designers are advocates for future people even though we do not know who they are or what their values will be. Such a stand implies that urban designers are prepared to argue that the public forgo immediate rewards by not consuming all possibilities and resources in order to avoid precluding future options. The design implications are that we should strive for open-ended designs and not necessarily ones that work best now. The issue, both substantive and procedural, is how best to identify these options. Urban designers, like all professionals dealing with the future, work under uncertainty about the best courses of action to take, which is why there is often disagreement among designers themselves. They draw on separate knowledge bases, attitudes, and intentions. They are also trying to corner markets for their own expertise.

COMPETING GOALS AND OBJECTIVES IN URBAN DESIGN

One position on urban design described in this book is that the comprehensive goal is to create patterns of the built world that presumably have a high utility for their sponsors, inhabitants/users, and themselves. Urban designs rest on a series of judgments based in turn on predictions of how specific patterns will be used, which in turn are based on an understanding of the past—on our positive theory about how the world works and evolves. Judgments also involve the application of values to these outcomes. The positions designers take are always on behalf of somebody or some people rather than others. Even if an urban design goal is to enhance the quality of the biogenic environment for its own sake, it is based on a set of values that have implications for people. In any urban design there will be different opinions as to what should be done because each stakeholder will see the situation in terms of their own needs.

Competing Stakeholders

Almost inevitably the designer is faced with a variety of individuals and groups of people with differing needs and different degrees of political power in getting their needs met. Competing urban design goals arise because different people have different attitudes toward the reasons for building. There are many examples of this competition.

Sponsors, Users, and Designers

Sponsors, users, and designers look at the environment in different ways. They will have different goals in changing it because they have different needs. The goal of sponsors is certainly to make a financial profit sufficient to meet other needs that they have. One of the goals of users may be also be a financial one—to have a safe investment— but it will also be to have many of their basic, cognitive, and aesthetic needs met, although they are unlikely to be articulate about them. Designers too have a financial stake in the built environment. Changing it is the source of their livelihood, but a design is also the mechanism to fulfill their self-esteem as well as their cognitive and aesthetic needs. In any design of any consequence, com-

promises between different goals and objectives have to be made.

Any large-scale urban design project is likely to have different sponsors, different designers, and a variety of users. The groups may agree on overall goals, but the design objectives—the means for achieving the goals— will differ. Often, however, they will have competing goals. One of the urban design tasks is to reconcile the goals of competing users. There is no deterministic way of achieving this end.

Competing Users

Any urban design has different users. It is clear, for instance, that in many instances adults like to have a highly manicured environment, but children may not, because every time they do something, their behavior is considered inappropriate for the behavior setting and damaging to the environment. In a comparative study of neighborhoods in Stoke-on-Trent, London, and the Bedwell area of Stevenage New Town in England, Robin Moore (1986) found what parents would regard as the worst place, Mill Hill in Stoke-on-Trent, is the best for children and most enjoyed by them because it affords the variety of behaviors that either damage Bedwell or would be regarded as unacceptable in such a manicured environment.

How manicured should urban designs be? Has neatness become too much of a goal in design? Will a child dropping an ice cream spoil a sidewalk? Can a design accommodate a shopowner handwriting a sign without making the whole scheme appear to be visually disordered? If it will be a mess, does it matter? Will a person sitting on a ledge damage it? Is there a place for children to test their strengths against the environment without damaging it? Are we designing opportunities for self-testing out of the environment except on the highways? With whom should one design in mind? What is in the public interest? The questions loop back on themselves.

To overcome the difficulty of understanding a wide array of ways in which different cultures and subcultures manifest needs, a designer may make a commitment to a particular group of people and take on the role of an advocate for its interests. In this case, urban designers are likely to be competing with each other. For instance, many designers have a commitment to the development of intellectual aesthetic theories associated with the artistic elite, an activity for which high accolades are received (Broadbent 1990). A number of designers (e.g., Hart 1978, 1979; R. Moore 1987, 1991; R. Moore et al. 1987; Ward 1990) focus their attention on the way basic and cognitive needs are fulfilled by children within a particular culture. Others focus their attention on the needs of the elderly (e.g., Lawton 1975; Regnier and Pynoos 1987). In some ways the needs of each group now and in the future overlap, but in others they conflict and they also compete with the broader needs of society. These recognitions bring with them the requirement to invent new ways of providing for those diverse needs in order to resolve conflicts.

Competing Needs of Users and Operators of the Built Environment

Conflicts also often arise between designing to fulfill the needs of those people who will be using a space and designing for those people who will be operating and maintaining it. Does one design health services primarily with patients in mind, or doctors? Does one design a plaza for the ease of use by people—either for activities or aesthetic effects—or for ease of maintenance? The easy answer is "design with all these ends in mind," but almost always there are tradeoffs between designing to fit one set of needs well and fitting another set well.

There are many examples of buildings, and probably even more of the spaces between them (e.g., Plaza d'Italia in New Orleans), that look good when the mayor cuts the ribbon and makes a speech on opening day but become forlorn within a short time. They have not received the maintenance they need to keep them close to their opening day appearance. Often the methods and costs of maintaining them were not considered either by their sponsors or their designers. There are also many examples of places, particularly public ones, designed with ease of maintenance rather than the use of the place by people in mind. They are frequently dreary from the outset.

Competing Goals

As the result of different people having different needs, and different professionals having different advocacies, urban designers will always be working with competing goals. Simple examples illustrate this point. The design of a city required to have an efficient public transit system does not allow for the highways that afford high individual mobility. The need to design compact cities to reduce infrastructure costs of transportation and sewerage systems will not necessarily result in reduced energy requirements for buildings in hot humid climates such as that of New Orleans. Designing for accessibility may also conflict with the desire for people to live in single-family homes with large private backyards. Individual control over decisions, say about signs, may not result in a neighborhood that promotes civic pride. Old warehouses provide low-rent accommodation but often look like slums. Tree-lined streets provide shade and serve formal aesthetic ends but get in the way of infrastructure elements both below and above the ground.

Many such conflicts that have attracted public attention over the past two decades have occurred at the supra-urban design scale or outside the realm of professional concern of urban designers, although these conflicts are often within their concern as citizens. For instance,

the benefits of large-scale economic development of scarce resources might have to be weighed against regional water and air pollution costs, resource consumption, and such consequences as the potential destruction of the habitat of various species of fauna and the effects of hardwood forest depreciation on the biogenic environment of tropical areas. Highway development needs of a society may well compete with private property rights. The first of these examples is international in scope and the second is at least regional. A seemingly endless list of similar conflicts occurs in urban design—for instance, between the aesthetic tastes of the public and the nature and role of public art as seen by artists, or between the merits of historic preservation and new development. Questions arise about how to deal with streams in urban areas and in deciding on the type of vegetation to use in a park (native plants or exotic species). These examples are characteristic of the problems that an urban designer confronts. There are strong arguments for and against each of the many ways of answering such questions.

Human Needs versus Environmental Needs

Design objectives vary not only because of the variety of human needs that have to be met through design but because they compete with the perceptions of the needs of the biogenic environment. People have changed the nature of the biogenic environment to better meet what they perceive to be their individual needs. All human beings consume resources—some of which are sustainable and some simply depleted. Should human beings consume any nonrenewable sources? Often there is a tradeoff between improving the lot of human beings in the short run and the long-term negative effects on the biogenic environment. Better housing in many countries means that more land will be transformed from unbuilt-on land to urbanized land. Such actions will inevitably change the flora and fauna of the world. At the extreme, we may be dealing with the competition for survival of individual humans and species of flora and fauna. Where does one draw the line?

The issue of the type of plants to place in parks and other urban open spaces exemplifies changing attitudes of both professionals and many laypeople. It has increasingly become a concern in places such as Florida that native plant species are being overwhelmed by imported ones (see Chapter 18). Plants are brought in to solve particular problems and then thrive so well that they become problems in themselves. In addition, when people migrated to the United States they brought their animals and plants with them, often causing considerable damage to the natural environment of their new homes. Certain of these plants have had particular associations for people. Such associations are important in meeting their need for identity (see Chapter 13), yet the use of these plants may be detrimental to existing species of plants and to native birds and thus may reduce a sense of place. Which is more important, the associational meanings that are central to people's identity or the maintenance of the natural habitat in a particular state? Such a question can only be answered in terms of a world view, a global model. It will be a political answer.

Many of these conflicts can be amicably resolved through creative design. Many cannot. Time and again the urban designer and those ultimately responsible for making communal decisions have to take a stand on such conflicts without much empirical evidence to assist them. More frequently the decisions are unfortunately made independently by people with individual responsibilities without concern for their side effects. Implicit in these stands are quantified positions, but we are unable to discern them, and we are thus unable to explicate them. Maslow's model of human needs provides the basis for introducing questions about the appropriate functions that any proposed urban design should fulfill, but there remain some basic problems in applying it.

The Hierarchical Order of Human Needs

Human needs may occur in an hierarchical pattern, but in deciding what to design there is no rule telling the designer the degree to which a particular need should be addressed to make sure that it is sufficiently satisfied before moving on to the consideration of other needs. For instance, how much should one design for safety? Segregating pedestrians from vehicles—horizontally (with malls) or vertically (in tunnels or with skyways)—may provide considerable safety for people on foot, but it also interferes with the attainment of other needs. It is also expensive.

Using Maslow's model we can predict that if one designs wholeheartedly to meet a set of people's primary needs, then their concerns will shift to less pressing needs, but being specific is difficult. Some people have to tolerate environments with high crime rates because they have little choice if they are to survive. It is, however, also clear that people are prepared to tolerate such environments in order to fulfill esteem needs. They may feel safe enough in New York City, but this is not necessarily true in Washington, DC. There are also districts in Washington, DC, Detroit, and New York City, for instance, where people live because they have no viable choice, or because they have become habituated to the socially dislocated environment and cannot imagine themselves attaining a different situation. What position should urban designers take on the needs of the perpetrators of crime?

While designers have to address the full array of human needs of many different people, there is no rule telling them where to place their emphases other than that some needs are pressing and others not. Identifying the focus of attention in any situation is thus an issue that has to be dealt with every time one designs. We understand little about the relative importance of the built environment in people's lives in comparison to the social and economic environment. Thus it is difficult to argue with hard evidence for emphasizing urban design in comparison to social and economic planning in increasing the opportunities for people to enrich their lives.

The decision to emphasize one goal over another will always be a bone of contention for the designer. Any decision will be the subject of argument and debate. It will remain an issue on which different people will take different stands. The more basic the need the less the variables are of intellectual concern to the design profession. There is little that urban design can do about hunger other than to strive to ease accessibility problems and provide opportunities for urban farming, which is hardly a major solution. The design of a sheltering public realm in cities is, however, one that requires considerable thought. Less pressing needs, particularly aesthetic concerns, have traditionally been central to urban design thought. We now understand the complexity of their nature better than our predecessors did.

EXAMINING THE CITY

While there is a hierarchy of importance of people's needs, there is also a hierarchy of elements in the way human settlements are organized and considered to be organized. There are arguments over urban design objectives because there are different positive concepts of the elements of the built environment. There are a number of ways of decomposing the city into its elements (see Chapter 9). They are neither necessarily in conflict nor mutually exclusive. The way one disaggregates the components of the city reflects how one pays attention to the environment and in turn how one sets about designing it. Issues arise because the best way of analyzing the built environment in particular circumstances is not obvious.

To design for ease of orientation, the way of considering the elements of the built environment suggested by Kevin Lynch (1960)—as paths, edges, nodes, districts, and landmarks—may well be the most sensible. There is certainly considerable empirical evidence for doing so (Pocock and Hudson 1978; Passini 1984; Arthur and Passini 1990). If one is concerned with esteem and the role of urban design, it may be better to consider the built environment as consisting of a prestigious foreground and less prestigious background elements (Westerman 1990). Recently (e.g., Corner 1990) efforts have been made to understand the city as a series of layers: historical fabric, open space, ground plane surfaces, building types, planting, circulation systems, and behavior settings. This approach may be helpful in creating a city with vitality. The important thing for urban designers is to develop an ordering system in which the form-giving elements chosen depend on the degree to which they contribute to the overall character of the affordances of the patterns of the built environment for activities and aesthetic appreciation, and the degree to which they determine the overall form of a settlement. The solution must be situation-specific. It also has to be implementable within the invisible web of existing laws or else has to have them changed within the Constitution. The laws will no doubt be changed to better address the nature of future societies and will thus affect potential future designs.

The overall behavioral and visual framework of the city is established through its patterns of circulation and public open spaces. The way these elements work together with the organization of the third dimension—the façades of buildings—gives a city much of its visual character. So does the way the details of the environment are handled. The character also stems from the activities that take place and the nature of the people involved. Perceptions of the character, however, differ for different people. A child sees the details and perceives the sensation-yielding nature of the environment more than adults do (Lukashok and Lynch 1956).

Many of the best-loved U.S. cities and their precincts are known not for their visual orderliness but for the richness of life they afford. The character of any city thus also comes from the behavior settings that exist and the degree to which they are physically and socially accessible to its inhabitants. This factor, while recognized by most architects, tends to be forgotten in making design decisions. The focus ends up being on the visual quality, depending on current canons of architectural good taste.

The issue that confronts designers is where to place their emphases. What is really important? Is it the overall network of paths in Lynch's terms (1960), or is it the detailing of the sidewalks and entrances of buildings? Or is it the nature of the nodes? Or the way the civic buildings are organized in relationship to squares? Different designers have different positions on what the important factor is. Their positions are based on images of a good society and what they themselves are competent in designing—the promotion of their own professional ends. The design task is to deal with the multivariate environment in all its complexity, but inevitably some issues are emphasized over others.

Environmental Possibilities

Many architects take the position that every design has to be innovative—a visual departure from the norm. It is perceived to be better for a design to fail than to replicate an existing design, even if that design is highly successful. Other designers take the position that if it has worked in the past why change it for the sake of changing it? (see "Peter Eisenman versus Leon Krier" 1989.) Cities are always changing, but many ways of life and values remain constant. The Rationalist branch of the Modern movement in architecture and urban design deliberately broke from a past that it perceived to be antihuman and

irrelevant, but the new world that was created did not work as well as predicted. The Empiricist approach to urban design has tended, it has been suggested in this book, to be unnecessarily romantic and picturesque. The issue that urban designers have to face is: To what extent should they be innovative and to what extent traditional? To what extent should new geometries and new technologies be sought for the sake of newness?

One of the major frustrations felt, rightly or wrongly, by urban designers occurs when they perceive better ways of doing things that involve new modes of thought or new patterns of the environment to which people are unaccustomed. One of the major roles of the urban designer is to sell ideas—to bring people's attention to new ways of doing things. At the same time there is often a desire for novelty for its own sake. One of the main ways architects gain prestige is through devising new ways of doing things. Novel designs attract the attention of both an architect's peers and the press, professional and lay.

URBAN DESIGN MECHANISMS FOR MEETING HUMAN NEEDS

One of the basic questions in urban design, as in architectural or industrial design, is: "How tailormade should the layout of the environment be for a specific behavior pattern or for a set of aesthetic tastes?" This question leads to others: "Does one design for comfort or development?" "Does one deal with changing behaviors, changing technologies, and changing taste cultures, or does one simply design for the known present and allow the future to take care of itself?"

Meeting Design Objectives

While we have knowledge of the general mechanisms linking the fulfillment of human needs to their expression in physical form, their manifestation for all individuals and even for all groups of people is beyond the capacity of a single urban designer to understand. Needs are not static, they are modified by culture, and the way the same need, for example, for esteem, is met will vary from culture to culture and even from individual to individual within a culture. In addition, questions arise over the comprehensiveness of our knowledge and our ability to deal with the needs of different groups simultaneously.

Within a culture the same need may be met in a variety of ways. Membership in a group may be met through participation in a group's activities and simultaneously through the display of the symbols of membership. One mechanism may reinforce the other. There are often conflicts to resolve. In some societies the use of symbolic expression of status may be regarded as desirable, but some of its members may disagree. The Modern movement in architecture and planning tended to frown on the symbolic displays of the different socioeconomic statuses of people, but in the United States at least, it has become quite clear that symbolic displays are important to many people and have been the raison d'être for many urban design projects. One of the issues facing the urban designer is to what extent should needs be met in one way rather than another. The search for self-esteem is seen by some as the overriding goal of people in the United States today (Pfaff 1991). How best can this end be achieved? Should it be achieved? Does one assume everything associated with a particular group's self-esteem to be good for society? To what extent can a designer aid the meeting of needs using different mechanisms? How far should the designer take these possibilities? This question loops the discussion back to the beginning. How specific should the design be to the demands of the behavioral program? Indeed, how specific should the behavioral program be? (See also Chapters 21, 22, and 24.)

Few design objectives can be met in only one way. Most design objectives can luckily be met through a variety of design patterns or mechanisms. Some of these ways are better than others, but none can be regarded as correct or incorrect. Take one objective—say, to design at high density. There are a number of ways of designing housing at the same density; each will meet other objectives in a better or worse way. It is thus difficult to think of any design pattern in absolute terms as good or bad even though doing so makes designing easier.

Such questions arise in dealing with almost every aspect of urban design. Examples abound. For instance, a continuing public policy question facing the United States, where the automobile is the dominant means of transportation, is the degree to which to design and build competing transportation systems, and to advise and legislate new transportation and land-use arrangements that recognize the possibility of future fuel shortages. The present distribution of behavior settings and the nature of the links between them require a considerable consumption of nonreplaceable fuel if the automobile is the major means of transport. Should one simply let the market dictate the distribution of activities in space?

Assuming it were possible to precisely define a behavioral program—the range of patterns of activities and aesthetic tastes to be fulfilled by a design—how closely should one design the mechanisms and patterns of the environment to fulfill those needs? How well can we do so? We know that behavior patterns change over time and that aesthetic tastes change as well. It seems foolish to design very specifically for existing patterns of behavior. Yet some behavior patterns seem to be enduring, some buildings types seem to be almost infinitely adaptable (e.g., the rowhouse), and some patterns of the environment afford many activities (a city market square can be a parking lot for automobiles).

How open-ended should a design be? This question leads to others. To what extent should one design for the present, and to what extent should one leave decisions to be made later? Does one simply design for the present and for ease of demolition, so that the built environment can be changed easily to accommodate the changing manifestations of the needs of people? How enduring should urban designs be? The moral high ground these days appears to be that all waste is bad, but is designing for continually changing needs and/or their manifestations necessarily wasteful?

Most urban design endeavors have assumed that what is built will last forever. There have been some exceptions, such as in designing Olympic villages, where the use may change but the buildings will last; world's fairs, where both elements of behavior and the built environment will change; and amusement parks, where elements of the built environment will respond to changing ideas and possibilities. The plug-in city concept assumed that change in cities would be rapid, and certainly a glance at any economically prosperous city will indicate that it is undergoing substantial renewal. Designing for stability and change is one of the basic concerns of urban design.

Comfort and Development Needs as Design Issues

Both our physiological and psychological comfort depend to some extent on being with familiar people, in familiar places, and doing familiar things. A certain level of stress is, however, not necessarily a bad thing. It serves a motivational purpose. New situations and new experiences lead to physiological and intellectual development (or at least the maintenance of one's abilities) provided they are challenging. Inevitably they will be accompanied by some stress. As a result, such situations will not be as comfortable as they could be. The issue is whether the designer should be designing to make people comfortable or to challenge them to new explorations of themselves, their abilities, and their surroundings.

Some people seek change; others seek what is psychologically comfortable, although alternatives processes or environments would be beneficial to them. Many elderly people, for instance, do not wish to deal with anything new, even when it is in their best interest. A dilapidated house may seem or be said to be fine by a long-time resident of a place, even though it is "rationally" clearly dangerous. Avoiding the predicted stress that would be evoked by changing the house or by moving to another place is perceived to be worth the opportunity cost of "no change."

SEARCHING FOR AMBIGUITY IN DESIGN

The ideal urban design would meet everybody's needs simultaneously. The only way to approach this ideal would be for all designs to be ambiguous in the sense that they can be interpreted in different ways by different people, and be open to different uses by different people. This statement is easy to write, but more difficult to implement.

Ambiguity is achieved when the same pattern of the environment has more than one set of affordances, both for activities and for aesthetic appreciation. In a sense this goal is easy to achieve because all patterns are ambiguous. The difficulty is to be specific in order to achieve the range of affordances that are of *importance* to different sets of people in a single pattern (Rapoport and Kantor 1967). This observation is particularly true of different aesthetic preferences. The danger in trying to accommodate too large a range of activities and meanings within one pattern is that the pattern may afford them so poorly that it meets nobody's needs. This attempt to meet everybody's needs at a basic level has been one of the problems with *universal space;* it suits nobody well. The alternative is to seek different places for different people. How far should one go in seeking this end?

A pattern of the built environment can serve many purposes simultaneously (see Chapter 1). A street can be a playground, a parking area, a rainwater channel, and so on. One of the major concerns in urban design is to design to meet a variety of needs of different people simultaneously and to meet them well without one set of affordances impinging negatively on another. This statement is clearly an ideological one and applies to aesthetic considerations as well as to activity patterns. Bold designs praised by architects tend not to have a high level of ambiguity in this way. Multidimensional designs tend not to have the simplicity of form and idea that captures the imagination of designers.

THE ROLE OF THE URBAN DESIGNER

When a design is said to be a poor one, or "doesn't work," it usually means that the problem has been poorly defined.

Some designs do not work in anybody's eyes, but others work for some people and not for others, or comply with a particular set of aesthetic associations but do not fit into a currently prevailing architectural ideology.

If one accepts the discussion of Functionalism and human needs in Chapters 11 to 17, the biogenic environmental issues in Chapter 18, and that the objective of design is to meet present human needs without destroying the possibility of attaining satisfaction of future ones, it is clear that all generic designs must be understood in terms of the purposes they serve and whose purposes they are before they are applied. It also becomes clear that the design of the problem is as important as the design of the solution and that the two go hand in hand (Bazjanac 1974; Rittel and Webber 1984). As a result, the concern of urban design theory is to understand the procedural issues as much as substantive ones.

The role of the urban designer is as much as an *analyst* and a *mediator* as a designer. It is possible to be a totally disinterested party in the argumentative process of design only when the issues are not close to the heart. Many issues are and the designers must recognize that they are interested parties in shaping the future city. At the same time, however, in identifying the issues to be addressed and in making proposals, the urban designer will have to mediate between the different interests of different parties. This task will be done implicitly if not explicitly. To be able to do it explicitly the urban designer needs to have a thorough understanding of *procedural design theory*. Based on this understanding a normative position can be sensibly taken. Without it there is no professionalism to urban design.

Photograph by Joyce George

PROCEDURAL ISSUES IN ATTAINING A FUNCTIONAL ENVIRONMENT

Substantive knowledge about the environment, how it is used, and the meanings that it might afford different people, however well developed, can only inform the urban designer about the potential functions of urban form. It does not tell them what they might or should do with this knowledge. Positive substantive information is neutral in the sense that it tells what is and has been, and helps us predict the future, but it does not tell us what to design. It cannot. Decisions about the future are creative ones. Understanding the decision-making process enables us to understand the potential ways in which urban designers might get involved in the processes of urban change. Our present understanding of positive procedural theory in urban design is outlined in this, the third component of Part Two, Functionalism Redefined.

The topics described under the rubric Procedural Issues in Attaining a Functional Environment are as interwoven as those described under Substantive Issues. The label "procedural issues" is itself ambiguous. It can mean issues concerned with the implementation of projects or with the nature of designing. The phrase is used in the second way here following the principles of Herbert Simon (1954) because the second usage subsumes the first. The concern here is with the overall decision process from the design of the problem to the evaluation of the solution after implementation.

Urban design is part of the self-conscious development process of human settlements. The way the built world is developed by public and private interests is described in Chapter 20, The Development Process. The particular concern is with the potential roles of the urban designer working with the land and building development community, public or private. There are a number of basic differences between centralized and decentralized planning and design. There are also differences among various methods of financing development that lead to different urban design results. The intervention of urban designers in the standard economic and legal processes of urban development should always result in attaining a better built environment than if the building and rebuilding of cities were left to politicians, devel-

Homesteading, Brooklyn, New York

opers, and lawyers alone. Certainly, the type of urban design controls implemented has a major effect on urban patterns at both a macro and micro scale. An understanding of the processes of urban development and of urban design is fundamental to structuring and carrying out the overall designing process.

Empirical research into the designing process is in its infancy, but we do understand more about it than we often admit. Our present knowledge on how to deal with wicked problems is presented in Chapter 21, The Urban Design Designing Process. The understanding of design problems as "wicked" ones and the design process as a problem-solving process is central to the description of urban design presented in this book and its advocacy presented in Part Three. One of the factors that tends to differentiate urban design from architectural design is the time it takes from inception/conception of a problem to the implementation of a solution can be very lengthy under a number of jurisdictions in space and time. The individual parts of an urban design project—even total urban design—are built in phases with some intended components inevitably being changed after the earlier phases are completed and functioning. Some projects are even abandoned. The type of flexibility in design thought that such changes require creates both conceptual and practical problems that need to be considered when structuring or designing the design process to be used in a particular circumstance.

A number of models of the design process and various understandings of what constitutes a creative design process coexist. The basic dyadic model (i.e., one that assumes a professional and a client as a point of departure) presented in the chapter is not a new one. It is, however, one that has stood up well over the last two decades as a general description of the process. It is useful as a point of departure for understanding the process of designing, and as a basis for designing processes that are as appropriate to their contexts as possible. It is a Rationalist model biased by the existing Empirical research. It assumes that the process begins with setting goals and designing the program (or brief, as it is sometimes called). The process then continues with designing a set of buildings and their infrastructure requirements and/or design policies and development guidelines. The next step involves the evaluation of these products while they are still "on the drawingboard," followed by the implementation of one. The final step is the evaluation of the results. It is clear, if one looks at designing in this way, that each step requires creative thought, and that each step involves the selection of methods and techniques of analyzing, synthesizing, and evaluating. The whole process is value-laden and highly subjective. It need not, however, be capricious.

There are a number of coexisting attitudes about how the development of cities and urban areas should take place. While the overall structure of the design process may be the same whatever specific methods are used, the way one goes through it will differ depending on the nature of the development process and political context. However, one of the major issues facing all designers remains. What happens if that which is deemed to have been a good design process yields a solution that the designer feels to be poor? Or, alternatively, what happens if a good design can only be derived by a process, either of design or implementation, that the designer finds repugnant? The answer depends on one's attitudes toward society, clients, and the built and natural worlds. Many such issues arise during the designing. They are often highly emotional. The discussion in Chapter 22, Procedural Issues in Urban Design, brings attention to the dilemmas that urban designers frequently face.

The whole discussion of functionalism, substantive, and procedural issues in urban design in Part Two of this book raises more questions than it answers and may leave the impression that the problems confronting urban designers are unsolvable and can only be considered in a purely arbitrary, intuitive, and irrational way. This is not the case. Decisions have to be made, and if urban design is to benefit society, stands have to be taken under uncertainty—positions must be presented with uncertainty. The public demand is increasingly that these decisions be taken in public view. Indeed, many architects avoid dealing with urban design for this very reason. A stand on how urban design should be carried out in the United States based on the American experience is taken in Part Three of this book under the title Synthesis—A Neo-Functional Approach to Urban Design, which leads directly back to Part One of the book. ■

20

THE DEVELOPMENT PROCESS

The development process varies considerably in scale from an extension on a person's house to urban renewal schemes to regional plans. The urban design concern is with the private and communal decisions that shape the public realm of cities and suburbs. All urban design requires some financial investment and accrues some financial cost in order to achieve public benefits. In addition, the nature of the investment and taxation process in any locale very much affects the work of urban designers because it determines what can be built much as zoning ordinances do. Government intervention into the marketplace attempts to shape it to meet specific public ends. As a result, American cities and those everywhere very much reflect eras of government policies and programs.

Within the set of opportunities provided by the existing investment in infrastructure and buildings, the state of the local economy, and the set of laws (the invisible web), the future built environment is shaped by the public and private sector decisions that constitute the development process. As the nature of the process is often misunderstood by urban designers, there is considerable confusion over potential schemes and how they might be implemented. Most urban design ideology has been developed independently of an understanding of how cities are shaped in capitalist societies. The focus has been on ideal designs, not ideal design processes. Urban design innovations have come from strong-willed individuals, many of whom are from the development community, not the architectural. Much of the recent concern with the nature of the development process among urban designers stems from the need to understand what can be implemented and what remains a dream.

Many urban design plans initiated by the public sector are not implemented because property developers cannot be induced to participate in building the plans'

private sector components. Many developers' plans sit in their closets because they were too grandiose for banks to finance, or their designs, based on the quest for profit, were detrimental to the public interest as perceived by government officials. The public sector has also invested much time, effort, and money in building the infrastructure for potential schemes so as to encourage private investment by reducing the financial risk for developers in building projects yet schemes are unbuilt.

The public investment in infrastructure and other subsidies has encouraged many important developments. The revitalization of Quality Hill in Kansas City, Missouri, the development of Gateway Mall in St. Louis, Quincy Market/Faneuil Hall in Boston, the Horton Center in San Diego, and Grand Avenue in Milwaukee would not have taken place without it (Frieden and Sagalyn 1989; Marks 1990; Frieden 1990). Such developments have revitalized downtown areas of many American cities during the 1970s and 1980s in a way that some critics had thought impossible a decade earlier (Lowry 1980). There are, however, also many schemes where the infrastructure stands in isolation (e.g., Penn's Landing, Philadelphia), and still others that were fully implemented but stand underused or even unused because they were not in accordance with market realities (i.e., consumer preferences).

It is important to understand market realities because the sums invested in any urban design project and the financial side effects are substantial. The St. Louis downtown renaissance has been difficult to achieve. Between 1966 and 1986 over $3.2 billion (in 1988 dollars) was invested in the area despite the city's population decreasing from 857,000 in 1950 to 406,000 in 1989 as people moved to the suburbs and elsewhere. Of this investment 8.5 percent was in public funds. The financial benefits appear to have been important but the psychological ones may well be even more so, although they are difficult

Photograph by Deepti Nijhawan

1. Faneuil Hall/Quincy Market Development, Boston

2. Horton Center, San Diego

Figure 20-1: Financially Successful Public-Private Developments
Almost any urban scene in the United States will consist of components of public and of private investment. The financing of much urban design in recent years has been complex, with governments directly subsiding land costs and/or building costs with grants or making low-interest loans, and private enterprise building parts of the public infrastructure. Such well-known developments as Faneuil Hall/Quincy Market (1) and the Horton Center (2) in San Diego would not have been built without such collaboration.

to quantify. Gateway Mall has been built and many other civic improvements have been implemented, but many proposals have not been and the building of a skyway system has ground to a halt. Making even financially impractical proposals does enable future possibilities to be discussed, but financially poor investment does not help the community.

As a result of the building boom and the consequent oversupply of commercial office space in many American cities during the 1980s and the failure of the savings and loan industry, the availability of capital funds for development has lessened in the country. A further consequence is that all urban design proposals will be subject to close scrutiny during the 1990s at least. The implication for urban design is that economic, market, and attitude research will form the basis for the mixture of elements contained in urban design proposals. The result is likely to be a conservative set of design strategies in the foreseeable future. Urban designers will have to be highly innovative to ensure that the issues of design quality raised in this book are addressed in the face of economic stringency and skepticism.

All development, and thus all urban designs, involve some financial and political risk, but flying in the face of economic realities is foolhardy, particularly in capitalist economies such as the United States. Many risks have been taken in the past. The Quincy Market/Faneuil Hall development was based on hopes rather than any empirical experience, but it has had considerable successes (Frieden and Sagalyn 1989). The opposite can also be seen, for instance, in the process of "demalling" America now taking place (Houstoun 1990a). High hopes without much foundation in economic reality have resulted in some expensive experiments.

In many urban, suburban, and small town shopping areas of the United States, perhaps as many as 300 in all, a main street was closed to vehicular traffic to create a pedestrian mall. They include well-known urban examples such as Nicollet Mall in Minneapolis and 16th Street Mall in Denver and less well known ones in suburban areas (e.g., Oak Park and La Grange, Illinois) and smaller cities (Kalamazoo, Michigan; Fresno, California; Ithaca, New York; Boulder, Colorado; and Rockford, Illinois). Such malls were the precursor to the usually internal downtown shopping malls of the 1970s and 1980s (e.g., the Gallery in Philadelphia, Galleria in Houston, and Horton Center in San Diego, the last mentioned being open air) modeled on successful suburban ones. The urban design goal was to revitalize traditional downtowns so they could compete successfully with the suburban shopping malls (largely enclosed), which by 1974 had already captured 44 percent of the U.S. retail trade, excluding automotive products and building supplies. The objective was to upgrade existing retail areas through the provision of congenial, safe, middle-class shopping environments. The attainment of a congenial design is a relatively straight-

1. Fresno, California

2. Rockford, Illinois

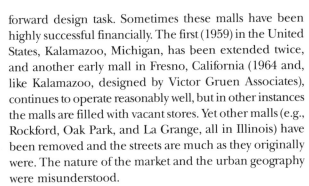

3. Rockford, Illinois

Figure 20-2: The Downtown Pedestrian Mall
The pedestrianization of a shopping street by closing it to vehicular traffic, paving it, and providing it with plantings and furniture was seen as a solution to the competition from suburban shopping malls, and the unpleasantness caused by the presence of vehicular pollution and crowded sidewalks. In some instances (1) the "malling" has been successful over a number of years but not in others. In Rockford, Illinois, however, the results were disappointing. The original shopping street, after being turned into a mall (2), has now been partially reconverted to a street (3). The market was misunderstood.

forward design task. Sometimes these malls have been highly successful financially. The first (1959) in the United States, Kalamazoo, Michigan, has been extended twice, and another early mall in Fresno, California (1964 and, like Kalamazoo, designed by Victor Gruen Associates), continues to operate reasonably well, but in other instances the malls are filled with vacant stores. Yet other malls (e.g., Rockford, Oak Park, and La Grange, all in Illinois) have been removed and the streets are much as they originally were. The nature of the market and the urban geography were misunderstood.

This result is particularly likely to occur when a typological approach to planning and design has been employed. A good idea in one place was thought to be the salvation to the problems in another place with many of the same characteristics. The type was applied without understanding the full nature of the situation, particularly its economic characteristics.

There are also many cities with weed-infested and trash-strewn vacant sites that have stood empty, waiting for redevelopment for twenty or thirty years. Individual sites were assembled by the public sector with public financing, using the power of eminent domain. The piecemeal sites were consolidated into large blocks of land for resale to the private sector for large-scale redevelopment. Many such urban renewal projects have been financially successful even if they failed to achieve their social goals. In many other cases, however, the market for redevelopment simply did not exist or redevelopers' plans were not politically feasible.

The position that many urban designers take is that understanding the nature of land development processes is outside their domain of interest. However, this lack of understanding reduces their potential role in creating the future city and places them at the whim of the development community. In purely capitalist countries such as the United States, or those with mixed economies such as Sweden, it is essential for policymakers and urban designers to understand the nature of the development process and the role of property developers in the building of the human habitat. Attaining this understanding is not an easy task, for each culture and even each administrative jurisdiction within a culture is likely to have its own development climate—its own entrepreneurial spirit. In this sense New York City differs considerably from Philadelphia and from New Orleans or Miami.

Without an understanding of the economic state of their cities, the development process, and the financing

1. Chicago

2. San Diego

3. San Diego

Figure 20–3: The Development Market and Urban Design
Many sites acquired by both the private and public sectors for urban renewal as long as thirty years ago still lie vacant (1). The infrastructure for other developments has been installed, but the private market has not been able to respond. While many projects have had a positive effect, acting as a catalyst for development around them, others have led to the failure of nearby businesses (2). Other developments have been stopped in midstream, incurring financial losses that have a ripple effect through their neighborhoods, the city and region, and sometimes the nation (3).

mechanisms available to developers, public officials may well propose schemes that will never be built because they are unmarketable, or will invest public money in projects that will fail economically when built. Or the public officials may simply go along with what developers say when they plead financial hardship in order to make greater profits. Also, they may be unable to communicate to developers their public interest concerns and how these can be considered in the design of a potential development. In cities such as San Diego, business community members are the planners because politicians have greater faith in what they say than in what the city planners say (Smith 1991). Conceptually the onus is on the public sector, not developers, to show leadership in improving the human habitat. If developers do show the leadership that is fine, provided they have the public interest as much as a corporate or personal profit concern. It is not, however, their defined role in capitalist societies. It is the role of city planners and urban designers.

The dynamics of urban development and the role of urban design movements in structuring American cities during this century were outlined in Chapter 2, Shaping the Twentieth-Century City. The purpose here is to focus on the role of developers in urban design and of urban

designers in the development process. Together with lawyers, politicians, and public interest pressure groups they are largely responsible for the physical shape and shaping of cities today.

THE PROCESS OF CITY BUILDING

The overall physical layout of a region consists of a set of subareas of varying sizes, each of which financially affords certain types of development. The affordances of a site for economically sound development depend on its natural character, its accessibility, the existing infrastructure, infrastructure possibilities, the taxation laws (and how they may be changed), zoning restrictions (and how they might be changed), and the people who live and work there or nearby. A variety of people scan the environment to see how it can be exploited for their own profit and in terms of their perception of the needs of the public and of the public interest. What they pay attention to depends on who they are and their motivations.

Property developers scan the environment for opportunities in terms of the potential profitability of a specific type of development. Developers with access to major capital markets will be looking at the environment in a different way from those who are capable of developing only a few units at a time. The former will be looking at large areas of land or sites where the location of new suburban areas or major buildings is possible, while the latter will be looking at smaller sites. Developers who specialize in a specific building type will look at the environment in terms of the developability of specific sites with that building type either to obtain economies of scale or simply because that is what they know how to do. For instance, those developers who build parking garages and developers who build shopping centers will be looking at the environment similarly but in terms of their experience in developing parking garages or shopping centers, respectively. In so doing their concern is not whether the intended use is the best one for the site but simply whether they can make a profit in building what they want to build there. Their concern for other potential uses extends only to whether or not they can be outbid for the site by another developer. They will be concerned primarily with their own self-interests.

Self-interest is a complex variable. The major changes taking place in suburban downtowns during the 1980s were due to more and more major business organizations seeking office space there so as to compete effectively in the marketplace for labor. Their self-interest is closely tied into the self-interest of those who wish to work near their homes and those who want to have the attributes and services of the traditional central business district (CBD) of a metropolitan area close at hand. Often this self-interest coincides with those of racists fleeing inner cities as they become populated predominantly by minorities. In this process they have often been aided by the public sector of a jurisdiction, which has seen the capturing of a component of the traditional CBD office market as part of their self-interest, although they have not always been prepared for the negative side effects in terms of traffic and associated costs (Leinberger and Lockwood 1986). Public officials in places such as Glendale, California, and Southfield, Michigan, perceived a market for office and retail developments when other suburbs of Los Angeles and Detroit, respectively, were hanging back or opposing development. By being aggressive in terms of planning and providing the basic infrastructure to make private development possible, Southfield has more office space than downtown Detroit, and Glendale has captured a sizable segment of the market that might otherwise have gone to adjacent areas. Whether or not it was in the public interest of the whole of the Los Angeles area for such a development to occur was not a question asked by Glendale authorities, or anybody else (Crooks 1985; Glendale Redevelopment Agency 1986a, 1986b). Now that it has occurred, other areas will have to adjust to that reality.

The public sector presumably is looking for opportunities to meet the needs of the citizens it represents as perceived in voting patterns. In different countries and in different areas and eras in the same country, public sectors vary in what they are prepared to do or are capable of doing. In socialist countries and countries with mixed economies, such as those of Scandinavia, governments have been much more forceful as developers than those of capitalist countries. During the 1950s, 1960s, and early 1970s the U.S. federal government was much more progressive and assertive in setting development priorities than it has been since then. It provided funds for specific types of infrastructure, housing, and community developments (Gallion and Eisner 1986; Frieden and Sagalyn 1989). Local governments tended to see their problems in terms of the types and amount of funding available, and those with aggressive leadership (e.g., New Haven, Connecticut) were able to secure a disproportionate amount of federal urban renewal and other funds for development until neighborhood groups began seriously questioning the fairness of programs. City and suburban governments still focus on problems in terms of the funds available, even though they may recognize the existence of many other problems. In the United States the types and amounts of funds available for subsidizing development, particularly in cities, are different in the early 1990s than in the heyday of urban renewal in the 1950s and 1960s. However, this situation may well change in the future as the political pendulum swings and the American political leadership and population becomes willing to deal with infrastructure and social problems that are beyond the capability of the private sector to address let alone solve.

One of the roles of the public sector has been to protect areas that are ripe (i.e., economically rewarding to the private sector) for being developed into housing, shopping, industrial, or other uses requiring buildings, and that have a natural attractiveness or can serve an important purpose in terms of public interests that cannot compete economically in the marketplace with the private sector. Often such areas have an economic benefit to the community as a whole because of the tourism they attract. During the 1980s pressure groups for preserving open spaces and existing developments have been increasingly vocal in stating their protectionist positions in the face of major population increases in the metropolitan areas of the world (Attoe 1988b).

The stated concern of public sector city planners and urban designers is to channel the forces that shape cities in ways that they perceive will better the lives of their inhabitants and the performances of the private sector. As mayors, city councillors, and civil servants look at the areas under their jurisdiction, the primary question is often not so much what should be built as what can be financed—what can be built now. The most immediate needs politically are the most pressing in terms of getting decisions made. In the United States and other purely capitalist countries, long-range and comprehensive plans tend to be shelved (Smith 1991). Immediate problems are the focus of attention. This attitude is prevalent among the design professions themselves. Their most basic need is to survive.

Developers and public officials alike compete or cooperate within a set of laws (or operate outside them) in building up the city as we know it. Whose interests urban designers represent very much affect their roles and potential roles in society and vice versa. They tend to be advocates for whomever pays them—their sponsors. If they represent the private sector, they look at the overall environment and its opportunities and design schemes in a different way than if they represent the public sector. Specifying the role they *should* play is a normative question addressed in Chapters 23, 24, and 25. At the very least, urban designers who understand the dynamics of the marketplace and the nature of the political environment have an expertise that lends them credibility in the eyes of others. In practice urban designers soon learn enough about the development process to survive, but many economically inappropriate designs continue to be built. Such designs are based on hopes not knowledge.

THE NATURE OF THE URBAN DESIGN DEVELOPMENT PROCESS

In a sense, everybody involved in the development of a new suburb or the redevelopment of an existing built-up area is involved in urban design. The concern here is with urban design as a professional activity. An understanding of the steps by which development takes place helps us to see the role and potential role of urban designers in shaping the outcomes of the process, whether publicly or privately initiated.

Urban design projects all need to be financed. They vary in character, depending on the state of the economy and whether it is the public or private sector, which leads and sets priorities for development. In the United States, the initiative has been with the private development of cities. As the economic base of cities shifts from manufacturing to diverse services, so the financing of the projects that are being developed is becoming more complex (Meltzer 1984). The shift creates multifaceted design schemes, particularly as the advocacy takes hold among urban designers for multiuse developments in reaction to the dullness of many Modernist environments. During the 1980s the types of urban design projects that had to be financed included urban renewal, waterfront festival markets, research and office campuses, housing developments, convention centers, and medical parks. Much of this development took place in suburban areas, but there was also considerable development of office buildings in the central areas of most American cities, partially in response to demand from 1980 to 1982 but also in response to the changes brought about by tax law revisions during the 1980s. These changes created opportunities for investments from Europe and Japan, where money could be borrowed at lower interest rates than in the United States.

The desire by major banks and investment institutions to develop global markets was an added pressure. All of these types of developments include elements that have traditionally been regarded as a part of the public domain but have relied heavily on private development for their implementation.

The financial feasibility of any urban design project, other than guideline writing (which can have major economic repercussions), depends very simply on the ability of its promoters to raise sufficient money to finance it and on its political payoffs. Financial feasibility depends on perceptions of how much the project will cost, the market that exists, and the price of money (i.e, interest rates), because these factors will dictate the rate of return on money invested. The political payoffs occur as politicians use their success in getting projects built or defeated as a means of garnering votes at election time.

Each group involved in financing a development works out what it is capable of providing in terms of equity and financial guarantees. The process of negotiation between public and private sectors is as argumentative as the design process as a whole is (see Chapter 22). Financial issues tend to be clearer than many other urban design considerations because one is dealing with tangible value—dollars. The argumentative process is nevertheless seldom a rational one because a whole set of intangible variables involving power, influence, and personality conflicts intervenes. Power rests in the hands of those with the assets but is shaped by how much the various parties involved want a project built. If the private sector wants a project built, power then lies in the hands of public officials to get what they think is important for the public interest in return. This has been the experience in the United States with the development of suburban downtown areas (Leinberger and Lockwood 1986; Lang 1987b; Garreau 1991). Those places where there is a demand for development are able to apply stringent design guidelines for developers to follow (e.g., Glendale, California). In the United States, when there is little market demand for development, it is difficult for the public sector to impose restrictions on how building should take place in the face of the political reality created by a city's financial need for development to enhance its tax base. In such circumstances, any development is regarded as desirable whatever its long-term social or financial impacts might be.

In the United States, as in much of Europe, government subsidies available to develop the infrastructure necessary for new urban design developments were severely reduced during the 1980s. This low level of public expenditure will not necessarily persist into the future, but it does show that government officials (in the 1990s at least) will have to be highly creative in developing financial packages for both the development and the operation and maintenance of projects. Infrastructure costs will have to be borne by state and local taxes, user charges, and bond financing. The implication is that governments will seek private sector financing to pick up the cost of providing public infrastructure. This means that the private sector has considerable control over public interests. This situation will change over time, but urban design ideas and the scope of projects built will always be buffeted by financing considerations as much as by prevailing public tastes, design ideologies, and political situations.

The Market

The market required to support a potential development consists of the population seeking services and their capacity to pay for them. The question the developer must ask is: "Is the market large enough to support this development?" The question the public sector asks is: "How is the public interest to be furthered by this development?"

The nature of the market as perceived by the private sector and the public sector differs. Both have images in their minds of the people who constitute potential purchasers and users of their products. The public sector is primarily concerned with developments that create a tax base to raise revenues, and that create other investment opportunities and/or support public services. It is also concerned with the needs of people who cannot get the services they need in the marketplace, either because there are two few of them to provide the critical mass needed for the service (e.g., an orchestra hall for aficionados of classical music) or because they cannot afford what the marketplace offers (e.g., housing for the poor).

In the private sector, the market for a particular type of development depends on the purchasing power of the community to be served, the physical structure of the surrounding areas, and the cost and availability of financing for the development. The market is not static. Public behavior and attitudes change the marketplace. The success of neighborhood restoration efforts and the whole process of gentrification of cities during the past two decades has shown that attitudes can and do change. There is a small but financially successful component of the population in the United Staters, Western Europe, and Australia who choose the lifestyle implicit in the layout of older inner-city neighborhoods that are disliked by the majority (Meltzer 1984). The preference is, however, more pronounced among the young, the unmarried, those people who favor the independent behavior of their children and variety of experiences for them, the elderly, and people with nonconforming lifestyles.

Changes in demand are partially due to the changing demographic structure of society, but there are changing values among almost all segments of the population. The aspirations of a society shift over time, depending on the society's self-image. Statesmen, politicians, advertisers, and people in the service professions (including the design fields) all vie to shape public values and thus the nature of

a culture. Urban designers play a similar role, particularly those visionary leaders of the field. The range of future possibilities of which people are aware affects their perceptions of their needs. In this sense, technological innovation will also provide new opportunities that follow demand, but such innovations will also create demand. The physical structure of the city reflects all these factors to a greater or lesser extent.

Urban Design Consequences of a Market-Driven Development Process

There are a number of urban design consequences of a market-driven development process that suggest that a greater public sector involvement in the development of cities is necessary in the future than exhibited in the United States during the past two decades. For reasons of economic and construction efficiency, projects in a market-driven urban design process tend to be large and easy to build. The quality of the projects is open to question, certainly in terms of the dimensions of human experience described in this book. They may be good enough to sell, but there will be opportunities lost for not doing something better. The increasing internationalization of the money market means that the focus on design will be on professional attitudes not local attitudes, and that there will be little front-end time allocated to research or design to deal with local peculiarities. The danger is that international urban design and building types will be used and public review processes avoided to the extent possible.

Another fear is that unless urban designers are vigilant, sites will tend to be cleared completely (whether they are urban or rural) prior to redevelopment, thereby destroying the very attributes that made them financially attractive in the first place. Problems, such as traffic congestion, resulting from development will to the extent possible be displaced onto neighboring jurisdictions. In existing cities and suburbs, such processes can result in a loss of a sense of place and feelings of powerlessness over their own lives by local people. This sense of loss and the lack of control are often expressed in vandalism and, in extreme form, in riots. It must, however, be remembered that the built environment and the development process are symptoms, not causes, of alienation. The lack of opportunities to participate in society is a cause. It results from an environment that is out of human scale as defined by ecological psychologists. Such alienation creates methodological problems in designing by stifling rational and logical debate for design ends and means.

The Public Sector Development Process

During this century much urban development has been initiated by the public sector, particularly in eras of comparative fiscal health. The Quincy Market development in Boston was initiated by Mayor Kevin White, but it was an architect, Ben Thompson, and a shopping center developer, James Rouse, who brought the scheme to fruition aided by considerable public investment (Frieden and Sagalyn 1989). Most of the urban waterfront development schemes of the 1970s and 1980s, such as Baltimore's Inner Harbor, resulted from perceived opportunities to improve the urban environment and to generate finances for city coffers through their catalytic effect (Attoe and Logan 1989; Torre 1989; Kelly and Lewis 1992). More recently, places such as Glendale, California, and Arlington, Virginia, have invested considerable public funds, using tax-increment financing to initiate financially successful downtown renewal efforts.

For such development the public sector has hired urban designers to provide an overall scheme and has provided the financing for infrastructure improvement. The actual work to construct facilities is then contracted out to the private sector. In this type of public-private interaction the public sector has provided the catalyst for urban renewal by subsidizing the private sector (Attoe and Logan 1989; Miles et al. 1991). The private sector bids on work that it perceives as profitable within the limits of the contract it establishes with the public sector. This process of development led by the public sector has been characteristic of much urban renewal in the United States since World War II. For better or worse, new approaches are also opening up.

There are four primary roles that the public sector now plays in the development process in the United States, although the first seems to be highly depressed at the moment: (1) to set social and physical development policies that establish a direction for development, (2) to create a political climate to evaluate development opportunities within the overall framework of a set of civic goals, (3) to muster and focus resources, and (4) to create a physical setting that makes development attractive. In carrying out these roles any political jurisdiction is in competition with other political jurisdictions. Cities compete with their suburbs, suburbs and neighborhoods with each other, metropolitan regions with other metropolitan regions. Each develops its own plans. There is generally little coordination among them, although the level varies from state to state.

Three types of plans are required for the public sector to fulfill its development roles: (1) an overall *physical plan* for its jurisdiction, with more detailed plans for each precinct within it, (2) a *capital improvement and financing plan,* and (3) a *strategic plan*—a step-by-step development agenda. All three plans have to recognize the dynamic nature of city form and the evolving nature of plans. Their relationship to each other in the overall planning process is shown in Fig. 20-4.

These public sector plans are part of the larger process of administering a political jurisdiction. Percep-

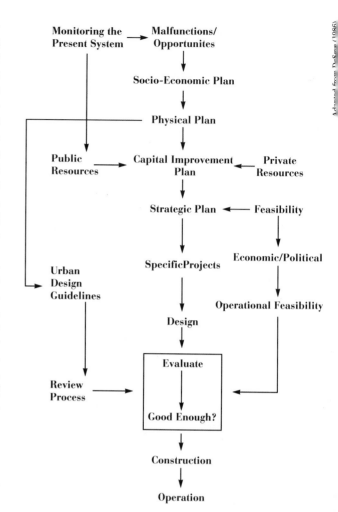

Figure 20-4: Steps in the Public Sector Planning Process

tions of opportunities and malfunctions in the present system lead to broad-scale socioeconomic policies. The physical plan comes out of the need to change the layout of the built environment to implement economic and social policies. It has to stem from some image of *what should be*—the normative question—and *what can be*—the financially and politically pragmatic question. The physical plan describes desired developments in the future. The capital improvement plan shows where the public sector proposes to develop and improve the public realm of the urban environment. Based on these plans the private sector can make decisions provided it knows that they will be implemented.

For a plan to serve a society well it has to be based on the resources available to implement it, unless the plan's sole purpose is to inspire people to dream about future possibilities. In the United States most governmental jurisdictions have a credit rating provided by the capital markets that tells how much capital can be raised for specific projects. Orderly financing is essential for a city to do well. For each capital project a source of financing and a schedule for obtaining that financing needs to be delivered. The capital improvement plan must spell out the sequence in which the development of the public environment will take place. The ability of a community to keep developing its infrastructure is an indicator to developers of the public sector's ability to accomplish its ends.

The strategic plan lays out the responsibilities of each of the components of the public and private sectors involved in the development, the deadlines for achieving particular ends, and a review process whereby the public sector can monitor the progress of projects to see whether they are complying with original intentions and with existing urban design guidelines. The plan also has to include specific criteria for development, including the types of development sought in terms of the activities to be housed, the rate of return on public investment, and the tax benefits expected. The urban design plan for the city and for precincts within it should also be part of the strategic plan or derived from it. The goal is to have open and clear discussions on all sides about the intended qualities of the future built environment, the behavior settings that comprise it, and the aesthetic ends it is to achieve so that both public and private sector participants understand their own and each other's expectations and obligations.

The basic difference between the public and private sectors in development is that the former has some notion of civic progress in mind in seeking development, whereas the latter has profit. Nevertheless, much philanthropic work is still carried out to raise the self-esteem of individual developers or to fulfill their self-actualization, cognitive, or aesthetic needs, as the redevelopment of cities such as Pittsburgh, Pennsylvania, and Portland, Oregon, shows (Smith 1991). Private sector developers in general, however, have to show a reasonable and tangible return on investment to obtain financing from banks and other lending institutions. The public sector has to be able to perceive and demonstrate the tangible benefits of development proposals to both its electorate and its capital markets, but it can also argue for its ends based on intangible improvements and secondary consequences. Raising tax revenues is, however, always a problem, especially when the tangible results of doing so are not easily discernible by the public.

The Private Sector Development Process

The traditional approach to development by the private sector has been to look for investment opportunities that have a high probability of financial success. Individual developers vary considerably in personality and social concerns. Some are risk takers and others are financially very conservative, preferring to avoid failure rather than to be innovative. The last characteristic explains why so much urban design is very conservative. Some

developers are very responsive to local communities' viewpoints, others are not. Nevertheless, the general approach to looking at the world is the same for all developers (and landowners) in the United States. A region of the world, a country, a city, or a neighborhood is looked at as a series of development opportunities, each with its associated opportunities and risks. Land is seen as a commodity.

The development process is a complex one, involving a number of steps: (1) scouring the existing environment for opportunities for development, (2) predicting what the real estate market will be, (3) preparing feasibility studies, (4) projecting development costs, (5) projecting what the cash flow in terms of expenses and incomes will be over time, (6) obtaining short-term and long-term financing, (7) finalizing plans, (8) contracting, and (9) managing the operation of the development. Carrying out the process successfully requires considerable economic foresight.

A large-scale development, such as a new town, requires considerable front-end investment by the developer before any return on capital is received. Case studies of the World Trade Center in New York (Ruchelman 1977), Columbia, Maryland, developed by James Rouse (R. Brooks 1974), Las Colinas, Texas, developed by the Carpenter family (Las Colinas Association 1986), and those developments studied by Bernard Frieden and Lynne Sagalyn (1989) clearly illustrate this point. The front-end expenses involve the purchasing of land, planning the development, developing the road, water, sewer and other infrastructure systems, mapping out sites for development, writing urban design guidelines for site development, negotiating sales of property, and reviewing individual development plans. The phasing of development becomes crucial. If it is delayed, the developer incurs real costs and the community incurs opportunity costs—tax revenues that might have been received as a consequence of development and thus spent on other projects and/or services are foregone. Developers' concerns for the *functionality* of the ultimate built environment in the terms described in this book vary considerably depending on what they perceive the nature of the market to be and on their own self-images.

All developers today are very much concerned with safety and security issues and the quality of the appearance—the symbolic aesthetics—of the facilities and the buildings they develop. The actual form this concern takes depends on the population targeted as the market. In this sense, developers have been more sensitive to user needs than many architects and urban designers who are concerned with the intellectual aesthetics of their designs (see Broadbent 1990). Developers have sought to "uplift the spirit" of the people to whom they will be selling or renting property. It has been financially profitable to do so. There are many examples of how they have gone about achieving this end.

Photograph courtesy Ann Strong

1. The Suburban Environment

2. Williams Square Buildings, Las Colinas, Texas

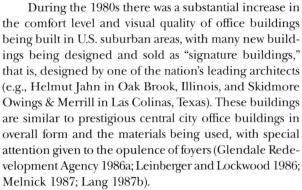

3. Commerce Square, Philadelphia

Figure 20-5: Aesthetics and the Marketplace
The speculatively built environment in the United States has needed increasingly to fit in with cultural images of high quality. The standard suburban housing development is very much a response to what people are used to seeing and what they believe can be sold again easily (1). To capture the type of businesses that were once exclusively in central cities, developments in suburban downtowns now have many of the characteristics of traditional central city buildings. This new era of development is exemplified by Las Colinas, Texas (2), with its new office buildings. The goal is to achieve the aesthetic effect of prestigious central city buildings (3).

During the 1980s there was a substantial increase in the comfort level and visual quality of office buildings being built in U.S. suburban areas, with many new buildings being designed and sold as "signature buildings," that is, designed by one of the nation's leading architects (e.g., Helmut Jahn in Oak Brook, Illinois, and Skidmore Owings & Merrill in Las Colinas, Texas). These buildings are similar to prestigious central city office buildings in overall form and the materials being used, with special attention given to the opulence of foyers (Glendale Redevelopment Agency 1986a; Leinberger and Lockwood 1986; Melnick 1987; Lang 1987b).

There are also opportunity losses in this process. The emphasis is on the individual building or complex, on what one can get away with rather than contribute to society, on not cooperating with others for mutual benefit (even often when the financial rewards are there). Developers naturally enough wish to retain total control over the design, construction, and operation of their projects. They are, however, learning that to develop within the context of an appropriate set of design guidelines (i.e., financially feasible and clearly understandable and acceptable definitions of the public interest) will reduce approval time and, in the long term, result in greater capital gains by maintaining the overall quality of an area (DeSeve 1986). This willingness to act with and support guidelines is clearly the experience of planners and urban designers in places such as Glendale and Walnut Creek, California, and Bellevue, Washington—suburbs of Los Angeles, San Francisco, and Seattle, respectively (Lang 1987b). This observation does not mean that developers will not challenge guidelines when they get in the way of what they want to do, but that the challenges will be more logical. This situation increases the whole quality of public debate over design ends and means.

Designers as Developers

There are a number of instances when the designer, usually an architect, is the developer or quasi-developer of a project. The nature of the architect as developer takes several forms. In some countries (e.g., France) the chief architect of a new town, acting on behalf of the government, is a quasi-developer using public money (Rubenstein 1978). Much housing development and design in London was undertaken by its county council. In the United States public sector, in contrast, architects are seldom

involved in actually designing projects, although publicly employed city planners may be responsible for the design of land-use distributions and urban designers may be responsible for the creation of design guidelines. When we think of the architect as developer we are usually considering work in the private sector. Most such work consists of single buildings, often relatively small ones. Architects can also use their services in a joint venture with other partners in lieu of an equity contribution.

When architects act as developers, it is the architects or those they hire who initiate the development, obtain financing, do the design, supervise the construction, and let or sell a project. There are few large-scale examples of this approach. The Quincy Market development in Boston may be more typical. It is an architect-initiated design idea. In this case, it was architect Ben Thompson who had the original vision and sought out developer James Rouse to lend his development expertise and marketing knowledge and to act as developer of the scheme (Frieden and Sagalyn 1989). Conceptually, the architect as developer approach is attractive to architects because they perceive that they would have considerable control over the final project. When the architect is the developer the arguments during the designing process are internal to the architectural organization. Almost inevitably, however, architects operating in this way become advocates for their developer persona. In this process the dynamic nature of the arguments and the broader societal concerns in urban design become lost. Thinking changes from being professional to being commercial.

Probably the best-known developer/architect in the United States, one who has worked at a scale large enough for it to be considered total urban design, is John Portman, designer of the Renaissance Center in Detroit and developer of the Peachtree Center in Atlanta (Portman and Barnett 1976). Even when not the developer as well as the architect, Portman's work has a strong development orientation. He is very much concerned with the quality of his design as both architect and developer, but even so, many public interest concerns get discarded in the design process. One of the social objectives of the Renaissance Center was to revitalize central Detroit. While it has increased the tax base of the city, and a number of new office buildings have been built across the street from it, the development is an isolated project separated visually and psychologically from the city (see Fig. 2–13(1)). It is not, nor was it designed as, an integral part of the city. The implementation of that goal was not ostensibly Portman's responsibility to oversee. His responsibility was to the developer and to ensure his design resulted in a set of buildings that turn a profit. Portman's recent financial problems in Atlanta show the difficulty of wearing too many hats. The difficulty arises from being on too many sides of the argumentative process when designing everything—from finances to building complexes—to design them all well. Presumably these difficulties can be overcome.

FINANCING URBAN DESIGN PROJECTS

Much of the debate over ends and means in urban design is concerned with the financial feasibility and the prediction of sources and costs of money. There are two basic fiscal concerns in financing urban design projects: (1) the capital cost of building a project, and (2) the operating cost of running and maintaining a project once built. While the former is always of concern, the latter has too often been neglected, with sad consequences. Projects have become rundown because they have been too expensive to maintain. In these cases it has not been possible to pass the operating costs on to their users. In working out the market for these projects or services, the operating costs of the project were not considered or were underestimated, or the sources of the expected financing failed to materialize.

Capital Costs and the Development Process

Capital costs include the price of land, the structural improvements required to make it developable, the cost of building, and all the associated administrative costs in bringing a project to completion. One of the main contributors to the cost of a project is the cost of money for financing the development. The costing and pricing structure of a development depends on the financing mechanisms available, including interest rates and loan terms.

One of the major changes that has taken place in the United States during the last decade is in the nature of capital markets. The change is having a profound impact on the nature of development and thus on the work of urban designers. It explains why so much recent urban design is *financially pragmatic*. Finances for investment are being moved around nationally and internationally. Much of the development in the United States is financed by Canadian and British sources. Much of the development in Britain and Canada is financed through American resources. There is a considerable investment in all three countries by Japanese organizations. Local reliance on local sources still exists, but much investment money is from "out of town." This trend affects the development of cities and urban design in two basic ways: the financiers look for development opportunities internationally and architects work internationally. While clearly working within their own professional cultures, both groups are working in local cultures with which they are unfamiliar. Architects do not have a proven record of paying more than lip service to cultural issues (Brolin 1976; Wolfe 1981), but those working in the Empiricist tradition are showing an increasing concern for the cultural appropriateness of their work. Often, however, the dominant design concern is with self-esteem of the sponsors of the project and other considerations are bypassed. Thus in many instances the concern with being fashionable is prime.

The developer's concern in any economic climate is for the *surety* and *security* of potential developments. Surety refers to the likelihood that a project will be built, and security means that the project will yield the return on capital that its proponents claim and at worst will certainly not lose money. Urban designers in the United States may not be primarily concerned with these issues, but they will certainly become aware of them as they design a project of any note. As the design process takes them through several iterations of proposing building programs and built form solutions, evaluating them, or having them evaluated in terms of the security and surety they provide the developer, they will come to know these issues.

Developers have to convince their financial backers that their projects will go ahead without delays, and in turn will seek assurance from local governments that their projects will not be delayed. In areas where there is low demand for development, the developers can claim that proposed projects, and the financial package behind them, will be moved to other jurisdictions if they are not given priority treatment. Developers are highly successful at claiming financial hardship if they do not get things their own way in jurisdictions where there is little development taking place. In politically volatile situations, in contrast, projects may be arbitrarily shelved as one government gives way to another simply because the project represents the work of an earlier regime.

Governments usually find it easier than developers to raise capital. Their credit is based on their ability to raise revenues from taxes in the future. Developers, on the other hand, have to raise finances on a project-by-project basis and have to have some equity in the project to be able to obtain loans. They seek to lower the required equity and to have as low an interest rate on a loan as possible. Governments aid and subsidize developers by such procedures as building the infrastructure of a development, guaranteeing mortgages, agreeing to lease space in a project, or structuring a pooled commercial paper program backed by a letter of credit (DeSeve 1986). In essence, the private sector is now frequently required to subsidize the public sector.

The private sector can aid the public by absorbing the cost of infrastructure development and providing public facilities not only in terms of public open space but also in terms of services. Indeed, they are increasingly required to do so through a variety of *linkage* programs. These programs tie the right to develop an area or a building to the provision of some public necessity such as low-income housing, a school, or a creche. In some cases these facilities have to be provided on site, and in other cases a cash payment is made to the public sector agency to provide them elsewhere.

The basic idea is to use incentives rather than prohibitions—carrots rather than sticks—for developers to help a locale meet what it perceives to be public interest ends. Examples include the forgiving of taxes to rehabilitate historic properties, loosening parking and building code requirements (particularly in dealing with the preservation of buildings in historic districts), and, probably as commonly, allowing the building of taller buildings to get public facilities in return.

Designing Operating and Maintenance Procedures

A number of powerful arguments can be made for the failure of the Modern movement's urban design ideas, particularly in the area of housing, as a failure not so much of design but rather of the management of a development once constructed (Arias 1988). There are certainly some urban design considerations in making schemes function well over time: designing with maintenance in mind, the process of management itself, and the continued investment in the maintenance and evolution of a development as needs change while at the same time designing to meet the full range of needs a project is to fulfill.

A number of housing projects developed during the late 1930s (e.g., Father Panic housing in Bridgeport, Connecticut) were considered to be major successes as subjectively assessed by their residents during the projects' early days of operation. As less money was put into their maintenance, so their facilities were reduced in scope and the whole social program (in terms of people, facilities, and their operation) on which the developments were based started to crumble. The subjective evaluations of the new generation of residents is that the living situation in the housing is very poor. In the late 1980s in Bethesda, Maryland (see Fig. 2-3(2)), where the development community had already invested heavily in new buildings in accordance with detailed design guidelines and where the opportunities for further development are few, developers were promising much in public interest terms to get an opportunity to develop a project at all. There have been expressions of concern about developers' abilities to keep their promises about maintaining the projects and the public amenities they provide once they are built because of the cost involved. The perception is that the costs will ultimately be transferred to the public sector by default (Fulton 1985). In the current economic and political context these costs would be difficult to bear.

In a number of cases unacceptable and/or illegal management procedures regarding tenant steering and/or quotas have been used to keep projects in good order (as perceived by both their residents and by outside authorities). This situation places the public, urban designers, and managers of projects in a quandary. On the one hand, the physical and social design is fine, but on the other hand the basic management procedures that keep it that way are unacceptable. The position taken here is that the management procedures have to be changed, but it is a difficult decision to reach, particularly if one predicts that the project as a sociospatial scheme will fail as a result (see Chapter 23).

Where an understanding of how much a project is going to cost to maintain, socially and economically, has gone into its planning, it will survive well. This thoroughness was exemplified in the planning of Rockefeller Center, New York (Balfour 1978; Krinsky 1978). Such an understanding depends on the careful design of the source of a project's funding, the accurate prediction of its life expectancy, and the selection of management procedures as well as the nature of the design. The size of the public realm does not have to be substantial to clearly be in the public interest. Such considerations are as important as understanding the capital costs of development. Increasingly they are becoming part of an urban design plan (Bartholomew 1991).

IN THE FUTURE

In the foreseeable future, the United States is most likely to see the continued development of techniques of public and private partnership in urban and suburban development. Governments are going to seek new techniques of financing developments and will be seeking private sector support in defraying what have heretofore been public sector responsibilities to finance development, particularly infrastructure costs. The private sector must also recognize that public sector investments affect its profits and that it has a responsibility to plow these profits back into the attaining of the public good, because that will aid the private sector in the long run by creating good investment opportunities. Urban development is a circular and endless process. Edmund Bacon, once executive director of the City Planning Commission in Philadelphia, portrays it as in Fig. 20–6 (Bacon 1969).

As the quality of the environment becomes more important to people, government roles are likely to expand in setting directions, acquiring land, and constructing site improvements, including site rehabilitation. In the immediate future local governments are likely to pass these costs on to the public via the private sector rather than through increases in taxes. Governments will also regulate development through the implementation of zoning ordinances and the use of design guidelines. They will promote specific ends through bonus systems, incentive zoning, and linkage programs. There will be an increased role for urban designers and an increasing need for an empirically based design approach. Design guidelines will have to have a clear purpose and the principles to attain those purposes must be clearly understandable and based on evidence that they will achieve their purposes. The government may guarantee mortgages and provide tax incentives, but it should know what the social and economic return for the public will be.

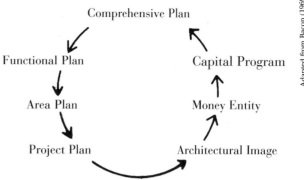

Adapted from Bacon (1969)

Figure 20-6: Urban Design as Part of the Urban Development Process

The private sector will be the initiating force for many development proposals. Instead of simply responding to a government's request for proposals, it will initiate proposals for the development of areas of cities and suburbs alike. Such initiatives are already taking place to a greater and greater extent, as many municipal governments in the United States find themselves in financial trouble. Thus, urban development and redevelopment will continue to be a joint public-private venture. There is a major need for more thinking about the roles of the public and private sectors in urban design. The position taken here is that the public sector should (i.e., ought to) regain its role in setting public policies for the future. Recent surveys (e.g., Zehner 1990) show that few public agencies in Australia are looking very far ahead at present. Anecdotal evidence suggest that this situation prevails in the United States as well.

THE ROLE OF THE URBAN DESIGNER

Urban designers, city planners, landscape architects, and architects can clearly play a number of roles in the development process in the 1990s, depending on how much they understand about the development process. Two of the roles are as urban designers per se—one as the representative of private sector interests, and the other as the promoter and defender of public sector interests. In the former position, urban designers shape proposals that are likely to maintain the socioeconomic status quo; in the latter, there is more of a choice. Urban designers can be "soft cops" (Goodman 1971), reinforcing the existing power structure in order to get things done easily—the pragmatic attitude. Alternatively, they can represent the broader public interest with a concern for the long-term viability of designs (where this is desirable), and for the needs of under- and nonrepresented people, by bringing concerns that normally fall outside the discussion of the functionality of proposed projects into the debating forum (see also Chapters 23 and 24).

It is also clear that in other countries urban designers work within different sociopolitical settings and have different roles than in the United States. In many countries, architects working in the public sector do much urban and architectural design. They are responsible for many total and all-of-a-piece urban designs. In purely socialist countries they do it all. In countries with mixed economies, the potential roles are more diverse. In all instances, the urban designer gains political power by understanding the development process. This understanding is important in order to reasonably consider the tradeoffs between embarking on one project rather than another. Developing one project often precludes investment in others. In addition, all new projects affect their surroundings, changing the land values and the development opportunities that exist there (Attoe and Logan 1989). They will create ripple effects, except where they are located in surroundings that are irreversibly decaying. In that case the surroundings may bring the project down.

The proponents of urban design will have to address a series of questions other than purely design ones in the future:

- How will any infrastructure investment/public capital improvements change land values and economic opportunities?
- What methods of public/private investment can best bring about desired developments?
- How will any proposal help retain desirable behavior settings and attract new ones?

- What economic and social programs need to accompany physical design ones (and vice versa)?
- How can people's basic and cognitive and aesthetic needs be met economically and efficiently in design? How best can a truly functional environment be achieved?

In general, greater emphasis will have to be placed on the financial functionality of proposals. In such a political climate, it is essential that urban designers bring attention to a variety of ways of achieving desirable ends on all the dimensions of human experience, otherwise economic pragmatism may shift from the greed of the 1980s to simple necessities in the 1990s.

MAJOR REFERENCES

Attoe, Wayne, and Don Logan (1989). *American Urban Architecture: Catalysts in the Design of Cities.* Berkeley and Los Angeles: University of California Press.

DeSeve, G. Edward (1986). "Financing Urban Development: The Joint Efforts of Government and the Private Sector." *The Annals, The American Academy of Political Science* 53: 58–76.

Frieden, Bernard J., and Lynne B. Sagalyn (1989). *Downtown, Inc.: How America Rebuilds Cities.* Cambridge, MA: MIT Press.

Johnson, Robert E. (1989). *The Economics of Building: A Practical Guide for the Design Professional.* New York: John Wiley.

Miles, Mike E., Emil E. Malizia, Marc A. Weiss, Gayle Berens, and Ginger Travis (1991). *Real Estate Development: Principles and Process.* Washington, DC: Urban Land Institute.

21

THE URBAN DESIGN DESIGNING PROCESS

Positive procedural theory—design methodology—is concerned with developing externally valid descriptions and explanations of the design process, the methods used, and the results obtained using different methods. Its refinement has been hampered by the lack of empirical research. As a result, much of what we hold to be the content of design methodology is drawn from research in other fields (e.g., psychology, business administration) and from anecdotal information from design professionals. The growing body of research on the nature of architectural practice (e.g., Blau 1984; Gutman 1988; Cuff 1991), on architectural designing (e.g., P. Rowe 1987 and Lawson 1990), commentary (e.g., Schön 1983), case studies (e.g., Ruchelman 1977; Frieden and Sagalyn 1989; Langdon with Shibley and Welch 1990), reflections on the nature of urban designing (e.g., Shirvani 1985), and what it should be (e.g., Cutler and Cutler 1982) does enable some observations to be made about the dynamics of the process and how it enhances our understanding of the intricacies of urban design.

There are a number of comprehensive models of the urban design process (e.g., Bailey 1973; Cutler and Cutler 1982; Shirvani 1985) and also many models of generic design processes biased toward architecture (e.g., Koberg and Bagnall 1977). Many of the models are normative in character specifying the types of studies and methods that should be used by the urban designer. The general models tend to be positive ones, although on closer examination they have a high ideological content to them. The purpose here is to review the general nature of the design process so that the character of the decisions that the urban designer has to make can be identified.

THE NATURE OF THE OVERALL DESIGN PROCESS

There are a number of ways to describe the nature of urban designing. One way would be in terms of the institutions involved. The concern here is, however, with the role of the urban designer vis-à-vis other participants in the process of urban change—on a dyadic model of urban design dealing with the professional-client relationship.

Inevitably any design process is divided into a number of phases, each with its own products. The nature of the urban designing process depends on how this division takes place, and on the degree to which the phases are conducted independently or simultaneously, haphazardly or systematically, in a piecemeal or a systematic manner, and on the products required at the end of each phase.

The Phases of the Urban Design Process

The phases of the urban design designing process, like any other design process, have been identified and given various names by different scholars. However, they are remarkably similar in nature, indicating a high degree of agreement on their general characteristics (see Lang 1987a). Borrowing from Herbert Simon (1960, 1969) they will here be called the *intelligence phase,* the *design phase,* the *choice phase,* the *implementation phase,* and the *operational* or *postoccupancy evaluation phase.* Each phase is in itself a design process involving the same basic intellectual activities: analysis, ideation (i.e., divergent production of ideas), synthesis, prediction, evaluation, and decision. The whole

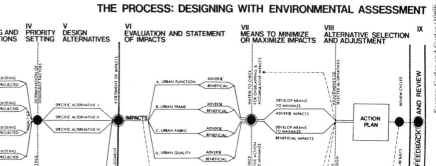

Figure 21-1: The Urban Design Process as Seen by Lawrence and Sherrie Stephens Cutler

design process can be seen as a spiral iterating through these processes in sequence (see Fig. 21-2), but there is a utility in thinking of the overall process as a set of phases because specific conclusions are drawn and products produced during each (see also Chapter 9). The emphasis placed on each of the basic intellectual activities and the specific methods used to carry them out also vary from phase to phase as does the focus of the designer's attention. It shifts from ideas to forms to evaluations in a cycle of decision-making (Zeisel 1980).

The product of the intelligence phase is a program, or brief. The product of the design phase is a sketch design or, increasingly, a set of designs. The product of the choice phase is different in character; it is a decision. The decision may be to abandon, revise, or to go ahead with a project. The products to this point are in the symbolic world—plans on paper. The product of the implementation phase—a total design, illustrative site design plus guidelines, infrastructure plan, and growth (or decline) management plan—is in the real rather than the symbolic world. The product of the postoccupancy evaluation phase is information. This information can be used to further develop our positive theories about design and design processes, or it might initiate a whole new cycle of decision-making.

The design process is always argumentative. Designers argue with themselves and among themselves about the nature of the problem, the solution, and the evaluation process. It is argumentative because design problems are *wicked* ones (Bazjanac 1974; Rittel 1984; Rittel and Webber 1984). One can go on and on asking questions about the problems and exploring alternative ways of resolving a design. There is no rule for determining when to stop the exploration and no definitive set of measures to use in evaluating a design. The process of design is an

iterative one in which the designers more and more closely approach an acceptable solution (Zeisel 1980). It is a process of developing images of solutions—of making conjectures—and testing them. Creative designers are those who manage to get beyond a merely acceptable solution—that is, "satisficing" one (Simon 1960). The amount of time available dictates when particular stages of the design process will be complete. Almost inevitably designers want more time to design. These observations apply to the whole process and to each part of it.

Empirical substantive knowledge adds rationality to the arguments made during the process by enabling topics to be discussed with some clarity and even objectivity. Without it there is considerable confusion, as words and descriptive terms have subjective not specific meanings. Indeed, some critics claim that there is a conspiracy in the art world to perpetuate the confusion since it gives power to the artist (see George Orwell's commentary, 1954).

While the process of design follows a general sequence from the intelligence to postoccupancy evaluation phases, there is much jumping back and forth in the process as dead ends to lines of thinking are met or new possibilities are considered. As a result one gets the feedback and forward loops shown in Fig. 21-3. Indeed, it may well be that no progress in the design process is possible without an image of a potential solution at the beginning. The way individual designers go through the process and the methods used depend on their normative stance—the design ideology or *procedural style* used (Simon 1970).

Programs and Paradigms

There are two basic approaches to the design process that are often seen to be, and often are, in opposition to each other. In practice they are usually amalgamated to

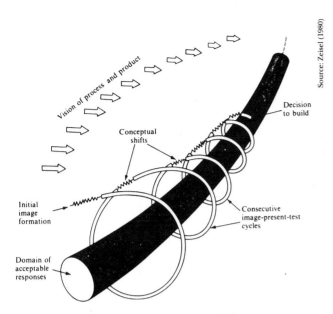

Figure 21-2: The Design Development Spiral

some extent. The first is the process most used by architects—the *typological approach*—and the second is a *problem-solving* approach. They do indeed represent two very different intellectual attitudes toward the design process, but they are not necessarily mutually exclusive ways of designing in practice.

Colin Rowe identifies the key difference between the two in his paper "Program versus Paradigm" (1983). Those architects who advocate the typological approach to design are saying that there are certain design types, or paradigms, that have evolved over long periods of time that meet people's needs, and that these can be adapted through incremental improvements and changes to fit present situations. Those architects who advocate the problem-solving approach to urban design believe that this process locks designers into a way of looking at cities and buildings that a priori imposes a definition of what needs to be done in a situation rather than an analysis of the situation leading to the *design* of a program that requires resolution in physical form. Some of the most notable "design failures" have stemmed from the typological approach to design, but these failures result from a widespread failure to understand the nature and appropriate use of types (Marmot 1982) and a concern for what other architects might think about a design rather than dealing with the issues at hand. Problem-solving approaches rely on associative predictions from positive theory as the basis for deciding what should be done. It is as good as the positive theory of which the designers are aware. A look at the nature of each of the stages of the design process shows the advantages and limitations of typological and problem-solving design patterns in their pure forms. Design almost inevitably involves a mixture of the two processes; what differentiates designers one from another is where they place their emphases (see also Colquhoun 1967).

Public Participation in Urban Design

Some designers firmly believe that the whole process of urban design should be carried out intuitively in a "black box" manner. This position still underlies most architectural education. Others believe that the process should be open to scrutiny and carried out in a "glass box" manner. This latter approach is increasingly demanded of practicing urban designers in the United States because, except for some total urban designs, their work is in the public arena, deals with the public realm, uses public funds, and thus has to be open to scrutiny.

Many urban design projects in the United States may be initiated in the public sector, but they are developed in private professional offices. Many projects, particularly in suburban development, may be wholly initiated and carried out within the private sector subject to government approvals. In contrast, in much of Western Europe and in other countries throughout the world, the whole process may be carried out by government architects. The phases and intellectual activities of the design process are essentially the same in either case and the process may involve much public participation or none. The person or people who control the final decision to implement a scheme may differ. It is seldom the designer who has the political power, but the power that comes with having expertise to argue for a design should be neither underestimated nor abused.

The two polar opposite ways of running the urban design process in terms of its openness are: with full public participation throughout the process, and where design professionals do the analysis, synthesis, and evaluation "uncontaminated" by the politics of public participation before presenting the scheme for approval by public agencies. Between the two extremes are a number of intermediate positions in which some parts of the process are open to participation and others are not. Designing with full public participation assumes that those who are going to be affected by a project know much about the issues involved; the aloof approach assumes that the designers have the experience and expertise and can learn little from the community (Halprin 1969; Rittel 1984; Bazjanac 1984; Batchelor and Lewis 1985; King et al. 1989).

The approaches that emphasize the openness of the process go under various names: the *community design process*, *RSVP cycles* (Halprin 1969), *co-design* (King et al. 1989). The process had strong advocates in the 1970s (e.g., Mitchell 1974; Rittel 1984) and is often perceived to be associated with the thinking of that era and to be passé as a way of working. In many ways, it has been absorbed into standard urban design practice. Almost all urban design schemes in the public sphere involve some public participation, and many private sector developments do as well. Many schemes are still developed with a high degree of public participation (J. Stern 1989; Scott Brown 1990), and much urban design in the United States is

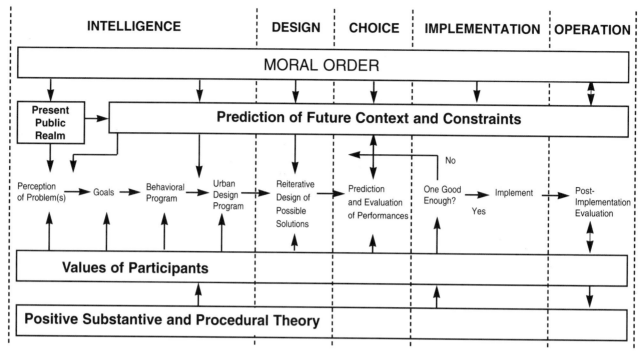

Figure 21-3: A General Model of the Design Process

legally required to be carried out in this manner. *Advocacy design* is based on community input and conducted on behalf of politically or economically powerless groups (Hatch 1984; J. Stern 1989).

Much urban design in the United States in recent years has been concerned with privately developed suburban residential areas. The plans are based largely on what the developer has done before, on market studies, or on studies of what other developers are doing. They will almost certainly involve some public hearings, but the people who participate are not those who will be potential future residents; rather, they are the people who live in surrounding areas and who are likely to be affected by the new development or who perceive that they will be affected. Their concern is with the side effects of the development rather than the development itself.

THE INTELLIGENCE PHASE: DESIGNING THE PROGRAM

The urban design process like any other decision-making process begins with the perception of either a problem or an opportunity. If one considers human settlements as a whole, the intelligence phase begins with the monitoring of the social and built environment to identify discrepancies between the present way of doing things, the appearance of a place, and those patterns of the environment that could potentially better meet people's needs. In such cases there is a "misfit" between the *functioning* of the present environment and some desired alternative, known,

imagined, or believed to exist. While such a recognition may often be an intuitive insight into the problems and opportunities that exist in a place, site, or activity system, it can also involve systematic analyses. Whether they are conscious or subconscious, these intellectual activities form the core of the opening stage of the overall urban design process (Koberg and Bagnall 1977; Shirvani 1985).

The built environment is constantly being monitored by a wide variety of people in terms of their own personal or professional interests. Developers scan it for opportunities to invest profitably. Highway engineers monitor the flow of vehicular traffic along the city streets. Their identification of a misfit will likely be based on some measure of speed or volume of traffic flow. This measure may be at odds with what motorists, adjacent pedestrians, or residents think is desirable. Householders may monitor the environment to safeguard their own investments and quality of life. Individuals see opportunities and promote ideas. One of the roles of urban designers, particularly those employed in the public sector or either directly or as consultants, is to scan the environment for problems that need to be solved, or opportunities that can be exploited, in order to make the human habitat a better place, a better functioning place, in which to live. In this sense urban designers are the promoters of partisan goals even if they see them to be in the public interest.

There are two usual situations which an urban designer confronts: a specific geographic area, and a set of activities and an aesthetic expression that need to housed.

1. Riverwalk, San Antonio, Texas

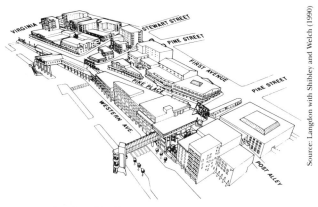

2. Pike Market Place, Seattle

3. Quincy Market Area, Boston

Figure 21-4: The Perception of Opportunities

Individual citizens, sometimes laypeople and at other times design professionals, perceive opportunities for civic improvements where others do not. Turning what was essentially an open sewer into a beloved riverside walk in San Antonio (1; see also Fig. 11-7(2)) and retaining Pike Market Place (see also Fig. 17-12(3)) to maintain a local character in Seattle (2) were the work of individuals with both foresight and energy. The situation was similar with the Faneuil Hall/Quincy Market development in Boston (3). In the last two cases an architect played a prominent part.

In both cases, the perception of the problem is inevitably in terms of the needs of specific sets of people or the biogenic environment. There is a third situation, in which the urban designer is part of a broader problem-solving team that asks what can be done to improve the lives of people.

In the first case, where a site is being examined for its potentialities (the functions it might serve), there are likely to be strong advocates for specific future uses (or more likely against specific uses). The site's potential uses depend on the biogenic characteristics of the site, its location, the market that exists, and the needs of specific groups of people. Urban designers may see the site in terms of a known development elsewhere, developers in terms of what they are used to developing, and local people in terms of the effect any development will have on their lives. The role of a government agency is to consider the site's potentials in terms of the public interest, but the agency is more likely to be responding to specific pressure groups and their constituents, and, particularly in a time of fiscal stringency, to the funds available to promote specific developments and the potential tax revenues they will yield for municipal coffers. Such agencies will be very much influenced by elected public officials, whose perceptions of the situation will depend both on their personal interests and on those of their electorates. Here there are major differences in attitudes between those officials elected at large and those elected by wards. Those elected by wards tend to focus on local problems. It is difficult to achieve strong large-scale urban design goals in civil divisions whose governments are elected on this basis (Smith 1991).

In the second case, where the behavioral program (i.e., the functions that a place has to serve) has already been designed, the urban designer's task is more limited. The problem is to move from general goal statements to specific statements on the characteristics of patterns of the built environment that are required to house the activities and simultaneously be aesthetically appropriate. Having a strong positive theoretical base and a carefully organized set of design types that meet specific goals on which the designer can draw makes the task less capricious than it has often been in the past.

In the third case, when the urban designer is part of a team advising decision makers (usually politicians) about the state of a city or region in a holistic way, urban design becomes a truly collaborative art (Lang 1990). The whole design process also becomes more complex. The program is designed out of an analysis of people's needs, the affordances of a place, and the analysis of the resources available to cater for them. Adjustments to people's behavioral as well as the physical environment may be necessary for the program's goals be met—few goals are met simply by changing the physical environment.

In all three cases, there are specific sets of people involved who have their own sets of goals. Identifying who these sets of people are and clarifying their goals is the point of departure for the problem-solving approach to urban design. The difficulty is that some people who should be involved do not participate until they have a design to which they can react; other people are inarticulate about their goals. One of the roles of the urban designer is to get people to articulate their needs and to bring possibilities to people's attention. In all three cases, the program is designed from the bottom up—from the perception of problems to a program. It is a partial solution to the problem situation at hand. It will specify not only the goals of a development, but also the more specific objectives that the development is to fulfill in terms of performance criteria for both the activities to be housed and the aesthetic values to be fulfilled.

The perception of a problem situation always depends on a comparison of one situation with something else. There are two basic approaches to making such comparisons in urban design: the typological and the problem solving (or the paradigmatic and programmatic). In the former, the measure used is another place—city, precinct, street, plaza—that is perceived to work well. The second uses a performance indicator or set of indicators as comparators. The first tends to look at the world as a set of physical patterns, the latter as a set of performances and settings—as behavior settings and geometries.

The Typological (or Paradigmatic) Approach to Problem Definition

One of the standard ways in which urban designers identify problem situations is to compare the present situation, what they see before them, with other standard models, generic solutions, and/or existing precedents. "The typological approach [has] revived a traditional way of looking at function and re-established precedent as a point of departure for designing" (Kelbaugh 1990). There have been many efforts to identify these precedents for different components of the city and even for towns as a whole. For instance, there are books on housing types (Sherwood 1978), urban spaces (R. Krier 1979, 1990), and towns (Rossi 1982). Also, recent efforts have been made to design generic solutions to recurring urban and suburban problems for urban designers to use. The promotion of pedestrian pockets (Kelbaugh 1989; Calthorpe 1991) and urban villages (PAS 1991) as ways to design suburbs takes the generic neighborhood unit schemes of the 1920s into the 1990s. In using precedents and generic solutions, urban designers follow a typological approach to problem identification (and solution development).

Designers using the typological approach will look at a site and think of existing developments elsewhere or generic solutions with a character that they would like to emulate because they are memorable or have worked well. At its best the process first involves identifying another place with similar characteristics in terms of location and surroundings but that "works better" (i.e., one that affords more or different activities, is more aesthetically pleasing, or is simply a nicer place in which to be). The process then considers the application of what exists on that other site to the present situation in a modified form (to show that it is not simply copied) and because the geometry of the context differs. The type may be a use one or a formal one, or it may be a zoning ordinance or a set of design guidelines. The point is that a precedent is used.

The very idea of what a city, town, or urban place should be is a type that guides much urban design. Using types as the basis for design, like using any previously acceptable experiences, can, however, paralyze the imagination because we try to keep using them (Birch and Rabinowitz 1968; Laing 1971). For many American urban designers the image of a town that they have is a European one. Their proposals attempt to make the American city into a preautomobile European one. Most urban design ideas based on this image remain on the drawing-board. If implemented, they are often totally out of cultural context. There are, however, types that are unique to twentieth-century United States. Some have evolved unselfconsciously (e.g., the suburban shopping strip) and others have been consciously sought (e.g., for the Denny Regrade neighborhood in Seattle).

Many visionary urban designers have sought to develop new types that address twentieth-century uses of the city and its surroundings. Already noted here are the two new generic solutions for neighborhood design developed earlier in this century—the horizontal neighborhood of Clarence Perry (Regional Plan Association 1927; Stein 1957; Gallion and Eisner 1986) and the Unité d'habitation of Le Corbusier (1953, 1960). In the United States there has been the largely unselfconscious development of the mini-city (Muller 1981), or urban village, as a new type of suburban downtown. The strip (Venturi, Scott Brown, and Izenour 1977; Ramsey 1986) and, during the 1980s, the mega-church are two other automobile-era types that have been developed—the former unselfconsciously, the latter highly self-consciously. One of the most frequently used types in recent urban design is the new waterfront (Torre 1989). Yet another, the downtown pedestrian mall (Houston 1990a), was mentioned in Chapter 20.

Many waterfront designs for the cities of the United States follow the leadership of Baltimore, the first major city in the United States to revitalize and reuse its obsolete waterfront (Kelly and Lewis 1992). The solution has come to be known as the "festival market approach to waterfront design." Similarly, the idea of the pedestrianization of

Main Street of cities and neighborhoods to create more pleasant shopping environments has led many urban designers to perceive that the problem of their cities is that Main Street was not pedestrianized.

Developers follow a similar process when they scan the environment for opportunities to develop what they have experience in developing—the development, or building, type they know: tract housing, regional shopping malls, prestigious Class A office buildings, middle-income tract housing, and so on (see Chapter 20). Some developers do deal with a number of building types and some with all-of-a-piece as well as total urban designs. James Rouse was the developer of Columbia, Maryland, Faneuil Hall/Quincy Market in Boston, and the Market Street Gallery in Philadelphia as well as many suburban shopping malls; Ernest Hahn developed Horton Center as well as suburban shopping centers (Frieden and Sagalyn 1989). Government agencies and authorities acting as developers have been responsible for much urban design work. For example, the Port Authority of New York and New Jersey was the developer of the World Trade Center in New York City (Ruchelman 1977), the New York State Urban Development Corporation was responsible for the development of the new town of Radison (formerly Lysander) in upstate New York and for the new-town-in-town of Roosevelt (formerly Welfare) Island in New York City (see Figs. 8-8(2,3)), and various municipal housing agencies have been responsible for the development of housing complexes throughout the United States. Much of this housing consists of a number of tower blocks surrounded by rowhouses—a standard type developed in the 1950s and applied with success in many places and with failure in many others (see Fig. 3-18).

In a typological approach to problem identification urban designers have standard designs that they use as comparators to present situations. The program is implicit in the type used. Many situations faced by an urban designer are indeed similar in nature, particularly within a specific culture. However, the solutions inherent in the type may not be the best ones for the problems at the new site. The use of types is an essential mechanism for urban design analysis so that typology is a prerequisite for understanding programming for urban design (Colquhoun 1967). The point that must be remembered is that both problem and solution are implicit in the type, with the resulting danger that urban designers often see the solution in terms of the type and not in terms of the problem requiring attention (Alexander, Ishikawa, and Silverstein 1968). The strength of a typological approach to design lies in the reuse of successful solutions.

The Problem-Solving, or Programmatic, Approach to Problem Identification

A problem-solving, or programmatic, approach to urban design focuses on the situation at hand and the *design* of a detailed program as a point of departure for design. The program specifies the functions to be provided—the activity and the aesthetic objectives that have to be met—and the criteria against which any physical design will be measured. Usually the constraints—financial, political, and social—within which the design has to work will also be identified here. Sometimes, if not often, the constraints may be self-imposed and unnecessarily truncate the search for creative ways of providing for the functions that require fulfilling. The actual project, scheme, or guidelines will be created in response to the program and constraints.

The first step in the problem-solving approach to urban design is to identify a situation worth addressing. There are three broad categories of problems in urban design: (1) the demolition, removal, or containment of functions present in the environment that are undesirable, (2) the attainment of some desired functions, and (3) the prevention of undesirable functions from happening. All three types of problems are likely to be wicked ones in which the specification of the exact nature of the functions is an open-ended process. Creative problem definition involves being able to look at the social and biogenic environments in new ways, to get outside one's professional shell. Often a reductionist approach has been used to cut the problem down to a manageable size (i.e., reducing the number of functions to be considered) and in so doing loses its essence. Yet problems have to be seen within the resources and constraints that affect the finding of a solution. Premature consideration of these restrictions on what one might do may prematurely eliminate possible solutions. The programming process thus has to be open to a number of options to be effective.

A problem-solving approach to design can involve working directly with the people whose concerns are affected in a particular situation and considering their needs, or it can be carried out by professionals alone. Either way, the city is seen as a functioning entity with misfits between the way it operates and the way it should be operating in somebody's terms. The programming goal is to specify the performances required to reduce this discrepancy as an advocate for a person or set of people. All designs involve a number of advocacies. These advocacies are operationalized in a set of design objectives.

Design objectives are specific statements of what a design is to achieve. Whereas a goal may state that a design is to be attractive visually, an objective is an operational definition of what that means—a measure, qualitative or quantitative, that one can use to recognize that the goal has been met. The design of objectives as the basis for the design program begins with the statements of intentions of the various sets of people involved. The process involves obtaining and analyzing information and then synthesizing it into design objectives. The difficult (or interesting) aspect of the process is that the various people involved in the process will agree on some objec-

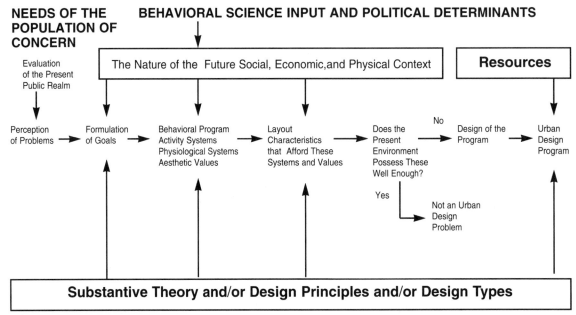

NEEDS OF THE POPULATION OF CONCERN

BEHAVIORAL SCIENCE INPUT AND POLITICAL DETERMINANTS

Figure 21-5: A Model of the Intelligence Phase

tives but will disagree on others. The process of designing objectives thus involves considerable discussion and argumentation. The people involved have an unequal distribution of power to make decisions depending on the degree to which they control what can be done. This control stems from political or financial clout, or from professional expertise (or reputation).

The final design of the program is implicit in the implemented design of the project. It is seldom if ever exactly the same as the product produced at the end of the intelligence phase. That product might be regarded as an interim program that is changed by the act of designing potential solutions to it. A rigorous program is nevertheless the point of departure for actual physical design, even though the act of designing a building complex or set of design guidelines changes the program by raising issues that were not previously apparent.

The People Involved in an Urban Design Project

In any situation involving the work of urban designers, there are likely to be entrepreneurs, sponsors of developments, potential users, and other design professionals participating in and making decisions. In a large-scale urban design situation there may be many players in each role. The public interest is represented by zoning laws and building codes that already exist in a situation but, more dynamically, by specific pressure and special interest groups that get involved in the overall debate regarding ends and means (Wheaton and Wheaton 1972). The zoning laws and many other bureaucratic regulations are bent considerably by public officials in order to get a project that they desire built (Frieden and Sagalyn 1989).

Sponsors

Self-conscious urban design projects are initiated by some entrepreneurial act. It was noted above that in the United States the entrepreneur is likely to be a developer, although governmental agencies and local community groups and individual citizens often initiate projects. In socialist countries, in contrast, the government or one of its agencies will more likely be the developer. Sometimes urban designers, acting in what they perceive to be the public interest, initiate a project, but it is usually on behalf of a specific group of people, community group, or public agency (see Fig. 21-4).

Sponsors provide the funds for a development. They may be lending institutions such as banks expecting a return on their investments or governmental bodies subsidizing a project by building the public realm and/or partially paying the interest component of loans with tax revenues. Traditionally, the public, through tax funds, has paid for the public infrastructure of projects, although in much suburban and new town development developers have passed the infrastructure costs on to future inhabitants in the price they charge for land and homes. In addition, as described in Chapter 20, the cost, maintenance, and control of the public infrastructure in urban renewal projects are now often being passed on to the private sector. Occasionally a sponsor will be a patron of the arts who gives a designer or set of designers a free rein to do what they believe will enhance the city. In much of the admired urban design work of the past, it has been a patron with autocratic power who has sponsored major urban design works (e.g., Pope Sixtus V in Rome and Napoleon III in Paris). Particularly powerful politicians can act in much the same way in the United States (e.g., Governor Nelson Rockefeller in Albany, New York).

1. Architects' and Planners' People

Source: The Department of City Planning, San Francisco

2. Watching the Mummers Parade, New Years Day, Philadelphia

Courtesy of the Philadelphia Museum of Art

3. Image of an American Woman by Japanese Artist Hiroshige (1860)

Figure 21-6: Images of the Users of the Public Realm
In any design we take a stand on whom we bear in mind and whom we omit. Urban designers have been criticized for having too limited a view of users as exemplified by the people they include in their drawings (1; see also Wood, Brower, and Latimer 1966; Ellis and Cuff 1989). It is clear that user-clients display a variety of behaviors and perceive the utility of the environment from their own points of view (2, pun not intended). If we do not know about the nature of people we use our own intuitions (e.g., 3).

Users

The concept of "user" is a tricky one. The operational definition of who the users are for a future development is difficult to specify. Users will vary from those who will ultimately inhabit a site to passersby. Some people are more important than others. There are those people for whom the project is designed and those who have to maintain it. People come and go. The first inhabitants of a development will move on to be replaced by others. Implicit in all designs, however, is a definition, for good or ill, of who the users are, their needs, and relative importances. Often the model of the users that emerges is simply that of a potential consumer (see Frieden and Sagalyn 1989). This is the model used as the basis for much financially pragmatic urban design, particularly new retail complexes.

Professionals

The professionals involved in any urban design project cover the whole spectrum of consultants: architects, traffic engineers, landscape architects, and so on. Each tends to see the problem in terms of specific professional interests. Urban design is seldom the work of an individual designer. Interdisciplinary efforts increase the num-

ber of variables considered. The urban design task is twofold: setting directions and managing the overall team. The role of urban designer has traditionally been played by architects but, in the sense described here, it could be filled by any professional. When working effectively urban design involves the mutual support of people with expertise in a number of areas (Baldwin 1975). There is often much blaming of other professionals when mistakes are made. Such an attitude does not help anybody.

Methods

Each component of the programming process involves some method of working. A number of ways are used to understand the needs and their manifestations of the people who are involved in the development of a scheme as either users or sponsors. In a problem-solving approach to design, the concern is to find out what people are doing now, their behavioral tendencies (see Alexander and Poyner 1970), aesthetic preferences, and interpretation of their needs for the future in order to specify the functions that the built environment should afford. The methods used involve observation, interview (the basic way of understanding people's hopes and aspirations), and the logical application of positive theory to changing circumstances

(Zeisel 1980; Bechtel, Marans, and Michelson 1987; Lang 1992). The development of these approaches during the 1970s and 1980s has given a considerable boost to the quality of design programs in architecture and, by extension, in urban design.

There have been similar developments in the design of market analyses as well as legal and contextual studies. Market studies specify what can be sold but tend to focus on past examples rather than future possibilities and the normative question of what ought to be developed (Franck and Ahrentzen 1989; Preiser et al. 1991). Legal studies focus on the rights of different people and have to be seen within a cultural context. Contextual studies tend to focus on identifying the various existing infrastructure systems of the city (e.g., transportation networks), the characteristics of the built environment that afford a sense of place, and, increasingly, the nature of the local biogenic environment.

Throughout the intelligence phase partial images of potential built environments will be shaping the design program by raising questions and directing explorations. These images are dealt with largely intuitively. Images of problems and solutions will vary from person to person. Some of the images will be well developed, others will be very vague. Some people will have a well-developed ability to understand the implications of social and economic decisions on design, and vice versa; others will not. A well-developed understanding of positive architectural theory helps architects to stay in command of their potential contributions by understanding the design implications of various social and aesthetic scenarios.

The product of the intelligence phase is a *design program*. Once considered to be simply statements of the number of units of specific uses with certain sizes that need to be built, urban design programs are becoming considerably richer in content and now cover the full array of functions to be served in much the same manner described earlier in this book. They specify the goals and objectives of a project, the people who are to be served, their needs, and often preliminary guidelines for meeting their needs—from survival to cognitive and aesthetic needs. They are more and more thoughtful statements of design intentions based on increasingly externally valid methods of analysis and design (Moleski 1974; Sanoff 1977, 1989; Robinson and Weekes 1983; Preiser 1985).

THE DESIGN PHASE: DESIGNING THE DESIGN

The objective of the design phase of any urban design process is to create potential physical solutions to one or another of the four basic types of designs that an urban designer has been and is likely to be engaged to do in the future. They have been identified already: design of guidelines, design of infrastructure with or without guidelines, design of all-of-a-piece designs, and design of total designs. The design phase will differ in character but not in basic intellectual processes depending on whether the designer is doing one or the other task. The design of guidelines is after all a means for achieving a physical form, or rather a set of acceptable physical forms.

The use of types shifts the concern from the nature of problems to letting a type determine the design configuration of an urban area, a building or open space, or a sequence of these (Kelbaugh 1990). The problem-solving approach has in operation been similar. The concern has been with identifying patterns of the environment that meet specific ends and the synthesis (not combination) of these patterns into design wholes. The difference between typological and problem-solving approaches to urban design is really at the scale of pattern used. The typological approach relies on wholes and hopes that both the whole and the parts that comprise it fit the problem; the problem-solving approach works out the parts and hopes that in the act of synthesizing these parts into wholes that both the wholes and the parts meet specific needs.

If the design task is to create a total urban design, the process involves the development of sketch plans of possible solutions for evaluation during the choice phase. Sometimes this task will be carried out by one designer, but usually it is a collaborative effort among many professionals. However, the basic design idea may stem from one mind and be identified with the person whose idea it is or often with the head of the design team that produced it.

Implicit in the design of design guidelines is a set of potentially acceptable design solutions. To be able to design guidelines, there must be some image of the potential built environments in mind. Thus these images have to be turned into potential designs first. The design of design guidelines therefore involves three basic steps: (1) the design and acceptance of a set of overall schemata for the site, (2) the abstraction of the essential components of these schemata, and (3) the writing of design guidelines to ensure that these essential characteristics are achieved. The first step involves both design and choice activities (i.e., the design of possible schemata, the prediction of how these schemata will perform, the evaluation of their performances, and the decision that one design, or design direction, is appropriate for the site). Thus this first step is essentially the same as in a total design. The difference is in focus of attention. In a total design the details of the design—buildings and the spaces between them—are under the control of the designer or design team, whereas in designing through the use of guidelines only the essential *characteristics* of the ultimate public realm—the spaces between buildings as defined by their façades—are controlled. The rest is left up to later individual designers.

The problem-solving approach to the design phase focuses on giving physical form to the program without imposing an a priori solution on the situation. It is a bottom-up approach to design. It involves the design of forms to resolve partial problems (i.e., some functions) and then the synthesis of these partial patterns into a whole solution or set of potential solutions. Each step may involve backtracking because the best solution to a component of the problem may not be the best one down the line when synthesized with other partial solutions. Designers have to avoid the premature truncation of lines of design exploration by the early design decisions they make if creative solutions are to be achieved.

The Basic Intellectual Processes in Designing

Most designs emerge from an amalgam of habitual and creative thought. Even the most creative of designers do not approach problems de novo (Colquhoun 1967). They approach the act of designing with a vocabulary of patterns in their heads—patterns of design guidelines and design precedents. Designers are used to doing things in a particular way, and their work is recognized because it uses the same patterns of space and structure and the same materials as in their other designs. It is their style (Simon 1970).

Creative designs are often thought to comprise those designs that are departures from the normal visual forms that we expect to see. Thus Rationalist designs with their purity of form were, and still are, regarded by many mainstream architects as creative alternatives to the Victorian city, even if they were dull places in which to live. They suggested new ways of dealing with open space and buildings and the form of the environment and were therefore closer to the fine arts in thought processes. Empiricist designs have seldom been considered in this way because of their traditional reliance on existing patterns.

Creative designing involves two basic intellectual processes: divergent thinking and convergent thinking. Divergent thinking involves the generation of possible ideas or design patterns, and convergent thinking the synthesis of these ideas—the bringing together of ideas. The former may be considered to be the pure creative effort, but the latter involves the processes of predicting how patterns will function and then evaluating or recognizing the utility of those patterns. Convergent thinking is the truly creative act in designing since it involves identifying not only patterns that are new but ones that also have utility in terms of the problems they address (Wade 1977).

Urban designers use many processes to enhance divergent thinking. They may be used self-consciously or unselfconsciously (Lawson 1990). The methods include morphological analysis, metaphorical thinking, and brain-storming (individual and group). These processes have been well documented (Broadbent 1973; De Bono 1973; Koberg and Bagnall 1977; Zeisel 1980; Lang 1987a), and they are beginning to be better understood and enhanced through empirical research. Convergent thinking—the act of synthesis—is largely an intuitive process conducted by trial and error, by conjecture and refutation. Implicit in synthesis are also the processes of predicting performance and weighing possible combinations and permutations of elements—of judging. Creative thinking is enhanced by postponing such judgments until a completed design is available for review.

All the research on creativity shows that there is a strong relationship between productivity and creative thinking. The goal of the design phase is to generate as many potential solutions as is practically possible. This task is a psychologically difficult mental activity. A number of urban designers prefer to generate one design and to defend it (Bacon 1969). According to this view the design should only be changed as a result of a rejection by decision makers during the choice phase of the process. Clients are, however, increasingly asking for more than one genuine design for simultaneous evaluation. To aid creative problem-solving the possibilities have to be based on different design ideas. The comparison helps everyone involved to better understand both problems and solutions.

Ordering Principles—Wholes and Parts

There seem to be two basic procedural approaches to the development of the ultimate geometry of whole urban design schemes. They involve synthesizing the scheme: from the inside out (i.e., from the parts to the whole with the basic building blocks setting the ordering agenda for the higher-level units), and from the outside in (i.e., following some space-filling algorithm given the whole and given the relationship—a geometric ideology, the movement patterns, or sun angles—between the parts). The perception is that in following the first approach no overall coherence in the design emerges—there is no overall visual idea to it. In the latter approach there is a geometric order that is transferred from the overall design down through each step of the hierarchy. In this case, the perception is that in the search for geometric purity the experiential qualities of the built environment get lost. The basic question in both cases is, however, essentially the same—how to develop a relationship between parts and wholes—the nature of the ordering system.

A variety of analogies and metaphors has been used to give an overall order to urban designs. Cosmological ordering systems have already been mentioned. In them, some image of the universe, often in the form of a mandala, is used as the basis for design. In the case of Jaipur, India, it was a 3-by-3-square grid (see Fig. 10–8(1)). An adaptation of the idea was used by architect B. V. Doshi in his design for the extension of the city in the mid-1980s. Similar forms without a cosmological analogy have also been used by architects, particularly Neo-Rationalists, to give an organizing idea to their buildings and their proposals for urban designs.

1. TWA Terminal, Kennedy Airport, New York

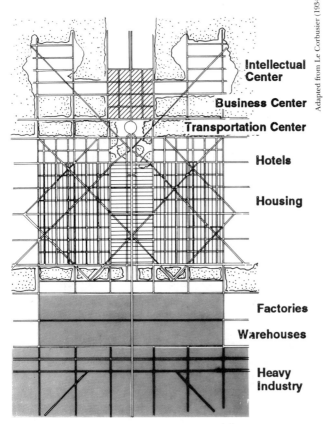

2. Lucio Costa

3. The Radiant City

Intellectual Center

Business Center

Transportation Center

Hotels

Housing

Factories

Warehouses

Heavy Industry

Collection of the author. Source unknown

Adapted from Le Corbusier (1934)

Rationalists have been concerned with the development of geometric systems (see also Chapter 10) in which the whole is subdivided into parts, or parts built up and adapted into a whole, based on some mathematical or proportional system. Le Corbusier, for instance, developed the Modulor as a proportional system to relate parts to wholes, using the Fibonacci series to approximate the relationship between parts of the human being—a biologically inaccurate but mathematically elegant model of people (Le Corbusier 1954). Peter Eisenman, in his design for House III, worked in the Rationalist mode by subdividing a square prism based on a 3-by-3 grid system. He superimposed a 45° 3-by-3 grid on the prism followed by a diagonal shear in the building (Gamble 1989). Leon Krier, in his design for St. Quentin en Yvellines (see Figs. 4-5(3,4)), relied on the continuities of diagonal lines to give an order to the diverse parts of the complex.

Empiricists in contrast have sought a behavioral basis for organizing parts into wholes. A number of systems have emerged: the elements that give a cognitive coherence to wholes in terms of the Gestalt principles of visual organization of forms (e.g., Lynch 1960), the sequential experience of vistas systems of Thiel (1961) and Lawrence Halprin (1965), and the geometrical necessities of the movement systems in terms of their actual performance characteristics and in human experiential terms (rather than as a pure exogenous orthogonal geometry that the Rationalists have tended to use). In this sense no externally imposed artistic idea, such as City Beautiful geometries, is used as an organizing principle unless it emerges endogenously, from within, as an issue of concern. One frequent commonality to urban design following both lines of thought is the gridiron road plan as an organizing mechanism, simply because it is a rational geometry that also makes considerable empirical sense as a land subdividing system.

The goal in both approaches is to build up a hierarchy of parts into wholes and then larger wholes or to disaggregate a whole into parts and subparts, each of which has its own coherence. The Rationalists seek a purity of form (i.e., a pure geometry) at each level of the

Figure 21-7: The Use of Analogy and Metaphor in Urban Design
The history of design is replete with examples of the use of metaphors and analogies as the basis for generating new ideas about a wide range of products. Their use has probably been more successful in individual buildings as works of art (1) than in city design. Some city designs are based on natural analogs of organic or human form, such as Lucio Costa's (2) plan for Brasilia (see Fig. 2-18). Le Corbusier sought the precision of naval architectural thought and used a machine analogy as the basis for his thinking, but he also used a biological analogy of head, heart, and body in urban design (3).

hierarchy. The building blocks that Empiricists use tend to be behavior or activity settings, and their concern is with the overall behavior setting system at each level in the hierarchy nested within higher-order levels. The result is usually, but not necessarily, a less geometrically well-ordered environment than the Rationalists seek.

THE CHOICE PHASE: EVALUATING DESIGNS ON THE DRAWINGBOARD

The purpose of the *choice phase* is to evaluate potential designs before they are implemented. They are, literally or figuratively, on the drawingboard whatever urban design type one is considering. The phase involves a number of intellectual activities: the prediction of performance of possible solutions, the evaluation of these performances, and the decision that one scheme should be implemented or that none is good enough—that there is no satisficing solution (Simon 1960). In the last case, the whole project might be abandoned or the design process might be taken back to the intelligence phase to redefine the problem or to the design phase to seek another solution.

Evaluating guidelines before they are actually implemented is difficult. Any evaluation is based on a prediction of how the guidelines will work when implemented—i.e., what kinds of results will occur when different architects design within them. The best test is to see what kind of designs they produce when used by a creative architect and when they are used with the worst-intentioned developer or architect team. This kind of test can be simulated by the designers of the guidelines themselves or by some other architects, and then submitted to a jury or panel of experts for evaluation. Seldom, however, are there sufficient resources for conducting such a process. In the future, computer-based design algorithms may be used to test the kinds of designs that result from different sets of guidelines. Today, however, we usually rely on a jury's black box predictions and evaluations—the whole process is largely hidden. In the case of choosing between two possible schemes for Horton Center, the "jury"—a selection committee, the mayor, and the business community as well as the city planners—made their decision on the basis of their perceptions of the financial viability of the competing developers not on the proposed designs (Frieden and Sagalyn 1989).

Prediction of Performance

Two types of predictions of performance—of the functionality of a design—are now usually required of almost any urban design proposal: how the total design or design guidelines will work in context when implemented, and how the design will affect its context when implemented—an environmental impact prediction. Such predictions all involve the simulation of how a project will work, how the context will shape this performance, and how it will be shaped by it.

Predicting how a design on the drawingboard will work when implemented is difficult. Drawings and iconic models give some idea of what an urban design scheme will look like in place. Advances in computer graphics enable a person to get a feeling for the sequential experience of moving through a complex at various speeds. Simulations of certain aspects of an urban design's performance, such as the total distance people will have to go to carry out activities, or the total energy consumption to maintain people's physiological needs, are well developed, and placing models of buildings in wind tunnels give some indication of how a specific configuration will shape wind flows. Much, however, remains up to experts to predict based on past experiences or on the accumulated positive knowledge of the design fields.

One of the difficulties architects face in dealing with their own urban design proposals is that they are selling them to the public in the same manner as any other salesperson sells a product. Because they want certain outcomes to occur—that is, they want their schemes to work in certain ways and to have a certain appearance—they predict it. There are a number of ways of getting beyond this approach. The most common way is through the use of case studies—a typological approach—which laypeople can understand better than abstract theory.

The use of case studies for comparison is essentially a typological approach to evaluation. The argument is that because similar schemes in similar circumstances have worked before they will work here and now. It is a powerful argument. The danger is that, because the designer wants the scheme to work, the other cases or situations will be perceived as similar when they are not. This is a universal problem in design (Alexander, Ishikawa, and Silverstein 1968).

Another approach favored by designers is to use an analogy to explain their designs and an analogical system to predict what the outcome of their designs will be. One of the most popular analogies has been the natural one—to consider the city as an organic system. Changes to the artificial environment are considered in biological terms. Such analogies can be a very colorful (e.g., Buckminster Fuller's "Spaceship Earth"), but they are only as good as the quality of the analogy. The most powerful technique is *associative prediction*. In associative prediction, positive theory and models based on empirical research are used as the basis for stating how a scheme will work. Positive theory, however, is based on the past and has many limitations. These limitations must be recognized, but associative prediction remains the most accurate technique for predicting the performance of potential designs.

While all prediction techniques are flawed, in urban design, as in any other designing, designers have to stick their necks out to state how they believe their proposals will function. Making predictions intuitively has not been

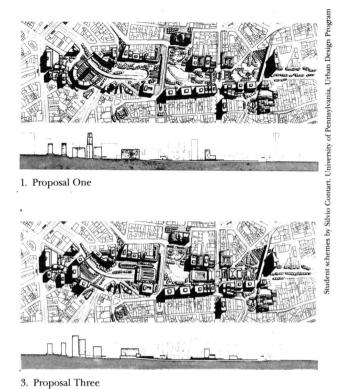

1. Proposal One

2. Proposal Two

3. Proposal Three

Student schemes by Silvio Contart. University of Pennsylvania, Urban Design Program

Figure 21-8: Evaluating Designs on the Drawingboard
The illustrations here show three possible solutions to a design problem. Choosing the best among them (or even that one is good enough) involves both predicting how each will perform in the future on both tangible and intangible variables as well as applying a set of evaluations to these predictions. In addition, urban designers are concerned (or are required to be concerned) about the impact of proposals on the overall urban sociogenic and biogenic environments—on the side and catalytic effects of proposals. Much will remain in the realm of conjecture.

very successful with complex projects in the past, and few clients (sponsors and users) are now willing to make decisions without strong supportive evidence. Even with such evidence, most predictions are today considered within a framework of probabilities not certainties.

Some aspects of a proposal can be measured quantitatively and with accuracy. For instance, the monetary cost of a project and the return on capital invested can be predicted, although even here there have been a number of projects with major costs overruns and less use than predicted. There have also been projects that have been financially successful beyond anybody's dreams. Other aspects of the performance of a design are difficult to pinpoint let alone quantify. The less tangible variables, such as the increase in civic pride of the inhabitants of a place as the result of a major accomplishment, are difficult to operationalize. Much is still taken on faith and hope (Frieden and Sagalyn 1989; Smith 1991).

The prediction in quantified terms of the impact of a proposal on its surroundings has proven to be difficult to do accurately, although environmental impact statements are mandated for many projects in the United States as in a number of other countries. These studies tend to focus explicitly on the biogenic environment, partly because the issues of traffic generation and environmental pollution are of current political concern and partly because these impacts can be measured. The less tangible effects on the culture and attitudes of people are difficult to assess.

Without doubt, the desire to get a project built leads to distortions in the prediction of the cost, the impact of a project, and the evaluation of these factors given other possible projects. There are number of people who want specific schemes to be built—building trade unions, the architect, the person in whose honor a building will be built, politicians, and so on. The controversies over the building of the Philadelphia Convention Center in the late 1980s exemplify the differences in prediction made by different parties over the financial performance of a building in its urban context. Some parties predict a major financial disaster for the city in the future, while others predict financial success. The evaluations of proposed projects are thus clearly open to argument. The utility of doing cost-benefit analysis and using a glass box approach to the evaluation is that the variables that are and are not included in the evaluations become seen and open to debate.

Evaluation

Evaluations of the predicted performances of an urban design are frequently left up to the intuitive judgment of a jury and the consensus that evolves during the discussion and argument among its members. The jury may be a panel of experts or may consist of the range of people to be affected by a proposal. This type of evaluation process is a black box one in which all the jurors make their own predictions of performance and evaluate the proposals according to their own value systems.

NUMERICAL RANKING	NAME OF PROJECT	A. RESIDENTIAL provision of dwellings	B. PEDESTRIAN 1. links out from Metro	B. PEDESTRIAN 2. pathways on private land	B. PEDESTRIAN 3. places for public activity	B. PEDESTRIAN 4. streetscape materials	B. PEDESTRIAN 5. magnet uses	B. PEDESTRIAN 6. encourage walking	B. PEDESTRIAN 7. other enhancement	C. EFFECTIVENESS 1. building massing	C. EFFECTIVENESS 2. efficient interior	C. EFFECTIVENESS 3. orientation	C. EFFECTIVENESS 4. environmental quality	C. EFFECTIVENESS 5. other enhancement	D. MANAGEMENT provision of organization	TOTAL SCORE	DIFFERENCE	
1.	Chevy Chase Garden Plaza	8	7	1	1	2	6	2	4	1	2	2	1	2	3	42	12	
2.	Artery Organization Headquarters Building	9	7	7	4	1	4	4	6	2	1	1	2	1	5	54	4	
3.	7475 Wisconsin Avenue	9	1	2	5	6	1	1	5	4	4	4	5	5	6	58	10	
4.	Gateway Building	9	8	7	3	3	2	3	8	3	3	3	4	8	4	68	11	
5.	4600 East-West Highway	9	2	7	7	7	3	6	9	5	5	8	7	3	1	79	4	
6.	Community Motors	6	5	5	7	4	6	7	9	6	7	5	3	6	7	83	3	
7.	Franklin C. Salisbury Building	9	4	3	2	5	8	5	9	7	6	6	6	9	7	86	14	
8.	Air Rights Hotel	5	3	6	6	8	5	7	9	8	9	9	9	9	7	100	4	
9.	Woodmont Air Rights	9	6	4	6	8	7	7	9	9	8	7	8	9	7	104		
	Totals	73	43	42	41	44	42	42	68	45	45	45	45	52	47	674		

Courtesy of the Montgomery County Planning Commission, Maryland

Figure 21-9: Bethesda, Maryland, Project Evaluation Method

Recently efforts have been made to open up the process—to implement a glass box approach to evaluation. This approach is exemplified by the Montgomery County (Virginia) Planning Commission's "beauty contest" (Fulton 1985). Competing proposals were evaluated against a checklist of variables weighted in terms of importance, given the goals of the proposals (see Fig. 21-9). More elaborate methods for evaluating schemes based on cost-benefit analysis have been proposed, but they have proven to be difficult to implement. Increasing demands for public accountability of urban design proposals are, however, likely to lead to more detailed glass box approaches to evaluation in the future.

The general process of evaluating schemes is to check whether they meet the criteria established during the programming process. The difficulty is that not all criteria are equally important, not all the people served are equally important, and not all objectives will be equally well met. The goals' achievement matrix proposed by Morris Hill (1972) provides an intellectual framework for considering all these factors—people and goals of different importance and tangible and intangible variables (see Fig. 24-6). Ultimately, however, the evaluation process is, like the rest of the design process, highly argumentative and often volatile.

Decision

Deciding to go ahead or to reject an urban design proposal may depend on a rational analysis of the evaluations, but often it seems to be a highly capricious process because it is closely tied into different rationalities—the rationality of the political process, for example. Because urban design takes place in the public domain, the official(s) holding the authority to consent to a project may change from the intelligence phase to the choice phase. In this case, the proposal may be associated with past politicians and so is shelved, not on its merits, but as a representation, or symbol, of a past regime. In other words, the definition of the functions to be served by a design—the problem—has changed since the design process began.

There are also different attitudes toward the results of evaluations, however thoroughly and clearly they might have been made in terms of the various people involved. Associated with every evaluation is a probability that the predicted outcomes will occur. This probability is not necessarily explicitly stated, but it is there nevertheless. Different decision makers have different attitudes toward these probabilities. The rational decision may be to select the design that has the best outcome given the most likely future, but this criterion is often not used. Some decision makers are highly conservative and the fear of failure may dictate their decision criterion. This is particularly true of financial failure. Given the monetary losses of a number of recent developments throughout the world, this attitude is understandable. Other people are willing to take risks, to gamble, and to trust to luck. Much depends on how the failure will directly affect the decision maker.

It is also possible that what appears to be a sound project may lead to a major disaster if it fails. The worst possible outcome may be so bad that, despite an almost zero possibility of it occurring, the choice of that proposal is rejected. This is the position on nuclear power stations that is still hotly debated in the United States. Few such extreme examples exist for urban design. In urban design the potential diasters are likely to be financial ones.

THE IMPLEMENTATION PHASE

Many urban design proposals have never been implemented. Among the many reasons for this failure are they may have been purely exploratory efforts, whimsical ego trips by designers, fiscally impossible or politically inopportune proposals, and projects in which the perceived psychological consequences of change were beyond the emotional capacity of people to tolerate. Nowadays, specific implementation procedures are often worked out as part of the intelligence phase of the project. Indeed, as pointed out in Chapter 4, ease of implementation has become a major decision criterion and thus a major part of the problem definition in the intelligence phase. The concern in considering how a proposal can best be implemented is with identifying the political and financial viability of a project, and with identifying and securing financing and often a commitment of people to purchase or rent parts of the completed scheme prior to ground being broken for its construction.

Assuming that a design has been accepted as a result of a thorough choice phase, the steps involved in getting a work in place differ if one is involved in implementing guidelines or implementing a total design. The intellectual processes are, however, essentially the same.

All-of-a-Piece Urban Design

A decision has to be made during the intelligence and design phases as to whether the infrastructure is to be publicly funded, paid for by the developers of individual projects, or built incrementally by developers as their individual projects are built. Guidelines have to be accepted as official policy by some regulating authority that has the power to control developments within its geographical or functional jurisdiction. Otherwise, compliance with guidelines relies on the good will of individual developers and their architects and the ability of administering agencies to delay approvals on unrelated grounds, thereby incurring a considerable cost to the developer. The process is seen as a bargaining one. Sometimes the power is held by the general developer of a site, who has set the guidelines for the developers of components of the overall project. This situation exists in the implementation of Las Colinas, Texas (Las Colinas Association 1986) and at Seaside, Florida (Duany et al. 1987; Dunlop 1989; Patton 1991; Mohney and Easterling 1991). More frequently, however, guidelines are written for local or state governments (Shirvani 1985; Zotti 1991) as for example, for the theater district and midtown Manhattan (Barnett 1974) or for Battery Park City (Barnett 1987; Fisher 1988) in New York City.

In many countries the power to institute urban design policies is delegated to administrative units of governments, but even in these cases there are often opportunities to appeal the policies to a political body or to the courts. In the United States, a municipal council usually has to accept urban design guidelines as the policy for the development of a city's physical layout. The power to supervise their use is delegated to an authority established to develop an area of a city or to a licensing body. Appeals to their rulings generally go to a zoning board. Alternatively, the power to both approve and supervise the implementation of guidelines may be delegated by a municipal government to a review board. This board may be a panel of experts selected by a mayor with professional advice, or it may be part of the ongoing administration of planning and zoning applications in a local government. How such processes should best be carried out in local government has been of concern to planning theorists for a long time (see Kent 1964).

Once development packages and guidelines have been accepted as policy for specific sites, development proposals are sought from potential developers. The evaluation of their design proposals is usually at least a two-step operation: first, evaluation by a review board to see whether the designs comply with the guidelines and fulfill the requirements of the development package, and second, a comparative assessment of competing proposals, if any, based on criteria established during the programming process—the intelligence phase. Once proposals have been accepted, their compliance with the guidelines as they are being constructed has to be monitored. This responsibility may be delegated to the urban designer or remain the prerogative of the review board of the public agency responsible for giving permission for the project to be built.

Total Design

Once a proposal for a total design has been accepted, it becomes an architectural design problem. Working drawings and specifications are developed, subject to further review by building inspectors and licensing departments of local governments, contractors are engaged, and the project is built. It seldom occurs as simply as this scenario suggests. Many unforeseen events occur during the implementation phase—governments change, unanticipated site conditions are discovered, a sponsor goes bankrupt, a competing project goes ahead, contractors refuse to build in a particular way because that is not how they have done it in the past. All these events change the nature of the problem and result in at least a partial revision of the project.

Urban design schemes are often implemented in a number of steps, or phases. It has been found to be important that each phase can work on its own and ideally not interfere with, nor be interfered with by, the next phase that is being implemented or constructed. Some-

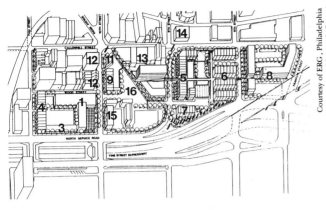

Courtesy of ERG., Philadelphia (Environmental Research Group)

Figure 21-10: Urban Design Schemes as a Set of Phases
Any urban design proposal of consequence has many separate components. The scheme illustrated here requires a series of possibly independent actions in order to bring it to fruition. Some are purely administrative; others involve architectural design development and implementation. It is difficult to predict in advance which components will be implemented first, for in a capitalist economy much depends on financial exigency or its catalytic effect. Also, any possible sequence of steps needs to be based on the assumption that each will work as an entity if the scheme falters at the end of any development phase, and that the development of subsequent steps will not have a negative effect on the earlier ones. Many urban design master plans remain on the shelf after the first step is completed; others have totally different second and subsequent phases than originally envisioned.

times only the first phase of a proposal is built, so that component of the proposed overall project has to work on its own or with very different second phases than were originally envisioned. University campuses are replete with examples of ill-fitting sequences of development (see P. Turner 1984). Indeed, much current university campus design focuses on remedying problems established during the expansionist period of the 1960s.

THE POSTOCCUPANCY EVALUATION PHASE

The ultimate test of any urban design effort is the quality of the built environment that ensues. The ultimate test of a total design is the built configuration and what it really does afford people in place. Once a project is completed and inhabited, it will certainly be evaluated by its users. Their feelings about it will depend on the costs and rewards of being there (Helmreich 1974). A scheme may be reviewed by critics and almost certainly at least casually evaluated by its designers themselves. The nature of architects' and critics' evaluations is partial and mostly concerned with visual appearances. A cynic has said that buildings have to be built so that they can be photo-

graphed for architectural journals. Users' evaluations are likely to be broader in nature and based on their own experiences. They are unlikely to be concerned with architectural ideas.

Some architectural critics (e.g., Grady Clay, Ada Louise Huxtable, Paul Goldberger, William Morgan, Martin Pawley) are extraordinarily insightful people and their reviews have shaped architects' thinking about the city and urban design as well as the design of individual buildings. Their commentaries are, naturally enough, biased by their own values, although a number of reviewers are able to examine schemes from many points of view. Over time too what reviewers pay attention to has varied (Belgasem 1987). With few exceptions, the architectural press now reviews schemes primarily in terms of their geometries—their formal aesthetics—and the intellectual aesthetic theories that generated them. The failure to do more systematic analyses of inhabited projects from a variety of perspectives has had opportunity costs in terms of building better positive theory on which to base future decisions. Learning from past experiences in a more rigorous fashion in order to understand the strengths and weaknesses of a design has become very much part of the Empiricist and empirical research agenda, as has, to a lesser extent, the analysis of the methods used to achieve a design.

During the past twenty years there has been a major growth in the number and quality of postoccupancy studies. New methods of observation and interview have been developed to pinpoint issues that casual questioning has failed to detect (Preiser, Rabinowitz, and White 1988). Most recent postoccupancy studies have not been done by the architects or architectural firms involved in the design or project. There is little direct incentive for them to do so. They would not only have to pay for the studies, but the results might leave them open to liability claims. Most studies have been done by analysts hired by building administrators to deal with problems that have arisen in buildings or by researchers interested in developing design theory.

The results of the studies have shown the difficulty of drawing singular conclusions about a scheme because of the variety of opinions held by different people about the same project, given their own aesthetic tastes, the way they use the built environment, and their states of mind (Gutman and Westergaard 1974). The studies have also shown that many architectural award-winning schemes are liked by nobody but other architects (Bycroft 1989). Above all they have shown that "failures" result not from the form-designing abilities of architects, but from their weaknesses in defining or designing the program—in understanding or designing the problem in terms of the full range of human needs that have to be fulfilled. One of the questions about the future of architecture and urban design as professional activities is the degree to which designers wish to develop the skills to be problem identifiers rather than simply form givers.

CONCLUSION: THE URBAN DESIGN DESIGNING PROCESS

The process of urban design is clearly a complex one in which many people participate. It is also clearly an argumentative one. The design of the process itself has become a major design task, and our understanding of the consequences of designing following one route rather than another is limited because insufficient research exists on the process; our positive procedural theory is poorly developed. Consequently, designers must work under uncertainty not only because of the unpredictability of the consequences of applying many new types of forms to cities, but also because of the limitations of our knowledge about the best way of going about a design in particular circumstances. Yet there is much that we cumulatively do know.

An understanding of patterns of the environment and what they afford is necessary to carrying out the design process well. Inventing new patterns to meet new problems or to solve old problems in new ways is essential to creative urban design. A knowledge of existing types—generic solutions—is critical to the process of urban designing in three ways, provided the context in which they work is known, what "working" means is known, and the problems they solve are understood. The use of types provides a vocabulary of partial solutions as the basis of design, and it avoids having to reinvent the wheel. Also, if properly used, it helps to avoid repeating the mistakes of the past. Types need to be used within a problem-solving framework in which the program is rigorously designed. It is not "program versus paradigm" but, as Colin Rowe (1983; Lang 1985) suggests, "program and paradigm" that is the approach necessary for creative urban design within specific cultural contexts. The quality of any urban design will, however, always be open to debate.

Understanding and evaluating any project can be done from a number of viewpoints: (1) in terms of one's own experience, (2) in terms of the experiences of a number of users, and (3) in terms of the designer's intentions. At every step in the process of design, urban designers confront issues that have to be resolved. The choices they make among different ways of laying out a city or an urban precinct have lasting impacts. Every choice involves the application of a set of values. Urban design is clearly a highly political act.

MAJOR REFERENCES

Ackoff, Russell L. (1978). *The Art of Problem Solving*. New York: John Wiley.

Bechtel, Robert, Robert Marans, and William Michelson, eds. (1987). *Methods in Environmental and Behavioral Research*. New York: Van Nostrand Reinhold.

Cuff, Dana (1991). *Architecture: The Story of Practice*. Cambridge, MA: MIT Press.

Dalton, Linda C. (1989). "Emerging Knowledge about Planning Practice." *Journal of Planning Education and Research* 9, no. 1:29–44.

De Bono, Edward (1973). *Lateral Thinking: Creativity Step by Step*. New York: Harper.

Koberg, Donald, and Jim Bagnall (1977). *The Universal Traveler*. 2d ed. Los Altos, CA: William Kaufman.

Lang, Jon (1987a). "Procedural Theory." In *Creating Architectural Theory: The Role of the Behavioral Sciences in Architectural Design*. New York: Van Nostrand Reinhold, pp. 31–72.

——— (1992). "Methodological Issues and Approaches: A Critical Appraisal." In Ernesto G. Arias, ed., *International Studies on the Meaning and Use of Housing: Methodologies and Their Applications to Policy, Planning and Design*. London: Gower, pp. 51–69.

Rittel, Horst (1984). "Second Generation Design Methods." In Nigel Cross, ed., *Developments in Design Methodology*. New York: John Wiley, pp. 317–329.

Rowe, Colin (1983). "Program versus Paradigm," *Cornell Journal of Architecture* 2:8–19.

Shirvani, Hamid (1985). *The Urban Design Process*. New York: Van Nostrand Reinhold.

——— (1990). *Beyond Public Architecture: Strategies for Design Evaluation*. New York: Van Nostrand Reinhold.

Zeisel, John (1980). *Inquiry by Design: Tools for Environmental Behavior Research*. New York: Cambridge University Press.

22

PROCEDURAL ISSUES IN URBAN DESIGN

A number of procedural issues have to be confronted by urban designers in almost all the situations they face. The basic issues have to do with philosophical positions on the nature of the process itself. Secondary ones concern designers' attitudes toward the specific methods and techniques used and their consequences. The way the issues are resolved affects the qualities of a design and the satisfaction of the various stakeholders with it. This chapter is largely about the basic issues, but the secondary ones impinge on them and so need to be identified as well. If urban designers (and their clients) had completely rational minds and comprehensive knowledge, most of the issues would be easy to resolve, but this is not the case. Implicitly or explicitly, urban designers nevertheless take stands on them all.

PROCEDURAL PARADIGMS

While there is general agreement on the nature of the structure of the decision-making process, the basic intellectual processes involved, and even of the general methods for enhancing creative thinking, there are also a number of fundamental procedural questions that divide urban designers into ideological camps. Indeed, it is probably more revealing to recognize the differences between urban designers in terms of the processes of designing they use than the forms they generate. Procedural paradigmatic differences represent fundamental sociopolitical attitudes. These attitudes pervade the methods used in programming, designing, and evaluating, and even the methods an urban designer is willing to learn about.

Rationalism and Empiricism

The placing of Rationalism and Empiricism as opposing ways of thinking about urban design has been a thread running throughout this book. Rationalism is the approach to research and design that is founded on logical reasoning rather than information derived from observation.

Empiricism stresses the role of observation as the basis for developing designs for the future. Much urban design involves both types of processes, but urban designers working (or writing manifestos) at the extremes are clearly evident throughout this century (Broadbent 1990).

Although Rationalist and Empiricist approaches to urban designing are structured in much the same way, they suggest radically different programming, designing, and evaluating procedures because they begin with very different value orientations. Rationalists have generally advocated radical change. They have sought to achieve a particular model of a Platonic world that is rational to them. Many such proposals have come from architects. Empiricism has advocated a much less dramatic set of changes; it has advocated an Aristotelian approach to design (see, e.g., Peattie 1981a). It has focused on the problems to be solved, but even within the problem-solving mode of thinking there are different approaches.

Almost every commentary on design processes contains an observation such as "[designing] embodies a critical reflection on, a value judgment of, the inheritance and context to which they pertain" (Steiner 1990, cited in Corner forthcoming). How does one decide what ideas, ways of life, buildings, landscapes, and so on are worth keeping and what should be abandoned? How does one take Empiricist observations into future? How does one relate Rationalist thinking to the realities of human existence? Does one assume that the marketplace is the best arbiter of people's needs and the functions the built environment should perform, and thus the best measure of the success or failure of schemes?

Typological and Problem Solving Approaches to Design

Another question that has been running through this book is: What is the best way for urban designers, particularly Empiricists, to work? Is a paradigmatic approach to urban design better than a programmatic approach to design? Are there circumstances in which one is better than the other? These two last questions are difficult to answer. Each approach has strong proponents, although there has been a general movement toward a problem-solving approach, particularly from those people approaching urban design from a social rather than a formal or intellectual aesthetic perspective.

Much depends on the self-image of the urban designer and the degree to which the designer believes in broad participation in making decisions. Is the urban designer an artist or an environmental designer? The artist leans toward Rationalism and typological development of designs; the environmental designer leans toward Empiricism and a problem-solving, or programmatic, approach to design. Ultimately, the urban designer works within the limits set by a society, but there is considerable freedom of choice in how to organize the urban design activity.

FUNDAMENTAL ETHICAL DILEMMAS: ENDS AND MEANS IN URBAN DESIGN

A series of ethical dilemmas often faces the urban designer whatever procedural paradigm is followed. They have to do with whose interests the designer represents and the ends and means of an urban design effort. The easiest way to deal with them is to ignore them, but a stand on them is at least implicit in any designing process.

The urban designer is hired by a sponsor to carry out work in the public domain. Who do professionals represent? Certainly the sponsor. Does the urban designer worry about all the citizens of a city or a select few? Who represents vagrants and vandals? What are designers' responsibilities toward their own professions and the values of their peers? Every design implies a stand on these questions. The urban designer certainly plays a mediating role between various interested parties in the outcomes of a project.

The overriding dilemmas arise from questions over the real or imagined competing qualities of products and processes. There are a number of such dilemmas. First, urban designers can use processes of design that they regard as good but that yield a design that they regard as poor. Second, the reverse can also happen: What the designer feels is a morally reprehensible process, including the bending of legal requirements, can yield a good design. A third situation occurs when the quality of the design can only be maintained by a social or administrative process that is regarded as morally unacceptable. The reverse of that situation can also occur—an acceptable administrative process can lead to the failure of a design.

In the first case, there is usually a conflict between the way the designer has assigned relative importance to the variables of concern during the programming process and their relative importance in evaluation. The criteria for evaluation have shifted from what the urban designers believe ought to be done to what they like or want to do.

In the second case, it usually means that a client or a client group has been slighted during the process. The third case raises questions about the domain of urban designers' responsibilities. Should an urban designer be concerned with how a project is to be administered once it is complete? This issue arises more and more now with the privatization of public space. Who should have access to it? Who controls it? If, as the result of a particular group having access to a particular place, it will lose its character and fail economically and close down so that nobody can enjoy it, should one say that excluding those people is acceptable administrative behavior? If quotas for specific types of people are believed to be necessary to maintain what is deemed to be, say, a good racial or age mix in a residential area among its inhabitants, should one support a quota system at all, let alone one based on race or age? Many such issues arise in urban design. Some are easier to resolve, particularly on paper, than others.

On ethical/political grounds a number of people argue for a glass box approach to design. Many designers insist, with little if any supporting evidence, that a black box approach to design yields better results. If this is correct, does the end justify the exclusion of a genuinely participatory approach to design? After all in the long run it is the product that counts, or is it? As some politicians, municipal officials, and designers say: "You can't make an omelet without breaking eggs!"

ISSUES RECURRING THROUGHOUT THE DESIGN PROCESS

Some issues occur throughout the designing process. Indeed, almost any part of an evolving design is open to revision as one goes through the steps of programming, design and evaluation, and even implementation, and as the definition of the problem shifts in character. The concern here is, however, with issues that confront the designer throughout the process. The primary ones are how to deal with the changing world as one goes through the process and with the constraints of time itself on the way the process is conducted. Other questions arise over what methods should be used at each phase of the design process and how to represent evolving designs.

The Temporal Factor in Urban Design

Designing takes time. There is almost always a desire by clients to reduce the amount of time (and money) allocated to it. Implementing schemes takes time. Design always involves looking into the future. Two very different procedural issues of concern result. "How does one deal with the observation that one is dealing with a changing world?" and "How best can one generate a design under the limitations of the time available to do so?" With wicked problems there are always innumerable questions to ask and an endless array of potential solutions to a design problem (Rittel 1984).

Designing for a Changing World

The process of creating a master plan, a set of guidelines, or even a total urban design takes a long time to complete well. During the designing period, as well as in the future during which the design is to function, the world changes in many ways simultaneously. The people involved at the beginning of the design process may differ from those involved at the end of it and from those who ultimately benefit from it. The context may change: politicians may be defeated in an election, buildings adjacent to one's site may be demolished, a competitor may build the same type of project next door. Some things can be predicted with a high degree of accuracy, probably more than we like to believe for the world is not an entirely capricious place; however, other things fall outside the scope of experiences and knowledge of the urban designer and are not easy to predict (except with hindsight). Procedurally, how should one deal with this situation in urban design?

One way is simply to disregard changing contextual variables. When this option is chosen urban designers assume that their projects will indeed be catalysts for changing the surroundings to fit in with the designs rather than the reverse. If every urban design endeavor adopts this position, the city, or any other human settlement, will end up being a collage of unrelated and competing rather than mutually supportive developments. Major social and opportunity costs will be involved. To some people in the United States this outcome is the right one as it involves a minimal public intervention into property decisions. Other people wish to avoid such an occurrence. One approach to urban design is thus to design so that whatever happens in the surroundings will fit the scheme and vice versa. The question then is: "How does one go about achieving this end?" Indeed, "Is it conceptually possible?"

Designing under Time Constraints

All design takes place under a time and a financial constraint. It is never possible to describe a problem situation exhaustively; it is never possible to examine all possible solutions. The cost in time and money of diligently working through the decision process is high, even when such a process is likely to have long-term benefits. Cost cutting in public agencies for planning and urban design work is very much a fact of life (Hamblen 1991). Developers want to minimize costs. Often implicit in such cost-cutting procedures is deferring opportunity costs so that they are borne by people in the future.

Like all other designers, urban designers develop techniques for cutting corners. They have a set of heuristic devices that truncate the design process. They work until they seem to have something good enough. Creative people do better than that, but their search for better answers is still always truncated. The easiest way to trun-

cate both the design of the problem and the design of its solution, yet to explore design possibilities, is to use a typological, or paradigmatic, approach to design and thus to rely on generic or past types, existing design principles, and design standards. At best this approach is only likely to achieve a *satisficing* scheme. Many issues are thus avoided, variables neglected, and avenues of exploration untried.

There are four effects of time constraints on the design process itself: (1) greater reliance is placed on intuition, (2) the number of variables being considered is reduced, (3) possible lines of exploration for solutions are eliminated, and (4) the care with which ideas are represented is reduced. When operating under severe time constraints, where should urban designers' efforts be placed? Can a highly reductionist approach to design be avoided? Almost inevitably a typological approach to designing has to be employed in such circumstances.

Design professionals are businesspeople. They have to stay in business to survive. They get work by cornering segments of the marketplace. One way they do this is by having their own style—the process of design and the set of patterns that they use and with which they tend to be identified. Developing a new style, while potentially rewarding, is also fraught with difficulties. To what degree should urban designers push for deviations from the norm of their own designs and others that presently exist? Time constraints tend to lead to poorly thought-through solutions, particularly when a novel end product is sought. Time constraints are less important when a standard solution suffices.

Methods/Techniques

There are many combinations of analytical, synthetic, and evaluative methods, or techniques, available for urban designers to use. Each one represents a biased look at the world. The techniques we use for describing the world—for modeling the world—affect what we look at. Modeling the world in terms of land uses and behavior settings may seem to be very similar processes. After all they are both dealing with activities. Analysis of behavior settings give a temporal view of the world and its uses a much finer grain than does land-use analysis. Similarly, the techniques that we use for ascertaining people's hopes about the future and the ways in which we simulate (represent) potential designs to meet their needs affect the choices we make for the future. We can never describe the whole realm of human experience. What methods should we choose to simplify it? What are the issues that arise as a consequence? Each method is *chosen* by the urban designer in carrying out professional work, even if only by default.

The specific methods urban designers use at each phase of the design process is part of their problem-solving style (Simon 1970). Often the choice of process is not based on what needs to be looked at, but rather on those methods the designer knows that are neither stressful nor time-consuming to use. Deviating from existing ways of working is stressful. There has thus been a reluctance to design new methods for dealing with what is appropriate or even to examine the array of available techniques. We end up designing by habit. This reluctance frequently explains the discrepancy between what we profess the design process should be and what it is. Few urban designers know the full range of methods available to them. A criticism that can be leveled at us is that we hide behind the shield that we are dealing with intangibles in order to avoid having to be specific about what we are doing. Creating new methods to deal with questions of analysis, synthesis, and evaluation is part of the ongoing development of the field. Nevertheless, in the same way that we shall never have complete substantive knowledge, we shall never have complete procedural knowledge.

Since the 1960s many methods of analysis, synthesis, and evaluation for environmental design have been taken or adapted from other design fields, such as those in engineering and the business world (see, e.g., G. Moore 1970; Broadbent 1973; Koberg and Bagnall 1977; Cross 1984; Heath 1984). Indeed, one of the major changes in the practice of urban design has been a methodological one. Considerable debate still exists about the utility of the new techniques (Land 1992). While they have enriched our view of the world, urban designers will always choose methods of working uncertain that they are the best ones for achieving their purposes. We shall always be operating with models of reality. Which approaches to modeling realities are best?

Modeling (or Representing)

One process involved throughout the design process affects what we pay attention to and what we do: it is the process of *modeling*, or as many architects prefer, *representing*, reality. We work on an artificial reality (see also Simon 1969). Each step of the design process involves representing reality. In the intelligence phase we are modeling the existing world and its behavior, the identification of fits and misfits in it, what people aspire to have, own, and achieve, and the ends that will fulfill their aspirations. During the design phase we are modeling the new behavioral and physical worlds—the former as images in our heads and the latter in drawing and iconic model form (see Fisher 1989). During the choice phase we are using a model of values to assess the quality of a design.

The way in which we model humans and other organisms, human needs, and human settlements patterns can be a conscious choice. Often the choice is made subconsciously—the model has frequently been an impoverished one (Ellis and Cuff 1989). The methods we select bias how we look at the world, which in turn biases the methods we select. We do much intuitively and we do

much in a black box, which helps to avoid serious debate about what we are doing and the stress that accompanies it. We also use such techniques because they seem to yield better results, or at least results closer to our hearts. A look at each phase of the design process raises questions about the wisdom of this position.

THE INTELLIGENCE, OR PROGRAMMING, PROCESS

The overall structure of the intelligence phase was described in Chapter 21. Monitoring the environment as it changes, identifying misfits between what is happening and should be happening in somebody's or some group's view, identifying what requires to be changed, recognizing the well-functioning elements of the environment to protect, and establishing and designing a program for dealing with them are the basic activities of the phase. The misfits may have to do with the way the environment provides for present needs or predicting future needs and functions. There are two basic questions about the programming process: Who does it? What are the methods used? Implicit in the second question is: "How does one identify the variables of importance?"

Increasingly the designer of the program and the designer of the project itself are different people or even different organizations. The arguments for such a differentiation are twofold. First, the designers of solutions/ projects tend to define the program in terms of what they want to do—their own self-interests—rather than what needs to be done. Second, as demands for environmental quality increase, so the process of programming has become more sophisticated and an area of professional specialization. This growth in specialization in the design fields has been occurring steadily, with the architectural profession spinning off city planning and landscape architecture and now construction management into separate professions. Programming may follow.

Programming clearly calls for the use of a variety of methods that fall outside the expertise of the generalist architect or landscape architect (Moleski 1974; Sanoff 1977, 1989, 1991; Zeisel 1980; Palmer 1981; Moleski and Lang 1982; Robinson and Weekes 1983; Preiser 1985; Peña, Parshall, and Kelly 1987). How best can the present biogenic and sociogenic environments be described? How best can clients be defined? How should one go about developing a model of future needs? How best can these needs be translated into a statement of physical design requirements? Where during the overall design process should we be considering constraints? Every time we choose one particular method we are biasing the definition of the problem. This bias is inevitable. The issue is: "Which biases should be built in?" A number of procedural issues result from raising such questions during the intelligence phase. How does one define the client? Who are the most important clients to consider? How does one define the public interest? *Advocacy design* has been developed specifically to assist people without much political clout in getting their ends met (Davidoff 1964; R. Goodman 1971; J. Stern 1989).

Defining the Client

A human needs approach to the design of functional environments provides the basis for asking questions about the nature of ourselves and the people with whom, or for whom, we are designing. The questions still arise: "Whose needs should be identified?" "Whose needs are paramount?" "What methods are best for answering these questions?"

A variety of people are involved in creating an urban design. As pointed out earlier, at the least there are users, sponsors, and designers. Each group has its own interests. If an urban designer accepts a user-oriented approach to design, then a number of procedural questions arise, because in designing the public realm there are many different potential users. They vary in physical abilities, they are at different stages in their life cycles, there are gender differences, and different people attend to different aspects of the world around themselves. The basic issues are: "Which groups are important and how best should one be concerned with their interests, with other people's interests, and, at the same time, with fulfilling the needs of the designer(s)?" The model of the users' needs is likely to change as the programming and design process evolves. In the design of Kresge College, for instance, Charles Moore found that the values of students with whom he was designing at the outset differed from those with whom he worked later, and considerable reprogramming was necessary to develop a more general design.

It is usually clear who the sponsors of a project are. In some instances, the user-clients are also relatively easy to ascertain. This is particularly true when one is dealing with improving an existing built environment. Often, however, one is dealing with the production of a new complex of buildings, a new set of facilities, a new residential area. The future users are not there to speak to about their hopes and aspirations. Market studies may yield what can be sold, but the broader questions of design quality implicit and explicit in the arguments presented in this book can easily be missed. What one has to do is to develop analogs and surrogates of the likely users and ask questions about what their needs are, how these needs might be manifested, and how they might best be satisfied. There are two basic approaches for doing this: (1) to find people similar to the intended inhabitants of a development and to observe their uses of similar places and/or to interview them about their activities and aesthetic values, and (2) to extrapolate from the positive theories that are available regarding people and environment to predict what is needed. Some combination of the two seems preferable. The alternative is simply to let the market decide or to rely on one's intuition. Are these the best ways? They are certainly the easier ones.

Defining the Public Interest

One of the purposes of urban design—the very reason for its emergence—is to impose strictures on what the individual architect or landscape architect can do in response to the perceived social and visual chaos that arises as the consequence of individual designers making decisions on behalf of their sponsors without concern for the overall quality of the environment. The same observation can be made about any number of other variables from traffic flows to climatic conditions to children's play spaces. It has been and is often perceived to be in the public interest to have a scheme, a settlement pattern, that is more than a sum of its parts. How far should the urban designer go in restricting the range of things architects can do for their clients or in pushing them in a particular direction to achieve what is perceived as a public good? How does one measure the public good? It is largely an intangible variable. How does one deal with perceptions of socially desirable goals when they compete with what people *say* they want?

There are two basic approaches to defining the public interest: (1) to accept what the public, either directly or through their political representatives, says is the public interest, and (2) to rely on the designers' and planners' expert knowledge of what should be the public's interest. The second approach has been the one generally used, although the first has been the point of departure for the development of a number of city plans (Wheaton and Wheaton 1972). Few so derived public interest goals have been achieved in the United States because of the primacy of individual interests. It has been perceived to be in the public interest to let individual interests reign. The issues thus remain. Should short-run interests be postponed in favor of some potential long-range concerns, which may or may not be important? What should the advocacy of urban designers be? Much depends on how we model human needs and how the broader sociogenic and biogenic environment functions.

Defining Human Needs

Maslow's model of human needs appears to have universal applicability, but much about its operation remains a mystery. We do know that the manifestations of needs vary from culture to culture. The way of attaining esteem in one culture may be simply through being older and having had more experience with the world; it may have no material manifestation. In another culture it may depend on the display of possessions. In one culture it may be the house that is the element of display; in another, houses may be indistinguishable from each other, but jewelry may be the mechanism. These issues are substantive ones; the procedural issues have to do with the methods of assessing needs.

Behavior and Mental Images as the Basis for Design?

All the people involved in any design process are likely to have images of the good world and their own attitudes toward it in mind as they consider future options. Two major procedural problems are raised by these images: (1) different people will have different images when talking about the same thing (Brolin 1981), and (2) there is likely to be a discrepancy between what people do and what they say they will do, or, in retrospect, what they said they would do and what they actually do (Michelson 1976). The first can be resolved to some extent by representing the images in drawings and photographs. The second is more of an issue because it cannot be resolved through any representation of the images.

In carrying out any participatory design process, there will frequently be a discrepancy between what is observed about users' behaviors and aesthetic values and what the users or potential users say they will like and will use in the future. Concerns arise from deciding to base urban design programs on what designers perceive to be future behaviorally congruent environments for sets of users in contrast to what people say they will use and enjoy (see also Chapter 19). If one relies on what people say, there is a major danger of designing something that fits, or is congruent with, that mental image and that turns out not to be what they really wanted. On the other hand, their perceptions of themselves are likely to be more accurate than the designers' images, however good the positive theory on which they are based. As in dealing with all wicked problems, no definitive set of techniques is available for resolving such potential discrepancies. We argue them through.

Measuring Needs Satisfaction

Implicit in the Neo-Functionalist approach to design is that the lowest-order needs in Maslow's hierarchical model must be met first before designers shift their attention to dealing with higher-order needs, but we also know that meeting a need shifts the focus of people's concern up the scale. How should designers develop a procedure for deciding to what extent they should focus on complete fulfillment of one need before moving on to consider the next, but less pressing need?

According to Maslow (1987) a basic need does not have to be 100 percent satisfied before the next higher need in the hierarchy emerges as a focus of concern. Few people if any have all their needs satisfied to their full contentment. Maslow believes that a more realistic view of the hierarchy of needs is to expect lower-order needs to be filled to a greater extent than upper-order ones. The

1. East River Project, Harlem, New York—Proposal 1

2. East River Project, Harlem, New York—Proposal 2

Figure 22-1: Behaviorally Congruent and Mentally Congruent Environments

The impact of user input into the design process is aptly represented by these two proposals made in the 1960s (1) and early 1970s (2) for the same project by the same architects (THE Hodne/Stageberg PARTNERS Inc.). The original proposal was based on observations of lifestyles of its prospective clients. They, however, wanted a development akin to the more prestigious ones in New York. The first scheme was based on behavior patterns and the second on mental images; the first emphasized affordances for activities and the second meeting esteem needs through an appropriate symbolic aesthetic.

example he gives is for the average American citizen, say, to have 85 percent of physiological needs filled, 70 percent of safety needs, 50 percent of affiliation needs, 40 percent of esteem needs, and 10 percent of self-actualization needs. The manifestation of a need is not something that happens suddenly; it emerges over time. "For instance, if prepotent need A is satisfied only 10 percent of the time, the need B may not be visible at all. However, if this need A becomes satisfied 25 percent of the time need B may emerge 5 percent, as need A becomes satisfied 75 percent need B may emerge 50 percent, and so on" (Maslow 1987, p. 28).

With any given population mix that has limited resources and a wide variety of needs at different levels and manifested in different ways, how should the urban designer decide where to place emphasis? Alexander and Poyner (1970) argue that the difficulty in answering such a question illustrates the limitations of the human needs approach to design. They suggest that urban designers should focus on behavioral tendencies of the populations of concern instead. Their proposal is one way out of the dilemma, but even if the urban designer has success in designing to meet those tendencies, people's perceptions of their needs will shift!

Constraints on the Achievement of Human Needs

What we strive for is also very much affected by our perception of what is attainable within our competency and resources. Thus the designer has to be concerned with identifying design possibilities. Presenting alternatives outside the realm of possibility to the public is not helpful, but how does one establish the domain of possibilities?

The methodological issue is: "How do we distinguish between something that is really impossible and something that might be possible although it does not seem to be?" At the extremes it is easy, but some proposals that seemed to be financially absurd have been implemented, whereas many proposals have raised people's hopes only to dash them. It is fine to raise people's aspirations, including our own, but the failure to deliver projects has established a poor reputation for city planners and urban designers in a number of situations, so much so that potential clients become skeptical of our intentions and our designs. The recent surge in the number of financially pragmatic projects has been the result of recognizing this problem. Implicit in such projects is, however, a simplified program.

Richness of Programs?

The end product of the intelligence phase is a program that has to be fulfilled during the design phase. It might be better considered as an interim program, for the act of designing will almost certainly raise new questions.

In recent years, such programs have become richer in content, covering not only spatial requirements but also aesthetic goals, performance criteria, and the financial constraints under which the design has to be generated. The programs may even contain partial solutions.

The increase in scope of programs is due to the perception that the failure in architectural and urban design has been at the stage of establishing goals and identifying design principles to be followed rather than in the ability to generate built forms—the design ability per se. The programming process has long been recognized as crucial, particularly by leading designers, but the question now arises: "How detailed should the programs be?" The answer will be situation-specific and will emerge from considerable debate among the people involved in the programming process. Can the issue be resolved in other than a political power struggle? Is there a rational method for doing so?

DESIGNING

A number of questions inevitably come up during the design phase. One has already been considered: "How best can one simulate the layout of the environment and the experiencing of it?" Other questions that are central to the design phase also apply to programming: "What are the best techniques for generating new ideas given the time constraints under which one is operating?" "Do the design principles that have been developed in the past for urban design schemes of various types hold for both today and the future?" "How best can urban designers break away from habitual ways of working and avoid the negative effects of past experience on creative thinking?"

A number of techniques for aiding creative thinking have been borrowed from other fields (Koberg and Bagnall 1977). They include psychoanalytical techniques such as brainstorming and associational thinking, mathematical techniques such as linear programming, and a growing number of computer-based algorithms drawing on queueing theory. Morphological analysis, it was noted earlier, whether recognized as such or not, is the basis of much recent Deconstructionist work. Each of these techniques has specific utilities because each addresses special design problems. There are also major biases against using them at all. The leaders in the design fields have a tremendous investment in the maintenance of the procedural status quo. Some are, however, willing to seek new and better ways of working; others are not and rail against new knowledge and new approaches. So the prevalent technique is still largely intuitive reasoning, a powerful technique indeed. Intuition too, however, has major limitations, particularly in dealing with new situations.

There are a number of value questions that tug at the designer's mind. How does one decide how much to strive to meet the design professions' current ideas of what good design is? It is difficult to deal with peer group pressures. How much should one seek novelty? Is it worthwhile to use any other than an intuitive and/or paradigmatic, or typological, approach to design given the time constraints under which most designs have to be generated? How strong a personal artistic statement should one make in urban design?

EVALUATING DESIGNS ON THE DRAWINGBOARD

At present, most evaluations of proposed designs while they are still on the drawingboard are conducted by peer evaluations in the design office and then submitted for the sponsor's review. Predictions of performance and the impact of a proposal on its surroundings and the decision that a scheme is acceptable or not all take place intuitively in a black box manner except for a few quantifiable variables. The demand for a more open process places considerable pressure on traditional ways in which an urban designer presents ideas and, more generally, works. Most designs are presented in the form of orthographic projections, perspectives and axonometric or isometric drawings, and small-scale iconic models made of cardboard or plastic and often uniform in color or all white. Professionals are the only ones who can really understand these models, and even so they often evaluate the model as a design rather than as a model of a future building complex. There is also a tendency to focus on those aspects of a design that are displayed in the model.

There are a number of procedural issues that arise from this observation of how the evaluation process takes place. The first is the recurrent one of how best to represent, or simulate, a potential design. The second is the ideological question of who should evaluate the proposal and the relative importance given to various evaluations. The third is about evaluation techniques—what is being evaluated and how it is evaluated. And the fourth has to do with the impact of the proposed design on its surroundings—what is being measured and how it is measured.

During recent years there has been a growth in explorations about how to best represent a design (Thiel forthcoming). They include a variety of techniques aimed at understanding (and enhancing) the experiential quality of what is proposed. They represent a bias toward the users' interests and assume that the architects' intellectual aesthetic ideology is less important than the results as experienced when built. Most of these new techniques focus on the visual simulation and particularly the sequential experiencing of the proposed world as an observer moves through it. These new processes promise much because laypeople have difficulty visualizing what schemes will be like from drawings. If their ability to visualize results is enhanced, the quality of debate about the quality of potential designs will itself be raised. The difficulty is how to simulate the many nonvisual aspects of the performance of a design.

Many processes can be mathematically modeled, for example, the structural performance, the consumption of energy to maintain a comfortable interior biogenic environment, the efficiency of people's circulation within a project, and the capital and maintenance costs of the scheme. Wind tunnels can be used to predict changes in the movement of air as the result of a new building or set of new buildings. Many other processes, however, can as yet only be simulated in the mind's eye (or nose).

The same observations can be made about methods for assessing the impact of a new urban design scheme on its surroundings. While it is not inevitable that somebody's interests get hurt as the result of implementing an urban design proposal, in a project of any importance or complexity such a consequence is likely. For instance, existing businesses and people's lives may be severely disrupted by urban renewal. Some people may be put out of business, and some residents required to move. Issues of compensation arise. How does one measure the intangibles?

While it can be argued that every impact a scheme will have on the surroundings should be identified, urban designers have neither the time nor the skills to do so. The question is: "What range of variables should be taken into consideration?" Certain variables, such as financial impact, can be dealt with quantitatively, although not necessarily accurately, but the effect of any urban design proposal or building on the architectural quality or livability of the surroundings is more difficult to portray and assess. As urban designers and architects are made to be legally responsible for carelessness in their work, so the importance of dealing with such questions increases. New methods will be designed. The lessons of the Cityspire Building in New York will be learned.

The fine incurred by the Cityspire Building for causing "unnecessary noise" surprised the architects for two reasons: (1) that a fine for such an infringement on neighbors' privacies was even possible, and (2) that the design of the building's dome would cause such a noise from the winds. This noise presumably was predictable within the realms of known science. The possibility of such an outcome was simply not investigated. Other variables to which we seldom pay attention are regarded simply as fortunate or unfortunate aspects of life. Should they be heeded? If so, how? For instance, grieving for a lost home or a city neighborhood that has been demolished for a major new project is difficult to measure. Outward displays of emotion are often sincere, but they can also be a ploy to attain higher levels of compensation. Inner feelings do not attract attention.

IMPLEMENTING

There are two basic implementation concerns: (1) getting the design into place, or, if guidelines, administering the guidelines, and (2) maintaining a project as a well-functioning scheme or part of a city when in place. Implicit in both is a concern for financial feasibility, the obligations of different parties to bear the costs, and their right to reap the financial benefits.

Total Urban Design

In any large-scale urban design project considerable time elapses from the inception of construction to its completion. Schemes are phased and financial arrangements are made according to each phase. Determining these phases and arrangements is part of the design process. Issues arise over the degree to which the process should be open-ended, the legitimacy of using private funding for public purposes, and who takes responsibility for the overall process and for each part of it.

In most total urban design schemes, the developer, whether in the private or public sector, pays. If the private sector pays, the costs are passed on to the direct users of the complex. If the public sector pays, the result may be the same, but it is much more likely that a component of the broader tax-paying public pays part of the bill. The degree to which the public sector should subsidize private sector investments that are perceived to be in the public interest and, even more so, the reverse is a continuing political issue that has major implications for what can be built in different geographic locations and political jurisdictions.

All-of-a-Piece Design and Urban Design Guidelines

In implementing an all-of-a-piece design through the use of design guidelines and in city building through a combination of zoning incentives and guidelines, review boards evaluate whether or not a work meets specified standards. A number of questions arise. Who should the members of the review board be and what qualifications should they have? How strictly should guidelines be interpreted and enforced? How does one deal with a scheme that fails to meet a set of guidelines but promises to be a major addition to the city in its own right—something that no one had previously considered? Does one support the integrity of the process or set a precedent for later developers and their designers who claim that their own schemes fall into the same category? Any deviation sets a precedent.

It is clear that master plans and guidelines have to be reviewed as circumstances change. The process of urban designing is an ongoing one. There is undoubtedly a tendency to change the master plan and guidelines for purely political reasons unrelated to the quality of the physical environment. The guidelines then become a vehicle for achieving other social ends. Is this a legitimate use of urban design work? If not, how can one prevent it from happening?

Future Management

To operate well, a scheme not only has to meet its goals, it also has to be managed well. How does one go about assessing whether management in the future will be sound? That promises will be kept? There is much that we have to take on trust.

While a future urban design does not necessarily have to be easy to operate, the procedures for doing so must be clear and be implementable given the resources available. Designing for operational costs has been frequently neglected in assessing the potential functioning of a scheme while it is still on the drawingboard. In considering the operation of a complex in the future, what methods should be used to predict such things as the costs of energy and the cultural conditions within which a scheme will have to operate? Should one be conservative—the pragmatic solution—or optimistic about future changes being in a fruitful direction? Does one assume that necessity will be the mother of invention—that new solutions to emerging problems will be developed? Does one assume, for instance, that crime rates will continue to rise in the United States or that social conditions will improve? Conservative attitudes in developing maintenance procedures may prevent failures but may also incur opportunity costs.

EVALUATING A PROJECT IN PLACE— POSTIMPLEMENTATION EVALUATION

The postimplementation evaluation of designs and design policies is infrequently but nevertheless increasingly regarded as an integral part of the designing process. The argument is that unless such evaluations are done, the utility of neither the substantive nor the procedural theory used as the basis for designing will be effectively understood. In this case, urban designers will learn little about the effectiveness of various types of guidelines, design methods, or design principles in meeting specific functional objectives.

As design problems are wicked ones, society as a whole, the people directly involved, and designers have to accept that there will always be misfits between the needs of a set of people and what is actually achieved. Total and continual satisfaction for everybody is impossible. The levels of satisfaction will vary over time in response to changes in moods, changes in status, and changes in the other day-to-day situations that people face in the world. Robert Gutman and Barbara Westergaard (1974), in their review of evaluations of the Richards Memorial Laboratories designed by Louis Kahn, noted that many subjective opinions about the quality of the building as a research laboratory had little to do with the building itself, but rather with people's states of mind at the time. The procedural need is to have a method for disentangling people's feelings about the quality of the environment from feelings about themselves.

Conflicts also arise over evaluating a scheme in terms of the original goals set. A world full of cognitive opportunities will almost certainly involve some stress for people. Is this an acceptable design goal? Is the stress perceived to be in the people's own interests? A cognitively rich environment may conflict with people's needs for esteem. What levels of comfort and challenge should the built environment afford? How does one disentangle the various aspects of the environment in evaluating it? Is the pragmatic principle of "whatever sells is good" a sound postimplementation evaluation technique? Success or failure has to be seen in terms of the fits and misfits of a development for particular groups of people. Whether the misfits are substantial enough to warrant changing a design depends on the politics of the situation—the interest groups involved, the harm incurred, and the resources available.

The concerns loop back to those raised about the beginning of the process. Who should conduct such evaluations? Who should pay for them? On whose terms should the evaluation be made? It must be recognized that for some critics negative evaluations of other people's work fulfill their own needs for prestige. What do you evaluate? When do you evaluate? The last is probably the least controversial question intellectually. It is clear that studies should be done over time. The case of Habitat in Montreal is instructive. Twenty-five years after being built it is working well, as perceived by its residents specifically and by the rental market generally. Immediately after it was built attitudes toward it would have resulted in a very different conclusion. Few people wanted to live there (Rybczynski 1990).

There are few incentives to do postoccupancy evaluations of specific projects except on behalf of the design professions (and society) as a whole. The occupants and users of a design know what works and does not work. If there is strong evidence that certain aspects of a design do not work, the architect fears being sued for malpractice. The impact of guidelines is likely to be more subtle. Yet without studies of designs and guidelines the learning curve of the profession is severely reduced. Much has been learned from those studies already done (e.g., Lansing, Marans, and Zehner 1970; Cooper Marcus 1975; Zeisel 1980; see also Schneekloth 1987 and Wener 1989).

CONSEQUENCES FOR URBAN DESIGN

Design problems are indeed wicked ones. The design process is an argumentative one. There is neither a right nor a wrong way of resolving many of the issues identified here, at least not with our present knowledge, but some ways yield better results than others. All designers work through the process using their own values (which may be to base designs on other people's values) and the values that they are allowed to use by the marketplace for their services. Each designer has a practiced, if not a clearly professed, position on the way one goes through the process. One such effort to specify in general terms how a designer *should* deal with the issues identified here is contained in Part Three of this book, which presents a normative model of urban designing.

In facing the issues described here, urban designers have to consider two sets of consequences in the self-conscious development of a normative position. The first set concerns the immediate implications for urban design and the second the implications for the future design of specific methods for conducting inquiries and generating answers. The first consequence is that urban designers need to be fully aware of the strengths, limitations, and biases of the methods they select for carrying out any part of the design process. They need to be able to logically defend the biases in light of the project they are designing, its context, and the purposes it serves. Designers need to be aware of who gains and who loses by the techniques used. They need to recognize their own advocacies. The obverse to this also holds. Urban designers need to select methods that deal with the issues and advocacies that are important. The difficulty is that what may be important in the long run may not be politically important in the short run.

The design of designing methods has become a topic of professional development during the past twenty years. A number of designers have been striving to design better models of human experiences and better techniques of analysis, synthesis, prediction, and evaluation. The designing of methods is a highly creative act, possibly demanding higher creative skills and powers of observation than designing the environment! Progress is slow for three reasons: (1) the difficulty of dealing with what are traditionally regarded as intangible variables, (2) the complexity of the interlinkage of variables, and (3) the paucity of researchers who are involved in studying the process of design in comparison to, say, architectural history. The design fields do not have a strong research tradition in design methodology. Perhaps the one factor inhibiting the development of better techniques is the intellectual and political commitment that many designers and educators have to the failure of the enterprise lest their artistic mystique be threatened. This commitment has the simultaneous effect of sharpening the quality of the research that is being done while inhibiting it from taking place at all.

MAJOR REFERENCES

Gutman, Robert (1977). "Cast of Characters: Architecture, the Entrepreneurial Profession." *Progressive Architecture* 58, no. 5:55-58.

Gutman, Robert, and Barbara Westergaard (1974). "Building Evaluation, User Satisfaction and Design." In Jon Lang et al., eds., *Designing for Human Behavior: Architecture and the Behavioral Sciences.* Stroudsburg, PA: Dowden, Hutchinson, and Ross, pp. 320-329.

Lang, Jon (1992). "Methodological Issues and Approaches: A Critical Appraisal." In Ernesto G. Arias, ed., *International Studies on the Meaning and Use of Housing: Methodologies and Their Applications to Policy, Planning and Design.* London: Gower, pp. 51-69.

Peattie, Lisa (1981a). "First Stage: The Platonic City versus the Aristotelian City." In *Planning: Rethinking Cuidad Guayana.* Ann Arbor: University of Michigan Press, pp. 41-72.

PART III

SYNTHESIS: A NEO-FUNCTIONAL APPROACH TO URBAN DESIGN

San Juan Capistrano, California

The thesis of this book is that the knowledge base from which design professionals derive their design principles should be empirically built. It needs to be based on a research agenda focusing on people's motivations, the sociogenic and biogenic environments in which they live, and the decision-making processes that shape their lives. It is clear from Part II that since the early days of the twentieth century when the Modernist architectural manifestos were written much has been added to our knowledge of the meaning of Functionalism and the way the built environment relates to human needs. While this knowledge enlightens us considerably, the urban designer, in conjunction with the others involved in the development of the human habitat, still has to make decisions about the future. The future has to be made. The nature of future human settlements will depend on the resources available to a society and the public attitudes that exist within it, but also partly on the nature of the processes, including urban design, that it uses for making decisions.

Implicit in this book has been a set of values based to some extent on those espoused by the Modernists. The underlying one is that the world can be made a better place. The meaning of "better," however, depends on a set of perceptions about society and how it is evolving. The way a better built environment should be purposefully evolved also depends on our perceptions of who should have control over future decisions. One perception is a laissez-faire view—all people should be able to do what they want, largely without outside interference. In this view cities should evolve without urban design, except for total designs on a scale that property developers can finance successfully. This position is clearly untenable if one believes that the opportunity costs to society that such a process incurs are too large. On the other hand, too much central control over the processes that shape human environments deadens the spirit and thwarts the attainment of a whole set of human needs.

The purpose of this synthesis is to present a view of what urban design should be. In it an integration of a number of prevailing views is presented. The observation is that the design of the built, or artificial, environment does and should emerge from an ongoing process. Any model of a self-conscious design process has to be based on a set of values and a general set of goals. A description of the process means little if these values are not understood. For this reason, Chapter 23, Fundamental Attitudes for Urban Design, presents the basic principles for designing rather than for specific urban forms. The procedural theory advocated here and by a number of people is based on these attitudes. It is presented in Chapter 24, A Normative Procedural Model for Urban Design, which is the heart of this synthesis.

The point of departure is that the argument between those advocating urban design as art and those advocating urban design as problem solving is unnecessary. It is also unnecessary for there to be a split among the people advocating an ecological or a typological empirical approach to design research and theory building and those people advocating phenomenology or hermeneutics, provided all are concerned with the "real" world of people and their sociogenic and biogenic environments. Each approach has much to offer; each has its limitations. There needs to be an integration of approaches, each recognizing what it does have to offer and its limitations (see also Robinson 1990).

The layout of buildings, neighborhoods, and cities is an important part of life. There are many other factors that are often more important in determining the quality of life. There is a need for urban designers to celebrate what they have achieved and can achieve, but also to recognize their limitations. Above all it is important to recognize that urban design is a process that operates without complete knowledge of the world and certainly without complete control over it. Urban designers will always be making decisions under uncertainty. They will always be dealing with too many variables to consider simultaneously. They will always be reducing the problems they face to a manageable size; they will eliminate some variables and work on others.

One of the fundamental dilemmas that urban designers face, as mentioned in Chapter 22, is to decide what to do when the process they believe should be followed for ethical reasons does not yield a design that they believe to be a good one. Another occurs when the mechanisms, such as design guidelines and design controls, that they believe to be necessary to attain a good design are deemed to be unfair or unethical even though they may attain what are perceived to be good results. The position described in this part of the book (as any position on urban design) is a controversial one. It is that the quality of the process has precedence and that we, as a society, will have to put up with opportunity costs in terms of the design result to avoid using processes that are unethical. This stance imposes on urban designers the need to be able to argue effectively for their schemes based on open evidence that their claims are justified.

Any process of urban design involves taking stand after stand. It is a political process. We have to take a stand on who the clients of concern are, on a set of goals, on a design program, and on a design or set of designs. The process involves repeated analyses, divergent production of ideas, syntheses, evaluations, and decisions. The process involves frequent predictions of how designs will perform in predicted future contexts. We cannot know with certainty how the designs will work in the future; we cannot know future sociopolitical contexts. Good theory will help us better predict how the specific urban design patterns we might propose will work. This is the basic thesis of this book. ■

23

FUNDAMENTAL ATTITUDES FOR URBAN DESIGN

Urban design is clearly a complex task, and there is naturally enough a desire on the part of many who are concerned with it to make it simpler and more manageable—to bring it into their own realm of expertise. The easiest way to do this is to deal with fewer issues—to narrow the scope of the problem. A position that could be taken is the pure Rationalist one: urban design is only concerned with the visual geometry of urban places. Another way is to simplify the design process. Adopting a naïve, typological approach to design achieves this end. Such an approach has strong advocates, particularly within the architectural profession in the United States, which, unlike landscape architecture, has generally but by no means universally dealt with complexity by narrowing the scope of its concerns rather than broadening its intellectual horizon. Urban design has to be different in theory and practice. It must draw on many of the developments in the field and on the experience of those directly involved in it, as well as on the developments in landscape architectural philosophy during the past twenty years. The objective in this chapter is to present a synthesis of the fundamental attitudes that an architect or landscape architect, or any other design professional, should take regarding urban design if the human-needs–based concept of functionalism described in this book is to have any utility for society. It is an expansionist, integrationist view.

While the issues that have to be considered in urban design are vast, and some reduction in its scope of concern is necessary to bring urban designing within the realm of professional practice, the basic position described here is that there is much more knowledge available to urban designers than they currently use. If they can draw on it, they can at least join as equals with members of other disciplines and professions in the intellectual debate about the future distribution and internal organization of human settlements, and in particular about the nature of

the public and parochial realms within them. They do have, or can have, a special expertise in thinking about the social and built structure of cities and urban places in a four-dimensional manner that other professionals, developers, and politicians do not bring to the table or drawingboard. The question is: "What attitudes should guide their development of prescriptions for the future given our current understanding of human needs and the development and design processes in the United States?" A point of departure is to examine current views on urban design and their utility as synthesizing approaches.

CURRENT STATEMENTS ON URBAN DESIGN

As noted, urban design in the United States is concerned with the design of the public realms of human settlements and the implications of the nature of the private realm for the public—what these realms are and what they can and should be given our understanding of human needs and the need to have a well-functioning biogenic environment. The concern is with the city's infrastructure and the relationships among the elements of the built environment. These relationships are four-dimensional, for they consist of the three-dimensional relationships of built form as they are used, appreciated, and evolve over time. The changes made in the physical fabric of places are in response to the changing needs of individuals and societies and the resolution of conflicts among them.

The basic goal of urban design is to help society create well-functioning environments—ones that meet the needs of people. The specific issues being addressed will vary from place to place, from culture to culture, and from one time to another, but the basic goals will remain the same. What attitudes should urban designers adopt in going about their work? Should they simply serve the socioeconomic status quo or strive for change? Views differ. The answers depend on what is needed to enhance the well-being of society.

During the course of this century there have been two sets of manifestos on urban design. The first set has to do with the nature of the product—the nature of urban and building forms. These manifestos are normative, substantive statements on designs. The second set consists of procedural statements, some universal and some peculiarly American. There is much that is common to all of them. The basic point is that in urban design *the human being as the measure of all things should be renewed as the guiding principle in environmental design* [italics added] (Preiser, Vischer, and White 1991).

In the earlier chapters of this book a distinction was drawn between Rationalist and Empiricist approaches to urban design, and a number of substantive paradigms that coexist today were described: Neo-Modernism, Neo-Traditionalism, Deconstructionism, and Discrete urban design (see Chapters 2 and 3). Implicit in each is a set of attitudes toward people and society.

There are two components to the normative procedural models of design: statements on the attitudes urban designers should hold as the basis for design, and, less clearly, statements of what constitutes a good design process. The concern in this chapter is with the first. These attitudes will then be used as a basis for the discussion of the second component in Chapter 24. Positions on both substantive and procedural matters have been clearly described in a number of manifestos written in the 1970s, 1980s, and into the 1990s as empirical research has advanced our knowledge.

"The Charter of Machu Picchu" (1979) is a Rationalist approach to urban design focusing on the nature of the designed product, the NATO group at the Architectural Association in London also has a clear image of the end product they want, while "A Humanist Design Manifesto" of a number of the educators at the University of California at Berkeley (Appleyard et al. 1982) elaborates an earlier position taken by Roger Montgomery (1975). Christopher Alexander (1991) and his colleagues (Alexander et al. 1977, 1987) have been reconsidering the whole nature of urban design and along with people such as Kevin Lynch (1984), Bernard Huet (1984), and Wolfgang Preiser, Jacqueline Vischer and Edward White (1991) have been rethinking the nature of good cities, urban places, and buildings. They draw heavily on empirical studies. Allan Jacobs and Donald Appleyard (1987), in contrast, describe more specifically the problems both in society and in the built environment that urban designers should address. The concern here is with the fundamental attitudes that urban designers should use as a basis for designing—for carrying out the process. Almost inevitably the reaction to the Athens Charter (*The Town-Planning Chart,* Fourth C.I.A.M. Congress, Athens, 1933; see Sert and C.I.A.M. 1944 and Le Corbusier 1973) is a point of departure in creating a position on urban design today.

The Charter of Machu Picchu

An international group of architects, city planners, and urbanists met in Peru in 1977 under the auspices of the Universidad Nacional Federico Villareal to discuss the role of the design professions in improving the quality of urban life ("Charter of Machu Picchu" 1979). The convening was a response to the perception of the decline in concern and sense of direction about urban design issues among the design professions. The purpose was to update the 1933 Athens Charter.

The authors of the "Charter of Machu Picchu" advocate the effective use of resources and the unity of people, city, and surroundings. The charter decries the segregationist land-use policies of C.I.A.M. and the abuse of technological development in urban design. It advocates greater use of public transportation, and the preservation of cultural values and historical heritage. It also decries the continued architectural view of urban design simply as the ordering of buildings in geometric space. Their normative position is: "In our times the main problem of contemporary architecture is no longer on the visual play of pure volumes, but the creation of spaces in which people can live." The charter adds: "The emphasis is no longer on the container, but the contents, no longer on the isolated building, no matter how sophisticated and beautiful, but on the continuity of urban texture." While many architects profess this position, fewer practice it or are working in sociopolitical environments in which they are able to practice it. They are advocates for their art or for sponsor clients who seldom have public interest concerns.

While the charter advocates a human needs approach to design, its authors show a reluctance to accept the perceptions of needs other than their own as the basis for defining the functions that the built environment should help fulfill, or for developing the social program to be used as a basis for design. The document shows that its signatories were very much aware of the urban issues that were emerging in the late 1970s, but that they seemed removed from the study of cities, urban life, or how the built environment relates to human development (see "Four Commentaries on the Charter" 1979).

The NATO Group at the Architectural Association

During the mid-1980s, the Narrative Architecture Today group (NATO) in England took essentially the same intellectual position as the Rationalists among Modernists. The Modernists' position was that if the city is not working, change everything. The NATO group's position is that if Modernism is not working, change everything. The group recognized that the Modernists' emphasis on order led to sterility, and so they advocated that cities be untidy. More reasonably, they stated that designers should think of cities as a patchwork of events with an interweaving of

Congrès Internationaux d'Architecture Moderne, Declaration of Aims, 1928

On Architecture:... We particularly emphasize the fact that to build is an elementary activity in man, intimately associated with the evolution and development of human life...

It is only out of the present that our architectural works should be derived...

The intention which brings us together is that of attaining a harmony of existing elements— a harmony indispensable to the present— *by putting architecture on its real plane, the economic and sociological plane;* therefore architecture should be freed from the sterile influence of Academies of antiquated formulas...

Animated by this conviction, we affirm our association and our mutual assistance towards the end that our aspirations may be achieved.

To us, another point of view is that of economics in general, since it is one of the material bases of our society...

The conception of modern architecture associates the phenomenon of architecture with that of the general economy...

The most efficacious production is derived from rationalization and standardization. Rationalization and standardization directly affect labor methods, as much in modern architecture (its conception) as in the building industry (its achievement).

Town Planning: Town planning is the organization of the functions of collective life; it applies just as well to rural places as to urban agglomerations.

It cannot be conditioned by the pretensions of an established aestheticism; its essence is of a functional nature.

The functions it embraces are four in number: (i) dwelling, (ii) work, (iii) recreation and (iv) transportation (which connects the first three functions with one another).

The chaotic subdivision of land as a result of real estate speculation should be corrected.

Present technical means, which multiply ceaselessly, are the very key to town planning. They imply and propose a complete change in existing legislation; this change should be commensurate with technical progress...

Figure 23-1: The Basic Tenets of the Athens Charter

diverse functions. In some ways this position parallels that of the Deconstructionists, and the images that the two groups presented of the future city are not all that dissimilar.

While evocative of a line of reasoning and as a challenge to coexisting normative models, there are major limitations to the line of thinking presented by the NATO group. The problem with any substantive urban design paradigm is that the program it assumes is largely implicit in the design and not open to a debate. Such paradigms tend to be based on a simplistic set of ideas for a limited range of people. They tend also to be based on a highly deterministic architectural philosophy of "function follows form" rather than "form follows function."

Current Empiricist Views of the Good City

There are a number of views of what an Empiricist city should be that are based on observations of how people behave and the aspirations they have. Some of these views are clearly represented in specific end products. Leon Krier's plan for Poundbury in England (see Fig. 23-3(2); Broadbent 1990) is one physical representation of it, as are the works of Neo-Traditionalist designers in the United States (see Chapters 2 and 3). In contrast, Kevin Lynch (1984) presents a set of performance criteria for good city form and Christopher Alexander and his colleagues (1977) a series of patterns for cities although no overall image. More recently (1987), recognizing that urban design is an ongoing process and that no city ever reaches an end state, they present a series of tenets for urban growth.

Lynch's five criteria for defining good city form have already been introduced (see Chapter 19). They are that the form of a city should have *vitality* in terms of people's biological needs, provide for a *sense* of orientation in space and time, and have behavior settings that fit people's aspirations, and to which they have *access* and over which they have *control*. These dimensions are to be fulfilled with *efficiency* and *justice*.

The physical representation of the ideal city that emerges from the work of Lynch, of Alexander and his colleagues, and of people such as Jane Jacobs (1961) would have many of the attributes that Krier plans for Poundbury, although it would not be as picturesque. The scale of elements that they advocate is considerably smaller than in the Modern city, while density is achieved through multiplicity of units in relatively low buildings with carefully orchestrated, small open spaces. These images promise much, but their proponents did not think of them as always appropriate to the meeting of human needs nor for dealing with conflicts between opposing sets of needs. They can best be regarded as exemplars of how human needs can be met in specific circumstances rather than as universal images. The series of manifestos that have come out of the School of Environmental Design at the University of California at Berkeley is more provocative in terms of suggesting the attitudes designers should take in dealing with the present American city and processes of

A New Theory of Urban Design of Christopher Alexander, Hajo Neis, Artemis Anninou, and Ingrid King

Seven Detailed Rules of Growth:

1. Piecemeal growth: To "guarantee a mixed flow of small, medium, and large projects"— preferably in equal quantities by cost

2. The growth of larger wholes: "Every building increment must help form at least one larger whole . . ."

3. Visions: "Every project must first be experienced, and then expressed, as a vision which can be seen in the inner eye (literally)

4. Positive urban space: "Every building must create coherent and well -shaped public space next to it"

5. Layout of large buildings: "The entrance... main circulation, main division...into parts...interior spaces...daylight, and...movement within the building, are all coherent and consistent with the position of the building in the street and the neighborhood

6. Construction: "The structure of every building must generate smaller wholes in the physical fabric...in its structural bays, columns, windows, building base, etc...in its entire physical construction and appearance"

7. Formation of centers: "Every whole must be a center in itself, and must also produce a system of centers around it"

Figure 23-2: Christopher Alexander and His Colleagues' Theory of Urban Design

urban and suburban development as a point of departure for urban design. Much of the discussion in this book has been based on these manifestos.

The Berkeley Manifestos

The manifestos developed at the University of California at Berkeley during the 1970s and 1980s focus more on the attitudes that urban designers should adopt than on the products of urban design. In 1975, Roger Montgomery, noted: "In urban design today, we face a crisis of legitimacy that mirrors the multilayered crises that cripples our larger society." In his strongly worded "Manifesto on Urban Design," Montgomery (1975) decries the often lifeless urban designs, based on naïve politics, prepared in the service of power elites. He argues for the urban design to become urban designing, "object giving way to process, artifact to activity." He argues for an active participation of those to be affected by a design in its creation. Urban designers have to be concerned with city building, not only city buildings.

In a similar vein during the early 1980s, a number of faculty members at the University of California assembled "A Humanist Design Manifesto" (Appleyard et al. 1982). Implicit in it is a response to the C.I.A.M. position (Sert and C.I.A.M. 1944) but it was more directly related to the contemporary design scene. In it the faculty (Donald Appleyard, Peter Bosselmann, Galen Cranz, Kim Dovey, Russell Ellis, Susan Goltsman, Randy Hester, Dan Iacofano, Eva Lieberman, Roslyn Lindheim, Richard Lloyd, Clare Cooper, Thomas Priestley, and Fried Whitman) decried the move in architecture toward "looked-at" buildings and places as objects rather than as "lived-in" environments. They suggested a series of actions for designers that they believe are essential for creating a more humanistic design: *Fight for Environmental Justice, Empower People, Use What We Know, Enhance Community, Break Down Bigness, Free Pedestrians, Extend the Design Process, Tell the Truth, Learn to Listen, Abolish Aesthetic Monopolies.* "The designer's prize is the user's prison."

Later in the 1980s Allan Jacobs and Donald Appleyard (1987) took this statement a step further. They identified a set of problems that urban designers should be addressing: poor living conditions, the giantism of projects and the loss of control by people of their own environments, the large-scale privatization of public places and the loss of public life, the centrifugal fragmentation of cities, the destruction of valued places, the placelessness or lack of identity of places, the unjust distribution of environmental quality, and the nature of design professionalism. These may or may not be the issues of concern in a particular place. The position advocated here is that the problems to be addressed have to come out of the situation being considered. The advocacy ultimately presented in this chapter is for the primacy of the process of designing over any preconceived idea of the problems to be addressed or solutions needed. The paradox is that without some image of what they are, the design process cannot proceed (Na Nangara in progress).

Jacobs and Appleyard also identify the goals of urban life: the city should be a place where people can live comfortably, and have identity and control, access to opportunity, and imagination and joy. Cities should provide for community and public life, be energy self-sustaining, and provide accessibility for all. They maintain that all good cities should have these qualities. The position to be described here is similar: *cities should provide for human needs* while sustaining the biogenic environment. The hierarchical concept of functionalism based on Abraham Maslow's work provides a framework for thinking and asking questions about the evolution and manifestation of human motivations over time. For instance: "Does the demise of public space really signify the demise of public life, or is it simply taking on another form as communications technology changes?" (Brill 1989). The position taken here is that the Jacobs and Appleyard manifesto on urban design should be regarded as a statement of issues to be confronted now; their form will evolve over time. They should not be regarded as static statements of what should be urban designers' concerns in the United States.

Urban Design Issues in the United States Today

What are an urban designer's responsibilities? This will vary by designer and situation. *Urban design should be seen as a service to society,* and *urban designers must take on the responsibility for the social consequences of their designs.* Urban designers need to understand their own value positions, to be articulate about them, and to understand the positions of others. They need to be active participants in debates about the future of cities. They need to base the arguments on knowledge, not belief (B. Jones 1962). At the same time urban designers will face a number of recurrent substantive and procedural issues (as outlined in Chapters 19 and 22) that are highly emotionally charged and based on images of the rights of individuals and groups, the distribution of resources and power in society, and, more generally, about what a good life is.

In almost any situation, an urban designer will be taking stances on the issues already raised in this book. For instance, designs will reflect positions on such issues as the degree of integration or segregation of activities, populations, land and building uses that are desirable, and on the current roles that individuals and groups play in society. Should society be egalitarian or socially hierarchical? What is the appropriate size of institutions? Should all environments be barrier-free? Should one be designing for comfort or for development? How far should an urban designer go in being concerned with safety needs when they start to impinge on the livability of the environment? Whose meanings should elements of the built environment possess? To whom should meanings be directed? These issues are broadly debated in society, but the stances taken on each will affect an urban designer's work.

All people should be able to participate in the mainstream of life to the extent they wish unhindered by social or physical barriers. While the most basic needs should be met first, the goal of urban design is to enhance behavioral opportunities and enrich life through the provision of environ-

mental cues that support individual and group identity without being detrimental to the needs of others. This position is, however, a very general humanist one. The details depend on the specific circumstances. Specific urban designs should stem from a knowledge-based user-oriented process of designing. Designers must be capable of designing environments for and in terms of other people's needs and values even though the qualities of such environments fall outside the designer's own taste culture. This demand is perhaps the most difficult for designers to accept, however rational they perceive the argument for it to be.

ATTITUDES FOR URBAN DESIGNERS

While there are many generic solutions and design standards that can be applied to specific design problems, no single substantive model for the future city or how it should perform is universally applicable. We must now look toward shaping the processes that shape cities. The process will be governed by a set of attitudes. The prime one will be about how to deal with the future, but the positions taken inevitably stem from perceptions of the nature of human beings and of society.

Attitudes Toward the Future

Urban design deals with change. It responds to changes and creates changes in human habitats. It deals with creating a future. On what intellectual foundation should future visions be based? The fundamental differences between Rationalism and Empiricism in urban design has been (in practice if not in basic philosophical stances) toward how and what designers should think about the future. Many aspects of urban life and form are changing. Urban designers should not moralize about ways of life unless a lifestyle is doing social harm or inhibiting the lives of other people. Yet we should also avoid assuming that present patterns, empirically observed, will persist into the future, although many patterns are indeed enduring. Thoughts about the future nevertheless need to be based on who we are now.

Accepting this view means that the positions urban designers should take are:

1. *That the fundamental role of urban designers is to bring society's attention to the possible future nature of the public realm, its relationship to the private realm, and the possibilities that might be achieved.*
2. *That future visions of the city need to take who we are now, as individuals and as a society, as a point of departure.*
3. *That while many aspects of the American social system are self-consciously designed (e.g., civil rights), future social systems used as a basis for urban design will develop largely unselfconsciously in an evolutionary process.*

4. *That in most situations facing the urban designer, the design of social systems is outside the scope of the designer's professional concern.*
5. *Urban designers need to fully understand and be able to articulate the social and psychological consequences of their proposals and how they support or hinder the achievement of specific activity patterns and fulfill specific aesthetic objectives.* Not all consequences will be predicted accurately, but being wrong is not a privilege that urban designers, any more than any other designers, have (Bazjanac 1974; Rittel 1984; Rittel and Webber 1984).

Paradoxically the urban designer should *fight for social justice* even though any move toward autocratic centralized power tends to enhance the ability of urban designers to implement proposed schemes (see also "Attitudes Toward the Societal Culture" below). This statement may imply that radical social changes are necessary in the United States, and consequently radical urban designs, but such radical social changes seldom have major implications for urban design. The same urban forms serve many but certainly not all social systems. Changes in communications technologies have had a major effect on urban form, but the technologies that are likely to affect urban design during the next fifty years are most likely already here. They need to be understood. Dealing with the biogenic environment may have more radical consequences for urban design. The empirical knowledge is not yet available, however, to draw that conclusion.

The Urban Designer as a Visionary

Visionaries are concerned with what might be. They look ahead to possible social and physical worlds. Utopian thinking does have a role in urban design (Reiner 1963; Fishman 1982, 1987). Many of the urban design ideas that we regard as commonplace now were once regarded as revolutionary. Empirical research itself will not lead to major new images of what the future might be like. Such images are created.

There are many injustices in American society, especially for the poor and even more particularly for racial minorities, and thus many opportunity costs in the way things are. New social organizations are possible, other forms of behavior settings than those presently existing could, for instance, provide children everywhere, but particularly those trapped by poverty, with opportunities for active rather than passive participation in life. Some new aesthetic ideologies will be adopted. What such models really afford people needs to be understood before they are accepted. In looking ahead, it is also wise to remember the Aristotelian position (Jones and Sparrow 1980; Peattie 1981a). It is well expressed by Patrick Geddes: "Civics as an art has to do not with imagining an impos-

sible no-place where all is well, but making the most and the best of each and every place, especially of the city in which we live" (quoted in Boardman 1978). That is certainly the role of the practitioner.

The Urban Designer As a Practitioner

The practitioner, it has already been noted, is involved in the day-to-day political world of elected officials, civil servants, pressure groups, professional aesthetic ideologies, and deadlines. Much as been accomplished in urban design since World War II. New towns and suburbs have been built and urban renewal projects have gone ahead in almost every country of the world (see Chapters 2 and 3). It is not hard to be critical of urban designs because misfits are much easier to identify than what works well.

Practitioners learn much from their own experience. The most thoughtful also learn from the accumulated experience of the field. They are aggressive observers of the urban scene, and they "learn to listen" and listen to learn. They must be concerned with the public interest and with looking ahead. These strictures are not easy to follow. They require the leaders of the field to have high motivation, dedication, and energy. Those leaders also need to contribute to the cumulative knowledge of the field through their own experiences. They have to disseminate the results of their work (Proshansky 1974). With some exceptions (e.g., Barnett 1974, 1982, 1986, 1987; Duany 1989) practitioners have a poor track record for doing more than describing what they have done. Even though many have been fine educators in academic institutions their basic ideas are not disseminated beyond the bounds of their students. They operate in the real world of severe time constraints. They have little time or energy for regarding their work as research, but they need to do so.

Attitudes Toward People

The prime concern in urban design must be for the dignity of people. Much of the argument about urban design in recent years has been for a greater concern with the wider range of needs of a broader range of people than considered in the past. The concern has arisen because of changing perceptions of people and their rights in society, and a consideration of what these rights might and should be in the future. The arguments are becoming well developed, for instance, for a greater concern for the needs of a wide array of minority cultural groups. As a result or perhaps coincidentally, much environmental psychological research has focused on such groups and their needs. For instance, there has been research on the social and family organizational needs arising from the existing and changing roles and aspirations of men and women in society (Popenoe 1977; Wekerle, Peterson, and Morley 1980; Saegert 1981; Hayden 1984; Wekerle 1984;

R. Peterson 1987; Mozingo 1989; E. Wilson 1991). Similar discussions are concerned with the image and role of children (Ariès 1962; Bronfenbrenner 1970; Pollowy 1977; Hart 1978, 1979; G. Moore et al. 1979; Chawla 1991), the elderly in health (Lawton 1975) and illness (Lawton 1977; Calkins 1988), and the handicapped (Bednar 1977; Welner 1990). The needs and manifestations of needs of various groups of people such as those mentioned have to be seen within cultural contexts (Leighton 1959; Rapoport 1969, 1977, 1984; Brolin 1976; Low and Chambers 1989).

These design concerns have been clearly expressed at the level of housing (e.g., Cooper and Sarkissian 1986 and Lang 1989a), the design of open spaces (e.g., Francis 1987b), plazas (e.g., Gehl 1987), and neighborhoods (Hester 1975). The impact on the mainstream of the architectural profession has been negligible (see e.g., Gosling and Maitland 1984a, 1984b and Broadbent 1990). There are those who believe that changing the entrenched thinking of architects about the design process is impossible (Montgomery 1966, 1989; Francescato 1989)—that designs will only change when architects have new pattern types on which to base them. Indeed, the position being taken is that empirical research must be aimed at generating new generic types for architects to copy. Although generic types are important, urban designers must take a broader view of the nature of people and their needs than in the past (see also Preiser et al. 1991), and must understand how generic types function and what needs they do and do not satisfy.

It must also be recognized that few laypeople are articulate about design possibilities or their own needs, and that almost inevitably the urban designer is dealing with the competing needs and goals of different people. As a result the positions that are increasingly being taken by urban designers are:

1. *That the design of the problem to be addressed (i.e., the programming process) must take the diversity of people into account.*
2. *That the urban design process has to be conducted with people as well as for them.*

These two positions almost inevitably mean:

1. *That the goal in urban design is to strive for ambiguity in built form.*
2. *That designs must be open-ended.*
3. *That the requirements of populations with the more basic needs should be met first.* Care should be taken with objectifying this concern, for often the best results are achieved through indirect action by taking care of the needs of others and allowing the multiplier effect to work rather than addressing the issue directly.
4. *That new environments must be designed to be barrier-free—socially and physically; existing environments should be retooled to be so.*

Roger Montgomery (1975) states the overall position: "Urban designers must always ask in whose interests they act, always being careful to seek not only the manifest interests that lie on the surface of things, but also the latent interests hidden behind the façade of the everyday world."

Attitudes Toward the Societal Culture

In a sense all human habitats are a reflection of the cultures that produced them. A criticism of the built environment is a criticism of the broader *societal culture* in which it exists and the intellectual and administrative framework of the processes for shaping the built environment. As such it is also a criticism of the *professional culture.*

In many countries there is a considerable disparity between the quality of life and the control over their own lives of the wealthy and the poor, the politically powerful and the politically impotent. Although the Rationalists argued for major social changes, urban designers have almost inevitably supported the powerful in society and their needs as well as the status quo in terms of the nature of a culture. They have gone along with the roles of various groups in society as they are at present. Urban designers have been advocates for the people who sponsor them (R. Goodman 1971). At the same time, the design ideologies that have shaped parts of the city during this century have served a dual purpose. They have supported the efforts of their sponsors but also the efforts to create cultural change. Modernism was certainly based on different models of culture than those that existed in the United States and Europe at the beginning of the twentieth century.

What views should an urban designer espouse today? Jaquelin Robertson, an architect and urban designer, takes the following position:

1) generally build within and not against a cultural and national context, unless there is a profound reason otherwise
2) reinforce the found order
3) articulate and enhance social ceremony
4) use implied architectural conventions

These positions need to be sharpened. They apply largely to dealing with societies and nations other than one's own. They remove the architect from dealing with major social issues. A basic question does arise: "How does one recognize a *profound* reason to take issue with the current order?" Another question is: "Where does one take a stand on the goals of a society versus the goals of an individual?"

In the United States, where the Constitution calls for equal opportunity for all people, the present cultural system has great inequalities in the distribution of opportunities and resources. In designing for the future, does the urban designer make decisions based on the normative model of the United States or on the present reality? Similar questions can be asked about any society, and the nature of the roles and aspirations of people within it. In the United States today, there may well be greater opportunities for all people than in many other societies, but there is a major, possibly growing, schism between the opportunities for the rich and the poor. Should urban designers simply wash their hands of such concerns on the grounds that they fall outside their domain of responsibility?

In taking a position on social issues, urban designers must recognize the limited role of the built environment in shaping human behavior (see Chapter 1). One must also recognize that while cultures evolve largely unselfconsciously, they can be pushed in specific directions, as the civil rights campaign showed and as advertisers recognize today. The hope is that such a cultural evolution will result in a society with greater justice and greater opportunities for all people to pursue their own ends provided they do not harm others. The position taken here is that urban designers should:

1. *Recognize the essential, political nature of urban design.*
2. *Recognize that their work takes place within existing social structures, but they are obligated to:*
   a. *Argue for social justice for people regardless of gender, age, and cultural origin requirements.*
   b. *Design physical layouts that do not inhibit social change unless such changes are antisocial ones.*
3. *Always regard themselves as defenders of the public interest.*

Urban designers need to recognize the limitations of present definitions of the public interest and that the various pressure groups define it in different ways. Nevertheless, they need to consider posterity's potential needs when they are designing. They have to be able to deal with such ambiguities.

Attitudes Toward Nature

In much of the world, and the United States in particular, the landscape and built environment reflect the Judeo-Christian (and Islamic) attitude that people have dominance over nature. Some Eastern philosophies, on the other hand, see people as part of nature, although there is scant exhibition of this attitude in recent professional practice or in the unselfconscious development of Asian cities. Indeed, one might often think that the philosophical positions were reversed.

Many countries contain people with very different attitudes toward the natural world that reflect the many subcultures. Some regard trees an essential component of the environment; others regard them as a nuisance. Those designers of the Anglo-American tradition have traditionally favored the English landscape garden approach to the design of parks; those out of the Continental tradition, the baroque. Anglo-Americans have shown a primary concern for appearance in landscapes with a secondary concern for their amenity for activities. Americans have historically, however, been more directly exploitive in terms of using the landscape for financial profit. This attitude has changed considerably in recent years.

Spurred on by Ian McHarg's ecological view of nature touched with the paintbrush of the English landscape garden tradition in *Design with Nature* (1969), there have been a number of explorations of the role of the natural environment in the human habitat. These explorations include Randolph Hester's environmental or conservation aesthetic (1975, 1989), Michael Hough's search for a design theory based on evolutionary change (1990a, 1990b), and Anne Spirn's search for a new urban aesthetic based on the natural processes of urban areas (1984, 1989).

The point of departure for the position described here is that urban life is here to stay for the foreseeable future. Cities have a major utility for people, and urban and suburban life is enjoyed and sought after by many. Given these observations, the positions for urban designers to take in the future are:

1. *Urban areas have to be designed with the consequences for the natural environment in mind. This means that the amenity level that wealthy people can afford in their inner city or suburban lives must be extended to others, and unremediable distortion of the natural processes of the biogenic environment must be avoided.*
2. *Energy resources should be conserved—urban design should be designed with climate and efficiency of circulation in mind.*
3. *Urban open areas must be perceived as mechanisms to deal with environmental pollutants as well as providing for the recreational and aesthetic functions required by people within cities, towns, and suburbs.*
4. *Special attention must be paid by societies to the redevelopment of existing built-up areas rather than extending cities into the unbuilt-on environment and virgin land.*
5. *Exposure to the natural elements of the environment is important because it gives people a sense of time and place, and thus this exposure must be enhanced.*
6. *The quality of life of the fauna that enhance the quality of human lives must itself be enhanced.*

Designing with nature in mind raises issues more complex than may be seen at first glance. Migrating birds, resident songbirds, and animals such as squirrels give pleasure to many people and spark the curiosity of children. Cities can be designed with them in mind. There are other species that may be important in enhancing the quality of the natural world but have little direct impact on people; nevertheless, they are and should be considered part of the natural cycle of life. There are yet other species in cities, such as rats, that serve no apparent part in enhancing human lives. Pigeons are in a more ambiguous position. In some ways they are pests but in others they are a feature of urban landscapes. Measures should be taken to eliminate pests unless the side effects of such measures have a detrimental effect on human lives or the species that do enhance human lives. In this last case people will have to tolerate pests in their own interest!

Attitudes Toward the Built Environment

Designers' attitudes toward the built environment are closely associated with their attitudes toward people and nature. Maslow's model of the hierarchy of human motivations and an understanding of the affordances of existing and potential patterns of the built environment provide an intellectual framework for considering the range of purposes that the built environment has to possess in order to serve human beings.

Implicit in this book are a number of positions on the built environment and design:

1. *Urban design must be concerned with the processes of environmental change—design must be open-ended.*
2. *Bold unidimensional design may be important in some situations, but by and large the built environment has to serve a multiplicity of purposes simultaneously.*
3. *The goal of urban design, as already noted for other reasons, is to strive for ambiguity in form.* Ambiguity means that the forms that are chosen/or designed serve many purposes and can be used and interpreted in many ways by different people. It does not mean that forms have no meaning or are vague in meaning. In general, but not inevitably, this position is likely to lead to less bold forms. They will have less "architectural content." These statements lead to two conclusions:
4. *The general aesthetic goal of urban design should be to be discrete.* Departures from this attitude should only be for very specific purposes. Cities should largely be seen as backdrops and settings for life. While panoramic views are exciting, environments should be designed to be participatory ones, not simply panoramas to be seen in aerial views.
5. *Communal (i.e., public and quasi-public) buildings should be the foreground buildings in the city.* Built environments in which the buildings are undifferentiated—where everything is a background building—are dull. Nowadays, some of the most visually exciting buildings in the United States are indeed private office buildings. They have become the foreground buildings while public buildings are regarded as the background infrastructure necessary to sustain individual actions. This phenomenon very much reflects American life and values—where individual rights are more important than communal ones. Perhaps the time

has come to reflect on the character of both American society and life because problems arise when there is a lack of decorum in the environment—when everything strives to catch the eye. The general urban design principle, however, should be to create discrete urban environments where the hand of the urban designer is largely unseen.

Attitudes Toward Technology

One of the fundamental differences between Rationalists and Empiricists in Modern architecture and urban design was in their attitude toward harnessing technology. The Rationalists dreamed of possible technologies, the Empiricists tended to accept current levels of technological development as the basis for design. In our contemporary architectural theories there are also different positions toward technological development. Some architects stick to ways in which they are used to designing rather than considering new technological developments; some use what appears to be advanced technology but their buildings are really simply symbols of advanced technology rather than technologically innovative; and some strive to build using technologically advanced materials and structural systems.

It is also clear that recent advances in the transportation of goods, people, and utilities are merely marginal developments of the systems introduced to cities in the first part of this century. There has, however, been considerable speculation on the changes in urban life and form likely to be brought about by new communications mechanisms. We live in what is regarded as an age dominated by technology, but urban designers should be careful of taking the position that because some action is technologically feasible it is clever to do it. In societies where technological novelty is regarded as a good thing, however, such an end is culturally appropriate provided people are not hurt by it!

The basic positions being taken by many urban designers today are:

1. *Technology is a means to an end.*
2. *New technologies should be embraced provided their potential side effects are understood.*
3. *Efficiency in means of construction is a worthwhile goal* provided that *the utilitarian and symbolic significance of something inefficient is not high (e.g., it may be worthwhile giving up some efficiency in construction in order to use techniques that provide a sense of worth to the builders).*

It is impossible to predict the full impact of emerging building or communications technologies on potential urban designs, but we do need to ascertain precisely what their advantages and repercussions are before embracing them simply to appear to be modern. However, we often have to make decisions under uncertainty.

Attitudes Toward the Design Process

Few if any designers deny the utility of intuitive or even purely emotional thinking as a creative force. Many, however, wish to believe that intuition and subconscious processes are sufficient and indeed that there is no alternative. The arguments described in this book are clearly opposed to that position, which seems to be associated with the "gifted gentleman" view of the architect (see Saint 1983). Among design professionals, urban designers at least have to be able to structure the overall design process so that what they are doing is clear to other professionals and the lay public. The processes that they are using for designing programs and briefs, for designing built forms, for evaluating the design options, and for making proposals must be open for examination. The position taken here is that *a glass box approach to design has to be used.*

Thus designers *need to be able to design the process of design,* and *to be open and articulate to laypeople about the process and the methods they are using.* This position can only be operationalized if urban designers are aware of the substantial body of positive procedural theory that has been developed over the last three decades. It also assumes positions on the overall structure of the decision-making process, the professional-client relationship, and on the programming, design, and evaluation methods that urban designers should use.

The Overall Structure of the Design Process

The design process is an argumentative one that begins with the perception of a problem, iterates through many steps (see Chapter 21), and ends with postoccupancy evaluation. The process of design for the overall human habitat consists of an endless loop of many design processes that involve different people and that occur simultaneously, overlapping each other. Both of these assertions are positive statements. The normative position outlined here is:

1. *Urban designing should be regarded as a problem solving process.*

2. *Typological approaches should be regarded as techniques for elucidating problems and considering potential solutions and no more than that.*

3. *Problem identification is the most important step in the overall process.*

4. *The design of potential solutions should be regarded as part of the process of problem definition.*

5. *The overall process is one of conjecture and testing of problem definitions and potential solutions.*

Implicit in these positions is an argument for a programmatic rather than a paradigmatic approach to design, but this very statement has an internal contradiction. A programmatic approach is a procedural paradigm!

Program versus Paradigm

The debate between proponents of programmatic and paradigmatic approaches to design has already been mentioned. Programs are statements of what ought to be done prior to actually designing a product, while paradigms can be regarded as types, patterns, or exemplars of solutions and designs. Both have biases.

Colin Rowe (1983) notes that all programs are biased. Indeed all analyses are biased by the set of questions one asks. Programs are themselves designed. They are partial solutions to problems. Inherent in any paradigm, or generic type, is a set of problems it can solve (or opportunities it can exploit). All design actually involves both ways of working—there has to be some program as a point of departure and designers' heads are full of potentially applicable paradigms (Colquhoun 1967; P. Rowe 1987; see also Gutman 1988 and Cuff 1991). In every paradigm there is an implicit program that needs to be recognized before an application of the paradigm is seriously considered (Lang 1988). The position taken here is that *good programming is fundamental to designing well.* Design failures are failures to understand the issues at hand. All design processes are, however, argumentative ones and operate under uncertainty.

The Professional-Client Relationship

During this century there have been examples of urban design where the paying client and designer are the same—the developer as designer of total urban designs probably comes the closest (see Chapter 20). Usually there is a multiplicity of clients (see Chapter 21). Today, urban design is seldom done for a patron of the arts but usually for committees, and often the urban designer has little contact with the ultimate users of the project (Zeisel 1974). Increasingly, the position being taken openly is one that many architects have long claimed to be theirs:

1. *That the relationships among sponsor, user, and urban designers should be a collaborative one.*

2. *That the urban designer should be an advocate not only for the represented interest groups but also for the unrepresented.*

3. *That the urban designer should argue for the public interest in all designs or, if unclear about the position that should be taken, should make sure that a clear statement of the public interest is used as a basis of the programming process.*

Methods and Techniques

The techniques and methods for carrying out analyses, syntheses, predictions, and evaluations vary among designers. The major difference is between those designers who advocate qualitative intuitive approaches and those who argue for more open systemic and systematic if not quantitative approaches.

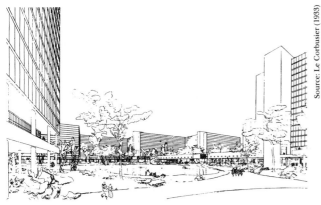

1. The Modernist City: Proposal for Antwerp (1933)

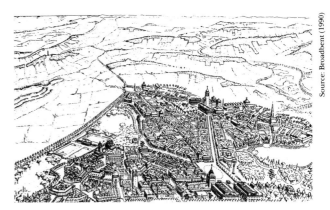

2. The Neo-Traditional City: Poundbury, Dorchester, England (1989)

3. The Discrete City: Mission Bay, San Francisco (1989)

Figure 23-3: Urban Design Paradigms
The basic paradigm guiding urban design is the laissez-faire city with the public realm being a byproduct of private actions. The Rationalist city, however, remains a powerful image for designers (1). The commentary on the noncity with its far-flung individuals needing little face-to-face contact has produced no clear image as yet. In contrast, there is the neo-traditional city (2). The coexisting image that of the discrete city (3). The argument in this book is for designs to be dependent on the problems requiring resolution rather than on a pre-ordained image.

The basic position being articulated today is that: (1) *a rigorous, glass box technique is preferred, provided it deals with the problems at hand,* and (2) *quantification is neither to be feared nor glorified.* The effort to quantify values of variables and relationships makes the designer look at the world more sharply. It builds an understanding of the entities and their attributes being considered in the design process. As a fetish should not be made of intuition, neither should it be made of quantification. The limits of our ability to quantify variables should be understood. Thus, (3) *tangible and intangible variables need to be dealt with simultaneously and with concern appropriate to their importance during the overall design process.*

SYNTHESIS: THE INTEGRATION OF INTELLECTUAL TRADITIONS

The design of cities is clearly a function of many decision makers working in their own self-interest. Urban designers are among them. There is, however, no such profession. People who call themselves urban designers are drawn from the traditional design professions of architecture, landscape architecture, and city planning, and also from nondesign fields. Some may have special education in urban design but many will not. Each looks at the city through the glasses of the professional concerns about which he or she is educated, either formally or through personal experience. The prescription described in Chapter 6 of this book is that a holistic approach to urban design must be developed (see also Preiser et al. 1991). Understanding the multifunctionality of the elements of the built environment in terms of the human needs it serves leads to a number of conclusions.

1. *Present approaches to urban design need to be integrated.* The two streams of thinking about the purposes of urban design—as art and as environmental design—need to be brought together. It has also been argued that the strengths of the Rationalist approach to urban design need to be subsumed under a broad Empiricist approach. The labels "Neo-Functionalist" and "Neo-Modernist" are appropriate for such a view because they suggest that the goal of any design is to be functional. The normative position here might also be called a *behavior deterministic theory* because it assumes that the nature of human experience in its fullest sense is the basis for establishing the functions to be served by the public realm of cities or other human habitats.

There is also a need to integrate problem solving with typological approaches to design. Program and paradigm need to work hand in hand. Paradigms bring attention to aspects of a problem situation; they can also mislead one, but there is no need to reinvent the wheel every time a designer looks at a blank sheet of paper. Existing "solutions" should, however, be looked at with extreme caution.

2. *The layout of the environment needs to be designed with its multifunctionality in mind.* The built environment serves many purposes—it is clearly multifunctional. While so-called unifocal urban designs may be more powerful and of simpler geometries, they should be restricted to situations that really call for them. Most built environments have to serve many purposes and users. The goal is to create urban patterns that are ambiguous—they afford many uses and meanings. Places so designed will survive. Many places also need to be flexible— they can be changed to other uses on a temporary basis. The city as a whole has to be a functioning whole adaptable to "permanent" changes.

One of the more general goals of urban design is to provide settings that can evolve over time. In one sense this attribute is a characteristic of all places. Any place can be demolished and a new one built. The argument for an environment in which the elements are of a small scale is that individual elements can be removed or changed on a piecemeal basis without damaging the whole (Alexander et al. 1975, 1977; see also Preiser et al. 1991). In people's minds the whole thus remains similar. A place that provides for memories as well as other contemporary functions serves many purposes (Rossi 1982).

3. *Urban design needs an integrated theoretical base.* New knowledge is being developed all the time. We have to have the capacity to incorporate it into our information base for designing. It is being developed by researchers in all the design fields as well as environmental psychologists and by scholars in the traditional fields of the social and physical sciences. The model of the structure of design theory presented in Fig. 6–2 provides an overall framework for identifying our concerns but it is a tentative one. Without such a model, however, it is difficult if not impossible to integrate the research being done into a form that has practical utility.

The Role of the Urban Designer

Implicit in all the commentary in this chapter is an image of the role for the urban designer or, more likely, a team of urban designers. In the late 1960s Horst Rittel (Bazjanac 1974) stated that there was a symmetry of lack of knowledge between users and professionals. This is a useful point of departure for thinking about the role of the urban designer in society, but it is not the position taken here. As a positive statement describing the state of the design profession at the time he wrote, Rittel's observation may well have been accurate. It certainly no longer has to be that way.

One of the statements in the 1982 (Appleyard et al.) Berkeley manifesto was *"Use what we know."* During the past thirty years our substantive and procedural knowledge has increased substantially. There has been a major increase in our understanding of how people use and enjoy the environment, methods of finding out in particular situations what is important to people, and the conceptual models for considering the nature of functionalism. Much of this knowledge is scattered in research reports, journal articles, and in many books, but efforts have been made to synthesize it into a form understandable to architects and landscape architects (e.g., Saarinen 1976; Alexander et al. 1977; Porteous 1977; Rapoport 1977; Spirn 1984; Cooper Marcus and Sarkissian 1986; and Lang 1987a). There is much that we do know, and we need to use it.

Designers can be experts on many matters, not because of their superior intuition and experience, but because of their knowledge. We can show leadership in thinking about the future layout of cities and places. We can bring attention to what might be, as well as how to achieve it. We also need to recognize the limitations of knowledge and to *tell the truth.* In so doing there are many roles for design professionals in urban design (see Chapter 25).

The Limitations of Urban Design

Although the quality of the layout of the environment is a major contributor to the quality of life afforded in human settlements, there are limitations to what can be achieved by changing it. City planners discovered this reality forty years ago and social scientists have constantly reinforced this observation (e.g., Gans 1968 and Michelson 1976). There are also limitations to what can be achieved by the type of cooperative work that urban design entails.

Cities are structured for many purposes. The built environment serves many purposes and is a catalyst for many others. In thinking about the layout of the environment and the quality of life, the overall role of the former has to be seen in perspective. The layout of the environment shapes the more basic functional needs of human beings rather than the higher-order ones. In addition, all kinds of affordances are provided by almost any pattern of the environment, as the changing use of the same patterns over time attests.

The danger of making any statement promoting urban design, as this book has done, is that urban design work becomes seen as the panacea for all the ills of the city (or rural) habitat in much the way that the Modernists believed. It is a position deeply embedded in architectural thinking and much lay thinking but cannot be justified. Le Corbusier's slogan "Architecture or Revolution" needs to be uttered with great caution. Yet the role of the built environment in people's lives should not be underestimated.

There is much that we understand. There is also much that we do not understand. However much we understand there are limits to the human ability to deal with it (Harris 1967). At the same time, empirical evidence can be used extensively to improve the quality of design, but we need to differentiate between what is based on evidence and what is conjecture. All designing is, in essence, the creation of hypotheses about what will work in the future and the important dimensions on which "working" is based.

Urban designers will always have to make predictions about how designs will work and judgments on what should be done. The knowledge base used by an urban designer is not value free; decisions cannot be. *"Urban designers must turn their attention to ways in which values are constructed and the special role of the designers themselves in this social process"* [italics added] (Montgomery 1975). They need to know how values shape all work.

CONCLUSION: A POSITION ON PROCESS AND ON PRODUCT

It was noted in Chapter 22 that urban designers may design the process of design and carry it out only to find the product is unsatisfactory in their eyes. This places the designer in a dilemma, particularly when facing a review board or jury that has little understanding of the issues being considered. It is particularly a problem for the architect or urban designer who has been socialized to believe that certain patterns of the environment are inherently good either because they follow a certain rule or because there is a precedent for them that is held in high esteem by the profession.

The attitude to take is neither to dismiss the feelings about the designed product out of hand simply because the process was a good one nor to decry the design process. Intuitions are powerful instruments; they can also be highly misleading. The need is to examine the proposed product to ascertain what is wrong with it, and to examine the process to see why it has led to the design that was generated. If the process is still deemed to be a good one then the product should be accepted.

A process of designing based on a sound theoretical knowledge of the nature of the environment, the nature of the client group, and the relationship between built form and people and using a collaborative design process is the basis for urban designing for the future. Past solutions *may* have been well and good when they were built and may still function

well today, but the urban designers have to trust the process of design they use, provided it too is based on a sound theoretical knowledge of design procedures. The information is there (Koberg and Bagnall 1977; Cutler and Cutler 1982; Bechtel, Marans, and Michelson 1987; Preiser, Rabinowitz, and White 1988; King et al. 1989; Sanoff 1989, 1991; Lawson 1990). It may still be fragmentary. It is nevertheless there to be used.

There may be a tendency, whether purposeful or not, for urban designers to shape the design process so that the physical outcome is what the designer likes and defends based on the veracity of the process. *The basic requirement of all professionals in all fields is to be honest not only to other people but to themselves.*

MAJOR REFERENCES

"Charter of Machu Picchu, The" (1979). *Journal of Architectural Research* 7, no. 2:5–9.

Hayden, Dolores (1984). *Redesigning the American Dream: The Future of Housing, Work, and Family Life.* New York: Norton.

Huet, Bernard (1984). "The City as Dwelling Space: Alternatives to the Charter of Athens." *Lotus International* 41:6–16.

Jacobs, Allan, and Donald Appleyard (1987). "Toward an Urban Design Manifesto." *American Planning Association Journal* 53, no. 1:113–120.

Lang, Jon (1985). "Problems, Paradigms, Architecture, City Planning and Urban Design." *Journal of Planning Education and Research* 3, no. 2:26–27.

——— (1988). "Understanding Normative Theories of Architecture." *Environment and Behavior* 20, no. 5:601–632.

Le Corbusier (1973). *The Athens Charter.* Translated from the French by Anthony Eardley. New York: Grossman.

Lynch, Kevin (1984). *Good City Form.* Cambridge, MA: MIT Press.

Preiser, Wolfgang, Jacqueline C. Vischer, and Edward T. White, eds. (1991). *Design Intervention: Toward a More Humane Environment.* New York: Van Nostrand Reinhold.

Rowe, Colin (1983). "Program versus Paradigm." *Cornell Journal of Architecture* 2:8–19.

Scott Brown, Denise (1982). "Between Three Stools: A Personal View of Urban Design and Pedagogy." In Ann Ferebee, ed., *Education for Urban Design.* Purchase, NY: Institute for Urban Design, pp. 132–172.

Sert, José Luis, and C.I.A.M. (1944). *Can Our Cities Survive? An ABC of Urban Problems, Their Analysis, Their Solutions.* Cambridge, MA: Harvard University Press.

Venturi, Robert (1966). *Complexity and Contradiction in Architecture.* New York: Museum of Modern Art.

24

A NORMATIVE PROCEDURAL MODEL FOR URBAN DESIGN—AN EMERGING EMPIRICIST CONSENSUS

The goal of urban design is to create behaviorally congruent, biogenically sensitive built environments that are robust enough to evolve as the demands on them change. This end should be achieved with equality of opportunity and with justice for all. The meaning of this statement and the emerging process required to achieve it have to be understood within the set of attitudes described in Chapter 23. While the positions described here are by no means universally accepted, they are becoming more and more widely held as procedural paradigms for urban design against which individual efforts and projects can be measured.

The major shift from the attitudes of the Modernists is in the attitude toward user groups from a benign paternalism to recognizing them as active collaborators. A second shift is to openly recognize the political nature of urban design. A third is to recognize that design problems are wicked problems and that urban design is an open-ended process. A fourth is that urban design should be concerned with designing a well-functioning built environment based on an understanding of human motivations and the needs of the biogenic environment rather than on guesswork and simply personal experiences.

The urban design process in essence is the same as any other design effort, for it is one of a family of decision-making processes. It is biased by its concerns. Like city planning, urban design focuses on the public realm and the public interest. Like architecture, it is concerned with the quality of individual buildings, but it is also concerned with the quality of the built environment. Like landscape architecture, it is concerned with the quality of open spaces and the impact of development on the bio-genic environment. Urban design's nature—its place in the market system—does create special obligations in the United States.

When urban designers work for private developers (or public agencies for that matter) whose concerns for the public interest are often limited to what can be sold, they should still be obliged to be concerned with the broader public interests and with the interests of the potential range of users of a project. This is a difficult position to take given the nature of the working world—the task environment. It is thus tempting to look for easier positions.

One easier and possibly legitimate position to take is that the obligation of urban designers is only to the sponsors of their projects. Given this argument, they are advocates for their sponsors' needs. In this case it is up to the public sector alone to define the public interest and if it fails to do so then that failure is part of the culture in which design takes place. This position is not, however, congruent with the image of urban design that is most widely accepted in theory if not practice in the United States. The opportunity costs for society and for the professional activity of urban design as the result of taking this position are high. The obligation of the urban designer is to work for the broader concerns of society using the best empirical knowledge available.

There are few instances when it is possible to fully implement the model of urban designers' aspirations and obligations described in this chapter. There are constraints of finance and time that truncate the design process. There are limitations of the human imagination and powers of rational thinking that lead us to develop a variety of shortcuts, or heuristic devices, to reduce the complexity of the processes explicit and implicit in this model. Too great a deviation from or simplification of the model will, however, result in many lost opportunities for society.

Urban designers are part of and contributors to the political process of their societies. The normative public participation theories of the 1960s and 1970s have moved much of the environmental decision-making process away from the dictation of designs by elites to a direct democracy. Much, however, remains unchanged (Montgomery 1989). The objective of this chapter is to describe an idealized process within the framework of our present understanding of the design process as outlined in Chapter 21, The Urban Design Designing Process. In doing so a number of stands have to be taken.

URBAN DESIGN AND THE POLITICAL PROCESS

When the urban design process is seen for what it is—as a political process from its inception when goals are defined to the point when results are evaluated—it is essential that a clear statement of social goals and a social schema is developed, either before or simultaneous with the exploration of potential physical forms for the future built environment. *The role of urban designers in any discussion or design of social goals is: (1) to argue for the full range of human needs to be considered in any debate about goals and means, and (2) to bring the attention of politicians, other decision makers, and the public to the physical design implications of different social policies, and the social implications of physical form proposals (i.e., what they do and do not afford in terms of activity patterns and displays). The prediction of these impacts should be based on empirical information. When there is no empirical basis for making predictions urban designers need to make it clear on what evidence their conclusions are based. The process has to be an open one—in both the formal and informal political arenas.* The topics for debate have been concisely summarized by Ray Studer (1988) in Fig. 24–1. Clearly, arguments arise over "what ought to be" but they also arise over "what is."

The Formal Political Process

Major changes in the social fabric of American society can only come about through changes of opportunities induced through marketplace offerings, through changes of heart reflected in the political stances taken by legislators, and through the pressure exerted formally or informally by specific individuals and groups of people. If urban designers are to argue for social justice (to the extent that the layout of cities, their precincts, and urban places makes a difference), then they should have two sets of concerns about their political role in society. The first has to do with urban designers acting as a political pressure group so as to ensure that such issues are considered

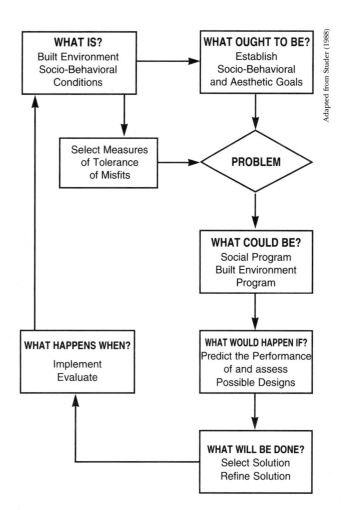

Figure 24–1: Built Environment Decision-Making Issues

Adapted from Studer (1988)

when government policy changes that will affect the structures of human settlements are made. The second has to do with their professional work with reference to existing political and administrative structures within government.

Elected officials and the pubic alike seldom fully appreciate the difficulty of designing the policies and schemes for making cities and other human settlement well-functioning places. At present urban designers do not act as a unified political pressure group because no single body represents them nor is there agreement on ends to be achieved. The pressure they can exert comes from their representation in existing professional bodies and as individual practitioners. The difficulty that urban designers have in promoting a societal concern for a well-functioning environment (in both sociogenic and biogenic terms) is that the existing design professions and individual design professionals have their own agendas, which are often opposed to a concern for high-quality urban designs. As people become more aware of environmental concerns an increasing number of urban designers, particularly landscape and community architects, have been encouraging societies to look critically at the urban physical environment to understand what it does and does not afford people and the biogenic environment and what it could afford them. The promotion of partisan goals by urban designers must, however, be done with an understanding of the relative importance of urban design in relationship to other human welfare concerns on the political agenda.

The working environment of the practicing urban designer is affected by the role of urban design in city government and the role of consultants in relating to governments. Issues regarding the location and role of urban design in city government are essentially the same as in city planning as a whole. At present the concern with physical environmental quality issues is fragmented and spread across many governmental jurisdictions representing different geographical areas. Within each jurisdiction the concern is divided among many different departments and agencies. In a capitalist society such as the United States, where urban design leadership can come from either the private or public sectors, this situation needs to be changed for two reasons: to get greater coordination in perceiving issues that need to be considered, and in developing policies across geographic and political boundaries; and to streamline the review of proposals submitted for approval. The existing agency structure within governments leads to sectional jealousies in defining issues and also to inordinate delays in reviewing schemes to determine if they meet required urban design guidelines and other criteria. Delaying proposals that do not meet the criteria is, however, a successful tactic in getting developers to conform to the ordinances and design guidelines that have been created to achieve specific public interest ends.

Consultants have to work with many agencies and coordinate the effort themselves. In the United States as elsewhere, there is strong competition among professionals within the public sector. Coordination seems easier to achieve from the outside rather than from within government because of entrenched organizational structures. Outside consultants can at least develop coordinated design teams. Within government, winning arguments and controlling resources are often more important than serving the public interest. *There is a need for governmental agencies to be structured to deal with problems rather than along traditional professional lines if urban design is to be carried out in the public interest within the public sector.* A number of political reformist movements exist, but the high personal rewards that individual politicians and public agency members get from the current structures makes reform difficult. *Those of us concerned with urban design need, as individuals and as members of existing professions, to recognize the implications of potential changes in the administrative location of urban design efforts within municipal governments and to fight for those changes that are in the public interest—those that deal with problems and opportunities comprehensively.*

The Informal Political Process

All urban design work involves collaborative action, although the degree and the nature of the collaboration will vary from situation to situation. Any collaborative urban design process involves informal politics. The distribution of power among the stakeholders in the situation being addressed will differ based on who holds the purse strings, who has professional expertise, who has political power, and who is persuasive. In the United States, as in most societies, the people who hold the purse strings have considerable power. Urban designers have a considerable variety of expertise and areas of concern, both of which have political significance.

Future urban designers will need to be highly knowledgeable about the environment as a multivariate system, rather than just viewing it as a geometry with an absolute aesthetic quality based on their own taste culture. There are many urban designers with a broad knowledge base. While the goal of collaborative efforts in design is partially a political end in itself, the fundamental purpose of using a participatory, Neo-Functional approach to designing is to ensure that different perceptions of the problem and of potential solutions are laid on the table for open discussion and debate.

Each phase of the design process will require people with different strengths to provide intellectual leadership in making decisions. For instance, in predicting how a proposed urban configuration will function in different possible future conditions, some people will have a well-developed expertise on the proposal's micro-climatic effects while others will have an understanding of its social and economic multiplier effects. The quality of the overall management of the design process is thus likely to make or break the process.

The Leadership Role

Urban design must be recognized for what it is, a collaborative process, for it to function successfully. It must involve collaboration between and among: (1) public and private sectors, (2) the design professions, (3) professionals and clients, (4) sponsors and users, (5) different researchers, and (6) researchers and designers (Lang 1990). Successful collaboration (i.e., one that results in the goals of the project being met) is impossible unless there is a common understanding of the nature of the design process and of the empirical basis for design decisions, but it also requires strong leadership.

The leadership of any urban design team has to come from those with the appropriate managerial skills. It is unlikely to be a person who has been trained purely as a manager who does not understand the nature of the design process and design issues. Future urban design leaders are likely to come from any of the design fields or from other professions. In collaborative work, it is too often those people who shout the loudest and whose goal it is to win the argument who prevail. What is needed is someone who can delegate authority and who can hold together a design team of often highly egocentric people (Warfield and Hill 1973).

There are two leadership roles: intellectual leadership in setting directions, and group maintenance leadership. The abilities to carry out the roles well do not necessarily have to reside in the same person, as the names of many of the architectural firms who are noted for the quality of their work attest. However, intellectual leadership without the ability to hold a team together is unlikely to be fruitful. *Leaders should be selected for their ability to hold a group together and to draw on the abilities of different people during the overall decision process.* This kind of leadership is important in structuring the overall process and dealing with changes as the process moves through its various phases. In open, glass box design processes, it is essential that this leadership role be carried out by a person or people who have firm convictions but who are not defensive in open debate about ends and means.

A Participatory Urban Design Process

The design process has to be a participatory one. Participation can mean a number of things. *Active participation involves considerably more than professionals telling or educating people about a proposal. It involves their ongoing role in the debate about ends and means.* The Maslow model of human needs provides the urban designer with a mechanism for focusing attention on the concerns of urban design. It is particularly important as the basis for opening up the discussion of issues, possible futures, and possible designs. *The act of designing the program itself, of pulling the strands together, of synthesizing it, is best left to a few professional individuals.* Its review should be part of the full participatory process. Such a process can only occur if the full consequences of what is proposed are understood not only by professionals but also by laypeople. While a full understanding can only happen if a solution to the program (i.e., a design) as well as the program is at hand, the program itself can be evaluated against theoretical models and case study information. In practice the programming and design phases will often merge, but the need is still to recognize the separate purpose and intellectual foundations of each.

In defining the goals of a project, it is of primary importance that urban designers help the people concerned in the process formulate what they want and/or what they ought to want in their own interest and in the public interest (Halprin 1969, 1974; King et al. 1989). Interviews with people, either those directly involved or matched surrogate populations, must be used to yield information on people's perceptions and beliefs about their desired futures (see also Sanoff 1977, 1978, 1989). Using the framework of human needs considerations described in Part II of this book enables the designer to focus on ends and means.

The model of human needs, empirical evidence, and theories of the person-environment relationship provide a framework for the professional to wonder what can be done. Theory, however, provides generalizations so relying purely on it would lead to a top-down approach to design. The danger is that the local details that bring theory to life will get lost in the discussion. A bottom-up approach to design involving the specifics of a situation must also be used. The information required for this approach can only come from the local context. A participatory design process helps considerably to yield it.

A number of problems with the participatory approach to urban design must be compensated for in the design process. There is often, for instance, a discrepancy between people's beliefs about how they will behave in the future and what they actually do when that future comes to be (Michelson 1976). There are a number of approaches to resolving this. One can observe behavioral tendencies and trends that may harbinger what is to come (Alexander and Poyner 1970). Observations of the changes made by people to their own environments also yield good insights on what they are striving to achieve (see Perin 1970). A variety of gaming techniques are also available to aid the process of goal formulation (Sanoff 1977). Ultimately, the stand taken on the appropriate goals results from an open argument among the people involved.

The statements of the activity system, territorial, privacy, and community criteria, the degree of control and developmental opportunities that should be provided, and the aesthetic principles that form the behavioral system model to be used in an urban design program are all ultimately political statements. The specification of radical departures from existing cultural norms (i.e., people's habituation levels) is done at high peril.

It has been hard to attain genuine participation in the urban design process in the past because people have had difficulty visualizing urban design proposals—that is, understanding drawings and other graphic devices used by planners and designers (see the discussion on representation of ideas below).

STRUCTURING THE URBAN DESIGN PROCESS

Urban design has to be a systemic and systematic process open to public examination. It must, however, be recognized that our ability to carry out such a process is limited by both our intellectual and financial resources and the human energy required to implement it. Such a process is the *ideal*. Modeling or designing the process on this ideal is essential if the goal is to deal with problems of society in a multivariate, democratic manner.

The process of design should not be forced neatly into the sequence of steps shown in Chapter 21, although the overall framework of decision making is well represented by that model (see Fig. 21–3). It is clear that all the issues that need to be considered in developing a proposal (whether for the creation of a total design, an all-of-a-piece design with design guidelines to achieve it, or a growth management plan) are seldom if ever clear before an effort is made to design a solution to them. This observation applies to each phase of the design process. Designing the program and designing possible solutions to it go hand in hand (Robinson and Weekes 1983). The advocacy today is nevertheless generally for a detailed and broad effort in designing the program as a point of departure for any urban design activity. This advocacy is reflected in the books that describe the overall urban design process in greater detail than is done here (Cutler and Cutler 1982; Shirvani 1985). It is an advocacy for a programmatic rather than a paradigmatic approach to design.

The steps of the urban designing process are interwoven in many ways, and designers, through experience, develop a number of personal heuristic devices for cutting through them. Using habitual processes and existing urban design paradigms for defining and designing the problems to be addressed and in designing solutions is, however, to be avoided. Situations need to be looked at afresh. Designing a systematic model of the overall design process to address a particular situation is essential for designing creatively in context. It forces one to look at situations anew. *Although the essential structure of the design process is that shown in Fig. 21-3, the detailed design process and the methods and techniques to be used have to be designed (or selected) for each particular situation.*

The best way to operate a design process that enables the problem situation and potential solutions to be thoroughly explored is probably *a depth-first approach*—where programming and design become an interactive process (Palmer 1981; see also T. Moore 1988). While the first step is to develop a comprehensive program, the effort then is to push through to the design phase quickly to generate a potential solution. The process of programming and design is then reiterated, as the design spiral described by John Zeisel (1980) suggests (see Fig. 21-2). This approach seems to be more fruitful than a breadth-first approach of a "totally" saturated in-depth analysis, and the simultaneous carrying forward of a variety of programs and solutions. Rather, the way to work is to push through to a solution and then to go back to goal formation and programming, to extend and/or change the criteria to be used as a basis for design and then to design another potential solution. Whether one uses a depth-first or a breadth-first approach to design, the goal is to generate a number of potential solutions for examination with an understanding of the strengths and weaknesses of each. This position implies that designers develop programming as well as design skills well beyond that which they generally are willing to possess. The knowledge base for doing so is available. This does not mean that difficulties will not remain.

One major difficulty in working this way occurs when the designer (or client) falls in love with the first potential solution generated and will not give it up even when evidence mounts that it will not meet the problems at hand. *Potential urban design solutions should be regarded as analytical tools that elucidate problems rather than as solutions to be defended.* A collaborative evaluation of potential solutions enables new issues to be confronted and new possibilities to be examined. The goal of such a process is to elaborate the problem during each iteration until a stage is reached when an iteration brings an improvement in neither defining the problem nor defining a solution. In practice, the number of iterations is constrained by the time available to carry them out.

Most of us find this way of working a difficult one. We have been educated to be single-minded and highly defensive about our work. As a result, the easiest way to deal with having to generate several high-quality solutions is to have a number of teams working simultaneously in parallel, each one generating a single design. The pros and cons of each can then be discussed.

Dealing with Uncertainty

A point made repeatedly throughout this book is that urban designers have to make decisions under uncertainty—there is a risk involved (Byrne 1984). One way of dealing with uncertainty is simply to ignore it and to assume that what we want to occur will occur—the *gambler's fallacy*. Good predictions require a strong positive theoretical base. Urban designers must recognize not only the depth of their knowledge but also its shortcomings, yet not be hamstrung by either the knowledge or the lack of it. They, like any other designers, must have confidence in their knowledge and abilities yet the intellectual strength to recognize the limitations of both (Harris 1967).

It is not always easy to recognize and admit to oneself, let alone others, what one does not know. Theoretical frameworks provide a way not only to organize information but also to recognize the gaps in it (Rittel 1971; see also Chapter 6). One of the saving graces of designing the physical layout of the environment is that there are many configurations that achieve similar ends. We can get away with many mistakes, but that does not give us the right to do so (Bazjanac 1874).

In dealing with uncertainty one should draw on and present the best evidence that one can. The design process should rely on empirical information and theory. The designer should strive for open-ended design—design that can easily be changed and adapted and that is able to evolve. If the idea behind a design is robust enough and important enough to decision makers in the future, they will hang on to it and continue to implement it. Many of the most important urban designs are based on strong ideas that can be comprehended by people, as designers recognize. Thus the recent plan for Des Moines, Iowa, by Mario Gandalsonas and Diana Agrest is highly imageable (Gallagher 1991). The search for a clear idea should not, however, override the reality of the situation nor should its permanence automatically

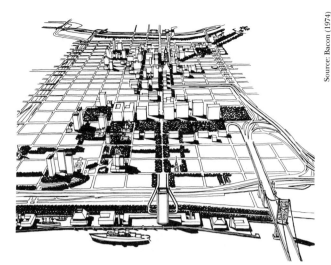

Source: Bacon (1974)

1. Edmund Bacon's Schema for the Development of Center City, Philadelphia

2. Inner Harbor, Baltimore, Maryland

Figure 24-2: The Importance of an Urban Design Idea
Having a formal central design idea gives a powerful cohesive image to an urban design scheme. An example of such an idea was Edmund Bacon's proposal for Philadelphia, which, although the details have been changed, has been largely implemented (1). A formal central idea is characteristic of major urban design paradigms—the City Beautiful, the neighborhood unit, the city as a movement system, the Neo-Traditional town. Sometimes the idea gets formalized into a type (e.g., festival market (2)) and sometimes an architecture. Almost all urban designs need to have a synthetic concept—an organizing principle—that holds them together.

be assumed to be the goal of a design. In many situations, adaptability or even "abandonability" may be more important.

DESIGNING THE PROGRAM— A NEO-FUNCTIONAL APPROACH

An urban design program consists of a set of statements defining goals and design objectives embodied in the description of a desired behavioral system and assertions

about what the built environment should afford in order to fulfill the functions required of it. Programming thus involves making a series of decisions starting from a general statement of desirable activity systems and aesthetic ends, to specifications of how and where they should occur in space and be reflected in designs. The need is to establish a collective vision of the future.

The type of program that is needed as the basis for future urban design work is thus radically different from the statements of square measures of space of many present building programs. *An urban design program should not be regarded as simply a specification of the number of open spaces to be built and the nature of their defining walls if any. Rather, it should be a statement of the behavior settings that should exist and the nature of the performance requirements for their milieus in terms of the physiological pleasantness and the territorial, privacy, and community needs they have to fulfill. It should specify the nature of the displays that the milieu should contain and the constraints under which a design will have to function.* This concept of a program is somewhat different both in spirit and content from those specified in guidebooks on architectural programming (see, e.g., Palmer 1981; Peña, Parshall, and Kelly 1987; and Salisbury 1990). The typical content of an urban design program should be something like that shown in Fig. 24-3.

Different professionals will be concerned with different aspects of defining the program. City planners will be involved in specifying the requirements for overall land-use design, urban designers and landscape architects in the three-dimensional qualities of the environment. It is clear that the design of the program will be an interactive process among the stakeholders. The goal is to specify what has to be done at different scales of design. In making clear specifications, conflicts between different objectives, and thus the needs of different subpopulations, will arise and have to be debated. There are also likely to be clashes between the alternative objectives of a specific population. The classic example of this is the desire for more open space per household and a greater efficiency in circulation. The better the information available to the participants in the argument, the more the need for give and take is likely to be understood and compromises effected.

That urban design programs are designed was the observation made in Chapter 21. Specifying goals, objectives, and the means of achieving any desired end is a creative act. A model of the overall structure of the phase is shown in Fig. 21-5. It can be carried out in a number of ways. It should be based on the normative position that design should be a collaborative effort, and that designs should fit the needs of people rather than people having to meet the needs of the design.

The overall goal of programming is to operationally define the nature of the problem being addressed. *The concern of the urban designer in establishing a design program is with: (1) defining opportunities for new behavioral systems, (2)*

The Overall Purpose of a Possible Project
    The Perimeters of Concern
    The Context
        Social
        Physical

The Stakeholders Involved
    Who they are
        The Sponsors
        Users
        The Public Interest
    Their relative importances
    Their goals
    The Existing Context
        Sociogenic
        Biogenic

The Social Agenda: Goals and Objectives
    Sponsors Needs
    Users Needs
        The Basic Needs of Stakeholders
        The Cognitive Needs of Stakeholders

The Desirable Behavioral System Model
    Activity Systems
    Aesthetic Values

The Desirable Physical System Model

**The Present Physical Environment and
the Desirable Physical System Model**
    Fits and misfits between the two
    The tolerable limits for misfits

The Resource Available
    Financial
        Public
        Private
    Cultural and Human

Specifications of Changes Required
    Behavioral Changes
    Changes Required of the public realm
        To afford activity systems
        To afford aesthetic objectives

Figure 24-3: Typical Contents of an Urban Design Program

identifying problems in the existing behavioral system, (3) recognizing potential problems due to changes either in the behavioral system or in the layout of the built environment, and (4) changing standards of expectations of how well the structure of the built environment should fit the behavioral system. All these actions have to be carried out within the overriding goal of enhancing the quality of the biogenic environment. Indeed, one of the purposes, the partisan goal of urban designers, is to raise people's expectations of how well the built environment should function on all the dimensions of human experience. Somebody, however, has to engage the urban designer to become involved in these activities.

Getting Involved

Urban designers get involved in a particular effort in a number of ways. Sometimes they initiate the process by identifying a problem, then find a sponsor and resolve the problem. While this process has been initiated successfully by single individuals (e.g., Pike Market, Seattle; see Langdon et al. 1990), it is more likely to occur when the urban designer is an employee in the public sector. In private practice they are much more likely to be hired to address a problem situation identified by others than to initiate a process. *While it is clearly also in their own self-interest, urban designers should seek involvement on behalf of public interests.*

The first step for the urban designer is to decide whether to embark on a project or not (Koberg and Bagnall 1977). In doing so the designer may well have to accept many attributes of the situation that are personally dismaying. It is difficult for a designer to reject a project on ethical grounds knowing someone else will do a worse job, or when they have no other work. *Unless a project is going to be directly harmful to a population without the people affected receiving any compensation, urban designers should enter the fray and do the best job they can.*

DEFINING THE CLIENTS— THE STAKEHOLDERS

Because it is focused on the design of the public realm, urban design is in turn directly concerned with the public's interest and the public interest. The public's present demands may not be in the long-term interests of society. *The prime concern early on in the design process should be with defining the public interest and understanding what it means to be designing the layout of an environment in the public interest.* The public interest, it has been noted already, is difficult to define because there are different perceptions of what the goals of society should be. Implicit in every urban design work, however, is a statement on what the public interest is.

In the United States as in all societies, the goals of the sponsor of a project, either public or private, must be met. *The advocacy here, however, is for a user-oriented approach to design.* The users of any scheme may be homogeneous or heterogeneous on any number of dimensions: basic cultural ethos, stage in life cycle, aesthetic values, and so on. Urban designing should deal with the full range of clients.

A political decision has to be made on the moral order, or social principles, to be used as the basis for defining what the design objectives should be. The obligation of the urban design professional is to mediate *among interests and to bring the design implications of the various stances to the debate over ends and means.* The easiest way to resolve conflicting goals in a capitalist economy is to let the marketplace decide. Taking such a stance means that people with financial power decide the future. *Urban designers should recognize that there has to be a market for a project; however, while developers' complaints about hardships in meeting public interest goals should be considered, their complaints and goals should certainly not be automatically accepted.*

Urban designers have little control over highly political decisions such as those establishing social ends except at a project level, but it is up to them to be advocates for the broad range of clients' interests to be met either directly through a project or through its catalytic effect. Inevitably compromises among the objectives of various clients have to be made, but if urban designers are not concerned with social ends no other design professional will be.

Identifying the Range of Clients

A differentiation has been made between the paying and nonpaying client (Zeisel 1974). Paying clients or their appointees are usually readily identifiable because they have veto power over whether a project goes ahead or not. The broader concerns of society are represented, however poorly, at the outset of the decision process by existing codes and zoning ordinances. The characteristics of potential users who are going to be renting or buying a place can also be identified. The users of the public realm, as individuals, are difficult to identify, but the research on behavior settings shows that broad conclusions can be drawn about their needs within specific cultural contexts (Bechtel 1977; Bechtel, Marans, and Michelson 1987). Such a statement inevitably requires a prediction based not simply on an extrapolation of what is, but on a rational statement of what might be!

Sponsor Clients

In any society, capitalist or socialist, if an urban design scheme is to be implemented it has to fulfill the basic goals of its sponsor. In a capitalist society, if the paying client is a private sector developer, urban designers may be in one of two situations. They may prepare a scheme so that the sponsor can judge if it is financially beneficial to pursue it and if it is legally plausible. Or urban designers may prepare a design that is actually intended to be implemented as a total urban design or as infrastructure development with or without guidelines for the overall project's development. There are many permutations of these situations. The obligations of the urban designer are essentially the same in all of them.

An urban designer's obligation to paying clients is to inform them of the financial costs and benefits of moving in a particular direction. The designer's obligation to society is to place social costs and benefits on the agenda. The disincentive for urban designers to do this is that they may lose their sponsors. Difficulties arise when paying clients are antagonistic to all design possibilities other than the ones they are used

to considering. Although most developers are open to the discussion of public interest concerns, there are limits to their ability to subsidize them without financial rewards for doing so. When a scheme is actually to be implemented the obligations of the urban designer are broader. There needs to be a much greater concern with users' participation, directly or indirectly, in the decision-making process. There is a concomitant need for a more detailed concern with public interest goals and means.

If the public sector is the sponsor then the situation facing the urban designer is different. The public sector is supposed to deal with the public interest but often it is defined in terms of a single issue (e.g., providing a specific number of housing units). In this case, the broad scale issues of environmental quality can easily get lost. Public officials, based on their own experiences, also have a set of biases about what makes a good environment and what situations are bad. Many of these biases, like everybody else's, are based on inadequate knowledge and intellectual laziness. The role of an elected politician is to represent the electorate sufficiently well to be reelected. Politicians are thus often placed in the difficult position of having to deal with their own experiences, the prejudices of their constituencies, professional advice, and the broader public interest. This situation holds particularly in political jurisdictions where the elected officials represent specific wards rather than when they are elected at large (Smith 1991). *Urban designers are obligated to bring the broader concern with human needs and its implications for the attainment of a well-functioning environment to bear on the public debate.*

User-Clients

An urban designer's obligations extend beyond designing simply for the minimal standards established by the marketplace in terms of users' needs. The role of the urban designer is to bring the attention of users and potential users to the experiential opportunities provided by different patterns of the environment, including those outside the realm of the users' own experience. Users, if they are identifiable, have the same obligations to the professional. The debate among users, sponsors, and professionals becomes the vehicle for each group to educate the others about needs, means, and resources. Participation in the design process also enhances the fulfillment of users' need for esteem—one of the goals of a Neo-Functional approach to urban design.

Clients have an excuse for their limited knowledge of how the environment actually works and what different possible patterns of the built environment that are geometrically and technologically plausible (see Chapter 10) afford in terms of activities, symbolism, and aesthetic appreciation. While there is much that professionals do not understand, we have no easy excuse. Experts are often treated with skepticism because they have a perceived record of mistakes. Users need evidence and logical arguments that they can understand to support positions being taken by experts. The model of Functionalism presented in this book is one means of structuring the knowledge base required of urban designers to bring it to bear on urban design issues.

The Range of User-Clients

One of the major issues in any urban design situation is deciding on the range of users that should be considered. To some extent this is a chicken-and-egg situation. If a residential area is designed to be inhospitable to children, few parents will decide to live there. The same applies to any group. If an area does not provide for the needs of disabled, they will try to find areas that are barrier-free (although in many instances this search will be fruitless). Any design implicitly assumes a set of users. The issue is the degree to which populations, and thus areas of cities and building complexes, should be segregated by population or user type. Part of the attractiveness of precincts of cities is that they have population characteristics that are unique to them. *Urban designers should argue for richness of environmental experiences and opportunities as the basis for design. This implies that people should be exposed to many other types of people. The normative position is also that the people involved should themselves decide. These two positions are often in conflict, raising questions about what the public interest really is.* The process has to be legitimate.

Often it is only those users who are going to buy or rent a portion of a completed urban design who are the focus of design and participatory concern. This situation is understandable. They are the ultimate financiers of a scheme through the places they purchase or the rents they pay, and often their main concern is whether their purchase can easily be resold. The public realm will, however, be used by many people. *Those users with financial interests in a project must be a prime concern for urban designers and architects, but the broader range of users and users' needs must be considered too.* Such a stance involves a prediction.

A number of methods have been and are used for making such predictions (Bross 1953). One can observe similar situations. For instance, in designing residential areas, the range of inhabitants of particular types of housing areas can be recorded. The problem is that such observations tell us what is and not what can or should be built (see Fig. 24–1). Using a strong body of positive theory (i.e., extrapolating—making conjectures—from what is known) enables us to make speculations on what might be with a reasonable hope that the result when implemented will function well. Ultimately, statements of what ought to be are based on perceptions of a moral order. We need to get away from a moral order that says simply that we should design what can be sold.

Heterogeneity versus Homogeneity as Urban Design Goals

Present planning policies, what the marketplace offers, people's choices, and entrenched prejudices often lead to precincts of cities that are homogeneous in character. This observation applies to both residential and employment centers. It reflects the saying "birds of feather flock together." Many such places in cities and suburbs are much loved and meet the individual needs of their residents and other users. They do not necessarily meet them for society as a whole. Such fragmentation of the environment allows people who are out of sight to be out of mind. The result may be a less stressful society but it will also be a less caring society.

Neither homogeneity nor heterogeneity of building uses and people in urban design is good or bad, but the normative position described here is that a variety of opportunities in the public realm is an end worth achieving. Possibly having a "mosaic of cultures" (Alexander et al. 1977) is the solution. Many existing cities in the United States provide it, but public policy decisions have allowed these cities to decay and become both socially and physically inhospitable. Presumably this result has been broadly perceived by politicians to be in the public interest given the range of demands on public resources.

Establishing the Public Interest as a Client

When they are working for private sector clients, architects are concerned about public interest issues only to the extent that designs meet code requirements. Often it is not even at this level—the goal is to avoid dealing with codes and cities often do not enforce them (e.g., Denver's landscape requirements for parking lots). *Urban designers must deal with three sets of public interest concerns: (1) that a project's qualities meet the needs of all the subgroups involved, (2) that the affordances of the public realm of a proposed project are in the public interest, and (3) that the impact of the proposal on its surroundings and on society is in the public interest.* Social justice issues are difficult to establish in any society, but the American stance is that in capitalist societies, where competition is the norm, the survival of the fittest is regarded to be in the public interest—as achieving the greatest benefit for all.

An urban design project is likely to have an effect on its immediate surroundings and may even have effects on areas at a considerable distance from it. For instance, the development of new mini-cities, new suburban downtowns on the periphery of cities, has had a major effect on the central business districts (CBD) of existing cities because they change the behavioral opportunities of the overall metropolitan area. Such decisions are justified by saying that they improve the overall performances of the system for people, and that such competition is beneficial. In a purely competitive society this is what must be expected. It is up to those who are advocates for the CBD to respond as they have done successfully in cities such as Minneapolis, Minnesota, and Portland, Oregon, by improving the quality of their own environments.

When tax money in the public coffer is used to make a particular site more desirable (e.g., by building highways to make it accessible) the question of what is in the public interest needs to be asked. Issues arise such as the side effects of building a project on the overall sociogenic and biogenic environments, and society's obligations to those who receive no gain but are left to bear the costs of the developer's profits themselves. These questions have been partially recognized by the demand for environmental impact statements for major projects. It is tempting for urban designers in dealing with such complexities to throw up their hands in despair, but there are several ways of moving ahead that at least partially meet public interest concerns (Wheaton and Wheaton 1972). Handling these issues is certainly beyond the expertise of a single urban designer, but they are not so complex that they and their implications for urban design cannot be substantially understood. It comes down to dealing with unrepresented as well as represented values in the argumentative process of design.

Represented Values and Positions

There are vocal proponents for some interests, none for others. There are many organizations with special interest that hold their ends to be in the public interest. There are lobbies, for instance, for the interests of real estate, education, medical practitioners, senior citizens, some elements of the poor, architecture as art, public art, and the biogenic environment. The environmental movement is particularly strong at the moment, although Proposition 128, an all-encompassing set of conservation measures in California, was overwhelmingly defeated in late 1990. Yet those issues still remain in the long-range interests of the public, assuming that the empirical observations of biologists, climatologists, and other environmentalists are correct (Ingersoll 1991).

One set of represented values is that held by urban designers themselves. The concern of many urban designers with an ordered environment has been noted, but their interests have historically been wider (see also "The Professional Culture as a Client" below). While there is no empirical study of these positions, the leaders of the planning movements have generally stood for greater equity and justice for all. This position was the basis for the design of many of the housing, health, welfare, recreation, and education reforms of the twentieth century in the United States. Urban designers need to continue to fight for these ends professionally. The establishment of the public interest comes from bargaining among these forces. It is a political process. The problem is that many important issues fall outside the realm of concern of many pressure groups because nobody raises them.

Under- and Unrepresented Values and Positions

All people are diminished when the weaker members of a society are trampled on. This observation does not mean that the under- or unrepresented views are right or that their interests are necessarily paramount, but rather that their views and needs should be articulated as they see them, not as others see them. Although there are strong lobbyists for the interests of the elderly, the poor, children, the handicapped, and even taste cultures other than those of the elite, when it comes to a specific scheme, these concerns often get lost in the debates over architectural design ends because they are not directly represented. *There is considerable empirical research on the special needs of many segments of the population. Urban designers should be aggressive in seeking out such sets of needs rather than simply allowing those that emerge to be the ones that are considered.* This position does create a dilemma for urban designers because of their simultaneous obligation to their sponsors for whom, generally, the fewer people whose interests have to be considered, the better. There are, however, even trickier issues with which urban designers have to contend.

There are a number of broad issues with which the urban designer must be concerned if opportunities for future populations are to be safeguarded. Some have to do with the health of the biogenic environment, but there are also many other such concerns that will be outlined briefly later under the rubric "The Future as a Client."

The Biogenic Environment as a Client Although there are strong environmental activist groups very much concerned with the effect of potential developments on the biogenic environment, and although stronger laws are being written to protect it, the biogenic environment should nevertheless be regarded as an unrepresented client, because the scope of concerns is broader than generally considered by the environmentalists. *The primary position that urban designers are taking is, quite rightly, that human interests are paramount.* In serving human interests, a part of the biogenic environment will be consumed. Ideally, the resources should be renewable ones, but inevitably some changes will take place. Open land, for instance, will be taken up and transformed into a manicured or built environment. *All people are diminished by the unremediable destruction of the natural environment. "Design with nature"* is an appropriate slogan for the urban designer as much as *"form should follow function."* The concern extends beyond the desire for a salubrious environment for human life, which has been a prime concern of planning and design movements in the past, to having a healthy and self-sustaining natural system.

This statement has not only biological but symbolic aesthetic implications that may well conflict with the fulfillment of many human needs as they are presently manifested and certainly with economic demands on land. The urban form consequences of taking such a position will differ considerably between desert, temperate, and other climatic zones with different terrains. It will almost automatically give a sense of regionalism to many schemes. It is thus argued here that achieving these ends is in the public interest, and total urban designs, urban design guidelines, and growth management strategies should all be designed with these ends in mind.

1. University of Washington, Seattle

2. Medical School Dormitories, University of Louvain-la-neuve, Brussels

3. Nelson Rockefeller Empire State Plaza, Albany, New York

Figure 24–4: Open-Ended Design
Most building complexes are changed over time to meet changing needs. The University of Washington in Seattle may have a basic City Beautiful plan but its elements have been built at different times (1). A number of architects have designed systems to afford the easy changing of elements. The medical school dormitories at the University of Louvain-la-Neuve designed by Lucien Kroll are a well-known example (2). The goal in urban design is often to have a unity in design (3), but the process needs to consider how to maintain this unity when subsequent changes are made.

The Future as a Client There is much that we cannot predict about future ways of life and values of people, future technological changes, and future economic conditions. *Urban designs have to be open-ended and subject to personalization and change over time without losing a coherent character.* Open-ended design that leaves a variety of possible options for later changes may have short-run costs associated with it. For example, allowing potential future public transit corridors to remain open in Columbia, Maryland, means that opportunities for immediate development are lost. In this instance, the corridors act as parkland and if they are not required in the future they will remain as such or be available for other uses (R. Brooks 1974).

A number of architects have developed systems for dealing with future change. John Habrakan (1971) argues for designing the infrastructure of buildings and letting people fill them in on their own. Lucien Kroll developed this option in the design of the dormitories for the University of Louvain-la-Neuve medical school in Brussels. Such a situation is largely the norm of urban design, but it usually occurs by happenstance. More broadly, the open-endedness of design is important when thinking about long-term and large-scale multifunctional projects that will be built in a number of phases (see "Implementing

Urban Design" below). The university campus is a prime example of such a project, but so are large-scale urban renewal schemes such as Charles Center in Baltimore and, more recently, Bunker Hill in Los Angeles and Peachtree Center in Atlanta. Design guidelines can offer some control over how future phases of a project are carried out, but open-ended designs tend not to have the formal unity that designers have traditionally sought.

In some instances, specific future changes will form part of the design specifications in the program. Where the built environment is to be temporary (e.g., in world's fairs) it should be designed with demolition (either wholesale or partial) and conservation of materials in mind. Better still, it should be designed with a new life in mind (e.g., an Olympic village becoming a university or a housing area). In a broad sense almost everything that is built is temporary. The built environment is changed to meet future needs. *Some buildings and landscapes should be retained as a memory and symbol of continuity, but change is the norm. The consequence for urban design is that the sequencing and phasing of development for change should be part of design thinking and be reflected in guidelines that are proposed to shape the built world.* The guidelines too will be changed in the future as society's needs and values change, but their overall goals are likely to remain constant.

The Professional Culture as a Client   Urban design is a professional activity if not a profession. Urban designers are likely to be members of a profession. Most of them in the immediate future are likely to be architects, landscape architects, and city planners, although many are members of other professions that have shown considerable leadership in setting the policy direction for urban design work (e.g., Susan Schick in Glendale, California, and Pierre Le Compte in Louvain-la-Neuve in Belgium are both lawyers who have played crucial roles in award-winning urban designs).

One of the reasons for the existence of professions is to control a corner of a market. One of the advantages of urban design as it is presently constituted is that it is the meeting place of many design professions and of artists. *One of the obligations of the designer is to change the professions to better meet the needs of society rather than attempting to change society to better meet the needs of the professions.* Each profession has its own concerns, reward structure, and standards. These are fine and good in their place. They are inevitably narrower than the concerns that urban designers should display. Distorting the definition of urban design problems so that they meet the needs of a profession does a disservice to society and in the long run to the design professions themselves.

The Relative Importance of Different Client Groups

Implicit in any design is a hierarchy of importance of client groups and their needs. In the acts of programming, designing, and evaluating potential schemes a stand is taken. Very seldom are such positions taken openly. *In a glass box approach to design the relative importance of the various stakeholders in any urban design process should be explicitly stated.* This stance is easier to state than to implement.

Clearly, fulfilling the basic motivations of the sponsors of a scheme is crucial to its success. Without sponsors' acceptance a scheme cannot go ahead. In terms of the public interest this means that there must be a perceived market for the project and a real and perceived willingness on the part of the public sector to enforce design guidelines established to meet public needs—to have all developers build within them. The same is true of other legal embodiments of public interest positions.

The direct participants in the process—the sponsors, urban designers, and various other client groups—will have different powers based on the degree to which they are involved, have the expertise, and have financial or political clout. They can establish through open discussion whose interests are paramount and take a stand on them. *The urban designers should bring the needs of the unrepresented and underrepresented into the discussion.* Any position on who is important will, however, emerge rather than be carefully planned. *A basic procedural task of the urban designer, it was stated above, is to mediate between interests to the extent that* *they are articulated and to be an advocate for the un- or underrepresented.* This process is continuous because the perception of the relative importance of the people involved in any urban design project is likely to change as the process moves ahead.

Designing Design Goals and Objectives

Once a preliminary statement on the range of interest groups involved in a potential scheme has been established, defining the operational goals of a scheme is the most global decision that any designer has to make. In urban design the first order of business is to establish a sense of direction based on the design of a social agenda—a behavioral program—or the acceptance of an existing one.

The Social Agenda and Behavioral System Model

A Neo-Functional approach to programming implies that the purpose of establishing urban design goals and objectives is to define the performance, or functions, that a design or set of design guidelines has to achieve when implemented. This task can be an open-ended one. To narrow it, one of the first steps in the design process is to establish the domain of concern. This definition is usually made by default. *The scope of concern in a specific situation should be explicitly stated.* It will no doubt change as the design process proceeds. In a particular situation the concern is likely to include discussions on the physical design patterns and what they should afford people and/or the biogenic environment, or discussions of the policies for the design for a specific area and what they afford. Asking what the area should afford inevitably expands the perimeter of concern to deal with social questions.

The scope of concern, spatially and intellectually, is likely to shift as the design progresses in response to issues as they arise, but a point of departure is required. Much is defined by what the urban designer is hired to do. The perimeter of concern is defined exogeneously (i.e., from outside). *The obligation of urban designers is to think broadly about their concerns—more broadly than their sponsors. Urban designers need to be outward-looking.*

The initial focus of attention of urban designers is with establishing the overall functions that the four-dimensional character of the city, precinct, total, or an all-of-a-piece urban design has to afford. The specification of these functions is essentially the statement of a design's goals. The goals, and particularly their definition in a behavioral system model, are likely to shift as the design process proceeds because much is conjectural at the outset. Nevertheless, a point of departure is needed. *The urban designer's concern, in addition to the specific concerns of the project, must be with the catalytic effect of any design situation on the surrounding areas and with decisions and potential decisions in those areas on the one under consideration.*

The goals of the physical design effort have to be perceived as serving agreed-upon social goals. In much urban design work the concern is with specifying which elements of urban development should be controlled and how they should be controlled. This is particularly true when the basic concern is with developing guidelines for future developments. The urban environment, it was noted in Chapters 2 and 9, consists of thematic situations, in which the individual architect should have a freedom of action to do something idiosyncratic, and the nonthematic component, which will constitute the background. In that sense the built environment consists of figures and grounds. Goals have to be established for both.

Urban design goals are general; design objectives are specific statements of intention. Goals, it has already been noted, are often so general that everybody agrees on them. Goals have to be operationalized by describing them in terms of an activity network that has to be accommodated and the aesthetic values that will form the basis for the display character of the layout of the environment (see Studer 1969). *In defining and designing objectives, the potential implementation processes and financial resources for accomplishing an end also have to be borne in mind. Ideally, however, one should postpone using possible implementation techniques as a constraint on establishing design ideas until potential ideas have been explored. Such an action enhances creative problem solving. However, as the available implementation techniques are often part of the problem, considering them should be part of the program. No empirical, inductive method can exist for any of these processes. They are acts of* design.

Human Motivations, Needs, and Design Programs

The general model of human needs and programming issues raised by the Neo-Functional approach to urban design advocated in this book is shown in Fig. 7–3. As described in Chapter 23, all needs should be taken into consideration, but the first concern is with the most basic needs.

Human needs are operationalized in the behavior system model. *If many of the failures of past designs are to be avoided, the design program must recognize the culturally appropriate way of carrying out activities and appropriate aesthetic values.* The identification of these activities and values is an empirical question. Observational and interview techniques for describing and explaining the present activity systems and aesthetic values have been widely described (Hester 1975; Michelson 1975; Zeisel 1980; Bechtel, Marans, and Michelson 1987; Marans and Ahrentzen 1987; Krampen 1991; Sanoff 1991). They represent approaches to design analysis and synthesis that have empirical substance. Activity systems analysis and design should be done within a behavior setting framework because the concept links activity systems and milieu temporally. *Designing the behavior settings and aesthetic values that ought to exist is a* design

question. *It is the heart of programming. It is possible to make many accurate observations and to find out from people what they perceive their needs to be, but such statements still have to be translated into design requirements, or specifications.* Thus such observations as those shown in Fig. 24–5 about people's behavior and the requirements for meeting them in a newly designed environment can be met in a variety of designs other than the one shown. This method of working is, however, the essential one for urban design.

The Necessity of Urban Design

If the urban design problem involves the creation of a new urban area or open space system, a physical design is clearly a necessity, but in dealing with the existing city many politicians and most designers have an "edifice complex"—the belief that all problems can be solved through changing the built environment, through erecting buildings, especially housing, constructing roads, and building parks (Sarason 1972).

The behavior system model that is used as a basis for designing the performance requirements of the physical system exists within a biogenic and sociogenic environment. If the activities and aesthetic values that form the behavior system can be carried out or exist in the present built environment well enough (given acceptable tolerances), then no urban design problem exists. There has to be a state of dissonance between the desired behavioral system and the existing affordances of the layout of the environment for a change to be required in the built environment.

To be able to carry out this assessment a physical system model has to be developed. The objective of this model is different from a final design proposal. It is a statement of the affordances required of the built environment in order for the behavior system to be possible, not a statement of a design intention. Even though the behavior system may be possible, the built environment may still require changes in order to better afford the behavior system. The degree of tolerance for incongruity between behavior and physical system models varies considerably from culture to culture, and it also has to be seen within a model of the costs and benefits of making changes. In resource-poor situations the degree of tolerance has to be high. In addition, the degree of tolerance differs for each variable. In the United States there is generally very little tolerance for physical discomfort but considerable for visual disorder and public squalor in comparison to Europe.

The final step in the programming phase is to specify the changes that are required and the relative importance of each change. This is not an easy task because the changes that are required are neither mutually exclusive nor independent of each other. In any design process, but particularly in a participatory one, relative importances are argued for using whatever evidence may be available

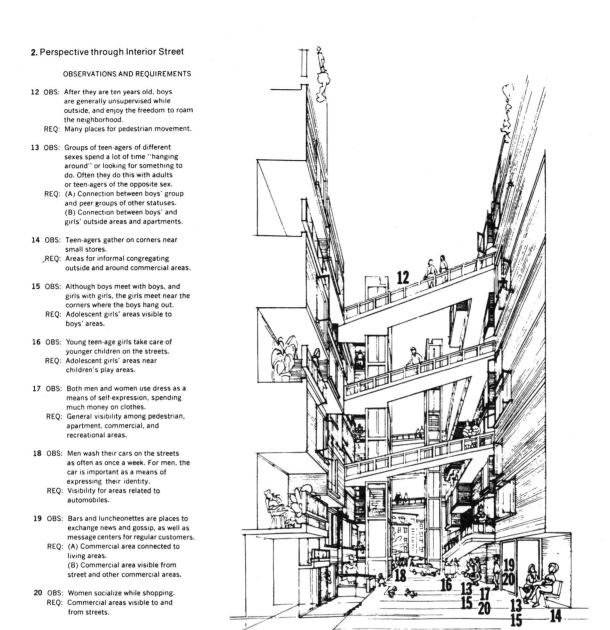

2. Perspective through Interior Street

OBSERVATIONS AND REQUIREMENTS

12 OBS: After they are ten years old, boys are generally unsupervised while outside, and enjoy the freedom to roam the neighborhood.
REQ: Many places for pedestrian movement.

13 OBS: Groups of teen-agers of different sexes spend a lot of time "hanging around" or looking for something to do. Often they do this with adults or teen-agers of the opposite sex.
REQ: (A) Connection between boys' group and peer groups of other statuses.
(B) Connection between boys' and girls' outside areas and apartments.

14 OBS: Teen-agers gather on corners near small stores.
REQ: Areas for informal congregating outside and around commercial areas.

15 OBS: Although boys meet with boys, and girls with girls, the girls meet near the corners where the boys hang out.
REQ: Adolescent girls' areas visible to boys' areas.

16 OBS: Young teen-age girls take care of younger children on the streets.
REQ: Adolescent girls' areas near children's play areas.

17 OBS: Both men and women use dress as a means of self-expression, spending much money on clothes.
REQ: General visibility among pedestrian, apartment, commercial, and recreational areas.

18 OBS: Men wash their cars on the streets as often as once a week. For men, the car is important as a means of expressing their identity.
REQ: Visibility for areas related to automobiles.

19 OBS: Bars and luncheonettes are places to exchange news and gossip, as well as message centers for regular customers.
REQ: (A) Commercial area connected to living areas.
(B) Commercial area visible from street and other commercial areas.

20 OBS: Women socialize while shopping.
REQ: Commercial areas visible to and from streets.

Source: Brolin and Zeisel (1970)

Figure 24–5: Field Observations and the Design of Behavior Settings

for making rational decisions and the relative power of the individual participants in the process. The decisions have to be seen with reference to the people they benefit and those they do not—the hierarchy of importance of the stakeholders in a project.

DESIGNING THE DESIGN

Much creative thought is required in programming well. Goals, the behavior system model, and the physical system model are all designed. The procedural objectives in the design of these models are, however, different from that in the generation of an actual proposal for the built environment. The goal of the design phase is to generate a specific physical product. It is a task best left to designers to accomplish without interruption using whatever techniques they wish to use. The description of the act of design here does not have the ideological nature of the description of the act of programming. The ideological stance taken here is that now widely if not universally accepted as a necessary part of creative thinking. It has considerable empirical support. *The objective of the design phase of the decision process is to generate a number of possible implementable futures that will form the basis of participatory evaluation in the choice phase of the overall process.*

Based on the observation of what urban designers do today (see Part I), there are four general types of products of urban design: (1) a total design, which may vary in scale from a small building complex to a university or office campus to a whole new town, (2) an all-of-a-piece design, in which some buildings and the infrastructure initiate a project and guidelines are written to guide the remainder of it, (3) an infrastructure system design, within which buildings and open spaces will be placed, and (4) a set of design policies or guidelines for shaping the three-dimensional nature of a city as it goes through phased redevelopment, and for maintaining aspects of the present city. There can be many combinations of elements of these possibilities. Paralleling any such effort should be a plan for managing the system when it has been implemented.

All these situations involve designing a number of completed schemes in model form. An end product—some future state or set of states of the social and built environments—is foreseen. Specific physical end states are only likely to be reached in total designs. In other types of urban design the concern is with the performance of any physical end state that might be reached. To design guidelines for a situation one must first design a number of illustrative site plans and sections (to understand height and thus spatial closure relationships) indicative of the range of acceptable, geometrically possible outcomes. Defining what are acceptable physical design futures must come out of a glass box participatory review process. Guidelines can then be developed based on the principles inherent in the designs in order to actually achieve desirable end products during the ongoing process of city building (see Fig. 9–8).

The Meaning of an Empiricist Approach to Designing

Turning a program into actual design proposals for the built environment is a creative not an empirical act. If one thinks ecologically the process can, however, draw on an empirical understanding of several things. First are the affordances of different patterns of the surfaces of the milieu for different behavior patterns. Second are the affordances of the properties (including the surface textures, pigmentation, opacity, and rigidity) of the different potential surfaces for activities. Third, the sensory, formal, and symbolic aesthetic affordances of different patterns of the milieu both at a macro- (e.g., at the scale of a plaza) and a micro-level (e.g., at the scale of textures and colors) must be understood. Fourth are the structural properties of materials and their affordances for assembly into technologically sound patterns. Fifth, the geometric possibilities of combining different forms to create larger entities for specific purposes need to be understood. In thinking typologically, the designer can draw on precedents and generic solutions as the basis for a hill-climbing (incremental improvement) approach to design. *In thinking ecologically and empirically the designer must rely on positive theory to draw inferences about future possibilities. Inevitably the designer has to make rational decisions based on logical reasoning. If this reasoning has an empirical base there is a greater probability that a behaviorally congruent environment will be achieved than if a purely Rationalist approach is used.*

Integrating Ecological and Typological Approaches in Designing

It has been observed that many if not all designers feel most comfortable using a mimetic approach to design that involves the adjustment of precedents and generic solutions to particular situations, and then adding their own aesthetic elaborations or embellishments to the type within the resources available to do so. This approach to design has often, it has already been pointed out, led to very poor designs that are in nobody's interest (see Marmot 1982). It does not have to be this way. For an urban designer to be without a knowledge of types, paradigms, or generic solutions is foolish, but the knowledge must be in conjunction with an understanding of the affordances of their configurations and the circumstances in which they have meaning.

Urban designers have to be familiar with types of urban forms, open spaces, communications media, transportation modes, and buildings as they exist within different cultural and terrestrial contexts. They have to understand the generic forms of buildings and the open-space elements that constitute the built environment. In establishing this understanding, the designer will almost inevitably learn the principles of the relationship between form and function in terms of human lives and purposes.

One standard way of designing is to manipulate a generic solution to a class of problems to fit the situation at hand. A number of generic solutions have been introduced in this book including the Fort Worth plan for downtowns (see Fig. 3–5). Three generic residential area designs—the neighborhood unit, the Unité d'habitation, and the pedestrian pocket—have been mentioned a number of times. They have been much used as the basis for generating many other designs, sometimes with success in terms of expected outcomes and sometimes not. Columbia, Maryland, is based on the neighborhood unit idea, and although it does not fulfill all the expectations of its proponents the schema creates a pleasant enough environment. In Chandigarh, the neighborhoods, or zones, while providing an overall organizing principle, have little meaning as a neighborhood. Similarly, the Brown-Kock-Kennedy-Demars-Rapson design for 100 Memorial Drive near MIT in Cambridge, Massachusetts, has stood up well over time for its middle-income inhabitants, but the application of the Unité in whittled-away form to mass housing design has largely been a disaster in terms of what the type affords its inhabitants (see Fig. 6–6). One of the basic difficulties with the use of generic solutions is that the problems in a situation are seen in terms of the solution and not the situation itself. On the other hand, many problems with which an urban design has to deal are generic ones.

The approach to design advocated here is principally the problem-solving one, starting with the establishment of goals and objectives and then fitting design patterns to those objectives based on an abstract theoretical knowledge of the nature of the environment and the person-environment relationship—an ecological approach. Typological knowledge can aid this process, provided types and the classification system on which they are based are understood. A defense for a design that uses precedents is a powerful one. The danger is that apparent precedents are not true ones!

Generic Solutions and Design Standards

From time to time, new generic solutions to a class of problems, either new or existing, are created. Indeed, this is sometimes regarded as the most useful end product of empirical research and is reflected in the recent emergence of guidebooks for design based on research (e.g., Cooper Marcus and Sarkissian 1986; Regnier and Pynoos 1987; Cooper Marcus and Francis 1990). Generic designs are statements of both programs and solutions. Thus a neighborhood unit plan specifies the character of community and design pattern together. Design standards are similar in character. They bring attention to particular problems and solutions.

Their ease of application has led to certain scheme types becoming generic solutions, although they were not developed as such in the first place. For example, the general model of how to deal with an obsolete waterfront has its precedent in places such as Baltimore's Inner Harbor (see Figs. 16–4(1) and 24–2(2)). Based on the past experience of the misuse of general paradigms there has been a reluctance to propose generic solutions for urban design use. The pedestrian pocket idea is, however, one recent solution (see Fig. 16–7(3)) as is the woonerf (see Fig. 8–2). Much empirical research has focused more on describing specific patterns of the built environment and what they afford. The work of Christopher Alexander and his colleagues (1977) is an exemplar but by no means a unique example.

Some problems are indeed generic, and there is no need to reinvent the wheel every time one faces them. The turning radii of motor vehicles of various types are well established but not generally carried in the head of architects. Standards are useful in this instance (e.g., De Chiara and Koppelman 1975, 1978). Similarly, standards have been developed for such general situations as housing for the elderly (Regnier and Pynoos 1987). Not only are there standards for patterning elements of the built environment, but also for design procedures such as the use of morphological analysis (Koberg and Bagnall 1977). In this chapter the use of the goals achievement matrix as an ideal type of approach to the evaluation of schemes is suggested (see Fig. 24–6).

The use of generic solutions and design standards as a short-cut to generating designs is legitimate when the problems being addressed are the same as those in the generic solution or standard. The definition of the problem should be generated independently of the use of a generic solution. Such a procedure reduces the probability of the generic solutions or standards being inappropriately used. Generic solutions and design standards are, as their names imply, broad-brush statements of how to deal with recurrent situations. *It would be foolish not to use types and generic solutions if they apply. Deviating from them simply for the sake of novelty is equally foolish.* The failure of Swedish housing authorities to continue using successful types simply because they had already been used is an example how such an attitude can result in poor environments for people.

Divergent and Convergent Production in Designing

The creative act involves thinking divergently—producing ideas—and convergently—synthesizing them into wholes. An array of techniques from brainstorming to morphological analysis to computer-based design algorithms can aid designers in this task (Broadbent 1973; Koberg and Bagnall 1977; P. Rowe 1987).

The process of design involves systematically correlating and identifying congruences between elements of the proposed behavior system and patterns of the layout of the built environment in much the same way that Christopher Alexander and his colleagues suggest (1977). The objective is to specify the nature of the space-defining elements, and the objects and machines of the public realm in terms of their quantities, qualities, materials, and geometry. *The most important elements in terms of the functioning of the environment have to be discussed first, followed by the less important.* The ultimate act of designing is, however, an act of synthesis and not of simple assembly. Inevitably, well-functioning solutions to components of a problem have to give way to less well functioning ones in order to meet the requirements of yet other components of a problem. The act of synthesis is an argumentative process with designers arguing among themselves and with other collaborators during the act of designing.

Creative designers are those people who can see/ understand a large number of the affordances required of the built environment, who are constantly examining potential ways of combining the affordances, who recognize the potentialities of new combinations of the elements of the environment, and envision new elements and geometries of built form and understand their affordances for human behavior in its multifaceted manifestations. They have a high tolerance for the ambiguities in their work.

Representing Designs

The way one represents or models a proposal biases both the designing and understanding of it. One of the difficulties in establishing a truly participatory design process is that laypeople find many standard drawing types (e.g., orthographic, axonometric, and isometric projections) and even iconic models and perspective drawings difficult to understand. In addition, many attributes of a design are described (i.e., modeled) verbally, and the images people have of what the words signify differ considerably. There are almost no ways around this communications problem, particularly in situations where time is short. People rely heavily on the designer's expertise in envisioning what proposals will be like.

If one of the obligations of urban designers is to bring people's attention to future possibilities, then the choice of presentation techniques for proposed designs must be based on their utility as models that predict well what the future will be like. Models should be regarded neither as designs that meet artistic standards nor as products in themselves, as they often are. Existing prototypical designs or places with features similar to those of a proposed design can also be visited so that people can experience what a place is like. However, such prototypes are often nonexistent or too distant to be visited. The need is to have good models on which evaluations can be based (see also the discussion on "Predicting the Performance of a Design in Context" below).

Any representational technique brings attention to some aspects of a problem or a solution and not others. A model is often used as a sales device rather than as a model of what will actually occur. Many urban design schemes are represented in axonometric or bird's-eye and other perspective forms. Iconic models can be examined from various viewpoints. Computer graphics techniques enable the simulation of movement through a scheme. Perhaps computer-based models of virtual reality will provide significant advances in the four-dimensional perception of potential future spaces in the public realm. Today much remains in verbal form.

The design of the management process for maintaining both the behavioral program (which in many instances may require strong subsidies to survive) and the built environment is likely to be represented in algorithmic form in words and flow diagrams.

EVALUATING DESIGN PROPOSALS ON THE DRAWINGBOARD

Urban design proposals need to be evaluated based on how well they afford the behavioral and physical systems desired, the resources they consume to implement, and their management and operating requirements when implemented. In addition, their side effects, positive and negative, on the broader sociogenic and biogenic environment must form part of the evaluation. Proposals vary in how they combine strengths and weaknesses in dealing with a multivariate situation. One proposal may have inherent weaknesses but also have a highly positive catalytic effect on its surroundings. The reverse may be true of

another design. One proposal may well serve the needs of one group of people but not another. The fiscal behavior of different proposals may have varying long- and short-term costs and benefits.

In Chapter 21 it was noted that several intellectual processes are involved in the choice phase of the design process. A major process is predicting the performances of a social agenda, the physical system that will house it best, and the outcomes of a design proposal. A second intellectual process is evaluating these performances. A third one is making the decision that one design proposal is better than the others and is acceptable or not. Such an evaluation must be based on the original goals of the project established during programming and that have evolved during the ensuing debates over ends and means.

Predicting the Performance of a Design in Context

Three interactive sets of predictions must be made in order to describe how a design will function in the future: (1) the nature of the future sociocultural context in which the design will exist and its effect on the proposal if it were to be implemented, (2) the performance of the project in that context, and (3) the nature of the effect of the proposal on its environment biogenic, and sociogenic.

Predicting the Future Sociocultural Context

Any proposal if implemented will function in a social, economic, and physical context. Some factors in the environment will be remarkably stable, some will change in some ways that are predictable with a high degree of accuracy and in others that may be highly capricious. Some of these changes will not affect the quality of a proposal, some will enhance it, and others will detract from it. It is tempting to deal with the potential capriciousness of changes outside one's jurisdiction or control by treating a proposal as an island that can withstand any changes outside it. While sometimes an urban design proposal may literally be for an island (e.g., Roosevelt Island, New York), it is still affected by what is going on around it.

There are three primary environmental concerns: the catalytic effect of a proposal on the land uses and building types around it (see below), changes in the economic climate, and changes in the social context that will affect a design once implemented. While all predictions of the future involve some risk, elements in the environment do occur in specific patterns. There are considerable data on the sequence of changes in the population and economic climate of cities that can be used to predict in the short run. Information on planned changes in the infrastructure of cities and building permit applications can be ascertained from public agencies so that some inkling of supportive and competitive projects can be ascertained. Any information will, however, be incomplete. Decisions have to be made under uncertainty.

Making accurate predictions about future lifestyles, insofar as they will affect a future urban design, is difficult. It seems that where possible Americans have become increasingly materialistic and comfort seeking and desirous of sensuous experiences. They are by no means unique in this respect (see, e.g., Ninan and Singh 1984 on India). How long this trend will persist is open to considerable conjecture. All these observations reinforce the argument for open-ended, robust urban design.

Predicting the Performance of a Design

A whole range of modeling techniques using empirical data is available to designers to predict how their schemes will perform. One way that has long been used is simply a drawing of the project as a simulation of its future appearance. There are other modeling processes.

The performances of design proposals must be predicted multidimensionally. The process involves many judgments. Usually these judgments are made by experts—a jury or a review board. In some matters the prediction of performance of a proposed design is relatively straightforward. These matters include the cost of the scheme, its impact on traffic flows, and its effect on the biogenic environment. Predicting the effect on wind patterns can be made reasonably accurately in wind tunnel tests. Predicting the appearance of a scheme can be done not only through the use of drawings but also through computer-aided sequential-experience modeling techniques, although laypeople still have difficulty in seeing what a future building will actually look like from computer graphics simulations. Simulation modeling of movement patterns can be developed, and econometric models can be used for predicting the economic impact of a project. One of the most frequently used techniques is to compare the present situation with analogical ones or with case studies of similar situations. Knowing how analogical situations and case studies work enhances the making of predictions about how the present proposals will work provided the analogies and case studies are good ones (i.e., ones that correspond to the present situation). One of the problems with analogies is that they can be very colorful and capture the imagination but operate very differently from the situation under consideration (i.e., they are not good analogies). Much is still done in our heads and presented verbally.

Associative prediction, which extrapolates from empirical theories about the world and how it functions, is the most powerful approach to prediction that we have available to us (Bross 1953). It is, however, only as good as the positive theories on which it is built.

Predicting the Effect of a Proposal on the Environment

Any new total design, component of an all-of-a-piece design, or set of design guidelines will have an impact not only on its site but also on adjacent areas. The impact will be directly on the biogenic environment, on the affordances for economic, cultural, and recreational activities, and thus on the lives of people. Introducing a high-income project into a low-income area will tend to lead to the gentrification of the area. The reverse may also be true. Introducing a new shopping center into a city or its suburbs will affect present shops, particularly if there is neither population growth nor an increase in disposable income in the potential market.

Environmental impact statements are legally mandated in many countries. Such statements tend to focus on specific effects of a project on the biogenic environment—air and water pollution mainly—and not the full range of concerns raised in Chapter 18. Urban designers should be equally concerned with the sociogenic environment. If the effects on either the biogenic or sociogenic environments are negative, then people should be compensated for their loss or the proposal should be abandoned. Such decisions have to be made in specific cultural contexts. For instance, in the United States if the general expectation is that all entrepreneurial activities are risks, then only the negative effects of publically funded urban design efforts should be regarded as requiring compensation. This position hardly seems fair. Social justice issues, however, have to be perceived within a culturally accepted moral order. Often there are debates about the tenets of a moral order and considerable difference between the professed moral order and the practiced one.

Evaluating Proposals

Evaluation involves the application of a value system to the predicted performances of a design proposal. The people affected by or involved in the design must be the ones who evaluate the results of its predicted performances. For a participatory process to be meaningful the predictions, their probabilities, and the procedures for making them must be clear. Otherwise logical debate is impossible. An open participatory discussion requires the cost and benefits of each proposal to be displayed. The most rigorous method of making this display is with a goals achievement matrix such as that suggested in the early 1970s by Morris Hill (1972). The system recognizes the variation in the values of goals of people with different stakes in the outcome of a design (see Fig. 24–6). Thus each goal and each set of stakeholders is given a different weight. The system also recognizes that some goals can be measured in quantitative terms while others can only be dealt with verbally. The matrix becomes a display sheet that enables the relative merits of possible solutions to be debated with some clarity. The logistic difficulty is to develop the display sheet. Intellectually it is a sound model, and we need to develop an ability to approximate such rigor in evaluation schemes.

The importance of having a detailed program in which the goals of the design are clearly specified becomes very apparent in attempting to carry out such an evaluation. The framework also makes those people doing the evaluation consider the relative importance of different objectives and of the people who will be affected by a proposal. The matrix becomes a display of the pros and cons of a proposal and the focus of debate among the parties involved over which of a number of schemes should go ahead. It becomes clear that without specific statements of what a design is to achieve, a logical discussion of a design proposal is impossible. With one, a logical discussion is still not guaranteed!

Deciding on a Course of Action or Design to Implement

Urban design involves a constant stream of decision making from the moment a process begins until it ends. Ultimately it involves making a commitment to implement one particular design or set of guidelines. It is often a difficult decision to make because the monetary and human consequences are large. *The decision to implement one scheme from an array of possibilities should not take a cost-benefit analysis at face value.*

Empirical knowledge of how to design and conduct cost-benefit studies has progressed substantially over the past two decades, but nevertheless there remain many shortcomings. All decision making involves some risk that the design objectives will not be met. The ultimate decision maker on whether a project goes ahead is likely to be the sponsor of a scheme or a public regulatory agency. Sometimes, particularly if bond financing of projects is necessary for implementation, the proposal may be the subject of a public referendum. However thoroughly the design process has been carried out on behalf of all concerned, the ultimate decision of whether to implement a proposal may be a capricious one. If the decision is no, the process goes back to an earlier stage of the design process or is abandoned, depending on the nature of the issues that need readdressing.

In autocratic societies the decision of what should be built may be passed on to the urban designer, but even then there is likely to be somebody who has veto power over the design. In such societies, power is centralized and the urban designer is likely to be working closely with the decision makers. Albert Speer's work for Berlin between 1937 and 1943 was so closely associated with Adolf Hitler that Hitler is often regarded as the co-designer. In democratic societies the power to make decisions is more diffuse. The role of the urban designer in the United States must be to ensure that the participation in making decisions is as wide as possible if the concept of a participatory democracy is to be fulfilled.

IMPLEMENTING URBAN DESIGN

Implementing an urban design proposal involves bringing to realization the design proposed in the imaginary

Source: Hill (1972)

THE GOALS-ACHIEVEMENT MATRIX

Goal Description: Relative Weight:	*a* 2			*β* 3		
Incidence	Relative Weight	Costs	Benefits	Relative Weight	Costs	Benefits
Group a	1	A	D	5	E	-
Group b	3	H		4	-	R
Group c	1	L	J	3	-	S
Group d	2	-		2	T	-
Group e	1	-	K	1		U
		Σ	Σ			
Goal Description: Relative Weight:	*γ* 5			*δ* 4		
Group a	1		N	1	Q	R
Group b	2		-	2	S	T
Group c	3	M	-	1	V	W
Group d	4		-	2	-	-
Group e	5		P	1	-	-
		Σ	Σ			

Figure 24–6: The Goals Achievement Matrix Method of Project Evaluation

world on paper. There are many urban design proposals that have never been implemented. While some were explorations of ideas and were never intended to be implemented, many that were intended to be have not been. If implementation is intended then the array of procedures to be used and the resources available should, as noted earlier, have been specified as part of the problem definition and program development phase of the designing process. It must also be noted that in some cases the nature of implementation procedures to be used can only be designed once a proposal has been made.

There are a number of cases of what are now deemed to be worthwhile projects where, if the full difficulty of implementing them had been known at the outset, the project would almost certainly have been shelved. An Australian example illustrates this point well. If politicians had been aware that building the Sydney Opera House would cost $127 million Australian rather than $7 million Australian, it is doubtful whether it would have been built. If the full benefit to Sydney and Australia had also been predicted at the outset, it may have gone ahead anyway, but the ability of the public and their elected representatives to imagine long-term benefits is also often limited. The failure to predict costs was matched by a failure to predict its full benefits.

Time and Implementation Procedures

With the exception of some total urban designs, urban design schemes are not built all at once. All-of-a-piece designs are implemented over time in a number of stages and are likely to be changed as the process goes forward. University master plans change considerably between the implementation of the first buildings and open spaces and later ones (see Turner 1984). Any empirical observations will show such a result is typical if not universal. Roosevelt Island in New York City is being developed in a series of phases with substantial changes occurring along the way. What should the urban designer do about the nature of implementing an urban design project or proposal?

Each phase of the implementation process should result in a scheme that works independently in terms of the logic of the financial aspects of the development process and the quality of life of those using the project. Each phase should be able to work as a completed whole if the overall master plan is discontinued after a phase and if future designs other than those proposed for a particular part of the scheme are implemented. The design of each phase should not preclude other options unless this is its very intention. A strong design idea that can be perceived by people other than simply the designer is likely to persist under varying future conditions. The master plan for Rice University in Houston has remained remarkably consistent over the course of this century and has been respected by the architects and sponsors of recent design additions to the university. Very often, however, the second phase of a large-scale project will be delayed and a new overall plan developed. This new plan may well depart from the original simply to show that a different designer and often different sponsors are involved. Frequently, however, new problems or opportunities will have arisen and must be addressed.

The Range of Implementation Procedures

Implementing any large-scale urban design project involves many processes and difficulties, some of which can be foreseen, but others not. The acquisition and assembling of land parcels is often a major problem, however much it is in the public interest to do so, as the federal urban renewal programs of the 1950s and 1960s recognized. Obtaining funding for a project, particularly public funding, is another problem. In countries where there is no land market, a central authority can acquire land by decree. In the United States, the accumulation of small parcels of land into larger ones is almost certain to involve stealth and negotiated sale and often quasi-legal maneuvering, even when conducted in the public domain (Frieden and Sagalyn 1989). In the United States as in many countries, governments have the right to acquire land by using the power of *eminent domain*. Sometimes the whole process of land acquisition has been completed before urban design programming is seriously begun; at other times the processes go hand in hand. *One of the obligations of urban designers is to fight to ensure that people are not penalized by land acquisition efforts. Individuals have to be appropriately compensated for hardships they endure. Similarly, people who receive windfall benefits should be taxed on them.* Implementing such a normative position may be politically impossible, and questions about how much an urban designer should attempt to be a reformer of the tax and legal systems is open to debate. Certainly the tax system in the United States is a major determinant of land purchase and investment decisions and thus of urban form.

Coordinated urban design projects are easier to implement if: (1) they are large scale, (2) the land on which they are built is held in large parcels under common ownership, particularly public ownership, (3) there is pressure for development, (4) there are resources available to fund development, (5) there is political support for the projects, and (6) they are opportune (see also Westerman 1990). Most visionary schemes have recognized the first and second but have tried to create the other four conditions.

In total and all-of-a-piece designs, developers with their financing arrangements in place have considerable control over what is done, but even in this situation there will be some review board to whom they must submit their plans for approval. In democratic societies, the power to implement other than total urban design proposals relies on legal mechanisms and on the range of implementation procedures available within them. In the United States, the procedures are essentially those that presently exist and were described in Chapter 3, Urban Design Today. They are:

> Zoning Controls
> > Prescriptive Zoning
> > Incentive Zoning
> Restrictive Covenants
> Design Guidelines

In designing and using these approaches the public sector usually dictates the terms.

In most places the process of having these procedures accepted as public policy and implemented and administered are well developed and clear. The way that zoning is implemented, the way applications for building permits and licenses have to be reviewed, and the way appeals from negative reviews are handled are all legally established. The only points to be made here are that if the mechanisms are not in place, they need to be designed within the legal framework of the jurisdiction under concern; many of the procedures are open to considerable corrupt actions; and in many jurisdictions controls give way easily to developers' pleas of economic hardship.

Urban designers are, like other citizens, required to fight corruption. It is, however, easy to get caught up in a corrupt system in order to achieve desired ends. In some cultures what appears to be legally corrupt seems to be the behavioral norm. A dilemma arises when the laws are deemed to be corrupt. *The obligation of an urban designer remains to fight for social justice and an ethical design and implementation process.*

The Rights of the Individual and the Community

In implementing any scheme, particularly the redevelopment of urban areas, a number of people are likely to be displaced or a proposal may have a negative impact on their lives, even though the community as a whole may prosper. This problem is particularly acute with the placement of noxious facilities (i.e., those which are socially or biogenically undesirable).

In a society such as the United States, which stresses individual rights over communal rights, advocates of the latter have sometimes been labeled "communists," although, as problems intensify and the need for cooperative action becomes clearer, this attitude will no doubt change. *Urban designers need to be prepared to go to court in defense of schemes in the public interest, but also to argue for the interests of those impacted negatively by any proposal.* In some cases, the very idea of a project is the negative factor, regardless of any other impact it might have on the quality of anybody's life. In this case, the urban designer's role is an educative one. As Violett-Le-Duc noted a century ago:

> we shall do wisely even to regard [popular judgment] as sovereign in the last resort, for the very sufficient reason that after all, if we erect public buildings, it is the public which makes use of them and pays for them. I am quite ready to admit that we must enlighten that judgment although it is never so far astray as some are willing to support.

Urban design by its very nature puts the community first. It stresses the benefits to be gained, directly or indirectly, by communal action. Decisions have to be fought out in the political arena and often in the courts of law. Using empirical evidence, by understanding and being able to explain a project's strengths and limitations based on associative predictions, gives political power to the designer. Frequently it is still insufficient to win cases.

EVALUATING THE COMPLETED PROJECT

Traditionally the systematic verification of how well an urban design scheme works when implemented has not been a major concern of the design professions, as was explained in Chapter 21. *One of the obligations of urban designers is to analyze the results of their work or, better still, to hire others to evaluate the results of their work, and to disseminate the results.* This places the urban designer in a major quandary. In whose terms should the results be evaluated? Who pays for the evaluation? Who does it? What are the rewards for the urban designer? The answers have to stem from an understanding of the purpose of a scheme.

An urban design work should be evaluated in terms of the stakeholders directly involved but also in terms of the public interest. For some it may work well and for others not so well. If the problem situation is of any complexity, then a design solution is extremely unlikely to work well on all dimensions for all people. It should be one of the roles of the academic community to constantly evaluate the results of design in a multidimensional manner *simply as a theory-building task.* The goal is not to censure any designer but rather to build the knowledge base for future designs. *Critics in the professional and lay press also need to look at designs*

in terms of the public interest and various stakeholders rather than simply in terms of architects' intellectual aesthetic ideologies.

Design professionals receive awards from their peers for design quality. Awards and prizes can give deserved recognition to design professionals, but many award-winning schemes are held in high esteem only by the professional elite. *Any system of accolades for urban designers should be based on a rigorous multidimensional evaluation rather than on the opinions of a panel of professionals looking at photographs of a project.* At present, many evaluations use exactly this approach; few are rigorous. The methodology and methods for empirical reviews of projects after construction are well developed (Preiser 1988). Such reviews must focus not only on the product but also on the process whereby it was achieved if the full positive theoretical basis for urban design actions is to be improved.

The process of evaluation involves asking a number of questions: What actual behaviors are going on? Are they the ones used as the basis for programming and design? Are there intolerable dissonances between what is going on and the desired behaviors? Are these dissonances attributable to the built environment? If the dissonances are within acceptable limits, the design is acceptable. If there is no dissonance for anyone, the design is implausibly successful!

OPERATING AND MAINTAINING THE SYSTEM

The level of maintenance of a project is perceived by users as a major contributor to its quality. The costs of operating and maintaining the built environment and the activities it houses (particularly those that require social subsidization) are high—sometimes very high. There are many examples of designs that worked when they were first implemented, but after a short time started to deteriorate either through wear or tear or because little thought had been given to the management of the system, social and physical. Raised planter boxes are provided in many city streets, only to have the trees and flowers within them wither and die and be replaced by discarded bottles, cans, and other trash and garbage. Paving stones crack and surfaces get dirty. Once a place is seen to be uncared for, it seems to attract a greater lack of caring because it is seen as being under nobody's jurisdiction—nobody's caring. Attitudes toward maintenance vary considerably in the United States. The nature of the culture in which a scheme is to function must thus be understood. Some cultures are highly tolerant of dirt and disrepair; others are not. In some cultures cleanliness is next to godliness. Many urban designs in the United States are based on the assumption that people in general act according to this precept. In some cities they do but in others the consequences suggest another stance should have been taken.

The process of maintaining and managing a system must be considered in defining the problem to be addressed and in designing

1. Society Hill, Philadelphia

2. Almost Any City, USA

3. Market Street East, Philadelphia

alternative solutions. The resources available for maintaining a system need to be considered at the inception of the decision-making process. A management plan must be part of any urban design scheme and must be reflected in the design itself.

Kevin Lynch noted that well-maintained places tend to be loved by their inhabitants, and that design professionals can improve their ability to design such places (Banerjee and Southworth 1990). In order to achieve this end people themselves have to be involved in making decisions about their own environments. Lynch's dictum is worth repeating: *Planning and design must begin with community participation, local control, and individual engagements with the immediate environment.* There is a major danger in considering an urban design simply to be another consumer product (Schurch 1991).

CONCLUSION

Urban designers have a choice. Either they can adopt the expansionist view of their task as described here and advocated by a number of people today or else they can withdraw into treating urban design like large-scale architecture. It is certainly easier to keep their domain of concern limited to the interests of the sponsors of their work. It is clear that the position taken here is that this stance would be unfortunate.

The process of urban designing has to be designed to fit the circumstances—the task environment and societal culture—in which it is taking place. An abstract model such as that presented here provides a framework for asking what should be done anywhere and for understanding the degree to which any process is in the public interest. It also enables us to recognize what our own role in society is. There is much that can be accomplished to improve the habitat of human beings through urban design, however, much requires policy decisions to which designers can contribute but that fall largely outside the professional expertise of the design professions, however well developed their knowledge bases might be.

Figure 24–7: Operating Urban Designs and Environmental Quality
Well-maintained environments contribute to a sense of well being (1). The cost of operating and maintaining the public realm can be very high. Many urban design proposals seem to assume that the money supply is infinitely elastic and that people are gentle with the environment around them. Designers need to perceive how people will use the affordances of the environment (2) and how the results of their behavior affects perceptions of environmental quality. The task is to design environments that are behaviorally rich and at the same time robust or, alternatively, to make maintenance procedures part of the design (3).

MAJOR REFERENCES

Baldwin, Maynard M., ed. (1975). *Portraits of Complexity: Applications of Systems Methodologies to Societal Problems.* Columbus, OH: Battelle Memorial Institute.

Cutler, Laurence Stephan, and Sherrie Stephens Cutler (1982). *Recycling Cities for People: The Urban Design Process.* 2d ed. Boston: Cahners Book International.

Hatch, C. Richard, ed. (1984). *The Scope of Social Architecture.* New York: Van Nostrand Reinhold.

Mills, Miriam, ed. (1990). *Conflict Resolution and Public Policy.* New York: Greenwood.

Preiser, Wolfgang F. E., Harvey Z. Rabinowitz, and Edward T. White (1988). *Post-Occupancy Evaluation.* New York: Van Nostrand Reinhold.

Shirvani, Hamid (1985). *The Urban Design Process.* New York: Van Nostrand Reinhold.

Studer, Raymond (1969), "The Dynamics of Behavior-Contingent Physical Systems." In Geoffrey Broadbent and Anthony Ward, eds., *Design Methods in Architecture.* London: Lund Humphries, pp. 59–70.

——— (1988). "Design of the Built Environment: The Search for Usable Knowledge." In Elizabeth Huttman and Willem van Vliet, eds., *Handbook of Housing and the Built Environment.* New York: Greenwood, pp. 73–96.

PART IV

CONCLUSION:
THE FUTURE OF URBAN DESIGN

Westlake Plaza, Seattle

Urban design as an activity has a long history but a short one under that rubric. As a recognized field of design endeavor it is thirty years old, having begun to establish its own identity, in the United States at least, in the 1950s. Late in that decade the growing interest in urban design as an intellectual and professional activity distinct from architecture and city planning led the Association of Collegiate Schools of Architecture to focus on the topic in its seminars. A conference on urban design criticism held in Philadelphia in January 1959 attracted such luminaries as Nanine Clay, David Crane, Jane Jacobs, J. B. Jackson, Louis I. Kahn, Kevin Lynch, Ian McHarg, Lewis Mumford, I. M. Pei, G. Holmes Perkins, Gordon Stephenson, William L. C. Wheaton, and Catherine Bauer Wurster. In 1962 the association asked David Crane to organize a seminar on urban design at the Cranbrook Conference. It led to the publication of The Architect and The City *(1962). The field has developed considerably since then, as more has been learned about the built environment, the human purposes it serves, and the effect of different built patterns with their infrastructure systems on the biogenic environment. Its empirical content has grown.*

Empiricism in urban design is not new. It has a long history too, but the current effort to build a knowledge-based discipline derived from a research program on people and their built environments is as recent as the term "urban design." The twenty-first annual conference of the Environmental Design Research Association (EDRA), held at the University of Illinois at Champaign/Urbana, was entitled "Coming of Age" as recently as 1989. A gap between the knowledge being generated by researchers and its practical application does exist, but it is beginning to be closed as researchers learn how best to enhance the practicability of their work by generating design principles understandable to practitioners and as practitioners learn how to use the research literature.

Urban design and environment and behavior studies have both come of age and are at a point of analyzing what they have and have not accomplished. The utility of the accomplishments and intellectual foundations of both are, however, constantly under challenge. The legitimacy of environment and behavior studies as a unique endeavor within the behavioral sciences is constantly being challenged. After all, psychology deals with both the external and the internal, or mental, environment of human behavior, even though the latter is strictly speaking a contradiction in terms. The legitimacy of urban design as a unique field among the design professions is also challenged. Much of the discussion is irrelevant to improving urban design.

There is a continuing need for design professionals with an understanding of cities, the built environment, and human behavior to address the problems of urban and suburban development. There are considerable gaps in our present knowledge of how built environments and their sociogenic and biogenic environment interact, but we have learned much in the past thirty years. Much of the knowledge remains in a piecemeal state as does professional practice. This situation needs to be overcome if urban design is to be effective. Urban design should be regarded as an integrative discipline and an integrative professional activity. It should be an area of synthesis among all the design professions. It has, however, evolved its own literature and specific methods and techniques, so it may well continue on its own evolutionary path. This independence may not be in the best interests of society.

The degree to which urban design can be regarded as a discipline and as a profession in its own right is discussed in Chapter 25, Urban Design as a Discipline and as a Profession. Such a discussion also enables the urban design roles of people drawn from the various design professions to be discussed, for each has a contribution to make to the creation of the future urban environment. Leadership in urban design, however, will serve society best if it comes from those people who have a synthetic vision that extends beyond their own professional expertise to an integrative view of the contribution of other disciplines and to the enhancement of the quality of life of all people.

The Modern movements, despite their failings, set urban design in a sound direction. We need to continue their task by building an intellectual footing for urban design as an integrative discipline and an integrative professional activity. Much has already been accomplished and much more can be if the strengths and weaknesses of past endeavors are understood. This knowledge can help urban designers to make sound decisions about the future and to understand what their proposals can and cannot achieve. Ultimately, however, creating the future is a political endeavor to which urban designers drawn from the traditional design disciplines can make an important contribution only if their ideas have a sound empirical basis and are accompanied by creative thought about future possibilities. ■

25

URBAN DESIGN AS A DISCIPLINE
AND AS A PROFESSION

"*Urban design* is a relatively new term for an activity of long standing" is the way this book began. As an activity it will continue, although its name may change in response to new challenges. The focus of attention of what we now call urban design has been with the age-old activities of consciously shaping and reshaping (or forming and reforming) human settlements directly through physical design or indirectly through the establishment of rules that others must follow.

In the late 1960s, *urban design,* as the name for a field, replaced *civic design,* a label associated with the urban concerns of the School of Architecture at Liverpool University. Civic design implies perhaps a primary design focus on major municipal buildings, city halls, opera houses, and museums and their relationship to open spaces in the manner of the City Beautiful tradition. *City design* has also been used, especially by Kevin Lynch, but it implies a primary focus on the overall nature of the city. Philip Thiel's *envirotecture* may be a better label to describe the broad concerns of the design fields as a group (Thiel forthcoming).

This book has described the intellectual concern about the nature and goals of urban design in the United States since the beginning of the century but primarily since World War II. Led by an interdisciplinary group of people, but predominantly architects, the growth of urban design as a field of intellectual inquiry and professional action over the last thirty years has been remarkable. Urban designing is an increasingly complex task as the range of human activities grows in size, communications processes become more diverse, new ways of putting geometries together are found, and the rate of physical changes being made in cities speeds up. The growth of

knowledge makes the task of design considerably more difficult because it both opens up new options and highlights the ambiguities and contradictions in the tasks we face. Moreover, except in a few instances, the traditional ordering principles such as the cosmological rules or even the compositional principles of Rationalist architecture used historically to justify design ends and means have little intellectual weight in arguments about what constitutes a good design. New urban design principles have to be generated. In the United States today, urban designers' work is and has to be seen as forming part of the democratic decision-making process shaping future cities, suburbs, and other human habitats.

Since the early 1980s the scope of concern of the practicing architect as urban designer has narrowed in the United States (as elsewhere). The focus has been on large-scale site planning for development projects in the private sector, with the primary goal being to enhance the developer's profitability. Many much-admired and lively schemes have resulted in a profit for the private sector but have also been clearly in the public interest. At the same time, there are many dull, even antisocial schemes, and much of the social and public interest concerns of past urban design efforts have unfortunately been lost. This loss parallels the general decrease in concern of society as a whole with social equity issues in the broader policy-making arena. On the other hand, the concern of urban designers with the design of design guidelines and linkage programs maintains the public policy line of thought that initiated the concern with environmental quality issues and that in turn initiated urban design thirty years ago. In 1977, John M. McGinty, president of the American Institute of Architects, echoed this concern:

I honestly don't think that individual buildings matter any more. Pennzoil Place is beautiful, but who cares? You get into your car and drive past ugly parking lots and junky furniture stores on Main Street to get there. You drive into a subterranean parking lot and walk through grimy tunnels. Or you walk above ground on sidewalks that are not wide enough. By the time you get to the Pennzoil building you don't care whether it is beautiful or not. How you get there and what you look at on the way are as important as having beautiful buildings in a city. Houston is a sorry place to be in and walk in. It's like a museum of buildings. It's the total urban fabric of a city that's important (cited in Thiel, forthcoming).

Columbus, Indiana, with its stock of buildings by many of the world's leading architects is a pleasant enough city, but it too has learned that the finest buildings in the world, piece by piece, leave many opportunity costs in terms of the overall quality of a city. Its civic leaders have become more concerned with urban design quality.

Certainly the central areas of most American cities tend to be in better condition now than in 1977, when McGinty made his comments. Much of this is due to the economic climate of the 1980s, the filling in of gaps resulting from the premature demolition of buildings during the 1950s, 1960s, and 1970s, and the improvement in the quality of many individual buildings, but much has been due to concerted city planning and urban design efforts. In thinking about the future in the United States, a special question arises: "Are individual property rights so important that the benefits of overall cooperation and a concern for social equity in the development of human settlements can only be measured in enhanced property values for tax collectors and return on capital invested to developers?"

The answers to such questions are not empirical ones. They are ideological, although they can be informed by empirical knowledge. They are the kinds of questions that will always arise. In order to be able to address them sensibly, urban design theory, and practice as its behavioral correlate, need to be organized in a manner that can be best brought to bear on the problems of society. The time has come to ask whether urban design needs to be seen as a discipline and a profession in its own right if it is to promote quality of life issues in the built environment—or if urban design is to be the public interest concern of architecture. If it needs to be, can it be?

DISCIPLINES AND PROFESSIONS

A discipline is a branch of knowledge. A profession is either an occupation or a group of people in that occupation. It also implies that the group of people have a specialized set of skills and a unique body of knowledge (Larson 1991). Architecture is both a discipline and a profession (see Anderson 1988). Much knowledge about architecture has little relevance to the design of buildings today but remains quite rightly part of the discipline. Also, much of an architect's professional activity (many architects would claim most of it) draws very little on the disciplinary knowledge of architecture, but instead draws on that of other fields—the management sciences, for instance. Even the act of building design itself draws heavily, in practice if not in academia, on the various branches of engineering and their basis in the discipline of physics.

The same kinds of observations can be made about civil engineering, landscape architecture, and city planning—the other major environmental design fields. They are acknowledged to be both disciplines and professions. The emergence of urban design as a professional activity raises questions about its legitimacy as a field in its own right and about whether it exists as a discipline. Certainly the other design professions regard it as part of their own domains. Whether or not it benefits society to have another specialization as a discipline and a profession in its own right is another question. Urban design certainly cannot be an exclusive profession.

URBAN DESIGN AS AN INTEGRATIVE DISCIPLINE

Paralleling the growth in empirical research on the nature of cities and urban places has been a growth in substantive urban and urban design theory based on an enhanced understanding of the person-environment relationship. There has also been a concomitant growth in our understanding of the designing processes—procedural theory. Much of this growing body of knowledge and ideas is shared with other fields—urban studies and environmental psychology on the positive theory side, and urban planning, landscape architecture, and to a lesser extent architecture on the normative side.

The theoretical content of the field of urban design as envisioned in this book, while overlapping those of other fields, is, as a synthesis, unique. Whether it should be regarded as a discipline in its own right is an open question. Much depends on the future scope of concern of other disciplines, particularly the environmental design disciplines of architecture, civil engineering, city planning, and landscape architecture. Traditionally urban design has been most closely allied with architecture and city planning by filling the intellectual and professional gap between them. As architecture reduces the domain of its concerns and methods of working, and as city planning continues to be concerned mainly with transportation and land-use planning, to the extent that it deals with other than social and economic issues, so urban design has become increasingly an entity on its own.

Architecture as a discipline, as a branch of knowledge, has focused on the nature of buildings and on the forming principles used by members of the profession in designing them. In recent years, the profession seems if anything to have narrowed its range of concerns in response to the increased complexity in building that arises from new uses and new means of construction. Programming has been taken over by independent specialists. In many places the developing field of building is taking over the construction, construction supervision, and management role traditionally held by the architect. The focus of concern of the discipline of architecture has remained firmly on the *design* aspect, architecture's unique contribution, and thus mainly on intellectual aesthetic issues. Architecture has not developed a broad environmental concern, although individual architects are becoming increasingly concerned with environmental issues in site design and the selection of materials. It has been reluctant to embrace new empirical knowledge about the physiological or psychological consequences of its work except where forced to do so by critics, clients, laws, regulations, and design guidelines.

A broad array of citizens and professionals has been concerned with the nature of the biogenic environment, particularly those living in areas of the United States where there is a shortage of land. As population pressures have increased in places that hitherto had wide open spaces, so has the concern with environmental health. Regarding urban designing as part of the process of environment change, of environmental adaptation, is a recent attitude that grows out of the basic changes in the landscape architecture profession and the growth in its scope of concern from garden design to include regional planning on an ecological and biological basis. Concomitant with this development has been the concern with the social ecology of the patterns of both agricultural landscapes and human settlements, and with the search for new forms of settlement patterns and legal tools to protect the biogenic environment. There is a sense of urgency about these issues as populations increase and more land is turned from rural to urban uses, and also, paradoxically, as abandoned agricultural land returns to woodland or grassland in a number of areas of the United States.

The bodies of knowledge of the design fields overlap considerably, and their positive substantive theory draws heavily on both the natural and social sciences. The natural sciences provide insights into the nature of materials, structures, and technology, and the social sciences into the understanding of activity systems, the distribution of activities in space within cultural frameworks, and aesthetic theories. Design methodology, the study of design processes, is common to all decision-making fields, although the specific techniques of analysis depend on the focus of concern and the substantive theory one uses as a basis for design.

The unique concern of urban design is its focus of attention on urban form and forms. This focus has come about by default rather than forethought. It has developed as a result of a need to address problems that other professionals and laypeople were not addressing. As a result it is now beginning to conduct research and develop substantive theory in areas that are important to its own intellectual development. Like architecture, urban design has until recently little in the way of a research tradition other than descriptions of historical precedents. This situation is changing. Whether or not urban design really becomes a discipline in its own right depends largely on what directions architecture, landscape architecture, and city planning take in the future. The drive for each design profession to claim urban design as part of its professional responsibility is understandable. A concern for urban design is a concern for the quality of life and future lives.

A concern for life is exemplified by the empirical research on places, and on people's behavior in and appreciation of them. A concern for exploiting our abilities in dealing with the future has been a primary one of the Rationalists. Such a statement denies neither a concern for the future among Empiricists nor the concern of Rationalists with life, but is rather an expression of how each group sought its ends. There is a need for urban design as a discipline to integrate the two lines of thought—research on who and what we are and what we might become with a concern for exploring future possibilities that extend our present understanding of what might be.

What is likely to happen is that a whole new discipline, possibly the envirotecture mentioned above, will serve as the intellectual basis for all the design specializations. Urban design is an integrative act. It depends on a broad understanding of environmental issues, possibilities, and consequences of developing different possible futures. Social pressures in the long run will almost inevitably lead to a greater common concern among the existing design professions for quality of life issues and thus with human habitats. This will also mean the breaking down of traditional professional boundaries and jealousies. The pressure for change at present is somewhat surprisingly coming from developers who want to see an integrated approval process for their projects. There is a need for a professional ecumenicalism as well.

URBAN DESIGN AS AN INTEGRATIVE PROFESSION

Thirty years ago *urban design* was an almost completely unknown rubric among design professionals. Since then it has become a recognized field of professional activity at least. There are a number of professional organizations devoted to the development of urban design expertise and to the promotion of urban design as a professional activity. Journals focus on urban design, descriptively in terms of the proposed and completed projects, and theoretically in terms of the intellectual basis for design. A number of professional firms promote themselves and their skills as urban designers. Public agencies advertise for urban designers and people with urban design skills. There are a number of educational programs in schools of design around the United States (and increasingly around the world) devoted to the teaching of urban design skills. Does all this make for a profession?

Urban design is an area of mutual interest among all the design professions. At the same time, doing urban design well requires a unique body of knowledge and skills in addition to those associated with the traditional design professions. Aspects of its professional work are also unique. Yet it has been and should remain an applied collaborative effort. The problems urban designers face are too complex to be dealt with by individuals alone. With the increasing challenge that the quality and logic of the work of architects and urban designers face in courts of law, so the demand for professional expertise grows. The "gentleman architect" is increasingly an image of the past not only because of the increasing number of women entering the design professions, but also because of the failure of "good taste" as a persuasive argument in either courts of law or with the public at large.

Bit by bit an increasingly educated society is directly, or indirectly through the questions people ask, demanding that urban design work be professionally competent. The demand parallels those made of other professions, such as medicine. Thus designers must know about the natural and social sciences pertinent to the design of the human habitat and use this knowledge as a basis for design. This knowledge is highly diverse, as has been shown in this book. For example, just understanding the effect of wind patterns on the built environment and the built environment on wind patterns is an increasingly detailed field of study. Understanding how to use the flushing power of winds to simultaneously cleanse the air and make public places pleasantly comfortable is a highly specialized area of knowledge and design skill. In a few places this understanding is already contributing to urban design practice, and through it to the quality of urban life, particularly urban street life (see Chapter 11). The act, or art, of urban designing pulls many such strands together.

Urban design will remain a collaborative art. People with urban design skills, whether acquired through specialized training or assertive personal experience, will continue to be in demand. As human settlements continue to grow in size and population densities increase, making planning and design based on causal observations of the world difficult to defend, the demand will remain. Urban design has clearly developed an area of applied expertise with its own body of knowledge, as this book has demonstrated. It has at least one unique professional facet. This aspect is, as Jonathan Barnett (1982) notes, "the designing of cities without designing buildings"— the writing of design guidelines that shape cities and their

precincts by shaping buildings and the public realm. For urban design guidelines to have plausibility in court, they will have to be based on expert knowledge, not personal whimsy. They can be. While the creation of guidelines to shape the public realm of cities may be the unique aspect of urban design, it is by no means the only role that urban designers will play in the future.

Urban Design and the Problems of the World

As noted in Chapter 3, The Nature of Urban Design Today, architects have been settling for a more limited role in dealing with the social and economic issues confronting the world (Goldberger 1989b). Indeed, the architectural profession has seen its role in the design and implementation of single building design shrink as the building and the construction processes have become more complex. This retrenchment in terms of urban design recognizes that the design of buildings and the quality of the physical environment have little impact on the totality of the major problems facing the world, but it fails to recognize urban design's potential role in creating a better world—in dealing with the multivariate impact of the built environment on people's lives.

The experience of the total and all-of-a-piece designs— the housing projects, the new towns, and new-towns-in-town—of the first three decades after World War II has clearly shown us that major social problems cannot be reduced to housing problems or lack-of-open-space problems, as we design professionals (often abetted by our clients) have been wont to believe. At the same time, the way that cities have been developed during the 1980s through the efforts of the private sector in the absence of any overall concern with the monitoring of urban quality has not contributed to the improvement of life for as many urban dwellers as it might have or as well as it should have.

A number of roles in the overall urban design effort need to be fulfilled if the continuing opportunity costs of current practices are to be reduced. One potential function of urban designers is to provide leadership and advice to decision makers about the nature of the changing three-dimensional quality of the built environment, and in particular about the public realm. They might also bring to the public's attention the social consequences if design decisions regarding the built environment are made on a piecemeal basis. For some a reduced but more glamorous artistic role might be appropriate in simply giving geometrical compositional ideas to other decision makers. Different designers concerned with cities will no doubt see their functions differently given their own perceived areas of expertise, interests, and values (Bruegmann 1982; Scott Brown 1982; Alexander et al. 1987; Ostler 1987; Mackay 1990). The danger arises if they claim too much expertise or can only see the world in terms of their own professional competence and fail to see themselves as one of a number of decision makers—if they fail to see urban design as a collaborative effort.

The Decision Makers

In democratic societies decision-making powers are highly diffuse. The decisions establishing the overall goals of society are ostensibly made by the members of a society themselves (or at least, those who are citizens) acting through elected politicians. Most such societies allow the marketplace to be the major arbitrator of competing goals and means for establishing the nature of the society. This observation was made in Chapter 2, Shaping the Twentieth-Century City. In some countries, the public sector has intervened more strongly than in others in establishing priorities for qualities of city form. In those societies, the professional designer as policymaker, or, more likely, as the advisor to policymakers, plays a larger role than in the United States, where power is spread more diffusely among individuals, who can do what they want within certain legal limits. Thus professional designers have had a greater impact on the design of the cities in West Europe than on those in the United States.

The design professions have traditionally followed social currents rather than created them. The Modernists—both Rationalists and Empiricists—were dealing with the social concerns of the first half of the twentieth century, and many urban designers today have simply been following the social currents of consumer pragmatism in the broader society. This situation will continue unless designers take a more openly political stance in society. They would have to be much stronger advocates for environmental quality than they are now. They would have to be much more willing to step on politicians' toes than they are now. There needs to be a resurrection of the crusader spirit on behalf of the quality of human settlements, such as that demonstrated by people such as Michael Harrington (1962) on the part of the poor and Ian McHarg (1969) on the part of landscape architecture, and perhaps Greenpeace today.

During the 1980s the U.S. public sector, particularly in cities, was primarily concerned with short-run monetary returns. In terms of the design of cities, the prevalent attitude encouraged larger-scale development of large buildings by developers as entrepreneurs. The leadership in the design of cities has come from the private sector. City governments have largely abdicated their planning role. Historically, the public sector made policy proposals and developers made building proposals within them. Today developers make building proposals and the public sector responds. The initiative for shaping the future physical city now lies largely in the developers' hands for good or for ill.

The major decision makers in society remain the politicians, landholders as well as the developers, and the people who fund development—bankers in the private sector, governmental agencies in the public. The degree of power they hold shifts over time. The power to make the major design decisions in cities is held by relatively few people—*the power elite*. The myriad smaller-scale decisions that give a city much of its character are made by many people. The function of the urban designer can be to give coherence and shape to all these decisions in the public interest, as advisor or designer to both the public and private sectors of the economy. Designers could also fill any number of less onerous roles, depending on their expertise.

The political power of design professionals comes from their own expertise. The more empirically based their knowledge, it has been argued in this book, the more powerful their arguments. Transportation planners and other planners in technical fields had until recently considerable power to do as they wished because they were able to describe in detail the performance requirements of their concerns. Now, however, the social consequences of their plans, in terms of land use, the distribution of populations, and social dislocations, are subject to considerable debate, and the criteria they have traditionally used to evaluate and promote their schemes have been severely questioned.

Some architects have provided strong leadership in urban design by trying to understand urban issues and suggest solutions. The mainstream of architecture, however, lost credibility, and thus political power, by its insistence that it knows best because of its innate creative ability and not because of the depth of its knowledge. The formalist Rationalist approach to design is legitimate provided its limited functional utility in terms of enhancing the quality of people's lives is understood and no higher utility is claimed. Urban designers' power to make decisions, or rather to shape decisions, comes from their reputation and expertise, and from their ability to argue persuasively for their proposals. Relying on arguing ability alone will be a major long-run error.

Integrating Professional Expertise

Few people have been specifically educated in urban design. The number of graduates of urban design programs throughout the world is negligible, and some of those graduates have returned to building design, an activity with more immediate rewards. Most of those design professionals directly involved in urban design today have learned about urban issues the truly empirical way—by experience—although they may have missed other than what is immediately necessary to enable a decision to be made.

They have had to learn about the development process because so much urban design has been developer-driven. They have had to be more sensitive to the broader functional concerns of urban form than in the past because of their participation in the political infighting that accompanies the development and implementation of urban design proposals. They have not, however, been concerned about making highly multifunctional designs because there has been neither political pressure to do so nor has their education, formal or experiential, equipped them to address broad social and technical concerns (Scott Brown 1990). Designers are, however, clearly developing an awareness of the growing body of empirical research, particularly that which can be turned into design principles easily (e.g., Lynch 1960; Newman 1972; and Whyte 1980).

It is clear that in the future, most people working in urban design will be drawn from the traditional design disciplines. Many of them will deal with urban design strictly through their own disciplinary foci. They will continue to be advocates for their own interests. Somehow these strands of interest need to be pulled together by some urban designers at least, if the potential contribution of designers to society, as both a social and design force, is to be met.

The Urban Designer as Image Maker and Formal Artist: The Architectural View

The creation of what has been labeled *hollow form*—a design for its own sake (Hester 1989)—has traditionally been associated with much architectural thinking. When architects look at and criticize the city today their concern is still largely with the city as a geometrical pattern and as a setting for the display of buildings. This kind of work has to be integrated into other urban concerns.

The urban designer as pure form giver without any clear social concern, has a number of potential functions. One basic function is as an architect or building designer to bring to creative life a building that is being designed to meet a set of urban design guidelines. If a design program is based on a detailed understanding of the social, cultural, and economic problems to be resolved and a commitment to resolve them, urban design guidelines at their best can give only an outline of what needs to be done. They can be interpreted in many ways. The ability to provide creative solutions to building designs that must meet urban design guidelines was clearly illustrated in the work of a number of major architects—Robert Stern, Frank Gehry, and Robert Venturi—at Fan Pier in Boston (Barnett 1987). If this ability can be extended to the membership of the profession as whole, the quality of cities will be increased.

A second role as form giver is more closely related to urban design per se. It is the traditional one of presenting urban visions or design ideas on how to organize the spatial pattern of the city (Bacon 1974). The public realm is ultimately architecture after all—it has a physical form. The goal is to create an inspired and recognizable physical framework for people's lives. Architectural visions can spark ideas about the potential form of places, but like their predecessors the visions are likely to be bold schemes solving a limited set of problems that remain unbuilt (Sky and Stone 1976). Sometimes the set of problems that they solve is important enough that all others might be neglected.

The Urban Designer as Applied Ecologist: The Landscape Architectural View

One of the major effects of the built environment and its inhabitants is on the natural world—on the biogenic environment—and ultimately on human well-being. Buildings change the micro-climate, paving changes water runoff patterns, human endeavors pollute the air, and so on. The list is almost endless, as suggested in Chapter 18. Since the 1970s, the profession of landscape architecture has undergone radical change. It has been thrust into the forefront of the environmental design disciplines, as the public has become more aware of the depredation of the biological environment. The goal has been to design for regional and local ecological fitness, bearing in mind the consequential impacts of design decisions on the inanimate natural environment (McHarg 1969; Hough 1984; Spirn 1984). The focus of attention has often been on serving the interests of the natural environment per se.

Many landscape architects as urban designers have had, as have architects, a limited model of the human being in mind—it has been largely a biological model. While generalizations are dangerous, landscape architects in the United States have also tended to bring a preconceived environmental aesthetic drawn from traditional garden design—the English landscape garden for those out of the Anglo-American tradition and the formal garden for those out of the Continental, Rationalist tradition—to the design of cities and urban spaces.

More recently the concern among landscape architects has been to design with the needs of people in mind as well (Hester 1989; Spirn 1984, 1989). This concern stems from the recognition that the ends served by ecological landscape architecture are as political as those of any other professional design movement. In addition it has been a basic tenet, now much criticized, that the creation of more open space in human settlements solves social ills. The design of parks as recreation areas has evolved as political pressures have changed and as images of the functions that parks serve have changed. As a consequence, there have been a number of eras of park design: the pleasure ground, the reform park, the recreation facility, and the open-space system (Cranz 1982).

The contribution of landscape architects to future urban design thought promises to be a major one as the public becomes more concerned about the health of the biogenic environment. Many now have two areas of expertise that can be brought to bear on urban design. The first is an understanding of the role of the natural environment in the city, and the effect of the city on the natural world, and the second is the design of public places. The second role will be substantially enhanced as the field adopts a more generous model of the human being and an attitude toward problem solving characteristic of the parks movements and their strong social concern (e.g., Hester 1975, 1989; Cooper Marcus and Francis 1990).

The Urban Designer as Infrastructure Designer: The Civil Engineering View

The urban designer as infrastructure designer is most closely associated with the civil engineering and to some extent city planning professions. The primary concern has been with the design of infrastructure systems and related land uses. The focus of concern tends to be on the city as a set of communications channels. It has been argued in this book that the quality of a city is largely a function of the quality of the public infrastructure—streets and open spaces—and the distribution of facilities. Thus this role is crucial as the advocacy for broadening design concern from the narrow Functionalism of the Rationalists to that described in Chapter 7 and, more generally, to that which is indicated in Part Two. Indeed, urban design is and will continue to be concerned primarily with enhancing the quality of the capital web of settlements (Crane 1960; Buchanan 1988). Public policy needs to be as well.

The Urban Designer as a Social Force: The City Planning View

City planning has long had a social concern, to improve the quality of people's lives. The failure of the Modern movement led to city planners focusing on an Empiricist approach to planning, but the three-dimensional quality of the city became neglected as they strove to deal with fundamental social and economic problems (see Introduction). The necessary rediscovery of the physical city and the focus on form and function as an interrelated system will lead to a rethinking by city planners of the nature of their role in urban design. Urban design actions inevitably follow city planning decisions, but they should also shape them, although much recent total and all-of-a-piece urban design seems to have taken place in a city planning vacuum.

The urban designer is involved with other decision makers in helping societies self-consciously create a future. Inevitably any urban design scheme shapes that future by the behaviors it affords and does not afford. In Chapter 1 it was noted that because a behavior is afforded by a particular pattern of the built environment it does not

mean that it will occur, but those behaviors not afforded cannot take place. The design of a social agenda sets the parameters for urban design.

An urban designer like any other citizen can also play an activist role in shaping social ends. This role has been more closely associated with visionaries than with practitioners, but the Community Design movement has had social objectives in mind (see Chapters 2, 3, and 4).

Creating a Synthetic Vision

For urban design to make a major contribution to the betterment of society in the future all four images covered in the last section need to be integrated. Each of the traditional design professions has much to offer its clients, the public, in the design of cities and their parts, either directly through public sector work or indirectly through the work they do for developers. Society would probably be better served if city planners, urban designers, landscape architects, and civil engineers came under one umbrella. To be able to carry out the role of urban designers described in this book what is needed is people with an integrationist viewpoint to provide synthetic visions.

It is irrelevant which profession provides the leadership. Leadership is likely to come from the individuals who are the most concerned. The problem has been that those who are concerned do not necessarily have the scope of knowledge to provide that synthetic vision. Leaders are needed who know enough about the overall set of issues to know what they know, what they do not know, and how to bring people with different areas of knowledge and skills together. They must also have enough self-confidence to use other people who have the expertise to ascertain what problems should be addressed in a particular situation.

Given current expertise, city planners and landscape architects are more likely than other design professionals to develop policy leadership in urban design, although the identification of specific problems and opportunities is likely to come from anybody. Architectural teams are apt to play the leadership role in putting total and all-of-a-piece designs together because architects have competence in designing buildings. Designing the infrastructure and formulating guidelines for buildings that shape the public realm require people who understand both architecture in its narrow sense and environmental design and problem solving in a broad sense. As in the past, the central role for professionals specializing in urban design will be highly dependent on the nature of clients to be served.

POTENTIAL CLIENTS IN THE FUTURE

John Zeisel's (1974) distinction between the paying and nonpaying clients of urban designers, it has been noted, is a useful one. It is an important distinction because it illustrates the multiplicity of obligations facing urban designers in designing for the future. Designers have a major obligation to be the advocates for the people paying them, but they also have a professional obligation to the users of their schemes and to society as a whole. In reality, the so-called nonpaying clients end up paying for design quality through rent, taxes, or psychological stress. Despite lip service to the concept of user participation they are not usually involved directly in the decision-making process. They need to be.

The Paying Client: The Development Community

The development community consists of two major groups: entrepreneurs and their financial backers. In the public sector, the entrepreneurs are governmental agencies and politicians. Their financial backers are taxpayers (although increasingly it is the private sector). In the private sector, the entrepreneurs are developers and their financial backers are bankers and other lending institutions. They act as surrogates for the actual people who will pay—purchasers and renters—for the products they produce with their architects.

The Public Sector

The public sector, although it is not unique in this, has historically been the entrepreneur acting on behalf of the public interest in the public realm. It has promoted the development of the capital web of cities and the celebration of historic events and important people through public memorials. It has been a patron of the arts. The public sector has been concerned with the elements of form that are seen to be beneficial to society as a whole, but that would not pay for themselves directly through user fees or for which it is administratively impossible to collect fees. This concern must continue, but unless citizens are willing to pay for the system through taxes on property, income, and consumer goods of various types, little progress will be made. People have to be made aware that their own self-interest is at stake. In the United States such an awareness is likely to arise only when people perceive the probable impacts to be immediate.

The paying client in the public sector is operationally the politician and the civil servant. The former is supposed to give direction, and the latter to either execute or supervise the implementation of that intention. One of the major objectives of politicians is to get reelected. Their degree of concern for urban design varies with that of their constituents, but some politicians have been strong advocates for design quality and their cities reflect it (Smith 1991). Getting changes in the built environment is a major symbol of a public official's concern. It can also be a distraction from dealing with the basic problems of the city. Not only architects, but many elected officials have a strong belief in architectural determinism.

In recent years in many places, as has been already noted, the public sector has passed on the cost of the development of the public realm to the private sector. The public interest in this instance can be safeguarded in two basic ways: by establishing appropriate guidelines for development, and by elected officials or their designates being critically reactive to proposals from the private sector. In this sense what has emerged is a growing collaborative effort between public and private sectors in the building of the public realm. The price that has been paid is that the genuine public realm has often been neglected (Buchanan 1988; Hitt 1990). This does not have to be the case.

The Private Sector

It was noted in Chapter 20 that it is easy to develop a stereotyped image of the entrepreneurs and sponsors of the private sector. The stereotype of developer is that of a person whose only concern is with maximizing profit, and thus with building those projects that will make a quick profit. Developers, however, tend to build what they know how to build in the way they want to build even if it means foregoing potential profits. They tend to be prima donnas as much as architects are. They scan the city for opportunities to build what they want. They do not ask the question: "Is this the best thing for this place?"

There are two potential groups of financial backers: bankers and taxpayers. The stereotype of bankers is of people who wish to minimize risks and thus favor conservative design programs and solutions—the known over the unknown. The stereotype of taxpayers is one of people who want to minimize tax payments; they are weighed down by their own self-interest and are only concerned with the design of the environment when it affects them directly. Indeed, politicians thrive on arousing the ire of voters about taxes. As with many stereotypes, there is an element of truth to these descriptions; they can also be highly misleading.

Developers' thinking is considerably broader than the stereotypes suggest, and individual developers have their own special concerns. They are often very much concerned with the quality of the built environment, if only in their own self-interest. People such as James Rouse in Columbia, Maryland, have a strong social and aesthetic concern for their work (R. Brooks 1974; Tennenbaum 1990). Developers have been strong supporters of urban design guidelines in places such as Glendale, California, where the utility of the guidelines in maintaining design quality is easy to understand, and Houston, where zoning is a recent innovation. Developers often provide public amenities, in their own self-interest certainly, but also in the broad interest of the public. They can often be persuaded to do the latter if they can see that broad benefit and if there is also a tangible reward for them to provide the amenity. Indeed the whole incentive zoning system is based on this proposition.

It is clear that a concern for the design of the built environment varies considerably from person to person, but also from people to people, taxpayer to taxpayer. In some cities there is a major concern with the built environment. In Chicago there is a broader-based understanding of architecture, but not urban design, than in most U.S. cities. In San Francisco, and probably more so in Portland, Oregon, there is considerable public support for urban design measures that might harm the city financially but that will retain much of the physical design qualities for which it is renowned (Smith 1991). It is not surprising that San Francisco has been a leader in establishing urban design guidelines among American cities. Chicago, in contrast, has been concerned with promoting individual buildings, particularly skyscrapers—the taller the better.

The Nonpaying Client

The nonpaying client consists of many potential groups. They vary from users, to residential action groups, to national special interest groups. Four groups are and will continue to be of major concern in urban design: the actual users of a development, whether a building, building complex, neighborhood, open space, or a city; the public interest; the peers of the professionals involved; and inevitably the individual designer.

Users

The users of developments, it was stated earlier, are nonpaying in the sense that they do not hire the architects or urban designers. Often they have no contact with the professionals involved in designing for them. The result is an administrative gap between professional and user-client. The users are represented in the process by other people: public agencies or marketing experts who purportedly know how the users' needs are manifested and should be met. There also is and will continue to be often a social gap between professionals and users (see Chapter 21 and Zeisel 1974). The knowledge base for design and design process introduced in this book will enable the designer to ask sensible questions about needs, ends, and means rather than relying on his or her own view of society. The concern should be with the ultimate beneficiaries of a design, as was stated in Chapter 24. While many architects claim that they know better and that consulting the user is pointless, in a recent survey 85 percent of American architects said they believe that user input improves design quality (Dixon 1988). What is not clear is what the architects in the survey understood by user input.

It is difficult to justify designing without the user in mind except by evoking the *art defense*—urban design as a

work of artistic endeavor. Such designing occurs often enough for many expressions of concern (Perin 1970; Brolin 1974; Cooper and Sarkissian 1986). The difficulty architects face is that they are also tugged by professional norms of what the outcome should look like, the professional prize system, and their own likes and dislikes.

The Public Interest

It is easy to claim that urban designers should be serving the public interest. Defining what the public interest is, or designing a method to ascertain it, is a difficult task, as noted a number of times in this book. The question is: "Who represents the public interest?" Many groups advocate design ends that they believe are in the national interest.

It is now recognized that different participants in the development of cities have competing goals and concepts of the public interest, and that planners' and architects' definitions have been based on narrow professional, class, and social origin biases. The marketplace has been the institution where conflicts between these goals have been resolved. The consequence has been that those people with wealth have considerably greater ability to shape the course of events in their own interests than do others. The role of social and physical planners and urban designers is then to devise policies that deal with merit goods, which the marketplace fails to consider. Environmental quality is one of these goods.

If one accepts that the quality of the built environment of cities depends on what it affords different people, then the public interest concerns can be summarized as: (1) the welfare of the public, (2) the health of the biogenic environment but not to the neglect of the state of the human environment, (3) the preservation of environmental elements that are likely to be of importance in the future, and (4) the concern for those who are not represented or who are underrepresented in the decision-making process—specific minority groups, children, the poor. It is in the public interest, it is claimed here, to promote certain ends: to increase behavioral opportunities and the richness of life—the everyday environment should, in this sense, be an educational tool for all people; aesthetic ends, in terms of both fine arts and the pleasure derived from the environment by diverse populations (see Chapters 16 and 17). These ends are all poorly defined, and resolving them will continue to be a highly charged political process.

Defining the public interest will involve bargaining among vying parties. Urban designers' functions in this bargaining process are partly *mediating* and partly introducing potential futures into the discussion. The art defense for what urban designers might believe to be in the public interest is not a strong one. Urban designers have a much stronger role if they can accurately predict the outcome of decisions based on empirical knowledge.

Professional Peers

One of the major rewards for design professionals is for their work to receive awards, accolades, or praise from the professional society of which they are members (Montgomery 1966; Blau 1984). It not only increases the designer's self-esteem but is often good for business, although the opposite has also been perceived to be true.

One of the embarrassments that the architectural profession has had to face over the last thirty years is the number of award-winning or highly praised schemes that have run into trouble because they are perceived by those who use them as poor designs (Bycroft 1990). The reason for the discrepancy is that different evaluation criteria are used by professionals and users for judging a building or urban place (see also Gutman and Westergaard 1974). The professions naturally enough evaluate them as objects in terms of their own canons of contemporary aesthetic acceptability. Users evaluate a scheme's utility for their needs in terms of their own activities and aesthetic values. Both groups are sure that their positions are the correct ones. The question of whose values should be the ones to use in evaluating design will remain a fundamental political question (see Chapters 21 and 24).

The Urban Designer

Urban designers use their own work in a number of ways: for self-promotion, financial rewards, and self-satisfaction. The first two are necessary to stay in business—after all, urban design is a business—and the last has more intangible reasons. Urban designers get satisfaction from their work in various ways: accolades from their peers, inner satisfaction, and winning arguments.

The image of the architect Howard Roark (who did major Rationalist urban design work) presented by Ayn Rand in her novel *The Fountainhead* and explained in the philosophical position stated in *Atlas Shrugged* is a powerful one: "My philosophy, in essence, is the concept of man as a heroic being, with his own happiness as the moral purpose of his life, with productive achievement as his noblest activity and reason as his only absolute." It is similar to the portrayal by Tom Wolfe (1981) of the Rationalists among urban designers working in America. One would hope that professional happiness for urban designers can come from doing good work for all concerned, including themselves.

Professionals and Clients— An Integrative Approach

The potential future roles for the urban designer depend on how urban designers relate to the public and private sectors, but also on their knowledge and aspirations as well as the obligations they assume and society dictates to them. While a stance for a collaborative design approach has been an issue in this book (see Chapter 24), much will depend on what urban designers and their clients know.

The Designer as Expert

All architects, landscape architects, and other design professionals involved in the process of environmental change have expertise. When design professionals assume the mantle of expert, their efforts are to promote a design in their tastes and values—an *etic* approach to design (Vernez Moudon 1990a). It ends up as a give-em-what-I-want attitude on the part of the urban designer. It is a highly egocentric view of the design process, but one also inculcated in much design education (Mitchell 1974). If those educated in building design wish to play the role of expert in urban design, then they must have a much better understanding of the functions of the built environment and of human needs than they now have. This knowledge will serve two purposes: it will enable them to know what they do and do not know, and to ask sensible questions and understand how much they do have to rely on their clients' knowledge and also its limits. In many instances there will be a "symmetry of lack of knowledge" between professionals and clients (Bazjanac 1974, Rittel 1984).

The Designer as Midwife

At the beginning of the 1970s, Horst Rittel (Bazjanac 1974; Rittel 1984), reflecting on the architecture and urban design of the 1950s and 1960s, suggested that professionals' claims of expertise were exaggerated and that the clients did not know much better either. He suggested that the role of midwife rather than expert would be a more appropriate self-image for architects and urban designers.

Midwifery is an honorable occupation. The architectural analog assumes that clients are better judges of their own ends, and that the designer's role is to see the process through, eliminating problems that arise and suggesting ways of easing pains. The function of the urban designer is thus to work with a community to elicit its needs and values and then, using his or her expertise, to assist the community to turn these ideas into a design. This is an *emic* approach to design—one relying on users' values. Taken to its extreme form, this approach can end up as a give-em-what-they-say-they-want approach to design. The position taken here is that this view is as limited as to the potential role of the urban designer and of the domain of knowledge available to him or her as that of a designer claiming total rationality and comprehensive knowledge.

The designer-as-midwife concept of the function of the urban designer is seen as something that grew and died in the 1960s. If anything it has evolved into the much more thoughtful Community Design movement in which the architect and client relationship is seen as a collaborative one.

The Designer as Collaborator

The Community Design movement falls outside the mainstream of the professional design because it is not primarily concerned with architects' taste cultures. It has nevertheless flourished as one branch of professional activity, as described in Chapter 3, The Nature of Urban Design Today. The movement has dealt primarily with residential areas and populations that are generally seen as having little political power because they are neither voting blocks nor wealthy enough. The idea can, however (as indicated in Chapter 24), be extended into all areas of urban design because the Community Design movement is essentially a collaborative design movement.

The collaborative design process involves the cooperation of a variety of design professionals each with their own expertise, users, and sponsors in the evolution of a design (Halprin 1969, 1974; Mitchell 1974; Hatch 1984; King et al. 1989; J. Stern 1989). For collaboration to work well, there must be an understanding of the overall picture—a synthetic view. The collaborative design process requires much of urban designers because it is an approach that requires low ego involvement in designing, and it is an active process of user involvement rather than a passive one and can be psychologically exhausting. The approach relies heavily on the designer's expertise in bringing users' attentions to the issues of concern and listening assertively to their responses. Where the potential users of a project are unknown, the process involves working with surrogate populations. Design solutions emerge through cooperation in an argumentative process. The function of the urban designer is fourfold: (1) to elicit a community's goals, (2) to bring attention to potential ways of achieving those goals, (3) to help the community evaluate the possibilities by elucidating the strengths and weaknesses of each approach, and (4) to help the community to implement the agreed-on solution. Ideally, there is a fifth function: to evaluate the completed scheme.

THE FUTURE FUNCTIONS OF THE URBAN DESIGNER

There is a recurrent echo to the theme of this book. If there is to be a functional empirical urban design it is clear that the professions concerned with the design of human settlements must work collaboratively (Lang 1990; Westerman 1990). While the mainstream of professional activity of architects, the design of individual buildings, may well continue as it will, urban designers must focus on architecture and urban design as a professional public service. That is a current ideological position that has shaped this book (see Chapters 23 and 24). Urban design must be concerned with the public realm, whether it is under private or public control. It must be concerned with the public interest despite the difficulties in defining what it is.

The Public Sector Role

The urban designer can act in two ways for the public sector: as a public employee and as a private con-

sultant working for a public agency, probably a city planning agency. In the latter situation they may have more freedom to act in the public interest than in the former, where they are likely to be wrapped up in the partisan concerns of public officials. In either case, the purpose is to provide information and advice to elected public officials. In this role the urban designer's functions are to establish, in consultation with city planners and elected officials, the goals for city development; to provide guidelines within which specialist architects will design specific buildings, landscape architects public open spaces, and artists, art work; and to coordinate and evaluate the work of designers working within the guidelines established.

In developing these guidelines and designs, the normative position described here (and one that should shape the whole way the urban design process is conducted in the future, as was described in Chapters 23 and 24) is that the urban designer must be concerned with the community as a whole, and particularly with its less vocal members, with the short- and long-term consequences of design decisions; and with the potential needs of future generations. The function, and obligation, of the urban designer is to bring to public attention the physical design consequences of adopting one social design over another, the design possibilities for the future that might otherwise be missed, and particularly the state of the public realm for different groups of people in order to improve it or maintain its good qualities. The concern is with the future, both short term and long term.

The Private Sector Role

The role of urban designers in the private sector is trickier to define. On one hand, they are advocates for private interests and are concerned with mechanisms for avoiding public interest constraints. Indeed the demand for former public agency officials in the private sector is based on the assumption that they know how to get around rules and regulations. On the other hand, urban designers have their own professional obligations. A cynic would say that the latter give way to developers' needs to maximize their own profits. "How could an architect do otherwise when developers dangle large fees in front of them for designing condominium towers" (Goldberger 1989b).

The urban designer may be doing a total design for a developer or, just as likely, designing an overall schema, an illustrative site plan for a development, and the guidelines for individual architects and landscape architect to follow. The developer has the ultimate control and acts as reviewer with or without the urban designer's advice. In carrying out either of these roles, urban designers must fight for public interest objectives. This role is considerably easier when the public sector has developed clear public interest objectives and provides incentives for the private sector to work toward achieving them.

The ideological position that has been described in this book is that the urban designer in particular should fight segregationist policies that are often implicit in designs. These designs, whether the segregation is by age group, national origin, income, or land use types, have sold well. Except for very special groups, such as threatened ethnic minorities and groups going through severe cultural shock, the position taken here is that such designs are antithetical to a good society. Although there is some empirical evidence to support the social utility of this position, it is a political one. There are some contradictions in this position, as was shown when procedural design issues in urban design were discussed in Chapter 18. It was stated there that procedural issues in a democratic society take precedence over product quality!

CONCLUSION: URBAN DESIGNING AS AN ONGOING PROCESS

Many possible ideological positions on urban design have been omitted from this book. Others have been mentioned only in passing. Little has been said about specific patterns that the cities, suburbs, or their components should take. No new generic patterns have been offered. No integrative vision of the future city has been proffered. The position on urban design that has been described here assumes that two slogans serve urban designers well: "form follows function" and "the future beckons us."

Much of the argument of the book revolves around the definition of "function." It has been considerably broadened from the architectural norm. Given the definition, the concerns of urban design are considerably broader than they have been assumed to be by the mainstream of architectural thought, but they are not dissimilar from much current thinking. Indeed, the definitions have been borrowed from other theorists. Designing too has been seen in a somewhat different way than the norm, and although there is much that we do not understand it is not the mysterious process we have been wont to consider it. Urban designing has been viewed from a position held by a number of scholars and practitioners, but it also deviates from the architectural norm.

Urban designing is and needs to be considered to be one of the highly value-laden argumentative processes in which a society engages to shape its future. As such, urban designers have a social responsibility that extends beyond that of artists (except those concerned with public art) and individual architects. The former have responsibility to themselves and the latter to individual clients. Urban designers need to understand the social consequences of their work.

Urban designers must recognize the political nature of their work and that they need to seriously take the principles of democratic action and the recognition of individual rights and freedom of action as the basis of their work, both in theory and practice. They must also recognize that they are working within the twin and often contradictory tugs of designing within the public domain of the United States, namely, to add value to real estate and to serve the public interest.

In achieving these ends urban design is at its best a collaborative art. It is concerned with environmental change and the idea that environmental changes will yield as much public benefit as they can. All the design disciplines and professionals are involved in urban design from the viewpoint of their own self-interests. If progress is to be made, there needs to be a recognition of combined interests. Ultimately, urban design is the ongoing process of shaping cities, their precincts, and their public realms. The state of any of these elements in any human habitat is the result of an ongoing urban design process whether it is self-conscious or unselfconscious.

In a democratic society, the self-conscious design process has to be one that is open to examination, explanation, and debate. Architectural design for individual clients working within urban design guidelines and other bylaws may well remain the opaque process that many architects prefer, although the public utility of this attitude is not obvious. Urban designing has, however, to be a glass box process. To be a successful glass box process, urban design must be based on clearly transparent bodies of substantive and procedural knowledge. Much knowledge is there for us to use. Much remains to be understood. It behooves us to use what we know and to search for better understanding.

MAJOR REFERENCES

Anderson, Stanford (1991). "Themes for a Symposium on Ph.D. Education in Architecture." In Linda Groat, ed., *Post-Professional and Doctoral Education*. Ann Arbor: University of Michigan, Architecture and Planning Research Laboratory, pp. 8–12.

Ferebee, Ann, ed. (1982). *Education for Urban Design*. Purchase, NY: Institute for Urban Design.

Kostof, Spiro, ed. (1977). *The Architect: Chapters in the History of the Profession*. New York: Oxford University Press.

Lang, Jon (1990). "Urban Design: The Collaborative Art of Shaping Cities." In Tamas Lukovich, ed., *Urban Design and Local Planning: An Interdisciplinary Approach*. Kensington NSW: University of New South Wales, Faculty of Architecture, pp. 2.1–2.16.

Larson, Magali (1979). *The Rise of Professionalism: A Sociological Analysis*. Berkeley and Los Angeles: University of California Press.

Scott Brown, Denise (1982). "Between Three Stools: A Personal View of Urban Design and Pedagogy." In Ann Ferebee, ed., *Education for Urban Design*. Purchase, NY: Institute for Urban Design, pp. 132–172.

Thiel, Philip (forthcoming). *Notations for an Experiential Envirotecture*. Seattle: University of Washington Press.

BIBLIOGRAPHY, CREDITS, AND INDEX

San Francisco

BIBLIOGRAPHY

Abelson, R. P. (1968). "Computers, Polls and Public Opinion—Some Puzzles and Paradoxes." *Transaction* 5:20-27.

Abercrombie, Stanley (1982). "Afterthoughts on the San Juan Retreat." In Ann Ferebee, ed., *Education for Urban Design*. Purchase, NY: Institute for Urban Design, pp. 173-174.

Abu-Lughod, Janet (1991). *Changing Cities: Urban Sociology*. New York: HarperCollins.

Acharaya, Pansanna Kumar (1927). *Indian Architecture According to the Manasara-Silpasastra*. Reprint. Patna: Indian India, 1979.

Ackoff, Russell (1978). *The Art of Problem Solving*. New York: John Wiley.

——— (1981). *Creating the Corporate Future*. New York: John Wiley.

Agnew, John A., and James S. Duncan, eds. (1989). *The Power of Place: Geographical and Sociological Imaginations*. Winchester, MA: Unwin Hyman.

Agnew, John A., John Mercer, and David Sopher, eds. (1984). *The City in Cultural Context*. Boston, MA: Allen and Unwin.

Albers, Josef (1963). *Interaction of Color*. New Haven: Yale University Press.

Alexander, Christopher (1964). *Notes on the Synthesis of Form*. Cambridge, MA: Harvard University Press.

——— (1969). "Major Changes in Environmental Form Required by Social and Psychological Demands." *Ekistics* 28:78-86.

——— (1972). "The City as a Mechanism for Sustaining Human Contact." In Robert Gutman, ed., *People and Buildings*. New York: Basic Books, pp. 406-434.

——— (1990). "The Architect Has No Clothes." *Progressive Architecture* 71, no. 4:11.

——— (1991). "Perspectives: Manifesto 1991." *Progressive Architecture* 72, no. 7:108-112.

Alexander, Christopher, Sara Isikawa, and Murray Silverstein (1968). *A Pattern Language Which Generates Multi-Service Centers*. Berkeley, CA: The Center for Environmental Structure.

——— (1975). *The Oregon Experiment*. New York: Oxford University Press.

——— (1977). *A Pattern Language: Towns, Buildings, Construction*. New York: Oxford University Press.

Alexander, Christopher, Hajo Neis, Artemis Anninou, and Ingrid King (1987). *A New Theory of Urban Design*. New York: Oxford University Press.

Alexander, Christopher, and Barry Poyner (1970). "Atoms of Environmental Structure." In Gary T. Moore, ed., *Emerging Methods in Environmental Design and Planning*. Cambridge, MA: MIT Press, pp. 308-321.

Allen, Lady (Marjory) (1968). *Planning for Play*. Cambridge, MA: MIT Press.

Altman, Irwin (1975). *Environment and Social Behavior: Privacy, Personal Space, Territory, Crowding*. Monterey, CA: Brooks/Cole.

Altman, Irwin, and Ervin H. Zube, eds. (1989). *Public Places and Spaces*. New York: Plenum.

AIA (American Institute of Architects)/New York Chapter (1990). "Report of the 60th Street Task Force." New York: AIA/New York Chapter.

American National Standards Institute (1971). *American National Standard Specifications for Making Building and Facilities Accessible to, and Usable by, the Physically Handicapped*. New York: ANSI.

American Planning Association (1989). "Urban Design." In *The Best of Planning*. Chicago: American Planning Association, pp. 478-531.

Anderson, Stanford, ed. (1978). *On Streets*. Cambridge, MA: MIT Press.

Anderson, Stanford (1991). "Themes for a Symposium on Ph.D. Education in Architecture." In Linda Groat, ed., *Post-Professional and Doctoral Education*. Ann Arbor: University of Michigan, Architecture and Planning Research Laboratory, pp. 8-12.

Angel, Shlomo (1968). "Discouraging Crime through City Planning." Berkeley: University of California, Center for Planning and Development Research.

Appleyard, Donald (1965). "Motion, Sequence, and the City." In Gyorgy Kepes, ed. *The Nature of Art and Motion*. New York: George Braziller, pp. 176-192.

——— (1969). "Why Buildings Are Known." *Environment and Behavior* 1, no. 3:131-156.

———— (1970). "Styles and Methods of Structuring a City." *Environment and Behavior* 2, no. 3:100–107.

Appleyard, Donald, with M. Sue Gerson and Mark Lintell (1981). *Livable Streets*. Berkeley and Los Angeles: University of California Press.

Appleyard, Donald, Kevin Lynch, and John Myer (1964). *The View from the Road*. Cambridge, MA: MIT Press.

Appleyard, Donald, and Members of the Faculty, University of California, Berkeley (1982). "A Humanist Design Manifesto." Photocopied.

Arcidi, Philip (1991). "Paolo Soleri's Arcology: Updating the Prognosis." *Progressive Architecture* 72, no. 3:76–79.

Arens, E., and P. Bosslemann (1989). "Wind, Sun and Temperature—Predicting the Thermal Comfort of People in Open Spaces." *Building and Environment* 24, no. 4:315–320.

Arens, E., P. Bosslemann et al. (1989). "Developing the San Francisco Wind Ordinance and Its Guidelines for Compliance." *Building and Environment* 24, no. 4:297–303.

Arens E. et al. (1984). "Sun, Wind and Comfort." University of California at Berkeley, College of Environmental Design, Institute of Urban and Regional Development, Environmental Simulation Laboratory.

Arias, Ernesto G. (1988). "Resident Participation and Residential Quality in U.S. Public Housing: Towards a Substantive Understanding of Participation." Unpublished Ph.D. dissertation, University of Pennsylvania.

Ariès, Phillippe (1962). *Centuries of Childhood: A Social History of Family Life*. Translated from the French by Robert Baldick. New York: Knopf.

Arnheim, Rudolf (1965). *Art and Visual Perception*. Berkeley and Los Angeles: University of California Press.

———— (1966). *Towards a Psychology of Art*. Berkeley and Los Angeles: University of California Press.

———— (1977). *The Dynamics of Architectural Form*. Berkeley and Los Angeles: University of California Press.

Arnold, Henry F. (1980). *Trees in Urban Design*. New York: Van Nostrand Reinhold.

Arthur, Paul, and Romedi Passini (1990). *Wayfinding: People, Signs and Architecture*. New York: McGraw Hill.

ASCORAL (Assembly of Constructors for an Architectural Revolution) (1945). *Les Trois Etablissements Humains*. Paris: Denoël.

Ashihara, Yoshinobu (1983). *The Aesthetic Townscape*. Translated from the Japanese by Lynne E. Riggs. Cambridge, MA: MIT Press.

Attoe, Wayne (1981). *Skylines: Understanding and Molding Urban Silhouettes*. New York: John Wiley.

————, ed. (1988a). *Transit, Land Use and Urban Form*. Austin: University of Texas, Center for the Study of American Architecture.

———— (1988b). "Historic Preservation." In Anthony J. Catanese and James C. Snyder, eds., *Urban Planning*. New York: McGraw Hill, pp. 344–365.

Attoe, Wayne, and Don Logan (1989). *American Urban Architecture: Catalysts in the Design of Cities*. Berkeley and Los Angeles: University of California Press.

Audirac, Ivonne, Anne H. Shermeyen, and Marc T. Smith (1990). "Ideal Urban Form and Visions of the Good Life: Florida's Growth Management Dilemma." *American Planning Association Journal* 56, no. 4:470–482.

Avin, Uri (1973). "Le Corbusier's Unité d'habitation: Slab for All Seasons." Unpublished master's thesis, University of Cape Town.

Aynsley, R. M. (1989). "The Politics of Pedestrian Level Urban Wind Control." *Building and Environment* 24, no. 4:291–295.

Aynsley, R. M., W. Melbourne, and B. J. Vickery (1977). *Architectural Aerodynamics*. London: Applied Science Publishers.

Bach, Wilfred (1971). "Seven Steps to Better Living in the Urban Heat Island." *Landscape Architecture* 61, no. 2:136–138, 141.

Bacon, Edmund (1967). "The City as an Act of Will." *Architectural Record* 141, no. 1:113–128.

———— (1969). "Urban Process: Planning With and For the Community." *Architectural Record* 145, no. 5:129–134.

———— (1974). *The Design of Cities*. Rev. ed. New York: Viking.

Bailey, James, ed. (1973). *New Towns in America: The Design and Development Process*. New York: John Wiley.

Bakema, Jacob B. (1982). *Thoughts about Architecture*. London: Academy Editions.

Balint, Michael (1955). "Friendly Expanses—Horrid Empty Spaces." *International Journal of Psychoanalysis* 36:225–244.

Baldon, Cleo, and Ib Melchior with Julius Shulman (1989). *Steps and Stairways*. New York: Rizzoli.

Baldwin, Maynard, ed. (1975). *Portraits of Complexity: Applications of Systems Methodologies to Societal Problems*. Columbus, OH: Battelle Memorial Institute.

Balfour, Alan (1978). *Rockefeller Center: Architecture as Theater*. New York: McGraw Hill.

Baltzell, E. Digby, ed. (1968). *The Search for Community in Modern America*. New York: Harper & Row.

Bandini, Micha (1984). "Typology as a Form of Convention." *AA Files*, no. 6 (May):73–82.

Banerjee, Tridib, and Michael Southworth, eds. (1990). *City Sense and City Design: Writings and Projects of Kevin Lynch*. Cambridge, MA: MIT Press.

Banham, Reyner (1960). *Theory and Design in the First Machine Age*. New York: Praeger.

———— (1976). *Megastructure: Urban Futures of the Recent Past*. New York: Harper & Row.

Barker, Roger (1968). *Ecological Psychology: Concepts and Methods for Studying the Environment of Human Behavior*. Stanford, CA: Stanford University Press.

Barker, Roger, and Paul Gump (1964). *Big School, Small School: High School Size and Student Behavior*. Stanford, CA: Stanford University Press.

Barker, Roger, and Phil Schoggen (1973). *Qualities of Community Life*. San Francisco: Jossey-Bass.

Barnett, Jonathan (1974). Urban Design as Public Policy.

New York: Architectural Record Books.

———— (1982). *An Introduction to Urban Design.* New York: Harper & Row.

———— (1986). *The Elusive City: Five Centuries of Design, Ambition and Ideas.* New York: Harper & Row.

———— (1987). "In the Public Interest: Design Guidelines." *Architectural Record* 175, no. 8:114–125.

Barré, François (1980). "The Desire for Urbanity." *Architectural Design* 50, no. 11/12:5–7.

Bartholomew, Richard (1980). "Urban Design Education: Some Basic Questions." *Urban Design International* 1, no. 2:50.

———— (1991). Personal Interview.

Barzilay, M., C. Hayward, and L. Lombard-Valentino (1984). *L'Invention du Parc: Parc de la Villette.* Paris: Ed. Graphite.

Batchelor, Peter, and David Lewis, eds. (1985). *Urban Design in Action.* Raleigh: North Carolina State University, American Institute of Architects and School of Design.

Baumeister, Reinhard (1895). *The Cleaning and Sewage of Cities.* Translated from the German by J. Goodell. New York: Engineering Press.

Bayard, M. D. (1989). *Business and Industrial Park Development Handbook.* Washington, DC: Urban Land Institute.

Bazjanac, Vladimir (1974). "Architectural Design Theory: Models of the Design Process." In W. R. Spillers, ed., *Basic Questions of Design Theory.* New York: American Elsevier, pp. 3–20.

Beaujeu-Garnier, Jacqueline, and G. Chabot (1967). *Urban Geography.* Translated from the French by G. M. Yglesias and S. H. Beaver. London: Longman Green.

Bechtel, Robert (1977). *Enclosing Behavior.* Stroudsburg, PA: Dowden, Hutchinson, and Ross.

Bechtel, Robert, Robert Marans, and William Michelson, eds. (1987). *Methods in Environmental and Behavioral Research.* New York: Van Nostrand Reinhold.

Bednar, Michael J., ed. (1977). *Barrier-Free Environments.* Stroudsburg, PA: Dowden, Hutchinson, and Ross.

———— (1989). *Interior Pedestrian Places.* New York: Whitney Library of Design.

Belgasem, Ramadan (1987). "Human Needs and Building Criticism." Unpublished Ph.D. dissertation, University of Pennsylvania.

Bellevue, City of (c. 1984). *Design Guidelines: Building/ Sidewalk.* City of Bellevue, WA.

Benedikt, Michael (1984). *For an Architecture of Reality.* New York: Lumen.

Benevolo, Leonardo (1967). *The Origins of Modern Town Planning.* Translated from the Italian by Judith Landry. Cambridge, MA: MIT Press.

———— (1970). *History of Modern Architecture.* Translated from the Italian by H. J. Landry. Cambridge, MA: MIT Press.

———— (1980). *The History of the City.* Translated from the Italian by Geoffrey Culverwell. Cambridge, MA: MIT Press.

Benjamin, Andrew (1988). "Deconstruction and Art/The Art of Deconstruction." In Christopher Norris and Andrew Benjamin, eds., *What Is Deconstruction?* New York: St. Martin's Press, pp. 33–56.

Bentley, Ian, Alan Alcock, Paul Murrain, Sue McGlynn, and Graham Smith (1985). *Responsive Environments: A Manual for Designers.* London: Architectural Press.

Berleant, Arnold (1988). "Aesthetic Perception in Environmental Design." In Jack Nasar, ed., *Environmental Aesthetics: Theory, Research, and Applications.* New York: Cambridge University Press, pp. 88–108.

Berlyne, D. E., ed. (1974). *Studies in the New Experimental Aesthetics: Steps Towards an Objective Psychology of Aesthetic Appreciation.* Washington, DC: Hemisphere Publishing.

"Bernard Tschumi" (1988). *Architecture and Urbanism* no. 216 (September):10–67.

Betsky, Aaron (1990). *Violated Perfection, Architecture and the Fragmentation of the Modern.* New York: Rizzoli.

———— (1991). "Los Angeles: Recent Urban Design." *Architectural Record* 179, no. 1:27.

Birch, Eugenie Ladner (1980). "Radburn and the American Planning Movement: The Persistence of an Idea." *Journal of the American Institute of Planners* 46, no. 4:424–439. Also in Krueckeberg, *Introduction to Planning History,* pp. 122–151.

Birch, H. G., and H. S. Rabinowitz (1968). "The Negative Effects of Previous Experience on Productive Thinking." In P. G. Watson and P. N. Johnson Laird, eds., *Thinking and Reasoning.* Baltimore: Penguin, pp. 44–50.

Bird, Jon (1990). "Report from London: Distopia on the Thames." *Art in America* 78, no. 7:89–97.

Birren, Faber (1965). *Color Psychology and Color Therapy: A Factual Study of the Influence of Color on Human Life.* New Hyde Park, NY: University Books.

———— (1982). *Light, Color and Environment.* New York: Van Nostrand Reinhold.

Blake, Peter (1977). *Form Follows Fiasco: Why Modern Architecture Hasn't Worked.* Boston: Little Brown.

Blau, Judith (1984). *Architects and Firms: A Sociological Perspective on Architectural Practice.* Cambridge, MA: MIT Press.

Blau, Judith, Mark LaGory, and John S. Pipkin, eds. (1983). *Professionals and Urban Form.* Albany: State University of New York Press.

Bloomer, Kent, and Charles W. Moore (1977). *Body, Memory and Architecture.* New Haven, CT: Yale University Press.

Boardman, Philip (1978). *The Worlds of Patrick Geddes.* London: Routledge and Kegan Paul.

Boguslaw, Robert (1965). *The New Utopians.* Englewood Cliffs, NJ: Prentice-Hall.

Boles, Daralice (1989a). "Reordering the Suburbs: New Solutions to Urban Sprawl." *Progressive Architecture* 70, no. 5:78–91.

———— (1989b). "New American Landscape." *Progressive Architecture* 70, no. 7:51–55.

———— (1989c). "Aging in Place in the 1990s." *Progressive*

Architecture 70, no. 11:85–91.

Bosanquet, Bernard (1931). *Three Lectures on Aesthetics.* London: Macmillan.

Bottles, Scott L. (1987). *Los Angeles and the Automobile: The Makings of the Modern City.* Berkeley and Los Angeles: University of California Press.

Boudon, Philippe (1972). *Lived-In Architecture: Le Corbusier's Pessac Revisited.* Translated from the French by G. Onn. Cambridge, MA: MIT Press.

Boulding, Kenneth (1956). *The Image.* Ann Arbor: University of Michigan Press.

Bourassa, Steven C. (1990). "A Paradigm for Landscape Aesthetics." *Environment and Behavior* 22, no. 6:787–812.

Boyer, M. Christine (1983). *Dreaming the Rational City: The Myth of American City Planning.* Cambridge, MA: MIT Press.

———— (1990). "Erected Against the City: The Contemporary Discourses of Architecture and Planning." *Center: A Journal for Architecture in America* 6. New York: Rizzoli, 36–43.

Brill, Michael (1989). "An Ontology for Exploring Urban Public Life Today." *Places* 6, no. 1:24–29.

Broadbent, Geoffrey (1973). *Design in Architecture; Architecture and the Human Sciences.* New York: John Wiley.

———— (1978). "The Rational and the Functional." In Dennis Sharp, ed., *The Rationalists: Theory and Design in the Modern Movement.* London: Architectural Press. pp. 142–159.

———— (1990). *Emerging Concepts in Urban Space Design.* London and New York: Van Nostrand Reinhold (International).

Broadbent, Geoffrey, Richard Bunt, and Charles Jencks, eds. (1980). *Signs, Symbols and Architecture.* New York: John Wiley.

Brolin, Brent (1976). *The Failure of Modern Architecture.* New York: Van Nostrand Reinhold.

———— (1980). *Architecture in Context: Fitting New Buildings with Old.* New York: Van Nostrand Reinhold.

Brolin, Brent, and John Zeisel (1970). "Social Research and Design: Application to Mass Housing." In Gary T. Moore, ed., *Emerging Methods in Environmental Design and Planning.* Cambridge, MA: MIT Press, pp. 239–246.

Bronfenbrenner, Urie (1970). *Two Worlds of Childhood: U.S. and U.S.S.R.* New York: Russell Sage Foundation.

———— (1979). *The Ecology of Human Development: Experiments by Nature and Design.* Cambridge, MA: Harvard University Press.

Brooks, H. Allen, ed. (1987). *Le Corbusier.* Princeton, NJ: Princeton University Press.

Brooks, Richard O. (1974). *New Towns and Communal Values: A Case Study of Columbia, Maryland.* New York: Praeger.

Bross, Irwin D. J. (1953). *Design for Decision.* New York: Macmillan.

Brotchie, John, Michael Batty, Peter Hall, and Peter Newton, eds. (1991). *Cities of the 21st Century: New Technologies and Spatial Systems.* New York: Halsted.

Brower, Sidney N., Kathleen Dockett, and Ralph B. Taylor (1983). "Residents' Perceptions of Territorial Features and Perceived Local Threat." *Environment and Behavior* 15, no. 4:419–437.

Brownhill, Sue (1990). *Developing London's Docklands.* London: Paul Clapham.

Brownlee, David (1989). *Building the City Beautiful: The Benjamin Franklin Parkway and the Philadelphia Museum of Art.* Philadelphia: Philadelphia Museum of Art.

Bruegmann, Robert (1982). "Two Post-Modern Visions of Urban Design." *Landscape* 26, no. 2:31–37.

Buchanan, Colin Douglas (1963). *Traffic in Towns.* London: H.M.S.O.

Buchanan, Peter (1988). "What City? A Plea for the Place in the Public Realm; City Planning in Britain." *Architectural Review* 184, no. 11:30–41.

———— (1990). "Making Places in Spain." *Architectural Review* 188, no. 7:29–31.

Bucher, Lothar (1851). *Kulturhistorische Skizzen aus der Industrieausstellung aller Völker.* Frankfort.

Buder, Stanley (1990). *Visionaries and Planners: The Garden City Movement and the Modern Community.* New York: Oxford University Press.

Burnham, Daniel H., and Edward H. Bennett (1909). *Plan of Chicago.* Edited by Charles Moore. Reprint. New York: De Capo Press, 1970.

Burnette, Charles, Jon Lang, and David Vachon, eds. (1971). *Architecture for Human Behavior.* Philadelphia: AIA/Philadelphia Chapter.

Butt, John, ed. (1971). *Robert Owen: Aspects of His Life and Work.* New York: Humanities Press.

Bycroft, Peter (1989). "Behind the Façade: What Post-Occupancy Evaluation Tells Us about the Quality of Contemporary Architecture." Paper presented at the RAIA National Convention, Canberra, April 1989. Photocopied.

Byrne, Peter (1984). *Risk, Uncertainty and Decision-Making in Property Development.* New York: Spon.

Calkins, Margaret P. (1988). *Design for Dementia: Planning Environments for the Elderly and the Confused.* Owings Mills, MD: National Health Publishing.

Calthorpe, Peter (1991). "The Post-Suburban Environment." *Progressive Architecture* 72, no. 3:84–85.

Campbell, Joseph, with Bill Moyers (1988). *The Power of Myth.* New York: Doubleday.

Cantril, Hadley (1965). *The Pattern of Human Concerns.* New Brunswick, NJ: Rutgers University Press.

Caramel, Luciano, and Alberto Longatti (1988). *Antonio Sant'Elia: The Complete Works.* New York: Rizzoli.

Caro, Robert (1974). *The Power Broker: Robert Moses and the Fall of New York.* New York: Knopf.

Carper, Steve (1991). "Let it Snow." *Planning* 57, no. 4:29.

Carr, Stephen, and Kevin Lynch (1968). "Where Learning Happens." *Daedalus* 97, no. 4:1277–1291.

Carr, Stephen, Myer/Smith Inc. (1973). *City Signs and Lights:*

A Policy Study. Cambridge, MA: MIT Press.

Carstens, Diane (1990). "Housing and Outdoor Spaces for the Elderly." In Clare Cooper Marcus and Carolyn Francis, eds., *People Places: Design Guidelines for Urban Open Space*. New York: Van Nostrand Reinhold, pp. 171–214.

Cartwright, Timothy J. (1973). "Problems, Solutions and Strategies: A Contribution to the Theory and Practice of Planning. *Journal of the American Institute of Planners* 39 (May):179–187.

Castells, Manuel (1977). *The Urban Question: A Marxist Approach*. Translated from the French by Alan Sheridan. Cambridge, MA: MIT Press.

Catanese, Anthony J., and James C. Snyder (1988). *Urban Planning*. 2d ed. New York: McGraw Hill.

Cervero, Robert (1989). *America's Suburban Centers: The Land Use Transportation Link*. Boston: Unwin and Allen.

Chadwick, George (1971). *A Systems View of Planning: Towards a Theory of the Urban and Regional Planning Process*. New York: Pergamon.

Chandler, T. J. (1976). *Urban Climatology and Its Relevance to Urban Design*. Geneva: World Meteorological Organization.

Chapin, F. Stuart, Jr., and Edward J. Kaiser (1979). *Urban Land Use Planning*. Urbana and Chicago: University of Illinois Press.

"Charter of Machu Picchu, The" (1979). *Journal of Architectural Research* 7, no. 2:5–9.

Chawla, Louise (1991). "Homes for Children in a Changing Society." In Ervin H. Zube and Gary T. Moore, eds., *Advances in Environment, Behavior, and Design 3*. New York: Plenum, pp. 187–228.

Cherulnik, Paul D. (1982). "Impressions of Neighborhoods and Their Residents." In Polly Bart, Alexander Chen and Guido Francescato, eds., *Knowledge for Design: Proceedings of the Thirteenth International Conference of the Environmental Design Research Association*. College Park, MD:416–421.

Chidister, Mark (1989). "Public Places, Public Lives: Plazas and the Broader Public Landscape." *Places* 6, no. 1:32–37.

Ciucci, Giorgio, Francesco Dal Co, Mario Manieri-Elia, and M. Tafuri (1979). *The American City from the Civil War to the New Deal*. Translated from the Italian by Barbara Luigia La Penta. Cambridge, MA: MIT Press.

Claflen, George (1992). "Simulated Stimulation/Stimulated Simulation: Regionalism and Urban Design." Paper presented at the Association of Collegiate Schools of Architecture Conference. Photocopied.

Clark, Barbara (1979). *Growing Up Gifted*. Columbus, OH: Charles Merrill.

Cohen, Uriel, A. B. Hill, C. G. Lane, T. McGinty, and G. T. Moore (1979). "Recommendations for Child Play Areas." Milwaukee: University of Wisconsin-Milwaukee, Center for Architectural and Urban Planning Research.

Cole, Margaret Van B. (1960). "A Comparison of Aesthetic Systems: Background for the Identification of Values in City Design." University of California at Berkeley, School of Architecture. Mimeographed.

Collins, George, and Christiane Craseman Collins (1965). *Camillo Sitte and the Birth of Modern City Planning*. New York: Random House.

Collins, Peter (1942). "Parallax." *Architectural Review* 132, no. 789:387–389.

Colquhoun, Alan (1967). "Typology and Design Method." *Arena: Journal of the Architectural Association* 83, no. 913:11–14.

——— (1975). "Rational Architecture. Review of an Exhibition Offshoot of the Milan Triennale Architectura Razionale Exhibition Held at Art Net in London." *Architectural Design* 45, no. 6:365–370.

——— (1981). "Form and Figure." In *Essays in Architectural Criticism*. Cambridge, MA: MIT Press, pp. 190–172.

Conrads, Ulrich, ed. (1970). *Programs and Manifestoes on 20th Century Architecture*. Translated from the German by Michael Bullock. Cambridge, MA: MIT Press.

Conway, Donald, ed. (1977). *Human Responses to Tall Buildings*. Stroudsburg, PA: Dowden, Hutchinson, and Ross.

Cook, E. T., and Alexander Wedderburn, eds. (1903). *The Works of John Ruskin*. London: George Allen.

Cook, Peter, Warren Chalk, Dennis Crompton, David Green, Ron Herron, and Mike Webb (1991). *Archigram*. Boston: Birkhäuser.

Coolidge, John (1942). *Mill and Mansion: A Study of Architecture and Society in Lowell, Massachusetts*. New York: Columbia University Press.

Cooper Marcus, Clare (1974). "The House as Symbol of Self." In Jon Lang et al., eds., *Designing for Human Behavior: Architecture and the Behavioral Sciences*. Stroudsburg, PA: Dowden, Hutchinson, and Ross, pp. 130–146.

——— (1975). *Easter Hill Village: Some Social Implications of Design*. New York: Free Press.

——— (1978). "Remembrances of Landscapes Past." *Landscape* 22, no. 3:34–43.

Cooper Marcus, Clare, and Wendy Sarkissian (1986). *Housing as If People Mattered: Site Design Principles for Medium Density Housing*. Berkeley and Los Angeles: University of California Press.

Cooper Marcus, Clare, and Carolyn Francis, eds. (1990). *People Places: Design Guidelines for Urban Open Space*. New York: Van Nostrand Reinhold.

Copper, Wayne W. (1983). "The Figure/Grounds." *Cornell Journal of Architecture* 2 (Fall):42–53.

Cordray, Mark (1974). "Behavioral Choice: A Framework for Goals-Making, Programming and Evaluation in Physical Design." Unpublished student paper, University of Pennsylvania.

Corner, James (1990a). "A Discourse on Theory I: Sounding the Depths—Origins, Theory, and Representation." *Landscape Journal* 9, no. 2:61–78.

——— (1990b). "Layering and Strategies." *Landscape*

Architecture 30 (December):38–39.

——— (1991). "A Discourse on Theory II: Three Tyrannies of Contemporary Theory and the Alternative of Hermeneutics." *Landscape Journal* 10, no. 2:115–133.

Couperie, Pierre (1965). *Paris Through the Ages.* Translated from the French by Marilyn Low. New York: George Braziller.

Crane, David A. (1960). "The City Symbolic." *Journal of the American Institute of Planners* 26 (November):285–286.

Cranz, Galen (1974). "Using Parsonian Structural-Functionalism for Environmental Design." In William R. Spillers, ed., *Basic Questions in Design Theory.* New York: American Elsevier, pp. 475–484.

——— (1982). *The Politics of Park Design: A History of Urban Parks in America.* Cambridge, MA: MIT Press.

——— (1987). "Evaluating the Physical Environment: Conclusions from Eight Housing Projects." In Victor Regnier and Jon Pynoos, eds., *Housing the Aged: Design Directives and Policy Considerations.* New York: Elsevier, pp. 81–104.

Cronon, William (1991). *Nature's Metropolis: Chicago and the Great West.* New York: Norton.

Crooks, Cheryl (1985). "Glendale's Surprising Rebirth." *Los Angeles* (July).

Cross, Nigel, ed. (1984). *Developments in Design Methodology.* New York: John Wiley.

Crowther, Richard I. (1992). *Ecological Architecture: The Ecological Perspective for Design.* Stoneham, MA: Butterworth.

Csikszentmihalyi, Mihaly (1975). *Beyond Boredom and Anxiety.* San Francisco: Jossey-Bass.

Cudahy, Brian J. (1988). *Under the Sidewalks of New York: The Story of the Greatest Subway System in the World.* Rev. ed. Lexington, MA: Stephen Greene Press.

Cuff, Dana (1991). *Architecture: The Story of Practice.* Cambridge, MA: MIT Press.

Cullen, Gordon (1961). *Townscape.* London: Architectural Press.

Curl, James S. (1980). *A Celebration of Death.* New York: Charles Scribner's Sons.

Curtis, William (1982). *Modern Architecture Since 1900.* London: Phaidon.

——— (1986). *Le Corbusier: Ideas and Form.* London: Phaidon.

Cutler, Laurence S., and Sherrie Stephens Cutler (1982). *Recycling Cities for People: The Urban Design Process.* 2d ed. Boston: Cahners Books International.

Dahinden, Justus (1972). *Urban Structures for the Future.* Translated from the German by Geral Onn. New York: Praeger.

Dalton, Linda C. (1989). "Emerging Knowledge about Planning Practice." *Journal of Planning Education and Research* 9, no. 1:29–44.

Dane, Suzanne, ed. (1988). *New Directions for Urban Streets.* Washington, DC: National Trust for Historic Preservation.

Dantzig, George B., and Thomas L. Saaty (1973). *Compact City: A Plan for a Livable Urban Environment.* San Francisco: W. H. Freeman.

Darley, Gillian (1978). *Villages of Vision.* London: Granada Publishing.

Dattner, Robert (1969). *Design for Play.* New York: Van Nostrand Reinhold.

Davey, Peter, ed. (1987). "Public Places." *Architectural Review* 181, no. 1084:31–93.

——— (1989). "Three on the Waterfront." *Architectural Review* 185, no. 1106: 46–54.

Davidoff, Paul (1964). "Advocacy and Pluralism in Planning." *Journal of the American Institute of Planners* 31, no. 4:331–338.

Davidson, Judith (1991). "The Light that Made Milwaukee Famous." *Architectural Record* 179, no. 11:30–35.

Dear, Michael, and Allen J. Scott, eds. (1981). *Urbanization and Urban Planning in Capitalist Society.* London: Methuen.

Deasy, C. M. (1974). *Design for Human Affairs.* New York: Halsted.

De Bono, Edward (1973). *Lateral Thinking: Creativity Step by Step.* New York: Harper.

De Chiara, Joseph, and Lee Koppelman (1975). *Urban Planning and Design Criteria.* New York: Van Nostrand Reinhold.

——— (1978). *Site Planning Standards.* New York: McGraw Hill.

Del Rio, Vincente (1990). *Introdução ao desneho urbano no processo de planejamento.* São Paulo: Pini.

De Monchaux, Suzanne (1981). "Planning with Children in Mind: A Notebook for Local Planners and Policy Makers on Children in the City Environment." Sydney: New South Wales Department of Environment and Planning.

Dennis, Michael (1986). *Court and Garden from the French Hôtel to the City of Modern Architecture.* Cambridge, MA: MIT Press.

De Rivera, Joseph. (1984). "Emotional Experience and Qualitative Methodology." *American Behavioral Scientist* 27:677–688.

De Sausmarez, Maurice (1964). *Basic Design: The Dynamics of Visual Form.* New York: Reinhold.

Descartes, René (1934). "Discourse on the Method of Rightly Conducting the Reason." In *The Philosophical Works of Descartes.* Translated from the French by E. S. Haldane and G. T. R. Ross. New York: Cambridge University Press, pp. 87–88.

DeSeve, G. Edward (1986). "Financing Urban Development: The Joint Efforts of Government and the Private Sector." *The Annals, The American Academy of Political Science* 53:58–76.

De Solà Morales, Ignasi (1989). "Weak Architecture." *Otagano* 92 (Summer).

Deurksen, Christopher J. (1986). *Aesthetics and Land-Use Controls.* PAS Report No. 399. Chicago: American

Planning Association.

Devereaux, Kathryn (1991). "Children of Nature." *University of California, Davis Magazine* 9, no. 2:20–23, 38–39.

Dewey, John (1934). *Art as Experience.* New York: Putnam.

Diefendorf, Jeffrey (1990). *Rebuilding Europe's Bombed Cities.* New York: St. Martin's Press.

Dixon, John M. (1988). "P/A Reader Poll Design Preferences." *Progressive Architecture* 69, no. 10:15–17.

———(1992). "World on a Platter." *Progressive Architecture* 73, no. 7:86–88.

Doshi, Harish (1974). *Traditional Neighborhoods in a Modern City.* New Delhi: Abhinav Publications.

Downs, Roger, and David Stea, eds. (1973). *Image and Environment: Cognitive Mapping and Spatial Behavior.* Chicago: Aldine.

Draeger, Harlan (1991). "FAA Gives OK, Clear Way for World's Tallest Building Here." *Chicago Tribune* (April 4):1, 26.

Dreier, John (1936). "Greenbelt Planning: Resettlement Administration Builds Three Model Towns." *Pencil Points* (August):400–417.

Duany, Andres (1989). "Traditional Towns." *Architectural Design Profile 81*:60–64.

Duany, Andres, and Elizabeth Plater-Zyberk (1984). "The Town of Seaside." *Progressive Architecture* 65, no. 1:138–139.

Duany, Andres, Elizabeth Plater-Zyberk, and Chester E. Chellman (1987). "New Town Ordinances and Codes." *Architectural Design Profile* 79:71–75.

Duncan, James S., ed. (1982). *Housing and Identity: Cross Cultural Perspectives.* New York: Holmes and Meier.

Dunlop, Beth (1989). "Seaside: Coming of Age." *Architectural Record* 177, no. 8:96–103.

———(1991). "Our Towns." *Architectural Record* 179, no. 10:110–119.

Durgin, F. H. (1989). "Proposed Guidelines for Pedestrian Level Wind Studies for Boston—Comparison of Results from 12 Studies." *Building and Environment* 24, no. 4:305–314.

Eagleton, Terry (1990). *The Significance of Theory.* Oxford: Basil Blackwell.

Eaton, Leonard K. (1969). *Two Chicago Architects and Their Clients: Frank Lloyd Wright and Howard Van Doren Shaw.* Cambridge, MA: MIT Press.

Effrat, Marcia Pelly (1974). "Approaches to Community: Conflicts and Complementaries." In Effrat, ed., *The Community: Approaches and Applications.* New York: Free Press, pp. 1–32.

Egelius, Mats (1980a). "Ralph Erskine: Byker Redevelopment, Byker Area of Newcastle upon Tyne." In Yukio Futagawa, ed. *Global Architecture.* Tokyo: ADA Editions.

———(1980b). "Housing and Human Needs: The Work of Ralph Erskine (with Original Sketches by Ralph Erskine)." In Byron Mikellides, ed., *Architecture for People.* New York: Holt, Rinehart and Winston, pp. 135–148.

Eisenmann, Russell (1966). "Pleasingness and Interesting Visual Complexity: Support for Berlyne." *Perceptual and Motor Skills* 23:1167–1170.

Elazar, Daniel J. (1987). *Building Cities in America; Urbanization and Suburbanization in Frontier Society.* Lanham, MD: Hamilton.

Ellis, Charlotte (1987). "Paris Precedent." *Architectural Review* 183, no. 1092:78.

Ellis, John (1985). "Streets of San Francisco: The Downtown Plan." *Architectural Review* 183, no. 1056:50–54.

———(1987). "US Codes and Controls." *Architectural Review* 184, no. 1101:79–84.

Ellis, Russell, and Dana Cuff, eds. (1989). *Architects' People.* New York: Oxford University Press.

El-Sharkawy, Hussein (1979). "Territoriality: A Model for Design." Unpublished Ph.D. dissertation, University of Pennsylvania.

El Wakil, Abdel Wahid (1991). "Public Lecture." Royal Australian Institute of Architects, Sydney, 29 April.

Ely, Richard T. (1885). "Pullman: A Social Study." *Harper's Magazine* 70, no. 417:58.

Engels, Friedrich (1892). *The Condition of the Working Class in England in 1844.* Translated from the German by Florence Kelley Wischnewtzky. Reprint. London: Allen and Unwin, 1950.

ERG [Environmental Research Group] (1990). "Chestnut Hill: People, Environment, Issues, and Goals." Philadelphia: ERG.

Eriksen, Aase (1975). *Learning about the Built Environment.* New York: Educational Facilities Laboratory.

———(1985). *Playground Design: Outdoor Environments for Learning and Developing.* New York: Van Nostrand Reinhold.

Erikson, Erik (1950). *Childhood and Society.* New York: Norton.

Eslami, Manoucher (1985). "Architecture as Discourse: The Modern Idea of Method—Theory and Practice in Le Corbusier's Purist Period." Unpublished Ph.D. dissertation, University of Pennsylvania.

———(1988). "The Question of 'Architectural Object' in Modern Architecture: Le Corbusier's Cartesian Theory and Practice in His Purist Period." In Charles Hay, Peter Wong, Bryan Flesnor, and Alex Gotthel, eds., *VIA 9.* New York: Rizzoli:139–154.

Eubank-Ahrens, B. (1987). "A Close Look at the Users of Woonerven." In Anne Vernez Moudon, ed., *Public Streets for Public Use.* New York: Van Nostrand Reinhold, pp. 63–79.

Evenson, Norma (1966). *Chandigarh.* Berkeley and Los Angeles: University of California Press.

———(1970). *Corbusier: The Machine and the Grand Design.* New York: George Braziller.

———(1973). *Two Brazilian Capitals: Architecture and Urbanism in Rio de Janeiro and Brasilia.* New Haven, CT: Yale University Press.

———— (1979). *Paris: A Century of Change, 1878-1978.* New Haven, CT: Yale University Press.

Exline, Christopher H., Gary L. Peters, and Robert P. Larkin (1982). *The City: Patterns and Processes in the Urban Ecosystem.* Boulder, CO: Westview Press.

Fallows, James (1989). *More Like Us: Making America Great Again.* Boston: Houghton Mifflin.

Farrell, Terry (1985). "Post-Modern Urbanism." *Art and Design* 1, no. 1 (February):16-19.

Ferebee, Ann, ed. (1982). *Education for Urban Design.* Purchase, NY: Institute for Urban Design.

Ferriss, Hugh (1929). *The Metropolis of Tomorrow.* Reprint. Princeton, NJ: Princeton University Press, 1986.

Festinger, Leon (1962). *A Theory of Cognitive Dissonance.* Stanford, CA: Stanford University Press.

Fisher, Bonnie, and Boris Dramov (1987). *The Urban Waterfront.* New York: Van Nostrand Reinhold.

Fisher, Thomas (1988). "The New Urban Design: Building the New City." *Progressive Architecture* 69, no. 3:86-93.

———— (1989). "Presenting Ideas." *Progressive Architecture* 70, no. 6:84-93.

Fishman, Robert (1982). *Urban Utopias in the Twentieth Century: Ebenezer Howard, Frank Lloyd Wright, and Le Corbusier.* Cambridge, MA: MIT Press.

———— (1987). *Bourgeois Utopias: The Rise and Fall of Suburbia.* New York: Basic Books.

Fitch, James Marston (1965). "Experiential Bases for Aesthetic Decision." *Annals of the New York Academy of Science:*706-714.

———— (1972). *American Building 2: The Environmental Forces That Shape It.* New York: Schocken Books.

———— (1980). "A Funny Thing Happened. . . ." *American Institute of Architects Journal* 69, no. 1:66-68.

Fitzhardinge, Richard (1990). "The Humanists." Lecture presented at the University of New South Wales, March 20.

Fleischer, Aaron (1961). "The Influence of Technology on Urban Form." In Lloyd Rodwin, ed., *The Future Metropolis.* New York: George Braziller, pp. 64-79.

Fleming, Ronald Lee, and Renata von Tscharner (1987). *Place Makers: Creating Public Art That Tells You Where You Are.* 2d ed. Cambridge, MA: Harcourt Brace Jovanovich.

"Four Commentaries on the Charter." (1979). *Journal of Architectural Research* 7, no. 2:10-12.

Frampton, Kenneth (1983). *Modern Architecture 1851-1945.* New York: Rizzoli.

Francescato, Guido (1989). "Paradigm Lost: Exploring Possibilities in Environmental Design Research and Practice." In Graeme Hardie, Robin Moore, and Henry Sanoff, eds., *Changing Paradigms: Proceedings of EDRA20/1989.* Environmental Design Research Association, pp. 63-67.

Francis, Alan (1991). "Private Nights in the City Centre." *Town and Country Planning* 60, no. 10:302-303.

Francis, Mark (1987a). "The Making of Democratic Streets." In Anne Vernez Moudon, ed., *Public Streets for Public*

Use. New York: Van Nostrand Reinhold, pp. 23-39.

———— (1987b). "Urban Open Spaces." In Ervin H. Zube and Gary T. Moore, eds., *Advances in Environment, Behavior, and Design 1.* New York: Plenum, pp. 71-106.

Franck, Karen (1984). "Exorcising the Ghost of Physical Determinism." *Environment and Behavior* 10, no. 4:411-430.

———— (1987). "Phenomenology, Positivism, and Empiricism as Research Strategies in Environmental Behavior Research." In Ervin H. Zube and Gary T. Moore, eds., *Advances in Environment, Behavior, and Design 1.* New York: Plenum, pp. 59-67.

———— (1989). "Overview of Collective and Shared Housing." In Franck and Ahrentzen, *New Households,* pp. 3-19.

Franck, Karen, and Sherry Ahrentzen, eds. (1989). *New Households, New Housing.* New York: Van Nostrand Reinhold.

French, Jere Stuart (1983). *Urban Space: A Brief History of the City Square.* Dubuque, IA: Kendall/Hunt.

Freud, Sigmund (1949). *An Outline of Psychoanalysis.* Translated from the German by James Strachey. New York: Norton.

Fried, Lewis (1990). *Makers of the City: Jacob Riis, Lewis Mumford, James T. Farrell and Paul Goodman.* Amherst: University of Massachusetts Press.

Fried, Marc (1963). "Grieving for a Lost Home." In J. Duhl, ed., *The Urban Condition.* New York: Simon & Schuster, pp. 151-171.

Frieden, Bernard J. (1990). "Center City Transformed: Planners as Developers." *Journal of the American Planning Association* 56, no. 4:423-428.

Frieden, Bernard J., and Lynne B. Sagalyn (1989). *Downtown, Inc.: How America Rebuilds Cities.* Cambridge, MA: MIT Press.

Friedmann, John (1987). *Planning in the Public Domain: From Knowledge to Action.* Princeton, NJ: Princeton University Press.

Frieman, Ziva (1989). "A Non-Unified Field Theory." *Progressive Architecture* 70, no. 11:65-73.

Friend, John, and Allen Hickeling (1987). *Planning Under Pressure: The Strategic Choice Approach.* New York: Pergamon Press.

Fromm, Dorit (1991). *Collaborative Communities: Cohousing, Central Living and Other New Forms of Housing.* New York: Van Nostrand Reinhold.

Fromm, Erich (1941). *Escape from Freedom.* New York: Farrar and Rinehart.

Fulton, William (1985). "Bethesda Stages a Beauty Contest." *Planning* 52, no. 1:18-21.

———— (1990). "The Long Commute." *Planning* 56, no. 7:4-10.

Gadamer, Hans-Georg (1976). *Philosophical Hermeneutics.* Translated from the German by David E. Linge. Berkeley and Los Angeles: University of California Press.

———— (1981). *Reason in the Age of Science.* Translated by

Frederick G. Lawrence. Cambridge, MA: MIT Press.

Galanty, Ervin Y. (1975). *New Towns: Antiquity to the Present*. New York: George Braziller.

Galbraith, John Kenneth (1985). *The Scotch*. Boston: Houghton Mifflin.

Gall, Wayne (1990). "Breaking the Barriers: Restoration of an Urban Green Space." In David Gordon, ed., *Green Cities: Ecologically Sound Approaches to Urban Space*. Montreal: Black Rose Books, pp. 169–176.

Gallagher, Mary Lou (1991). "Des Moines and the Vision Thing." *Planning* 57, no. 12:12-15.

Gallion, Arthur, and Simon Eisner (1975). *The Urban Pattern: City Planning and Design*. 2d ed. New York: Van Nostrand Reinhold.

——— (1986). *The Urban Pattern: City Planning and Design*. 5th ed. New York: Van Nostrand Reinhold.

Gamble, John (1989). "Order and Process." Photocopied.

Gandelsonas, Mario (1988). *The Order of the American City*. New York: Princeton Architectural Press.

Gans, Herbert (1962). *The Urban Villagers: Groups and Class in the Life of Italian Americans*. New York: Free Press.

——— (1968). *People and Plans: Essays on Urban Problems and Solutions*. New York: Basic Books.

——— (1972). "Integrating New Towns." *Design and Environment* 3, no. 1:28-29, 50-51.

——— (1975). Foreword to Clare Cooper Marcus, *Easter Hill Village*. New York: Free Press, pp. ix-xxi.

Gapp, Paul (1990). "Turning the Planet into a House We Can Live In. *Chicago Tribune*, Section 13 (April 22):5.

Gardiner, Richard A. (1978). *Design for Safe Neighborhoods*. Washington, DC: U.S. Government Printing Office.

Garnier, Tony (1917). *The Cité Industrielle*. Reprint. New York: Rizzoli, 1990.

Garreau, Joel (1991). *Edge City: Life on the New Frontier*. New York: Doubleday.

Gastal, Alfredo (1982). "Towards a Model of Cultural Analysis for the Designing Process." Unpublished Ph.D. dissertation, University of Pennsylvania.

Gayden, Ernst L. (1979). "Design Model for the Energy Efficient City." In Rocco A. Fazzolare and Craig B. Smith, eds., *Changing Energy Use Futures*. New York: Pergamon Press, pp. 1142-1150.

Geddes, Robert, and James Dill (1989). "Practice in Theory." *Progressive Architecture* 70, no. 11:115-116, 118.

Gehl, Jan (1987). *Life Between Buildings: Using Public Space*. New York: Van Nostrand Reinhold.

——— (1989). "A Changing Street Life in a Changing Society," *Places* 6, no. 1:8-17.

Geist, Johann Friedrich (1983). *Arcades: the History of a Building Type*. Translated from the German by Jane O. Newman and John H. Smith. Cambridge, MA: MIT Press.

Gerosa, Piergiorgio (1979). "Architectonic Elements of the Urban Typology." *Lotus International* 24:121-128.

Getzels, Judith et al. (1988). *Zoning Bonuses in Central Cities*, PAS Report No. 410. Chicago: American Institute of Planners.

Ghirardo, Diane (1987). "A Taste of Money: Architecture and Criticism in Houston." *Harvard Architectural Review* 6:88-97.

——— (1989). *Building New Communities: New Deal America and Fascist Italy*. Princeton, NJ: Princeton University Press.

Gibson, Eleanor (1969). *Principles of Perceptual Learning and Development*. New York: Appleton-Century-Crofts.

Gibson, James J. (1950). *Perception of the Visual World*. Boston: Houghton Mifflin.

——— (1966). *The Senses Considered as Perceptual Systems*. Boston: Houghton Mifflin.

——— (1979). *The Ecological Approach to Visual Perception*. Boston: Houghton Mifflin.

Gibson, James J., and Eleanor Gibson (1955). "Perceptual Learning: Differentiation or Enrichment?" *Psychological Review* 62:32-41.

Giedion, Sigfried (1963). *Space, Time and Architecture*. 4th ed. Cambridge, MA: Harvard University Press.

Gilbert, James (1990). *Perfect Cities: Chicago's Utopias 1893*. Chicago: University of Chicago Press.

Girouard, Mark (1985). *Cities and People: A Social and Architectural History*. New Haven, CT: Yale University Press.

——— (1990). *The English Town: A History of Urban Life*. New Haven, CT: Yale University Press.

Givoni, Baruch (1973). "Architecture and Urban Planning in Relation to Weather and Climate." In S. W. Tromp and J. J. Boama, eds., *Progress in Bioclimatology*. Amsterdam: Swats and Zeitlinger, pp. 183-193.

Glendale Redevelopment Agency (1986a). *Urban Design Information*. Glendale, CA: GRA.

——— (1986b). Personal Interviews with Susan Shick, executive director, and Jim Rez, deputy executive director.

Goffman, Erving (1961). *Asylums*. Garden City, NY: Anchor.

Golany, Gideon (1976). *New-Town Planning: Principles and Practice*. New York: John Wiley.

Goldberger, Paul (1989a). "Building against Cities: The Struggle to Make Places." *New Art Examiner* 16, no. 5 (February):24-28.

——— (1989b). "Beyond Utopia: Settling for a New Realism." *New York Times* (June 25):Section H, 1,30.

Goldfinger, Erno (1942). "The Elements of Enclosed Space." *Architectural Review* 91, no. 541:5-8.

Goldsmith, Edward et al. (1990). *Imperiled Planet: Restoring Our Endangered Ecosystems*. Cambridge, MA: MIT Press.

Goldstein, Eric A., and Mark A. Izeman (1990). *The New York Environment Book*. Covelo, CA: Island Press.

Goode, David (1990). "Introduction: A Green Renaissance." In David Gordon, ed., *Green Cities: Ecologically Sound Approaches to Urban Space*. Montreal: Black Rose Books, pp. 1-8.

Goodman, Paul, and Percival Goodman (1947). *Communitas: Means of Livelihood and Ways of Life*. Chicago: University of Chicago Press.

Goodman, Robert (1971). *After the Planners*. New York: Simon & Schuster.

Goodsell, Charles T. (1988). *The Social Meaning of Civic Space: Studying Political Authority through Architecture*. Lawrence: University of Kansas Press.

Gordon, David, ed. (1990). *Green Cities: Ecologically Sound Approaches to Urban Space*. Montreal: Black Rose Books.

Gosling, David, and Barry Maitland (1984a). *Concepts of Urban Design*. New York: St. Martin's Press.

——— (1984b). "Urbanism." *Architectural Design Profile 51*. London: Architectural Design Publications.

Gottschalk, Shimon S. (1975). *Communities and Alternatives: An Exploration of the Limits of Planning*. Cambridge, MA: Schenkman.

Goudie, Andrew (1986). *The Human Impact on the Natural Environment*. 2nd ed. Cambridge, MA: MIT Press.

Gratz, Roberta Brandes (1989). *The Living City: How Urban Residents Are Revitalizing America's Neighborhoods and Downtown Shopping Districts by Thinking Small in a Big Way*. New York: Simon & Schuster.

Gray, Christopher (1953). *Cubist Aesthetic Theories*. Baltimore: Johns Hopkins University Press.

Greer, Norma Richter (1988). *The Creation of Shelter*. Washington, DC: American Institute of Architects.

Gregotti, Vittorio (1990). "The Weakness of Criticism." *Casabella* 562:2–3, 63.

Grigsby, William, and Louis Rosenberg (1975). *Urban Housing Policy*. New York: APS Publications.

Groat, Linda (1982). "Meaning in Post-Modern Architecture: An Examination Using the Multiple Sorting Task." *Journal of Environmental Psychology* 2:3–22.

——— (1988). "Contextual Compatibility in Architecture: An Issue of Personal Taste?" In Jack Nasar, ed., *Environmental Aesthetics: Theory, Research, and Applications*. New York: Cambridge University Press, pp. 228–253.

Groat, Linda, and David Canter (1979). "Does Post-Modern Architecture Communicate?" *Progressive Architecture* 60, no. 12:84–87.

Gropius, Walter (1962). *The Scope of Total Architecture*. New York: Collier.

Gruen, Victor (1964). *The Heart of Our Cities, The Urban Crisis: Diagnosis and Cure*. New York: Simon & Schuster.

——— (1973). *Survival of the City*. New York: Van Nostrand Reinhold.

Gutman, Robert (1966). "Site Planning and Social Behavior." *Journal of Social Issues* 22:103–115.

——— (1972). "Questions Architects Ask." In *People and Buildings*. New York: Basic Books, pp. 337–369.

——— (1977). "Cast of Characters: Architecture, the Entrepreneurial Profession." *Progressive Architecture* 58, no. 5:55–58.

——— (1988). *Architectural Practice: A Critical Review*. Princeton, NJ: Princeton Architectural Press.

Gutman, Robert, and Barbara Westergaard (1974). "Building Evaluation, User Satisfaction and Design." In Jon

Lang et al., eds., *Designing for Human Behavior: Architecture and the Behavioral Sciences*. Stroudsburg, PA: Dowden, Hutchinson, and Ross, pp. 320–329.

Habrakan, N. J. (1971). *Supports: An Alternative to Mass Housing*. Translated from the Dutch by B. Valkenberg. New York: Praeger.

Hakim, Besim S. (1986). *Arabic-Islamic Cities: Building and Planning Principles*. London: KPI.

Hall, Edward T. (1966). *The Hidden Dimension*. New York: Doubleday.

Hall, Peter G. (1980). *Great Planning Disasters*. London: Weidenfeld and Nicholson.

——— (1988). *Cities of Tomorrow: An Intellectual History of City Planning and Design in the Twentieth Century*. New York: Basil Blackwell.

Halprin, Lawrence (1963). *Cities*. New York: Reinhold.

——— (1965). "Motation." *Progressive Architecture* 46, no. 7:126–128.

——— (1969). *The RSVP Cycles: Creative Processes in the Human Environment*. New York: George Braziller.

——— (1974). *Taking Part: A Workshop Approach to Collective Creativity*. Cambridge, MA: MIT Press.

Hamblen, Matt (1991). "Montgomery County at the Crossroads." *Planning* 57, no. 6:7–12.

Handy, Susan (1991). "Neo-Traditional Development: The Debate." *Berkeley Planning Journal* 6:135–144.

Harrington, Michael (1962). *The Other America: Poverty in the United States*. New York: Macmillan.

Harris, Britton (1967). "The Limitations of Science and Humanism in Planning." *Journal of the American Institute of Planners* 35, no. 5:324–325.

Hart, Roger (1978). "Children's Explorations of Tomorrow's Environments." *Ekistics* 45:387–390.

——— (1979). *Children's Experience of Place*. New York: Irvington.

Hatch, C. Richard, ed. (1984). *The Scope of Social Architecture*. New York: Van Nostrand Reinhold.

Hatton, Brian (1990). "The Development of London's Docklands." *Lotus International* 67:55–90.

Hawley, Amos (1950). *Human Ecology: A Theory of Community Structure*. New York: Ronald Press.

Hayden, Dolores (1976). *Seven American Utopias: The Architecture of Communitarian Socialism*. Cambridge, MA: MIT Press.

——— (1984). *Redesigning the American Dream: The Future of Housing, Work, and Family Life*. New York: Norton.

——— (1989). *The Power of Place*. Los Angeles: The Power of Place, Inc.

Heath, Tom F. (1984). *Method in Architecture*. Chichester: John Wiley.

——— (1988). "Behavioral and Perceptual Aspects of the Aesthetics of Urban Environments." In Jack Nasar, ed., *Environmental Aesthetics: Theory, Research, and Applications*. New York: Cambridge University Press, pp. 6–10.

Hedman, Richard, and Andrew Jaszewski (1984). *Funda-*

mentals of Urban Design. Washington, DC: Planners Press.

Heidegger, Martin (1971). *Poetry, Language, Thought.* Translated from the German by Albert Hofstadter. New York: Harper & Row.

Heider, Fritz (1958). *The Psychology of Interpersonal Relations.* New York: John Wiley.

Helmer, Stephen (1980). *Hitler's Berlin: The Speer Plans for Reshaping the Central City.* Ann Arbor: University of Michigan Research Press.

Helmreich, Robert (1974). "The Evaluations of Environments: Behavioral Research in an Undersea Habitat." In Jon Lang et al., eds., *Designing for Human Behavior: Architecture and the Behavioral Sciences.* Stroudsburg, PA: Dowden, Hutchinson, and Ross, pp. 274-285.

Helson, Harry (1964). *Adaptation Level Theory: An Experimental and Systematic Approach to Human Behavior.* New York: Harper & Row.

Hepworth, Mark E. (1990). "Planning for the Information City: The Challenge and Response." *Urban Studies* 27, no. 4:537-558.

Herdeg, Klaus (1983). *The Decorated Diagram: Harvard Architecture and the Failure of the Bauhaus Legacy.* Cambridge, MA: MIT Press.

Hershberger, Robert G., and Robert C. Cass (1988). "Predicting User Responses to Buildings." In Jack Nasar, ed., *Environmental Aesthetics: Theory, Research, and Applications.* New York: Cambridge University Press, pp. 197-211.

Hertzberger, Herman (1980). "Shaping the Environment." In Mikellides, *Architecture for People,* pp. 38-40.

Hesselgren, Sven (1975). *Man's Perception of the Manmade Environment: An Architectural Theory.* Stroudsburg, PA: Dowden, Hutchinson, and Ross.

Hester, Randolph T., Jr. (1975). *Neighborhood Space.* Stroudsburg, PA: Dowden, Hutchinson, and Ross.
——— (1989). "Social Values in Open Space Design." *Places* 6, no. 1:68-77.

Hilbersheimer, Ludwig (1940). *The New City.* Chicago: Paul Theobold.

Hill, Morris (1972). "A Goals-Achievement Matrix for Evaluating Alternative Plans." In Ira M. Robinson, ed., *Decision-Making in Urban Planning.* Beverly Hills, CA: Sage, pp. 185-207.

Hillier, Bill, and Julienne Hanson (1984). *The Social Logic of Space.* Cambridge, Eng.: Cambridge University Press.

Hinshaw, Mark (1983). "The Private Sector Builds a Public Place: Sixth Street Pedestrian Corridor, Bellevue, Washington." *Urban Design Review* 6, no. 4:6-7.

Hitt, Jack, ed. (1990). "Whatever Became of the Public Square?" *Harper's Magazine* 281 (July):49-60.

Hochberg, Julian (1964). *Perception.* Englewood Cliffs, NJ: Prentice-Hall.

Holden, A. (1988). "The Crusader Prince." *Sunday Times* of London (October 30):C1-C2.

Holston, James (1989). *The Modernist City: An Anthropological Critique of Brasilia.* Chicago: University of Chicago Press.

Hopf, Peter, and John A. Raeber (1984). *Access for the Handicapped: The Barrier-Free Regulations for Design and Construction in all 50 States.* New York: Van Nostrand Reinhold.

Hough, Michael (1984). *City Form and Natural Process: Towards a New Urban Vernacular.* London: Routledge.
——— (1990a). "Formed by Natural Process—A Definition of the Green City." In David Gordon, ed., *Green Cities: Ecologically Sound Approaches to Urban Space.* Montreal: Black Rose Books, pp. 15-20.
——— (1990b). *Out of Place: Restoring Identity to a Regional Landscape.* New Haven, CT: Yale University Press.

Houstoun, Lawrence O., Jr. (1990a). "From Streets to Mall and Back Again." *Planning* 56, no. 6:4-10.
——— (1990b). "Weather Report." *Planning* 56, no. 12:19-21.

Howard, Ebenezer (1902). *Garden Cities of Tomorrow.* London: Sonnenschein.

Huet, Bernard (1984). "The City as Dwelling Space: Alternatives to the Charter of Athens." *Lotus International* 41:6-16.

Hughes, Robert (1980). *The Shock of the New.* London: British Broadcasting Corporation.

Ihde, Don (1986). *Experimental Phenomenology.* Albany: State University of New York Press.

Ingersoll, Richard (1991). "Unpacking the Green Man's Burden." *Design Book Review* 20:19-26.

Irving, Robert Grant (1981). *Indian Summer: Lutyens, Baker and Imperial Delhi.* New Haven, CT: Yale University Press.

Isaac, Alan R. G. (1971). *Approach to Architectural Design.* Toronto: University of Toronto.

Itten, Johannes (1965). "The Foundation Course at the Bauhaus." In Gyorgy Kepes, ed., *The Education of Vision.* New York: George Braziller, pp. 104-121.

Izumi, Kiyo (1968). "Some Psycho-Social Considerations of Environmental Design." Mimeographed.

Jackson, Daryl (1987). "Propositional Modernism and Evolutionary Urbanism." *Architecture Australia* 77, no. 10:57-59.

Jackson, John B. (1980). *The Necessity for Ruins, and Other Topics.* Amherst: University of Massachusetts Press.

Jackson, Kenneth, and Camilo José Vergara (1989). *Silent Cities.* New York: Princeton Architectural Press.

Jackson, Peter (1989). *Maps of Meaning: An Introduction to Cultural Geography.* London: Unwin Hyman.

Jacobs, Allan B. (1980). *Making City Planning Work.* Chicago: American Planning Association.
——— (1985). *Looking at Cities.* Cambridge, MA: Harvard University Press.

Jacobs, Allan B., and Donald Appleyard (1987). "Toward an Urban Design Manifesto." *American Planning Association Journal* 53, no. 1:113-120.

Jacobs, Jane (1961). *The Death and Life of Great American Cities*. New York: Random House.

——— (1969). *The Economy of Cities*. New York: Random House.

Jacobs, Steven, and Barclay G. Jones (1962). "Urban Design through Conservation." Unpublished manuscript, Berkeley, CA.

Jakle, John A. (1987). *The Visual Elements of Landscape*. Amherst: University of Massachusetts Press.

Jellicoe, Geoffrey, and Susan Jellicoe (1987). *The Landscape of Man: Shaping the Environment from Prehistory to the Present Day*. Rev. ed. New York: Van Nostrand Reinhold.

Jencks, Charles (1986). *What is Post-Modernism?* London: Academy Editions.

Johnson, Eugene, ed. (1986). *Charles Moore: Buildings and Projects 1949-1986*. New York: Rizzoli.

Johnson, Philip, and Mark Wigley (1988). *Deconstructivist Architecture*. New York: Museum of Modern Art.

Johnson, Robert E. (1989). *The Economics of Building: A Practical Guide for the Design Professional*. New York: John Wiley.

Johnston, Jacklyn (1990). "Establishing Ecology Parks in London." In David Gordon, ed., *Green Cities: Ecologically Sound Approaches to Urban Space*. Montreal: Black Rose Books, pp. 177-184.

Jones, Barclay G. (1962). "Design from Knowledge Not Belief." *AIA Journal* 38, no. 6:104-105.

Jones, Barclay G., and David E. Sparrow (1980), "Major Themes In Planning Thought." Mimeographed.

Joselit, David (1990). "Public Art and the Public Purse." *Art in America* 78 (July):142-151.

Jukes, Peter, ed. (1990). *A Shout in the Street: An Excursion into the Modern City*. New York: Farrar Straus Giroux.

Jung, Carl G. (1968). "Approaches to the Unconscious." In Carl G. Jung, ed., *Man and His Symbols*. New York: Dell, pp. 1-94.

Kalia, Ravi (1987). *Chandigarh: In Search of Identity*. Carbondale and Edwardsville: Southern Illinois University Press.

Kaminski, Gerhard (1989). "The Relevance of Ecologically Oriented Theory Building in Environment and Behavior Research." In Ervin H. Zube and Gary T. Moore, eds., *Advances in Environment, Behavior, and Design 2*. New York: Plenum, pp. 3-36.

Kandinsky, Wassily (1926). *Punkt und Linie zu Flache*. München: Langen.

Kantowitz, Barry, and Robert D. Sorkin (1983). *Human Factors: Understanding People-System Relationships*. New York: John Wiley.

Kaplan, Abraham (1964). *The Conduct of Inquiry: Methodology for the Behavioral Sciences*. Scranton, PA: Chandler.

Kaplan, Marshall (1973). *Urban Planning in the 1960s: A Design for Irrelevancy*. Cambridge, MA: MIT Press.

Kaplan, Sam Hall (1990). "The Holy Grid: A Skeptic's View." *Planning* 56, no. 11:10-11.

Kaplan, Stephen, and Rachel Kaplan (1982). *Cognition and Environment: Functioning in an Uncertain World*. New York: Praeger.

Kappraff, Jay (1990). *Connections: The Geometric Bridge between Science and Art*. New York: McGraw Hill.

Kay, Jane Holtz (1991). "Building a *There* There." *Planning* 57, no. 1:4-8.

Katju, K. N. (1953). "A Tale of Two Cities," *Journal of the Indian Institute of Architects* 19, no. 4:13-15, 22.

Kelbaugh, Doug, ed. (1989). *The Pedestrian Pocket Book: A New Suburban Design Strategy*. New York: Princeton Architectural Press.

——— (1990). "A Sense of Limits...from the Last Decade." In American Institute of Architects, eds., *American Architecture of the 1980s*. Washington, DC: American Institute of Architects, pp. 341-342.

Keller, Suzanne (1968). *The Urban Neighborhood: A Sociological Perspective*. New York: Random House.

Kelly, Brian, and Roger K. Lewis (1992). "What's Right (and Wrong) about the Inner Harbor." *Planning* 58, no. 4:28-32.

Kent, T. J. (1964). *The Urban General Plan*. San Francisco: Chandler.

Kepes, Gyorgy (1944). *Language of Vision*. Chicago: Paul Theobold.

———, ed. (1966). *Sign, Image, Symbol*. New York: George Braziller.

Khan-Magomedov, S. O. (1987). *Pioneers of Soviet Architecture*. London: Thames and Hudson.

Kiernan, Stephen (1987). "The Architecture of Plenty: Theory and Design in the Marketing Age." *Harvard Architecture Review* 6:102-113.

King, Stanley, with Merinda Conley, Bill Latimer, and Drew Ferrault (1989). *Co-Design: A Process of Design Participation*. New York: Van Nostrand Reinhold.

Kirchhoff, Gerhard, ed. (1989). *Views of Berlin*. Boston, MA: Birkhäuser.

Klee, Paul (1953). *Pedagogical Sketchbook*. Translated from the German by S. Moholy Nagy. New York: Praeger.

Klotz, Heinrich (1988). *The History of Post-Modern Architecture*. Translated from the German by Radka Donnell. Cambridge, MA: MIT Press.

Knack, Ruth E. (1989). "Repent, Ye Sinners, Repent." *Planning* 55, no. 8:4-13.

Knight, Barry, and Gary Gappert, eds. (1989). "Cities in Global Society." *Urban Affairs Annual Review* 35. Newbury Park, CA: Sage.

Koberg, Don, and Jim Bagnall (1977). *The Universal Traveler: A Soft-Systems Guide to Creativity, Problem Solving and the Process of Design*. 2d ed. Los Altos, CA: William Kaufman.

Koeningsberger, Otto (1960). *Master Plan for the New Capital of Orissa at Bhubaneswar*. Cuttack: Orissa Government Press.

Koffka, Kurt (1935). *Principles of Gestalt Psychology*. New York: Harcourt Brace.

Köhler, Wolfgang (1929). *Gestalt Psychology*. New York: Liveright.

Kohn, Franck Fox (1975). *Defensible Space Modifications in Row House Communities*. New York: Institute for Community Design Analysis.

Kolb, David (1990). *Postmodern Sophistications*. Chicago: University of Chicago Press.

Kolb, David A. (1984). *Experiential Learning: Experience as the Source of Learning and Development*. Englewood Cliffs, NJ: Prentice-Hall.

Koolhaas, Rem (1978). *Delirious New York: A Retroactive Manifesto for Manhattan*. New York: Oxford University Press.

Korman, R. (1986). "Reshaping the Urban Windscape." *Engineering News Record* 216 (3 April):30-33.

Kostof, Spiro, ed. (1977). *The Architect: Chapters in the History of the Profession*. New York: Oxford University Press.

———— (1985). *A History of Architecture: Settings and Rituals*. New York: Oxford University Press.

———— (1991). *The City Shaped: Urban Patterns and Meanings*. Boston: Little Brown.

Krampen, Martin (1991). "Environmental Meaning." In Ervin H. Zube and Gary T. Moore, eds., *Advances in Environment, Behavior, and Design 3*. New York: Plenum, pp. 231-268.

Kricken, John, and Philip Enquist (1986). "Four Recent Suburban Projects from SOM, San Francisco, California." *Urban Design Review* 9, no. 2:20-22.

Krier, Leon (1978). *Rational Architecture*. Bruxelles: Archives d'Architecture Moderne.

———— (1980). "Projet pour une Nouvelle Ecole de Cinq Cents Enfants." *Archives d'Architecture Moderne* 19.

———— (1985). *Albert Speer: Architecture 1932-1942*. Bruxelles: Archives d'Architecture Moderne.

———— (1987). "Master Plan for Poundbury Development in Dorchester." *Architectural Design Profile* 79:46-55.

———— (1990). "Urban Components." In Andreas Papadakis and Harriet Watson, eds., *The New Classicism: Omnibus Volume*. New York: Rizzoli, pp. 197-203.

Krier, Rob (1979). *Urban Space (Stadtraum)*. Translated from the German by Christine Czechowski and George Black. New York: Rizzoli.

———— (1990). "Typological Elements of the Concept of Urban Space." In Andreas Papadakis and Harriet Watson, eds., *The New Classicism: Omnibus Volume*. New York: Rizzoli, pp. 213-219.

Krinsky, Carol H. (1978). *Rockefeller Center*. New York: Oxford University Press.

Kroll, Lucien (1987). *The Architecture of Complexity*. Translated from the French by Peter Blundell Jones. Cambridge, MA: MIT Press.

———— (1980). "Architecture and Bureaucracy." In Byron Mikellides, ed., *Architecture for People*. New York: Holt, Rinehart and Winston, pp. 162-170.

Krueckeberg, Donald A. (1983). "The Culture of Planning." In Donald A. Krueckeberg, ed., *Introduction to Planning History in the United States*. New Brunswick, NJ: Rutgers University, Center for Urban Policy Research, pp. 1-12.

Krupat, E. (1985). *People in Cities: The Urban Environment and Its Effect*. Cambridge, MA: Cambridge University Press.

Kuhn, Thomas (1962). *The Structure of Scientific Revolutions*. Chicago: University of Chicago Press.

Kultermann, Udo, ed. (1970). *Kenzo Tange 1946-1949: Architecture and Urban Design*. London: Pall Mall Press.

Kundera, Milan (1990). Quoted by Calvin Maclean in "Director's Notes" for "Jacques and His Master." The Commons Theater, Chicago, IL.

Kuper, Leo et al. (1953). *Living in Towns*. London: Cresset Press.

Ladd, Florence (1978). "City Kids in the Absence of Legitimate Adventure." In Stephen Kaplan and Rachel Kaplan, eds., *Humanscape*. North Scituate, MA: Duxbury, pp. 443-447.

Lagorio, Henry J. (1990). *Earthquakes: An Architect's Guide to Nonstructural Seismic Hazards*. New York: John Wiley.

Lai, Richard Tseng-yu (1988). *Law in Urban Design and Planning: The Invisible Web*. New York: Van Nostrand Reinhold.

Laing, R. D. (1971). *The Politics of Family and Other Essays*. New York: Pantheon.

Lamb, Richard (1991). "The Challenge of Ecology to the Design Professions: Invention and Intervention." *Exedra* 3, no. 1:16-24.

Lang, Jon (1979). "Socio-Psychological Factors in Tall Building Design." New York: American Society of Civil Engineers, Preprint No. 3720.

———— (1980a). "The Nature of Theory for Architectural and Urban Design," *Urban Design International* 1, no. 2:41.

———— (1980b). "The Built Environment and Social Behavior: Architectural Determinism Reexamined." *VIA* 4. Cambridge, MA: MIT Press:146-182.

———— (1984). "Formal Aesthetics and Visual Perception." *Visual Arts Research* 10, no. 1:66-73.

———— (1985). "Problems, Paradigms, Architecture, City Planning and Urban Design." *Journal of Planning Education* 5, no. 1:26-27.

———— (1987a). *Creating Architectural Theory: The Role of the Behavioral Sciences in Environmental Design*. New York: Van Nostrand Reinhold.

———— (1987b). "The New Suburban Downtowns: Prototypes for Future Development?" Paper presented at the ASCA Conference, Los Angeles.

———— (1988). "Understanding Normative Theories of Architecture," *Environment and Behavior* 20, no. 5:601-632.

———— (1989a). "The Cultural Implications of Housing Design in India." In Setha Low and Erve Chambers, eds., *Housing, Culture, and Design: A Comparative*

Perspective. Philadelphia: University of Pennsylvania Press, pp. 375-392.

—— (1989b). "Teaching Urban Design: The Penn Experience." Paper presented at the Universade Federal do Rio Grande do Sul, Porto Alegre, Brazil. Photocopied.

—— (1990). "Urban Design: The Collaborative Art of Shaping Cities." In Tamas Lukovich, ed., *Urban Design and Local Planning: An Interdisciplinary Approach.* Kensington NSW: University of New South Wales, Faculty of Architecture, pp. 2.1-2.16.

—— (1991). "Design Theory from an Environment and Behavior Perspective." In Ervin H. Zube and Gary T. Moore, eds., *Advances in Environment, Behavior and Design 3.* New York: Plenum, pp. 54-101.

—— (1992). "Methodological Issues and Approaches: A Critical Appraisal." In Ernesto G. Arias, ed., *International Studies on the Meaning and Use of Housing: Methodologies and Their Application to Policy, Planning and Design.* London: Gower, pp. 51-69.

—— (in progress). "The Architecture of Independence: A Case Study of India, 1880-1970."

Lang, Jon, Charles Burnette, Walter Moleski, and David Vachon, eds. (1974). *Designing for Human Behavior: Architecture and the Behavioral Sciences.* Stroudsburg, PA: Dowden, Hutchinson, and Ross.

Langdon, Philip (1988). "A Good Place to Live." *Atlantic Monthly* (March):39-60.

Langdon, Philip, with Robert G. Shibley and Polly Welch (1990). *Urban Excellence.* New York: Van Nostrand Reinhold.

Langer, Susanne K. (1953). *Feeling and Form.* New York: Charles Scribner's Sons.

Lansing, John B., Robert W. Marans, and Robert B. Zehner (1970). *Planned Residential Environments.* Ann Arbor: University of Michigan, Survey Research Center.

Larsen, Jane Warren (1987). "Bethesda: An Artist's Perspective." *New Art Examiner* (April):1.

Larson, Magali (1979). *The Rise of Professionalism: A Sociological Analysis.* Berkeley and Los Angeles: University of California Press.

Lasar, Terry Jill (1989). *Carrots and Sticks: New Zoning Downtown.* Washington, DC: Urban Land Institute.

Las Colinas Association (1986). Personal Interviews with Greg Watling, vice president and manager, and Ethan R. Bidne, director, architectural controls.

Lasswell, Harold (1979). *The Signature of Power: Buildings, Communications and Policy.* New Brunswick, NJ: Transaction Books.

Latham, Richard S. (1964). "The Artifact as a Cultural Cipher." In Laurence B. Holland, ed., *Who Designs America?* New York: Anchor, pp. 257-280.

Laurie, Michael (1979). "Nature and City Planning in the Nineteenth Century." In Ian C. Laurie, ed., *Nature in Cities: The Natural Environment in the Design and Development of Urban Green Space.* New York: John Wiley.

Lavin, Sylvia (1990). "The Uses and Abuses of Theory." *Progressive Architecture* 71, no. 7:113-114, 179.

Lawlor, Robert (1982). *Scared Geometry: Philosophy and Practice.* London: Thames and Hudson.

Lawrence, Roderick (1989). "Structuralist Theories in Environment-Behavior-Design Research." In Ervin H. Zube and Gary T. Moore, eds., *Advances in Environment, Behavior and Design 2.* New York: Plenum, pp. 37-40.

Lawson, Bryan (1990). *How Designers Think.* 2d ed. London: Butterworth Architecture.

Lawton, M. Powell (1975). *Planning and Managing Housing for the Elderly.* New York: Wiley Interscience.

—— (1977). "An Ecological Theory of Aging Applied to Elderly Housing." *Journal of Architectural Education* 31, no. 1:6-10.

Le Compte, William (1974). "Behavior Settings as Data-Generating Units for the Environmental Planner and Architect." In Jon Lang et al., eds., *Designing for Human Behavior: Architecture and the Behavioral Sciences.* Stroudsburg, PA: Dowden, Hutchinson, and Ross, pp. 183-193.

Le Corbusier (1923). *Vers une Architecture (Towards a New Architecture).* Translated from the French by F. Etchells. Reprint. New York: Praeger, 1970.

—— (1934). *La ville radieuse (The Radiant City).* Translated from the French by Pamela Knight and Eleanor Levieux. Reprint. New York: Orion Press, 1967.

—— (1948). *Looking at City Planning.* Translated from the French by Eleanor Levieux. Reprint. New York: Grossman, 1971.

—— (1953). *L'Unité d'Habitation de Marseilles (The Marseilles Block).* Translated from the French by Geoffrey Sainsbury. London: Harvill.

—— (1954). *The Modulor.* Translated from the French by Peter de Francia and Anna Bostock. Cambridge, MA: Harvard University Press.

—— (1960). *My Work.* Translated from the French by James Palmer. London: Architectural Press.

—— (1973). *The Athens Charter.* Translated from the French by Anthony Eardley. New York: Grossman.

Lee, Terrence (1970). "Urban Neighborhood as a Socio-Spatial Schema." In Harold M. Proshansky et al., eds., *Environmental Psychology: Man and His Physical Setting.* New York: Holt, Rinehart and Winston, pp. 349-370.

Leedy, Daniel L., Robert M. Maestro, and Thomas M. Franklin (1978). *Planning for Wildlife in Cities and Suburbs.* Washington, DC: U.S. Fish and Wildlife Service.

Lefebvre, Henri (1984). *Everyday Life in the Modern World.* Translated from the French by Sacha Rabinovitch. New Brunswick, NJ: Transaction Books.

Leff, Enrique (1990). "The Global Context of Greening Cities." In David Gordon, ed., *Green Cities: Ecologically Sound Approaches to Urban Space.* Montreal: Black Rose Books, pp. 55-66.

Leich, Jean Ferriss (1980). *Architectural Visions: The Drawings of Hugh Ferriss.* New York: Whitney Library of Design.

Leighton, Alexander H. (1959). *My Name Is Legion: Foundations for a Theory of Man in Relation to Culture.* New York: Basic Books.

Leinberger, Christopher B., and Charles Lockwood (1986). "How Business Is Reshaping America." *Atlantic Monthly* 258 (October):43–52.

Lennard, Suzanne H., and Henry L. Lennard (1987). *Livable Cities. People and Places: Social Design Principles for the Future of the City.* Southampton, NY: Center for Urban Well-Being.

———, eds. (1988). *Livable Cities I.* Carmel, CA: Center for Urban Well-Being.

———, eds. (1990). *Livable Cities II.* Carmel, CA: Center for Urban Well-Being.

Leopold, Luna B. (1968). *Hydrology for Urban Land Planning—A Guidebook on the Hydrological Effects of Urban Land Use.* Washington, DC: Geological Survey Circular 554.

Lesnikowski, Wejciech G. (1982). *Rationalism and Romanticism in Architecture.* New York: McGraw Hill.

Lesser, George (1957). *Gothic Cathedrals and Sacred Geometry.* London: Alec Tiranti.

Levi, David (1974). "The Gestalt Theory of Expression in Architecture." In Jon Lang et al., eds., *Designing for Human Behavior: Architecture and the Behavioral Sciences.* Stroudsburg, PA: Dowden, Hutchinson, and Ross, pp. 111–119.

Levinson, Nancy (1991). "Share and Share Alike: Cohousing Is Catching on in the U.S." *Planning* 57, no. 7:24–26.

Levy, John M. (1991). *Contemporary Urban Planning.* 2d ed. Englewood Cliffs, NJ: Prentice-Hall.

Lewis, Nigel C. (1977). "A Procedural Framework Attempting to Express the Relationship of Human Factors to the Physical Design Process." Unpublished student paper, University of Pennsylvania.

Littlejohn, David (1984). *Architect: The Life and Work of Charles Moore.* New York: Holt, Rinehart and Winston.

Lofland, Lyn H. (1973). *A World of Strangers: Order and Action in Public Space.* New York: Basic Books.

——— (1989a). "Social Life in the Public Realm." *Journal of Contemporary Ethnography* 17, no. 4:453–482.

——— (1989b). "The Morality of Urban Life: The Emergence and Continuation of a Debate." *Places* 6, no. 1:18–23.

Low, Setha M. (1987). "Developments in Research Design, Data Collection, and Analysis: Qualitative Methods." In Ervin H. Zube and Gary T. Moore, eds., *Advances in Environment, Behavior, and Design 1.* New York: Plenum, pp. 279–303.

Low, Setha M., and Erve Chambers, eds. (1989). *Housing: Culture and Design: A Comparative Perspective.* Philadelphia: University of Pennsylvania Press.

Lowry, Ira (1980). "The Dismal Future of Central Cities." In Arthur P. Solomon, ed., *The Prospective City: Economic, Population, Energy, and Environmental Developments.* Cambridge, MA: MIT Press, pp. 161–203.

Lozano, Eduardo E. (1988). "Visual Needs in Urban Environments and in Physical Planning." In Jack Nasar, ed., *Environmental Aesthetics: Theory, Research, and Applications.* New York: Cambridge University Press, pp. 395–421.

——— (1990). *Community Design and the Culture of Cities.* New York: Cambridge University Press.

Lüchinger, Arnulf (1981). *Structuralism in Architecture and Urban Planning.* Stuttgart: Karl Kramer.

Lucy, William (1989). *Close to Power: Setting Priorities with Public Officials.* Chicago: Planners Press.

Lukashok, Alvin K., and Kevin Lynch (1956). "Some Childhood Memories of the City." *Journal of the American Institute of Planners* 22, no. 3:142–152.

Lynch, Kevin (1960). *The Image of the City.* Cambridge, MA: MIT Press.

——— (1972). *What Time Is This Place?* Cambridge, MA: MIT Press.

——— (1976). *Managing the Sense of a Region.* Cambridge, MA: MIT Press.

——— (1977). *Growing Up in Cities: Studies of the Spatial Environment of Adolescents in Cracow, Melbourne, Mexico City, Salta, Toluca, and Warszawa.* Cambridge, MA: MIT Press.

——— (1982). "City Design: What It Is and How It Might Be Taught." In Ann Ferebee, ed., *Education for Urban Design.* Purchase, NY: Institute for Urban Design, pp. 105–111.

——— (1984). *Good City Form.* Cambridge, MA: MIT Press.

Lyotard, Jean-François (1984). *The Post Modern Condition—A Report on Knowledge.* Translated from the French by Geoff Bennington and Brian Massumi. Minneapolis: University of Minnesota Press.

Mackay, David (1990). "Redesigning Urban Design." *Architect's Journal* 192, no. 2:42–45.

Maharishi Sthapatya Ved Institute (1991). "An Introduction to Maharishi Sthapatya Ved: Urban Design, Architecture and Construction for Perfect Health and Ideal Living." Fairfield, IA: Maharishi Sthapatya Ved Institute.

Maillard, Lucien, ed. (1989). *L'Evénement Média, la Revue de la Grande Arche.* Paris: Envénment Média.

Maitland, Barry (1991). *The New Architecture of the Retail Mall.* New York: Van Nostrand Reinhold.

Maldonado, Tomàs (1989). "Is Architecture a Text?" *Casabella* 53, no. 560:60–61.

Mansfield, Howard (1990). *Cosmopolis: Yesterday's Cities of the Future.* New Brunswick, NJ: Rutgers University Center for Urban Policy Research.

Mänty, Jorma, and Norman Pressman, eds. (1989). *Cities Designed for Winter.* Helsinki: Building Book.

Marans, Robert W., and Sherry Ahrentzen (1987). "Developments in Research Design, Data Collection, and Analysis: Quantitative Methods." In Ervin H. Zube and Gary T. Moore, eds., *Advances in Environment, Behavior, and Design 1.* New York: Plenum, pp. 251-277.

Mariani, Riccordo (1990). "The Planning of the E42: The First Phase." *Lotus* 67:90-126.

Mariemont Company (1925). *Mariemont: The New Town, "A National Exemplar."* Mariemont, OH: Mariemont Company.

Markovich, Nicholas C., Wolfgang E. Preiser, and Fred G. Strum (1990). *Pueblo Style and Regional Architecture.* New York: Van Nostrand Reinhold.

Marks, Larry (1990). "Revitalization of Downtown, St. Louis, Mo." *AIA Urban Design Case Studies* 1, no. 1:1.

Marmot, Alexi (1982). "The Legacy of Le Corbusier and High Rise Housing," *Built Environment* 7, no. 2:82-95.

Martienssen, Rex D. (1956). *The Idea of Space in Greek Architecture.* Johannesburg: University of the Witwatersrand Press.

Martin, Evelyn (1991). "Between Heaven and Earth." *Planning* 57, no. 1:24-27.

Martin, Richard, ed. (1990). *The New Urban Landscape,* New York: Rizzoli.

Marx, Karl, and Freidrich Engels (1848). *The Communist Manifesto.* Translated from the German by Samuel Moore. Hammondsworth: Penguin, 1967.

Maslow, Abraham (1943). "Theory of Human Nature." *Psychological Review* 50:370-396.

——— (1966). *The Psychology of Science.* New York: Harper & Row.

——— (1968). *Toward a Psychology of Being.* Princeton, NJ: Van Nostrand.

——— (1971). *The Farther Reaches of Human Nature.* New York: Viking.

——— (1987). *Motivation and Personality.* 3d ed. Rev. by Robert Frager, James Fadiman, Cynthia McReynolds, and Ruth Cox. New York: Harper & Row.

Masotti, Louis H., and Jeffrey K. Hadden, eds. (1973). *The Urbanization of the Suburbs.* Beverly Hills: Sage.

Mayer, Albert (1967). *The Urgent Future: People, Housing, City, Region.* New York: McGraw Hill.

Mayer, Harold M., and Richard C. Wade (1969). *Chicago: Growth of a Metropolis.* Chicago: University of Chicago Press.

McCamant, Kathryn M., and Charles R. Durrett (1988). *Cohousing: A Contemporary Approach to Housing Ourselves.* Berkeley, CA: Ten Speed Press.

——— (1989). "Cohousing in Denmark." In Karen A. Franck and Sherry Ahrentzen, eds., *New Households, New Housing.* New York: Van Nostrand Reinhold, pp. 100-126.

McClelland, David, John W. Atkinson, R. A. Clark, and E. L. Lowell (1953). *The Achievement Motive.* New York: Appleton-Century-Crofts.

McHale, John (1961). *R. Buckminster Fuller.* London: Prentice-Hall International.

McHarg, Ian (1969). *Design with Nature.* Garden City, NY: Natural History Press.

McNulty, Robert et al. (1986). *The Return of the Livable City: Learning from America's Best.* Washington, DC: Acropolis Press.

Meier, Richard L. (1962). *A Communications Theory of Urban Growth.* Cambridge, MA: MIT Press.

Melnick, Scott (1987). "The Urbanization of the Suburbs." *Building Design Construction* 28, no. 3:70-77.

Meltzer, Jack (1984). *Metropolis to Metroplex: The Social and Spatial Planning of Cities.* Baltimore: Johns Hopkins University Press.

Menzel, H. (1957). "Public and Private Conformity under Different Conditions of Acceptance in the Group." *Journal of Abnormal Psychology* 55:398-401.

Messinger, Alexander, and Robert G. LeRicolais (1972). "New Vistas for New Cities." *Architectural Design* 43, no. 3:144.

Meyer, Hannes (1928). *Hannes Meyer.* London: Schnaidt Tirani.

Michelson, William (1968). "Most People Don't Want What Architects Want." *Transaction* 5, no. 8:37-43.

———, ed. (1975). *Behavioral Research Methods in Environmental Design.* Stroudsburg, PA: Dowden, Hutchinson, and Ross.

——— (1976). *Man and His Urban Environment: A Sociological Approach.* 2d ed. Reading, MA: Addison-Wesley.

Mikellides, Byron (1980a). "Architectural Psychology and the Unavoidable Art." In Byron Mikellides, ed., *Architecture for People.* New York: Holt, Rinehart and Winston, pp. 9-26.

——— (1980b). "Appendix on Human Needs." In Mikelledis, *Architecture,* pp. 191-192.

Miles, Mike E., Emil E. Malizia, Marc A. Weiss, Gayle L. Berens, and Ginger Travis (1991). *Real Estate Development: Principles and Process.* Washington, DC: Urban Land Institute.

Miller, Donald L. (1989). *Lewis Mumford: A Life.* New York: Weidenfeld and Nicholson.

Mills, Miriam, ed. (1990). *Conflict Resolution and Public Policy.* New York: Greenwood.

Mitchell, Howard E. (1974). "Professional and Client: An Emerging Collaborative Relationship." In Jon Lang et al., eds., *Designing for Human Behavior: Architecture and the Behavioral Sciences.* Stroudsburg, PA: Dowden, Hutchinson, and Ross, pp. 15-22.

Mohney, David, and Keller Easterling, eds. (1991). *Seaside.* New York: Princeton Architectural Press.

Moholy Nagy, Sybil (1968). *The Matrix of Man.* New York: Praeger.

Moleski, Walter (1974). "Behavioral Analysis and Environmental Programming for Offices." In Jon Lang et al., eds., *Designing for Human Behavior: Architecture and the Behavioral Sciences.* Stroudsburg, PA: Dowden, Hutchinson, and Ross, pp. 302-315.

Moleski, Walter, and Jon Lang (1982). "Organization Needs

and Human Values in Office Planning," *Environment and Behavior* 14, no. 3:319–332.

Moll, Gary, and Sara Ebenzeck, eds. (1989). *Shading Our Cities: A Resource Guide for Urban and Community Forests.* Covelo, CA: Island Press.

Moneo, Raphael (1978). "On Typology." *Oppositions* 13 (Summer):23–45.

Monkkonen, Eric H. (1988). *America Becomes Urban: The Development of U.S. Cities and Towns 1790–1980.* Berkeley and Los Angeles: University of California Press.

Montgomery, Roger (1966). "Comment on 'Fear and House-as-Haven in the Lower Class.'" *Journal of the American Institute of Planners* 32, no. 1:31–37.

——— (1975). "A Manifesto on Urban Design." University of California at Berkeley, School of Architecture. Photocopied.

——— (1989). "Architecture Invents New People." In Russell Ellis and Dana Cuff, eds., *Architects' People.* New York: Oxford University Press, pp. 260–281.

Moore, Gary T., ed. (1970). *Emerging Methods in Environmental Design and Planning.* Cambridge, MA: MIT Press.

——— (1979). "Knowing about Environmental Knowing: The Current State of Research on Environmental Cognition." *Environment and Behavior* 11, no. 1:33–70.

Moore, Gary T., C. G. Lane, A. B. Hill, U. Cohen, and T. McGinty (1979). *Recommendations for Child Care Centers.* Milwaukee: University of Wisconsin-Milwaukee, Center for Architecture and Urban Planning.

Moore, Robin C. (1987). "Streets as Playgrounds." In Anne Vernez Moudon, ed., *Public Streets for Public Use.* New York: Van Nostrand Reinhold, pp. 45–62.

——— (1991). *Childhood's Domain: Play and Place in Child Development.* Berkeley, CA: MIG Communications.

Moore, Robin C., Susan M. Gottsman, and Daniel C. Iacofano, eds. (1987). *Play for All Guidelines: Planning, Design and Management of Outdoor Play Settings for All Children.* Berkeley, CA: MIG Communications.

Moore, Terry (1988). "Planning Without Preliminaries." *American Planning Association Journal* 54, no. 4:525–528.

Morris, A. E. J. (1979). *History of Urban Form: Before the Industrial Revolution.* New York: John Wiley.

Morris, Charles (1938). *Foundations of a Theory of Signs.* Chicago: University of Chicago Press.

Morris, E. K., and E. Levin, eds. (1982). "Typology in Design Education." *Journal of Architectural Education* 35, no. 2:whole issue.

Moudon, Anne Vernez, ed. (1987). *Public Streets for Public Use.* New York: Van Nostrand Reinhold.

——— (1990). "Normative/Substantive and Etic/Emic Dilemma in Design Education." Unpublished manuscript. University of Washington: College of Architecture.

——— (1992). "A Catholic Approach to Organizing What Urban Designers Should Know." *Journal of Planning Literature* 6, no. 4:331–349.

Mozingo, Louise (1989). "Women and Downtown Open Spaces." *Places* 6, no. 1:38–47.

Muller, Peter (1981). *Contemporary Suburban America.* Englewood Cliffs, NJ: Prentice-Hall.

Mumford, Lewis (1938). *The Culture of Cities.* New York: Harcourt Brace.

——— (1961). *The City in History: Its Origins, Its Transformations, and Its Prospects.* New York: Harcourt, Brace and World.

Murray, Henry A. et al. (1938). *Explorations in Personality.* New York: Oxford University Press.

Nadler, Gerald (1970). "Engineering Research and Design in Socioeconomic Systems." In Gary T. Moore, ed., *Emerging Methods in Environmental Design and Planning.* Cambridge, MA: MIT Press, pp. 322–331.

Nager, A. R., and W. R. Wentworth (1976). "Bryant Park: A Comprehensive Evaluation of Its Image and Use with Implications for Urban Open Space Design." New York: City University of New York, Center for Human Environments.

Na Nangara, Yongyudh (in progress). "A Psychological Study of Design Behavior: The Correlation between Preconceptions and Outcomes in Architectural Design." Ph.D. dissertation, University of Pennsylvania.

Nasar, Jack (1988a). "Architectural Symbolism: A Study of House Style Meanings." In Denise Lawrence and B. Wasserman, eds., *Paths to Co-existence: Proceedings of EDRA 19.* Riverside, CA: pp. 163–172.

———, ed. (1988b). *Environmental Aesthetics: Theory, Research, and Applications.* New York: Cambridge University Press.

National Capital Development Commission (1965). *The Future Canberra.* Sydney: Angus and Robertson.

National Main Street Center (1987). *Main Street Guidelines.* Washington, DC: Preservation Press.

Nealy, Craig (1983). "Burlington, Vermont Urbanization Strategy." *Cornell Journal of Architecture* 2:136–137.

Neisser, Ulrich (1976). *Cognition and Reality.* San Francisco: Freeman.

Neutra, Richard (1954). "Practical Cities Must Not Be Full of Irritations." *American City* 69, no. 4:122–123.

Newcomb, T. M. (1968). "Interpersonal Balance." In Robert P. Abelson, E. Aronson, W. McGuire, T. M. Newcomb, M. Rosenberg, and P. Tannenbaum, eds., *Theories of Cognitive Consistency: A Sourcebook.* Chicago: Rand McNally.

Newman, Peter W. G., and Jeffrey R. Kenworthy (1989). *Cities and Automobile Dependence: A Sourcebook.* Brookfield, VT: Gower Technical.

Newman, Oscar (1972). *Defensible Space: Crime Prevention through Urban Design.* New York: Macmillan.

——— (1975). *Design Guidelines for Creating Defensible Space.* Washington, DC: U.S. Department of Justice.

——— (1976). "The Use of Color and Texture at Clason Point." In Tom Porter and Byron Mikellides, eds.,

Color for Architecture. New York: Van Nostrand Reinhold, pp. 49–53.

——— (1980a). *Community of Interest.* New York: Anchor.

——— (1980b). "Whose Failure is Modern Architecture?" Mikellides, *Architecture,* pp. 49–58.

Newton, Norman T. (1971). "The City Beautiful Movement." In *Design on the Land: The Development of Landscape Architecture.* Cambridge, MA: Belknap, pp. 413–426.

New York, City of (1976). "Plazas for People, Streetscape and Residential Plazas." New York: Department of City Planning.

——— (1981). "Midtown Development: Final Report." New York: Department of City Planning.

Nicolin, P.-L. (1977). *GA: Carlo Aymonimo/Aldo Rossi Housing Complex at the Gallaratese Quarter.* Milan, Italy 1969–1974. Edited by Y. Futagawa. Tokyo: ADA Editions.

Nielsen, Sanja M. (1984). "Information Resources: An Expert's List of Books You May Need." *Architectural Record* 172, no. 9:39–43.

Nilsson, Sten (1975). *The New Capitals of India, Pakistan and Bangladesh.* London: Curzon Press.

Ninan, T. N., and Chandar Uday Singh (1984). "The Consumer Boom." *India Today* 9, no. 3:82–90.

Nohl, Werner (1988). "Open Space in Cities: In Search of a New Aesthetic." In Jack Nasar, ed., *Environmental Aesthetics: Theory, Research, and Applications.* New York: Cambridge University Press, pp. 74–97.

Norberg Schulz, Christian (1965). *Intentions in Architecture.* Cambridge, MA: MIT Press.

——— (1971). *Existence, Space, and Architecture.* New York: Praeger.

——— (1980). *Genius Loci: Towards a Phenomenology of Architecture.* New York: Rizzoli.

Norris, Christopher (1988). "Deconstruction, Post-Modernism and the Visual Arts." In Christopher Norris and Andrew Benjamin, eds., *What Is Deconstruction?* New York: St. Martin's Press, pp. 7–31.

Oc, Tanner (1991). "Planning Natural Surveillance Back into City Centres." *Town and Country Planning* 60, no. 8:237–239.

Okamoto, Rai Y., and Frank E. Williams (1969). *Urban Design Manhattan.* Prepared for the Regional Plan Association. New York: Viking.

Olds, A. R. (1987). "Designing Settings for Infants and Toddlers." In Carol S. Weinstein and Thomas G. David, eds., *Spaces for Children: The Built Environment and Child Development.* New York: Plenum, pp. 117–138.

Olgyay, Victor (1963). *Design with Climate: Bioclimatic Approach to Architectural Regionalism.* Princeton, NJ: Princeton University Press.

Olin, Laurie (1991). Personal Communication.

Olsen, Donald J. (1986). *The City as a Work of Art.* New Haven, CT: Yale University Press.

Olwig, K. R. (1986). "The Childhood 'Deconstruction' of Nature and the Construction of 'Natural' Housing Environments for Children." *Scandinavian Housing and Planning Research* 3:129–143.

Orwell, George (1954). "Politics and the English Language." In *Shooting an Elephant.* New York: Harcourt Brace, pp. 77–92.

Ostler, Tim (1987). "Whither Urban Design?" *Architects' Journal* 185, no. 18:20–21.

Ostroff, E. (1978). *Humanizing Environments.* Cambridge, MA: World Guide Publishers.

Overy, Paul (1969). *Kandinsky: The Language of the Eye.* New York: Praeger.

Owen, Robert (1825). *A New View of Society.* New York: Dodd and Manter.

——— (1821). "Report to the County of Lanark." Reprint. New York: AMS Press, 1975.

Palmer, Mickey A. (1981). *The Architect's Guide to Facility Programming.* Washington, DC: American Institute of Architects.

Papadakis, Andreas C. (1991). "Paternoster Square and the New Classical Tradition." *Architectural Design* vol. 62, no. 5/6:whole issue.

Papadakis, Andreas C., C. Cooke, and A. Benjamin, eds. (1989). *Deconstruction.* New York: Rizzoli.

Park, Robert E., Ernest Burgess, and Roderick D. Mackenzie (1925). *The City.* Chicago: University of Chicago Press.

Parr, Albert E. (1967). "The Child and the City: Urbanity and the Urban Scene." *Landscape* 16, no. 3:3–5.

——— (1969). "Lessons of an Urban Childhood." *American Montessori Society Bulletin* 7, no. 4.

Parsons, K. C. (1990). "Clarence Stein and the Greenbelt Towns. *Journal of the American Planning Association* 56, no. 2:161–183.

Parsons, Talcott (1966). *Societies.* Englewood Cliffs, NJ: Prentice-Hall.

PAS (Planners Advisory Service) (1991). *Reinventing the Village:* Chicago: PAS.

Pass, David (1973). *Vällingby and Farsta: From Idea to Reality.* Cambridge, MA: MIT Press.

Passini, Romedi (1984). *Wayfinding in Architecture.* New York: Van Nostrand Reinhold.

Pathak, Jitendra (1980). "Human Behavior and Community Design." Unpublished student paper, University of Pennsylvania.

Patton, Phil (1991). "In Seaside, Florida, the Forward Thing Is to Look Backward." *Smithsonian* 21:82–93.

Pawley, Martin (1971). *Architecture versus Housing.* New York: Praeger.

——— (1990). *Theory and Design in the Second Machine Age.* London: Blackwell.

Peattie, Lisa (1981a). "First Stage: The Platonic City versus the Aristotelian City." In *Planning: Rethinking Cuidad Guayana.* Ann Arbor: University of Michigan Press, pp. 41–72.

——— (1981b). "The Political Basis of Urban Design." In *Planning: Rethinking Cuidad Guayana.* Ann Arbor: University of Michigan Press, pp. 93–111.

Peets, Elbert (1927). "The Genealogy of L'Enfant's Washington." *Journal of the American Institute of Architects* 15, nos. 5, 6, and 7:115-118, 151-154, 187-191.

Peña, William, Steven Parshall, and Kevin Kelly (1987). *Problem Seeking: An Architectural Programming Guide.* Washington, DC: AIA Press.

Pepper, Stephen C. (1949). *The Basis of Criticism in the Arts.* Cambridge, MA: MIT Press.

Pérez Gómez, Alberto (1983). *Architecture and the Crises of Modern Science.* Cambridge, MA: MIT Press.

Perin, Constance (1970). *With Man in Mind: An Interdisciplinary Prospectus for Environmental Design.* Cambridge, MA: MIT Press.

——— (1977). *Everything in Its Place: Social Order and Land Use in America.* Princeton, NJ: Princeton University Press.

"Peter Eisenman versus Leon Krier" (1989). *Architectural Design Profile 81. Architectural Design* 59, no. 9/10:6-18.

Petersen, Arne Freimuth (1988). *Why Children and Young Animals Play and Its Role in Problem Solving.* Copenhagen: Commissioner Munksgaard.

Petersen, Steven (1979). "Urban Design Tactics." *Architectural Design Profile 20. Architectural Design* 49, no. 3/4:76-81.

Peterson, Jon A. (1976). "The City Beautiful Movement: Forgotten Origins and Lost Meanings." *Journal of Urban History* 2, no. 4:415-434. Also in Donald Krueckeberg, *Introduction to Planning History,* pp. 40-57.

——— (1979). "The Impact of Sanitary Reform upon American Urban Planning, 1840-1890." *Journal of Social History* 13, no. 1:83-103. Also in Krueckeberg, *Introduction to Planning History,* pp. 13-39.

Peterson, Peggy (1969). "The Id and the Image: Human Needs and Design Implications," University of California, Berkeley, School of Architecture. Mimeographed.

Peterson, Rebecca Bauer (1987). "Gender Issues in the Home and Urban Environment." In Ervin H. Zube and Gary T. Moore, eds., *Advances in Environment, Behavior, and Design 1.* New York: Plenum, pp. 187-218.

Pfaff, William (1991). "Puritanism, Fascism and the U.S. University." *Chicago Tribune,* Section 4 (May 26):3.

Pickford, Ralph W. (1972). *Psychology and the Visual Arts.* London: Hutchinson Educational.

Pocock, Douglas, and Ray Hudson (1978). *Images of the Urban Environment.* New York: Columbia University Press.

Pollowy, Anne-Marie (1977). *The Urban Nest.* Stroudsburg, PA: Dowden, Hutchinson, and Ross.

Pommer, Richard, David Spaeth, and Kevin Harrington, eds. (1988). *In the Shadow of Mies, Ludwig Hilbersheimer, Architect, Educator, and Urban Planner.* Chicago: Art Institute of Chicago.

Popenoe, David (1977). *The Suburban Environment.* Chicago: University of Chicago Press.

Porter, Tom, and Byron Mikellides, eds. (1976). *Color for Architecture.* New York: Van Nostrand Reinhold.

Porteous, J. Douglas (1977). *Environment and Behavior: Planning and Everyday Urban Life.* Reading, MA: Addison-Wesley.

Portman, John, and Jonathan Barnett (1976). *The Architect as Developer.* New York: McGraw Hill.

Portoghesi, Paolo (1979). *Postmodern: The Architecture of the Post Industrial Society.* New York: Rizzoli.

——— (1982). *After Modern Architecture.* Translated from the French by Meg Shone. New York: Rizzoli.

Prak, Niles Luning (1968). *The Language of Architecture: A Contribution to Architectural Theory.* The Hague: Mouton.

——— (1984). *Architects: The Noted and the Ignored.* New York: John Wiley.

Pressman, Norman (1987). "The Survival of Winter Cities: Problems and Prospects." In Gary Gappert, ed., *The Future of Winter Cities.* Newbury Park, CA: Sage, pp. 49-70.

Preiser, Wolfgang, ed. (1985). *Facility Programming: Methods and Application.* New York: Van Nostrand Reinhold.

Preiser, Wolfgang, Harvey Z. Rabinowitz, and Edward T. White (1988). *Post-Occupancy Evaluation.* New York: Van Nostrand Reinhold.

Preiser, Wolfgang, Jacqueline C. Vischer, and Edward T. White, eds. (1991). *Design Intervention: Toward a More Humane Architecture.* New York: Van Nostrand Reinhold.

Proctor, Mary, and Bill Matuszeski (1978). *Gritty Cities: A Second Look at Allentown, Bethlehem, Bridgeport, Hoboken, Lancaster, Norwich, Paterson, Reading, Trenton, Troy, Waterbury, Wilmington.* Philadelphia: Temple University Press.

Proshansky, Harold (1974). "Environmental Psychology and the Design Professions." In Jon Lang et al., eds., *Designing for Human Behavior: Architecture and the Behavioral Sciences.* Stroudsburg, PA: Dowden, Hutchinson, and Ross, pp. 72-97.

Proudfoot, Peter (1991). "Deconstructivism and Architectural Science." *Architectural Science Review* 34, no. 2:55-63.

——— (forthcoming). *The Secret Plan of Canberra.* Kensington, N.S.W.: UNSW Press.

Pushkarev, Boris S., and Jeffrey M. Zuphan (1979). *Urban Space for Pedestrians.* A Report of the Regional Plan Association. Cambridge, MA: MIT Press.

Rainer, George (1991). *Understanding Infrastructure: A Guide for Architects and Planners.* New York: John Wiley.

Ramsey, Richard (1986). "Spennard Commercial District Development Strategy." *Urban Design Review* 9, no. 2:16-19.

Rapoport, Amos (1967). "Whose Meaning in Architecture?" *Interbuild/Arena* 14 (October):44-46.

——— (1969). *House Form and Culture.* Englewood Cliffs, NJ: Prentice-Hall.

——— (1977). *Human Aspects of Urban Form: Towards a Man-Environment Approach to Urban Form and Design.* New York: Pergamon Press.

——— (1982). *The Meaning of the Built Environment: A Non-Verbal Communications Approach*. Beverly Hills, CA: Sage.

——— (1984). "Culture and the Urban Order." In John Agnew, John Mercer, and David Sopher, eds., *The City in Cultural Context*. Boston: Allen and Unwin, pp. 50–75.

——— (1986). "The Use and Design of Open Spaces in Urban Neighborhoods." In Dieter Frick, ed., *The Quality of Urban Life: Social, Psychological, and Physical Conditions*. Berlin: Walter de Gruyter, pp. 159–175.

——— (1991). *History and Precedent in Environmental Design*. New York: Plenum.

Rapoport, Amos, and Robert E. Kantor (1967). "Complexity and Ambiguity in Environmental Design." *Journal of the American Institute of Planners* 33, no. 4:210–221.

Rasmussen, Steen Eiler (1937). *London: The Unique City*. Rev. ed. London: Jonathan Cape.

——— (1959). *Experiencing Architecture*. Cambridge, MA: MIT Press.

Regional Plan Association (1927). *Regional Survey of New York and Its Environs*. New York: Russell Sage Foundation.

Register, Richard (1987). *Ecocity Berkeley: Building Better Cities for the Future*. Berkeley, CA: North Atlantic Books.

Regnier, Victor, and Jon Pynoos (1987). *Housing the Aged: Design Directives and Policy Considerations*. New York: Elsevier.

Reid, Paul (1990). "Urban Spaces: Theories and Practices." In Tamas Luckovich, ed., *Urban Design and Local Planning: An Interdisciplinary Approach*. Kensington: University of New South Wales, Faculty of Architecture, pp. 5.1–5.5.

Reiner, Thomas (1963). *The Place of the Ideal City in Urban Planning*. Philadelphia: Univesity of Pennsylvania Press.

Reissman, Leonard (1964). *The Urban Process: Cities in Industrial Societies*. New York: Free Press.

Ralph, Edward (1987). *The Modern Urban Landscape*. Baltimore: Johns Hopkins University Press.

Reps, John (1965). *The Making of Urban America: A History of Planning in the United States*. Princeton, NJ: Princeton University Press.

——— (1991). *Washington on View: The Nation's Capital Since 1790*. Chapel Hill: University of North Carolina Press.

Riboulet, Pierre (1985). "Concerning the Composition of the Capital at Chandigarh." In Association Française d'Action Artistique, *Architecture in India*. Paris: Electa Moniteur, pp. 91–98.

Richards, J. M. (1962). *An Introduction to Modern Architecture*. Harmonsworth: Penguin Books.

——— (1966). *A Guide to Finnish Architecture*. London: Hugh Evelyn.

Richter, Alexander, and Kurt Forster (1988). "Daniel Libeskind: Edificio per uffici, abitarione e spazi pub-blici." *Domus*, no. 696 (July/August):46–55.

Ricoeur, Paul (1975). *The Rule of Metaphor: Multidisciplinary Studies of the Creation of Meaning in Language*. Translated from the French by Robert Czerny. Buffalo and Toronto: University of Toronto Press.

Riesman, David (1950). *The Lonely Crowd: A Study of the Changing American Character*. New Haven, CT: Yale University Press.

Rietfeld, Rijk (1983). Personal communication.

Rittel, Horst (1971). "Some Principles for the Design of an Education System for Design." *Journal of Architectural Education* 26, no. 4:16–26.

——— (1984). "Second Generation Design Methods." In Nigel Cross, ed., *Developments in Design Methodology*. New York: John Wiley, pp. 317–329.

Rittel, Horst, and Melvin Webber (1984). "Planning Problems Are Wicked Problems." In Nigel Cross, ed., *Developments in Design Methodology*. New York: John Wiley, pp. 135–144.

Ritzdorf, M. (1987). "Planning and the Intergenerational Community." *Journal of Urban Affairs* 9, no. 1:79–87.

Roberts, Robert (1971). *The Classic Slum: Salford Life in the First Quarter of the Century*. Manchester: Manchester University Press.

Robertson, Jaquelin (1985). "Hasn't most of the built world always been a disparate slum with but a few places of light and beauty? Yes—and no, not quite." In Chris Johnson, ed., *The City in Conflict*. Sydney: The Law Book Co., pp. 43–60.

Robinette, Gary O., ed. (1977). *Landscape Planning for Energy Conservation*. Reston, VA: Environmental Design Press.

——— (1985). *Barrier-Free Exterior Design: Anyone Can Go Anywhere*. New York: Van Nostrand Reinhold.

Robinson, Charles Mulford (1901). *The Improvement of Towns and Cities, or The Practical Basis of Civic Aesthetics*. New York: Putnam.

Robinson, Julia (1990). "Architectural Research: Incorporating Myth and Science." *Journal of Architectural Education* 44, no. 1:20–32.

Robinson, Julia, and J. S. Weekes (1983). "Programming as Design." University of Minnesota School of Architecture. Mimeographed.

Roddewig, Richard J. (1981). *Preservation Ordinances and Financial Incentives: How They Guide Design*. Washington, DC: National League of Cities.

Roddewig, Richard J., and Cheryl A. Inghram (1987). *Transferable Development Rights Program*. PAS Report No. 374. Chicago: American Planning Association.

Rodger, Allan, and Roger Fay (1991). "Sustainable Suburbia." *Exedra* 3, no. 1:4–15.

Rogers, Carl (1980). *A Way of Being*. Boston: Houghton Mifflin.

Ronner, Heinz, and Sharad Jhavari (1987). *Louis I. Kahn: Complete Work 1935-1974*. Basel: Birkhäuser.

Rossi, Aldo (1982). *The Architecture of the City*. Translated from the Italian by Diane Ghirardo and Joan Ockman. Cambridge, MA: MIT Press.

Rouard, Marguerite, and Jacques Simon (1977). *Children's Play Spaces: From Sandbox to Adventure Playground.* Translated from the German by Linda Geiser. Woodstock, NY: Overlook Press.

Rowe, Colin (1983). "Program versus Paradigm." *Cornell Journal of Architecture* 2:8–19.

——— (1990). "Urban Space." In Andreas Papadakis and Harriet Watson. *New Classicism.* New York: Rizzoli, pp. 187–188.

Rowe, Colin, and Fred Koetter (1978). *Collage City.* Cambridge, MA: MIT Press.

Rowe, Peter (1987). *Design Thinking.* Cambridge, MA: MIT Press.

——— (1991). *Making a Middle Landscape.* Cambridge, MA: MIT Press.

Royal Australian Institute of Architects and BHP Steel, Sheet and Coil Products (© 1990). "Architecture Students Biennale Design Awards and Exhibition." Canberra: The RAIA and BHP Steel.

Rubenstein, James (1978). *The French New Towns.* Baltimore: Johns Hopkins University Press.

Ruchelman, Leonard I. (1977). *The World Trade Center.* Syracuse, NY: Syracuse University Press.

Rudofsky, Bernard (1964). *Architecture without Architects: An Introduction to Non-Pedigreed Architecture.* New York: Museum of Modern Art.

——— (1969). *Streets for People: A Primer for Americans.* New York: Doubleday.

Rusch, Charles W. (1969). "On the Relationship of Form to Behavior." *Design Methods Group Newsletter* 3 (October):8–11.

Rybczynski, Witold (1990). "With Wear and Tear, Habitat Has Become a Home." *New York Times* (August 5):H 28, 30.

Rykwert, Joseph (1988). *The Idea of a Town: The Anthropology of Urban Form in Rome, Italy and the Ancient World.* 2d ed. Cambridge, MA: MIT Press.

Saarinen, Thomas F. (1976). *Environmental Planning: Perception and Behavior.* Boston: Houghton Mifflin.

Saegert, Susan (1981). "Masculine Cities, Feminine Suburbs." In Catherine R. Stimpson, ed., *Women and the American City.* Chicago: University of Chicago Press: pp. 93–108.

Saint, Andrew (1983). *The Image of the Architect.* New Haven, CT: Yale Univesity Press.

Salisbury, Frank (1990). *Architect's Handbook for Client Briefing.* London: Butterworth.

San Francisco, City of, Department of City Planning (1971). *The Urban Design Plan for the Comprehensive Plan of San Francisco.* San Francisco: San Francisco Department of City Planning.

——— (1982). *Guiding Downtown Development.* San Francisco: San Francisco Department of City Planning.

——— (1983). *The Downtown Plan: A Proposal for Citizen Review.* San Francisco: San Francisco Department of City Planning.

——— (1985). *The San Francisco Downtown Plan.* Final Report. San Francisco: San Francisco Department of City Planning.

——— (1988). *Urban Design: An Element of the Master Plan of the City and County of San Francisco.* San Francisco: San Francisco Department of City Planning.

——— (1989). *Residential Design Guidelines.* San Francisco: San Francisco Department of City Planning.

——— (1990). *Mission Bay: The Plan.* San Francisco: San Francisco Department of City Planning.

Sanoff, Henry (1977). *Methods of Architectural Programming.* Stroudsburg, PA: Dowden, Hutchinson, and Ross.

——— (1989). "Facility Programming." In Ervin H. Zube and Gary T. Moore, eds., *Advances in Environment, Behavior and Design 2.* New York: Plenum, pp. 239–286.

——— (1991). *Visual Research Methods in Design.* New York: Van Nostrand Reinhold.

———, ed. (1978). *Designing with Community Participation.* Stroudsburg, PA: Dowden, Hutchinson, and Ross.

Santayana, George (1896). *The Sense of Beauty.* Reprint. New York: Dover, 1955.

Sant'Elia, Antonio (1973). "Manifesto of Futurist Architecture." In U. Appolonio, ed., *Futurist Manifestoes.* New York: Viking.

Santrock, John W. (1989). *Life Span Development.* 3d ed. Dubuque, IA: Wm. C. Brown.

Sarason, Seymour (1972). *The Creation of Settings and the Future Societies.* San Francisco: Jossey-Bass.

Sasuki, Peter (1976). "Germans and Turks at Germany's Railroad Stations: Inter-ethnic Tensions in the Pursuit of Walking and Loitering." *Urban Life: A Journal of Ethnographic Research* 4:387–412.

Schafer, Roger (1974). "Marseilles—A Housing Consultant's Look at Le Corbusier's Unité d'Habitation." *Architecture Plus* 2, no. 1:86–91.

Schmandt, Jurgen, Frederick Williams, Robert H. Wilson, and Sharon Stover, eds. (1990). *The New Urban Infrastructure: Cities and Telecommunications.* New York: Praeger.

Schneekloth, Lynda (1987). "Advances in Practice in Environment, Behavior and Design." In Ervin H. Zube and Gary T. Moore, eds., *Advances in Environment, Behavior, and Design 1.* New York: Plenum, pp. 307–334.

Schneider, Gerhard (1986). "Psychological Identity of and Identification with Urban Neighborhoods." In Dieter Frick, ed., *The Quality of Urban Life: Social, Psychological, and Physical Conditions.* Berlin: Walter de Gruyter, pp. 203–218.

Schneider, Jerry B., and Anita Francis (1989). *An Assessment of the Potential of Telecommuting as a Work Trip Reduction Strategy: An Annotated Bibliography.* Council of Planning Librarians Bibliography 246.

Schneider, Kenneth R. (1979). *On the Nature of Cities: Toward Enduring and Creative Human Environments.* San Francisco: Jossey-Bass.

Schön, Don (1983). *The Reflective Practitioner: How Professionals Think in Action*. New York: Basic Books.

Schroeder, Herbert W., and L. M. Anderson (1984). "Perception of Personal Safety in Urban Recreation Sites." *Journal of Leisure Research* 16, no. 2:178–194.

Schubert, Otto (1965). *Optik in Architektur und Städebau*. Berlin: Verlag, Gebr. Mann.

Schultz, Stanley K. (1989). *Constructing Urban Culture: American Cities and City Planning, 1800–1920*. Philadelphia: Temple University Press.

Schumacher, Ernst F. (1973). *Small Is Beautiful: Economics as If People Mattered*. New York: Harper & Row.

Schurch, Thomas W. (1991). "Mission Bay: Questions about a Work in Progress." *Planning* 57, no 10:22–24.

Scott, Allen J. (1988). *Metropolis from the Division of Labor to Urban Form*. Berkeley: University of California Press.

Scott Brown, Denise (1976). "On Formalism and Social Concern: A Discourse for Social Planners and Radical Chic Architects." *Oppositions* 5:99–112.

——— (1977). "Suburban Space, Scale, and Symbols." *VIA* 3:41–47.

——— (1982). "Between Three Stools: A Personal View of Urban Design and Pedagogy." In Ann Ferebee, ed., *Education for Urban Design*. Purchase, NY: Institute for Urban Design, pp. 132–172. Also in *Urban Concepts*, pp. 9–20.

——— (1990). *Urban Concepts*. London: Academy Editions.

Scully, Vincent J. (1962). *Earth, the Temple, and the God*. New Haven, CT: Yale University Press.

Seamon, David (1987). "Phenomenology and Environment-Behavior Research." In Ervin H. Zube and Gary T. Moore, eds., *Advances in Environment, Behavior, and Design 1*. New York: Plenum, pp. 37–70.

Selyunin, Vasily (1990). "The Stolen Sea." Translated from the Russian by Jonathan Bastable. *The Australian Magazine* (April 14–15):6–16.

Senkevitch, Anatole (1974). "Trends in Soviet Architecture 1917–1937." Unpublished Ph.D. dissertation, Cornell University.

Sennett, Richard (1970). *The Uses of Disorder: Personal Identity and City Life*. New York: Knopf.

——— (1977). *The Fall of Public Man*. New York: Knopf.

Sert, José Luis, and C.I.A.M. (1944). *Can Our Cities Survive? An ABC of Urban Problems, Their Analysis, Their Solutions*. Cambridge, MA: Harvard University Press.

Sharp, Dennis, ed. (1978a). *The Rationalists: Theory and Design in the Modern Movement*. London: Architectural Press.

——— (1978b). "Introduction." In Sharp, *The Rationalists*, pp. 1–6.

Shaw-Eagle, Joanna (1986). "The Fine Art (?) of Developing Bethesda." *New Art Examiner* (November):40–42.

Shearer, Alistair (1983). *The Traveler's Key to Northern India: A Guide to the Sacred Places of Northern India*. New York: Knopf.

Sherwood, Roger (1978). *Modern Housing Prototypes*. Cambridge, MA: Harvard University Press.

Shirvani, Hamid (1981). *Urban Design Review: A Guide for Planners*. Washington, DC: Planners Press (Chicago: American Planning Association).

——— (1985). *The Urban Design Process*. New York: Van Nostrand Reinhold.

——— (1990). *Beyond Public Architecture: Strategies for Design Evaluation*. New York: Van Nostrand Reinhold.

Shvidkovsky, O. A., ed. (1971). *Building in the U.S.S.R. 1917–1932*. New York: Praeger.

Simon, Herbert A. (1960). *The New Science of Management Decision*. New York: Harper.

——— (1969). *The Sciences of the Artificial*. Cambridge, MA: MIT Press.

——— (1970). "Style in Design." In John Archea and Charles Eastman, eds., *EDRA Two: Proceedings of the Second Annual Environmental Research Association Conference, October 1970*. Pittsburgh:1–10.

Singh, Ajit (1984). *Tribal Development in India*. Delhi: Amar Prakashan.

Sitte, Camillo (1889). *Der Städte-Bau nach sienen künstlerischen Grundsätzent (The Art of Building Cities: City Building According to Its Artistic Fundamentals)*. Translated from the German by Charles T. Stewart. New York: Reinhold, 1945.

Skaburskis, Jacqueline (1974). "Territoriality and Its Relevance to Neighborhood Design: A Review." *Architectural Research and Teaching* 3, no. 1:39–44.

Skolimowski, Henryk (1978). "Rationality in Architecture and the Design Process." In Dennis Sharp, ed., *The Rationalists*. London: Architectural Press, pp. 160–173.

Sky, Alison, and Michelle Stone (1976). *Unbuilt America: Forgotten Architecture in the United States from Thomas Jefferson to the Space Age*. New York: McGraw Hill.

Smith, Herbert H. (1991). *Planning America's Communities: Paradise Found? Paradise Lost?* Chicago and Washington, DC: Planners Press.

Smithson, Alison, ed. (1969). *Team 10 Primer*. Cambridge, MA: MIT Press.

Smithson, Alison, and Peter Smithson (1967). *Urban Structuring*. New York: Reinhold Studio Vista.

——— (1970). *Ordinariness and Light*. London: Faber and Faber.

——— (1972). "Signs of Occupancy." *Architectural Design* 41, no. 2:91–97.

Soleri, Paolo (1969). *The City in the Image of Man*. Cambridge, MA:MIT Press.

——— (1981). *Fragments*. New York: Harper & Row.

Sommer, Robert (1969) *Personal Space: The Behavioral Basis of Design*. Englewood Cliffs, NJ: Prentice Hall.

——— (1974). *Tight Spaces: Hard Architecture and How to Humanize It*. Englewood Cliffs, NJ: Prentice-Hall.

Sorkin, Michael (1991). *Exquisite Corpse*. London and New York: Verso.

Southworth, Michael (1969). "The Sonic Environment of Cities." *Environment and Behavior* 1, no. 1:49–70.

——— (1985). "Shaping the City Image." *Journal of Planning Education and Research* 5, no. 1:52–59.

Spaeth, David (1981). *Ludwig Hilbersheimer: An Annotated Bibliography and Chronology.* New York: Garland.

——— (1985). *Mies van der Rohe.* New York: Rizzoli.

Spirn, Anne Whiston (1984). *The Granite Garden: Urban Nature and Human Design.* New York: Basic Books.

——— (1989). "The Poetics of City and Nature: Toward a New Aesthetic for Urban Design." *Places* 6, no. 1:82–93.

Srivistava, Rajendra K. (1975). "Undermanning Theory in the Context of Mental Health Care Environments." In Daniel H. Carson, ed., *Man-Environment Interactions, Part II.* Stroudsburg, PA: Dowden, Hutchinson, and Ross, pp. 245–258.

Stamp, Gavin (1988). "Romania's New Delhi." *Architectural Review* 184, no. 1098:4–6.

Stäubli, Willy (1966). *Brasilia.* London: Leonard Hill.

Steadman, Philip (1975). *Energy, Environment and Building.* Cambridge, Eng.: Cambridge University Press.

Steele, Fred I. (1973). *Physical Settings and Organizational Development.* Reading, MA: Addison-Wesley.

Stein, Clarence (1957). *Toward New Towns for America.* New York: Reinhold.

Stein, Richard (1977). *Architecture and Energy.* Garden City, NY: Anchor.

Steiner, George (1989). *Real Presences.* Chicago: University of Chicago Press.

Stern, Jennifer (1989). "Pratt to the Rescue: Advocacy Planning Is Alive and Well in Brooklyn." *Planning* 55, no. 5:26–28.

Stern, Robert M. (1990). *Urban Alternatives: Public and Private Markets in the Provision of Local Services.* Pittsburgh: University of Pittsburgh Press.

Stern, Robert A. M., with John Massengale (1981). "The Anglo-American Suburb." *Architectural Design Profile.* London: Architectural Design.

Stern, Robert A. M., with Raymond W. Gastil (1988). *Modern Classicism.* New York; Rizzoli.

Stewart, Cecil (1952). *A Prospect of Cities: Being Studies Towards a History of Town Planning.* London: Longman's Green.

Stilgoe, John R. (1988). *Borderland: Origins of the American Suburb 1820-1939.* New Haven, CT: Yale University Press.

Stollard, P., ed. (1991). *Crime Prevention through Housing Design.* London: Chapman and Hall.

Strauss, Anselm (1961). *Images of the American City.* New York: Free Press.

Stringer, Peter (1980). "Models of Man in Casterbridge and Milton Keynes." In Byron Mikelledis, ed., *Architecture for People.* New York: Holt, Rinehart and Winston, pp. 176–186.

Strong, Ann L. (1971). *Planned Residential Environments: Sweden, Finland, Israel, The Netherlands, France.* Baltimore: Johns Hopkins University Press.

Studer, Raymond (1969). "The Dynamics of Behavior-Contingent Physical Systems." In Geoffrey Broadbent and Anthony Ward, eds., *Design Methods in Architecture.* London: Lund Humphries, pp. 59–70.

——— (1988). "Design of the Built Environment: The Search for Usable Knowledge." In Elizabeth Huttman and Willem Van Vliet, eds., *Handbook of Housing and the Built Environment.* New York: Greenwood, pp. 73–96.

Suttles, Gerald D. (1972). *The Social Construction of Communities.* Chicago: University of Chicago Press.

Swalwell, Bruce (1976). "Human Needs and Environmental Support Systems." Unpublished student paper, University of Pennsylvania.

Swan, James A., ed. (1991). *The Power of Place: Sacred Ground in Natural Environments.* Brea, CA: Quest Books.

Taylor, Jennifer, and John Andrews (1982). *John Andrews: Architecture, a Performing Art.* Melbourne: Oxford University Press.

Taylor, Nicholas (1973). *The Village in the City: Towards a New Society.* London: Temple Smith.

Tennenbaum, Robert (1990). "Hail Columbia." *Planning* 56, no. 5:16–17.

Thiel, Philip (1961). "A Sequence-Experience Notation for Architectural and Urban Space." *Town Planning Review* 32:33–52.

——— (1964). "The Tourist and the Habitué: Two Polar Modes of Environmental Experience, with Some Notes on an Experience Cube." Mimeographed.

——— (1990). "Starting off on the Right Foot: An Incremental Approach to Design Education for Responsible Public Service." Photocopied.

——— (forthcoming). *Notations for an Experiential Envirotecture.* Seattle: University of Washington Press.

Thorne, R., R. Hall, and M. Munro-Clark (1982). "Attitudes Towards Detached Houses, Terraces and Apartments: Some Current Pressures Towards the Less Preferred but More Accessible Alternatives." In Polly Bart, Alexander Chen, and Guido Francescato, eds., *Knowledge for Design: Proceedings of the Thirteenth International Conference of the Environmental Design Research Association.* College Park, MD:435–448.

Thorns, David (1976). *The Quest for Community: Social Aspects of Urban Growth.* New York: John Wiley.

Thrall, Grant Ian (1987). *Land Use and Urban Form: The Consumption Theory of Land Rent.* New York: Methuen.

Tillman, Peggy, and Barry Tillman (1990). *Human Factors Essentials: An Ergonomic Guide for Designers, Engineers, Scientists, and Managers.* New York: McGraw Hill.

Timms, Duncan W. G. (1977). *The Urban Mosaic: Towards a Theory of Residential Differentiation.* Cambridge, Eng.: Cambridge University Press.

Tobin, Joseph, J., David Y. H. Wu, and Dana H. Davidson (1989). "How Three Countries Shape Their Children." *World Monitor* 2, no. 1:36–45.

Toffler, Alvin (1970). *Future Shock.* New York: Random House.

Tompkins, Peter (1973). *Secrets of the Great Pyramid.* London: Allen Lane.

Torchinsky, Bernard (1989). *Ricardo Bofill—Taller de Arquitectura.* New York: Rizzoli.

Torre, L. Azeo (1989). *Waterfront Development.* New York: Van Nostrand Reinhold.

Trancik, Roger (1986). *Finding Lost Space: Theories of Urban Design.* New York: Van Nostrand Reinhold.

Treib, Marc (1985). "Fragments on a Void—Arata Isozaki's Design for Tsukuba Center, Partially Revealed." *Landscape Architecture* 75, no. 4:70-77.

Tschumi, Bernard (1987). *Cinégramme Folie, le parc de la Villette.* Paris: Champ-Vallon and Princeton, NJ: Princeton University Press.

——— (1988a). "Parc de la Villette." *Architectural Design* 58, no. 3/4:43-60.

——— (1988b). "Notes Towards a Theory of Architectural Disjunction." *Architecture and Urbanism,* no. 216 (September):11-15.

——— (1990). *Questions of Space: Lectures on Architecture.* London: Architectural Press.

Tuan, Yi-Fu (1977). *Space and Place: The Perspective of Experience.* Minneapolis University of Minnesota Press.

Turner, John F. C. (1976). *Housing by People: Towards Autonomy in Building Environments.* New York: Pantheon.

Turner, Paul V. (1977). *The Education of Le Corbusier.* New York: Garland.

——— (1984). *Campus: An American Planning Tradition.* Cambridge, MA: MIT Press.

Tyng, Anne (1969). "Geometric Extensions of Consciousness." *ZODIAC* 19. Milan: Edrioni di Communita, pp. 130-162.

——— (1975). "Simultaneous Randomness and Order: The Fibonacci-Divine Proportion as a Universal Forming Principle." Unpublished Ph.D. dissertation, University of Pennsylvania.

ULI (Urban Land Institute) (1988). "Fair Lakes, Fairfax, Virginia." *Project Reference File* 18, no. 5 (January-March): whole issue.

Untermann, Richard K. (1984). *Accommodating the Pedestrian: Adapting Towns and Neighborhoods for Walking and Bicycling.* New York: Van Nostrand Reinhold.

Unwin, Raymond (1909). *Town Planning in Practice: An Introduction to the Art of Designing Cities and Suburbs.* London: Unwin.

van der Plaat, Deborah (1992). "Geometrical Symbolism and the Influence of Mysticism and Occultism on Organic Architecture." Unpublished working paper, University of New South Wales. Photocopied.

van Vliet, Willem, and Jan van Weesep, eds. (1990). *Government and Housing: Developments in Seven Countries.* Newbury Park, CA: Sage.

Varva, Bob (1987). "High Profile or Too High." *DuPage Profile* 1, no. 20:8-9.

Vayda, Andrew, ed. (1969). *Environment and Culture: Ecological Studies in Cultural Anthropology.* Garden City, NY: Natural History Press.

Vaz, J. L. (1954), "Architecture for Bhubaneswar, New Capital, Orissa." *Journal of the Indian Institute of Architects* 20, no. 2:3-4.

Ventre, Francis T. (1990). "Regulation: A Revitalization of Social Ethics." In John Capelli, Paul Naprstek, and Bruce Prescott, eds., *Ethics and Architecture.* VIA 10:51-81.

Venturi, Robert (1966). *Complexity and Contradiction in Architecture.* New York: Museum of Modern Art.

Venturi, Robert, Denise Scott Brown, and Steven Izenour (1977). *Learning from Las Vegas: The Forgotten Symbolism of Architectural Form.* Cambridge, MA: MIT Press.

Verge, Alix (1990). "Geometry: The Architect's Friend." Unpublished student dissertation, University of New South Wales.

——— (1992). Personal communication.

Veseley, Dalibor (1989). "On the Relevance of Phenomenology." *Pratt Journal of Architecture* 2 (Spring):59-62.

Vigoda, Ralph (1991). "From Community's Pariah to Its Pride." *Philadelphia Inquirer* (January 24):6.

Vignelli Associates (1990). "Design: Vignelli." University of New South Wales College of Fine Arts, Announcement of Lecture Series.

von Frisch, Karl (1974). *Animal Architecture.* New York: Harcourt Brace Jovanovich.

Wade, John (1977). *Architecture, Problems, Purposes: Architectural Design as a Basic Problem Solving Process.* New York: John Wiley.

Wall, Donald (1971). *Visionary Cities: The Arcology of Paolo Soleri.* New York: Praeger.

Walter, Eugene Victor (1988). *Placeways: A Theory of the Human Environment.* Chapel Hill: University of North Carolina Press.

Ward, Barbara, and René Dubos (1972). *Only One Earth: The Care and Maintenance of a Small Planet.* New York: Norton.

Ward, Colin (1990). *The Child in the City.* Rev. ed. London: Bedford Square.

Warfield, John, and J. Douglas Hill (1973). *An Assault on Complexity.* Columbus, OH: Battelle.

Watkin, David (1977). *Morality and Architecture.* Oxford: Clarendon.

Watson, Lee H. (1990). *Lighting Design Handbook.* New York: McGraw Hill.

Webber, Melvin (1963). "Order and Diversity: Community without Propinquity." In Lowden Wingo, ed., *Cities and Space: The Future of Urban Land.* Baltimore: Johns Hopkins University Press, pp. 23-54.

Weber, Adna Ferrin (1899). *Growth of Cities in the 19th Century.* Reprint. Ithaca, NY: Cornell University Press, 1963.

Weiler, Ann (1988), "My Urban Design Manifesto." Unpublished student paper, University of Pennsylvania, Urban Design Program.

Weinstein, Carol Simon, and Thomas G. David, eds. (1987). *Spaces for Children: The Built Environment and Child Development.* New York: Plenum.

Weiss, Marc (1987). *The Rise of the Community Builders: The American Real Estate Industry and Urban Land Planning.* New York: Columbia University Press.

Wekerle, Gerda (1984). "A Woman's Place Is in the City." *Antipode: A Radical Journal of Geography* 16, no. 3:11–19.

Wekerle, Gerda, Rebecca B. Peterson, and David Morley (1980). *New Space for Women.* Boulder, CO: Westview.

Welner, Alan H. (1990). "Environmental Accessibility for Physically Disabled People." In Frederic J. Kottke and Justus F. Lehman, eds., *Krusen's Handbook of Physical Medicine and Rehabilitation.* New York: W. B. Saunders, pp. 1273–1290.

Wener, Richard (1989). "Advances in Evaluation of the Built Environment." In Ervin H. Zube and Gary T. Moore, eds., *Advances in Environment, Behavior, and Design 2.* New York: Plenum, pp. 287–313.

Wertheimer, Max (1938). "Gestalt Theory," "The General Theoretical Situation," and "Laws of Organization," In William D. Ellis, ed., *A Source Book of Gestalt Theory.* London: Routledge and Kegan Paul, pp. 1–88.

Westerman, Hans (1990). "The Contribution of Various Professions to Urban Design." In Tamas Lukovich, ed., *Urban Design and Local Planning: An Interdisciplinary Approach.* Kensington: University of New South Wales, Faculty of Architecture, pp. 1.1–1.9.

Westin, Alan (1967). *Privacy and Freedom.* New York: Atheneum.

Weyergraff-Serra, Clara, and Martha Buskirk, eds. (1990). *The Destruction of the Titled Arc: Documents.* Cambridge, MA: MIT Press.

Wheaton, William L. C., and Margaret F. Wheaton (1972). "Identifying the Public Interest: Values and Goals." In Ira M. Robinson, ed., *Decision-Making in Urban Planning.* Beverly Hills, CA: Sage, pp. 49–60.

White, Morton G., and Lucia White, eds. (1964). *The Intellectual versus the City from Thomas Jefferson to Frank Lloyd Wright.* New York: New American Library.

Whyte, William H. (1980). *The Social Life of Small Urban Spaces.* New York and Washington, DC: Conservation Foundation.

——— (1988). *City: Rediscovering the Center.* New York: Doubleday.

Wicker, Allan (1969). "Size of Membership and Member's Support of Church Behavior Settings." *Journal of Personality and Social Psychology* 13:278–288.

——— (1979). *An Introduction to Ecological Psychology.* Monterey, CA: Brooks/Cole.

Wiebenson, Dora (1969). *Tony Garnier: The Cité Industrielle.* New York: George Braziller.

Wiedenhoeft, Ronald V. (1981). *Cities for People: Practical Measures for Improving Urban Environments.* New York: Van Nostrand Reinhold.

Wilford, Michael (1984). "Off to the Races, or Going to the Dogs." In David Gosling and Barry Maitland, eds., *Urbanism—Architectural Design Profile 51.* London: Architectural Design Publications.

Wilkinson, P. E., ed. (1980). *Innovations in Play Environments.* New York: St. Martin's Press.

Williams, Eddie N., ed. (1971). *The Social Impact of Urban Design.* Chicago: University of Chicago, Center for Policy Studies.

Williams, Stephanie (1990). *Docklands Guide.* London: Architectural Design and Technology.

Willmott, Peter, and Michael Young (1960). "Social Research and New Communities." *Journal of the American Institute of Planners* 33, no. 5:387–397.

——— (1973). *The Symmetrical Family.* London: Routledge and Kegan Paul.

Wilson, Edward O. (1978). *On Human Nature.* Cambridge, MA: Harvard University Press.

Wilson, Elizabeth (1991). *The Sphinx in the City.* London: Virago Press.

Wilson, William H. (1989). *The City Beautiful Movement.* Baltimore: Johns Hopkins University Press.

Wingler, Hans (1969). *The Bauhaus: Weimar, Dessau, Berlin, Chicago.* Translated from the German by Wolfgang Jabs and Basil Gilbert, edited by Joseph Stein. Cambridge, MA: MIT Press.

Wise, James (1982). "Deopportunizing Design: A Comprehensive Strategy for Deterring Vandalism." In Polly Bart, Alexander Chen, and Guido Francescato, eds., *Knowledge for Design: Proceedings of the Thirteenth International Conference of the Environmental Design Research Association.* College Park, MD:283–284.

Wisner, Ben, David Stea, and Sonia Kruks (1991). "Participatory and Action Research." In Ervin H. Zube and Gary T. Moore, eds., *Advances in Environment, Behavior, and Design 3.* New York: Plenum, pp. 271–296.

Wolf, Edwin, 2d. (1975). *Philadelphia: Portrait of an American City.* Harrisburg, PA: Stackpole Books.

Wolfe, Tom (1981). *From Bauhaus to Our House.* New York: Farrar Straus Giroux.

Wolschke-Bulmahn, Joachim (1992). "Fear of the New Landscape: Aspects of the Perception of Landscape in the German Youth Movement between 1900 and 1933 and Its Influence on Landscape Planning." *Journal of Architectural and Planning Research* 9, no. 1:33–47.

Wood, Edward W., Sidney N. Brower, and Margaret W. Latimer (1966). "Planners' People." *Journal of the American Institute of Planners* 32 (July):228–234.

Woodbridge, Sally (1987). "A New Plan for Mission Bay." *Progressive Architecture* 68, no. 6:37–38.

Woodward, Alison (1989). "Communal Housing in Sweden: A Remedy for the Stress of Everyday Life?" In Karen Franck and Sherry Ahrentzen, eds., *New Households, New Housing.* New York: Van Nostrand Reinhold, pp. 71–94.

Wright, Frank Lloyd (1958). *The Living City.* New York: Horizon.

Wrigley, Robert L. (1960). "The Plan of Chicago: Its Fiftieth Anniversary." *Journal of the American Institute of Planners* 26, no. 1:31–38. Also in Krueckeberg (1983) pp. 58–72.

Wyckoff, William (1988). *The Developer's Frontier: The Mak-*

ing of the Western New York Landscape. New Haven, CT: Yale University Press.

Wynne, Nancy, and Beaumont Newhall (1939). "Horatio Greenough: Herald of Functionalism." *Magazine of Art* 32 (January):12–15.

Zehner, Robert (1991). "Environmental Priorities and the Greenhouse." *Australian Planner* 29, no. 1:33–38.

Zeisel, John (1974). "Fundamental Values in Planning with the Non-Paying Client." In Jon Lang et al., eds., *Designing for Human Behavior: Architecture and the Behavioral Sciences*. Stroudsburg, PA: Dowden, Hutchinson, and Ross, pp. 293–301.

——— (1980). *Inquiry by Design: Tools for Environmental Behavior Research*. New York: Cambridge University Press.

Zelinsky, Wilbur (1973). *The Cultural Geography of the United States*. Englewood Cliffs, NJ: Prentice-Hall.

Zevi, Bruno (1978). "The Italian Rationalists." In Dennis Sharp, ed., *The Rationalists: Theory and Design in the Modern Movement*. London: Architectural Press, pp. 118–129.

Zotti, Ed (1991). "A Primer for Writing Design Guidelines." *Planning* 57, no. 5:12–14.

Zube, Ervin, and Gary T. Moore, eds. (1987, 1989, 1991). *Advances in Environment, Behavior, and Design 1, 2, and 3*. New York: Plenum.

Zucker, Paul (1959). *Town and Square: From Agora to Village Green*. New York: Columbia University Press.

Zwicky, Fritz (1948). "A Morphological Method of Analysis and Construction." *Studies and Essays* (Courant Anniversary Volume). New York: Interscience.

CREDITS

All photographs, diagrams, and drawings other than those listed below are by me, the author. Some photographs and illustrations have been given to me by students (mainly those of the Graduate School of Fine Arts at the University of Pennsylvania), colleagues, and friends, and I no longer know their sources. I have listed them as part of the "Collection of the author." I very gratefully acknowledge all such contributions. Every effort has been made to contact and credit copyright holders of the illustrations used in this book. If copyright proprietorship can be established for any illustration not specifically (or erroneously) attributed below, please contact the author at the School of Architecture, University of New South Wales, PO Box 1, Kensington, NSW 2033, Australia.

Figure I-1(1)	Courtesy of Marvin S. Krout.
Figure I-1(4,5)	Used by permission of Richard Fitzhardinge.
Figure I-2(2)	Used by permission of Santosh Kumar Misra.
Figure I-2(3)	Used by permission of Alix Verge.
Part I. Urban Design in Context (pg. 13)	Courtesy of Larry Marks.
Urban Design Today (pg. 15)	Courtesy of the Department of City Planning, San Francisco.
Figure 1-1(1)	Courtesy of Ann Strong.
Figure 1-1(3)	Collection of the author.
Table 1-1	Used by permission of Schenkman Books, Inc.
Table 1-2	James J. Gibson, *The Senses Considered as Perceptual Systems:* p. 50. Copyright © 1966 by Houghton Mifflin Company. Used by permission.
Figure 1-7(1)	Used by permission of Ruth Durack.
Figure 1-7(2)	Collection of the author.
Figure 1-8	Copyright © 1973 by the American Psychological Association. Used by permission of Powell Lawton.
Figure 1-9	Used by permission of Van Nostrand Reinhold.
Figure 2-1(3)	Collection of the author.
Figure 2-5(2,3)	Used by permission of the Chicago Historical Society, ICHi-22270, ICHi-02524.
Figure 2-6(1,2)	Used by permission of the Art Institute of Chicago, RX 17016.28.
Figure 2-8(2)	Used by permission of MIT Press.
Figure 2-9(1)	Courtesy of the Frank Lloyd Wright Archives.
Figure 2-9(2,3)	Copyright © The Frank Lloyd Wright Foundation, 1958.
Figure 2-10(1,2)	Used by permission of George Braziller.
Figure 2-10(3)	Courtesy of Dion Neutra, Architect, and Neutra papers UCLA collection.
Figure 2-10(4)	© 1993 ARS New York/SPADEM, Paris.
Figure 2-10(5)	Courtesy of Vicente del Rio.
Figure 2-10(6)	Used by permission of Alix Verge.
Figure 2-11(2)	From J. M. Richards, *An Introduction to Modern Architecture* (Pelican Books, 1940, rev. ed. 1962). Copyright © by J. M. Richards, 1940.
Figure 2-12(1)	Reprinted by permission of the Cosanti Foundation with credit to Tomaki Tamura.
Figure 2-12(2)	© Paul Rudolph. Reproduced courtesy of Paul Rudolph.
Figure 2-12(3)	Reprinted by permission of Praeger Publishers, the Greenwood Publishing Group.
Figure 2-13(2)	Reproduced from *Architectural Design* magazine by courtesy of the Academy Group, London, and Hammond Beeby Babka, Architects.
Figure 2-13(3)	Courtesy of the SWA Group, Sausolito, California.
Figure 2-14(1)	Used by permission of J. Dennis Wilson.
Figure 2-15(3)	Used by permission of Richard Fitzhardinge.
Figure 2-16(1)	Collection of the author.
Figure 2-16(2,3)	Courtesy of the National Capital Planning Authority, Canberra, Australia.
Figure 2-16(5)	Collection of the author.
Figure 2-18(1)	Used by permission of Praeger Publishers, the Greenwood Publishing Group.
Figure 2-18(2)	Used by permission of Vicente del Rio.
Figure 2-19(1)	Used by permission of MIT Press.
Figure 2-19(3)	Reprinted by permission of the Historical Society of Pennsylvania.
Figure 2-20(3)	Used by permission of Ruth Durack.
Figure 2-21(1)	Used by permission of Heinz Ronner and Shavad Jhavari, Birkhäuser Verlag AG, Basle.
Figure 2-21(2)	Collection of the author.
Figure 2-21(3)	Collection of the author.
Figure 2-22(2)	Photograph supplied by the Universität Bielefeld.
Figure 2-22(3)	Used by the permission of Geddes, Brecher, Qualls and Cunningham, Philadelphia.
Figure 2-23(2)	Used by permission of John Ballinger.
Figure 2-23(3)	Used by permission of James Blank.
Figure 2-23(4)	Used by permission of Deepti Nijhawan.
Figure 2-23(5)	Collection of the author.
Figure 3-2(2)	Courtesy of the Department of City Planning, San Francisco.
Figure 3-4(1)	© 1993 ARS, New York/SPADEM, Paris.
Figure 3-4(2)	© 1990 Columbia University Press. Reprinted with permission of the publisher.
Figure 3-4(3)	Used by permission of the Kahn Archives, University of Pennsylvania, Philadelphia.
Figure 3-5(1,2,3)	Copyright © 1964, 1992 by Victor Gruen. Reprinted by permission of Simon & Schuster, Inc.

Figure 3-6(1)	Copyright © 1981 by Lester Walker. Published by the Overlook Press, Woodstock, NY.
Figure 3-6(2)	Reprinted by permission of Princeton Architectural Press.
Figure 3-7(1)	Used by permission of Alix Verge.
Figure 3-7(2)	Used by permission of Deepti Nijhawan.
Figure 3-7(5)	Courtesy of the Department of City Planning, San Francisco.
Figure 3-7(6)	Used by permission of Ruth Durack.
Figure 3-8(1)	Reprinted by permission of Chapman & Hall, Limited, London, and Bernard Tschumi.
Figure 3-8(2)	Used by permission of Ruth Durack.
Figure 3-8(3)	Used by permission of Ruth Durack.
Figure 3-9(2)	Courtesy of the Boston Redevelopment Authority.
Figure 3-10(3)	Reprinted by permission of *Progressive Architecture*, Penton Publishing.
Figure 3-11(1)	Used by permission of Alix Verge.
Figure 3-11(2,3)	Used by permission of Ruth Durack.
Figure 3-12	Courtesy of the Department of City Planning, San Francisco.
Figure 3-13(1,2)	Reprinted by permission of Architectural Record Books, a McGraw Hill Company.
Figure 3-14	Reprinted by permission of Architectural Record Books, a McGraw Hill Company.
Figure 3-15(3)	Reprinted by permission of MIT Press.
Figure 3-16(1)	Used by permission of Vicente del Rio.
Figure 3-16(2)	Used by permission of MIT Press.
Figure 3-17(1)	Used by permission of Arata Isozaki.
Figure 3-19(1)	Courtesy of the New York City Housing Authority.
Figure 3-19(2)	Reproduced from *Architectural Design* magazine, courtesy of the Academy Group, London.
Figure 3-20(1)	Courtesy of the Francis Loeb Library, Graduate School of Design, Harvard University.
Figure 3-20(5)	Reprinted by permission of Princeton Architectural Press.
Figure 3-20(6)	Reprinted by permission of MIT Press.
Figure 3-22(1)	Used by permission of Alix Verge.
Figure 3-22(2)	Reprinted by permission of the Academy Group, London, and the Disney Corporation.
Figure 3-22(3)	Used by permission of Richard Fitzhardinge.
Figure 4-1(2)	Used by permission of Edward Durrell Stone, Architects, P.C.
Figure 4-1(3)	Reprinted by permission of Oscar Newman.
Figure 4-2(1)	Reprinted by permission of the American Institute of Architects/New York Chapter from the Report of the Sixtieth Street Task Force, 1990.
Figure 4-2(2)	Used by permission of Hanna/Olin Ltd., Philadelphia.
Figure 4-2(3)	Used by permission of Randolph Griffith.
Figure 4-3(1,2)	Courtesy of the Redevelopment Authority, Glendale, California.
Figure 4-4(1)	Reprinted by permission of MIT Press.
Figure 4-4(2)	Courtesy of John Blatteau, architect.
Figure 4-4(3)	Reprinted by permission of Chapman & Hall, Limited, London, and Leon Krier.
Figure 4-5(1)	Reprinted by permission of Chapman & Hall, Limited, London, and Carlo Aymonimo.
Figure 4-5(2)	Courtesy of *Cornell Journal of Architecture*.
Figure 4-5(3,4)	Reprinted by permission of Chapman & Hall, Limited, London, and Leon Krier.
Figure 4-6	Reprinted by permission of Academy Editions, London, and Bernard Tschumi.
Figure 4-7(1)	Reprinted by permission of T. Gordon Cullen.
Figure 4-7(2)	Copyright © 1977 Christopher Alexander. Used by permission of Oxford University Press.
Figure 4-7(3)	Reprinted by permission of Oscar Newman.
Figure 4-8(1)	Used by permission of Van Nostrand Reinhold and Richard Hatch.
Figure 4-8(2)	Courtesy of the Pratt Institute Center for Community and Environmental Development, Ron Shiffman, Director.
Figure 4-9(2)	Reprinted by permission of Van Nostrand Reinhold.
Figure 4-10(1,2,3)	Reprinted by permission of MIT Press.
Figure 5-2(2)	Used by permission of Ruth Durack.
Figure 5-2(3)	Used by permission of Steve King.
Figure 5-3(1)	Collection of the author.
Figure 5-3(2,3)	Reprinted by permission of the *Journal of the American Institute of Planners*.
Figure 5-4(2)	Used by permission of Lori Leland.
Figure 6-1(1)	Reprinted by permission of Van Nostrand Reinhold.
Figure 6-1(2)	Reprinted by permission of MIT Press.
Figure 6-1(3)	Reprinted by permission of the Kahn Archives, University of Pennsylvania, Philadelphia.
Figure 6-3(3)	Courtesy of Ann Strong.
Figure 6-4(2)	Used by permission of Mark Hinshaw.
Figure 6-5(3)	Used by permission of Marvin S. Krout.
Figure 6-6(3)	Reprinted by permission of the Alexandrine Press.
Figure 7-1(1)	Reprinted by permission of MIT Press.
Figure 7-3(3)	Collection of the author.
Figure 7-7(1)	Used by permission of Deepti Nijhawan.
Figure 7-8(2)	Used by permission of Deepti Nijhawan.
Figure 7-9(1)	Collection of the author.
Figure 7-9(2)	Used by permission of J. Dennis Wilson.
Figure 7-9(3)	Used by permission of Richard Fitzhardinge.
Figure 8-2(1)	Used by permission of Mark Francis.
Figure 8-3(3)	Collection of the author.
Figure 8-6(2)	Used by permission of Alix Verge.
Figure 8-7(3)	Courtesy of Marvin S. Krout.
Figure 8-7(4)	Collection of the author.
Figure 8-8(1)	Used by permission of Deepti Nijhawan.
Figure 8-9(1)	Used by permission of J. Dennis Wilson.
Figure 8-9(3)	Courtesy of the Department of City Planning, San Francisco.
Figure 8-10(3)	Collection of the author.
Figure 9-1(1)	Used by permission of Alix Verge.
Figure 9-1(3)	Courtesy of *Cornell Journal of Architecture*.
Figure 9-2(2)	Courtesy of the Department of City Planning, San Francisco.
Figure 9-2(3)	Reprinted by permission of MIT Press.
Figure 9-3(3)	© 1977 by Christopher Alexander. Reprinted by permission of Oxford University Press.
Figure 9-4(5)	Used by permission of Jennifer Taylor.
Figure 9-6(1,2,3)	Collection of the author.
Figure 9-8(1,2)	Reprinted by permission of Van Nostrand Reinhold.
Figure 9-8(3)	Used by permission of J. Dennis Wilson.
Figure 9-9(1)	Reprinted by permission of Van Nostrand Reinhold.
Figure 10-1(2)	Collection of the author.
Figure 10-1(3)	Reprinted by permission of Stanley Tigerman, Architect.
Figure 10-2(1,2)	Reprinted by permission of Praeger Publishers, Greenwood Publishing Group.
Figure 10-2(3)	Reprinted by permission of Indiana University Press.
Figure 10-6(1)	Reprinted by permission of *Planning*. Copyright © January 1992 by the American Planning Association.
Figure 10-7(1)	© 1960, The Estate of Buckminster Fuller. Courtesy of the Buckminster Fuller Institute, Los Angeles.
Figure 10-7(2)	Reprinted by permission of Praeger Publishers, Greenwood Publishing Group.
Figure 10-8(1)	Reprinted by permission of Van Nostrand Reinhold.
Figure 10-8(2)	Used by permission of Alix Verge.

Figure 10-8(3)	Reprinted by permission of MIT Press.
Figure 10-9(1,2)	© 1993 ARS, New York/SPADEM, Paris.
A Functional Sociogenic Environment (pg. 211)	Used by permission of Deepti Nijhawan.
Figure 11-2(2)	Used by permission of Alix Verge.
Figure 11-5(3)	Collection of the author.
Figure 11-6(1)	Used by the permission of Venturi, Scott Brown and Associates.
Figure 11-6(3)	Used by permission of Ann Strong.
Figure 11-7(2)	Used by permission of Jennifer Taylor.
Figure 11-9(3)	Collection of the author.
Figure 11-10(1,2,3)	Collection of the author.
Figure 11-11(1,2)	Collection of the author.
Figure 11-11(3)	Courtesy of the Department of City Planning, San Francisco.
Figure 12-3	Used by permission of Irwin Altman.
Figure 12-4(3)	Collection of the author.
Figure 12-6(1)	Used by permission of Hanna/Olin, Ltd., Philadelphia.
Figure 12-7	Used by permission of Oscar Newman and the National Institute of Justice, U.S. Department of Justice.
Figure 12-8(1)	Collection of the author.
Figure 12-9(1)	Collection of the author. Photograph by Donald M. Stephenson.
Figure 12-9(2)	Used by permission of MIT Press.
Figure 12-9(3)	Collection of the author.
Figure 12-10(1)	Used by permission of Venturi, Scott Brown and Associates.
Figure 12-11(1)	Used by permission of Wallace, Roberts and Todd.
Figure 12-11(2,3)	Used by permission of Oscar Newman.
Figure 13-2(1,2,3)	Collection of the author.
Table 13-1	Reprinted by permission of Schenkman Books, Inc.
Figure 13-3(1)	Reproduced from *Architectural Design* magazine, courtesy of the Academy Group, London, with permission of Robert A. M. Stern.
Figure 13-3(2)	Drawing from *Cohousing: A Contemporary Approach to Housing Ourselves* (Ten Speed Press, 1990). Used by permission of Kathryn M. McCamant and Charles R. Durrett.
Figure 13-3(3)	Used by permission of *Planning*. Copyright © July 1991 by the American Planning Association.
Figure 13-4(1)	Used by permission of Hanna/Olin, Ltd., Philadelphia.
Figure 13-4(2)	Collection of the author.
Figure 13-4(3)	Used by permission of Michael McKinley, Clare Cooper Marcus, and Van Nostrand Reinhold.
Figure 13-6(1,3,5)	Used by permission of Randolph Hester and Van Nostrand Reinhold.
Table 13-2	Reprinted by permission of Randolph Hester and Van Nostrand Reinhold.
Figure 13-7(1,2)	Reprinted by permission of Van Nostrand Reinhold.
Figure 13-7(3)	Collection of the author.
Figure 13-8(3)	Collection of the author.
Figure 13-8(5)	Used by permission of Chapman & Hall, Limited, London, and Charles Moore and William Turnbull.
Figure 13-9(2)	Adapted from Donald Appleyard, *Livable Streets.* © Board of Regents, University of California.
Figure 13-13(3)	Used by permission of Ruth Durack.
Figure 13-14	Courtesy of the Department of City Planning, San Francisco.
Figure 13-15(3)	Used by permission of John Ballinger.
Figure 13-15(4)	Used by permission of Deepti Nijhawan.
Figure 13-15(6)	Used by permission of Hanna/Olin, Ltd., Philadelphia.

Figure 14-2(1)	Courtesy of Architect Haines, Lundberg Waehler, successor firm to McKenzie Vorhees and Gmelin.
Figure 14-2(2)	Courtesy of the Department of City Planning, San Francisco.
Figure 14-3(1,2)	Collection of the author.
Figure 14-4(1)	Used by permission of Ruth Durack.
Figure 14-9(2)	Used by permission of Neil Hart.
Figure 14-9(4)	Used by permission of J. Dennis Wilson.
Figure 14-10(2)	Used by permission of J. Dennis Wilson.
Figure 14-12(1)	Used by permission of Alix Verge.
Figure 14-12(2)	Used by permission of Steve King.
Figure 14-12(3)	Collection of the author.
Figure 16-2(1)	Collection of the author.
Figure 16-2(2)	Used by permission of Steve King.
Figure 16-2(3)	Used by permission of Deepti Nijhawan.
Figure 16-4(1,2)	Collection of the author.
Figure 16-5(1)	Collection of the author.
Figure 16-5(2)	Used by permission of Clare Cooper Marcus and Van Nostrand Reinhold.
Figure 16-6(2)	Used by permission of David Allison.
Figure 16-7(3)	Reprinted by permission of the Princeton Architectural Press.
Figure 16-8(1)	Used by permission of Deepti Nijhawan.
Figure 16-8(2)	Collection of the author.
Figure 16-8(3)	Courtesy of the Frank Lloyd Wright Archives.
Figure 17-2(1)	Courtesy of Ann Strong.
Figure 17-3(2)	Courtesy of the Department of City Planning, San Francisco.
Figure 17-3(3)	Used by permission of Larry Marks.
Figure 17-5(3)	Collection of the author.
Figure 17-6(1)	Used by permission of J. Dennis Wilson.
Figure 17-7(4)	Courtesy of the Department of City Planning, San Francisco.
Figure 17-11(2)	Used by permission of Alix Verge.
Figure 17-12(1)	Collection of the author.
Figure 17-13(4)	Used by permission of Hanna/Olin, Ltd., Philadelphia.
Figure 17-13(5)	Used by permission of Deepti Nijhawan.
Figure 17-13(6)	Collection of the author.
Figure 17-14(2)	Used by permission of Steve King.
Figure 18-1(1)	© 1960, The Estate of Buckminster Fuller. Courtesy of the Buckminster Fuller Institute, Los Angeles.
Figure 18-3(1,3)	Reprinted by permission of the World Meteorological Association, Geneva.
Figure 18-3(2)	Reprinted by permission of Routledge, London.
Figure 18-4(1)	Used by permission of Ruth Durack.
Figure 18-5(1)	Reprinted by permission of MIT Press.
Figure 18-5(2)	Reprinted by permission of Van Nostrand Reinhold and Lawrence Halprin.
Figure 18-6(1)	Used by permission of Alix Verge.
Figure 18-6(2)	Reprinted by permission of Van Nostrand Reinhold.
Figure 18-7(2,3)	Reprinted by permission of Routledge, London.
Figure 18-8(1,2,3)	Used by permission of Mark Francis.
Conclusion (pg. 355)	Used by permission of James Blank, Photographer.
Procedural Issues in Attaining a Functional Environment (pg. 367)	Used by permission of Ron Shiffman, Pratt Institute Center for Community and Environmental Development.
Figure 20-1(1)	Used by permission of Deepti Nijhawan.
Figure 20-5(1)	Used by permission of Ann Strong.
Figure 20-5(2)	Used by permission of J. Dennis Wilson.
Figure 21-1	Courtesy of Laurence S. Cutter and Sherrie Stephens Cutler, AIA, co-authors, *Recycling Cities for People: The Urban Design Process.*

Figure 21-2	Reprinted by permission of John Zeisel.
Figure 21-4(1)	Used by permission of Jennifer Taylor.
Figure 21-4(2)	Courtesy of the Pike Place Market Preservation and Development Authority.
Figure 21-4(3)	Used by permission of Deepti Nijhawan.
Figure 21-6(1)	Courtesy of the Department of City Planning, San Francisco.
Figure 21-6(3)	Used by permission of the Philadelphia Museum of Art.
Figure 21-7(1)	Collection of the author; source unknown.
Figure 21-8	Courtesy of University of Pennsylvania, Graduate School of Fine Arts.
Figure 21-9	Courtesy of the Montgomery County Planning Commission, Maryland.
Figure 21-10	Reprinted by the permission of ERG, Philadelphia.
Figure 22-1(1,2)	Courtesy the AIA/Philadelphia chapter.
Figure 23-1	Reprinted by permission of Harvard University Press.
Figure 23-3(1)	© 1993 ARS, New York/SPADEM, Paris.
Figure 23-3(2)	Reprinted by permission of Chapman & Hall, Limited, London.
Figure 23-3(3)	Courtesy of the Department of City Planning, San Francisco.
Figure 24-1	Used by permission of Raymond Studer.
Figure 24-2(1)	From *Design of Cities* by Edmund Bacon. Copyright © 1967, 1974 by Edmund N. Bacon. Used by permission of Viking Penguin, a division of Penguin Books.
Figure 24-5	Reprinted by permission of John Zeisel.
Figure 24-6	Reprinted by permission of the *Journal of the American Institute of Planners*.
Part IV. Conclusion: The Future of Urban Design (pg. 451)	Courtesy of Hanna/Olin Ltd., Philadelphia

INDEX

INDEX